Colonial America

1607–1763

HARRY M. WARD

University of Richmond

PRENTICE HALL, *Englewood Cliffs, New Jersey 07632*

Library of Congress Cataloging-in-Publication Data

WARD, HARRY M.
  Colonial America, 1607–1763 / Harry M. Ward.
    p. cm.
  Includes bibliographical references and index.
  ISBN 0–13–142449–1
  1. United States—History—Colonial period, ca. 1600–1775.
  I. Title.
  E188.W33 1991
  973.2—dc20   90-7507
                                                              CIP

Editorial/production supervision: *Carolyn Serebreny*
Interior design: *Joan Stone*
Prepress buyer: *Debbie Kesar*
Manufacturing buyer: *Mary Ann Gloriande*
Cover design: *Ray Lundgren Graphics, Ltd.*

Cover Photo: *A Musical Gathering*, a group portrait by unknown artist. Courtesy
of the Nassau County Museum, Syosset, N.Y.

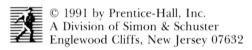 © 1991 by Prentice-Hall, Inc.
A Division of Simon & Schuster
Englewood Cliffs, New Jersey 07632

Printed in the United States of America
10 9 8 7 6 5 4 3 2 1

ISBN   0-13-142449-1

Prentice-Hall International (UK) Limited, *London*
Prentice-Hall of Australia Pty. Limited, *Sydney*
Prentice-Hall Canada Inc., *Toronto*
Prentice-Hall Hispanoamericana, S.A., *Mexico*
Prentice-Hall of India Private Limited, *New Delhi*
Prentice-Hall of Japan, Inc., *Tokyo*
Simon & Schuster Asia Pte. Ltd., *Singapore*
Editora Prentice-Hall do Brasil, Ltda., *Rio de Janeiro*

Contents

To Peg, Hiley, and Jack

Preface

This book treats the history of American colonial life, beginning with the founding of the colonies and concluding with America at the crossroads in 1763. The emphasis is on topical examination of the colonial experience. Learning of the contributions, triumphs, and travails of the colonists affords an understanding not only of the origins of American institutions and character but also of American identity and the value placed on freedom in America. The colonists faced the tasks of starting anew in a strange world, building communities and institutions, and defining ways of life. Borrowing from the Old World, they went in new and often innovative directions. By 1763, on the threshold of the American Revolution, colonial development had reached significant maturation.

Historical writing on the colonial period since the mid-twentieth century, specialized and exploratory, has offered fresh perspectives and interpretations. This work seeks to incorporate many of the conclusions and findings of modern colonial historians. While presenting a comprehensive overview, it calls attention to important areas that have been neglected in previous general histories of colonial America.

I wish to thank Steve Dalphin, Executive Editor, College Division of Prentice Hall, for encouragement from the inception of this project to its completion. Historians selected by the publisher have greatly aided in the improvement of this work with their critiques and suggestions. I am also grateful to Bruce Emmer for his fine editorial assistance and to Joan Stone, Production Supervisor, and Carolyn Serebreny, Production Editor, for their contributions toward enhancing the quality of the book.

Harry M. Ward

1

The Atlantic Frontier

The history of colonial North America begins in an age of reconnaissance. Europeans in the sixteenth century sought a passageway to Asia, chartered regions of new discovery, established northern fisheries, and, on rare occasions, attempted outpost settlements. They did so with the knowledge of the spheres of interest already staked out by the Spaniards and Portuguese to the south.

Even before the arrival of Columbus, America was not entirely unknown. Scholars and mariners had long wondered about the mysterious sea to the west, believing that its distant waves touched the shores of Asia. The preponderance of learned opinion from antiquity to the time of Columbus held that the earth was round. Various factors, however, delayed westward overseas exploration by Europeans. For several millennia the outreaches of Eurasia and Africa offered ample challenge for discovery. Sailing craft and nautical technology were scarcely adequate for extended ocean voyages. Warfare and social disequilibrium sapped the energies of petty and great states alike. The Middle Ages brought Europeans into commerce for the exotic commodities of the Far East. Venetian traders penetrated into central Asia, and the fabled journeys of Marco Polo into China, Burma, and India provided a whole new geographic perspective. The Crusades further drew Europe's attention eastward.

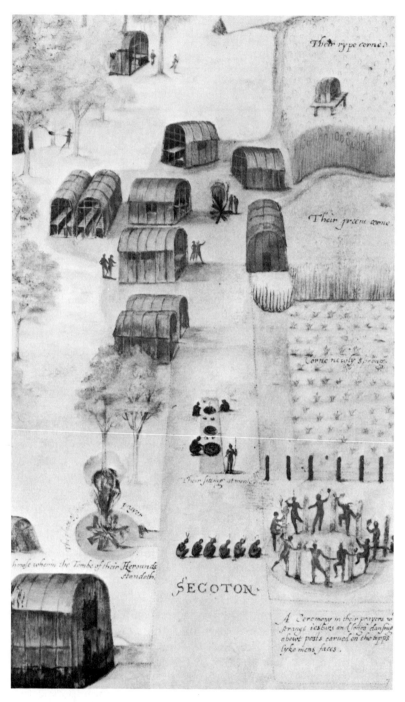

Secotan Village (1585) by John White. Reproduced by Courtesy of the Trustees of the British Museum

The *Geographical Outline* by Claudius Ptolemy (ca. 73–151), Greco-Egyptian astronomer, geographer, and mathematician, had a profound impact on Europe in the fifteenth century. The 1406 Latin translation was considered the authoritative work on global geography. Ptolemy's maps showed elongated contours for Europe, Asia, and Africa. Mistakenly depicting Asia much wider than it was in reality led Columbus to believe that it was possible to reach that continent by sailing west. Despite Europeans' reluctance to explore the full extent of the globe before Columbus's time, some bold mariners (not the least the Vikings) nevertheless ventured long distances into the Great Sea. But not until the beginning of the modern era did Europeans probe the far limits of the Atlantic Ocean on a grand and organized scale. If explorers, in their initial quests, did not discover fabled islands or even the Indies or Asia, they did happen upon a whole new part of the earth. Still, the calculations of the ancient geographers had in a sense been correct: Asia was linked with the American continents, whose Mongoloid inhabitants had migrated from Asia during the Upper Paleolithic age, about the same time that Cro-Magnon man dwelt in Europe. Columbus and sixteenth-century explorers refined early calculations and made known a wider world.

PRE-COLUMBIAN AMERICA

The first people to enter the New World were hunters who crossed from Siberia to Alaska. Skulls found in caves near Chungking and in northern China are similar to Amerindian remains from prehistoric times. A land bridge linked Asia and America at what is now the Bering Strait about 50,000 to 38,000 B.C. and also from about 26,000 to 8000 B.C. The melting of glaciers raised the ocean's water level (today about two hundred feet in the Bering Strait). At times a huge glacier sheet also stretched between the Atlantic and the Pacific.

A fascinating debate still continues as to when the Amerindians originally came to the New World. What are alleged to be crude stone artifacts from the Upper Paleolithic period have been recovered in the western part of North America and in Mexico. For example, campsites have yielded what may have been unsharpened bone and stone implements at Lewisville, Texas (dating to 37,000 B.C.), and Tule Springs, Nevada (30,000 to 26,000 B.C.). Detractors argue that the discoveries do not prove conclusively that such items were the work of Paleolithic man. Findings in Mexico, however, seem indisputably to confirm the presence of humans in North America as early as 20,000 B.C. Generally, it is estimated that the first Americans appeared at least by 24,000 B.C. and possibly as early as 50,000 B.C. As to eastern North America, which is believed to have been the last area in the northern Western Hemisphere to be inhabited by the

Indians, excavation at a cave in southwestern Pennsylvania has revealed the oldest occupation layer there to be sixteen thousand years old.

Archaeological evidence over the past half century has pushed the arrival of humans on the American continents backward in time, and other recent investigations have boosted Indian population at the time of Columbus's voyages. Anthropologist Alfred L. Kroeber concluded in 1939 that the population in the Western Hemisphere circa A.D. 1500 was 8.4 million and that of North America above Mexico just over one million. Estimates of the maximum Amerindian population for the Western Hemisphere now range from 50 to 112 million (Henry F. Dobyns) and for North America above the Rio Grande from 1.5 million (Arnell Gibson) to 12,250,000 (Dobyns). For eastern North America, however, calculations have not changed much since the famous report of James Mooney for the Bureau of American Ethnology in 1928: 55,600 for the North Atlantic states and 52,200 for the South Atlantic states. Indeed, the New World population in 1500 may well have exceeded that of western Europe. As historian Wilbur R. Jacobs, writing in 1974, observes:

> What is involved here is truly one of the most fascinating number games in history, one that may well have a determining influence upon interpretive themes not only of early United States history but also of the history of all the Americas. (p. 123)

Upon European contact, owing primarily to the white man's diseases but also, of course, to warfare and social disruption, the Indians of the Atlantic frontier rapidly dwindled in numbers. The known depopulation ratio of certain tribes after European contact has been used to project the rate of population decline for other tribes, for whom early data are lacking. Such calculations support the higher estimates of pre-Columbian Indian population.

Except for arctic regions, most of the Indians whom Europeans first encountered on the Atlantic frontier were of the Eastern Woodland culture. All were at the neolithic level of development. The Indians had no metal tools, although copper was used for ornamental purposes among some tribes. Population density was low.

From the Carolinas to Maine, the Indians whom the Europeans first met were of Algonquian linguistic stock. Toward the piedmont in Virginia and the Carolinas there were also Siouan tribes (including the Catawbas) and Iroquoian groups (Cherokees and Tuscaroras); from Florida along the Gulf Plains to the Mississippi were those of Muskogean stock (Creeks, Choctaws, Chickasaws, and Seminoles). The northern Iroquois, who lived in the eastern Great Lakes region from New York to the St. Lawrence, included the Five Nations (the Senecas, Cayugas, Onondagas, Oneidas, and, easternmost, Mohawks) and their rivals, the Hurons (in southern

Ontario). The Susquehannocks in south central Pennsylvania were also Iroquoian. Algonquian Indians occupied most of the northeastern Atlantic slope. Among Algonquian tribes with whom explorers and settlers had initial contacts were the Penobscots and Abenakis of Maine, the Naticks, Narragansetts, Wampanoags, Pequots, Patuxets, and Mohicans in Massachusetts and southern New England, the Montauks on Long Island, the Delawares (Lenapes) in New Jersey and eastern Pennsylvania, and the Powhatan Confederacy of Virginia.

Southeastern Indians relied more on domesticated crops and had greater productive technologies than northeastern Indians. Another difference was that in the south, Indians tended to be completely sedentary, living in their villages year round, while those in the north usually left their communities for seasonal hunting, fishing, and foraging. Social hierarchy was often more pronounced in the south.

Dwellings in the south usually consisted of mud-walled structures, with thatched roofs, covered with bark, mats, or skins. New England Indians favored domed wigwams of bark or mats strung over posts. The Iroquois, organized according to clans, built palisaded villages on about two acres of hilltop land. Given the Indians' skills at hunting, fishing, and agriculture, the first Europeans expected to enlist the Indians as procurers of commodities.

ATLANTIC CROSSINGS BEFORE COLUMBUS

Though conjectural, it is in the realm of possibility that a variety of pre-Columbian visitors made it to America. Besides the Norsemen, whose contact with the North American continent before the year 1000 is fairly well established, less reliable claims have been made for other alleged early travelers to America, among them the Phoenicians (480 B.C.), the lost tribes of Israel, the Chinese Hoei-Shin (crossing the Pacific in A.D. 49), Christians fleeing Nero's persecution in A.D. 64, Saint Brendan (ca. 600) and other Irish monks in the tenth century, an Icelandic abbot (purportedly the Quetzalcoatl of Aztec myth, around 1010), Prince Madoc of Wales (ca. 1170), the Zeno brothers of Venice (1380s), Henry Sinclair, a Scottish earl (1390s), the Portuguese João Vaz Corte Real (two decades before Columbus), and voyagers sent out by Bristol merchants on the eve of Columbus's discovery.

The Vikings have inspired a vast literature and speculation, not so much as to whether or not they scanned the coasts of North America but rather to what degree they penetrated into the continent itself and whether they colonized. Archaeological and literary evidence indicate that Norsemen planted a colony in Iceland about 874. One of the settlers there, Eric Thorvaldsson Raude ("the Red"), sentenced to exile for three years for manslaughter, using information from a sailor who had been blown off course, headed westward with his family for Greenland. There he founded a colony, which flourished until the 1400s, when it then disappeared. From 985 to 1261 Greenland was independent, though closely associated with Iceland; after 1261 both Greenland and Iceland were under the rule of Norway. Excavations have yielded the remains of two Greenland settlements, including graveyards.

The Norse expansion into the Atlantic was eventually recorded. The Greenlanders' saga, written about 1200, and Eric the Red's narrative, about 1270, suggested mainland landings and settlements. According to one story, Bjarni Heljolfsson, on his way from Norway to Greenland in 986, was blown off course and sighted a forested and hilly land. Leif Ericsson, oldest son of Eric the Red, in 1000 sailed west. He visited three different areas: Helluland ("Land of Flat Stones"), probably Baffin Island or northern Labrador; Markland ("Woodland") to the south, most likely Labrador or Newfoundland; and Vinland. Leif Ericsson's brother, Thorvald, camped in huts left by the expedition and was killed by the Skerllings (presumably Indians). Vinland, as described in the sagas, contained wheatfields growing wild and vines "wherever it was hilly." Though at first it was thought that *Vinland* meant "land of vines," a truer reading is "land of pasture." It has been long argued that Vinland was located in Maine or Cape Cod. Historians David B. Quinn and Samuel E. Morison, however, support the contention of archaeologist Helge Ingstad that Vinland was at the site of present-day L'Anse aux Meadows in northern Newfoundland, facing the entrance of the Strait of Belle Isle. From 1961 to 1968 Ingstad uncovered houses very similar to those excavated in Greenland. Two of the largest edifices measured seventy by fifty feet, with floors of hard clay, turf walls, and timbered roofs. Quinn, however, also argues that evidence supports a second Vinland at Cape Cod.

The sagas tell of follow-up ventures to Vinland. In 1009, Thorfinn Karlselfni, a wealthy Icelandic trader, led an expedition to Vinland consisting of three ships and 250 men and women. Among them was Freydis, the illegitimate daughter of Eric the Red. Freydis may have been the first woman of European extraction in America literally to fight for her rights. During a pitched battle with the Skerllings, she came across a dead Viking, "his skull crushed by a flat stone; and his sword lay beside him." Freydis picked up the weapon and "then she pulled out her bosom from under her bodice and ran the flat of the sword over it. Seeing this the Skerllings were panic-stricken, ran to their boats and fled away."

Unfortunately, many artifacts linking the Vikings to America are of dubious authenticity or outright frauds. Such celebrated items as the Kensington runic stone in Minnesota; the tower at Newport, Rhode Island; mooring stones on the Atlantic seaboard; and the "Vinland map" (purportedly dating to 1440) have been entirely discounted. A Viking ax, sword, and shield boss discovered in central Canada would suggest that Vikings headed deep into the interior of the continent, but that does not seem very plausible. Such articles, also found elsewhere, may simply have been family heirlooms of a later period. A tiny stone wheel, part of a spinning device, that turned up in Newfoundland is perhaps authentic and would suggest a settlement that included women.

Expeditions sent west by merchants of Bristol, England, in the 1480s in search of the legendary Isle of Brasil and the Island of the Seven Cities may have reached Newfoundland and Cape Breton Island. David B. Quinn's investigations lend credibility to this possibility, but definite proof is lacking.

English traders in the fifteenth century began a flourishing trade with Norway and its tributaries, including Iceland. The main reference to Bristol men reaching America before Columbus is in a letter from Englishman John Day, in Spanish, to the Grand Admiral of Spain (probably Columbus himself) in 1497 (a document not discovered until the 1950s), in which Day comments that "the cape of land" sighted by Gonçalo Velho Cabral, a Portuguese seaman, in the mid-fifteenth century, had already been found "by the men from Bristol. . . . It was called the Island of Brasil, and it is assumed and believed to be the mainland that the men from Bristol found." In any event, there is no conclusive evidence that English traders or fishermen were in the New World until after the Cabot voyages in 1497 and 1498.

A NEW ERA IN EUROPE

By the beginning of the sixteenth century, royal power was consolidated and enhanced in Portugal, Spain, France, and England. In Portugal, John II (1481–1495) suppressed a revolt by nobles in 1483 and along with his successor, Manuel I (1495–1521), increased the authority of the crown and promoted overseas empire. Ferdinand and Isabella, by their marriage in 1469, united the crowns of Aragon and Castile. The Hundred Years' War (1337–1453) had finally concluded between England and France. Louis XI (1461–1483) restored the influence of the French monarchy and encouraged economic revival. The Wars of the Roses in England ended with the ascension of the Tudor Dynasty in 1485, and Henry VII eliminated the remnants of feudal authority. With their crowns secure, the monarchs of the nation-states were prepared to seek out imperial advantage abroad.

The spirit of inquiry manifested during the Renaissance also fostered a quest for a wider world. Although the Renaissance sought chiefly to recover knowledge of the past, it aroused disinterested curiosity about the hitherto unknown. As Thomas Goldstein (1976) has written:

> The ultimate inner link between Renaissance and discoveries is implicit [in the] unique relationship towards time and space. The true Renaissance impulse behind the discoveries is the awakening to a world that had always been there, with a sudden keen urge to face and experience it. (p. 32)

Likewise, the Protestant Reformation set Europe along different paths. It provoked religious, political, and territorial rivalries, especially in the German territories, and also challenged the ecclesiastical authority of the governments of the nation-states. Though long simmering, the Reformation is said to have begun when Martin Luther posted his Ninety-five Theses on the castle door at Wittenberg on October 31, 1517, protesting the sale of indulgences by the church. The Lutheran revolt spread through many German states and into the Scandinavian countries. In England, Henry VIII severed the English church from the papacy, mainly so that he could remarry. The English church, with the sovereign at its head, retained essentially its Catholic form, leading to challenges from Puritans and other dissenters. John Calvin, emphasizing the doctrine of predestination, personal morality, and piety, established a theocratic government at Geneva, Switzerland. Calvinism, contending with both Lutheranism and Catholicism, spurred the founding of Reformed churches on the Continent and Presbyterian congregations in the British Isles. Radical and emotional religious groups also emerged on the Continent. Particularly those of the Anabaptist persuasion (see Chapter 13) were ruthlessly persecuted by both Catholics and Lutherans.

After the Wars of Religion in France (1562–1598), the French Protestants (Huguenots) won a limited right to worship in the Edict of Nantes (1598), which order, however, was revoked in 1685. The Thirty Years' War (1618–1648), fought largely between Protestant and Catholic princes, left terrible destruction and caused great loss of life, abetted by disease and famine. Amid the turmoil and persecution, religious minorities moved often in search of safe sanctuary. Many of them, when the opportunity presented itself, would seek refuge in the New World.

Another fundamental change was also affecting Europe. A static and localized economy was transformed by the commercial revolution (ca. 1400–1700), accompanied by new business methods and the desire to expand opportunities for profit. Accumulated surplus capital was invested in trading and shipping. Lending money by banks steadily expanded. The great financial house of the Fuggers of Augsburg engaged in extensive international banking. Florentine bankers substantially backed Portuguese overseas trade, and their Genoese counterparts invested in the first two voyages of Columbus.

The resumption of the advance of the Ottoman Empire after the fall of Constantinople in 1453 thwarted western Europe's expansion of trade with the Orient. Thus new trade routes bypassing North Africa and the Near East were sought. A crusading spirit was still strong in Spain and Portugal, reinforcing economic and imperial motives. Approaches to the Indies and Asia by sea beckoned.

Improvement in ship technology greatly enhanced oceanic navigation. Among nautical instruments that came into use were the log line (a block fastened to a line and run out from a reel) to measure the rate of a ship's speed, the compass, the astrolabe and quadrant for determining latitudes, and the traverse board, used for dead reckoning. New ship designs made extended voyages practicable. By 1500 vessels were longer and narrower, containing several decks and greater space for storage; hulls were more streamlined; the use of triangular lateen sails provided for more wind power; and a diversity of sails increased maneuverability.

EUROPEAN REDISCOVERY OF AMERICA

With trade routes blocked between western Europe and the Far East, Portugal sought commercial expansion in the Atlantic islands—the Canaries, the Madeira group, the Azores, and the Cape Verde Islands. Under the direction of Prince Henry (1394–1460), called "the Navigator," Portuguese caravels plied the West African coast. Raids against Moorish and other Muslim settlements, however, impeded discovery. After Henry's death, John II and Manuel I promoted more distant exploration. Bartholomew Diaz, in 1487 and 1488, reached the Cape of Good Hope and traveled a short distance along the east coast of Africa. Two years later, Vasco da Gama, with four vessels provisioned for three years, reached Mozambique and then sailed up the African coast and across the Indian Ocean to Calcutta, returning to Lisbon in August 1499 with samples of India's great wealth.

Portuguese success in discovering new avenues for trade stimulated interest in a western voyage to the Indies. Christopher Columbus (Cristoforo Colombo, in Italian; Cristobal Colón, in Spanish) had such an ambition. Initially a weaver, he soon took to the sea and was probably on vessels that sailed to England and Iceland. In 1477 Columbus settled in Lisbon and married the daughter of a Portuguese navigator. While employed as a sugar buyer trading with the Portuguese Atlantic islands for a Genoese mercantile firm, he had ample contact with pilots and navigators. Upon the death of his wife, Columbus dedicated himself to the mission of western discovery. Unable to secure assistance from King John II of Portugal, he was finally commissioned by Ferdinand and Isabella of Spain as "Admiral of the Ocean Sea" and viceroy and governor of all new lands he might discover. He would also share in any profits from the voyage. Three ships—*Niña*, *Pinta*, and *Santa Maria*—were outfitted for an expedition. On August 3, 1492, Columbus set sail on what, as J. R. Hale (1968) has noted, was "one of the most routine of explorers' voyages" (p. 62). With a fully stocked cargo, the ships, following the trade winds, had fair weather and traveled as much as 180 miles a day. After thirty-three days at sea, the vessels touched San Salvador (Watling Island) in the Bahamas (though a *National Geographic* team, in a recent investigation, analyzing currents and winds, insists that the landing was sixty-five miles to the southeast at the island of Samana Cay—a conclusion not accepted by other experts). Columbus then sailed for Cuba, which he thought to be the mainland of Cathay (China). On Christmas Eve, 1492, the *Santa Maria* ran onto a coral reef off the northeast coast of the island of Santo Domingo (now Hispaniola) near the present-day town of Bord de Mer de Limonade, Haiti. Its planking torn open, the ship had to be abandoned. Local Arawak Indians helped to unload the supplies and gave Columbus and his men two large houses in their village. Columbus named the site La Navidad; it was the first Spanish settlement in the New World. Leaving behind thirty-nine of his crew and instructing them to build a fort, Columbus set sail for home, first docking at Lisbon, in March 1493.

A second voyage (1493–1496) involved seventeen ships and fifteen hundred colonists. Columbus found his colony destroyed and the Spanish settlers dead; he reestablished a colony, naming it Hispaniola, on the south coast of Santo Domingo. Columbus explored Cuba, Jamaica, Puerto Rico, and the Leeward Islands before returning to Spain. He brought back with him Indians who were probably responsible for the first outbreak of syphilis in Europe, involving women from Barcelona and French soldiers in Naples. Another voyage (1498–1502) journeyed southward to Trinidad and reached the South American continent at the mouth of the Orinoco River. Back in Hispaniola, Columbus ran into a mutiny and was sent in chains to Spain. The final voyage (1502–1504), poorly equipped, visited the shores of Central America. Upon his death on May 21, 1506, Columbus had realized little of the fortune that he had expected in the New World.

Although insisting to the last that he had reached the Indies and Asia, Columbus did have the conception of having discovered *un otro mondo* (another world). At the time of his third voyage, he had written that he had been sent as an agent from God to travel "to the new heaven and world which till then had been hidden." On his return from the final voyage, Columbus, however, concluded that there were not "two worlds" as he had previously thought but one and the same world. It belonged to a Florentine to reintroduce to the imagination Columbus's earlier conception of two worlds.

At age forty, Amerigo Vespucci was a foreign agent to Spain for the merchant house of the Medicis, his major task being to equip vessels. Subsequently, Vespucci accompanied four expeditions (for Spain and then Portugal) to the Western Hemisphere, perhaps at one time serving as a captain of a ship. Publication of Vespucci's letters, first in Latin and then in French and German, especially the two printed as *Mundus novus*, brought him literary fame as a leading figure in the discovery of the New World. Columbus's letters had the misfortune of not gaining wide distribution. Martin Waldseemüller, a professor of geography at the College of Saint Die in Lorraine, included in his *Cosmographie introductio* (1507) maps calling the fourth part of the globe "America." Until the end of the sixteenth century, the name was applied only to South America.

Spanish and Portuguese rivalry over the New World contributed to efforts to establish principles of international relations governing westward overseas expansion. Portugal contended that Columbus's land discoveries lay within its sphere of interest. The Treaty of Alcaçovas in 1479 had recognized Portuguese monopoly of trade and settlement on the West African coast and also possession of all the Atlantic islands, except the Canaries, which belonged to Spain. Spain petitioned Pope Alexander VI for legalization of Spanish sovereignty in the New World. The papal bull *Inter caetera* of 1493 awarded Spanish control over "certain remote islands and even mainlands" discovered or to be discovered not held by a Christian prince. A new bull, a few weeks later, acknowledged Spanish rule over territory west of an imaginary line, one hundred leagues west of the Azores and Cape Verde islands. John II of Portugal accepted this determination, only requesting that the line of demarcation be 370 leagues (1,175 miles) west from the islands. Spain acceded, and the Treaty of Tordesillas to this effect was signed in 1494. Thus Portugal would have lands in the New World. In 1500, Pero Alvarez Cabral discovered the Brazilian coast and laid claim to the region for Portugal, since the area lay on the Portuguese side of the demarcation line. Portugal, however, did not found a colony in Brazil until the 1530s.

The papal bulls and the Treaty of Tordesillas could not be enforced regarding other nations, who could not be expected to surrender territory in the New World to Portugal and Spain. It would also be open to question whether Spain could assert claims to lands not yet discovered. Inevitably, as nations competed for space in the New World, only practical criteria governed: actual discovery, effective occupation, recognition of spheres of interest, and ultimately, might.

New Spain—the Caribbean, Mexico, Central America, and northern South America—prospered. Hernando Cortés conquered Mexico (1519–1521), and Francisco Pizarro subdued the Indians in Peru (1531–1534). Silver mines yielded immense wealth. The *repartimientos*, large land allotments, and the *encomiendas*, orders that conferred authority to exact tribute in labor from the Indians, aided mining and agricultural expansion. The Spanish quest turned even further westward. Vasco Núñez de Balboa in 1513 discovered the Pacific from the west side of the isthmus, and Ferdinand Magellan sailed around the tip of South America to the

Philippines; after his being killed by the natives, his crew continued the voyage to Spain, thus completing the first circumnavigation of the globe.

Spanish contact initially with North America, however, was one of exploration rather than colonization. Juan Ponce de León discovered Florida in 1512, in search of the magic isle of Bimini, and Alonzo de Piñeda in 1519 traversed the northern coast of the Gulf of Mexico. Pánfilo de Narváez landed in Florida in 1528 and marched north to present-day Tallahassee. He and all but two of his men, sailing for Mexico, were killed in a shipwreck. One of the survivors, Alvar Núñez Cabaza de Vaca reached the coast of Texas in a horsehide boat; then he journeyed across the Texas plains to New Mexico and Colorado and southward to Mexico, covering a distance of five thousand miles. De Vaca's journal, *Relación*, was the first book to describe western North America.

Among other Spanish North American explorers was Hernando de Soto, who traversed the Gulf plains and crossed the Mississippi into Arkansas (1538–1542); upon de Soto's death, his men returned along the gulf coast to Mexico. Inspired by de Vaca's telling of the rumored existence of the Seven Cities of Cíbola, long thought to have been an island but now believed to be in the interior of the new continent, Francisco Vásquez de Coronado crossed into the Great Plains as far as south central Kansas, finding not the fabled cities of gold but the sod-and-bison-hide huts of the Wichita Indians. Coronado's disillusionment dampened for a while Spanish interest in exploring the North American interior. Antonio de Espejo in 1582 and 1583 visited present-day New Mexico and Arizona. His finding of traces of gold led to the lengthy expedition of Juan de Oñate (1598–1606), which covered the southwest from Kansas to the Gulf of California. Oñate founded a settlement, San Gabriel, on the upper Rio Grande in New Mexico. In 1609 the Spaniards established Santa Fe.

In England, the Columbian voyages created interest in finding a passageway to Asia. Henry VII had taken merchants from Venice residing in England under his protection. One of these, John Cabot (Giovanni Caboto), a Genoese, and his sons successfully petitioned the king for letters of patent for a western voyage, whereby the king would receive one-fifth of any profits. Cabot, probably accompanied by his son Sebastian, set sail on May 2, 1497, aboard the *Mathew* with a crew of eighteen men. The voyage reached Cape Breton Island and most likely also Maine. Back in England, John Cabot reported that he had found the land of the Great Khan. On his second voyage, consisting of five ships, in 1498, Cabot reconnoitered the shores of Labrador and the American coast possibly as far south as Virginia. Storms took a heavy toll; Cabot himself disappeared, and only one of his ships returned to England. Ten years later, Sebastian Cabot sailed along most of the North American coast seeking a northwest passage.

France's claims to lands in North America began with the explorations

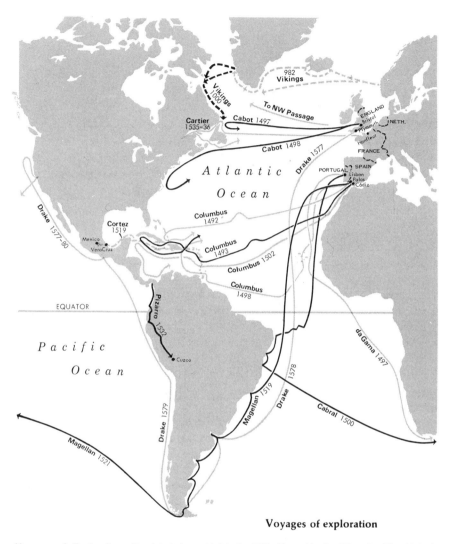

Voyages of exploration

of Giovanni da Verranzano, a Florentine navigator in the service of Francis I of France. In his 1524 voyage, in search of a northwest passage, he cruised along the North Atlantic coasts from the Carolinas to Nova Scotia and sailed into New York harbor and Narragansett Bay. Verrazano's report to the king is not only the first documentation of a voyage to New England but also a vivid description of that area. In 1528, while exploring the mouth of the Rio de la Plata in South America in an attempt to find a shorter passage to Asia than the route of Magellan, Verrazano was killed by Indians.

Jacques Cartier, bearing a commission from the admiral of France, in 1534 sailed to the Strait of Belle Isle and then southward to the Gulf of the St. Lawrence. In his second voyage (1535–1536) he proceeded up the river to the sites of Quebec and Montreal. Staying the winter in Quebec, he returned to France early the next summer. On the third expedition (1541), organized as a military endeavor to subdue a legendary Indian kingdom of Saquenay, Cartier again went to Quebec, where he established a post. The fabled kingdom, however, proved as elusive as that of the legend of Norumbega (supposedly in Maine), which would later lure English explorers. Cartier was reinforced by Jean-François de la Rocque, Sieur de Roberval, whom the king had appointed viceroy of Canada, Newfoundland, and Labrador. Unsuccessful in finding real gold or the Indian kingdom, both Cartier and Roberval were back in France by 1543. Roberval had left men at Cartier's post for the purpose of founding a colony, but the settlement disappeared from history.

The French Wars of Religion (ca. 1560–1598) deflected French overseas efforts. Jean Ribaut, however, led an expedition, consisting mostly of Huguenots, to Florida in 1562, leaving thirty persons behind to establish a post. This group was reinforced by René Laudonnière, who built Fort Caroline near the mouth of the St. Johns River. Again the primary objective was the quest for gold. In 1565, Ribaut brought over another three hundred settlers. The Spaniards considered the French colony an invasion of their territory, and to counter this threat, a Spanish expedition under Menéndez de Avilés destroyed Fort Caroline and killed its defenders; the Spanish commander then established St. Augustine and other posts in Florida. The French thereafter confined their interests to the northern part of the continent. French fisheries and fur trading were well established by the end of the sixteenth century. But it was not until 1608 that Samuel de Champlain founded the first permanent French settlement in the New World at Quebec. With emigration to New France severely restrained by the crown, the colony would develop slowly.

It would remain to the English, however, to provide large-scale immigration into North America, allowing conditions for the growth and expansion of English liberties. For the age of discovery and early settlements, Edmundo O'Gorman's (1961) observation is apt:

> It was the Spanish part of the invention of America that liberated Western man from the fetters of a prison-like conception of his physical world, and it was the English part that liberated him from subordination to a Europe-centered conception of his historical world. In these two great liberations lies the hidden and true significance of American history. (p. 145)

BEGINNINGS OF ENGLAND'S WESTERN PLANTING

During the half century after the Cabot voyages, England showed little interest in the New World. English merchants preferred short-run European investments rather than taking risks in exploiting lands unknown. Henry VIII was primarily concerned with England's internal problems and continental rivalry. The only documented English voyages of the period were those of John Rut (1527), who visited most of the North American coasts, and Richard Hore (1536), who explored the Newfoundland area. A midcentury depression and a deterioration in the Hapsburg alliance, however, revived interest in finding new markets.

A new form of business organization, the joint-stock company, facilitated the underwriting of large-scale trading ventures. English merchants had tried the regulated company, whereby each member contributed to a general fund for building forts and the like and pledged to abide by a common set of rules but was otherwise free to trade individually without sharing profits. Too often a merchant operated at the expense of the interests of the company as a whole. In the joint-stock company, however, each investor shared alike in both the risks and the overall profits (receiving dividends). Directors chosen from among the shareholders managed the company. Shares could be bought or sold. Each member would thus have limited liability in the taking of risks if a venture failed but could expect substantial financial gain if it succeeded.

Sebastian Cabot, upon his return to England in 1549, after thirty-five years' service in Spain, was instrumental in founding the first important English joint-stock company, the "Merchants Adventurers of England for the Discovery of Lands, Territories, Isles, Dominions and Seignories Unknown" (the Muscovy Company), chartered in 1553 and 1555. This group gave attention to opening a northeast passage to China. But disillusionment in attaining this objective brought Englishmen back full cycle to attempt a northwest route to the East.

Humphrey Gilbert was among those who promoted exploration of a northwest passage. His *Discourse of a Discoverie for a New Passage to Cataia*, published in 1576, had great impact and rallied public opinion to this idea. A joint-stock company was formed to send Martin Frobisher westward. His three voyages (1576, 1577, and 1578) went as far inland as Hudson Strait. Frobisher was somewhat distracted from his mission by searching for precious metals; the ore that he brought to England, however, was worthless. John Davis also led voyages (1585–1587) into the arctic region in search of a northwest passage.

Little did Frobisher or Davis dream that it would be almost four hundred years before a northern transit was made between the two oceans. The Norwegian explorer Roald Amundsen from 1903 to 1906 made the first crossing by way of sled and ship. In 1959 the United States Navy's nuclear submarine, the *Nautilus*, was the first sea vessel to travel entirely by water from the Bering Sea to Iceland and the first to circumnavigate North America (also using the Panama Canal). The nuclear submarine *Sea Dragon* in 1960 made the historic 850-mile east-west journey from Portsmouth, New Hampshire, by way of the Greenland-Labrador "slot," Davis Strait, Baffin Bay, and the Peary Channel route. In an east-west transpolar and isthmus voyage, the submarine *Silversides*, in 1989, was only the second vessel to circumnavigate the North American continent.

Deterred from finding a westward passage to Asia, England, as Spain had already done, turned toward carving out its own sphere of interest and the establishing of trade centers in the New World. Certain factors contributed to making such an endeavor. The age of Queen Elizabeth witnessed growing English insularity, the rise of national pride, and a crusading zeal to contend with Catholic Portugal and Spain. Demand in England was increasing for American timber, fish, and furs.

Promotional literature in England calling for a western planting abounded. The greatest of the western promoters was Richard Hakluyt, the younger (1552–1616). In 1582 he published *Divers Voyages Touching the Discoverie of America and the Islands Adjacent Unto the Same, Made First of All by Our Englishmen and Afterwards by the Frenchmen and Britons*, which recounted English navigational exploits and argued that England deserved a share in the New World. *The Principal Navigations, Voyages, and Discoveries of the English Nation* (published in 1589 and 1598–1600) further informed the public of England's increasing role in westward exploration. Hakluyt's *Discourse of Western Planting* (written in 1584, though not published until after his death) gives about every argument known on behalf of English western enterprise. Protestantism would be expanded by proselytizing the American natives. Prosperity would be restored through a revival of commerce and the drawing away of surplus population. Poverty in England would be alleviated. Spain would be weakened. By establishing colonies in the New World, England's naval and military power would be improved. Indeed, one of the most compelling arguments of Hakluyt and other propagandists was that a western planting would serve as a safety valve for distressed elements in the English population. Poverty affecting nearly a majority of the people, periods of economic depression, food shortages, scarcity of work, and social disorder during the half century after 1590, as historian Carl Bridenbaugh (1967) has noted, made for "a time of profound, unprecedented, and often frightening social ferment for the people of England" (p. 355).

English "sea dogs," such as Sir John Hawkins and Sir Francis Drake, while discovering the invulnerability of the Spanish Empire itself, found that through privateering and piracy, Spanish wealth could be preyed on. To counteract Spanish power, however, in the long run, outposts in the

New World were needed. It was also believed that Englishmen themselves might find their own El Dorado.

In the 1580s several ambitious Englishmen individually attempted New World colonization. Humphrey Gilbert obtained a patent from the queen for planting a colony in Newfoundland. Failing to reach America on his first voyage, Gilbert, in a second attempt in 1583, landed at Newfoundland, which he took possession of in the name of the queen. On his return, Gilbert and the ship that he was on were "swallowed up by the sea." Sir Walter Raleigh secured a new patent, which conferred on him rights of discovery and settlement and viceregal powers within two hundred leagues of any colony he should establish. In 1584, Raleigh sent Philip Amandas and Arthur Barbour on a reconnaissance voyage that surveyed the Florida and Carolina coasts and Chesapeake Bay. A second expedition sponsored by Raleigh, commanded by Ralph Lane, in 1585 put 180 men ashore at Roanoke Island at the Carolina Outer Banks. The next year Sir Francis Drake picked up the settlers and brought them back to England. In August 1587 another expedition sent by Raleigh left eighty-eight men, seventeen women, and eleven children at the same site. The governor of the new colony was John White, who, during the first attempt to establish a colony, had made a series of watercolor drawings portraying the environment and Indian life. Thomas Hariot, who had accompanied White to Roanoke, in 1588 published *Brief and True Report of the New Found Land of Virginia*; the Théodor de Bry four-language edition of Hariot's work (1590) contained engravings of White's paintings—an intriguing literary and pictorial advertisement for the New World.

After White returned to England, relief for the Roanoke colony was delayed because all ships and hands were needed in England to fend off the Spanish Armada. When White entered the Carolina waters with three small ships in 1590, all that he found was the palisade; etched on a post at the entrance was "CROATOAN," suggesting that the settlers had moved to a neighboring island inhabited by the Croatoan Indians. There was no display of a Maltese cross, which the colonists had been instructed to put up if they were in distress.

Various theories have been advanced as to the mysterious disappearance of the Roanoke colonists. Since the palisade was still intact and there were no signs of any emergency, it may be concluded that they went away voluntarily. In the next century several groups of Indians in the Carolinas had tribesmen with blue eyes and light-colored skin. Probably the best explanation of what happened to the Roanoke colonists is that they moved northward into the Chesapeake Bay region. Adding weight to this theory is that when the Jamestown colonists entered into the mouth of the James River, they spotted the smoldering ruins of an Indian village, called Chesepiooc, which had been visited by John White and other Roanoke voyagers and settlers. Powhatan and his Indians had just put the torch to the village and massacred its inhabitants. Archaeological research in the 1980s has located the Indian town on the south bank of Broad Bay, near Lynnhaven River. When the Jamestown expedition moved up the James, as George Percy observed at the time, "a Savage Boy" was sighted; the lad was about ten years old and "had a head of haire of perfect yellow and a reasonable white skinne, which is a Miracle amongst all Savages"— perhaps the lone survivor of the Roanoke group in the Indian massacre.

The English reconnaissance and planting of the sixteenth century had been expensive failures, but lessons were learned, the most important being that western ventures would most likely best succeed through pooling of limited resources, such as a joint-stock company. The Muscovy, Levant, and Eastland companies had brought English merchants wealth from the East. So, too, could a joint-stock company assist in the opening of profitable enterprise in North America. Outposts in the New World required permanent settlement and, to a large degree, a self-sustaining basis.

2

The Chesapeake Colonies

At the dawn of the seventeenth century, England prepared to exploit the resources of the New World. Although the long war with Spain concluded in 1603, it was imperative for a strong nation state to challenge that country's expansion overseas. The French had already created a trade and fishing emporium and were laying the foundations of New France. The Gilbert and Raleigh voyages and the untold number of English ships plying the northern fisheries and Indian trade awakened merchants to the possibilities of a western commercial empire. Promotional literature heralded the prospects of rewards from the establishing of outposts in America. English merchants had learned that cooperative endeavors, involving limited risk by individual subscribers, could earn large profits. The Roanoke experience had brought an awareness of the bounty of the Chesapeake Bay region. The abundance of fish and timber, the moderate climate, the expectation of discovering a variety of raw materials, perhaps even precious metals, and the use of Indians as a labor force were considered assets that would make a western planting a success. An outpost in the Chesapeake Bay region would be a means to support exploration that would surely lead to the discovery of a great passageway to the Pacific.

Captain Christopher Newport had scouted the Chesapeake Bay in the 1590s. Bartholomew Gilbert (who would be killed by the Indians) and

Martin Pring visited the Chesapeake shores in 1602 before heading for New England. Three years later, Captain George Weymouth journeyed to the region and brought five Indians back to England.

VIRGINIA

Bartholomew Gosnold, whom Captain John Smith called "the first mover of this plantation," and several of his friends set in motion organizational activity for the purpose of sponsoring a "venture" to Virginia, a name already given to the Chesapeake–Carolina Outer Banks area. Gosnold, however, would not become a member of the new company. Three groups of merchants (from London, Plymouth, and Bristol) contributed funds, and the king was persuaded to issue a charter and letters of patent. Thus the Virginia Company, though never incorporated, was born. It actually consisted of two groups, one representing the Plymouth and Bristol merchants and the other those of London. The London investors had territorial rights to the area between 34 and 41 degrees north latitude (Cape Fear River to New York Bay) and the west country associates to a region between 38 and 45 degrees (Potomac River to Maine). In the overlapping belt (Pennsylvania, New Jersey, Delaware, and Maryland), neither group could settle within one hundred miles of the other. The arrangement provided for a 52-man royal council to supervise the Virginia associates in London and a body of seven persons to conduct local affairs in the New World. The identity of the members of the resident council was not revealed until the expedition was at sea. The councilors selected were Bartholomew Gosnold, Edward Maria Wingfield, Christopher New- port, John Smith, John Martin, George Kendall, and John Ratcliffe. Instructions, prepared by Richard Hakluyt, called for settlement on an island up a navigable river that could offer protection against any Spanish naval assault. The Virginia pioneers were to build and fortify a town, clear and prepare ground for planting, and engage in exploratory missions.

On December 20, 1606, three little ships, the *Susan Constant*, *Discovery*, and *Godspeed*, lifted anchor in the Thames. Not until February, however, did the Virginia venturers set sail from England. Of the 105 persons who went over as colonists, about half were gentlemen, and the remainder consisted of their servants, about a dozen artisans, and a few boys. Traveling the southern route by way of the West Indies, the three vessels, commanded by Christopher Newport, reached the capes of the Chesapeake Bay on April 26, 1607. The southern point of land, where the ships briefly anchored, was named Cape Henry after the prince of Wales, and the one that jutted into the sea from the northward was dubbed Cape Charles, after the prince's younger brother, the duke of Albany. A party was sent to explore the northern shores of the mouth of the James at Point Comfort.

On May 13 the expedition reached a narrow pear-shaped peninsula about sixty miles up the river. Here, on the 1,500-acre peninsula, it was decided to erect a fortified town to be called Jamestown. Work began immediately to construct a fort and a triangular stockade. Two watchtowers were built to overlook the river. The Jamestown location had disadvantages in that much of the land in the area was swampy and tide covered one-third of the peninsula. It was also deep into the Indian country.

Since a priority of the mission to the New World was discovery—a search for precious minerals as well as for a passage to the Orient—Captain Newport wasted no time in ascending the river, which was named after the king. With twenty-two men, including Captain John Smith, he reached the fall line at the present site of Richmond. "By reason of the rockes and isles," Smith explained, passage up the river was blocked for about six miles. Nevertheless, the area was briefly explored for a short distance beyond the falls. But learning of fierce Indian tribes that had recently migrated to near the fall line, it was decided to go no further. Remarkably, however, there were festivities with the Indians of Powhatan town at the falls. The Englishmen put a cross on one of the islets, claiming the country in the name of the king. The Powhatan Indians at the site were typical of the Southern Woodland culture. Linguistically they were Algonquian. The Indians impressed the Englishmen as a noble breed—indeed, throughout the seventeenth century the early writers marveled at the fine physical attributes of these natives of tawny complexion who had developed a high state of agriculture and fishing. The Powhatan Confederacy, fashioned by Powhatan himself, consisted of some three dozen tribes in 161 villages scattered along the banks of the major rivers. Eventually Newport and his men returned to Jamestown. An attempt later in the year to plant a post on the James River below Powhatan town was frustrated by the growing resentment of the Indians located at the falls and the increased incidence of hostile behavior on the part of Indians around Jamestown.

During the first year, Captain John Smith explored along the bay and the James, York, and Chickahominy rivers. Already a veteran of thrilling adventures in the Austrian army and as a captive in Turkey, Smith demonstrated a bold recklessness in dealing with the Indians. There is no corroborating evidence of Smith being saved by Pocahontas; the legend appeared only after Pocahontas's death in Smith's *Generall Historie of Virginia, New-England, and the Summer Isles* (1624).

As the Englishmen had no intention of becoming solely agriculturalists, too much effort was spent on attempting to secure food from the Indians and searching for gold. Disease took a heavy toll. Provisions spoiled, and the brackish drinking water was dangerous. The Indians became more resistant. By September 1607, half the venturers were dead.

Newport returned home and brought back settlers and provisions in

Conjectural View of Jamestown (ca. 1614). Courtesy of the Colonial Williamsburg Foundation

January 1608. Despite other relief provided by Newport from England over the next several years, conditions worsened. Early in 1608 fire swept through the fort. Rats consumed much of the food supplies. Settlers gave more attention to producing manufactures such as glass, pitch, and soap ashes in an effort to find a profitable exportable commodity than they gave to farming. The colonists continued to rely mainly for their subsistence on supplies from abroad and what they could obtain from the Indians. Smith, as president in 1608 and 1609, provided leadership, but bickering among the councilors impeded effective control. Injured in a gunpowder explosion, Smith returned to England at the end of 1609.

Two hazards most of all thwarted any successful economic development during the early years: the high mortality rate and the indolence of the settlers. Edmund Morgan, in a seminal essay addressing the labor problem at Jamestown, attempts to explain the mystery why there was so much idleness when the colonists faced starvation. He finds the answer not so much in the quality of the settlers (too many gentlemen), the disease factor, or the communal system, but rather in the work habits they brought over with them from England. There was much idleness and underemployment in sixteenth- and early seventeenth-century England. Low wages brought low productivity. Division of labor meant that people working at one task or craft would not perform work alien to their special skills. Work was spread around, even in the houses of correction. Furthermore, the Jamestown settlement resembled a military expedition, which discouraged attention to menial work.

John Smith's Map. Collections of the Virginia Historical Society

Recent historians have emphasized poor water as a major cause for the high mortality rate. The early records give ample evidence that the colonists suffered from typhoid, dysentery, and other diseases as well as saltwater poisoning. The settlers used the James for drinking water, and they also dug shallow wells, tapping the high water tables, which were also contaminated. Jamestown was located on the river where fresh and salt water met, resulting in brackish water. Conditions were worst in summertime, when the level of salt in the water was at its highest. The brackish water was ideal for the breeding of bacteria and mosquitoes. The Indians knew the benefits of scattering population, particularly during summertime, to the upper fresh streams. So did Captain John Smith. In May 1609, President Smith sent one-third of the settlers up the James and the other third below at the Nansemond River. Fifty of the 460 settlers died by October, but none at the falls or at the Nansemond, which emptied into the James. If Smith's policy had been continued, the high death rate would in large degree have been arrested.

The Jamestown settlers also suffered from malnutrition. From descriptions by early writers it appears that the colonists contracted pellagra, caused by a deficiency of niacin and protein. A good part of the time the settlers had to rely on an unsupplemented maize diet. As historian Karen Kupperman (1984) has written, the niacin in corn "is bound to indigestible constituents and is therefore not available" (p. 32). Victims of pellagra become anorexic and apathetic.

Much has been made that the Starving Time, during the winter of 1609–1610, when the population was reduced to sixty, resulted from lack of food. Actually, besides some deaths at the hands of Indians, the major factor for the mortality was that the five hundred newcomers who arrived in late summer carried with them the plague and typhus. Debilitated by disease and famine, the settlers decided to abandon Jamestown in the spring of 1610. They headed down the river, hoping that at the coast they might be picked up by a ship. But fortunately the arrival of three relief vessels, carrying 150 persons, including the newly appointed governor, along with livestock and provisions, allowed for recovery.

In 1609 the Virginia Company made a determined effort to save the colony. A new charter provided for a tighter governmental rein. One "able and absolute" governor, who would reside in the colony, was appointed. The Virginia Company was now separated from the Plymouth adventurers. The company became fully a stock company, selling shares publicly for the first time. Each share was valued at 12 pounds 10 shillings, and each person "on adventure" in Virginia was given a share. The royal council in England was disbanded, and the company, through an elected treasurer and stockholders' meetings, would govern its own affairs. Most significant, the idea of an outpost was abandoned, and the colony, emphasizing agriculture, was to be entirely self-sufficient. More effort was to be made to diversify the economy and spread out settlement.

The new governor, Thomas West (Lord De la Warr), arrived in June 1610 and immediately declared martial law. When De la Warr left for England in March 1611, the colony was put under the administration of Sir Thomas Dale, who was designated deputy governor and marshal. Dale implemented a military code set forth in the *Lawes, Divine, Morall and Martiall*, which he and William Strachey had written in England. A communal arrangement was to be strictly observed until 1616, at which time private property would be allocated. The Dale code, as the new stipulations were called, gave the settlers no choice but to work. Punishments were severe. There were twenty capital offenses, ranging from stealing a chicken to persistent nonattendance at church.

Dale sought to expand the frontiers of the colony. He knew that both for survival and for defense against the Indians the population should be distributed over a wider area. In 1611, Dale brought three hundred men up the James to what was then a peninsula but is now Farrar's Island. There he laid out the foundations for the town of Henricus. Skirmishes were fought with the Indians, who now perceived the imperial

Pocahontas. Collections of the Virginia Historical Society

threat posed by the Englishmen. The town nevertheless got a start, with fifty houses, a church, and even a hospital. A masterstroke in buying a few years of quiet in Indian relations was the kidnapping of Pocahontas, the daughter of the Indian emperor, Powhatan, in 1613. Pocahontas was sent to live on the outskirts of the new town with the Reverend Alexander Whitaker. While a hostage, Pocahontas converted to Christianity, assuming the name of Rebecca, and in 1614 she married widower John Rolfe, who had established a plantation along the northern bank of the river. Rolfe obtained the reluctant approval from the colony's authorities for the marriage. Some prominent Virginians, even as late as the end of the century, condoned miscegenation with the Indians, as evidenced by Robert Beverley's history of the colony, though the practice was to be outlawed in 1691.

Pocahontas had already been well known to the Jamestown settlers. At age 14 she accompanied her father to the village in 1610. She delighted the inhabitants by doing cartwheels. The next year she, her brother, and a party of braves delivered parched corn to the settlers, at which time she dined at the governor's house and attended church. Rolfe, Pocahontas, and their one-year-old son, Thomas, traveled to England in 1616. In London the Indian princess was a celebrity and was received by King James and Queen Anne at the Court of Saint James. On the return trip home in March 1617, Pocahontas died of a pulmonary ailment. Pocahontas deserves credit not only for helping to bring about peace with the Indians but also, by her presence in England, for stimulating financial backing for the Virginia Company and contributing to the success of the lotteries (begun in 1612) held on behalf of the Virginia venture.

Powhatan died a year after his daughter. Indian resentment grew, but not in the open. The Indians viewed English expansion as a threat to their culture and way of life. Professing peace and compliance to the English will, Powhatan's successor, Opechancanough, bided his time.

Meanwhile, the colony found a profitable export commodity. John Rolfe introduced in 1612 a strain of tobacco, grown from seed imported from Trinidad, that proved superior to that grown by the Indians. The next year he exported the new variety to England. Tobacco helped put the colony on firm ground, though it contributed to deteriorating relations with both Indians and members of the company in England. Alluvial Indian lands were expropriated for growing the crop. Despite the king's disdain for the "stinking weed," even himself having issued as early as 1604 *A Counter Blaste to Tobacco,* and the Company's insistence on the diversification of crops, Virginians concentrated on tobacco production.

In 1616 the communal system was abandoned. "Ancient" settlers were awarded one hundred acres each; newcomers were to receive fifty acres. The "headright" system was also put into effect: Anyone paying for passage to Virginia would receive fifty acres for each person transported. "Particular plantations" were also introduced, whereby organized groups could acquire large tracts, which became known as hundreds. Within four years there were fifty such plantations. Tenants were engaged to work at the hundreds and also on company lands, usually for a period of seven years.

Between 1618 and 1623 the Virginia Company sent 4,500 colonists to Virginia. The Church of England raised funds for an Indian mission in the colony—the moneys to be used chiefly for establishing a college on a 10,000-acre tract above Henricus town. There were to be three schools: one for the children of the planters, an Indian school, and a university.

The colony government now shifted away from military organization and martial law. Instructions issued in 1618 to the governor, collectively often referred to as the Great Charter, included a provision for the calling of an elected assembly. Thus the first representative assembly in America met in the "quire of the church" at Jamestown from July 30 to August 4, 1619. Governor George Yeardley presided over twenty-two burgesses, two of whom were elected from each of the colony's constituencies. Most enactments were in the form of local ordinances. Regulations were put on planting and trade. Sumptuary legislation included punishments for drunkenness, ranging from an admonition by a minister for the first offense, to the third-offense sentence of requiring the offender "to lye in boltes 12 howers in the house of the Provost Marshall and pay his fees." Gambling brought a fine and confiscation of the winnings. Each curse word cost five shillings. Taxation was according to the clothes worn to church. Attendance at Sunday worship was mandatory. The Virginia Assembly consisted of the governor and his council and the burgesses. Successively the Assembly met in November 1621, February-March 1624, and May 1625. Sanctioned by the king, it met again in March 1628 and thereafter on an annual basis.

Despite the institution of private property and a more vital form of self-government, the Jamestown colony faced difficult times. The lottery in England, which had given much needed financial support, was canceled by the king in 1621. More effort was made to introduce exotic crops and industry. Vagrants, boy and girl beggars off the streets of London, were sent over by the company. Mortality was extremely high. Dissidents appealed to the king to nullify the Virginia Company's charter (which had been reissued in 1612). The king sent over his own investigators, who returned with a negative report documenting maladministration and waste. It was recommended that the king assume control of the colony.

But it was an Indian massacre of settlers that most discredited the Virginia Company. A white-sponsored Indian revitalization movement, to make the natives Christian and "civilized," only aroused further enmity toward the colonists. Yet George Thorpe, who was in charge of the missionary work and the college, and Virginians overall simply assumed that the Indians' impressive amiability would continue—until their long-simmering resentment exploded in a bloodbath.

In early March 1622 one of the chiefs, Nemattanew, was killed by the whites, allegedly for having murdered a settler and then wearing the victim's clothing. On Good Friday, March 22, as most Virginians were sitting down to breakfast, Indian bands simultaneously descended on the communities and plantations throughout the colony. Opechancanough had long planned the atrocity. The Indians, their intentions unsuspected, gained easy access to family households. Whites were hacked to death and many were dismembered, including humanitarian George Thorpe. In all, 347 of the colony's inhabitants died. Jamestown was saved only by a timely warning from an Indian servant boy named Chaco. After the carnage, detachments of armed settlers over the next two years relentlessly hunted down Indians, wreaking vengeance in kind. The major English tactic was "feedfight"—firing and wasting crops and food supplies on several fronts. The massacre of 1622 was clear proof to critics that the Virginia Company could not ensure the safety of the colony.

At home the company was beset by factional strife, accentuated by the rivalry of a country party (favorable to Edwin Sandys and the earl of Southampton) and the court party (headed by Thomas Smythe and Robert Rich, earl of Warwick, and backed by the king). Sandys became president (treasurer) of the company in 1619. Though he served but a year, his administration, now supported by the less experienced members, sought to promote an ambitious program of diversification. A tobacco contract in 1622 worked out between the company and the king supposedly provided reciprocal benefits: The company enjoyed a monopoly on imported tobacco in England and Ireland; the raising of tobacco was prohibited in these two countries; the king received one-third of the profits from tobacco imported; the crown bore one-third of the charges in handling the imported tobacco; and Spanish tobacco, except forty thousand pounds annually, was excluded. With both sides soon discontented, the tobacco contract was terminated the following year. Sale of tobacco in England was left to individual owners or their consignees.

In November 1623 a suit of quo warranto against the Virginia Company was docketed in the Court of the King's Bench. The company had to show justification for the continuance of its charter. The court declared against the company in 1624, whereupon the rights pertaining to the administration of the Virginia colony reverted to the king. Virginia then became a royal colony, which form would last to the American Revolution. Essentially, the government inaugurated in 1619 continued, except the king now appointed the governor and council. In 1625, Sir Francis Wyatt arrived as the first royal governor. Actually, as a royal colony, Virginia faced more relaxed supervision than when under the auspices of the company, since the crown could not devote full attention to the affairs of the colony. Efforts by Charles I to renew the tobacco contract with the colony, though never materializing, were significant in furthering the development of representative government, as the king sought approval from the burgesses.

The late 1620s and 1630s were times of transition. Governors earned censure from Virginians by trying to control expansion. Governor John

Harvey was deposed in 1635, largely because of this reason, his heated temper, and his favoring Catholic Maryland in its dispute with a member of the Virginia council, William Claiborne, over jurisdiction over Kent Island in Chesapeake Bay. Harvey, however, would be sent back as governor in 1639.

Boom times, with everyone trying to cash in on the tobacco market, led to a rip-roaring society similar to that of the later American western mining frontier. By the end of the 1630s, the boom was over, and Virginians began to struggle with the regulation of tobacco production and its quality. A new breed of well-heeled immigrants began to come over at midcentury.

Expansion and stability in government were evident with the establishment of eight shires (counties) in 1634: James City, Henrico, Charles City, Elizabeth City, Warwick River, Warrasqueake, Charles River, and Accomac (on the eastern shore). By 1640, with the population at eight thousand, settlement had reached the fall line of the James. Lands had opened up along the Rappahannock and Potomac rivers. By 1660, when settlements dotted the whole of the Tidewater region, there were twenty counties with a population of 35,000.

The appointment of Sir William Berkeley as governor in 1642 signified the beginning of an era of good feelings. Berkeley allowed unfettered expansion, removed the poll tax, permitted Dutch merchants to carry tobacco from the colony, and, along with the council, refrained from interfering with any taxes voted by the burgesses.

Indian war returned when Opechancanough, using much the same stratagem as in 1622, conducted a surprise attack colonywide on April 17, 1644, costing the lives of five hundred settlers. But the Indians were defeated for good, their towns burned and crops destroyed. Opechancanough was captured and killed. By a treaty with Necotowance, Opechancanough's successor, in 1646, the Indians abandoned all land between the York and James rivers and from the falls of these rivers southward. The Virginia Indians now became tributaries. Their numbers dwindled sharply during the last half of the century; by 1700 the Powhatan tribesmen (from an estimate of nine thousand in 1607) numbered only about twelve hundred, and the entire Indian population of the colony (about eighteen thousand in 1607) was reduced to around two thousand.

An English fleet dispatched by England's new ruler, Oliver Cromwell, in 1652 forced the submission of the colony, which under Berkeley had been staunchly royalist during the English Civil War. Beyond the imposition of a commission that governed the colony for several years, Virginia suffered no punitive measures. With the collapse of the Cromwellian regime in England, Virginia recovered its full status as a royal colony, including its governor, Berkeley, who would now become more the autocrat. Berkeley was supported by the older planters against a rising new planter class, based largely in the frontier regions, that increasingly felt excluded from power and privilege.

MARYLAND

John Hammond, who wrote *Leah and Rachell, or the Two Fruitfull Sisters of Virginia and Mary-land* (1656), extolled the promise of life in the Chesapeake region:

> The Country is very full of sober, modest persons. . . . By their labours is provided corne and Tobacco. . . . Of the increase of cattle and hoggs, much advantage is made [by] shipping . . . to the Barbadoes, and other Islands. . . . By trading with Indians for Skine, Beaver, Furres and other commodities oftentimes good profits are raised.

Indeed, the whole Chesapeake area was viewed as a land of opportunity. Virginia and Maryland shared common patterns of economic, social, and cultural development. Maryland, however, by the nature of its founding and the character of immigration into the colony, would exhibit much greater political turmoil than its sister colony. The major reason for the delay in settlement of the upper Chesapeake region was that the area was controlled by the Virginia Company. Though narrowing the north and south boundaries (east-west limits were from sea to sea), the Virginia charter of 1609 still gave the Jamestown colony a leeway of two hundred miles north and south of Point Comfort, which therefore included the area that would become Maryland. Had the Jamestown colony been a going concern at the beginning of settlement, it is likely that the Virginia Company would have expanded its interests into Maryland. With the king taking over the Jamestown colony, the Virginia Company was deprived of jurisdictional rights in the New World, and the crown could dispose of the lands that had belonged to the company as it saw fit. Indeed, it would become a consistent policy of the later Stuart kings to grant lands to individuals singly or in partnership rather than to companies. One favorite of Charles I, George Calvert, who in 1625 was named baron of Baltimore, would be the successful grantee of lands lying beyond the Potomac.

Calvert, a Yorkshire gentleman, served in Parliament and in 1619 became a principal secretary of state, which office he resigned when he converted to Catholicism in 1624. Calvert purchased interest in a syndicate pledged to founding a colony in Newfoundland and in 1623 himself received from the crown a patent for the whole southeastern coast of that region. Calvert fitted out an expedition in 1628 and made an effort to found a colony, which he called Avalon. He spent the winter at Avalon, but considering the weather too cold, he abandoned the project. On his return home he visited Virginia, with a view toward planting a settlement within the bounds of that colony, but irked at his reception, he decided to apply for lands farther up the Chesapeake. He asked the king for a charter giving him permission to plant a colony in the yet unsettled northern part of the territory that had belonged to the Virginia Company.

Besides economic motives, religion influenced Baltimore's decision. English Catholics, numbering only fifty to sixty thousand, had experienced severe persecution and disabilities. Between 1588 and 1603, sixty-one priests, forty-seven laymen, and two women had been executed. Many others had been tortured. The Jesuits endured the harshest penalties. Convicted of high treason solely for their religious beliefs, certain members of the order had been hanged, drawn, and quartered. The penal laws enacted during the reign of Elizabeth forbade liberty of worship for Catholics. Recusants—Catholics who refused to give allegiance to the Church of England—were fined twenty pounds sterling a month or had two-thirds of their property confiscated for not attending Anglican worship. Catholics were barred from serving in all civil and military offices. James I had reinstated the penal laws and banished all Catholic missionaries. Charles I, who married the French princess, Henrietta Maria, relaxed the enforcement of the anti-Catholic laws. Nevertheless, Catholics, like Protestant dissenters, were uncomfortable with the condition of religious freedom in England. Baltimore hoped that his new colony would be a refuge for Catholics. But he would discover that because of the lessening of persecution of Catholics and the contentment of the Catholic landed gentry with their economic status quo, not many of his coreligionists were inclined to brave settlement in the New World.

The king accepted Baltimore's proposal, and a charter was issued on June 20, 1632. Lord Baltimore, however, had died two months before, on April 15. His son, Cecilius Calvert, the second Lord Baltimore, thus became the beneficiary of the charter.

At the time, the Maryland charter was the most extensive grant to an English subject, conferring on Calvert authority almost independent of the crown. Baltimore would have the rights of the bishop of Durham, who had governed a county at England's northern border after the Norman Conquest with near-royal powers. Calvert could grant lands, erect manors, and establish courts. Maryland would be a great fief, an *imperium in imperio*. There were several limitations, however. Though absolute lord, Baltimore had to guarantee that the rights of his subjects were the same as of citizens in England. Legislation required the advice and consent of all freemen. Furthermore, all churches should be consecrated and dedicated to English ecclesiastical laws. This was not considered an infringement on the rights of Catholics but rather a tactic to prevent Catholicism from becoming the established church.

Gaining financial support from only a few Catholic gentlemen,

Baltimore invested much of his own fortune in getting his proprietary colony started. Initially, his role was much that of a real estate agent. He published *Account of the Colony of the Lord Barron of Baltimore* (1633), hoping to attract settlers for his new domain. The location of the new colony was to be from the ocean to the "first fountain" of the Potomac and from that river to 40 degrees north latitude. What Baltimore did not know was that the river cut sharply northward, greatly limiting the size of the colony.

On November 22, 1633, the *Ark* and the *Dove*, carrying the first governor of the new colony, Leonard Calvert (brother of Lord Baltimore), and 138 passengers, set sail from Southampton, England. Aboard were two Jesuits (Andrew White and John Altham), two priests, eleven lay brothers, seventeen gentlemen-adventurers, who were mostly Catholic, and an assortment of servants, laborers, yeomen, and craftsmen, most of whom were Protestant. After a four-month voyage by way of the West Indies, the *Ark* and the *Dove* entered the Chesapeake, first anchoring at Point Comfort, Virginia, on February 24, 1634, and then several weeks later at St. Clement's (now Blakiston) Island, at the mouth of the Potomac River. Here "on the day of the Annunciation of the Most Holy Virgin," March 25, as Father White recorded the event,

> we celebrated the mass for the first time, on this island. This had never been done before in this part of the world. After we had completed the sacrifice, we took upon our shoulders a great cross, which we had hewn out of a tree, and advancing in order to the appointed place, with the assistance of the Governor and his associates and other Catholics, we erected a trophy to Christ the Saviour, humbly reciting, on our bended knees, the Litanies of the Sacred Cross with great emotion.

Soon thereafter a site for a settlement was decided upon, six miles up the St. George's River (later renamed St. Mary's River), a tributary of the Potomac. Here the local Indians, the Yaocomicos, had a village, which they agreed to surrender in return for hoes, hatchets, and other tools. The Englishmen called their new settlement St. Mary's; it would be the capital of the colony for sixty-one years. The colony was named in honor of both the Virgin and the queen, Henrietta Maria.

Since Baltimore, as proprietor, could dispose of all lands as he saw fit in accordance with the laws of England, he envisioned a scheme of mixed land tenure: manorial estates and individual small freeholds. It was expected that manorial grantees would form a class wedded to the interests of the proprietor. Until 1676, when the practice was discarded, some sixty manors were established. Manorial estates consisted of one thousand or more acres. Baltimore allotted two thousand acres to first adventurers who brought with them five men (aged sixteen to fifty). The grantee would preside over a manor, with power to hold courts leet (criminal) and baron (civil, to the amount of forty shillings); there is only slight evidence, however, that this court structure was implemented. The manorial land inducement was soon changed to two thousand acres for bringing over ten laborers, upped in 1642 to twenty settlers. Quitrents (fees owed to the proprietor) were to be paid annually on manorial estates, amounting originally to six hundred bushels of wheat and later two pounds sterling. Individuals received one hundred acres for transporting themselves, and an equal amount of land for a wife and each servant; fifty acres was allotted for each child. This headright was reduced to fifty acres overall after the first decade; in 1683 it was abolished altogether. By 1642 quitrents were fixed at two shillings per hundred acres for all holdings.

The first Maryland assembly met in February 1635, with the freemen attending in person or giving their vote by proxy. Although the records have been lost, it is known that English statutes regarding felonies were adopted. For whatever reason, however, Baltimore did not approve the legislation. The assembly next met in 1638. Laws sent over by Baltimore were rejected. The freemen claimed the right to initiate legislation. Fourteen bills were passed and sent to Baltimore, who again exercised a veto. Baltimore, however, was now convinced that his subjects were bent on enacting their own laws and therefore conceded to them the right to initiate legislation. He also gave his brother, Governor Leonard Calvert, the authority to approve or reject laws in his name. For the assembly convening in 1639, the freemen chose two burgesses from each jurisdiction. Thus Maryland had a representative democracy, with a government resembling that of Virginia and the New England colonies—a governor, a council, and elected delegates. Though the Maryland legislature was dominated by Catholics during the early years, any influence from the Jesuits was thwarted. The Jesuits themselves refused to serve in the legislature, and Baltimore, fearful that they intended to create their own separate domain, in 1641 forbade them to acquire land from the Indians or as gifts.

From the beginning, Baltimore was mindful of the need for religious harmony. His instructions to the early Catholic settlers entreated them not to engage publicly in discussions of religion. When he made William Stone, a Protestant, governor in 1648, Baltimore put into the oath of office the obligation of preventing any professing Christian from being molested because of his faith. In 1649, Baltimore sent over an "act concerning Religion," which the assembly passed into law. This famous toleration act, despite its severe penalties, was a landmark in religious liberty at the time. The act stipulated that all Christians were guaranteed "free exercise" of their religion. But on the negative side, anyone who blasphemed or denied the divinity of any member of the Trinity was to be put to death. Blasphemy against the Virgin or any of the saints was punishable by fine or whipping. Baltimore and the Maryland assembly majority were aware that the rise of Puritan influence at home and in

Maryland threatened the rights of the Catholic minority. Under Puritan domination in Maryland, the act was revoked in 1654 but restored in 1657. The spirit of the act proved more pervasive than the letter of the law. No penalties were ever meted out for blasphemy of the Virgin and the saints. Several Puritan provocateurs, however, in February 1658 saw to it that Dr. Jacob Lumbrozo, a Jew, was charged with denying the divinity of Christ. The case was dropped, and subsequently Governor Philip Calvert proclaimed a general amnesty regarding the punitive features of the Toleration Act affecting religious faith. Lumbrozo became a naturalized citizen and in 1663 sat on a jury. There were indeed to be a number of blasphemy prosecutions during the seventeenth century, but only for words uttered, and none were treated as capital offenses.

Unfortunately, during most of the seventeenth century, the Maryland proprietary witnessed insurgencies. William Claiborne, a Virginia councilor, even before the arrival of the Maryland colonists had established a trading post on Kent Island in the upper Chesapeake, claiming it within the bounds of Virginia. Despite the fact that the island fell within the limits of the Maryland grant, Claiborne refused to recognize Maryland's sovereignty. In 1635 armed conflict between Claiborne's Virginians and Marylanders left four dead. Though the crown reaffirmed Kent Island as being under the jurisdiction of Maryland, Claiborne in the mid-1640s, taking advantage of strife elsewhere, briefly regained possession of the island. During the English Civil War, Richard Ingle, championing the Parliamentary cause, raised the standard of rebellion in Maryland between 1644 and 1647, as did William Fuller in 1654. Governor Josias Fendall joined in a movement to overthrow proprietary government in 1660 and 1661 and make the lower assembly supreme, but this effort soon collapsed.

The internal dissension of early Maryland was but one indicator of the colony's fragility. Like Virginia, waterborne diseases caused a high mortality rate. By 1642 the population numbered less than four hundred. Several dozen persons were clustered at five settlements, organized as hundreds (within one county, St. Mary's): St. Michael's, St. Mary's, St. George's, St. Clement's, and Mattapany (on the Patuxent River). In 1660 the population only amounted to twenty-five hundred, and fifteen years later, thirteen thousand.

Indians proved less troublesome in Maryland than in Virginia. The Maryland natives were of Algonquian stock and widely dispersed among small tribal villages. Along the western shore, the Doegs, Mattawomans, Chopticos, and Patuxents were in a confederacy dominated by the Piscattaways. Similarly, the Nianticokes held sway over the Choptanks, Pocomokes, and Wiacomicos on the eastern shore. Except for a few minor forays by eastern shore Indians at Kent Island, the Maryland Indians were peaceful. Like the Powhatans across the Potomac, the Maryland natives either moved away (as the Yaocomicos had at the beginning of colonization) or were decimated by disease by the second half of the century. The Susquehannocks (of Iroquoian stock), located along the northern bay, with firearms provided by the Dutch and Swedes, did cause some trouble in the 1640s. Two small expeditions were mounted against them. But the Susquehannocks, too, declined in numbers and became demoralized. Only during the later expansion of the frontier did the colony contend with a formidable external Indian threat.

Tobacco became the staple crop. As in Virginia, there were boom times in the 1630s, followed by problems arising from a glutted market. The manorial system failed, owing primarily to the scarcity of labor. Servants who had completed their contracted time of service and poor immigrants refused to accept permanent feudal status on the manorial estates. Nevertheless, a powerful class of landlords emerged. Maryland in the seventeenth century was characterized by wide economic and social disparity. Many of the poor settlers moved to Virginia, the Carolinas, and even to Maryland's own western frontier. While a steady influx of indentured servants would underscore the rigidity of Maryland's class structure, eventually the freed bondsmen would swell the ranks of yeoman farmers, affording greater equilibrium to Maryland society.

3

New England

A desire for the completion of the Reformation impelled English noncon-formists to found covenanted communities in the New World. Some Prot-estants hoped that the English church could be reformed within; others wished to separate from it. In England both the church and the state increasingly pursued policies imposing uniformity, leaving little latitude for people who wished to change the ecclesiastical order and give new directions to faith and practice. Moreover, both the Puritans and the separatists who founded the New England colonies deplored the corrup-tion in church and state and disorder in English society. As John Winthrop wrote on the eve of his departure for America in 1629, "This land growes weary of her Inhabitants. . . . We are growne to that height of intemperance in all excesse of riot." All the churches of Europe "are brought to desolation," and "the fountains of learning & religion" were corrupted. Thus "a place" in America would be "a refuge for many" whom God "means to save out of the general callamatie." In the new land, the Puritans intended to construct and nourish a new church and a holy commonwealth.

In a lay sermon aboard the *Arbella* in 1630, Winthrop summed up the mission: "Wee shall be as a citty upon a hill. The eies of all people are uppon us." As historian Perry Miller has noted, taking his theme from Samuel Danforth's election sermon of May 1670, the Puritans went on an errand into the wilderness. It was an errand on behalf of Reformed Christianity, Miller (1956) observes,

> and while the first aim was indeed to realize in America the due form of government, both civil and ecclesiastical, the aim behind that aim was to vindicate the most vigorous ideal of the Reformation, so that ultimately all Europe would imitate New England. (p. 12)

The errand was an end unto itself—to seek a better quality of life and thereby witness to the world.

The Puritans had an apocalyptic sense of history; their holy experiment was the best and last hope for the world for inculcating God's will for mankind. The Pilgrims, too, shared the Puritan vision of establishing a holy community, but, of more humble condition and insecure, they preferred to work out their destiny with a sense of isolation.

PURITANS AND SEPARATISTS

Puritanism as a word appeared in the mid-1500s to designate a reform movement within the Church of England, and, in a wider connotation, the variety of Protestant dissent against any formal ecclesiastical polity, practice, or doctrine. Certain English congregations ministered communion only to worshipers who "were kept pure from popery." Under the reign of Mary I (1553–1558), some of their leaders voluntarily went into exile in Switzerland and the Rhineland. Returning after five years, these "Marian exiles" had become greater advocates of a simplified religion. The spread of Puritanism reflected a demand among the rank and file of the English people for a return to primitive Christianity, more strictly based on Scripture, and to a church more oriented to local congregations.

Puritans opposed Catholic practices retained by the Church of England, among them the donning of the surplice and the square cap, making the sign of the cross in baptism, interrogation of infants, confirmation, and reading from the Apocrypha. The Puritans also insisted on better discipline, Sabbath observance, and the prohibition of holding more than one religious office. Doctrinally, Puritans objected to the Elizabethan establishment's placing the Thirty-nine Articles and the Book of Common Prayer on the level near to that of the Scriptures, or at least not "contrary to the word of God." Many of the dissident preachers engaged in itinerant preaching or held salaried lectureships, often supported by private patronage.

While not repudiating Anglican theology, the Puritans emphasized the Scriptures as revealing God's will and salvation by faith. The preaching of William Perkins at Cambridge molded the thought of Puritan leaders.

God, Perkins intoned, offered a covenant of grace to mankind, all of whom were tainted by original sin. At the core of this covenant, dating back to Abraham, man must first have faith, then walk with God and serve Him. Though the covenant was not a contract as such (more a free gift from God rather than any bargain, which would be beneath the dignity of God), it was assumed, as Perkins noted, that "God freely promising Christ, and his benefits exacts again of man, that he would by faith receive Christ, & repent of his sins." Continually striving to live according to God's will was evidence that one had been predestined to salvation. The Puritans took to heart Romans 8:30: "Whom he did predestinate, them he also called: and whom he called, them he also justified: and whom he justified, them he also glorified." Thus in accepting God's grace, man progressed toward salvation in four stages: effectual calling; justification, whereby one is considered just in God's eyes; sanctification, witnessing a strengthening of righteousness; and glorification, a transformation after death into the image of Christ. Though Puritans were strict predestinationists, they believed that salvation was within the reach of all by virtue of the covenant of grace.

Certain factions appeared in the religious reform movement in England. The main body simply wanted to take over the church establishment, making the desired reforms. On the right were the Presbyterians, who wanted to change the polity of church government by having each congregation elect representatives to larger bodies and thence to a central body, a republican rather than a democratic solution. On the left were Brownists (separatists), Baptists, and other groups who would admit only visible saints into the church and who insisted on complete church autonomy. All of those who may generally be called Puritans stressed preaching, a learned and godly ministry, piety, and following the Bible in detail.

The English separatist movement dates from the teachings of Robert Browne, who founded the first separatist church at Norwich in 1580. The separatists not only rejected ecclesiastical authority but also regarded the Church of England as corrupt and unscriptural. True believers must separate from the state church and covenant publicly with one another to enter into the perfect church. Each church was to be autonomous, with the congregation electing all its officers—pastor, teacher, elders, deacons, and deaconesses. The Lord's Supper was the seal of union.

After the defeat of the Spanish Armada (1588), such dissenters as the separatists were considered the chief enemies of the monarchy. Though during Elizabeth's reign the growth of dissenting sects was largely ignored, there were instances of repression. Two separatists—Henry Barrow, a barrister, and John Greenwood—were hanged together at Tyburn in 1593. After Elizabeth's death there seemed to be reason for religious dissidents to be even more apprehensive. James I, on his way to London to assume the throne in January 1604, convened a gathering of the church hierarchy and representative Puritans at Hampton Court. The Puritans presented the Millennary Petition, signed by one thousand persons, expressing loyalty to the king but also listing grievances. After listening for an hour, the king rose and declared: "I will have one doctrine and one discipline, one religion in substance, and in ceremony." For those who were of a different mind, he continued, "I shall make them conform themselves, or I will harrie them out of the land, or else doe worse." Some radical Puritan groups had already fled to the Continent. For separatists who yet remained, the prospect of freedom for religious worship under James I seemed bleak—but that freedom they would have.

THE PILGRIMS AND PLYMOUTH COLONY

A separatist church of about one hundred members was founded in 1606 at Scrooby, in Nottinghamshire. John Robinson, a nonconformist graduate of Oxford, tended the flock. Except for a few members, such as William Brewster, who had attended Cambridge, and John Carver, a Yorkshire merchant, the congregation consisted mostly of tenant farmers and tradesmen. Brewster was bailiff and receiver for the manor, a property belonging to the archbishop of York. The Scrooby group held religious services in the manor house chapel. William Bradford, a seventeen-year-old orphan who was living with his uncle and grandfather, walked ten miles to attend the Sunday gatherings. Bradford had inherited a small farm. Fearing persecution (Brewster had already been arrested and fined), John Robinson and half of the congregation decided to immigrate to Holland.

In 1607 the little band settled in Amsterdam, where they worshiped with an English congregation, who called themselves the Brethren of the Separation of the First English Church. After a year and a half, the Scrooby exiles moved to the university town of Leyden, a beautiful city situated on thirty islands at the mouth of the Rhine. It would seem that the refugees had found an idyllic location in which to establish their own religious community. Twenty-one houses were built on one lot, and the group bought a house near the university for a meeting place and home of Pastor Robinson. There was plenty of work in the various trades; Bradford became a twiller of cloth made from cotton and linen. Most of the Scrooby exiles became Dutch citizens in order to join the guilds. But they were unhappy. Not unlike first generations of American immigrants at a later period, they felt like intruders in an alien society. War was about to break out in Europe, and, as Bradford recounted, it was feared that the young men would be required to be soldiers. The Dutch were also viewed as too fun-loving a people. If the Scrooby refugees stayed in

Holland, "their posteritie would be in danger to degenerate and be corrupted." The exiles now looked toward America.

After two years of negotiation, Deacon Robert Cushman in 1620 secured a patent from the London branch of the Virginia Company to settle within the limits of the Virginia colony. Not until January 1, 1624, did the separatist group receive a patent to locate in New England, a grant conferred by the Council of New England (successor to the defunct Plymouth Company, the northern counterpart of the Virginia Company). The Pilgrims never intended to reside near the Jamestown settlement, and they wanted to be as far away as possible from corrupted Englishmen and any place where the Anglican church was established. The lower Hudson River, at the northernmost limit of the southern Virginia Company's grant, would be ideal, and this appears to have been the destination. Fortunately, London merchants were willing to invest in the overseas enterprise. A joint-stock company was formed, and seven thousand pounds, at ten pounds a share, was raised from seventy adventurers. Furthermore, each colonist over sixteen years old received a share. Similar to the Virginia colony experiment of 1609–1616, all property and profits would be held in common for seven years, after which time private property would be allowed and dividends paid.

In July 1620, Bradford and about 30 of the Leyden congregation of 238 boarded the *Speedwell* at Delft Haven, Holland, for a journey to Southampton, England, the rendezvous for those going on the voyage to America. As Bradford was to write:

> So they lefte the goodly and pleasante citie, which had been their resting place near 12 years; but they knew they were pilgrimes, and looked not much on those things, but lift[ed] their eyes to the heavens, their dearest c[o]untrie, and quieted their spirits.

Though the separatists who emigrated never called themselves pilgrims, they were, in the Christian sense, wayfarers in the world.

The *Speedwell*, "leaking and open as a sieve," had to be abandoned in England, and all persons scheduled to go on the expedition to the New World had to board the *Mayflower*, a 180-ton high-pooped vessel. For the journey there were 102 persons, of whom only 41 were Pilgrims (17 men, 10 women, 14 children); the rest were crew, servants, and "strangers," among whom was Miles Standish, a short, stocky, redheaded former soldier. The Standishes in England had been traditionally Catholic, and it is of note that Miles Standish, who would become the military leader of the colony, never joined the Pilgrim church. After 65 days of stormy and rough seas (having set out from Plymouth, England, on September 16), the *Mayflower* reached Cape Cod on November 19; then, after spending a half a day sailing down the peninsula, "they fell amongst deangerous shoulds and roring breakers, and they were so farr intangled ther with as they conceived them selves in great danger"; therefore, "they resolved to bear up againe for the Cape." On November 21 the Pilgrims went ashore at the tip of the cape at what is now Provincetown.

Just before debarking, the Pilgrims drew up the Mayflower Compact, signed by all the adult males over twenty-one years old, with the exception of two sailors and four servants. Given the lack of a charter or any governmental sanction from the English government, the document is significant in that it established a political corporation ("civil Body Politick") and made provision for future legislative enactment "as shall be thought most meet and convenient for the general Good of the Colony." John Carver, age fifty-four, was elected the first governor.

A month was spent in exploration. There were few Indians. A dreaded plague (probably smallpox) had all but wiped out the natives on the peninsula and in the immediate northern coastal area. On occasion, however, the Pilgrims did meet a few "lusty" Indians, who let their arrows fly at the direction of the Englishmen. On December 21 the *Mayflower* anchored at Plymouth harbor, and here it was decided to build the colony. A clearing was made from the beach to a hill. Eighteen house lots (eight feet wide and twenty-four feet deep) were laid out on one side of a street, with open fields on the other side. During the brutal winter, with disease rampant, nearly one-half of the company died. But hopes were revived in March 1621. Massasoit, a sachem of the Wampanoags to the south, arrived and agreed to peaceful relations. To the marvel of the Pilgrims, two English-speaking Indians, Samoset and Squanto, also appeared. Squanto showed the settlers how to plant corn, how to fertilize it with herring, and how to tap maple trees for sap. Squanto, a Patuxet tribesman, had a most interesting story. He had been to Europe twice: First he traveled with George Weymouth to England in 1605 and returned with Captain John Smith in 1614. He was then taken captive by Captain Thomas Hunt and sold into slavery in Spain, where he was befriended by friars; making his way to England, he lived several years with John Slanie, treasurer of the Newfoundland Company, who sent him back to the New World. To the Pilgrims, to find a cockney-speaking Indian in the wilderness eager to aid them was indeed an act of Providence. From the Indians the Pilgrims also learned how to trap animals and fish. The summer's corn crop was adequate. After the harvest, wrote Edward Winslow in a letter published in *Mourt's Relation* (1622), the Pilgrims held a thanksgiving feast. Winslow gave the only eyewitness description of the event:

> Our harvest being gotten in, our governor sent four men on fowling, that so we might after a special manner rejoice together after we had gathered the fruit of our labors. They four in one day killed as much fowl as, with a little help beside, served the company almost a week. At which time, amongst

Reconstructed village of Plimoth. Courtesy of Plimoth Plantation Inc.

other recreations, we exercised our arms, many of the Indians coming amongst us, and among the rest their greatest king Massasoit, with some ninety men, whom for three days we entertained and feasted, and they went out and killed five deer, which they brought to the plantation and bestowed on our governor, and upon the captain and others.

During the 1620s the Pilgrims built their community with little care of the outside world. The only threats to the colony were those of newly arrived Englishmen settling to the north of the town and an alleged hostile plot of Massachusetts Indians and their allies. Thomas Weston brought over an unruly group from England and established Wessaguset (Weymouth). These settlers soon fell on hard times and apparently treated the Indians unfairly. Wituwamat, a Massachusetts brave, planned to annihilate the settlement and possibly to attack Plymouth town as well. Miles Standish led an armed band to Wessaguset, at a time when Wituwamat and other Indians were there. Standish put to the sword Wituwamat and several of his companions and hanged Wituwamat's eighteen-year-old brother. This was enough to deter any Indian attack, if even one was really intended. In 1625, Captain Wollaston and a group settled near present Quincy, Massachusetts. Thomas Morton assumed the leadership at this trading post and called it Mare Mount (Merrymount). A maypole was erected at the site, and the Pilgrims were shocked at the reports of unchecked ribaldry:

Drinking and dancing aboute it many days togeather, inviting the Indean women, for their consorts, dancing and frisking togither, (like so many fairies, or furies rather,) and worse practises. As if they had anew revived and celebrated the feasts of the Roman Goddes Flora, or the beastly practieses of the madd Bacchinalians.

Morton, the "lord of misrule," and his ne'er-do-wells sold firearms to the Indians and interfered with the Plymouth trade. In June 1628, Miles Standish, or "Captain Shrimpe," as Morton called him, broke up the settlement and sent Morton back to England. Morton would return and face even stiffer punishment from the Massachusetts Bay colony authorities.

There were also economic problems. With a food shortage in 1623 and with persons seeming to have slight motivation to work, the communitarian arrangement was dissolved, and private plots of land were assigned to the "oldcomers." The Pilgrims also accused the London adventurers of cheating them. Finally, in 1627 the Pilgrims came to terms with the London subscribers, who gave up all rights pertaining to the colony for eighteen hundred pounds, payable in 200-pound installments. Bradford and other leaders then assumed responsibility for payment of the debt, for which they secured a monopoly of the fur trade and fisheries. The debt, however, was not completely discharged until 1645.

The Plymouth group had initially been bound together by three contracts: religious (the Scrooby church covenant), political (Mayflower Compact), and business (contract with the London merchants). For government, the Plymouth colonists followed the form of a trading corporation. During its history (1620–1691), Plymouth colony had no charter from the English government or other grounds for legal existence. Upon the death of John Carver in 1621, William Bradford became governor and served intermittently until his own death in 1657. The governor and a board of assistants (only one at first, eight assistants by 1633) formed the General Court. The colony quickly expanded southward and westward (by 1691 there were twenty-one organized communities). Beginning in 1638, two deputies from each town joined the General Court, which functioned in a legislative, executive, and judicial capacity. An annual court of election was held to select the governor and assistants. There was no statutory requirement for the freemanship before 1656. A county system was adopted in 1685.

Because the settlers were poor and without capital, the Pilgrim colony pursued essentially a subsistence agricultural and fishing economy. Fur-trading endeavors met with slight success because of competition from English and foreign neighbors. Lacking the confidence of the Puritans at the Massachusetts Bay colony, the Pilgrims pursued no ambitious goals. But to their immense credit, they allowed a much greater diversity and liberality in affairs of state and church than their Puritan counterparts.

MASSACHUSETTS BAY COLONY

Efforts at colonization by the Plymouth Company (the group within the Virginia Company permitted to settle between 38 and 45 degrees) met with little success. Merchants from Bristol, Exeter, and Plymouth sponsored four expeditions between 1606 and 1608. Only the last, headed by George Popham and Raleigh Gilbert, resulted in an attempt to found a colony on the Sagadahoc River in Maine; after a year, however, the settlers returned to England. The failures led to the disruption of the Plymouth Company. It was re-formed in 1620 as the Council of New England under a new charter, which conferred rights to settle all territory between 40 and 48 degrees, from sea to sea. In 1622 the Council of New England bestowed on John Mason and Sir Ferdinando Gorges all land between the Merrimack and Kennebec rivers; in 1629 the grant was divided, with Gorges receiving the area north of the Piscataqua River and Mason that to the south. No settlement under this arrangement, however, began until the 1630s.

Meanwhile, other companies were chartered for the purpose of colonization along the New England coast. In 1623 the Dorchester Company of Adventurers established a fishing station at Cape Anne; the post was soon abandoned, and the company went bankrupt in 1626. A few settlers stayed behind. Under the auspices of the New England Company, John Endecott and others in 1628 founded a settlement, Naumkeag, also along Cape Anne. The next year the New England Company was reconstituted as the Massachusetts Bay Company, modeled after the earlier Virginia Company. The Massachusetts Bay Company received a charter from the king. The crown conferred on the company title to land approximately between the Charles and Merrimack rivers from sea to sea, which patent rights encroached on the Mason grant by the Council of New England. A governor and board of directors (assistants) could administer the affairs of the colony, provided that laws and ordinances did not conflict with those in England. Of the twenty-six members of the company, some were unhappy with staying in England. As the charter specified no location for the meeting of the government of the company, twelve members convinced the others that the charter should be taken to America. This was intended both to prevent non-Puritans who might later become shareholders from gaining control of the company and to ensure Puritan control in America of the new colony. Thus the Cambridge Agreement was signed on August 26, 1629, whereby the twelve more militant Puritans agreed to emigrate to America on condition that they carry the charter with them and that the government of the company be conducted in the New World. The prospective colonists consented to assume most of the financial burden of the company. Those who stayed behind became passive shareholders.

Under the new arrangement, John Winthrop led an expedition to

John Winthrop. Courtesy of the Massachusetts Historical Society

New England. Winthrop, a lawyer and Suffolk squire, had in 1618 succeeded his father, Adam, a self-made businessman and country gentleman, as lord of Groton Manor. Winthrop served as a justice of the peace and in 1627 was appointed attorney at the Court of Wards and Liveries. He had several motives for wanting to go to America. The crackdown by Archbishop William Laud on religious dissent had already resulted in several of his friends being imprisoned. Winthrop lost his position at the

Court of Wards and Liveries, and heavily in debt, he found it difficult to provide for his large family. Yet the religious motive was paramount as there would not be much opportunity to acquire immediate wealth in America. Other country gentlemen and merchants coming to America with Winthrop, however, ensured adequate financial means for the success of a colony—an advantage that the Pilgrims had lacked.

In April 1630 the *Arbella*, a 350-ton ship, and eleven other vessels sailed from Southampton with 700 persons, 240 cows, and 60 horses. Two more ships put out from Plymouth and Bristol. By the end of 1630, seventeen ships had reached Massachusetts Bay. Despite the ample resources, though few supplies were obtained from the Indians, two hundred persons died the first winter, owing largely to scurvy and typhus. A relief ship arrived in February, bringing provisions, including lemon juice, which put an end to the scurvy. Boston, Medford, Watertown, Dorchester, Roxbury, and Lynn were founded. Naumkeag, renamed Salem, also became part of the colony. The large number of Puritans coming to New England during the 1630s and 1640s (known as the Great Migration) spurred further expansion. By 1643 the colony contained twenty towns and sixteen thousand people. The town planting detracted from the trading company identity. Another divergence from the commercial corporation idea was the encouragement of private and individual trade. Furthermore, new freemen (thirteen hundred by 1641) were brought into the political body on the basis of church membership rather than by virtue of holding a share in the company. An oath to the Massachusetts government—not to king—was also required for the franchise. Similar to Plymouth, a governor (and deputy governor) and a board of assistants governed the colony initially. The expansion of the colony, however, soon necessitated a more federal type of government. In 1632, Rev. George Phillips and Elder Richard Brown led a tax revolt in Watertown, protesting a new tax intended to be applied for the erecting of fortifications. The malcontents claimed that the assistants were not truly representative of the people. As a result of the controversy, two deputies from each town now met with the assistants. The General Court followed the example of Plymouth. Counties, however, were established earlier in Massachusetts (1636), eventually leading to the assistants, when functioning as a court, having only appellate jurisdiction.

A heated judicial dispute of the early 1640s resulted in a bicameral legislature. So disruptive was the controversy that the assistants were pitted against the deputies. It all began when the wife of Goodman Richard Sherman accused Robert Keane, one of Boston's most powerful and wealthiest citizens, of slaughtering a cow belonging to her. Not only did Mrs. Sherman fail in her suit, but she also lost a defamation judgment. With litigation renewed and reaching the General Court, the majority of the deputies sided with Mrs. Sherman, while the assistants favored Keane.

The first Town House, Boston, on site of present Old State House, head of King Street. Courtesy of the Boston Society/Old State House, Boston, Massachusetts

John Winthrop, who supported Keane, argued that the assistants should have the power to vote down any enactment or decision by the deputies; otherwise, there would be no mixed government. "A Democratie," he said, "is among most Civill nations, accounted the meanest and worst of all formes of Government." At a special General Court in March 1644, a compromise was accepted: The deputies would withdraw and form a separate house, but the assistants would serve as the upper house of the legislature.

Contributing further to the transformation from company to political corporation, the General Court issued the so-called Body of Liberties in 1641, expanded and published as *The Book of the General Lawes and Libertyes Concerning the Inhabitants of the Massachusets* in 1648. This code drew from English local, common, and statute law and criminal provisions in the Old Testament.

Unquestionably, the Puritan founders of the Massachusetts Bay colony intended to create a holy community unfettered by any interference from English authorities. The crown, however, was aware of the colony's separatism. Acting on a suit of quo warranto (aimed at vacating the Massachusetts Bay Company charter) brought by Archbishop Laud and the Commission for Regulating Plantations (of the Privy Council), the Court of King's Bench in 1637 ordered the Massachusetts Bay Company to return its charter to the king. Charles I announced that he was assuming control of all New England and appointed Sir Ferdinando Gorges governor general of the whole territory. But there were drawbacks to making good this claim, since the court's decision was weak, the company's officials had not been summoned, and the royal treasury lacked revenue to support a Gorges administration. The seventy-year-old Gorges nevertheless attempted to come to New England, but his ship broke up at launching. No further effort was made to consolidate the New England colonies directly under the crown until the 1680s. Interestingly, though, the Massachusetts authorities, fearing some intervention, fortified Castle Island at the entrance to Boston harbor, trained militia, and collected arms. In 1637 a ship not clearing at Castle Island was fired on and a passenger was killed. John Endecott at Salem refused to fly the British standard with its cross of St. George. Cutting out the offending symbol, he then allowed hoisting the emblem with the hole in the middle. Surely, Winthrop and associates would not have dared to make a bid for independence in the face of an armed force sent by the king. But the defiance of royal authority was evident throughout the period when the colony was under Puritan rule. Massachusetts laws omitted any references to the king. With the unsettled conditions in England during the era of the Civil War (1640s and 1650s), the colony could afford to go its own way.

Though the government and the church were separate in Massachusetts, they shared the common mission of maintaining a godly commonwealth, which inevitably brought forth opposition. One dissident, Robert Child, who advocated a presbyterian system for the church, penned the *Remonstrance* in 1646, which criticized the disenfranchisement of non–church members, the veto power of the assistants, and the church polity. For his protest Child was fined and deported to England. Other dissidents ruffled the Puritan regime and, cut off from the community, sought a refuge of liberty along the wilderness frontier.

EXILE SETTLEMENTS: RHODE ISLAND AND NEW HAMPSHIRE

Although John Winthrop would always have a liking for the amiable Puritan preacher who arrived in Boston in February 1631, he and other magistrates quickly discerned that views expressed by Roger Williams threatened the established authority. By winning annual awards as a student, Williams, poor son of a merchant tailor, had been able to matriculate at the Charterhouse School and Cambridge. After receiving his baccalaureate degree, he became a nonconforming minister. In 1629 he accepted a post as chaplain to Sir William Masham, soon thereafter answering a "New England call." With his wife, Mary Barnard, formerly a maid, Williams expected to reside in Boston. He refused, however, to serve as teacher at the first church in Boston because the congregation was too "unseparated" (members had not renounced the Anglican communion, which allowed participation by the unregenerate). After briefly assisting at the Salem church, Williams went to Plymouth, where he caused resentment by claiming that the colony did not have a valid land patent and by criticizing certain members of the church for having attended Anglican services during visits to England. Though not forced out of Plymouth, Williams returned to Salem, where he became an unofficial assistant to the pastor.

Williams now ranged more freely with his grievances. The Massachusetts colony, he pointed out, had no right to its lands, and indeed there was no right to establish government under the company charter. Furthermore, the state should not punish anyone for violation of the First Table of the Ten Commandments (Sabbath breaking, idolatry, blasphemy, and heresy), except in cases involving disturbance of the peace. Williams believed the New Testament superseded the Old. Because the New Testament makes no mention of coercion against conscience, Williams contended that civil government had no authority in religious matters. He considered rendering an oath an act of worship and prayer, and hence it was a "profanation" to require unregenerate persons to swear allegiance to the colony.

Examined several times by the General Court, in January 1636, Williams was sentenced to be deported to England. Pleading illness, he won a stay, whereupon he and his pregnant wife fled to the Narragansett Indian country. Fortunately, Williams had already made a treaty with this tribe and the Wampanoags for setting up Indian missions. After spending the winter with the Indians, Williams, now joined by others, moved to the peninsula in upper Narragansett Bay. On land purchased from the Indians, the refugees in June founded the town of Providence.

Providence became a receptacle for persons of all religious faiths, including Baptists, Quakers, and Spanish and Portuguese Jews. Williams himself was briefly a Baptist and then, finally, a Seeker, which sect believed in no institutional church. Whatever may be said of Williams, he eloquently appealed for freedom of conscience. In London in 1644 he published *The Bloudy Tenent, of Persecution, for Cause of Conscience*, which rebutted John Cotton's *Keyes of the Kingdom of Heaven*, a defense of church and state in Massachusetts. Until Cotton's death in 1652 the two men conducted a running debate. In *The Bloody Tenent Yet More Bloody* (1652), Williams touches a theme similar to that of his famed English contemporary, John Milton. "It is humane and Christian Wisdom," said Williams, "to listen to a serious Alarm against a Common Enemy: Prove the Alarm false, it may be but troublesome: Prove it true, it may be Destruction to have despised it." Williams's own best testament, perhaps, is seen in a comment made in 1662, in the context of advising his neighbors concerning the division of lands:

> I have one only motion and petition, which I earnestly pray the town to lay to heart. . . . It is this, that after you have got over the black brook of some soul bondage yourselves, you tear not down the bridge after you, by leaving no small pittance for distressed souls that may come after you.

Though historians, such as Perry Miller, James Ernst, and Samuel Brock-unier have argued that Williams had a broad vision of social democracy, other writers, such as Alan Simpson, regard Williams's principles to be solely expressive of the Christian experience.

One who challenged the Massachusetts authorities more introspectively but yet aimed at the marrow of Puritan doctrine was Anne Hutchinson. Mrs. Hutchinson, whose friends included Henry Vane (governor in 1636 and himself to become an exile), held weekly sessions in her home for the purpose of evaluating Sunday sermons. She also had the annoying habit of distinguishing in public persons whom she regarded as "sealed" with the covenant of grace from those simply under a covenant of works. Moreover, she asserted that God, through the Holy Spirit, spoke to her inwardly—thus challenging the Puritan view that God at this time in history revealed himself only through the Scriptures.

Considered an antinomian (one who, justified by faith, had no need for scriptural or moral law), Anne Hutchinson was charged with "traducing the ministry" and more especially with breaking the Fifth Commandment, which, as John Winthrop declared, "commands us to honour Father and Mother, which includes all in authority." At her trial in 1637 before the assistants and deputies, acting in a judicial capacity, she was asked how she knew that she was moved by the Holy Spirit. Anne replied: "How did Abraham know that it was God that bid him offer his son, being a breach of the Sixth Commandment?" Governor Thomas Dudley responded, "By an immediate voice." To which Anne retorted: "So to me by an immediate revelation!" Mrs. Hutchinson was found guilty by all the General Court save three, one of whom abstained. She and her brother-in-law, Rev. John Wheelwright, convicted separately for uttering sedition and contempt in his sermons, were sentenced to banishment; seventy-five of their followers were disenfranchised.

In spring 1638, Anne Hutchinson, with her husband and children, trekked to Rhode Island. The Hutchinsons purchased land from the Indians on Aquidneck Island and founded Pocasset (Portsmouth). When her husband died in 1642, Anne and the six youngest children moved to Long Island; in late summer the next year she and five of her children were killed by Indians.

John Wheelwright journeyed to the headwaters of the Piscataqua River, where he founded Exeter. In 1639 thirty-five settlers there entered into an agreement for self-government similar to the Mayflower Compact. By 1643, however, Massachusetts had extended its jurisdiction over Exeter and its three neighboring towns (Portsmouth, Dover, and Hampton). Since the proprietor of the area, John Mason, had died in 1635, Massachusetts considered that his title to the New Hampshire lands was vacated. In 1680 the crown separated New Hampshire from Massachusetts and made it a royal colony.

More refugees came to Rhode Island. William Coddington, who had joined the Hutchinsons at Portsmouth, founded Newport in 1639. Four years later Samuel Gorton established Warwick. Gorton, a non-Trinitarian, had suffered extremely at the hands of the Puritan authorities, being long kept in chains and even under a conditional sentence of death.

Newport and Portsmouth federated in March 1640, establishing a General Court, consisting of a governor, deputy governor, and four assistants. Largely from fear of future aggression from the Puritan colonies, Roger Williams went to England to secure a charter. In place of the king, who had fled, Parliament issued "a free Charter of civil incorporation and government" to the colony, "to be known by the name of the Incorporation of Providence Plantations on the Narragansett Bay in New England" (March 1644). The colonists were given "full power and authority to rule themselves." Thus the inhabitants of Rhode Island received the first free charter for a colony granted by the English government. In 1647 the freemen of the four towns—Newport, Providence, Portsmouth, and Warwick—met to accept the charter and to bind themselves into a colony government. The General Court consisted of a president and four assistants from each town. Freedom of conscience was guaranteed, and the towns had the right to legislative referendums and initiatives. The charter was reconfirmed by Charles II in July 1663, whereupon the name of the colony was changed to Rhode Island.

CONNECTICUT AND NEW HAVEN

As early as 1633 the fertile Connecticut River valley attracted settlers. Dutch traders had a post, Fort Good Hope (at present Hartford), until driven off by Plymouth traders. Beginning in 1635 whole or partial congregations from Watertown, Roxbury, Dorchester, and Newton (Cambridge) moved into the valley. The three new river towns of Windsor, Wethersfield, and Hartford joined in 1637 to form a colony, establishing a General Court, and two years later entered into a formal written constitution, the Fundamental Orders of Connecticut. The preamble of the document stated that the people covenanted among themselves in order "to assotiate and conjoyne our selves to be as one Publike or Commonwealth," to maintain "liberty and purity of the gospell," and to exact discipline in church and civil affairs. Eleven "fundamentals" provided for the usual form of New England government, though the franchise would be limited simply to "admitted inhabitants." Agawam (Springfield), founded by William Pynchon in 1636, elected to stay within the jurisdiction of Massachusetts. By 1662 there were fifteen towns in the Connecticut colony.

Although Connecticut shared Massachusetts's goal of creating a Puritan commonwealth, it had a broader theoretical base. Thomas Hooker, the colony's early political and religious leader, in the second election sermon (May 1638) made light of any special claim of persons being called to the magistry; rather, "the foundation of authority" derived from "the free consent of the people. . . . By a free choice the hearts of the people will be more enlarged to the love of the person and more ready to yield obedience." Hooker, in his *Survey of the Summe of Church Discipline* (1648) and letters to John Winthrop, reinforced his views on popular sovereignty, though it must be kept in mind that he was primarily concerned with religious rather than political polity.

In 1662, Governor John Winthrop, Jr., secured for the colony a royal charter that confirmed its autonomy and, like Rhode Island's charter, required only that laws not be contradictory to those in England. The colony's southern boundary was Long Island Sound, thus allowing for the annexation of the New Haven colony.

Though the shortest-lived of the New England colonies, the New Haven colony was formed on an ambitious scale. John Davenport, who had been vicar of St. Stephen's Church in London, along with Theophilus Eaton, a merchant, led a group to Boston in 1637, expecting to form a settlement within the Massachusetts Bay colony. But arriving at a time of internal dissension in the Massachusetts colony and wanting to establish an independent community in which they could develop their own commercial enterprise, the Davenport-Eaton company moved to Long Island Sound, at the mouth of the Quinnipiac River, where they founded the town of New Haven. A plantation covenant served the needs of the some seventy freemen for a while; in June 1639, however, it was decided to adopt John Cotton's *Moses His Judicialls* as the basis for colony government, thereby having provision for a governor, deputy governor, assistants, and deputies from the town and also a legal system reflecting the Mosiac code.

New settlers from the north aided in the expansion of New Haven. In October 1643 representatives from Guilford, Milford, and Stamford joined those from New Haven to extend New Haven's government into a federated system. Fairfield, Medford, Branford, and Greenwich also came under the jurisdiction of the colony, as did several towns on Long Island.

Some New Haven inhabitants crossed the Hudson to found villages in New Jersey. The colony, envisioning a future in oceanic commerce and the carrying trade, engaged in shipbuilding in New Haven and on Long Island. An effort to build a trading colony at the junction of the Delaware and Schuylkill rivers came to naught because of intervention by both the Swedes on the Delaware and the Dutch of New Netherland. Still there were great plans for commerce. Some New Haven residents became citizens of New Netherland in order to enhance trade connections. But misfortune plagued the colony. Agents sent to England failed to obtain either patent rights or a charter from the English government. Attempts at industry, such as an ironworks, did not succeed. The colony never fully recovered from the loss of its great ship (the "phantom ship") during an ocean crossing in 1646; it was laden down with furs and other precious commodities and carried several of the colony's leaders. The colony evidently gave refuge to two regicides (judges who had condemned Charles I to beheading and were not amnestied by Charles II). Understandably, the new king had no desire to favor New Haven, and it was of little surprise when he included New Haven in the Connecticut charter (1662).

CONFEDERATION OF THE PURITAN COLONIES

In the New World, Puritan leaders learned that their godly communities could not always function with harmony and splendid isolation. There were threats, internal and external. Non-Puritans came into the New England communities. Nearby Dutch and French settlers and the Indians threatened security. As the colonies rapidly expanded, an Indian menace, once negligible, became a major problem.

New Englanders had their first Indian war in 1637. After the murder of John Oldham of Plymouth and several seamen on Block Island, John Endecott, with ninety men from Massachusetts, raided the island, killing fourteen Indians and burning houses and fields. The Pequots, who lived along the mouth of the Connecticut River, retaliated by attacking the fort at Saybrook and other settlements upriver. John Mason and John Underhill, with a Connecticut and Massachusetts force, destroyed a stronghold of the Indians, killing five hundred of them. The Pequots not at the scene of this carnage were later captured and reduced to the status of mission Indians. Under the dispensation of the gospel by Rev. John Eliot and others they became known as the "praying Indians." The Pequot War brought to the Puritans a sobering realization of the potentiality of other Indian conflict.

The four Puritan colonies sought to institutionalize cooperation in the form of a confederation. Two representatives from each of the magistrates of the colonies of Plymouth, Massachusetts, Connecticut, and

New Haven, meeting in Boston in May 1643, agreed to create an intercolonial agency for the common goals of the member colonies and adopted "Articles of Confederation." The preamble of the Articles gave reasons for confederating.

> Whereas we all came into these parts of America with one and the same end and aim, namely, to advance the Kingdom of our Lord Jesus Christ and to enjoy the liberties of the Gospel in purity with peace; and whereas . . . we are further dispersed . . . and whereas we live encompassed with people of several nations and strange languages which hereafter may prove injurious to us or our posterity. And forasmuch as the natives have formerly committed sundry insolence and outrages upon several Plantations . . . and seeing by reason of those sad distractions in England . . . and by which they know we are hindered from that humble way of seeking advice, or reaping those comfortable fruits of protection. . . . We therefore do conceive it our bounden duty, without delay to enter into a present Consociation amongst ourselves, for mutual help and strength in all our future concernments: That, as in nation and religion, so in other respects, we be and continue one.

The style of the union was to be the "United Colonies of New England." Rhode Island, of course, was not invited; that colony was considered anarchical, and "Mrs. Hutchinson and those of Aquiday island broached new heresies every year."

The confederation was to be "a firm and perpetual league of friendship and amity for offence and defence, mutual advice and succor upon all just occasions both for preserving and propagating the truth and liberties of the Gospel and for their own mutual safety and welfare." The eight commissioners of the United Colonies met annually and also, during crises, in extraordinary sessions. In September 1643 they held their initial meeting.

During its first decade the confederation exercised important authority, more freely than would have been otherwise were it not for the "sad distractions" in England. The major accomplishment was the signing with Peter Stuyvesant of the Treaty of Hartford (1650), which set a line of demarcation between New England and New Netherland. The first Anglo-Dutch War (1652–1654), however, proved to be a stumbling block for the confederation. Three of the four colonies (six commissioners), the requisite number for declaring offensive war, voted to attack New Netherland. Massachusetts, the largest member of the confederation by far, steadfastly balked at this decision, claiming that final authority in such matters rested with the General Courts. As a result, the confederation did not enter the war. But the covenant of the confederation was breached, and thereafter the United Colonies of New England had minimal effectiveness. Throughout the 1650s and 1660s its main role was to dispense farm tools sent over by the Society for the Propagation of the Gospel (in England) to the Indians and to supervise the Indian mission work. In

1672, with New Haven having been absorbed by Connecticut, the three remaining Puritan colonies ratified a new set of Articles of Confederation that this time recognized the ultimate authority of the General Courts.

The confederation, nevertheless, had one more important role—the conduct of war during the Indian uprising of 1675. King Philip's War began with an attack by Wampanoags on the Plymouth town of Swansey, June 23 and 24, 1675. These Indians, particularly their leader, whom the colonists had dubbed "King Philip," had chafed under the stringent regulations placed on them by Plymouth colony. They had been ordered to disarm and to recognize dependence on the Plymouth authorities. The colony also sold lands that belonged by treaty to the Indians. The war spread to the Indians of western Connecticut and Massachusetts, resulting in a heavy toll in lives and destruction among the English settlers. The commissioners of the United Colonies put two "confederate" armies in the field, one for the western frontier and the other for the Plymouth–Rhode Island sector. King Philip, who himself had little to do with the general Indian uprising, was killed. The western Indians were defeated. One of the tragedies was the almost complete annihilation of the Narragansett Indians, who regarded themselves as neutral, though not by the English. Governor Josiah Winslow of Plymouth, with a large force, surprised the Narragansetts at their island fort, unprotected by a frozen swamp, at the Great Swamp Fight, December 20, 1675.

Meetings of the commissioners of the United Colonies ceased when Massachusetts lost its charter in 1684. As to be expected, the confederation was inoperative during the period of the Dominion of New England, when the crown attempted a consolidation of the northern colonies under royal administration. With the downfall of the Dominion of New England, the confederation was briefly revived, holding one last session in September 1689. The incorporation of Plymouth into the Massachusetts colony under the charter of 1691 left little need for the continuance of the confederation. Yet the half century of experimentation in intercolonial union served as a precedent (of admittedly debatable instructiveness) for future ideas of cooperation among the colonies.

4

The Completion of Colonization

The colonies received scant attention from England during its Civil War (1642–1649). Except for the passage of the Navigation Acts, the English government under the Commonwealth (1649–1653) and the Protectorate (1653–1660) offered few initiatives affecting the relationship between the colonies and the mother country.

The restoration of the monarchy in 1660, however, marked a new era in English colonization of North America. The British government now sought to consolidate gains in the New World, fill vacant territory between the French and Spanish possessions, imperialize colonial administration, afford further protection against foreign commercial competition, and achieve a greater mercantilist advantage for Englishmen in the realm by exploiting the economic resources of the colonies.

All the mainland English colonies, except New Hampshire, established during the remainder of the seventeenth century—New York (from the conquest of New Netherland), New Jersey, the Carolinas, and Pennsylvania (including Delaware)—were proprietary. Though a clear and assertive program was lacking, the process of royalization eventually succeeded happenstance among the new proprietaries (except Pennsylvania), aided by internal conflict in the colonies and the neglect of the proprietors themselves. Uniquely, Georgia, the last colony to be founded, underwent a brief trusteeship before becoming a royal province. The post-1660 colonies contrasted with those of an earlier time in that they were more heterogeneous in population.

NEW NETHERLAND AND NEW YORK

As if a precursor of events to come, it was an English navigator, Henry Hudson, who opened the way for Dutch colonization in North America. Under the sponsorship of the Dutch East India Company, Hudson took the *Halve Maen* ("Half Moon"), a little sixty-ton ship with an eighteen-man crew, on a search for the northwest passage. After cruising the coast from Cape Cod to Delaware Bay, he sailed up the Hudson (North) River. Recrossing the Atlantic, Hudson stopped off at England, where he and his ship were prevented from returning to Holland. The next year Hudson sailed for the English and disappeared from history when a mutinous crew set him adrift in Hudson Bay. The New Netherland Company, lasting from 1614 to 1618, sent out several expeditions to the Hudson River country. Hendrick Christiaensen supposedly erected a post (Fort Nassau) at the present site of Albany.

In June 1621 the Dutch States General granted a charter to the West India Company. This joint-stock company, with the States General a major subscriber, held exclusive rights for trade in the New World and parts of Africa and Australia. The prime goal of the Dutch West India Company was to create a colonial commercial empire rivaling that of Spain. In May 1624 thirty families, mostly Walloons (French-speaking refugees from southern Netherlands), began a settlement on Manhattan Island. A year or so later Peter Minuit, the company's first resident director general in America, purchased the island from the Indians for goods worth sixty guilders.

To promote colonization, the West India Company offered a patroonship (a land grant of four leagues along the coast or a river or two leagues on both sides of a river) to anyone who would bring more than fifty persons over age fifteen within a three-year period. A patroon was to have judicial and limited tax authority over settlers on his domain. Free persons and also indentured servants were to work the farms (*bouweries*) outside the town site (New Amsterdam). In 1639 two hundred acres were allowed per head of family. Of several conferred, the only patroonship to meet with partial success was that of Kiliaen Van Rensselaer, formerly a diamond merchant.

New Netherland expanded into Long Island and along the Hudson and Delaware (South) rivers. For a while the Dutch had to contend with the Swedish colony on the Delaware. In 1638 the New Sweden Company, employing chiefly Swedish and Finnish peasants, established Fort Christina

(Wilmington), the first permanent European settlement in the Delaware valley. New Sweden's limits extended to the falls at Trenton. As governor, Johan Printz, called "Big Tub" because of his massive weight of four hundred pounds, ruled New Sweden dictatorially from 1643 to 1653. His successor, Johan Rising, drove the Dutch from Fort Casimir on the Delaware in 1654; the Dutch, however, the next year, with seven ships and six hundred men, conquered the Swedish colony.

New Netherland, during its whole existence, came fully under the jurisdiction of the West India Company. In 1641, however, heads of families began choosing a Council of Twelve to administer the local government. This body was replaced by the Board of Nine Men when Peter Stuyvesant became director general. The board was purely advisory; its members were selected by Stuyvesant from a list of twelve persons nominated by freemen at large. The Indian wars of 1643–1645, 1659–1660, and 1663 sapped the strength of the colony. The cosmopolitan quality of New Netherland detracted from loyalty to both the company and the Netherlands. Housing about ten thousand persons in 1664, the colony was a melting pot for many nationalities, including Dutch, Norwegians, Danes, Bohemians, Poles, Germans, Italians, Scottish and Spanish traders, Portuguese Jews, and quite a number of Englishmen in the Dutch section of Long Island. Some eighteen languages were spoken. By 1700 one-quarter of the population of New York City (formerly New Amsterdam) was black.

The last director general of New Netherland, Peter Stuyvesant, brought an iron will and determination in his effort to bring order out of the chaos that had plagued the administration of his predecessor, Willem Kieft. As a young man, Stuyvesant had studied for the ministry in the Dutch Reformed Church at the small theological University of Franeker in Friesland but had been expelled for having "taken the daughter of his own landlord at Franeker, and was caught at it." He then became a clerk for the West India Company and eventually headed a company post at Curaçao. In 1644, Stuyvesant lost his right leg while leading a siege against the Spanish garrison on St. Martin's Island. As director general of New Netherland (1647–1664), he believed that the colony was incapable of self-rule.

Stuyvesant imposed some order on the rowdy colonists. In trying to govern entirely by himself, however, he aroused opposition from plain citizens and prominent leaders alike. Prodded by the home government, he had to back off from his policies of religious repression—banishment of Quakers, denial of non-Calvinists the right to worship, and withholding citizenship from Jews. He alienated the Board of Nine, which brought charges of tyrannical conduct and monopolizing the Indian trade. Because of the growing discontent, in 1653 Stuyvesant allowed the establishment

Peter Stuyvesant. Courtesy of The New-York Historical Society, New York City

of municipal government for New Amsterdam, consisting of two burgo-
masters (mayors), five schepens (aldermen), and a schout (sheriff).

The steady flow of New Englanders to Long Island posed the greatest
threat to Stuyvesant as governor and to the very existence of New
Netherland under Dutch rule. Connecticut laid claim to many of the Long

Island towns. In December 1653 a popular convention of delegates from Gravesand, Flushing, Newtown, Hempstead, Brooklyn, and Flatbush protested arbitrary government and drew up a document that fell just short of declaring independence. The *Humble Remonstrance & Petition of the Colonies and Villages in the New Netherland Province*, while acknowledging loyalty to the Dutch government, listed rights of free citizens and complained of lawmaking without representation. Stuyvesant ordered the convention to dissolve, telling the protesters, "We derive our authority from God and from the company, not from a few ignorant subjects."

The rising aspirations of English settlers on Long Island, however, could not be curtailed. The dissidents had a forceful leader in John Scott, the public attorney at Southampton. This agitator had an unusual career. At age ten, Scott, whose father was killed in the royalist cause, was caught cutting the saddles from the horses of Cromwell's troops, and though this was a capital offense, he was banished and indentured to a New England Quaker family. Later he fled to the West Indies, where he became a successful buccaneer, which activity would bring him to the American coast. On Long Island, Scott championed the settlers' cause not only against the Dutch but also against Connecticut's attempt to annex the towns of western Long Island. Captured by a band sent out by Governor John Winthrop, Jr., Scott was imprisoned at Hartford but escaped by lowering himself from a window with rope that his wife, feigning pregnancy, smuggled to him. In 1663, on the eve of another Anglo-Dutch war, Scott, who assumed the title of "president" of Long Island, organized six towns (Hempstead, Gravesand, Flushing, Middleburg, Jamaica, and Oyster Bay) into a "combination," whereby each town established its own government. Scott with some 170 men compelled several Dutch villages also to separate from New Netherland. Meanwhile, the revolters awaited a decision from the crown.

In March 1664, Charles II conferred on James, duke of York, all territory between the Connecticut River and Delaware Bay, including Long Island, for payment of 3,500 pounds. This proprietary grant, at the time of the outbreak of war between England and the Netherlands, gave all the more reason for a conquest of New Netherland. On August 19, 1664, three English men-of-war, with two thousand troops under the command of Colonel Richard Nicolls, passed the Narrows. English troops occupied Staten Island and blockaded the Hudson River. John Scott raised troops on Long Island, and Connecticut militia were also ready to assist. Nicolls sent notice that if the Dutch surrendered, he would "confirme and secure every man in his Estate, life, and liberty," even promising each Dutch soldier fifty acres of land; if there were no capitulation, there would be "the miserys of war." Stuyvesant had little choice. With Long Island in rebellion, supplies running low, and his citizens disinclined to fight and outnumbered, he quickly surrendered.

By the Treaty of Breda (1667) the Dutch conceded New Netherland to the British. Thus the Dutch colony was now English New York, although for eighteen months during the Anglo-Dutch war of 1672–1674 the Dutch held New Amsterdam. The Treaty of Westminister (1674), however, reconfirmed English possession.

Yet today there are constant reminders that the colony was once Dutch. Street and place names recall their Dutch heritage. Some prominent ones are Staten Island (named for the States General), Yonkers ("de Jonkeer's land"—Adriaen van der Donk was the *jonkeer* and patroon), Brooklyn ("Breuckelen"—broken ground), Flatbush (" 't Vlacke Bos"—wooded plain), Harlem (originally New Haarlem), and Flushing ("Vlissingen," the name also of a city in the Netherlands). Many of the street names given by the Dutch survive: for example, Wall Street (next to the stockade), Pearl Street (now three blocks from the East River but then at the waterfront), Broad Street, and Maiden Lane (so named because it was a path that Dutch girls used to carry their wash to a pond outside the town). The Bowery was Bouwerie Lane, a path that ran to the bouweries (farms). One curious note of the early British occupation was that part of the marketplace was fenced in and rented as a bowling area (Bowling Green); however, nine-pin bowling was outlawed when the English took over, so the Dutch bowlers simply switched to using ten pins.

Under English rule, New Yorkers did not immediately get the representative government they had expected. Richard Nicolls, the first governor, in 1665 issued the *Duke's Laws*, largely derived from New England codes. Instead of a representative assembly, laws were to be enacted by justices of the peace meeting annually as a Court of Assize, subject to the consent of the governor.

Governor Thomas Dongan, a Catholic, in 1683 issued the *Charter of Liberties and Privileges*, which, along with a bill of rights, permitted a representative assembly. Two years later, however, James II revoked this charter. With the overthrow of James II and also subsequently of the Dominion of New England, under which the government of New York was subjected, New York was established as a royal colony.

NEW JERSEY

The Dutch made the first European effort to settle in present New Jersey. In 1630, Michael Pauw and associates received a patroonship across the Hudson from Manhattan Island, which they called Pavonia. Only minimal effort was exerted to develop the patroonship. Indians destroyed settlements in the area in the mid-1640s and again in 1655. Stuyvesant built a stockaded village at Bergen in 1660.

Meanwhile, Charles I in 1634 gave the New Jersey–Delaware region to Sir Edmund Plowden and partners. Attempts to plant settlements along the Delaware in New Albion, as the land grant was called, met little success. Some New Haven and Long Island settlers drifted across the Hudson at midcentury, and several Swedish settlements were also established on the west bank of the Hudson.

New Jersey fell under the duke of York's proprietary grant after the conquest of New Netherland. The duke, however, conferred patent and governmental rights to New Jersey to Sir George Carteret and Lord John Berkeley. Headrights of 60 to 150 acres per person for a three-year period were offered to prospective settlers. Land occupancy bore a quitrent of one-half penny per acre. The two new proprietors issued the *Concessions and Agreements* in 1665, which document permitted the holding of an assembly, to consist of two delegates from each town and a council appointed by the governor. Religious freedom was guaranteed. Meanwhile, Governor Nicolls, in New York, not knowing of the change in proprietary ownership, granted land (the Monmouth grant) between the Raritan and Passaic rivers to a group of associates, mainly Baptists from Rhode Island and Quakers from Long Island; this action would lead to prolonged disputes in the future as to jurisdictional and landholding rights.

In 1674, Lord Berkeley sold his half interest in New Jersey to John Fenwick, acting for Edward Byllynge and three associates, one of whom was William Penn. Two years later Carteret and the Byllynge group signed the Quintipartite Deed, which divided New Jersey into West Jersey and East Jersey. At the same time, the Byllynge group issued the *Concessions and Agreements of the Proprietors, Freeholders and Inhabitants of the Province of West Jersey in America*, one of the most liberal of the colonial constitutions, which included a bill of rights and freedom of conscience.

Carteret retained East New Jersey, which, with the small farms and little trade, did not prosper. In 1682, a year after Carteret's death, East New Jersey was auctioned off to William Penn and twenty-four associates, most of whom were Quakers. Except for lowland Scots, the colony attracted few immigrants. The proprietors lacked capital.

By the 1690s, West New Jersey was under the control of the West Jersey Society, a group of men, mostly Anglicans, who had purchased Byllynge's share indirectly through his heirs. Near anarchy existed in both Jerseys. The proprietors lost control, and settlers refused to pay quitrents. In 1702 the proprietors of both Jerseys relinquished governmental authority, though retaining rights to collect quitrents, and the two regions were united as a royal colony.

THE CAROLINAS

Despite being heralded for its edenic environment, the land from Florida north to Albemarle Sound remained a no-man's-land for Europeans until the mid-seventeenth century. English, French, and Spanish explorers and privateers had often visited the coasts and outer banks. But distance, treacherous shoals, and hostile Indians were among the factors deterring colonization. For the English, the Roanoke experiment had ended in disaster. Lucas Vasquez de Ayllón, with five hundred colonists, attempted to plant a Spanish settlement in 1526. The exact site is unknown but is believed to be at the mouth of the Savannah River or at Winyah Bay (South Carolina). Beset with mutiny and Indian attacks, the venture was abandoned; only 150 survived to return to Hispaniola. Hernando de Soto, in 1539 and 1540, followed a course from Tampa to southern North Carolina before turning southwest toward the Mississippi. Angel de Villafaña, ordered to found a settlement at Port Royal Sound but not discovering any site that suited him, sailed northward to Cape Hatteras. When a hurricane sank two of his ships, he returned to Havana. Jesuits, led by Fray Bautista Segura, went to the Chesapeake Bay region in 1570. Their murder by Indians discouraged Spanish northward expansion along the Atlantic coast.

When Virginia became a royal colony in 1624, the rights of settlement held by the Virginia Company as far south as 34 degrees latitude (including the area of North Carolina and northern South Carolina) reverted to the crown. In October 1629, Charles I granted Sir Robert Heath territory between 31 and 36 degrees north latitude, from sea to sea. Plans to establish a colony, mainly of Huguenot émigrés, fell through. New England Puritans came to Cape Fear in 1662 and 1663 but for an unknown reason suddenly abandoned their settlement. By this time, however, Virginians had begun to filter down to the Albemarle Sound region.

In March 1663 eight of Charles II's most loyal supporters (Edward Hyde, George Monck, William Lord Craven, John Lord Berkeley, Sir Anthony Ashley Cooper, Sir George Carteret, Sir William Berkeley, and Sir John Colleton) received a charter for Carolina, which displaced the Heath patent. The king was to be paid a nominal twenty marks (a little more than twenty-three pounds) annually and was to acquire one-fourth of all gold and silver produced in the colony. Charles II, however, did not take seriously the eight courtiers' pledge to exercise "a pious zeal for the propagation of the gospel among the heathen." When told this, he burst out laughing and then picked up a spaniel dog, saying, "Good friends, here is a model of piety and sincerity which it might be wholesome for you to copy"; then tossing the animal to Edward Hyde, the earl of Clarendon, added: "There, Hyde, is a worthy prelate; make him arch-bishop of the domain I shall give."

The Carolina charter gave the proprietors all land between latitudes 31 and 36 degrees (the southern boundary was moved in 1665 to 29 degrees, some sixty-five miles south of St. Augustine, Florida). The charter, like Maryland's, contained a "bishop of Durham" clause and allowed for feudal powers, including the establishment of a nobility. Laws, however, were to be enacted only "of and with the advice, assent and approbation" of the freemen. The charter recognized freedom of worship.

The *Concessions and Agreements* (1665), essentially the same as issued by Berkeley and Carteret for New Jersey, provided for a governor and council, an elective assembly with sole powers of taxation, freedom of religion, and a liberal land policy. The proprietors could veto legislation and collect quitrents of one-half penny per acre. Incoming colonists were to receive one hundred acres of land, plus fifty acres more per manservant. Those completing indentured service were entitled to six acres. The proprietors, from the beginning, showed little interest in the internal operation of the colony, giving most of their energy, like real estate agents, to promotion of immigration to Carolina.

William Berkeley, governor of Virginia and one of the proprietors, took charge of the settlement at Albemarle Sound. He appointed William Drummond governor and also a council, which with delegates from the freemen were to make the laws for Albemarle (originally designated a county). Berkeley also directed the granting of lands. Immigrants from Virginia and Bermuda formed the early population. The first legislature for Albemarle met in 1665; thereafter, Albemarle went much its own way, separate from colonization to the south. A second attempt by New Englanders, now joined by Barbadians, to colonize at Cape Fear in 1664 failed in three years.

The proprietors issued the *Fundamental Constitutions* for Carolina in 1669, allegedly a collaborative effort of John Locke and Sir Anthony Ashley Cooper (named Lord Shaftesbury in 1672). The document established a model republican government and a feudal land system, but one without vassalage. The proprietors appointed the governor of the colony and had authority to disallow laws and to hear appeals. In the colony a grand council assisted the governor in proposing legislation; the assembly was continued, but members were required to have property valued at five hundred pounds. Only the assembly could reject laws. In 1693 the two groups began sitting as a bicameral legislature. A grandiose aim of the *Fundamental Constitutions* was to create a hierarchy of nobility based on landholdings. Counties contained 480,000 acres of land, divided into 12,000-acre-square tracts. Two-fifths of the lands were reserved for nobility; the remainder was intended as manorial lands or common freeholds. For each county, the eight proprietors each received 12,000 acres (96,000 in all), four landgraves were given 12,000 acres each (48,000) and two caciques got 24,000 acres each (48,000). The Carolina people, however, never accepted this feudal arrangement. The system was ended in 1693, and the titles of the twenty-six landgraves and thirteen caciques that had been created were allowed to lapse upon the deaths of the titleholders. Yet South Carolina in the eighteenth century, with the mix of large plantations and small farms, would resemble the landed scheme that was intended by the *Fundamental Constitutions.*

In 1670 immigrants from England and Barbados and a small band of Huguenots founded Charles Town on the west bank of the Ashley River. Plantations soon spread through the low-lying swamps along the Ashley and Cooper rivers toward the coast. In 1680, Charles Town (later renamed Charleston) was moved to the neck of land between the two rivers where they converged into the harbor. Malarial epidemics during the first decades ravaged the South Carolina low country, which probably had the highest mortality rate anywhere in the colonies. Attempts to produce exotic commodities, such as silk, wines, and raisins, despite being exempted from import duties in England for a certain period, came to naught. Later fortunes were to be made with rice and indigo.

South Carolina (so named officially in the colony's laws of 1696) contrasted with the scattered settlements at Albemarle, a "lubberland," as William Byrd II was to call northern North Carolina, where the people were poor farmers and often destitute. Albemarle (referred to as North Carolina after 1691), with no economic ties with South Carolina, was dependent on trade through Virginia.

Religious differences and discontent with the proprietors were major factors in the continual political turmoil in both Carolinas. In South Carolina, Anglicans held sway in Berkeley County (the Charles Town area), dissenters in Colleton County (southwest of the Stono River), and Huguenots in Craven County (north of Bull Bay). A Quaker-led party contended for control in North Carolina. Goose Creek men (Barbadians who had settled just north of Charles Town on a tributary of the Cooper River), were mainly Anglican and fought dissenters for control of the South Carolina government. Popular protests forced two governors out of office: James Colleton (South Carolina, 1690) and Seth Sothel (North Carolina, 1689; South Carolina, 1691). After 1689 the proprietors appointed a deputy governor for North Carolina; in 1712, North Carolina again had its own governor. From 1708 to 1711 two rival governments contested for power in North Carolina.

In 1721, two years after a peaceable coup toppled proprietary rule (see Chapter 17), South Carolina was made a royal colony. The proprietors, who were relieved not to have the responsibility of governing the recalcitrant settlers, negotiated with the crown for relinquishing their proprietary rights. In 1729, finally, seven proprietors sold their claims to the crown for 17,500 pounds; John Carteret held out but in 1744 agreed to exchange his one-eighth share for land in North Carolina. Thus in 1729, with seven of eight proprietors removed, North Carolina became a royal colony.

PENNSYLVANIA

Like John Winthrop, William Penn had a reformational vision for the New World. Writing to James Harrison, an agent for promoting his new colony, Penn explained:

> For my Country, I eyed the Lord in the obtaining of it . . . and desire to keep it; that I may not be unworthy of His love; but . . . serve His Truth and people; that an example may be set up to the nations; there may be room there, though not here, for such an holy experiment.

Unlike the Puritans, however, Penn sought immigrants of various Protestant persuasions from all the British Isles as well as from the Continent, though especially Pennsylvania was to be a haven for Quakers.

The Society of Friends was one of a number of radical perfectionist sects that appeared in seventeenth-century England. In 1647, George Fox founded the movement when he began preaching the belief that "every man is enlightened by the divine light of Christ." Under a scheme of organization Fox presented in 1668, the first yearly meeting of the Friends began in London in 1671. Called Quakers by outsiders, the Friends were regarded as subversive to both ecclesiastical and civil authority. They denied the sacraments, eschewed any form of priesthood and outward rites, and refused to pay tithes. They were pacifists, opposing all war and refusing to bear arms, and they would not swear oaths. English local courts could imprison anyone denying baptism and the Lord's Supper or violating religious statutes, such as the Conventicle Act (1664), which prohibited the assembly of five or more persons for any worship service other than Anglican. Not surprisingly, from 1661 to 1685 almost fifteen thousand Quakers were jailed in England. Even in the Massachusetts Bay Colony, four Quakers were hanged for returning to the colony after banishment. By the 1670s a large Quaker missionary movement was under way in Barbados, Jamaica, New England, New Jersey, and parts of the southern colonies.

The religious bent of William Penn, Jr. (1644–1718), may have originated in a son's rebelling against a headstrong father. William Penn, Sr. (1621–1670), had a naval career; he commanded a fleet during Cromwell's regime and captured the island of Jamaica in 1655. The elder Penn helped Charles II to secure the throne by turning over to him a fleet. A grateful Charles II knighted Penn, made him Lord High Admiral, and conferred on him a large estate in Ireland. Admiral Penn defeated a Dutch fleet in 1665.

William Penn, Jr., attended Oxford, from which he was expelled for religious nonconformity. His father sent him on a tour of the Continent to cure him of his religious inclinations, which for a while had the desired

William Penn (1644–1718) by Francis Place. Courtesy of
Historical Society of Pennsylvania

effect. Penn's study of law at Lincoln's Inn was cut short by the London
plague. Penn then managed his father's estate in Ireland, whereupon he
came under the influence of Irish Quakers. In 1667, in Cork on business,
Penn heard the preaching of Thomas Loe, whom he had known at Oxford,
and was converted to Quakerism. Penn would be imprisoned many times
for his writings and preaching. He was sent to the tower by the bishop of
London for writing *No Cross, No Crown*, which stated that all religion was
within the soul, not the church, and one's cross was the inner light. One
of Penn's trials led to an important constitutional precedent. Brought
before the court of quarter sessions in London, chiefly on charges of
violating the Conventicle Act for "speaking in Gracious Street" and inciting
unlawful assembly, the jury acquitted him on both charges. The court
would not accept the verdict, but the jurors refused to change their
decision. The court then fined the jurors, to be remitted if the verdict
was changed; four jurors refused to pay the fine and were imprisoned.

Upon appeal, the case of the jurors was heard before the Court of the King's Bench, whereupon the inviolability of a jury's verdict was upheld; said Lord Chief Justice John Vaughan, judges "may try to open the eyes of the jurors, but not to lead them by the nose."

William Penn, Jr., successfully petitioned Charles II for a grant of land north of Maryland in lieu of a 16,000-pound debt owed to his father for naval pay arrears and a loan. The king made him proprietor of all lands from 40 to 43 degrees north latitude and 5 degrees longitude west of the Delaware River. The charter of March 4, 1681, provided, like the other proprietaries, that the colonists be tenants, paying quitrents. Penn was to give the king two beaver skins annually and one-fifth of any gold or silver from the colony. Laws in the colony were to be made with consent of the freemen; Penn, however, could veto legislation, appoint officials, and issue pardons. The Pennsylvania charter was more restrictive than those given to the proprietors of other colonies: Specifically, the provisions stated that the Navigation Acts were to be obeyed, the Privy Council had the right to disallow the colony's laws, laws were not to be repugnant to England, the crown might hear appeals from the colony's courts, and, uniquely (a provision overlooked by patriots on the eve of the Revolution), taxes could be imposed on the colony by act of Parliament. Penn, in 1682, wanting to have an unimpeded water entrance into his colony, secured from the duke of York the eastern part of the peninsula between Chesapeake Bay and Delaware Bay (Delaware), though the duke of York had no legal right to make this grant.

Penn energetically promoted his colony, publishing advertisement tracts in several languages and twice visiting the Rhineland and Holland to drum up immigrants. Penn offered easy terms for land acquisition; a hundred acres could be purchased for five pounds, bearing a nominal quitrent of one shilling per hundred acres, and free homesteads were granted, though having a higher quitrent of one penny for each acre. A headright of fifty acres was also offered. Although settlement through large land companies did not succeed, Penn was able to bring over groups of pietist Dutch and Germans and Welshmen, not the least of whom were Dutch Quakers (Mennonites) and Germans, led by Francis Daniel Pastorius, who settled at Germantown. Influx of newcomers into Pennsylvania rivaled the massive immigration to New England in the 1630s and 1640s. By the end of 1683, sixty ships carrying four thousand newcomers had arrived at the colony. After but one year of settlement, Philadelphia had 150 houses. Penn, who himself resided in the colony from 1682 to 1684 and from 1699 to 1701, purchased land from the Indians through treaties, establishing peaceable relations that lasted until the mid-eighteenth century.

Four times Penn issued a constitutional charter for the colony—a *Frame of Government* in 1682, 1683, and 1695 and a *Charter of Privileges* in

1701. All inhabitants who acknowledged God and held "themselves obliged in conscience, to live peaceably and justly in civil society" were guaranteed religious freedom. Under the third *Frame*, the assembly acquired the right to initiate legislation (previously it could only reject or give assent to laws proposed by the governor and council). The *Charter of Privileges* recognized a supreme unicameral assembly; the council lost its legislative powers, and the only governmental authority retained by the proprietor was the appointment of the governor and members of council. Because of continued agitation from settlers in the Three Lower Counties (Delaware), the *Charter of Privileges* allowed these counties to have a separate assembly; the governor of Pennsylvania, however, would also be the chief executive for Delaware. To ensure Pennsylvania's contribution to frontier defense during King William's War, the English crown in 1692 made Benjamin Fletcher, governor of New York, also the governor of Pennsylvania. The colony was returned to the proprietorship in 1694 upon Penn's promise to have the colony provide its share of aid in the war against the French.

GEORGIA

The only American colony conceived as a means to alleviate social distress in England was Georgia. But this objective was never to be realized. The idea of a charity colony was owing largely to the leadership of Dr. Thomas Bray, who had already founded missionary societies of the Anglican church. In 1729, James Oglethorpe was appointed chairman of a parliamentary committee to inquire into "the State of the Gaols of this Kingdom." The committee's report noted that "in America there are fertile Lands sufficient to subsist all the useless Poor in England, and Distressed Protestants in Europe; yet Thousands starve for want of mere Subsistence"; the committee recommended the creation of a colony to receive English poor and debtors. Reinforcing the philanthropic motive were considerations of mercantilism and imperial defense. A Georgia colony could provide lumber, naval stores, and agricultural products; most important, it could compete with the Spaniards in the Indian trade for skins and furs.

In June 1732 the crown granted to a group of trustees for the period of twenty-one years all the territory between the Savannah and Altamaha rivers, westward to the Pacific. Unusually, the government of the colony was vested in a council of the trustees, residing in England. The trustees were forbidden to own land in Georgia or hold any office of profit pertaining to the colony. During the trusteeship period, rum and slavery were prohibited in the colony, and land ownership was limited to no more than five hundred acres. Full religious freedom was granted, except to Catholics. Although the trustees sent over a few debtors and some Irish convicts, most of the immigration from England consisted of poor artisans and laborers from London. Germans, particularly Lutheran Salzburgers and Moravians, and Scottish Highlanders formed the major segment of the early immigration. The first settlers founded Savannah, and four years later Augusta was laid out, soon becoming the center of the Indian trade. Oglethorpe, as "president" at Savannah, conducted affairs of the colony almost single-handed. His placing military posts on the Altamaha and St. Johns rivers provoked armed confrontation with the Spaniards during the early 1740s.

Georgia settlers complained of the absence of provincial and local government. In 1738 the citizens formally demanded the right to own slaves and fee-simple land ownership. The trustees returned the colony's charter to the king in 1752, at which time Georgia became a royal colony. Though the trustees had called for an assembly from towns of ten families or more in 1751, it was not until four years later that Georgia had a representative assembly. The conversion of Georgia into a royal colony, as intended after the expiration of the trusteeship, was consistent with English policy of strengthening crown control over administration of the American colonies.

5

Land and Agriculture

Land ownership and the prospects for agricultural productivity lured British and European immigrants to America. "Here every man may be master and owner of his owne labour and land; or the greatest part in a small time," asserted John Smith in his description of New England. The feudal system of service obligations did not take root in America, and actual ownership of land was universally in free and common socage. Various forms of leaseholding and tenancy, mainly by choice of convenience, were prevalent in the American colonies but distinguished as being on a voluntary and contractual basis. Nearly nine-tenths of colonial Americans engaged in some kind of agriculture, either subsistence farming or producing for internal or export markets.

LAND DISTRIBUTION

The New England township grants provided for ordered settlement, a system later forming the bases of United States public land policy. Although occasionally land was granted directly to individuals for special reasons, such as a reward for service or to promote industrial development, the common practice was to award land to groups who had petitioned for the right to settle a defined area, ranging from four to eight square miles. Upon approval by the colony's general court, a township was laid out. In the town, plat streets were marked, faced by narrow house lots, and space was reserved for a meetinghouse. The members of the group had use of a commons within the town for certain livestock. During the early colonial period, individual householders were assigned strips of farmland outside the town, much like the manorial system of the Middle Ages. Usually a lottery was used for the division of land. Members of the town corporation also had communal rights to meadowlands for pasturage and hay and also woodlands for further grazing and timber for domestic use. The original proprietors exercised authority in disposing of surplus land to newcomers. Those who could not obtain land, however, were sometimes tolerated to reside at the outskirts of the town as cottagers or laborers. Eventually the open-field system was abandoned, and villagers were assigned separate farms of one hundred to two hundred acres, enclosed by fences. Scarcity of land in time contributed to the growth of a landless class in the township and antagonism toward the proprietors. By 1698, in Massachusetts, proprietors were a separate body from the town government. Other New England colonies followed the example of Massachusetts. There was some divergence from the original village system, such as taking up amorphous patches of ungranted land, known as "pitches," an example being Connecticut's award of bounty lands to soldiers in 1697. Massachusetts continued the town grant system until 1762.

Conditions for securing land were more difficult in New York because of manorial grants and the engrossment of large areas by grantees who often engaged in bribery of the governor and council in order to receive their landholdings. Elsewhere in the middle colonies, land grants to individuals were easy to obtain. In northeastern New Jersey and in Pennsylvania, farms of one hundred to two hundred acres prevailed. Pennsylvania had a preemption policy of allowing squatters to select their own lands and paying later ten pounds per hundred acres. Maryland allowed the purchase of one hundred acres of uncultivated land for "caution money" (by the 1730s, five pounds). In the southern colonies, land, whether owned by a proprietary or the crown, was given to actual settlers, usually on condition of "seating" their property and payment of a small annual quitrent.

Tenancy, often a temporary step in upward mobility, was widespread in the colonies. It developed mainly in the eighteenth century. As James T. Lemon (1976) and Lucy Simler (1986) have shown, in southeastern Pennsylvania in the 1760s and 1770s, thirty percent of married taxpayers and of farmers were tenants. Tenancy was contracted on the basis of mutual obligations of the tenant and the landlord. Large landowners welcomed tenants as a means to improve their lands and also to meet terms of seating as a condition for receiving a grant. Many tenants were desperately poor but in time could prosper and, if they chose to do so, acquire their own farms. There were a variety of leaseholding arrangements, with land held for a short period or for a long span, such as several lifetimes, especially characteristic of New York manorial estates established in the seventeenth century. Renters were common in New England due to the shortage of land. Many renters and leaseholders were people who needed land for mercantile or industrial pursuits.

Outside New England and New York, the headright system, confined chiefly to the seventeenth century, accounted for both immigration and land distribution. Headrights began when the Virginia Company offered fifty acres of land to immigrants who paid their own transportation to the colony and the same amount of land to anyone who paid the cost of bringing over another person. Many of the large landholdings in Virginia were derived from the multiple acquisition of headrights. The headright system was subject to great abuse. Ship captains claimed lands by entering seamen as immigrants. Headrights were listed for nonexistent persons and also for more than one ocean crossing. The Maryland proprietor abolished the system about 1683. In 1699, Virginia prohibited land grants for importing Africans. By 1715 headrights ceased to be an important means of securing land in that colony. Similar to the headright system was the granting of land to immigrant groups who had been brought together through promotional activity.

Large land grants were awarded to individuals in New York and the southern colonies. Governors Nicolls and Dongan in New York initiated the practice of granting large estates as "manors" or "governorships," with the grantees having independent governmental jurisdiction through courts leet and baron. Quitrents were paid to the crown. Domains of great landed families made up most of the counties of Westchester, Dutchess, and Albany. Stephanus Van Cortlandt acquired 242,000 acres in Westchester County; Frederick Philipse's patent in Dutchess County amounted to 208,000 acres. The Livingston Manor in Albany and Columbia counties consisted of 160,000 acres.

Several immense tracts of land within an established colony were granted to certain individuals. The grant given to the earl of Granville (John Carteret) as compensation for his one-eighth share in the Carolina proprietary took in more than half of North Carolina, a strip sixty miles wide between 35°34″ latitude and the Virginia boundary. In 1673, Charles II gave all of Virginia south of the Rappahannock River to the earl of Arlington and Thomas Lord Culpeper, who for thirty-one years had the sole power of granting land in fee simple and were entitled to the collection of all quitrents. Technically, the governor and council could no longer make land grants. In 1681, Arlington disposed of his claim to Culpeper, who in 1684 surrendered all his rights of the land grant to the crown in return for a twenty-year annuity, to be paid from the poll tax in Virginia. But having a more lasting effect in Virginia was the Northern Neck proprietary. In 1649, Charles I granted to Lord Hopton a tract of some five million acres—the Northern Neck, the land between the Potomac and Rappahannock rivers. Hopton in 1689 assigned this grant to Lord Culpeper, whose grandson, Thomas Lord Fairfax, inherited the vast domain. Throughout the colonial period, the Northern Neck proprietary continued to grant "waste" and uncultivated lands on the basis of one shilling quitrent per fifty acres. Because of the low fee, many settlers, especially in the western part of the grant extending into the Blue Ridge Mountains and the Great Valley, were able to amass large holdings, much of which was used for speculative purposes.

Most of the colonies at one time or another sought to curtail the size of land grants. A Virginia statute of 1705 stated that no more than five hundred acres could be claimed in one tract, with each patentee required to have five servants or slaves; two hundred additional acres, however, could be obtained for ownership of each slave beyond five. But no more than four thousand acres could be awarded by one patent. By an act of 1710, failure to seat or plant resulted in forfeiture of the land grant. Subsequent laws retained the same principles. Yet the government was remiss in enforcing these laws, and the eighteenth century witnessed great expansion of individual planters' holdings. The large planters also came into possession of lands owned by farmers who could not survive the often low price of tobacco.

Speculative companies promoted the opening up of new lands. Among these were the Free Society of Traders in Pennsylvania (1681–1721) and the West Jersey Society (1691), which unsuccessfully sought to dispose of marginal lands, representing about one-fifth of the territory in New Jersey. At the mid-eighteenth century, groups of speculators received enormous land grants, especially those conferred by the Virginia government.

Military land bounties, the principal source for settlement of the trans-Appalachian frontier after the American Revolution, accounted for much of the frontier settlement during the colonial period. The colonies gave land to people who built a post on the frontier. War veterans were also given land. Thus Captain John Mason, for example, acquired one thousand acres for his service in the Pequot War. Massachusetts granted land to officers and soldiers who had fought in King Philip's War and also those who went on the Canadian expedition in 1690. Pennsylvania and Virginia provided land to veterans of the French and Indian War. The crown, by the proclamation of 1763, gave land to provincial soldiers in the same war. Because of confusion in staking out claims and making surveys, military land warrants for service in the French and Indian War were not issued until the American Revolution.

CROPS AND CULTIVATION

Knowledge of the Indian ecosystem aided early colonial farming. Both the Pilgrims and early Jamestown settlers took over abandoned Indian fields. The Indian practice of repeatedly burning forests left dead trees and ash-enriched soils, though such areas were soon overgrown with dense thickets. The colonists engaged in two methods of clearing land. Girdling, or "scotching," was a technique widely used until the mid-eighteenth century. A groove was cut around a tree, intercepting the sap. While the leafless trees were left to die, corn or garden crops were planted among them. Trees were taken down after they rotted. Standing trees contributed nutrients to the soil. The system had disadvantages in that the rotting made for a waste of wood, and roots still had to be removed before plowing. Felling trees with axes, usually in late summer, replaced girdling. During a dry spell in the following late spring, leaves and limbs were burned, thereby killing green roots of trees and accelerating the decay of stumps; also, on a short-term basis, this process provided ash fertilizer.

The colonists quickly adapted to Indian crop raising. They also borrowed Indian agricultural methods, such as intertillage, planting in hills, and using fish for fertilizer. The colonists also learned from the natives smoking and drying processes for preserving foods. It is estimated that one-third of the agricultural plants now grown in the United States originated with the Indians of the Western Hemisphere. Indigenenous to the Americas were maize (corn), potatoes (Irish and sweet), tobacco, peanuts, pumpkins, squashes, gourds, tomatoes, garden peppers, pineapples, watermelons, and a variety of berries, nuts, peas, and beans. The Europeans introduced wheat, barley, rye, oats, buckwheat, flax, various garden vegetables (such as cabbages, radishes, carrots, garlic, and onions), and two crops originating in the Far East—hemp and rice.

Indian corn (maize) was usually the colonial farmer's first crop, and it remained a diet staple throughout the colonies. One New England wife remarked that she had eaten "Indian pudding," or johnnycake, every day for four years. Corn was more easily ground and made into more forms of bread than any other grain. Moreover, corn yielded more food per acre, ripened earlier, and required less soil preparation than European grains. Initially, corn was planted according to the Indian method of placing four to six grains in hills measuring twelve by twenty inches located two to four feet apart. Squash, pumpkins, other low crops, and beans were seeded between the hills; the beans grew up the cornstalks. Eventually the settlers cultivated corn by plowing single furrows about six feet apart and then plowing cross rows; corn was planted at the intersections of the furrows.

Though grown in all the colonies, cereal grains were cultivated most extensively in the middle colonies and in the Virginia piedmont and valley. Virginia tobacco planters after the mid-eighteenth century increasingly turned to raising wheat in order to rotate crops and especially to take advantage of the soaring export market in flour. It was difficult to grow the grain in New England because of wheat blast (black stem rust), a mildew parasite fungus. Different varieties of wheat were grown. Often farmers put out both summer and winter wheat; if one crop failed (due to summer wheat lice, blast, or extended frost), the other might succeed. One way to enhance a wheat crop was to plow under earlier seedlings of buckwheat or oats, thus replenishing the soil before resowing for wheat. A major drawback in raising wheat was the difficulty in harvesting it. In one day, a man using a sickle could cut only an acre of wheat. The grain was threshed by flailing or by driving horses or oxen over wheat straw.

In some areas, rye, which grew best in sandy and gravelly soils, competed with wheat. One use for rye was as a base for whiskey. Barley, which provided malt for beer, and oats, the preferred barn fodder for horses, were also grown. Some planters, like Landon Carter of Virginia, frequently tilled several grain crops alternately in a single field. Fiber crops, flax (for linen), and hemp (for coarse fabrics and rope) were more suited to backcountry soils.

The southern colonies found valuable export commodities in the production of tobacco, rice, and indigo. Englishmen considered native North American tobacco too rank. Thus John Rolfe, with seeds from Trinidad, successfully introduced the porous-leafed Oronoco variety. Oronoco was best suited to the rich, heavy soils of stream bottoms. By the end of the seventeenth century, William Fitzhugh of Virginia introduced sweet-scented tobacco, which grew well in the sandy loams of the peninsula between the York and James rivers. Among the advantages of the cultivation of tobacco were its high yield per acre, its keeping qualities, its low weight, and its high exchange value.

A typical Chesapeake small farmer planted about three acres of tobacco along with ten to fifteen acres of corn or other crops. One acre yielded about a thousand pounds of tobacco. Large planters, of course, had more extended acreage in tobacco. The best time to sow tobacco was the middle of January. The small burned-over seedbeds were covered with branches. In early May the quarter-inch seedlings were transplanted to the main fields, in parallel rows. The crop was hoed three times. After eight to twelve leaves appeared, a plant was topped to prevent flowering; new leaf shoots were removed ("suckered"). At the end of July the tobacco was cut and allowed to lie in the field for a day; then the stalks were hung up in barns. After five weeks the tobacco was cured by smoke from slow fires. The tobacco was then bulked in piles, and after about two weeks of "sweating," the leaves were stripped from the stalks and "prized" into hogsheads for shipment. Tobacco hogsheads were rolled to the warehouse–

inspection stations on the rivers. About 1740, Rev. Robert Rose of Albemarle County, Virginia, developed the method of transporting tobacco hogsheads on streams by putting the hogsheads on two canoes (each fifty to sixty feet long) lashed together.

The most important crop in the Deep South was rice. Although rice planting was early encouraged by the Carolina proprietors, a superior-quality strain, from Madagascar, was not introduced until 1694 by Land-grave Thomas Smith. In the spring, rice seeds were planted eighteen to twenty inches apart and three inches deep in furrows. After planting, the field was flooded in order to be rid of grass and weeds. Carolinians took advantage of tidal waters but also brought in swamp waters to cover the rich lowland soils by means of dams, ditches, and reservoirs.

The Spaniards introduced indigo to America, and indigo plantations appeared in the British and French West Indies by the mid-seventeenth century. Indigo culture had been attempted in Virginia and South Carolina before 1700 but could not compete with better-quality indigo from the West Indies. Eliza Lucas Pinckney and other South Carolina planters successfully experimented with West Indian varieties of indigo about 1740. Cultivated on high ground not suitable for rice, indigo was easy to grow, despite the problems of weeds and grasshoppers. Indigo was very difficult to process, however, involving considerable skill in extracting dyestuff after fermentation and treatment in three different vats. The eventual goo, the "blue gold of Carolina," was dried and cut into pieces. By the eve of the American Revolution, South Carolinians were exporting annually one million pounds of indigo dye.

LIVESTOCK HUSBANDRY

"What made Indian and European subsistence cycles seem so different from one another had less to do with their use of plants than their use of animals," writes William Cronon (1983). "Where Indians had contented themselves with the burning the woods and concentrating their hunting in the fall and winter months, the English sought much more total and year-round control over their animals' lives" (p. 128). Livestock husbandry formed an essential part of the farms and plantations throughout the colonies. Most farmers had milk cows, beef cattle, hogs, and various fowl. Pork and beef were mainstays in the colonial diet.

Swine required almost no attention until the time of slaughter. Bearing owners' marks, hogs were usually left to fend for themselves in the woods, rooting for mast, such as nuts and acorns. After harvest, swine were rounded up, penned, and fattened for a few weeks on corn and vegetable crops such as potatoes before slaughter. Barreled pork was an exportable commodity in most colonies and was used to provision ships.

In colonial times, hogs were slaughtered at about eighteen months. Swine were trail-driven to market in some areas. In 1733, Governor William Gooch of Virginia commented, perhaps with some exaggeration, that "50,000 fat hogs are supposed to be driven into Virginia" from North Carolina each year.

Sheep were raised primarily for wool rather than as a food supply, although lamb and mutton did appear on the tables of southern planters. Stock grazing of sheep flourished among the bottomlands of the Connecticut River and in Rhode Island, Maryland, and the Carolinas. Large flocks were kept also on Long Island. Almost no sheep were raised in the far backcountry because of the prevalence of wolves. Southern plantation owners often kept flocks of sheep. A favorite breed was the Leicester longwool sheep. George Washington had a Leicester ram on his farm at Mount Vernon. Sheep grazed fallow fields. Landon Carter of Virginia had a sheep house and put flocks out in his rye fields. Carter recorded one time that he sheared 267 pounds of wool from 100 sheep.

Some colonists gave attention to horse breeding in the eighteenth century. The Virginia gentry, as racing enthusiasts, sought to build up bloodlines. Two famous breeds in the northern colonies were the powerful Conestoga draft horses developed by Pennsylvania Germans and, in Rhode Island, the Narragansett pacers, valued for their agility and speed. The Chickasaw horses in the Deep South derived from animals left by the de Soto and de Vaca expeditions of the sixteenth century.

A major factor contributing to livestock raising was the rapid expansion of English grasses. Unfortunately, wild rye and broom straw, the two dominant native grasses from Virginia to New England, contained a too high proportion of roughage to nutrients. English grasses common by the end of the colonial period were timothy (named for Timothy Hanson, who brought the seeds into Pennsylvania), bluegrass, crabgrass, greensward, and clover (red, white, and yellow). The European herb rape also provided forage. English grasses, however, could not grow in the area south of Virginia, which lacked a true winter period.

A typical colonial farmer had a small herd of "neat cattle"—milk cows, oxen, and beef cattle. Oxen were most often the beasts of burden, used for plowing and pulling heavy wagon loads. With random breeding from stock brought in from Europe, Louisiana, and the West Indies, there was no distinctive kind of cattle in the colonies, although "black cattle" were found from Maryland to Georgia. Much of the cattle were scrawny for having grazed on inferior fields and for being kept outdoors yearlong. Only among the Pennsylvania Germans was there intense care in raising cattle. The animals were housed and fed during the winter in large barns.

Beef, like pork, was prepared both salted and fresh. Important byproducts of beef cattle were hides tanned and oiled to make shoes, clothing, saddle harnesses, and various other leather goods, fat melted from membranes for use in candles and soap, and the horns, split and pressed into plates or combs.

Every farm and even many households in the towns kept dairy cows. Families made cheese and butter. Because of difficulty in transportation and easy spoilage, dairy products were seldom sent to market. Cheese and butter were made chiefly for local consumption. One Pennsylvania farmer, Aaron Robins, reported that he could produce thirteen hundred pounds of cheese from the milk of six cows during the spring of a year and, for a five-week period in the fall, two hundred pounds of butter.

A substantial range cattle industry developed in the colonies. One of the first stock raisers for market was John Pynchon, who in the mid-seventeenth century drove his cattle from the upper Connecticut River valley to Hartford for market shipment. Cattle raised on pastures near Hadley and Hatfield in Massachusetts by the end of the century were driven to Boston, as were stock from New Hampshire. With increased demand for dried beef in the eighteenth century, a sizable cattle industry existed from western Pennsylvania through the backcountry of Maryland, Virginia, and the Carolinas. The lush bluegrass of the Shenandoah Valley in Virginia, in lime soils not well suited for tobacco, led German and Scots-Irish settlers to turn to cattle production, often fattening livestock brought in by drovers. Elsewhere cattle before slaughter were fattened on corn or silage near their destination. Cattle from western Pennsylvania, Maryland, and Virginia made their way to market at Philadelphia, Baltimore, or Alexandria.

The Carolina frontier became the first great "cow country" in American history. The Carolina proprietors had sought to discourage cattle raising, but the settlers soon recognized the advantages for livestock husbandry offered by the mild winters and abundant range. Scottish Highlanders were among the first Carolinians to make use of the open range in the sparsely settled area between Albemarle Sound and the Neuse River. In South Carolina the thick marsh grasses were conducive to cattle raising. In the western hills, brush grass and tangles of pea vines provided ample forage. In western North Carolina, according to *American Husbandry* (1775), "vast herds of half-starved, stunted beasts," numbering into the thousands, roamed in the open range, each animal bearing the brands of individual owners. Like the later cattle kingdom of the nineteenth-century Far West, graziers conducted a yearly roundup, chasing cattle into natural corrals formed by forks of streams. Detained for a while at cowpens in forest clearings, cattle were driven to Charleston, Baltimore, or Philadelphia, often via the Great Wagon Road at the foot of the Blue Ridge Mountains, crossing the Potomac into Maryland and Pennsylvania and southward diagonally across the Carolinas through Salisbury to Charleston. In Virginia, because of rustling and the ill repute of drovers as "vagrants," the people in charge of a cattle drive had to register each head of cattle with a local justice of peace, providing a full description of each animal.

IMPROVEMENTS IN AGRICULTURAL METHODS

The evolution of better farm implements brought greater agricultural efficiency. The early colonists had tools that merely scratched the earth—wooden plows, hoes, mattocks, spades, picks, and shovels. Even then the huge wooden plows were scarce. It was twelve years before the Plymouth colonists had a plow, and there were only thirty-seven plows in all of Massachusetts in 1636. Farm neighbors often cooperated in using the same plow. One improvement was the introduction of a harrow, rectangular or A-shaped, consisting of several heavy beams with hardwood or iron teeth attached. Using handles at the end, the farmer raked and pulverized the soil. Another change was making plows more durable and smaller. By 1700, pieces of iron were nailed to the moldboards of plows, preventing wear too quickly and allowing for deeper furrowing. At the time of the American Revolution, the Carey or Dragon plow was in wide use; it was made of wrought iron and had interchangeable and replaceable parts.

The colonial farmer was often remiss in combating soil exhaustion. "The depth and richness of the soil," observed the Swedish naturalist Peter Kalm on his American tour in 1749, "misled" the settlers "and made them careless husbandmen." Like the Indians, colonial Americans sowed fertile "uncultivated grounds" as long as they produced a crop without manuring; then they turned the exhausted fields into pastures and cultivated

> new spots of ground covered since ancient times with woods, which have been spared by the fire or the hatchet ever since the Creation. This is likewise the reason why agriculture and its science is so imperfect here that one can travel days and learn nothing about land.

Similarly, Robert Beverley berated the agricultural neglect of his fellow planters: Virginia had a fertility of soil "equal to any Land in the known World . . . but I confess I am asham'd to say any thing of its Improvements, because I must at the same time reproach my Country-men with a Laziness that is unpardonable."

The persistent cultivation of corn (which after rice made the greatest demands on the soil), the rotation of fields instead of crops, and the insufficient use of fertilizers led to soil depletion. Usually one-third of lands were fallow each year. Tobacco, the staple of the Chesapeake area, which drew heavily on nitrogen, left the soil toxic. After three or four crops, tobacco fields were abandoned. Forests were cleared constantly for tobacco lands or "new lands."

Prejudice worked against the use of animal manures; it was believed that dung affected the taste of the crops. But this fear aside, it was difficult to collect manure when livestock was not penned. Some colonists, however, were attentive to fertilization. As they had learned from the Indians, New England farmers used shad and herring (particularly alewives) for fertilizer. The colonists discovered soil restoration through plowing under vegetable crops. Landon Carter noted in March 1757 that his field was "manured with pea vines." Some southern planters tried composted rice straw and swamp mud. Chesapeake farmers eventually employed the stock method of fertilization: penning cattle on tobacco lands and moving the fences weekly. Oyster shells were used as a lime fertilizer; after 1750 limestone was widely used.

Increasingly, farmers relied on planting fields, on a rotation basis, with leguminous forage crops, such as clover, thereby also providing hay for livestock. Kalm reminded colonists to cultivate root crops and legumes to restore fertility to the "butchered soil." Enlightened planters like George Washington, who read works of English agricultural reformers, such as Jethro Tull's *The Horse-Hoeing Husbandry* (1733), practiced rotation of crops and experimented with the cultivation of soil-restorative plants such as turnips, lucerne (alfalfa), and chicory.

Some colonists made thorough investigations of agricultural practices in order to determine what improvements could be made. Jared Eliot, a Connecticut minister and physician, published in 1760 *Essays upon Field-Husbandry in New-England*. He evaluated agricultural technology and assiduously called for a greater use of fertilizers and crop diversification. He advised Pennsylvanians to plant corn with "moderation" and "to intermix crops of pease, buckwheat, turneps, cabbages, potatoes, clover, and lucerne among those of maize, wheat, barley, oats, and flax; this would keep the land clean and in heart." It would also be wise after several corn crops to plant artificial grasses, "that they might have at once a good meadow, instead of that miserable management which they call a fallow." Thus "they would get meadows that would feed large herds of cattle, or yield at least a ton or a ton and half of hay per acre immediately." Many leading farmers and planters, including George Washington, Landon Carter, and Charles Read of Pennsylvania, kept meticulous notes on their agricultural endeavors. Colonial correspondence contained much information on agricultural improvements and experimentation. The budding field of botany, however, had only limited influence on colonists to engage in agricultural science or to raise rare plants. James Logan and John Bartram, early naturalists, nevertheless did make significant contributions to agricultural science, such as showing that alternate detassling of corn provided for cross-fertilization and thus better seed corn.

Although agricultural productivity slightly increased in the late colonial period, the average size of farms declined from 500 acres in 1700 to 130 to 140 acres. The greater productivity may be attributed not only to improvements in agricultural practices but also to the more intense use of cleared acres and the creation of new farms.

6

Industrial
Life

Expanding consumer demand, a rising standard of living, and openings in internal and external markets prodded colonial industrial development, remarkable for its variety and quantity of output. Although colonial production had to make do for the most part with the small-scale operations of households, shops, and farms and primitive mechanization, it reached the threshold of transition from a handicraft era to the age of modern industrialization. Extractive industries had the advantages of plentiful natural resources, limited operational requirements in production, world-wide markets, proximity to sea lanes, and the encouragement of both British and colonial governments. Commercial industrial growth, however, was impeded by a scattered and essentially rural population, insufficient capital and cash, lack of credit agencies, land luring away artisans, difficulties of transportation, and high freight rates.

FISHERIES

Fisheries, America's first staple export industry, were well established in North American waters nearly a century before permanent English settlement. The Grand Banks fisheries off Newfoundland were fully a part of the European Atlantic economy. In 1578 alone, 350 fishing vessels (mostly French and Spanish, about fifty English) were counted at the Grand Banks. With the founding of the English colonies, fishing became a mainstay of life. The middle and Chesapeake colonies did not develop any substantial commercial fishing, though they had some success harvesting oysters. New England dominated the northern fisheries, in a role enhanced by English victories over the French in the colonial wars.

Originally British West Country merchants, with ample capital, prevailed in colonial fishing. But New Englanders were quick to enter commercial fishing on their own. By using shallops (the building of which began in the early 1630s), small schooners, and other light craft, New Englanders were able to penetrate offshore fishing grounds where the larger English vessels could not. Coastal settlements gave important support to the local fishing industry. The small ships could conveniently put in at port to dry fish; this accessibility allowed for winter fishing, an option not available to the large ships of the British fishing fleet. Gloucester, Marblehead, and Salem soon became key fishing ports. As early as 1641, John Winthrop reported that Massachusetts fishermen had an annual catch of 300,000 cod. In the 1670s, New England fisheries moved up into the Gulf of St. Lawrence and offshore Nova Scotia (Acadia) and Newfoundland. By the end of the century, New England winter-cured fish had found markets in Spain, Portugal, the Mediterranean countries, England, France, the Canaries, and the West Indies. Soon about three hundred sail (thirty thousand tons of shipping) annually were delivering fish to Spain and Portugal. In the eighteenth century, the New England fishing industry integrated large ships with small craft. In 1741, Massachusetts had four hundred large fishing vessels and about as many small, undecked boats. It is estimated that one-tenth of New England adults engaged in commercial fishing, some only seasonally. In 1765, 31,000 persons served in the New England fishing fleets.

The best fish were sent to Europe, the "middling" sort were consumed at home, and the poor grade, or "refuse" fish, were delivered to the West Indies to feed slaves. The most prized catch was the "dun fish"—large, fat cod. Aboard a typical fishing vessel, fish were caught by hand lines and nets. Fish were cleaned, split, and salted on deck. At port, the salted fish were spread out on platforms ("flakes") and dried. Heads were saved for hog food. Tongues of cod were considered a great delicacy. Oil from the livers was used to treat leather (cod liver oil was not used for medicinal or nutritional purposes during the colonial period).

For local use, all along the Atlantic seaboard a wide variety of fish were caught in traps or weirs, especially herring, shad, salmon, and sturgeon moving up inland streams for spawning. Mackerel was prized for bait, alewives for fertilizer.

In southern New England and on Long Island, whaling rose to great prominence. The industry began in the early seventeenth century with the taking of drift whales stranded in shallow water. As drift whales became scarce by the 1680s, whaling extended to the high seas. New England whalers ranged from Cape Breton to as far south as the Falkland Islands. Oceangoing whalers, usually 50- to 180-ton boats, functioned as floating factories, able to stay long periods at sea; aboard were tryworks, consisting of iron pots in a brick furnace for the purpose of boiling oil from blubber. In the pursuit of whales, two small boats were lowered into the sea, one of which was held in reserve; each boat had a crew of six and one harpooner. Once a tired whale was brought to bay, it was killed with lances.

One important development in the mid-eighteenth century was distinguishing between humpback and sperm whales. The latter, which seldom came near shore, yielded a higher quality of spermaceti, a waxy substance found in the head cavities that was mixed with potash and used to make candles. Braintree and Providence had large spermaceti candleworks. Sperm whales also provided a higher grade of oil, used both as an illuminant and a lubricant. Whales were also valued for bone (for stays, stiffeners, and corsets) and ambergris, a secretive substance from the intestines, used as a nonevaporating base for perfumes.

Nantucket, Marblehead, Dartmouth (New Bedford), and Provincetown became leading centers of the whaling industry. On the eve of the Revolution, 230 of 304 whaling vessels from Nantucket and Dartmouth accounted for eighty percent of all marketed whale oil. The industry was favored by a British bounty on whale oil, which by 1740 had risen to forty shillings per ton.

The whole New England economy gained substantial benefits from fishing and whaling. The industries provided employment for the surplus manpower from the not too productive farms, garnered capital for investment, and stimulated the growth of other industries, such as naval stores, shipbuilding, and rope and sailcloth manufacturing.

SHIPBUILDING

Shipbuilding became a remarkably successful industry, engaged in by all the colonies, although capital construction was mainly confined to New England. The first vessel built by English settlers in North America was the thirty-ton *Virginia* at the Kennebec River in 1607. Small boats were launched during the early years of the Plymouth and Virginia colonies. John Winthrop and associates put the *Blessing of the Bay* to sea in 1631 for the purpose of trade with Dutch New Netherland. Later it and other ships plied the West India trade. One 120-ton vessel was launched at Salem in 1640, and in its maiden voyage brought home a cargo of Negroes and

cotton from the Bahamas and salt from the Tortugas. Shipyards proliferated in New England; every town along the Connecticut River had one.
From 1696 to 1713, in Massachusetts alone, some 1,118 vessels (69,468
tons) were constructed. Newport in 1712 had a dozen shipyards, and in
1718, Philadelphia could boast ten. Most vessels constructed were sloops
and other small boats of about thirty tons, carrying a crew of five or six
men, intended for the coastal and West India trade. Eventually larger
ships were built, especially two-masted schooners and large brigantines in
the 100- to 300-ton range. The average size of Massachusetts-built ships
about 1700 was 117.3 tons. Most likely the largest colonial-made ship was
the 720-ton merchantman constructed by John Jeffery over a period of
two years and launched at New London in 1725. This vessel sailed for
Portugal, where it was sold to English merchants. Frequently, American
built ships were sold at European ports. It was not unusual for British
merchants to send consignment goods to America, the proceeds from the
sale of which were used to build ships.

American builders stayed close to European technology, their main
innovations being new ship designs for speed and the development of the
schooner, a simple and flexible craft. Many merchant ships were constructed using the Dutch flyboat as a model, resulting in long and lightly
built vessels with nearly flat bottoms that permitted greater speed and
bulk capacity. In the eighteenth century, American-owned ships dominated
the coastal and West India trade. On the eve of the American Revolution,
ninety-five percent of ships trading between New England and the West
Indies were American-owned, and one-third of the British merchant fleet
was colonial-built.

FOREST INDUSTRIES

From the abundant forests came naval stores, board lumber, heavy timber
for masts, and woods for furniture and implements. Naval stores were
products of the New England white pines and the yellow pines of the
South. Parliament in 1705 and 1706 allowed for attractive bounties for
colonial-produced naval stores and placed them on the enumerated list
(meaning that they could only be sent to England or elsewhere within the
empire). Tar, a charcoal substance burned from dead and rotting pine
knots, was used for soapmaking, sealing vessels watertight, and protecting
rope from deterioration. Pitch, a more advanced stage of tar, served as a
lubricant. Resin, obtained from pine bark, was suitable as a varnish or
used for medicinal purposes. Turpentine, a distillation of pine wood, was
in demand in colonial times as a disinfectant; ship crews washed the decks
of their living quarters with turpentine. Potash was made by draining
water through wood ashes and boiling out lye from the remaining

substance; potash was used in the making of crown glass, soft soaps, drugs, dyes, and saltpeter; it was also used by itself as a scouring agent.

A Liverpool and Manchester syndicate operated a large potash works in Philadelphia in the mid-eighteenth century and had subsidiary plants elsewhere in the colonies, including Fredericksburg, Virginia. Potash works were found in many New England towns. After the mid-eighteenth century, the supply of pine dwindled in New England, and the naval stores industry then centered in the Carolinas. In the 1760s, North Carolina produced sixty percent of all naval stores exported from the colonies. South Carolina also exported large quantities of naval stores to Great Britain.

Heavy timber was in demand for shipbuilding. The British government paid bounties of a pound a ton on trees used as masts, yards, and bowsprits for ships in the Royal Navy. Timber reserved for masts measured twenty-four to thirty-six inches in diameter at the base and in length as many yards as inches in diameter. British policy, as early as 1688, prohibited the cutting of white pine trees of twenty-four inches or greater in diameter, although certain exceptions were allowed. Colonists both ignored and resisted enforcement of this program. Because of the difficulty in hauling masts, it was more profitable to cut up the large trees.

An early method for cutting timber was pit sawing, whereby a log was placed across a pit; one person below and one at ground level worked a whipsaw in an up-down motion. Eventually the colonists erected sawmills propelled either by water or by windmills. Despite the considerable investment and landholding required, sawmills dotted the landscape everywhere in the colonies. By 1766, the Cape Fear valley alone had more than fifty sawmills. Much in demand in the colonies and in the export trade were sawn lumber, shingles, and staves, especially for barrels and hogsheads. Lumber accounted for one-tenth of exports of the colonies.

FURS

A kind of forest industry, the fur trade consistently marked the far reaches of the receding colonial frontier. Trappers and traders jutted deep into the Indian country and zones of international friction.

Fur trading began in the earliest settlements. The Pilgrims traded for beaver along the Kennebec, Penobscot, and Connecticut rivers. The Dorchester and New England companies in the 1620s sent over colonists for the purpose of securing both fish and furs. The New England fur trade was important for nearly a half century. As pelts became scarce along the seaboard, fur trading extended into and beyond the Appalachian mountain ranges. Albany and Oswego were key points in the fur trade with the Indians of the Great Lakes area. With the Iroquois Confederacy neutral or as allies, the colonists were able to take advantage of the far-ranging trade activities of these Indians. Pennsylvania, Maryland, and Virginia traders challenged French fur-trading supremacy in the Ohio country. Carolina and Georgia traders penetrated deep into the southwestern Indian country.

Furs were in high vogue in England, the basis of luxurious garments and hats. English hatters in 1740 were producing nine times as many hats as in 1700; English mercantilist policy sought to maintain this success at the expense of hatmaking in the colonies. All kinds of furs were in demand—beaver, mink, fox, bear, muskrat, raccoon, deerskin, even wolf and rabbit. But it was the beaver pelt that was most prized as the leading component in felt hats. In hatmaking, the barbed hair of the beaver was worked into durable felt, which was used as a nap over other animal fur, such as rabbit, muskrat, or raccoon. The beaver hat passed through five styles during the colonial period, each reflecting a political change in England: high-crown, squarish, and broad-rimmed (James I and Charles I); plain and conical (Cromwellian period); feathered, broad-rimmed, flattish, and slouched, after the French style (Restoration); shallow-crowned with a wide brim curved up at the sides, resembling the clerical shovel hat (Glorious Revolution); and the basic style of the eighteenth century, three-cornered and cocked.

Furs were on the enumerated list in 1722. For New York, Virginia, and the southern colonies, fur trading was a profitable enterprise in the eighteenth century, involving considerable credit expansion and organizational activity. In New York between 1700 and 1775, furs accounted for twenty percent of exports. Deerskins became a leading staple for South Carolina and Georgia. Savannah, Augusta, and Charleston served as headquarters for the trade, and both colonies kept pelt and skin factories on the frontier. One-fifth of South Carolina's exports in the mid-eighteenth century were in deerskins. Victory over France in the last colonial war abetted rapid expansion of the English fur trade. In the 1760s fur-trading and military posts were established in the far Ohio country and as distant as the Straits of Mackinac.

IRON

Although copper and lead were mined in the colonial period, the only major metals industry was the production of iron. Seventeenth-century attempts at iron manufacture, however, were not very successful. The first ironworks in America, founded in 1619 at Falling Creek (near Richmond), Virginia, fell victim to the Powhatan Indian uprising of 1622. A report in England (1623) noted receipt from the Falling Creek works of a "fire shovel, tong and a little bar of iron." The versatile John

Winthrop, Jr., who tried his hand at diverse industries, including salt-making, quarrying, and sawmilling, joined with associates to form the Company of Undertakers for the Iron Work in the early 1640s. The Undertakers received a 21-year monopoly grant from the Massachusetts government. As a result, furnaces and rolling and slitting forges were established at Braintree and Lynn. Winthrop himself had a blast furnace at New Haven. Unfortunately, the Undertakers' operations were soon enmeshed with litigation alleging damages to neighboring properties. As Rev. William Hubbard wrote: "Instead of drawing out bars for the countrys use, there was hammered out nothing but contention and lawsuits, which was but a bad return for the undertakers." There were several other attempts in early New England to make use of bog iron deposits, of which the Raynham Works was the most successful, founded in the 1650s and lasting two centuries.

Most iron discovered was surface or bog iron, although rock iron was also used, dug through shafts and tunnels. During the early colonial period, blast furnaces were rare; instead, bloomeries were used, whereby iron ore was mixed with burning charcoal in a hole in the ground. Goatskin bellows increased the heat intensity; the molten metal settled at the bottom of the pit in lumps, called blooms. The typical blast furnace, coming into general use, consisted of a chimney furnace made of granite or other local stone and sometimes brick, about twenty-one feet in diameter at the base, with the inward sloping walls of the stack rising twenty to thirty feet. Alternate layers of fine ore and charcoal were piled in the furnace. Water-powered bellows at the bottom of the furnace supplied air blasts. The molten ore ran into trenches, called pigs, below the stack. Small furnaces, or forges, further refined pig iron into either cast or wrought iron.

One of the most famous colonial ironworks was Governor Alexander Spotswood's plant at the falls of the Rappahannock River. In 1714 and 1717 he brought in German Swiss artisans and established a company town that he called Germanna. Eventually Spotswood also had furnaces at three other sites. Though the German immigrants soon moved away, the Spotswood works lasted several generations after Spotswood's death in 1740 on a limited basis, employing slave labor. But the most grandiose ironworks scheme of all was that of the American Iron Company, founded by a London syndicate, which sent over Peter Hasenclever and five hundred German immigrants to operate ironworks at several locations in New Jersey; six years after Hasenclever's arrival in America in 1764, however, the ironworks went into bankruptcy and ceased operations. Two other large ironworks were the Salisbury Iron Works in Litchfield County, Connecticut, and the Principio Company in Maryland, at the head of the Chesapeake Bay.

"Iron plantations" were founded throughout Pennsylvania, and especially the Delaware, Schuylkill, and Susquehanna valleys became major iron-producing areas. On the eve of the American Revolution, there were eighty-one blast furnaces in Pennsylvania. A 1762 report to the Board of Trade noted eight furnaces and ten forges in Maryland. It is estimated that the British mainland colonies had more blast furnaces and forges than could be found in both England and Wales at that time.

MILLING

The most prevalent of industrial plants in the colonies were gristmills. One of the first buildings provided for by the early New England towns, in addition to a meetinghouse, was a gristmill. North and South, farms bordering strong streams often had mills. Court records are filled with references to riparian rights and damages, such as flooding, regarding privately owned mills. Country storekeepers frequently operated mills, advancing goods in return for grain. Overseas markets for flour increased substantially in the mid-eighteenth century.

The first colonial mills probably relied on power from undershot water wheels. Soon dams were used, allowing for greater water friction and control of the force of water currents. Tidal water flow also propelled some mills. In New Jersey and on Long Island, windmills were commonly employed. Millstones, at least twelve inches thick and four feet in diameter, were made from a variety of hard rock, such as sandstone or granite. Sometimes ballast rocks thrown overboard near shore by English ships were cemented together to make millstones. Milling presented hazards: Sparks could ignite explosive mixtures of flour, dust, and air, and there were dangers of being crushed by millstones or drowning while adjusting a deep-set water wheel. The colonial period saw considerable progress in mill technology, from the horizontal nongeared mill to the vertical mill employing rotary action and vertical shafts.

Planters and farmers brought their flour and cornmeal by wagon to river ports. Until the Revolutionary period flour milling was almost exclusively a rural enterprise. The early gristmills produced whole-wheat flour. Bolts to separate bran and skin from flour were not in general use until after 1750. Thus meal was sifted in homes by handpower until that time. Flour milling concentrated in American port cities was a development of the Revolutionary War period.

OTHER INDUSTRIES AND HOUSEHOLD GOODS

Colonists preferred to make their own beverages. Only rum was produced on a large-scale commercial basis. A distillation of molasses and poor-grade sugar, rum was in great demand among Chesapeake colonists and especially as a staple in the slave trade. It was also favored by workers in the fishing and timber industries as a supplement to a diet of pork and bread. A sectional industry, rum manufacturing was confined almost exclusively to New England and New York. By 1750 fully sixty-three rum distilleries were located in Massachusetts and thirty in Rhode Island. In the late colonial period, farmers and planters, particularly in the backcountry, had stills producing whiskey, some of which entered the commercial market. Breweries were often not very successful because difficulties of refrigeration meant that they could manufacture only for the local market. Apple cider was an important commodity in New England. One New England village of forty families in 1721 made three thousand barrels of cider.

Paper milling became important in the eighteenth century with the increase of newspapers and the proliferation of many other published materials. Perhaps the earliest paper mill was that at Roxborough, near Philadelphia, which began in 1693 but was soon swept away in a flood. Paper was made by grinding cotton or linen rags into pulp, which was then molded and pressed into sheets. By 1769 there were forty paper mills in New Jersey, Pennsylvania, and Delaware.

Tanneries made leather goods. Making leather was an arduous process, involving a series of tasks, including salting, washing, drying, soaking in lime, scraping, stretching, pickling, unhairing, and dipping in tannic acid. Tanners in Charleston, South Carolina, from 1760 to 1775 produced more than 41,700 sides of leather.

Every major colonial port had at least one ropewalk, which made cordage and sailcloth (or duck). Hemp was the ingredient for ropes and usually also for sailcloth (although linen and cotton were also used). For ropemaking, the natural glue was washed out of soaked, decomposed hemp; then the hemp fibers were separated and split. Spinning was accomplished by "walking" the fibers through a spreader, a drawing frame, and two sets of rollers.

Glassmaking, though early attempted at Jamestown and Salem, did not become a major industry during the colonial period, largely due to the intricate skills required and problems in obtaining the best materials. One large glass manufactory, however, was that of Baron Henry William Stiegel at Mannheim, Pennsylvania (1765–1774), specializing in glass tableware. As Victor S. Clark (1933) observes, Stiegel's glassworks was so large "that a coach and four could turn around within the brick dome of his melting-house" (p. 169). Caspar Wistar, also a German immigrant, in 1740 opened a glassworks on a plantation, which he named Wistarburg, near Salem, New Jersey. Richard Wistar succeeded to the management upon his father's death in 1752. The Wistarburg works produced mainly window glass, flint glass, and bottles and also experimented with colored glass.

Most clothing and preserved food and meats were made by members or servants of households. Whole families were often involved in making woolens—shearing, softening with hog's lard, carding, spinning, weaving, and dyeing. Similarly, households produced linen through a complicated process—washing and drying rotted flax stalks, stripping fibers, combing, sorting, spinning, and bleaching. Colonial authorities took measures from time to time to encourage clothmaking. Massachusetts in 1640 required that both boys and girls be taught spinning; in 1646, Virginia counties were ordered to send two children each to Jamestown, where they were to be employed in carding, knitting, and spinning. A textile factory-school opened in Boston in 1751 under the auspices of the Society for Promoting Industry and Frugality. Dr. William Douglass's 1750 estimate that Pennsylvanians manufactured nine-tenths of their clothing probably holds true for other colonies as well.

WORKSHOP CRAFTS

As the colonial period progressed, much of household manufacturing moved into a broader arena. Itinerant tailors, weavers, shoemakers, and other craftsmen performed tasks previously undertaken in households. Independent artisans set up shop. Families sent semifinished products to be completed elsewhere.

Skilled manual workers who earned over fifty percent of their income from nonfarm work are properly called artisans. Craftsmen were artisans who followed a specific trade. Several craftsmen sometimes banded together to establish a shop. Only loosely did the colonial craft system borrow from the medieval English guilds, namely in distinguishing degrees of workmen's status—master workman, journeyman, and apprentice. In reality, however, about the only difference between a master and a journeyman was that a journeyman had not set himself up in business. Apprenticeship (specialized training) did come under statute definition and regulation. Contract obligations governed the relationship between master and apprentice. A master agreed to give board, job training, and sometimes also the rudiments of education to an apprentice in return for work. Apprentices, as usually fixed by law, served until age twenty-one or for seven years. A typical work day for an apprentice was twelve to sixteen hours. There were two kinds of apprenticeship: voluntary and compulsory. As in England, a common practice among the colonists was to bind out children to learn a trade. Public authorities bound over orphans and other destitute children. At the completion of the bound service, whether entered into voluntarily or not, a young tradesman was by law entitled to "freedom dues," similar to the award given upon completion of indentured servitude. The gratuity was mainly in the form of clothes or other necessities and seldom cash or tools.

Most colonial craftsmen were not narrow specialists. This was especially true of metalworkers and woodworkers. Thus Paul Revere, a silversmith by trade, also functioned as a coppersmith, engraver, and dentist and as a manufacturer of branding irons for hatters and surgeon's implements. Woodworking is a good example of the subdivision of work within a trade. A general carpenter might also work specifically as a joiner, cabinetmaker, or wagonmaker.

Tradesmen's associations made few strides during the colonial period. In a few cities, benevolent societies did appear, giving most of their attention to providing benefits to the sick, widows, and orphans. Of the few attempts to establish guildlike organizations, the Carpenters Company in Philadelphia, founded in 1724, was the most prominent. This group kept a "Book of Prices," to which members were expected to adhere. The English guild system as such, however, did not take root for various reasons: Master craftsmen were usually themselves retailers and employers of labor; there was no clear distinction between master workmen and journeymen, and any person could set himself up as a master craftsman; statutory definition of master craftsman and guilds was lacking; and the cost of labor was high.

Concerted protest action was rare among craftsmen, although such efforts were occasionally undertaken to maintain monopoly or restrict competition from newcomers or itinerants. English common-law principles carried over into the colonies, and any cooperative resistance among laborers tended to be viewed as criminal conspiracy. Colonial labor protests were aimed chiefly at government regulation and price fixing, unlike the modern stance of employee versus employer. Hence little success could be expected of economic sanctions, such as strikes. One example from the late colonial period is indicative. In 1770, when New York City coopers refused to sell casks at the price set by the government, they were tried for conspiracy of trade and fined fifty shillings.

COLONIAL ECONOMIC REGULATION

Colony and local governments, in the public's interest, enacted numerous laws and ordinances promoting manufactures and regulating retail and labor conditions. Bounties, subsidies, loans, monopolies, patents, and land were granted to encourage production of both manufactures and raw materials in order to meet general consumer demand. Monopolies often conveyed the intent of patenting. This view, for example, was expressed in a 1641 Massachusetts enactment that stated that "there shall be no monopolies granted or allowed among us, but of such new inventions as are profitable to the country, and that for a short time." To some degree the colonies specifically experimented in patent law, though most colonial patents related to processes rather than machinery. The practice of granting monopoly privileges for encouragement of new industries had all but died out by the time of the American Revolution, as had already been the case in England.

Particularly during the early colonial period, thoroughgoing economic regulation prevailed. Colonial governments determined price and quality of commodities; storage and wharfage rates; fees and wages of millers, smiths, and the like; and markets. They also set weights and measures, granted licenses, and sought to prevent unfair practices such as forestalling and engrossing. Regulations were more extensive in New England than elsewhere in the seventeenth century, probably because of the Puritan emphasis on the sinfulness of man. Colonial legislatures also exempted certain manufactures and raw materials from taxation. Industrial workers were sometimes freed from taxation and public obligations. Though there was decided progress toward more of a laissez-faire economy, colonial regulatory policies were still pervasive up to and through the Revolutionary War period, especially with respect to quality and price controls.

Colonists were cognizant of their capacity for economic self-sufficiency. As Peter Kalm observed in his American tour in the mid-eighteenth century, in Pennsylvania "most of the inhabitants are manufacturers, and make almost everything in such quantity and perfection, that in a short time this province will want very little from England, its mother country." Benjamin Franklin wrote of the expanding American population, and though representing an agricultural viewpoint, he thought that the colonists could meet the challenge of supplying their own needs as well as those of England. But the perspective of Americans in the 1760s went far beyond notions of self-sufficiency or the proper economic role in the English imperial system. With continuing industrial growth, expansion of products entering the world market, and accumulation of domestic capital, Americans now looked toward being suppliers of commodities on their own terms.

7

Trade
and Empire

Commerce sustained an expansive colonial economy and contributed to a steady rise in the standard of living. From 1700 to 1775, population increased at the rate of three percent per annum in the American colonies, while per capita income grew on the average of nearly one-half percent annually. Though operating within the confines of the British imperial system, colonial trade serviced the empire as a whole, dominated the American internal market, and, on a limited basis, developed worldwide contacts.

Out of the chaos of the Civil War and economic stagnation, the English government in the mid-seventeenth century embarked on a course of enhancing both the economy and the power of the nation-state by promoting self-sufficiency within the empire. The welfare of the realm, however, would be the primary consideration. Mercantilist policy became the leading measure for defining the relationship between the colonies and the home country. In accordance with mercantilist theory, Great Britain should not only encourage development of industry at home but also obtain a favorable balance of trade, whereby sales overseas exceeded purchases. It was expected that in the settlement of accounts, specie (gold and silver) would be drawn into the mother country. The accumulation of precious metals would bolster the power of the state. Mercantilist policy sought to discourage importation of finished goods from the colonies as well as from foreign countries. Imports should support home industries. Although the colonies were to be in a state of economic dependency in relation to the mother country, the colonies should be encouraged to produce needed raw materials and any manufactures not readily made in England.

English mercantilist theorists abounded in late seventeenth and early eighteenth centuries. Josiah Child, for example, in *A Treatise concerning the East India Trade* (London, 1681), noted that "foreign trade produces riches, riches [produce] power, [and] power preserves our trade and religion." Andrew Yarranton, in *England's Improvement by Sea and Land* (London, 1677), observed:

> For as the honesty of all governments is, so shall be their riches; and as their honour, honesty, and riches are, so will be their strength; and as their honour, honesty, riches, and strength are, so will be their trade. These are five sisters that go hand in hand, and must not be parted.

ENGLISH REGULATION OF NAVIGATION AND TRADE

Before the mid-seventeenth century, a large part of the trade of the American colonies was carried by Dutch ships. Under the strong rule of Cromwell, the English government began the process of remedying this problem. A provision appended to a 1650 act on Virginians' allegiance to the Commonwealth required the licensing of all foreign ships trading with the English colonies. The Navigation Act of 1651 stipulated (1) that all goods from Asia, Africa, or America were to be sent to England or any of its territories only in vessels whereby the master and the majority of seamen were English, (2) that all goods from Europe could be carried to England or its territories only in English vessels belonging to persons of the country of origin, and (3) that other foreign goods could be brought into England only from the place of production or from the ports where first shipped. Penalties involved forfeiture of cargo and vessel.

"An Act for the Encouraging and Increasing of Shipping and Navigation" in 1660 sought a further exclusion of the foreign carrying trade. No goods regardless of origin could be imported into or exported out of English colonies except in vessels owned and built in the realm, Ireland, or the English colonies, and the master of such ships and three-fourths of the crew had to be English. Colonists were forbidden to deal directly with foreign merchants. The Navigation Act of 1660 also provided that certain enumerated articles (sugar, tobacco, raw cotton, ginger, indigo, and dyewoods) produced by the colonies could be sent only to Great

Britain, Ireland, or other English colonies. The only commodity of continental America affected was tobacco. The enumerated list would eventually be extended: In 1706, molasses, rice, and naval stores were added; in 1722, copper, beaver, and other skins; in 1764, coffee, pimento, coconuts, whale fins, raw silk, hides and skins, potash, and pearl ashes.

To insure England as the market for European goods destined for the colonies, Parliament in 1663 passed "An Act for the Encouragement of Trade" (the Staple Act), which required that any "Commodity of the Growth, Production, or Manufacture of Europe" to be imported into any English colony had first to be "laden and shipped in England." To enforce the navigation law of 1660, colonial shippers were required to post bond guaranteeing the destination of enumerated cargoes according to the law. In 1673 an act "for the better secureing the Plantation Trade" placed export duties, in addition to bonding, on vessels carrying enumerated articles that went from one colony to another, thus encouraging direct shipment to England. This act also empowered the Commissioners of Customs in London to appoint collectors of customs to be resident in the colonies; five were named, one each for Massachusetts, New York, Virginia, Maryland, and the Carolinas. The export duty was significant in itself, soon supplying the crown treasury with over 100,000 pounds annually from the tariff on tobacco alone.

Except during the Cromwell regime, when a parliamentary committee and a council of state had responsibility, general supervision over navigation and trade was exercised by Privy Council committees until 1696, when the Board of Trade assumed this function. Naval officers, customs officials, and colonial governors were charged with the enforcement of the navigation laws. In the 1690s, Edward Randolph was the first to hold the office of surveyor general of His Majesty's colonies in America. The Navigation Act of 1696 established a vice-admiralty court, an inferior branch of the High Court of Admiralty in London, for each of the American colonies. The vice-admiralty court consisted only of a judge, register, and marshal and had jurisdiction over violations of the navigation acts; there was no jury. Colonial courts, however, insisted that they had jurisdiction over cases arising from seizures in American ports and waters and frequently reversed decisions of the admiralty courts. Thus the vice-admiralty courts in America remained ineffective until the British government gave them added powers in the 1760s.

Four major acts of trade supplemented the navigation laws. The Woolen Act of 1699 forbade the export of wool, woolen yarn, or woolen cloth outside the colony where produced, including a prohibition from shipment in the intercolonial trade. Similarly, to afford protection to a depressed English industry, the Hat Act of 1732 interdicted the export of hats from the colonies to England, any foreign country, or another colony; the term of apprenticeship in shops was set at seven years; a master could employ no more than two apprentices; and Negroes were barred from hatmaking. "An Act for the better Securing and Encouraging the Trade of His Majesty's Sugar Colonies in America" (Molasses Act) of 1733 levied prohibitive duties on sugar, rum, and spirits imported from the foreign sugar islands: nine pence per gallon on rum and spirits, six pence per gallon on molasses or syrup, and five pence per hundredweight for sugar. Any violation of the law, including nonperformance of duty by a customs officer, brought a fifty-pound fine.

The interdependence that was supposed to be fostered by the mercantilist system is evident in the passage of the Iron Act of 1750. Iron manufacturing was an important industry in the English Midlands. Because of deforestation and dwindling mineral deposits, English iron manufacturers had to rely increasingly on importation of smelted iron. Large importations of iron came from Sweden. Iron deposits were plentiful in the colonies, and the colonial iron industry so expanded that it threatened to compete substantially with British finished iron products. Thus the Iron Act was a compromise measure that was expected to benefit both British and American producers. The act encouraged production of pig and bar iron in America by removing duties on American iron in Great Britain, but it forbade any further erection of slitting mills, plating forges, and steel furnaces in the colonies. Existing establishments would not be affected. The intent of the law was simply to check further growth of the manufacture of finished iron products in the colonies. Actually, the act caused almost no hardship to the colonial iron industry. The law lacked means of enforcement, and the colonial finished iron industry had reached a level that allowed more for retrenchment than expansion; meanwhile, producers of unfabricated iron had a favored market in England.

The other acts of trade also had a minimal effect on colonial commerce and industry. Wool remained largely a domestic industry regardless of imperial regulation. The Molasses Act was evaded by wholesale smuggling. Given the dominance of powerful northern merchants in colonial West Indian shipping, the appointment of leading colonists as customs officials and naval officers, and the localization and ineffectiveness of vice-admiralty jurisdiction, collusion to evade payment of the offensive duties was rife. Only the Hat Act caused inconvenience to a minor colonial industry. The British ministry avoided the pursuit of any stringent measures for enforcement of the trade acts; hence the period from the 1690s to 1763 is styled an era of "salutary neglect."

In many ways the navigation acts worked in the colonists' favor. Colonial merchants had secure English markets. The navigation laws guaranteed Great Britain as the first market for colonial exported staples. Preferential tariffs were permitted on most enumerated goods. Great Britain, on direct shipping routes to Europe, served as a convenient entrepôt for the northern European trade. Colonial tobacco enjoyed a monopoly in England, where local cultivation of tobacco was forbidden. Colonial ships dominated the American coastal trade and participated fully in the imperial Atlantic trade and elsewhere. The navigation acts stimulated American shipbuilding and removed the competition of foreign shipping. British fleets provided protection for American trading vessels.

One liability for the American colonies under both the navigation acts and acts of trade was some interference with intercolonial trade, most notably the plantation export duties on enumerated commodities. A negative effect on relations within the British Empire was the failure to recognize the colonists' status as the same as that of inhabitants of the realm. This awareness on the part of the colonists would become manifest when the British government, after 1763, attempted to restructure the "old colonial system" into one of tighter mercantilist supervision of the colonies.

OVERSEAS COMMERCE

American-owned and -operated ships figured substantially in colonial commerce. As James F. Shepherd and Gary M. Walton (1972) have noted, colonial vessels outnumbered British ships in intercolonial trade and overseas areas outside the British Isles, while British-owned ships dominated the trade between Great Britain and both the southern colonies and the West Indies. Direct shuttle patterns and route specialization typified colonial trade between the southern colonies and Great Britain. Triangular traffic often characterized commercial voyages from New England and the middle colonies. For example, New England vessels brought to Africa rum, trinkets, or other manufactures, which were exchanged for slaves, gold, and ivory; these commodities were then sold in the West Indies for molasses, coin, and bills of exchange, which the vessels carried back to their home ports. New England ships also transported wheat, fish, and forest products to southern Europe in exchange for wine, fruits, salt, and other items, which were then carried to England and swapped for manufactured goods. Similarly, ships from the middle colonies brought foodstuffs, livestock, and wood products to the West Indies; sugar and other tropical products were then transported to England, where they were exchanged for manufactures. Frequently, northern vessels broke West Indian voyages with stops at Charleston or other southern ports.

Although there were a great variety of goods in the colonial export trade, there was regional specialization. New England exports consisted mainly of fish, provisions, rum, forest products, and ships. New York primarily exported furs, cereals, provisions, fruits, and lumber. From Pennsylvania came pipe staves, pork, beef, fish, grain, and flour. Philadelphia accounted for more than one-half of colonial shipments of flour.

While tobacco remained the staple export of Maryland and Virginia, grain increasingly became an important export commodity in these colonies. North Carolina relied mainly on exports of naval stores and other lumber products, while South Carolina chiefly marketed rice, indigo, and pelts and skins. West Indian products were reexported from colonial ports.

Some exemptions from the navigation acts were allowed for colonial trade to areas south of Cape Finisterre, Spain, and colonial ships made their way especially to Lisbon, the largest urban market on the Iberian peninsula. American vessels, however, did not penetrate into the Mediterranean.

In the eighteenth century a marked shift in colonial overseas trade was the expansion of the southern European and West Indian markets. For example, as Shepherd and Walton have estimated in their quantified study of the colonial export trade, for the 1720s and 1730s, the value of colonial exports to southern Europe amounted to 50,000 to 60,000 pounds sterling per annum; to the West Indies, 125,000 to 150,000 pounds annually. By the 1750s the annual value of goods sent to southern Europe was 125,000 to 150,000 pounds and to the West Indies, 175,000 to 200,000 pounds. West Indian and southern European trade leveled out in the 1760s. Shepherd and Walton give the total value of colonial exports for 1768–1772 as 2,801,000 pounds: to Great Britain, 1,528,000 pounds; Ireland, 87,000 pounds; southern Europe, 406,000 pounds; the West Indies, 759,000 pounds; and Africa, 21,000 pounds. Although balance of payments in trade fluctuated owing to economic conditions at home and abroad, amount of surpluses, demand, and wartime factors, the colonies in the eighteenth century overall experienced little or no trade deficits (imports exceeding exports).

British exports to the colonies relied chiefly on textiles of all sorts, metal hardware, household goods and wares, gunpowder and shot, and paper. Leading commodities reexported from England to the colonies were tea, hemp, German and Russian linens, spices, and drugs.

INTERCOLONIAL TRADE

Foreign and West Indian goods brought over by oceanic vessels were distributed throughout the colonies by way of small craft plying the coasts and inland waterways and by transport overland. Locally produced commodities were sent from colony to colony. The relationship between inland consumers and producers and seaport merchants was much like that of the Chesapeake planters and commission firms in England and Scotland.

Boston, New York City, and Philadelphia each became an entrepôt for the distribution of imported goods in the northern colonies, as did Charleston and lesser ports, such as Norfolk and Alexandria, in the South.

Boston served as an exchange center for all of New England and eastern Long Island; New York City for western Long Island, eastern New Jersey, and New York; and Philadelphia for western New Jersey, Delaware, northern Maryland, and Pennsylvania. There was an active carrying trade in small vessels from Maine to Georgia. New England ships also had ports of call in New France. During the winter season, New England fishing boats were engaged in the colonial trade as far south as the Carolinas. It has been estimated that the North American coastal trade equaled one-fourth of the amount of the colonial overseas commerce.

New York City serves as a good example of the linkage of intercolonial commerce. It imported rice from Georgia and South Carolina, furs and naval stores from North Carolina, and grain from Maryland and Virginia. In return, it supplied bread, flour, cider, beer, a few slaves, and European and West Indian products. The New York colony had to supplement its native crops largely because most of its home-grown commodities were exported in the West Indian trade. Also, manufactures from New England and Great Britain, foodstuffs, tea, and Madeira wine were shipped via New York City merchants to the southern colonies. Trade from New York to New England included breadstuffs in return for fish, oil, and rum for shipment to southern Europe. New York merchants competed with New Englanders for the sale of British manufactures in Providence and Newport. Connecticut and New Jersey were both "tributary provinces" dependent on New York for the sale of their farm products (chiefly pork, beef, and flaxseed) and imported European manufactures. Boston and Philadelphia also conducted an intense rivalry with New York for the trade of these two colonies.

The colonies experimented with impost duties as a means of gaining trade advantages over their neighbors. In 1747, Connecticut placed a charge on anyone bringing into the colony more than fifteen pounds' worth of commodities from any other New England colony, New York, New Jersey, or Pennsylvania—five pounds for every hundred pounds' worth of goods imported. Importers from outside the colony had to pay an extra duty of seven and one-half percent. Because the demand was far greater than the supply, this scheme soon fell through. Massachusetts, New York, Pennsylvania, and Maryland all had imposts on goods from other colonies at one time or another, but most were short-lived because of retaliatory measures by the colonies affected.

Virginia's commercial restrictions sought mainly to reduce competition from tobacco planting in North Carolina. Virginia acts in 1679, 1702, 1705, 1706, and 1726 prohibiting entirely the importation of tobacco from North Carolina and forbidding ships in Virginia waters from taking it aboard were a major factor in driving the Carolina tobacco trade into the hands of Boston merchants.

South Carolina took advantage of the North Carolina trade that followed the natural waterways of the Pee Dee and Catawba rivers into South Carolina. South Carolina levied heavy imposts on North Carolina commodities via this route. Although the Board of Trade condemned this policy, nothing was done to remedy it. In 1751, North Carolina laid retaliatory duties on liquors coming from South Carolina. In the 1730s, South Carolina placed high duties on all pitch, tar, and turpentine coming in from other colonies and by 1763 also had duties on rum, biscuits, and flour from the northern colonies and on rum, sugar, and molasses from the West Indies. A problem of a different sort was that of Virginia traders taking out deerskins without a license in the Carolinas, which led South Carolina to pass a prohibitive tax on all Virginia goods coming into the colony.

A solution to the intercolonial economic rivalry would have been for Parliament to revoke the assemblies' powers of taxation over trade and to impose imperial duties at American ports. Or Parliament could have required uniformity in the colonies' regulation of trade. Strangely, English mercantilist writers seldom addressed these issues and even then only vaguely. But people who dealt with colonial trade problems at first hand in the colonies saw the situation in a different light. An anonymous Virginian wrote in 1701 that "to redress the Grievances that one Plantation may suffer by another" there should be "the Setling an equal Liberty of Trade" and to this end a "General Law" that could decide and adjust all controversies over trade and commerce in the colonies.

TRADE DURING WARTIME

The colonial wars generally stimulated the American economy, particularly during the French and Indian War (1756–1763). The colonists had ample opportunity to supply British army and naval units in America as well as provincial troops. Specie from the mother country was used in payment for military supplies. The impact of war on the British reexport market caused some hardship in the colonies, especially among tobacco planters. During wartime the Dutch became almost the exclusive purchasers of English tobacco; mixing their own poor-quality tobacco with that received from England, they caused a glut in low-grade tobacco in Europe. During King George's War and the French and Indian War, however, licensed English ships carrying tobacco were allowed to go to French ports, but they could not bring back any French goods. During the last colonial war, the so-called rule of 1756 was applied to Dutch shipping, which meant that French ports not opened to the trade of another nation in peacetime were considered to be closed to ships of that country during wartime.

Though all commercial intercourse between the American colonies and the enemy was prohibited during wartime, the colonists nevertheless engaged in trade with Canada, Cape Breton, and the French and Spanish West Indies. During the later part of the French and Indian War, French forces in Canada were chiefly supplied from Pennsylvania, New York, and New England. Flour, beef, and pork were exchanged for French rum, sugar, and molasses.

A major factor encouraging smuggling was that the French West Indies were not self-sustaining. Producing sugar, coffee, indigo, and the like, the French islands had to import most of their foodstuffs from the American colonies. In order to clamp down on smuggling in wartime, the colonial governors were allowed more discretionary authority over commerce than normally in peacetime, but in the exercise of these powers they often abetted trade with the enemy. Governors issued commissions known as "flags of truce" to exchange prisoners, but these were frequently a coverup for trade in provisions with the enemy.

Embargoes were placed on foreign goods and also at times on provisions and other commodities for the purpose of ensuring the availability of needed supplies for the military forces. The colonial embargoes, however, were usually uncoordinated, intermittent, and for short durations; thus it was difficult to sustain a coastwide embargo with broken links in the chain.

OVERSEAS MARKETING AND CREDIT

The channels of marketing and credit differed between the northern and tobacco colonies. Northern merchants were self-reliant for marketing and obtaining capital. Maryland, Virginia, and North Carolina planters relied chiefly on credit supplied by consignment of goods to British commercial agents.

Leading merchants in Boston, New York, and Philadelphia usually did not do business with middlemen. They transported their commodities in their own vessels and sold directly on the English market. The elimination of freight and commission charges contributed to a favorable balance of payments. As distributors of European and West Indian goods, northern merchants profited from sales and interest on credit they extended.

Under the consignment system, southern planters retained ownership of their commodities until they were sold in Great Britain. A British commercial agent charged a commission fee of two and one-half to three percent for his role in overseeing unloading, trucking, inspection, warehousing, and marketing. The agent also filled orders for the purchase of goods in England to be returned to the planter. The agent held balances in the form of bills of exchange that could be drawn on by the planter in Great Britain or the West Indies and offered advance funds, with future crops as collateral. The consignment trade had disadvantages: selling on the merchant's terms, the long delay in collection of payment for cargoes shipped, the easy opportunity for the English agents to falsify accounts, the long time that English merchant ships remained in American waters while obtaining a full shipload, and the expenses planters had to bear in transportation and in defraying taxes and charges advanced by the agent.

Because of the problems of long-distance marketing and buying, a new method of disposing the produce of planters emerged in the eighteenth century. The factorage (or factory) system, whereby resident factors (salaried or commission agents) represented British mercantile houses, allowed for planters to sell their goods immediately in the colonies. London factors dominated in the tidewater areas. As settlement moved into the piedmont, Scottish firms (many of them wholesale houses) established "stores" in the backcountry, which served as centers for the purchase of tobacco and the sale of imported goods. Besides providing spot cash to the planter, the Scottish factors, like the consignment agents, also extended credit. The Glasgow factors dominated the inland trade and were able to pay higher prices for tobacco than the London agents because of lower ocean transportation costs (due to current and winds, the westward voyage from Scotland to the colonies was two to three weeks shorter than from England), quicker turnaround for ships loading in full at the wharves of Scottish stores, and excessive markups on goods sold to planters. Some large planters, producing the better grades of tobacco, still preferred to do business in the consignment trade, which just before the Revolution amounted to one-fourth of Virginia tobacco shipped abroad. A good part of the six million pounds owed by American colonists to British creditors on the eve of the Revolution consisted of debts accrued from the consignment trade by Virginia, Maryland, and North Carolina planters.

The patterns of marketing differed somewhat in South Carolina from that of Virginia, Maryland, and North Carolina. Charleston merchants, whether representing London firms or operating on their own accounts, served as factors in buying planters' crops, making credit advances, and assuming the risks of bringing cargoes to the British markets. Facilitating the role of Charleston merchants as commercial agents was the city's connection with inland rivers and wagon roads that went into the settled parts of the backcountry—an advantage also enjoyed by Savannah merchants in the late colonial period.

PROBLEMS OF MONEY AND EXCHANGE

The achievement of convenient and standard media of exchange eluded Americans throughout the colonial period. The colonists devised various means to remedy the shortage of coin.

Barter of goods, the most rudimentary form of exchange, was often used in local transactions and constituted the primary way of doing business with the Indians. During the early colonial period, wampum was employed in trade with the northern coastal Indians. Wampum was in the form of cylindrical pieces of shell, drilled through the center; polished on stones, the shell fragments were strung on thread like beads. Blue wampum came from the eye of the quahog shell, white wampum from the periwinkle shell.

Colonists moved from barter to the use of commodity money, that is, allowing certain products to be received in payment of taxes and other public debts. A wide variety of commodity money ("country pay") was accepted by colonial governments at one time or another: such payment included beef, pork, peas, Indian corn, wheat, rye, barley, fish, and lumber in the northern colonies; flax and hemp in Pennsylvania and Maryland; tobacco in Virginia and Maryland; pitch and tar in North Carolina; and rice in South Carolina. As William B. Weeden (1890) noted regarding early New England:

> Cattle walked into the public treasury; if fat, they gave currency to property and wealth; if lean, they walked out again, repudiated by the wary tax-collector, because their spare shanks gave too much movement and too little solid value to this peripatetic currency of the public wealth. (vol. 1, p. 315)

The colonies most dependent on commodity money lacked a large trading center. Most colonies continued to use commodity money for payment of taxes, though Massachusetts ended the practice in 1694.

To compensate for the dearth of coin, Massachusetts in the seventeenth century experimented with its own mint—the only colony ever to do so. Ample South American silver was being obtained through the West Indies. In 1652, John Hull, who had been trained as a gold-and-silversmith, was hired as mintmaster to produce three-penny and six-penny pieces, but this issue was soon discontinued because of clipping of coins. A second minting cut two-, three-, and six-penny silver pieces, which became known as the willow, oak, and pine tree "shillings." Concentric rings at the edges of these coins deterred clipping, as did a 1679 law that made this offense punishable by having both ears cut off. That sturdy trees graced the face of the coins instead of any semblance of the English sovereign caused ire in the home government. The Massachusetts coins were discontinued in the 1680s.

Spanish milled dollars and pieces of eight (one-eighth of a dollar) and other foreign coins—Spanish, French, Dutch, and Portuguese—circulated legally in the colonies. The colonies attempted to maximize the value of foreign coins in order to draw money from the outside and to reduce the burden of debts. A royal proclamation in 1704, however, decreed the value of pieces of eight at six shillings in the colonies; to accept such coins at a higher valuation than the proclamation rate carried a penalty of six months' imprisonment and a ten-pound fine. Colonial assemblies circumvented this order by stating the value of silver by weight rather than expressing the value of the coin itself in shillings. To preserve a favorable influx of specie into the mother country, English coins, after 1663, were not permitted to be exported to the colonies, although the colonies could receive foreign coins and bullion. The colonies were also required not to prohibit exportation of coins to England.

A worthy substitute for specie was the bill of exchange. Much like a modern bank check, a bill of exchange was an order by a person to a correspondent to pay a specified sum of money to a third person named in the bill. Endorsements were permitted. The bills, frequently drawn on deposits held by British agents, circulated like cash. Another kind of paper passed like money was the "tobacco note." One form of such notes was certificates of ownership issued at warehouses for tobacco that had been approved at inspection; these warehouse notes changed hands like money, with one holder finally exporting the tobacco. Promissory notes, pledging payment in tobacco "at the next crop," also circulated.

Actual paper money in the colonies—and, for that matter, in the Western world—first appeared in 1690 when the Massachusetts legislature provided for the emission of seven thousand pounds in promissory notes, or bills of credit, secured by anticipated provincial revenues. The colony needed extra financial resources to pay for a military expedition to Canada. The bills of credit were made legal tender and receivable as payment for taxes and other public debts; upon their return to the Treasury, they were to be destroyed.

Between 1700 and 1715, all colonies except Pennsylvania, Maryland, and Virginia followed Massachusetts's example. South Carolina in 1702 issued bills of credit as legal tender backed by duties on liquors, skins, and furs. Virginia was the last colony to emit bills of credit, doing so at the start of the French and Indian War in 1755. Colonies resorted to bills of credit especially during war and its aftermath; such bills were usually secured by additional special taxes, and a time period was specified for their redemption. Depreciation occurred because of failure to vote or collect taxes to retire the bills, extension of the periods for redemption, or a too large issue. Thus it became a practice to retire bills of credit by including redemption of "old tenor" currency within the purview of emission of "new tenor" bills.

Increasingly, bills of credit were issued in the form of government loans secured by land. Loan offices issued the paper money in return for mortgages on land. The bills drew interest that was discounted when turned over to the government. Unlike bills of credit backed by tax revenues, land-secured notes broadened the borrowing capacity of farmers. Often persons failed to turn in notes within specified time periods. To make payments, they frequently needed fresh loans. Hence, like those based on tax receipts, these bills of credit were overissued and depreciated.

Paper money, however, was beneficial to the colonial economy in providing capital and stimulating trade. One factor contributing to keeping paper money in circulation was that depreciation was seldom rapid. Thus as it exchanged hands, a current holder would suffer only slight depreciation. Devaluation of money did not pose a great threat to the colonists because few incomes were fixed and there were no bank deposits.

The major currency problem was the discrepancy in the exchange rate between paper money and specie. No colony ever fixed a set ratio. There was constant bickering between colonists and British creditors, who were often compelled reluctantly to accept paper money, even though it was valued considerably lower than its equivalent in specie. Not surprisingly, British merchants pressured Parliament to restrict paper money in the colonies.

The issuance of private bills of credit was deemed one solution to the demand for more sound money. Such a proposal became a bitter political issue in Massachusetts in the 1730s. The scheme almost came to fruition. A land bank was organized in Massachusetts in 1740. Essentially, the private land bank's function was similar to the government's in issuing bills of credit backed by land. The plan was to issue notes of credit to subscribers at three percent interest, secured by mortgages and personal bonds. The land bank was to be capitalized at 150,000 pounds for twenty years. Repayments would go into a fund, from which commercial loans could be made, with interest from these providing dividends for the subscribers. Boston merchants also came up with the idea of a silver bank, with annual repayments in silver bullion; the notes were to be secured by bonds and surety (other than land). Parliament, however, by extending the Bubble Act of 1720, declared illegal all such schemes as land and silver banks.

During the eighteenth century, colonists divided over the question of paper money versus hard currency. William Douglass, an immigrant physician from Scotland, became the leading proponent of hard money. In *An Essay concerning Silver and Paper Currencies . . .* (1738) and *A Discourse concerning the Currencies of the British Plantations in America* (1740), he denounced paper money as defrauding creditors and as stimulating extravagance in public expenditures. Hugh Vance, a small merchant in Boston who was himself in debt, advocated the cause of paper money. In *Observations on the Scheme Projected for Emitting 60,000 Pounds in Bills of a New Tenor* (1738) and *An Inquiry into the Nature and Uses of Money . . .* (1740), he insisted that limited issues of secured paper money under government authority met all the requirements for a sound currency: stability, conveniency, common consent, and public approbation. Benjamin Franklin also enlisted on the side of paper money. In *A Modest Enquiry into the Nature and Necessity of Paper Currency* (1729), he observed that the scarcity of money led to high interest rates, a reduction in the prices of products in trade, the discouragement of craftsmen and laborers coming to America, and a greater consumption of English goods. With an ample currency, Franklin noted, people would less likely run into debt or sue one another for debts. Franklin favored the issuance of bills of credit through a provincial loan office; the bills would be secured by land, and borrowers would pay interest on the bills at a rate equal to rent on the land.

At last Parliament heeded the pleas of British creditors. The Currency Act of 1751, affecting the New England colonies, prohibited land banks, required regular retirement of existing issues of paper money, insisted on the retirement of paper as legal tender within two years, and banned future notes except those backed by tax revenues. The Currency Act of 1764 extended the 1751 law to all the colonies, with Virginia especially in mind. Parliament, however, in 1773 would modify its restrictions somewhat by permitting the emission of legal-tender currency for public debts in the colonies.

8

The New Immigration

Before 1680, nine-tenths of white colonial Americans were of English stock. The ethnic minority was primarily Scandinavian and Dutch. The Dutch assimilated slowly, retaining their language and customs well into the eighteenth century. The 1680s marked a radical change in the composition of immigrants to America. The vast majority of the new immigrants came from six regions other than England: Germany, Northern Ireland, Africa, Scotland, France, and Switzerland. After 1720 immigration was overwhelmingly non-English. On the eve of the Revolution, one-third of Americans were foreign-born. The total number of white immigrants from 1700 to 1775 is estimated at nearly 300,000.

Of course, with no general or categorized census during the colonial period (only local tax assessment lists, muster rolls, and the like), it is difficult to quantify ethnic population segments of colonial America. In 1931 the American Historical Association published a report of an American Council of Learned Societies committee in which the ethnic populations for 1790 were estimated according to names reflecting linguistic and national stocks. Though historians Forrest McDonald and Ellen Shapiro McDonald (1980) have since demonstrated that the 1931 report erred substantially in confusing Scotch-Irish with Scots and also in underestimating the Celtic element in the middle and southern colonies, it is useful as an attempt to discern ethnic composition by names. The report estimated that in 1790, people with the following ethnic identities were living in the United States: English, 1,939,396; Scots, 261,138; Scotch-Irish, 190,662; Irish, 116,248; Germans, 279,220; Dutch, 100,000; French, 73,750; Swedes, 21,100; Spaniards, 25,625; and unassigned, 219,805. The figures, of course, reflect the immigration shifts after 1763.

Although improvements in economic and demographic conditions led to a slackening of emigration from England, mercantilist considerations favored substantial immigration into the colonies. Population increase in the colonies would provide a widening market for English manufactures, expanded productivity of desired goods from the colonies, and greater security against foreign and Indian enemies. Poverty, economic blight, war, religious persecution, and political and social discontent impelled Europeans to migrate to the British mainland colonies. For the most part, colonists welcomed the newcomers, many of whom were indentured servants and redemptioners. The new immigration reflected both a "push" and a "pull." Above all, America represented a new life and opportunity.

THE GERMANS

The largest number of non-English immigrants were the Germans. Although scattered in farms and communities from New York to Georgia, they tended to keep much of the old country's ways. The first important arrival of Germans were those sponsored by William Penn. Pietists from Frankfurt-on-the-Main, led by Francis Daniel Pastorius and Johannes Kelpius, settled in 1683 at what was to become Germantown. More pietists—Mennonites, Dunkards, Schwenkfelders, and others—followed in the eighteenth century. After 1730 the majority of German immigrants were separatists from the state churches—Reformed, Lutheran, and Moravian. The flow of German immigration, assisted by the English crown and colonial entrepreneurs, steadily accelerated, many coming over as redemptioners.

German peasants viewed America as a place where there would be few taxes, high wages, and an absence of compulsion for military service. Promotional literature lured the Germans, as did the bright prospects in the promised land painted by "Neulanders," agents of ship captains, land companies, or merchants who posed as wealthy German settlers in America. But getting to America entailed great hardship. To borrow a term from Oscar Handlin, those who left their homeland passed through a "brutal filter." Unscrupulous supply agents combed the countryside, through one means or another separating emigrants from what little wealth or property they had. Upon reaching Rotterdam or Amsterdam for embarkation, personal belongings also managed somehow to disappear. Many of the émigrés, being impoverished, had to pledge future labor service in return for passage to the New World. Crowded aboard ship, allotted a space of only six by two feet between decks, often spending days lying on their backs, the emigrants suffered terribly, with a high mortality from scurvy, smallpox, and typhus. Children under seven seldom survived. Gottlieb Mittelberger wrote that the drinking water was "black, thick with dirt, and full of worms" and the biscuit contained "red worms and spiders." Lice were everywhere. Upon debarking, many of the newcomers faced the auction block, and those who were free had to figure out a way to start from scratch in the wilderness.

The great majority of German immigrants came from the Rhineland area. From the time of the Thirty Years' War (1618–1648), the Rhenish German provinces had suffered the ravages of war. Louis XIV, at the start of the War of the League of Augsburg, followed a scorched-earth policy in the Palatinate, leveling the whole cities of Mannheim, Speyer, and Worms, and during the War of the Spanish Succession (1702–1713) brought desolation to other Rhenish provinces.

During the War of the Spanish Succession, the British government offered asylum to Germans fleeing their homeland. By 1709 some eleven thousand German refugees were in London. But because of the burden in caring for them, the crown sought means to send them to America. Nearly three thousand Palatine refugees in England were sent under contract to the New York colony for the purpose of making tar and pitch. Most of the refugees were settled on the estate of Robert Livingston, fifty-five miles north of New York City. Because trees had to be treated for two years and because Finnish tar sold at half the price of American, the enterprise did not succeed initially. The Germans began to protest what they considered slavelike conditions. Thus Governor Robert Hunter had them moved to the Schoharie valley in 1712 and 1713. Some also went to the Mohawk valley. Many filtered down into Pennsylvania and the northern counties of New Jersey.

Eventually, Germans amounted to half the population of Pennsylvania. Seven thousand Germans landed at Philadelphia in 1717, and for half a century thereafter about two thousand a year debarked at that port. German communities dotted central Pennsylvania along the Susquehanna River. Moravian Brethren settled Bethlehem and Nazareth in 1741. With the Scotch-Irish blocking the piedmont area, Germans spilled down into the valleys of the Appalachian mountain range into Maryland along the Monocacy and Conococheague rivers, the Shenandoah valley in Virginia, and through the piedmont region of the Carolinas to Savannah, Georgia. They also crossed westward into the valley of the South Branch of the Potomac (in present West Virginia). Governor Alexander Spotswood brought over Germans for his Germanna ironworks. Groups of Germans, besides those moving down through the western valleys, settled in the southern colonies, notably Palatines and Swiss at New Bern, North Carolina, in 1710; Germans and Swiss led by Jean-Pierre Purry at Purrysburg, South Carolina, near the mouth of the Savannah River, in 1732; and Lutherans from Salzburg at Ebenezer, Georgia, in 1736.

Most of the Germans had been peasants in the old country and sought to duplicate farm life as they had known it. Thrifty and diligent, their work ethic mixed with fundamentalist Christianity, the German pioneers were content to engage in subsistence and intensive agriculture. The family farm was a way of life, and women and children worked in the fields. Germans decried the carelessness of other American farmers. As one German saying had it: "Wie einer den Zaun hält, hält er auch das Gut" (As one tends his fence, so he also tends his farm). The German barn, Conestoga wagon, and the hunting rifle were distinctive contributions. The German (*Deutsch*) or "Dutch" barn had two stories, a pitched roof, a backport for cattle, a threshing floor, and a hay loft. Germans near Conestoga Creek developed the Conestoga wagon, which would become the great vehicle of inland commerce. The wagon, eleven feet high and twenty-six feet long (including the tongue), weighed two to three thousand pounds and was pulled by four or six horses; the bottom was concave to keep goods from spilling out, and a canvas of linen or hemp covered high, arching hoops. The Germans brought with them weapons from the homeland, especially a firearm with spiraled grooves (rifling); in time the barrel of this weapon was elongated, becoming the Pennsylvania, or Kentucky, rifle. German communities sought to preserve the culture and language of the old country, aided by use of the Bible in German, worshiping in their own churches, and having their own German-language newspapers.

THE SCOTCH-IRISH

Like the Germans, the Scotch-Irish fled adversity in expectation of a better life. Always regarding themselves as Scots rather than Irish, the Scotch-Irish hailed from Northern Ireland. The better to tame Ireland, the English government had moved Lowland Scots into Ulster Province (the northernmost counties of Ireland—Donegal, Londonderry, Tyrone, Fermanagh, Armagh, and Cavan). From 1608 to 1697 some hundred thousand Scottish Presbyterians had been thus resettled. But the Scotch-Irish soon found themselves among the persecuted and disadvantaged. An act of Parliament of 1704 restored the sacramental test for officeholding, thus excluding Presbyterians from civil and military offices. Scotch-Irish Presbyterians were compelled to pay tithes to the Episcopal clergy; among other religious grievances were the denial of the validity of Presbyterian marriages and the requirement of an Anglican service for funerals.

Repressive trade laws also furthered discontent. The shipment of cattle and of meat and dairy products was prohibited out of Ireland, and the Woolen Act of 1699 forbade exports of raw wool or woolen cloth from Ireland to any country. When the land leases of the 1680s expired in 1717, absentee landlords imposed double and treble rents, forcing the eviction of many tenants. Disease, droughts, bad harvests, a high rate of sheep mortality, and decline of the linen industry added to the distress.

In the northern colonies above Pennsylvania, the Scotch-Irish formed an arc from the Maine coast through the backcountry, with enclaves such as Portland, Topsham, and Bath, Maine; Londonderry, New Hampshire; Somerset County, New Jersey; and Orange and Ulster counties, New York.

The Scotch-Irish, as latecomers, headed for the foothills of the Alleghenies in Pennsylvania, and then, by the 1730s, began moving southward into the western valleys of Maryland and Virginia and into the Carolina piedmont, mixing in with the Germans. Often as squatters on the frontier, the Scotch-Irish staked out homesteads, preferring, as in Ireland, hillsides rather than the better bottomlands. They let their cattle roam unfenced. The Scotch-Irish pioneers had a reputation for being slovenly in agriculture, and it was not unusual for them to move to a new farm every few years. Most of the Scotch-Irish population was rural, but some immigrants remained in urban centers as shipworkers and artisans. Others were servants, tenant farmers, and laborers. Hardheaded and proud, the Scotch-Irish were viewed as "a pernicious and pugnacious people." At the cutting edge of the frontier and disregarding Indian rights, they could behave savagely. Residing in remote areas, they had little political influence.

THE SCOTS

More so than other immigrants, the Scots represented a broader spectrum of social classes: exiled rebels, landowning families, professionals (physicians, lawyers, and tutors), merchants, skilled tradesmen, and tenant farmers. The defeats of Scottish armies by Cromwell between 1648 and 1651 and the failed Jacobite uprisings of 1715 and 1745 drove Scots to America either as voluntary exiles or under sentence of transportation. After the defeat of the army of Bonnie Prince Charlie at Culloden Moor in April 1746, the British government sought to destroy the clan system. Parliament forbade the wearing of Scottish national dress, deprived rebellious chieftains of power, and gave their lands to loyal chieftains and commissioners of the crown. Much like their brethren in Ireland earlier, Highland Scots in the 1760s faced rent racking and evictions. Population growth and scarcity of good land also contributed to the late Highland migration to America.

Many of the Scots who were exiled by royal authority in 1746 and 1747 settled in the Cape Fear region, founding Campbelltown (later Fayetteville). Other exiles found their way up the Hudson and Mohawk rivers in New York and also into the backcountry. Highland family and clan units usually came to America under clan chiefs or subchiefs. Lowland Scots came over individually, as merchants, farmers, professionals, and servants. Adam Stephen (1721–1791) was a good example of a Lowland Scot who set out to America to make his fortune. A physician trained at Edinburgh, he for the most part abandoned his profession and became a proprietor of a 5,000-acre estate in the Shenandoah valley, where he also raised livestock on a large scale and manufactured flour, firearms, and whiskey; yet he also held a high military command during the French and Indian War and served as a major general in the American Revolution. Other Scottish physicians practiced their calling; indeed, it was all but impossible to find a physician in the colonies who was not a Scot or who had not at least trained at a Scottish university. As before noted, Scottish merchants and factors dominated the inland Chesapeake tobacco trade.

MINOR GROUPS

Some French Protestants settled in New England and New Amsterdam before 1680. French-speaking Walloons from Belgium also came to New Netherland. After Louis XIV revoked the Edict of Nantes in 1685 (in effect decreeing Protestantism illegal in France), some fifteen thousand Huguenots came to the thirteen colonies.

In 1686, on land purchased from the Atherton Company, fifty Huguenot families founded Frenchtown, Rhode Island. Five years later, however, a mob from Greenwich forced the French immigrants to flee to New York City and Boston. Thirty Huguenot families established Oxford, near Worcester, in 1687 but abandoned the site in 1704. Many Huguenots settled in New York: New York City, Staten Island, Westchester County (founding New Rochelle in 1689), and New Paltz. Some eight hundred Huguenots made their way to Virginia in 1700 and 1701; about five hundred of them settled on a 10,000-acre tract at Manakin Town, an abandoned Indian site just above the falls on the James (Richmond, Virginia). William Byrd I gave them supplies to hold them over. These Huguenots prospered and married into English families. Large plantations replaced the village. The Huguenots fanned out into all of central Virginia. There were Huguenot settlements also along the Potomac, Rappahannock, and York rivers. A sizable number of persons of Huguenot extraction were living in Boston, New York, and Charleston by the end of the colonial period. Huguenots founded Dresden, Maine, in 1752. Some Huguenots from New England and New York migrated to the Carolinas.

The Huguenots assimilated easily into colonial society. Their dispersal, exogenous marriages, secular character of immigration, sojourn in other countries before coming to America (Holland, Great Britain, Switzerland, and Germany), and material success worked against the maintenance of group cohesion. Huguenot immigrants Anglicized their names, and most joined already established colonial churches. As planters, merchants, and skilled craftsmen, the Huguenots found great success. Jean, Benjamin, and André Faneuil prospered as merchants in Boston, and André's son, Peter, next to John Hancock, was the wealthiest man in that city. Pierre Manigault (d. 1729) was the patriarch of the wealthiest family in South Carolina; Henry Laurens (1724–1792), a rich planter and merchant, was a dominating force in the colony and during the Revolution served as president of the Continental Congress. Other families of Huguenot extraction that exerted important influence in early America were the Bayards, Boudinots, Bowdoins, De Lanceys, Jays, and Reveres.

One late injection of French culture in the colonies was the Acadians, "French neutrals," eight thousand of whom were expelled by the governor of Nova Scotia for purported disloyalty in wartime. Some were dispersed in the colonies, but most went to Louisiana. Their being Catholic caused a hostile reception in the colonies. The Virginia assembly refused in 1756 to provide funds to receive 1,150 of the exiles and instead had them sent to England.

Welsh groups, mostly Baptists and Quakers, settled in southeast New England and in Pennsylvania. John Myles, founder of the first Baptist church in Wales, distressed by religious restrictions imposed upon the restoration of the Stuarts, took some of his followers to Plymouth colony in 1663. At first unwelcomed by the authorities for attempting to settle at Rehoboth, these Welsh Baptists then secured a land grant from the colony and established the village of Swanzey (Swansea); some of the group then also founded Warren and Barrington (both located in Rhode Island after the boundary adjustment of 1741).

Welsh Quakers, many of them landed gentry, arrived in 1682 and 1683 to take up a 40,000-acre tract that they had purchased west of the Schuylkill River. The Welsh settlers had hoped to create a barony, with feudal privileges, but William Penn would not allow this. The "Welsh Tract" eventually consisted of the townships of Merion, Radnor, Goshen, Newton, Tredyffrin, and Uwchlan. In the 1730s, Welsh pioneers migrated into the Virginia piedmont and also settled on the Pee Dee River in South Carolina. The Welsh also found their way to the Black River country of North Carolina.

Swiss immigrants came to America for many of the same reasons as the Germans, whom they often accompanied. Swiss Mennonites settled in

Pennsylvania and filtered into the Shenandoah valley. Swiss joined Germans in settling at New Bern, North Carolina, and Purrysburg, South Carolina. Probably 25,000 Swiss came to the American colonies during the eighteenth century.

Because of their low profile and their arrival as individuals or in small groups, immigrants from southern Ireland are difficult to trace. The Irish Catholics suffered the same hardships under English rule as the Scotch-Irish. Those who left southern Ireland were mostly single males who were already alienated from family and cultural ties. Many arrived as indentured or convict servants. Most dropped the *O'* or *Mac* before their names, and because of the scarcity of Catholic churches, some converted to Protestantism. At the end of the American Revolution, there were only 24,000 practicing Catholics from all ethnic groups.

Italians trickled into the colonies with other groups or as servants. Some Huguenot and English families were of Italian extraction. It is known that Italians settled on the eastern shore of Chesapeake Bay and along the south bank of the James River. Land records for Nansemond County, Virginia, in 1702 refer to a portion of the county as "Banks of Italy" or "Italia."

In the 1760s, Scotsman Dr. Andrew Turnbull, who had resided in Smyrna in the Levant (Izmir, Turkey) and had married a Greek, attempted to plant a Mediterranean colony in East Florida, with financial backing from Dr. William Duncan and the former British prime minister, George Grenville. Over fourteen hundred colonists—Italians, Greeks, Aegean Islanders, Greek-Corsicans, and two hundred Minorcan stowaways—made it to Mosquito Inlet, seventy-five miles south of St. Augustine, where they founded New Smyrna. One-half of the venturers died within two years. But despite the mortality and a mutiny, the colony survived.

Sephardic Jews expelled from Spain and Portugal arrived at New Amsterdam on a French ship in 1654. They were later joined by German-speaking Ashkenazic Jews from central Europe. Through intermarriage the two groups were fused. The Carolina proprietors opened settlement to "heathens, Jews, and other Dissenters," and James Oglethorpe encouraged migration of Jews to Georgia. Jewish congregations were established in New York (1656), Newport (1677), Savannah (1733), Philadelphia (1745), and Charleston (1750). New York City, in 1695, had the first synagogue. Parliament granted full citizenship to Jews in the colonies in 1740. Colonial American Jews prospered in manufacturing, shipping, and merchandising. Few in numbers, the Jews made up for the lack of the corporate social structure they had known in the Old World by establishing synagogues, burial grounds, religious schools, and mutual charitable organizations.

NATURALIZATION

The opportunity to become citizens and to enjoy equal rights as English subjects under the crown lured immigrants to America. Until 1740, naturalization was granted chiefly by processes in the individual colonies. In Virginia aliens had merely to enroll in the local courts. New York in 1683 provided naturalization of all resident aliens who openly professed Christianity and took an oath of allegiance. A South Carolina act of 1691 stated that all French and Swiss inhabitants could become citizens upon registering with the clerk or secretary of the assembly within six months; after this act was disallowed by the proprietors in 1697, citizenship could be obtained by petitioning the governor and swearing allegiance to the crown. A New England town's grant of admission as a freeman automatically conferred citizenship. Proprietors and royal governors issued letters patent of denization. Most colonies also allowed for citizenship through special legislation. Parliament and the crown claimed the right to grant citizenship in the colonies; sometimes this status was conferred even before immigrating to America, as Charles II did for French Huguenots.

One issue proved troubling—whether a person naturalized by one colony was entitled to full English citizenship. Stated more broadly, was the granting of complete English citizenship a national function exclusively or also a local one? On the question of "whether a foreigner naturalized by an Act of Assembly in any of the plantations, can they thereby claim the priviledges of natural born subjects in this kingdom," the Board of Trade in 1736 reaffirmed a legal opinion of 1703 stating that aliens naturalized in a colony were English citizens of that colony only and aliens elsewhere.

An act of Parliament of 1709 sought to standardize the process of naturalization within the empire. To become full English citizens, aliens had to swear allegiance to and acknowledge the supremacy of the crown, prove that they had taken the Protestant sacraments during the previous three months, and refute in open court the doctrine of transubstantiation. This act, however, remained in force for only three years; Parliament then reiterated its previous position, that full citizenship was to be granted by Parliament and the crown upon petition.

Finally, in 1740, Parliament passed a law for naturalization in all the American colonies. The act required an applicant to have resided seven years in one colony; to produce a certificate, signed by two witnesses, stating that the applicant had taken the sacraments in an Anglican church for three months before; to proclaim Christianity before a colonial judge; and to subscribe to allegiance to the king and an oath of supremacy. Quakers and Jews, but not Catholics, were exempt from the sacramental requirements. Another exception was made in 1761 when Parliament permitted citizenship for all foreign Protestants who had served in British military forces in the colonies for two years and who took the required oaths and had received the Anglican sacraments within the previous six months. The act of 1740 proved to be an irritant to the colonists. The residency requirement meant a long delay, at least technically, in obtaining the rights to engage in trade, hold land titles, vote, or serve in public office. For a while the colonies continued to grant their own citizenship to aliens, but in 1773 Parliament banned local naturalization entirely.

The contrast between colonial and British views on naturalization underscored a separateness in the understanding of constitutional rights. The colonists claimed to have all the liberties of Englishmen in the realm by virtue of their charters and the nature of their immigration to America. Implied in these rights was self-government. Colonial Americans held to the idea of concurrent jurisdiction in granting naturalization.

ETHNIC DISCORD

Except for the Germans and African slaves, immigrants fit into the dominant English culture. Many immigrants came from the British Isles— Scotch-Irish, Scots, Welsh, and Irish—and others, such as the French Huguenots and Jews, had been Anglicized from having sojourned in Great Britain or the West Indies or had at least severed ties from the countries of their origin. Yet for economic and religious reasons and the existence of immigrant enclaves, there was prejudice against newcomers. Ostracism of immigrants, however, was engaged in by individuals and groups rather than by colonial governments. Official anti-immigration policies aimed primarily at restricting entry of vagrants, convict felons, and persons posing health hazards. Ship captains were often required to post bond vouchsafing the good behavior of convict passengers and guaranteeing that they would not become a public burden. To be sure, there were temporary measures intended to keep out certain groups, largely on religious grounds, but these were rare. For example, laws in Massachusetts before 1700 restricted or prohibited entry by Quakers and Catholics, and South Carolina and Maryland at the end of the seventeenth century passed acts limiting the immigration of Irish Catholic servants. Colonies also placed duties on imported slaves in order to regulate the traffic.

Some non-English ethnic groups faced disparagement and even hostility from other colonists because of poverty, unauthorized possession of land, economic competition, clannishness, alleged propensity for collusion with foreign and Indian enemies, and, above all, the potential of interpolating an alien culture and style of living upon English ways.

The "foreign peril" was a constant theme in colonial ethnic prejudice.

For small ethnic minorities like the Jews and the Scots, the resentment was not that of fear from cultural influence but rather a dislike of their alleged sharpness in getting an economic edge over their neighbors. The rancor against the Scots, mainly the factors and storekeepers, in Virginia on the eve of the Revolution reached a high pitch, and with the coming of the war they bore the brunt of punitive measures against presumed loyalists. A diatribe, published in the *Virginia Gazette* of October 20, 1774, conveys the indignation toward the Scots:

> A Scotchman, when he is first admitted into a house, is so humble that he will sit upon the lowest step of the staircase. By degrees he gets into the kitchen, and from thence, by the most submissive behavior, is advanced into the parlour. If he gets into the dining room, as ten to one he will, the master of the house must take care of himself; for in all probability he will turn him out of doors, and by the assistance of his countrymen keep possession forever.

Above all, it was the Germans in Pennsylvania who encountered the most xenophobia among the colonists, due to their large numbers, nuclear settlement, and determination to preserve old country ways. Benjamin Franklin was not immune to Pennsylvanians' fear of being overrun by the Germans. In 1751 he commented, "This will in a few years become a Germany colony." In 1753 Franklin observed:

> Now Germany is swept, scour'd and scrumm'd by the Merchants, who, for the gain by the Freight, bring all the Refuse Wretches poor and helpless who are burthensome to the old Settlers; or Knaves and Rascals that live by Sharking and Cheating them.

As he also wrote, the Germans "are generally so disagreeable to an English Eye" that "it wou'd require great Portions to induce Englishmen to marry them." It was the "teutonic peril" that worried Franklin the most. "Why should the Palatine boors be suffered to swarm into our settlements," he asked,

> and, by herding together establish their language and manners to the exclusion of ours? Why should Pennsylvania . . . become a colony of *Aliens*, who will shortly be so numerous as to Germanize us . . . and will never adopt our language or Customs, any more than they can acquire our complexion?

Yet the Germans had their own prejudiced views of colonial Englishmen. One Pennsylvania German wrote that the English nation "consists of proud and conceited people who denigrate all others, who oppress all those nations of whom they can be master." Germans deprecated the lack of authority and the deterioration of morals in the colonies. Yet their own isolation and determination to preserve their ethnicity can be viewed as a defense against cultural shock. Indeed, for those Germans who found themselves in fractionalized communities or as settlers in the interior valleys south of Pennsylvania, amalgamation into the mainstream of colonial life proceeded rapidly. One colonial traveler rued that "the language which our German people make use of is a miserable, broken, fustian salmagundi of English and German."

French Huguenots were linked in the colonial mind with "French papists" in Canada. At the end of the seventeenth century, they were accused of siding with the enemy. New York prevented them from settling on the frontier, and Pennsylvania authorities kept them under surveillance.

Only rarely, however, were there instances of mob actions against immigrants. As mentioned, a mob forced Huguenots to leave Frenchtown, Rhode Island, in 1691. In Boston, in July 1729, "a mob arose to prevent the landing of Irish," although the effort was unsuccessful. Rioters in Worcester in 1734 pulled down a Scotch-Irish Presbyterian church. In 1743 a mob attacked a Jewish funeral procession in New York City. On occasion local ruffians prevented Germans from voting in Philadelphia.

Physical space deterred interethnic tension. Black slavery absorbed prejudice. Difficulty in establishing schools because of poverty, geographic isolation, and scarcity of teachers impeded many immigrant groups from preserving their separate identity. Ethnic rivalry seemed to decline at the end of the colonial period, and what there was represented political and economic conflict rather than a clashing of cultures. Contention from Scotch-Irish settlers, for example, in the backcountry of Pennsylvania and North Carolina can be defined in a sectional and political context.

Strong ethnic identity did thrive in the few locales where immigrant population was large and dense and supported by close family ties and ethnic churches, schools, and press—primarily the German communities. On balance, however, the colonial American, as the French immigrant Hector St. John Crèvecoeur pointed out at the close of the American Revolution, was "that strange mixture of blood which you will find in no other country." It was in America, he said, that "individuals of all nations are melted into a new race of man."

9

Colonists in Bondage

First for survival and then for a productive economy, British colonization demanded cheap and abundant labor. Thus in the early Jamestown colony, the Virginia Company tried a communal system, put into effect quasi-martial law for six years, and finally introduced bonded servitude. In 1618 the City of London sent one hundred poor persons to Virginia to serve as tenants on the Virginia Company's lands for a term of seven years, after which these immigrants received freedom dues. The next year the Virginia Company sold such servants to planters at large. The use of servants was encouraged by a fifty-acre headright conferred on anyone who paid the passage of a person coming to America. The newcomer was obligated to serve time as a worker equal to the cost of bringing him over.

During the seventeenth century there was a great demand for servants in most of the colonies. By 1625 fully forty percent of the Virginia colony's inhabitants were servants. In 1628 the Massachusetts Bay Company brought 180 servants to Salem. Servants were among the Winthrop fleet two years later. By 1650 servants made up nearly one-third of the Massachusetts work force, though white servitude in the colony greatly declined thereafter. The Dutch West India Company brought tenant laborers to New Netherland. White servants were in especially high demand in the colonies from Pennsylvania southward. In the 1680s, one-third of the settlers in Pennsylvania were under indentured contract. For the period of 1607–1775, one-half of the estimated 350,000 white immigrants came over as servants. Toward the end of the colonial period, four-fifths of immigrant servants entered the Chesapeake Bay area, and one-fifth came into Pennsylvania. In addition to the white servant immigrants, some 260,000 Africans were brought to the British mainland colonies during the colonial period, one-half of whom arrived after 1740.

Initially, colonial Englishmen, observant of the Portuguese and Spanish experience in the New World, hoped to exploit the Indians for their labor as well as their goods. But as the Jamestown settlers discovered, the native Americans had to be treated primarily as foreign nationals rather than as participants in an English labor network. Englishmen nevertheless did attempt to establish to some degree Indian enslavement, justified by captivity in war.

In all the colonies, however short the periods, some form of Indian slavery or servitude existed. Seventeenth-century New Englanders forced some of the captives of the Indian wars into involuntary servitude and sold others overseas as slaves. Actually, with the exception of South Carolina, Indian slavery never fully caught on in the colonies. In the Carolina lowcountry, where in 1720 Indians in the slave labor force reached a high of seventeen percent, it was found that Indians were less adaptable to rice production than blacks and were also greatly susceptible to disease. Only four colonies—Virginia, South Carolina, Rhode Island, and New York—declared enslavement of American natives illegal. Virginia did so in 1691 by implication in a law authorizing free and open trade with all Indians. New York distinguished between free natives of the colony and those brought over from the Spanish West Indies. One main reason for the disuse of Indian slavery was its replacement by black slavery. But other factors also militated against Indian enslavement: the decimation of eastern Indian tribes by disease and war, the removal of Indian populations westward, the Indian's irregular work habits, geographic knowledge rendering escape easier than for black slaves, the fear that Indians might resort to savagery, and the English missionary perspective toward the Indians.

While pejorative views held by Englishmen and colonists of persons of color, tawny and black, and knowledge of the Spanish and Portuguese enslavement aided the subjugation of Indians and imported Africans in the British colonies, permanent enslavement of whites was never feasible, given the lack of slavery in the British Isles and on the Continent, the claims of free-will immigrants to the rights of Englishmen, and the legal conditions of white bound labor.

The colonists endorsed English ideas of temporary white servitude, either by government sanction or by contract. The Statute of Artificers in England (1562) legalized the assignment of minors by a parent or guardian to a person outside the household for training in industrial work for seven years or until age twenty-one; in the seventeenth century such apprenticeship applied to trades only under the guild system. English vagrancy laws also provided for a forced labor condition for specified periods. The apprentice system, whether formal or informal, was prevalent throughout the colonies, whereby parents bound out their children primarily to receive training or courts placed orphans into the custody of guardians. Other than apprenticeship per se, white bound labor in America fit into two general categories: voluntary (indentured servants and redemptioners) and involuntary (victims of kidnapping and people whose servitude resulted from punitive action). Certain trends in England—a rapid increase in population, a labor surplus, and a decline in real wages—in full sway until late in the seventeenth century, stimulated recruitment for servants coming to America.

INDENTURED SERVANTS

Indentured servants came in greater numbers during the seventeenth century, although the system continued until the early 1800s and was even revived under federal auspices around the time of the Civil War. Indenturers were almost exclusively from the British Isles.

Before embarking for America, recruits signed contracts, the terms of which were stated twice on a sheet of paper; with both sections signed by the parties involved, the document was folded (indented) and torn, each party receiving thereby a copy of the contract. The recruit agreed to go to America and give labor service of equal value to the cost of transportation. The contract stipulated that whoever was the consignee in America had to provide clothing, food, and shelter and often also, if so noted in the contract, specified training and freedom dues to the recruit. What distinguished indentured servitude from other foreign contract labor was that the recruits could name their own terms. The cost of purchase of an indenture covered transportation, equipment, clothing, and expenses entailed while awaiting departure. The servant typically promised to serve the master in the New World "well and faithfully in such employments as the master might assign." The indentured servant trade was particularly advantageous to the Chesapeake colonies, allowing English ships to transport a cargo of servants and return to England with tobacco.

The period of labor under an indenture varied according to age, skills, and terms of the agreement, though on the average amounted to three to five years' service. In the seventeenth century merchants and ship captains spent four to ten pounds bringing a servant to America and then sold the indenture for six to thirty pounds. Unlike English practice, contract labor could be sold from time to time. Typically, a male servant could be purchased for two to four pounds if only one year was left of indenture, thirteen to sixteen pounds with six years remaining. Female servants usually brought one to three pounds with one year left on the contract, up to a maximum of fifteen pounds for a balance of five to six years.

The indentured system had mutual benefits. The master obtained needed labor, often skilled, at low cost. The servant was guaranteed subsistence during initial settling and after a few years, now accustomed to a new country, could strike out on his own or put up his own "sign." Indentured servants, much like other contract laborers, came to America to escape unemployment or adverse market and agricultural conditions and also simply to "push fortune" or acquire property. A major factor in stemming the tide of indentured servants at the end of the seventeenth century was improvement of the situation in England—higher prices, flatter population growth, and increased employment.

Historians have revised calculations as to the quality of indentured servants. Until the mid-twentieth century, the prevailing view was much like that of Abbot E. Smith (1947/1965): The contract laborers coming to America were totally destitute, among whom were "rogues, vagabonds, whores, cheats and rabble of all descriptions, raked from the gutter and kicked out of the country" (p. 3). Mildred Campbell, David W. Galenson, and other historians now have a contrary assessment. Campbell (1959) analyzed emigration registers at Bristol (1654–1685) and London (1683–1694), and Galenson (1981) did the same for London (1682–1686, 1718–1759, and 1773–1775), Middlesex (1683–1684), Liverpool (1697–1707), and Bristol (1654–1685). The two authors conclude that indentured servants tended to be of the middling sort, representing a cross section of farmers and artisans. There is still a dispute, however, over the half of indenturers who gave no occupations. Can it be assumed that they were of the same work background or instead were among the unskilled and destitute poor? Galenson claims that a pattern emerged of more skilled servants coming to America: one-third skilled in 1680, eighty-five percent in the 1770s. He also notes a seventy percent literacy rate among the immigrating servants.

Campbell's model affords a close inspection of indentured servants leaving from Bristol. They were principally middling people from the West Country, an area ravaged by both armies during the English Civil War. These émigrés, as tradesmen and tenant farmers, had known great hardship. The cloth industry was impoverished. There were many Quakers and other nonconformists in the West Country. The Bristol registry reveals that among male indenturers, thirty-six percent were yeomen and husbandmen and twenty-two percent were artisans and tradesmen.

The very poor in England were reluctant to leave their immediate environs, mostly because of their social inversion, characteristic of the most unfortunate everywhere (for example, the Appalachian poor in modern America). Robert Southwell in 1669, as Campbell notes, commented that the English destitute class "are loth to leave the smoke of their own cabin if they can but beg neere it." As Thomas Ludwell wrote to his brother in Virginia, the poorest people preferred to "live meanly" and to "send their families to the parish to be relieved rather than hear of such a long journey." What little security there was in England was better than experiencing the perils of the unknown in America.

Most male indentured servants were young and single, between eighteen and twenty-four years of age, a time when tradesmen were completing their apprenticeships. Generalizing from the registration lists, it appears that about eighty-two percent of indentured servants leaving England were men and boys; only eighteen percent were women. Campbell finds that in the seventeenth century, thirty percent of the women servants were under twenty years old and fifty percent below age twenty-five. Women were usually classified as simply "single woman," "spinster," or "widow." Young women frequently enlisted in pairs or threesomes from the same village or family.

REDEMPTIONERS

The majority of servant traffic after 1730 was German and Scotch-Irish. The Germans particularly emigrated as redemptioners, without a contract. Like indentured servants, redemptioners had their passage paid for by ship captains or merchants who then sold them in America as workers for a specified time period. Ideally, they would find a relative or friend to make recompense. If not, two weeks after docking, the ship's captain would put the redemptioners up for sale. In Pennsylvania, each brought ten pounds in 1722, fifteen pounds in the 1750s, and twenty pounds in 1772. Unlike indentured servants, redemptioners tended to come over as families or sometimes as neighborhood groups. Family immigration, however, declined in the 1760s and 1770s, with more arrivals being young and single.

Since redemptioners did not have a written contract, the colonies regulated the time of service; five years was the most common term, though length was governed by age. Virginia in the 1660s required all noncontract servants to serve five years if older than sixteen and if under that age to be bound until age twenty-four. A Maryland law in 1638 also set the labor terms according to age: fourteen and under, eight years; fifteen to eighteen, seven years; eighteen to twenty-two, six years; and over twenty-two, five years; for female servants over twelve, four years, and those under age twelve, seven years. Thus redemptioners served according to the "custom of the country." Most redemptioners went to the middle and Chesapeake colonies. Between 1727 and 1776, some seventy thousand redemptioners arrived at Philadelphia.

At dockside, redemptioners were purchased individually or as a group. Most likely, the captain sold them in gangs of fifty or more to soul drivers, who literally drove them like cattle from place to place, auctioning them to the highest bidder. Soul drivers advertised their lot of human merchandise in the newspapers. Fairs and court days, which brought in people from all around the countryside, were considered the best times to sell redemptioners. Needless to say, family members were frequently separated. William Barker witnessed a sale of nearly a hundred redemptioners at Williamsburg in 1754 over a two-day period. "I never seen such Pore Raches in my Life," he noted,

> som all most naked and what had Cloths was as Black as Chimney Swipers, and all most Starved by the Ill usidge in the Pasedge By the Capn, for they are used no Bater than so many negro Slaves: they are Brought in hare and sold in the same manner as horss or cows in our market or fair.

Actually, the redemptioners, once sold, fared much the same as indenturers, governed by the same regulations and laws, and were also, according to the "custom of the country," given freedom dues.

INVOLUNTARY BOUND LABOR

Besides the apprenticeship of minors, there were five kinds of involuntary servitude: vagrants and dissolute persons, colonial debtors, victims of kidnapping, political prisoners, and convicted felons.

Vagrants and the dissolute were sent to the colonies in the seventeenth century. For example, in 1619, James I, exercising his royal prerogative, dispatched one hundred "dissolute persons" to Virginia as servants. English magistrates in 1692 ordered to be transported to Virginia fifty lewd women from a house of correction and thirty others who habitually walked the streets at night.

Servitude ordered by colonial courts for satisfaction of a debt was a rarity in the colonies. Nevertheless, a 1700 Pennsylvania law, disallowed in England but repassed, provided for servitude not to exceed seven years for debtors, unmarried and under fifty-three years of age, and a term not above five years for debtors who were married and not over forty-six years old. A law of the same colony in 1730 removed the threat of punishment through servitude if the debtor surrendered all goods to help satisfy the creditor.

With the increased demand for servants in America during the seventeenth century, kidnappers, or "spirits," preyed on the unwary—wandering children, simple-minded adults, or intoxicated persons—in the streets of English cities. Confined, the victims were sold as servants bound for America. Often the spirits were agents of respected merchants. To curtail this nefarious practice, Parliament in 1664 required the registering of all persons transported to the colonies and in 1671 made it a capital offense to steal children for the purpose of sending them to the colonies. Kidnapping nevertheless continued into the eighteenth century and inspired the later writing of Sir Walter Scott's *Waverley* and Robert Louis Stevenson's *Kidnapped.* Two suits by victims of kidnapping aroused great interest in England. Both plaintiffs had been whisked off to America as young lads, prospered in the New World, and then returned to England to exact retribution on their malefactors. Peter Williamson told of his experiences in *Life and Adventures of Peter Williamson,* and James Annesley, son and heir of the earl of Altham, did the same in *Memoirs of an Unfortunate Young Nobelman.* Williamson won an award of two hundred pounds; Annesley won his case but was unable to recover his inheritance.

At intervals, the British government banished what might be called political prisoners to the colonies. Disturbances against the Anglican church led to the deportation of eight hundred Scottish Covenanters between 1678 and 1685. Under the Conventicle Act of 1664, Quakers convicted for the third time of attending unlawful meetings could be shipped to the colonies. About a hundred such offenders were transported before Parliament repealed this provision in 1670. Over four hundred Scottish military prisoners were exiled in 1654; 150 of them were sold at Boston for twenty to thirty pounds each and then were employed in the ironworks at Lynne and sawmills in Maine, receiving land when freed. Others were transported to Virginia. Prisoners of the Monmouth uprising of 1685 and the Jacobite rebellions of 1715 and 1745, about three thousand in all, were sent to the colonies, mainly to Maryland and the West Indies.

From 1615 to 1718, on the basis of royal clemency, English felons were shipped to the colonies as servants. During the 1660s these convicts numbered about a hundred a year, going mainly to the West Indies and the Chesapeake area. The colonies, however, resisted the influx of these convict servants. Virginia in 1670 prohibited their admission, and Maryland did the same in 1676. Though the Maryland law was disallowed later, Virginia's interdiction was respected. South Carolina in 1712 established a fine of twenty-five pounds for the landing of each transported convict.

In England some three hundred crimes were felonies, and about 160 of these were capital offenses. Stealing an article valued at one shilling or more merited the death penalty. Successfully petitioning the king for a pardon or pleading benefit of clergy (for the first offense) mitigated somewhat the extremity of the British penal codes and lessened the need to deport criminals.

The transportation of convicted felons to the colonies received parliamentary sanction in 1717. Under the law, any person convicted of an offense within benefit of clergy could, by court order, be transported for service of seven years. Anyone convicted of an offense without benefit of clergy and subject to the death penalty could be sentenced to fourteen years' servitude in the colonies but would be put to death upon returning to England. The law effectively put an end to the use of benefit of clergy. An example of how the new system worked may be seen in the cases over an eight-year period at Old Bailey. Of 560 persons tried, 353 (sixty-three percent) were convicted of a felony or a misdemeanor. Of these, 60 were sentenced to death and 235 ordered to be transported. Half of those sentenced to death were pardoned on condition of being transported (this was still the prerogative of the king), leaving, therefore, only 7½ percent of those tried facing execution.

From 1717 to 1775 some fifty thousand convicts were sent to at least nine colonies, twenty thousand of them going to Maryland and ten thousand to Virginia. Transportees came from all over the British Isles (including sixteen thousand from Ireland and eight hundred from Scotland). The names of those transported were printed in the *Gentleman's Magazine*. Banished convicts were put under the charge of a local merchant, who was responsible for getting them aboard ship. The merchant contractors received five pounds for each convict. Like redemptioners, convicts were sold upon arrival, usually to soul drivers wholesale, with the buyer receiving a "conviction bill" for each convict, which substituted for an indentured contract. The convict, however, had no say in any negotiations. Interestingly, nearly one-half of the convicts arriving in Maryland and Virginia were women. Most of the transportees had been convicted as thieves.

Though usually shackled during the voyage, once entering servitude in America, convicts had the same freedoms as other servants, enjoying their own use of their free time. Actually, for a master, convict labor had two advantages over indentured servitude: at least two years more in service and a lack of freedom dues. Most transportees adjusted to their new life, but some resorted to their old ways and ran away. The newcomers also brought with them "jail fever" (typhus). Colonists feared that convict servants contributed to the corruption of the morals of youth; even Benjamin Franklin compared them to rattlesnakes. Maryland, New Jersey, and Pennsylvania each passed a law placing prohibitive duties on incoming convicts, but the latter two measures were disallowed in England, and the Maryland law proved unenforceable. In order to diminish the numbers of incoming transportees, Virginia in 1736 required that masters pay freedom dues upon expiration of a convict's service. One-half of the convict servants, whose ages usually ranged from fifteen to twenty-nine years old, were unskilled. Upon completion of service, if not before, some of the convict servants joined the ranks of riffraff elements on the frontier.

TREATMENT OF WHITE SERVANTS

Most indentured craftsmen and professionals pursued activities related to their vocations. Unskilled white servants usually wound up on the farms and plantations, performing a variety of agricultural tasks. While slaves were left to work the tobacco fields, white servants tended to the cultivation of grain. Women servants served as dairymaids, laundresses, spinners, and weavers, although those who were thought to be slatterns were put in the fields.

Upon completion of service, servants had the right to claim freedom dues, whether by indentured contract or by custom. In 1690 instructions to Governor Lord Howard of Effingham of Virginia required that the colony provide fifty acres of land to each freed servant. The colony in 1705 set freedom dues as ten bushels of corn, thirty shillings or "the value thereof in goods," and "one well fixed musket" of twenty shillings' value. Other colonies determined as freedom dues any combination of clothes, farm tools, corn or wheat, and money. South Carolina in 1730 gave fifty acres, free of quitrents for ten years. Maryland conferred the same amount of land in addition to clothing and implements. New York and Massachusetts had no special requirement, only that servants "not be sent away empty."

Unlike slaves, white servants had the full protection of English rights, although, because of their status, certain privileges were curtailed. Servants could not marry except by permission of the master, vote, or engage in trade. They could, however, hold property, sue in the courts, and register complaints against masters before the magistrates. In some colonies they were taken into the militia. A freed servant had a legal settlement in a community, thus making him eligible for poor relief. Yet in his legal rights, a servant was at a disadvantage. He had hardly the financial resources to become involved in litigation, and if he pressed a charge against a master, he had to contend with an elite establishment, to which his master most likely belonged.

Certain liabilities were applicable only to nonfree persons. Bastardy led to fines or whipping and extended terms of service for each of the servant parents; the child would also be bound out. Running away brought severe penalties. Extra time was added to the term of service for the escapee when captured. Corporal punishment could also be inflicted on runaways. A South Carolina act, for example, extended service one week for every day absent, not to exceed two years. It became the practice in the colonies that for a master to punish a runaway with whipping, he had to secure permission from a justice of the peace. The maximum number of lashes to be inflicted on runaways generally was not to exceed thirty-nine. Only Maryland made running away a capital offense, but this was never enforced. By statute, heavy fines awaited those who aided an escapee, such as giving shelter. The colonial newspapers were filled with detailed descriptions of runaway servants, forming a fascinating and varied profile of America's early underclass. Typical, for example, as Marcus W. Jernegan (1965) has noted, is an advertisement in the *Virginia Gazette* for the apprehension of James Murphy, a runaway Irish servant-schoolmaster. The culprit is described as follows:

> Somewhat long visaged, with sharp nose, much pitted with the small pox, flaxen hair, reddish beard, sometimes ties his hair behind with a string, a very proud fellow, loves drink and when drunk is very impudent and talkative, pretends much, and knows little, was sometime on the French service and can talk French. (p. 52)

Rewards were offered for apprehending runaways, and culprits had to reimburse the cost of capture, which further added to the penalty of extended service.

BEGINNINGS OF BLACK SLAVERY

Whether black slavery in the colonies derived chiefly from English adoption of slavery as already known in the European empires in the Western Hemisphere, from an unconscious decision evolving from the felt necessities of the time, or from racial prejudice are questions that modern historians are still pondering. Winthrop D. Jordan, for example, argues that Englishmen, at the beginning of colonization, had already acquired negative views of blacks as heathen and uncivilized and therefore considered Africans an inferior race. Edmund S. Morgan emphasizes a "populist" interpretation: Colonial authorities found it expedient to neutralize the underclass; by establishing slavery, the blacks and the poor and servant whites were kept separate, thus lessening the danger from discontent of the rabble. Whatever the causes of black enslavement, the introduction of temporary servitude early in the seventeenth century left options for finding a more enduring and controlled source of labor.

Few blacks were imported before 1680, and slavery was not fully institutionalized until the end of the seventeenth century. Its growth in the eighteenth century, however, was spectacular. By the end of the colonial period, slaves accounted for twenty percent of the work force and nearly forty percent of the population in Virginia and Maryland and fifty percent in South Carolina.

Many factors influenced colonists to turn to the enslavement of imported Africans. As mentioned before, the improvement of economic conditions in the British Isles led to a diminished supply of indentured servants. In the 1680s the cost for the use of indentured servants rose, while at the same time prices for slaves fell; though in the 1690s the price of slaves went back to previous levels, this was offset by improved wages in England. The expansion of tobacco production and the rice and indigo planting in the eighteenth century involved drudgery and health conditions not viewed as attractive by English would-be servants. Colonists were becoming more displeased with white servants, who could easily escape and were difficult to apprehend. Until 1699, in Virginia, importation of Africans carried headrights, just as for white servants. The mortality rate declined at the end of the seventeenth century, thus affording a better investment in a chattel for life, further enhanced by slave reproduction and the use of offspring in the fields at an early age. There were no limits on work for slaves, and masters could skimp on provisions more than with white servants. Blacks could be compelled to work in the fields. Opening a market for slaves directly from Africa made for a greater and cheaper supply of workers. The rise of the British slave trade promoted the use of slaves, coinciding with acquisition of capital by colonists, who now could afford long-term investment in slaves.

Slavery was introduced early in New England, New York (New Netherland), Pennsylvania (in the 1680s), and the Carolinas. In South Carolina, however, the number of slaves was negligible until after rice cultivation began in the 1690s. Except for the lower Cape Fear region, where rice production was significant, slaves in North Carolina worked primarily in forest industries. In New York blacks, many of them slaves, made up one-seventh of the population; three-fourths of them lived in agricultural areas in the southern counties around New York City. Some slave farm labor was used in New England, New Jersey, and Pennsylvania. But generally slavery failed to find a broad economic base in the northern colonies, and many of the slaves in that region were found in urban centers, working in households and at various trades. In New England slaves had a dual status, both as property and as persons before the law. Massachusetts declared in 1641 that a slave possessed "all the liberties and Christian usages which the law of God established in Israel doth morally require." Slaves in New England were generally referred to as servants, and many gained their freedom after about six years of service.

Slavery as such, however, gradually appeared in the Chesapeake colonies. In Virginia and Maryland the development of slavery went through three stages: de facto regulations to about 1660; statutory provisions from 1660 to 1705; and, in 1705, through legislative enactment, the collection of previous laws and established practices into a "black code." The first Negroes arrived in Virginia in 1619 as servants, with no reference to slavery. Over the next half century, however, black servitude was steadily transposed into slavery, with circumstances parallel to those in Maryland. Important steps in the evolution of slavery in Virginia may be noted. Until the 1630s there appears to have been no distinction between black and white servants. In 1639 all persons except Negroes could have arms and ammunition. The next year provision was made for black runaways to serve for life, and in 1662 children were to be bound according to the status of their mothers.

Two court cases show the decline in the position of blacks in Virginia. In 1655, Elizabeth Key sued for her freedom on grounds that at age five or six she had been indentured for nine years, a period long since elapsed, her father had been a free man and therefore according to common law she should also be free, and she had been baptized. A county court decision rendered in her favor was overturned by the General Court. A House of Burgesses committee then remanded the case for retrial in the county court. Nothing further is known except that Elizabeth married the white lawyer who had represented her. Fernando, of Portuguese extraction, sued for his freedom in 1667 in Lower Norfolk County Court on the basis that he "was a Christian and had been several yeares in England"; he also presented documents to prove his free status, but since these items were in Portuguese, no one could read them. The suit was dismissed, and then it was brought before the General Court, whose determination is not known. The significance of both cases is that they show a transition in the rights of blacks; what had previously been regarded as qualifications for freedom were now disputable. In 1667 it was enacted that conversion to Christianity did not confer freedom and three years later that all imported servants from overseas who were not Christian served for life. Subsequent laws limited black mobility and rights, provided means of control by whites, and denied slaves property and due process in the courts. The various restraints on black servants, as restated in the code of 1705, added up to slavery.

THE AFRICAN SLAVE TRADE

Most black slaves on the American mainland in the seventeenth century arrived by way of the West Indies. The Dutch West India Company introduced the slave trade in the American colonies when one of its ships brought slaves to New Netherland in 1626. The first known voyage by English colonists in the black slave trade occurred in 1637 when Captain William Pierce's *Desire* traded a cargo of Indian captives, dried fish, and liquors in the Bahamas for cotton, tobacco, and slaves. In 1644 three Boston vessels brought slaves from Africa. For the remainder of the century, only a few American vessels, mainly from New York, engaged in the African trade. It was British merchants, however, who first opened up a substantial African and West Indian colonial slave trade. Dutch competition was removed by the navigation acts, and there was great demand for slaves in the sugar islands and then also on the North American continent.

The Company of Royal Adventurers of Africa, chartered by Charles II in 1660, became involved in the Atlantic slave trade but because of financial difficulty soon surrendered its charter, being replaced by the Royal African Company in 1672. This firm, also chartered by the crown, received a monopoly to trade along five thousand miles of the West African coast. The company's ships brought textiles, salt, metal implements, liquors, firearms, and other English manufactures to Africa in exchange for gold, ivory, and dyewoods, which were shipped to England, and slaves, sent to the West Indies in return for molasses and sugar. Despite its exclusive trading privileges, the Royal African Company faced competition from international traders (Portuguese, French, and Dutch); the illicit traffic engaged in by the company's own ship captains, who sold slaves on their own account; the illegal activity of private traders ("interlopers"); and, to a limited extent, the trading in slaves by the East India Company, whose territory included East Africa. After 1688, when Parliamentary supremacy was fully established, the Royal African Company refrained from enforcing its monopoly, and in 1698 Parliament opened African commerce legally to independent traders. By the Treaty of Utrecht in 1713, England was granted the Asiento (contract) whereby it could import 4,800 slaves a year into the Spanish West Indies. The South Sea Company was organized for this purpose. The Asiento was not revoked until 1750.

Full colonial participation in the African trade began only as demand increased from southern planters. From 1711 to 1720 there were only eleven known American-managed African voyages—one from Virginia and ten from New York. In the 1720s, New Englanders entered significantly into the African slave trade. Rhode Island merchants gained ascendancy in this commerce. From 1709 to 1800, mainly through Newport but also through Providence and Bristol, Rhode Island merchants sponsored at least 934 African slave voyages. The small Rhode Island slaver, seldom more than one hundred tons, carried a human cargo of seventy-five to one hundred. Boston, Philadelphia, New York, and Charleston also engaged in the African slave trade. From 1715 to 1774, New York merchants conducted 151 African slave voyages.

Most of the slaves brought to the colonies directly from Africa were delivered in the southern colonies. Slave vessels went up the major rivers of Virginia, docking at large plantations, where leading gentry acted as agents for the sale of slaves. Thus Robert "King" Carter at his plantation along the Rappahannock brought neighbors aboard slave ships, selling the human cargo, usually in pairs, at a ten percent commission. In

Charleston, Henry Laurens, a partner in the firm of Austin and Laurens, was an agent for selling slaves, disposing of about seven hundred Africans a year, also for a ten percent commission.

Slave trading in Africa was conducted according to districts, originally defined by the Royal African Company: Senegambia (mostly present-day Gambia and Senegal), Sierra Leone, the east-west coast from Cape Mount to Assini (Ivory Coast and present Liberia), Gold Coast (Ghana), Bight of Benin (present Togo and Dahomey), Bight of Biafra (Niger delta and mouths of the Cross and Duala rivers), central Africa, southeast Africa (from Cape of Good Hope to Cape Delgado), and Madagascar. The Gold Coast had the greatest concentration of English forts (fortified stations or factories), tapping the gold as well as the slave trade from the interior. The largest English fort was Cape Castle, on the Gold Coast, employing fifty to one hundred persons; lesser forts usually had ten to twenty employees.

Africans offered for sale kinsmen who had been captured in war, were under sentence for debt or crimes, or had been kidnapped. The black prisoners were brought either to the forts or to vessels off the coasts (the floating trade) or were turned over to the bolder white traders who ventured up the rivers and streams and negotiated directly with chiefs and caboceers (men of rank). Adult male slaves could be purchased for one hundred gallons of rum, adult female slaves for eighty-five, and children for sixty-five. Slaves from different parts of Africa were thought to have special physical and characterial traits. Virginians and South Carolinians preferred the Mandingos of Gambia, believed to be of gentle nature even if not too trustworthy.

Historians have recently debated whether the colonial and British slave trade was truly three-cornered, in which slave vessels transported cargo over every leg of a route. One viewpoint is that ships, especially after 1750, carried on their return bills of exchange and ballast. However, it appears that most slave ships brought home products from the West Indies or the southern colonies. The slave trade was indeed triangular, with a middle passage, except for the direct trade between northern ports and Africa.

There is no denying the hardship and trauma of the middle passage. Slaves were startled to see the huge copper kettles, or "cabooses," upon boarding ship, fearing that their large size indicated cannibalism. The captives were fed a steady diet, lacking in protein, of a mash made of boiled ground corn or rice mixed with salt, pepper, and palm seed oil. Sometimes there was fried corn cake or black-eyed peas. Bad hygiene and poor ventilation in the cramped slave quarters in the hold of the ship caused a high mortality. Dysentery, measles, smallpox, scurvy, and yaws were all fatal. Exercising the prisoners on deck (only the men being chained) and scrubbing slave quarters with vinegar reduced the death rate during a voyage from twenty-five percent in the seventeenth century to ten percent in the later colonial period.

The rapid increase of slavery in the eighteenth century made colonists aware of the problems of too many Africans: A decrease in the value of slaves and especially a "darkening of half a continent" increased the possibility of slave insurrection. All the colonies except Connecticut and New Hampshire imposed duties on slaves. South Carolina and Connecticut forbade importation of slaves in the 1760s, but these laws as well as other colonial acts that allowed prohibitive duties on slaves were disallowed by the British government. The African slave trade by the end of the colonial period proved to be a divisive issue between the colonies and the home country. Parliament encouraged the trade and from 1729 to 1750 even appropriated ninety thousand pounds for maintenance of the African slave stations. There was yet no groundswell in British public opinion condemning the overseas slave trade. A writer of "The African Slave Trade Defended: And Corruption the worst of Slaveries," printed in the *London Magazine* in 1740, argued that it was not within the power of Britishers "to cure the universal Evil" of slavery; but "by purchasing, or rather ransoming the Negroes from their national Tyrants, and transporting them under the benign Influences of the Law, and Gospel, they are advanced to much greater Degrees of Felicity, tho' not to absolute Liberty." Colonial condemnation of England's promotion of the slave trade would be firmly expressed in the original draft of the Declaration of Independence, indicting the king for not using "his negative" in suppressing the "execrable Commerce" in slaves.

10

Black Slavery: Life and Resistance

Enslavement of Africans affected every phase of the economy, society, and institutions in the South. Inward and outward resistance, real and imagined, served as warnings of the danger of relaxing control over slaves. While the grip of slavery was beginning to shake loose in the North as the slave population stabilized, in the South it intensified. Racial tensions increased everywhere, and southerners and northerners alike faced the problem of reconciling chattel slavery and the natural liberty of human-kind, though few persons anywhere probed for solutions of the dilemma or even questioned the justifiability of slavery itself.

Black populations in the colonies are difficult to determine, but studies by Evarts B. Greene and Virginia D. Harrington (*American Population before the Federal Census of 1790*, published in 1932) and Robert V. Wells (*The Population of the British Colonies in America before 1776*, published in 1975) offer reasonable estimates. The number of blacks in New England was never large, less than three percent (16,000) of the total population on the eve of the Revolution: New Hampshire, 0.8 percent (1775); Massachusetts, 2.1 percent (1764); Connecticut, 2.6 percent (1774); and Rhode Island, 6.2 percent (1774). The proportion of the number of blacks in New York decreased from a high of 15.2 percent in 1723 to 11.8 percent in 1771. New Jersey averaged about eight percent blacks during the colonial period, and 0.6 percent of the population of Pennsylvania and Delaware is estimated to have been black in 1775. From 1730 to the Revolution, slaves composed about two-fifths of the population from Maryland to Georgia, though steadily increasing: at the time of the Revolution, about thirty-three percent in Maryland, forty-five percent in Virginia, twenty-six percent in North Carolina, fifty-five percent in South Carolina, and forty-five percent in Georgia.

THE SLAVE COMMUNITY

Slaves in the northern colonies were owned in small numbers by merchants, shopkeepers, and farmers, which allowed for greater freedom of mobility and mixing with the general population. This contrasted with the southern colonies, where, in the 1770s, one-half of the slaves lived on plantations with ten or more bond servants. Many northern slaves were artisans, household servants, and laborers, such as those employed in loading and unloading ships. In the South, on the self-contained plantations, slavery was structured into a vertical and hierarchical system: from the bottom up, field hands, drivers, artisans, house servants, overseers, and masters. New slaves from Africa (also known as raw, Guinea, or outlandish slaves) worked in the fields. Many had been sold to the small planters; others, however, attended the outlying fields of large plantation owners. In Maryland in the early eighteenth century, it was not unusual to find groups of four or five slaves living at campsites near the lands they attended. One factor contributing to the adaptability of raw African slaves to the plantation work force was that most had been accustomed to routine agricultural work in Africa, such as tending rice paddies or herding livestock; women had also worked in the fields in Africa.

Because of the scarcity and high cost of free skilled labor, plantation owners trained slaves as craftsmen. One skill many Africans possessed was woodworking. Assimilated slaves worked as artisans or as household servants and also tended the wharves, warehouses, and plantation industries. One British officer, James Grant, who had commanded troops in South Carolina during the Cherokee War (1759–1761) before becoming governor of East Florida, observed in 1768:

> The Planter has tradesmen of all kinds in his Gang of Slaves, and 'tis a Rule with them, never to pay Money for what can be made upon their Estates, not a Lock, a Hing or a Nail if they can avoid it.

American-born slave women worked as nurses, laundresses, cooks, seam-stresses, gardeners, and personal maidservants, although many were still used in the fields. Even small children performed work assignments, such as hoeing, feeding livestock, and shooing birds. As in the North, southern urban centers provided employment for slave artisans. In Charleston, for example, from 1730 to 1799 some 372 slaves were counted as engaging in fifty occupations.

A universal complaint of plantation owners was the difficulty of getting slaves to work to full capacity. Leading planters, such as Landon Carter or William Byrd II, constantly complained of negligence and indolence and averred that slaves were diligent only when closely supervised. It was suspected that slaves feigned illness; of course, disabilities disappeared on Sundays, the traditional day off, and on holidays. These were the kind of inward resistance that slaves, lacking any real incentives, were able to employ with limited liability. Some masters subjected slaves to lashings, but other slave owners, such as Landon Carter, thought that counterproductive.

Southern masters supplied their slaves with meager rations of coarse food in bulk, such as Indian corn, beans, peas, and rice. Slaves often could keep their own gardens, and they also supplemented their diets by foraging, fishing, and hunting (trusted slaves were allowed weapons for this purpose). What spare meat was infrequently furnished by the slave owner most likely consisted of fat, inferior cuts of pork, and old bacon. Slaves, both male and female, wore primarily loose smocks made of coarse cotton, linen, or woolen cloth. Landon Carter, in Virginia, required his slaves to purchase clothing from their garden produce. Slave quarters were typically cabins, about three hundred square feet, with dirt floors; furnishings included straw bedding, barrels for sitting, a few pots and pans, and millstones for grinding grain.

While some slaves, especially in the Deep South, had scant opportunity to interact with masters, many of whom seldom ventured away from the great house or were absentees, other planters kept a check on their slaves. A Virginia "patriarch" such as William Byrd II made daily rounds "to talk with his people" and even interfered in the domestic affairs of his slaves. The interpersonal dimension, however, in the relationship between master and slave, elicited, as Gerald W. Mullin and Latham A. Windley have shown, a defensive pattern of behavior from slaves. Mulattoes and the more acculturated bondsmen often revealed anxiety through stuttering and stammering.

To some extent slaves were able to find sustenance from nuclear families and a network of friends and relatives. Although slave marriages were not legally recognized, owners encouraged monogamous relationships between slaves, feeling that a man devoted to his wife and children was less likely to be rebellious. By the time of the Revolution, the ratio of women to men was nearly equal.

In one particular way the system of slavery in the South weakened family stability: Slave families were dependent for their support on masters and not on male slaves as heads of households. Slave women had almost total responsibility for raising children. Mothers were the authority figures in slave communities. Another change was a reduction in the lactation period for childbearing women. American-born slave women weaned children in one year, much less than the time period in Africa. It is estimated that the birthrate among American slaves was quadruple the rate in Africa.

Culturally, black bondsmen sought self-definition. Semblances of African rituals and totemism were carried over into slave religion. It was not uncommon for new slaves to believe in transmigration—that after death they would return to Africa. Suicides among the new slaves were usually acts of religious martyrdom in expectation of release from bondage and the return of their souls to the land of their birth. Singing and dancing kept alive reminiscences of African origins. Music and religion, for the most part, were left unregulated in plantation communities.

"Black English" also contributed toward a black identity. Most new slaves had great difficulty in learning English. Slaves developed a pidgin language for communication among themselves. In the plantation South, masters suppressed literacy and tended to reduce oral communication with slaves to a lower-level language, a sort of "baby talk." In the South Carolina lowcountry, new slaves were not expected to learn English. Northerners, however, were more prone to advocate literacy for black slaves. As Cotton Mather noted, "They are barbarous. But so were our ancestors. . . . Christianity will be the best cure for this barbarity. . . . It may seem unto as little purpose to teach, as to wash an Ethiopian. But the greater must be our application." Many slaves spoke, as a European traveler observed in the 1770s, a "mixed dialect between the Guinea and English." In the South Carolina and Georgia coastal areas, a Gullah dialect, persisting to this day, exhibited an affinity for using groups of words for nouns, verbs, adjectives, and adverbs.

In New England, in contrast to southern slave society, one feature contributing to black identity was the quasi-institutionalization of elections of black kings, governors, and judges. The voting was held when whites went to the polls. In Massachusetts masters traditionally gave slaves a three-day holiday to celebrate a black election. The black "officials" exercised extralegal authority and meted out punishment, which had the effect of complementing legitimate means of slave control. Such a pattern seems to have existed in New York, though not sanctioned by the white community, and hence it was a factor in assigning a spirit of rebelliousness to slaves.

SLAVE OFFENSES AND PUNISHMENT

Unlike white servants, slaves in the southern colonies could be disciplined as a master saw fit, though not to the extent of loss of life or limb. Masters, however, on grounds of self-defense, could exact punishment resulting in mutilation or loss of life. Also, killing a slave in correction was not a felony. A master could have a slave whipped, branded, chained, or punished in any number of ways deemed appropriate to the transgression.

A white person who murdered a slave could almost certainly escape the death penalty in the southern colonies. In South Carolina it was not even a capital offense, only punishable by a maximum fine of seven hundred pounds and certain civil disabilities. For example, in that colony in 1737, a master who killed his slave in a fit of passion was fined three hundred pounds and barred from public office. In Virginia, although there were a number of trials of white men who killed slaves, only in 1739 was anyone executed for this crime—an overseer and an accessory before the fact. In 1729, the General Court condemned Andrew Bourne to be hanged for whipping his slave to death, but for fear that execution of the sentence would encourage slave insubordination, he was pardoned.

The slave criminal codes of the colonies relied on corporal punishment or the extreme penalty of execution. In less than capital crimes, slaves, of course, could not pay fines, and since a slave represented both time and money, the objective was to return him to his master as quickly as possible. Slave capital crimes generally consisted of plotting or engaging in insurrection, murder, rape or attempted rape of a white woman, poisoning, manslaughter, housebreaking at night, burglary of articles of twenty shillings or more in value, destruction of certain types of property, or a repeated commission of a lesser crime. Indeed, punishment progressed in relation to the number of offenses. Petty larceny, according to the South Carolina code of 1712, for example, was punishable by forty lashes for the first offense, cutting off one ear or branding on the forehead for the second, slitting the nose for the third, and death for the fourth. Slave owners were compensated at public expense in the southern colonies and in New York, New Jersey, and Pennsylvania for slaves executed. In New England, however, there was no compensation, and hence masters frequently tried to save slaves convicted of capital crimes, usually attempting to get punishments for other than murder reduced to whipping.

Crimes by slaves were considered more horrid than those similarly committed by whites because of the implication of defiance and rebellion against white authority. Terrible retribution was meted out to slave felons. Castration was a legal punishment in Virginia, Pennsylvania, New Jersey, and the Carolinas. In New Jersey and Pennsylvania it was a penalty for the rape or attempted rape of a white woman. Georgia prohibited castration in its first slave code of 1755. Virginia did the same in 1769, except for the rape of a white woman. In South Carolina the penalty could be imposed for running away the fourth time or for striking a white person. A North Carolina law, in force from 1758 to 1764, provided castration for first felonious offenses committed by male slaves, except for rape and murder (punishable by execution). In most instances, limitation and prohibition of mutilation as punishment for felonious offenses were not the result of any growing concern for mitigation of the severity of the slave criminal laws. Rather, the alternative—execution—was usually prescribed in place of mutilation. Slave owners thus could receive compensation, which they could not for mutilation of slaves. Furthermore, there was the fear of potential danger from embittered mutilated slaves.

Slaves were legally burned alive in at least half the colonies, especially in New Jersey, New York, Virginia, and South Carolina, though the punishment was reserved chiefly for arson and the murder of a white person by poison. Rev. Francis Le Jau complained in 1709 that in Charleston "a poor Slavewoman was barbarously burnt alive near my door without any positive proof of the Crime she was accused of, wch was, the burning of her Master's House, and protested her innocence even to my self to the last." In New Jersey a slave was sentenced to have his hands "cut off and burned before thine eyes" and then to be hanged. It was a common practice in Virginia that after a slave had been hanged the head and sometimes the quartered remains were posted in public view, such as along roads leading into a town—the purpose, of course, was to strike terror among slaves.

Except in New England, slaves faced trials for felonies in special courts. The slave courts consisted usually of two justices of the peace and three to six "substantial" freeholders. In Virginia, where the practice was a little different, a sheriff notified the governor of any crime committed by a slave punishable with "death or loss of member," whereupon a commission went out to a county court to establish a court of oyer and terminer from about five of its members. In any of the special courts, slaves were tried without a jury, and the decisions of judges had to be unanimous.

The most effective way to minimize any danger that might arise from an assembly of slaves was to limit mobility. Generally, a pass, or "ticket," was required to leave one's immediate neighborhood or plantation. In Pennsylvania blacks could not travel more than ten miles from home. Furthermore, colonial statutes restricted congregating of blacks. In New York it was a misdemeanor, punishable by flogging, for four slaves to meet unless on business of a master.

As anxiety over potential insurrection increased in the early eighteenth century, colonies provided for slave patrols that aimed chiefly at preventing slaves from leaving a plantation or forming an unlawful assembly. If slaves away from a plantation did not have passes, the patrol would return them to their plantations, where they would be whipped. Patrols also inspected slave quarters in search of weapons or other contraband. Patrols were usually made up of young volunteer militiamen, who regarded "Negro hunting, Negro catching, Negro watching, and Negro whipping" as a sporting adventure.

RUNAWAYS

Runaway slaves faced harsh penalties. In Virginia (laws of 1723 and 1748) dismemberment was a punishment for a second or later try at escape— castration or cutting off part of a limb, usually a foot. The South Carolina code of 1712 also had graduated penalties: for males sixteen years or older, the first offense for staying out over twenty days, forty lashes; second, branding the cheek with an *R*; third, forty lashes and one ear cut off; fourth, for staying away thirty days, castration; and fifth, also for thirty days, cutting of the Achilles tendon or death. For women, in place of castration, an ear was to be cut off. Southern colonies used the ancient English practice of hue and cry, whereby running away was viewed as outlawry, and it was the duty of all citizens to apprehend the escapee dead or alive.

While slaves innately had the will to be free, they usually ran away for specific reasons: the shock of newly arriving from Africa, desire to be with family or friends located elsewhere, displeasure with a new owner, fear of punishment, apprehension of being sold, having been beaten, or finding a place of known refuge. Runaways might head for nearby woods, large towns, or places of difficult accessibility, such as the mountain fastnesses or the Dismal Swamp in southeastern Virginia and northern North Carolina. In 1728, William Byrd II "came upon a family of mulattoes that called themselves free" in the Dismal Swamp. Until 1763, Spanish Florida officially granted freedom to escaped English slaves.

From slave advertisements in newspapers, historians have profiled slave runaways during the later colonial period. In South Carolina most escapees were from lowland districts near Charleston, twenty-five percent of whom had occupations related to fishing or boating. One study (Windley, 1974) found that only thirty-seven percent of runaways in South Carolina were mulattoes (compared to sixty-three percent in Virginia), while another analysis (Philip D. Morgan, 1986) noted that only one-half of the South Carolina runaways were American-born. In Virginia the assimilated or "accommodationist" slave, the least suspected of rebelliousness, was the most likely to run away. Outlandish slaves, according to Gerald W. Mullin (1972), preferred defecting in groups, while American-born slaves generally ran off alone. Most plantation slaves, however, were merely truant, living for a few days at a time on the outskirts of the plantation. One-sixth of runaways in New England and the middle colonies were mulattoes. Almost all southern runaways had visible scars—tribal markings or brands of their masters.

SLAVE INSURRECTIONS

Much more serious than individual acts of protest or attempts to escape, slave conspiracies for collective resistance threatened the safety of a community. Black insurrection was viewed as aiming at Negro mastery as well as freedom. Insurrection, like other capital crimes committed by slaves, had the connotation of treason because it endangered the very existence of the established order. Generally in the colonial period, slave insurrection was defined as three or more persons armed and assembled with intent to obtain freedom through force. More often than not, however, there were only alleged conspiracies.

Although no blood was shed from any black insurrectionary activity in Virginia until the Nat Turner uprising in 1831, white residents of that colony had just enough provocation to keep up a close guard on slaves. Black and white servants of Gloucester County in 1663 planned to seize arms and march on the governor to demand their freedom; an informer revealed the plot, and several of the conspirators were executed. Slaves in Westmoreland County in 1687 allegedly planned to destroy plantations and kill whites; there must have been some doubt, however, as the putative leader was merely whipped and forced to wear an iron collar the rest of his life. Supposedly there was a similar plot in Middlesex County in 1691, but nothing definite is known. In 1709 and 1710 blacks in Isle of Wight, James City, and Surry counties planned to fight their way to freedom; again the plots were nipped early, with several ringleaders executed, one of them hanged, drawn, and quartered. In 1722 a posse in Westmoreland County rounded up alleged conspirators, who were then transported out of the colony. In 1729 a band of Negro and Indian fugitives headed for the Blue Ridge Mountains but were captured. Two conspiracies in Princess Anne County in 1730 led to the execution of four persons. In Maryland the only major conspiracy (1739) involved a gathering of two hundred slaves, who supposedly intended to capture Annapolis and murder the whites or, if failing to do so, take to the woods; at least one of the leaders was executed.

The concentration of blacks in districts near Charleston and their segregation from whites formed fertile ground for slave conspiracy. In 1713 slaves along Goose Creek planned to "get their liberty by force," but the scheme was discovered, and one slave leader was executed. Slaves in 1720 set off for St. Augustine, killing two whites on the way, but were captured at Savannah, and three slaves were hanged. There was a similar unsuccessful attempt in 1730, again with the leaders put to death. The insurrection in South Carolina that created the greatest terror and prompted a more stringent slave code was the Stono uprising of September 1739. Led by a slave named Jemmy, blacks along the Stono River, twenty miles southwest of Charleston, broke into a store, stole arms and ammunition, and killed the two proprietors, leaving their heads on the steps. Setting out for Florida with flags flying and with drums beating in hopes of rallying other slaves along the way, the group paused at the Edisto River. Lieutenant Governor William Bull accidentally ran across them, but, managing to escape, he was able to rally militia. In an ensuing battle, forty blacks and twenty whites were killed. The Ashley River militia pursued the insurgents who fled, caught up with them, killed twenty more slaves and then, according to one contemporary, shot, hanged, or gibbeted forty others. In June 1740 about two hundred slaves along the Ashley and Cooper rivers were thought to have entered into another conspiracy; subsequently, fifty of those considered to be implicated in the plot were hanged in batches of ten a day.

White residents of New York City, for over a generation, worked themselves up to a "great fear." Certain episodes fed the paranoia. For the murder of seven whites, four slaves and an Indian were hanged and a woman was burned at the stake at Newton, Long Island, in 1708. Four years later New Yorkers had a real shocker. New slaves from Africa and several Indians formed a secret brotherhood for the obliteration of whites, the conspirators binding themselves together by sucking blood from each other's hands. After setting fire to buildings at the edge of the city, the group killed ten whites who came out to fight the fires. Those who fled, however, soon sounded the alarm, and militia captured the band, except several who escaped or committed suicide. A special court tried twenty-seven culprits, of whom nineteen were executed. Since New York had a law that gave judges discretion in meting out sentences to fit the terror of a crime, besides thirteen who were hanged, three were burned at the stake, one was suspended in chains and starved to death, one was roasted over a slow fire, and one was broken on the wheel. New Yorkers did not get over the scare of 1712. A rumored plan for a bloodbath by slaves in New Jersey in 1734, which resulted in the execution of the ringleader, also served to feed the fear of slave insurrection in New York City.

By 1740, New York City was a thoroughly cosmopolitan city that lacked social cohesion. There were nine thousand whites and two thousand blacks, in addition to a large contingent of seamen, many of whom were foreigners. At the time New Yorkers were disturbed by the knowledge of an undeclared war being waged on the high seas between England and Spain (the War of Jenkins' Ear), and they feared a Spanish fleet would come into New York harbor. The winter of 1740–1741 was extremely cold, and, with the price of wheat high and bakers on strike, bread was scarce.

The allegation that a great Negro conspiracy was unfolding in New York City resulted from a combination of events. In spring 1741 there was a rash of robberies, and beginning a day after St. Patrick's Day, there were eight fires in six days at government buildings, including the governor's house, the troop barracks, and Fort George. A black was caught looting one of the burning structures. An investigation of what was believed to be arson and the robberies led to an alehouse on the riverfront kept by John Hughson and his wife. The Hughson establishment was known to entertain twenty to thirty slaves at a time as well as to cater to a criminal element. A fence for stolen goods was thought to be operating out of the tavern. The authorities moved quickly in making mass arrests.

From May 1741 to September 1742, the Supreme Court of Judicature, presided over by Daniel Horsmanden, the city's recorder, conducted a series of trials. Relying chiefly on the testimony of a sixteen-year-old Irish servant belonging to the Hughsons, Mary Burton, and William Kane, a white soldier also given immunity, the court returned 101 convictions. Seventeen blacks and four whites (two men and two women) were hanged, thirteen blacks were burned at the stake, and the other persons convicted were banished. Hughson, his wife, and Peggy Kerry, a prostitute, were hanged at one time; Hughson's body was left hanging in chains, and after a while the corpse bloated and dripped and turned black, which New Yorkers took as a sign that Hughson had indeed been in a conspiracy with the blacks. It was believed that blacks and some whites plotted to kill citizens of the city and to install a new government, with a black governor at its head. Most of the convictions were based on these assertions.

Hysteria at one time during the so-called New York Conspiracy was so great that many citizens fled the city. Very much part of the fear was the belief that the Negro plot also involved a Spanish conspiracy. In May 1741, Governor James Oglethorpe of Georgia sent a letter to Lieutenant Governor George Clarke of New York that he had

> some intelligence . . . of a villainous design of a very extraordinary nature
> . . . that the Spaniards had employed emissaries to burn all the magazines
> and considerable towns in English North-America, thereby to prevent
> subsisting of the great expedition and fleet in the West-Indies.

An implication of a Spanish conspiracy was made throughout the trials. Mrs. Hughson was cited as a "papist," and "Spanish negroes" were among those executed. The last "conspirator" to be put to death was John Ury, a white schoolteacher who claimed to be a nonjuring Anglican priest. Ury, however, was believed to be a Catholic priest acting as a Spanish spy. He conducted his own defense (no member of the New York bar was willing to defend any of the accused). As often with scapegoating, charges were eventually made against persons in high places. Only too late did the authorities realize that the primary accuser, Mary Burton, had been a liar. Thus the trials ended, with the court expunging the later perjured testimony of Mary Burton, who, upon receiving a reward to the amount of buying her freedom, disappeared. The 1741–1742 New York Conspiracy had all the earmarks of the Salem witchhunt of 1692, but this was apparently also true of much of the prosecution for slave conspiracies elsewhere.

MANUMISSION AND FREE BLACKS

There were few encumbrances on a master who wished to liberate a slave in the northern colonies, and this was also true in the South before slavery reached full legal status. Rhode Island in 1652 limited enslavement to a ten-year period. It became a practice in New England to reward blacks with freedom for years of faithful service. Slaves were also freed by wills, appeals to courts, and purchase of their liberty. Connecticut, Massachusetts, Rhode Island, New York, and Pennsylvania had laws requiring masters to post bond to guarantee that their freed slaves would not become a charge to the community. New Jersey (to 1769) and New York (1712–1717) also mandated that former masters pay twenty pounds annually to each of their freed slaves.

In Maryland slaves could be freed by deed and, until 1752, also by word of mouth and last will. Elsewhere in the South efforts were made to prevent an increase in the free black population. A Virginia law of 1691 said that no "Negro or mulatto" could be freed unless transported out of the colony at the expense of the former master. In 1723 a slave could be manumitted in Virginia only by license of the governor and council, and "meritorious service" was the sole admissible grounds for granting freedom. In North Carolina a county court had to approve manumission. North Carolina also prohibited free blacks from remaining in the colony, but after 1741 they could remain if so permitted by a county court. South Carolina waited until 1722 to regulate manumissions, at which time it was stipulated that newly freed persons had to leave the colony within twelve months (after 1735, six months), and manumitted persons staying beyond the specified period were to be reenslaved. Of the southern colonies, only Georgia made no provision for limiting manumission during the colonial era.

Free blacks met some form of repression everywhere. In New England they were ostracized and, though taxed, could not vote, own certain property, bear arms, or serve in the militia. New England freedmen also came under a curfew, unless possessing a pass, and could be compelled to work on streets and roads. New York and New Jersey prohibited blacks from owning land. In Connecticut freedmen could not reside or conduct business in towns without the consent of the local authorities. In the South free blacks could own property, but they were disfranchised in South Carolina (1705), North Carolina (1715–1737), and Georgia (1761). Colonial laws discouraged miscegenation, with penalties including flogging, banishment, and, for white parties, a period of servitude.

Free blacks in Virginia had a wide latitude of freedom in the seventeenth century. Freedmen in Northampton County on the eastern shore became prosperous farmers. They acquired land or leaseholds through incentives afforded by masters and freedom agreements. Their status, however, deteriorated because of the 1691 Virginia law requiring newly freed blacks to leave the colony, an increase in racial tensions, and a decrease in the free black population due to migration to Maryland. Free blacks in the northern colonies also did not fare well economically, many of them being retained in a quasi-servant capacity or moving into squatter communities on unclaimed land.

ANTISLAVERY

Colonial Americans inevitably had to confront the problem of reconciling slavery with Christianity. Even though Africans might be devoid of certain rational faculties, it was argued, they were still among the children of God. Colonial religious bodies slowly began to recognize the obligation of converting and churching the black bondsmen. Yet there was almost no effort among the churches to denounce the evil of slavery itself. In New England ministers often kept one or two household slaves. In the late seventeenth century, the writings of an English clergyman, Morgan Godwin, who had briefly visited the colonies, set the tone for the Anglican accommodation with slavery. He argued that Christianity improved the behavior of slaves and that Christian slaves were more productive and loyal.

The Society for the Propagation of the Gospel in Foreign Parts sent over missionaries to convert and teach the slaves (though not proceeding much beyond catechization). Even then, the actual churching of southern slaves did not gain momentum until the Revolutionary War era, mainly under the auspices of evangelical groups such as the Baptists and the Methodists. Although educating slaves was anathema to southern slave-holders, some efforts, chiefly in the North, were made in the late colonial period to give blacks the rudiments of learning. Cotton Mather in 1717 helped to found a charity school for blacks in Boston. Anthony Benezet, a Quaker schoolmaster, established a night school for blacks in Philadelphia. Dr. Bray's Associates (an English philanthropic group, named after the Reverend Thomas Bray, who died in 1730) attempted to found Negro schools throughout the colonies, being most successful in Philadelphia (1758). That blacks could embrace Christianity and education was seen as evidence by some that black bondsmen were entitled to the enjoyment of the natural rights of human beings.

Not until the end of the colonial period was there a movement for the abolition of slavery. Even Quakers, at one time, owned one-third of the slaves in Pennsylvania. The first recorded protest against slavery in the colonies was the petition of a small group of German Quakers from Germantown presented at a Philadelphia monthly meeting of Friends in 1688. The Germantown petitioners condemned slavery as violating the Golden Rule and compared the suffering of slaves to their own European experiences of religious persecution. George Keith, who led a schismatic faction of Quakers known as Christian Quakers, in 1693 published *An Exhortation & Caution to Friends concerning Buying or Keeping of Negroes*, which argued along the lines of the Germantown petition. Both the Germantown petition and the Keith tract at the time received a cool reception among the Quakers.

Samuel Sewall, the Massachusetts merchant and judge, stands out almost alone among New Englanders in announcing opposition to slavery. *The Selling of Joseph* (1700) was the first public plea in the colonies condemning slavery. "All men," Sewall said "are the Sons of Adam" and "are Coheirs; and have equal Right unto Liberty, and all other outward Comforts of Life." Since *"Liberty* is in real value next unto *Life*: None ought to part with it themselves, or deprive others of it, but upon most mature Consideration."

Some southern planters recognized the evils of slavery but saw no solution. William Byrd II thought that slavery had an especially debilitating effect on slaveholders, making them proud and less industrious; though he did not advocate freeing slaves, he did laud the exclusion of slavery from Georgia during the trusteeship period.

In the eighteenth century, Quaker condemnation of slavery mounted. In 1718, William Burling, a Quaker merchant on Long Island, appealed to his brethren to free any slave that might come into their possession. John Hepburn, a New Jersey Quaker, in 1715 published *The American Defence of the Christian Golden Rule*, which, through a dialogue between a "Negro-Master" and a "Christian," called attention to cruelty toward slaves. Ralph Sandiford, a Philadelphia shopkeeper, published a similar condemnation of slavery in 1729, as did Elihu Coleman, a Nantucket Quaker, the following year. As the Quaker communities slowly shifted against slavery, arguments rested not so much on moral considerations as on fears that slavery posed a danger of insurrection and a threat to spiritual purity. As the colonial period ended, Anthony Benezet became the most influential propagandist of the emerging antislavery movement. In 1759 he published *Observations on the Enslaving, Importing, and Purchase of Negroes*, the first of a series of tracts denouncing the slave trade, showing all of its horrors through eyewitness accounts. John Woolman, a tailor and shopkeeper from western New Jersey, in 1754 published *Some Considerations on the Keeping of Negroes*, which condemned slave ownership. "The Color of a Man avails nothing in Matters of Right and Equity," he wrote. Woolman contended that black slaves had helped to build up wealth and should therefore have a share of it. Woolman's other writings would reflect firsthand knowledge of slavery from extensive travels through the southern colonies.

By the mid-eighteenth century, Quaker yearly meetings and local monthly meetings began to take stands against slave ownership and the slave trade. Efforts of individuals would not let the issues die. Best known for unusual tactics is Benjamin Lay, an eccentric hunchback who had arrived in America from Barbados in 1735. His most notorious act occurred at the Friends' yearly meeting at Burlington, New Jersey, in 1738. Lay appeared in a heavy overcoat. Arising to speak, he threw off the garment to reveal a military uniform and a sword. He held in his hand a hollowed book, which he opened to show a bladder filled with red liquid (probably pokeberry juice). "It would be as profitable in the sight of the Almighty," he exclaimed, "if you should thrust a sword through their hearts as I do through this book!" Thereupon he stuck the sword through the book and bladder and sprinkled the "blood" on persons seated nearby.

In the 1740s many Quakers began to free their slaves. The Philadelphia yearly meeting in 1753–1754 denounced slavery as a sin and in 1758 urged a ban on the slave trade and the freeing of slaves already owned. Not all Quaker local meetings went along with this decision, and the Philadelphia yearly meeting avoided any further action on slavery for a number of years following. Nevertheless, by the time of the Revolution, the Quakers had paved the way for a broader antislavery movement in the North.

11

Women, Children, and Family

Gender and family relations followed English ways, though in the colonies there was greater latitude for diversity and liberalization. The colonists did not always adopt common law or equity guidelines of England, nor did ecclesiastical courts exist in the colonies. Social mobility, varied religious experiences, Dutch and other European influences, regional distinctions, and economic opportunity were among factors that shaped attitudes and practices relating to family and gender. The colonial family itself was often in a state of flux, due to the high mortality among children, early deaths of a spouse (twenty percent of men and women between the ages of twenty and forty), remarriage, or sending children away to school or foster homes.

LEGAL STATUS OF WOMEN

The prevailing view was that women should be kept in subjection to their husbands for their own good. As William Byrd II sardonically expressed it, "Female Passion" required that women be confined within "bounds . . . like a Mettled Horse from running away." The proper role of a woman was that of mother, housewife, and companion, and she constantly needed protection and intellectual guidance from her husband. From the Puritan religious perspective, woman had been the first to fall from grace, and the daughters of Eve, more so than men, had to be attentive in giving witness to their salvation. Yet Cotton Mather felt that more women experienced saving grace than men. Whether married or single, women had limited options for participation in society. They could not vote, and in most religious bodies they could not speak out or hold offices, even though they were accepted as full members.

A single woman (feme sole), including one whose marriage had been dissolved by death or divorce, was considered entirely competent in matters of private law, being permitted to own and dispose of property and to sue in the courts. Margaret Brent, a Catholic spinster who arrived in Maryland in 1638, not only looked after her own affairs and manorial estates but also acted on powers of attorney for her brother and others, served as a legal guardian for a young Indian princess, and was executrix of the estate of Governor Leonard Calvert.

For a married woman (feme covert) it was an entirely different matter. Under the colonial legal systems, as in English common and ecclesiastical law, a married woman and her property were under the control and supervision of her husband. The husband was his wife's overseer. As Marylynn Salmon (1986) has pointed out, the "benchmark" for the interpretation of the "unity of person" in marriage was embodied in a dictum of the English jurist William Blackstone:

> By marriage, the husband and wife are one person in law: that is, the very being or legal existence of the woman is suspended during the marriage, or at least is incorporated and consolidated into that of the husband: under whose wing, protection, and *cover* she performs every thing. (pp. 14 and 200)

After marriage, a woman lost the right singly to execute contracts or sue as a legal guardian, executrix, or administrator, but in most colonies she could do so jointly with her husband, with his consent. A married woman relinquished control over real estate and income. A husband was the sole guardian of the children and could will their guardianship, but if the husband died without mention of the future care of the children, the widow automatically became the guardian. A husband had the right to chastise his wife, but if he abused this, the wife could appeal to the courts, whereupon the husband might face a fine or a whipping. A 1650 Massachusetts law called for a ten-pound fine or a whipping for any man who struck his wife or wife who hit her husband. A husband was responsible for any minor crimes that his wife might commit; he had the choice of paying a fine or allowing his wife to be whipped.

In some instances, however, a married woman had some legitimate claims over property. In the Plymouth and New Haven colonies, a wife's permission was required before a husband could sell a house or land. Importantly, in all the colonies, a wife, through a premarital contract, could retain full possession and control of her dower, including that obtained from a previous marriage. Such a prenuptial agreement was a sure way of protecting a wife's own property. Massachusetts, however, did not make prenuptial contracts binding until 1762.

Under the Roman-Dutch law in New Netherland, a wife could own real and personal property, operate a business without her husband's permission, and sue and be sued. At marriage, the wife had the choice of living according to manus, with a status of a minor and the husband as legal guardian, or making a prenuptial agreement, whereupon she rejected all marital power and renounced community property, retaining full control of her own estate. A wife, however, had the option of renouncing manus at any time. After 1664 this arrangement was allowed to continue by virtue of New Netherland being a conquered Christian country, though it was eventually superseded by English colonial legal practices.

Despite the restrictions on femes covert, the colonies recognized the need for support of widows. Even colonies that adopted the English rule of primogeniture for a male parent dying intestate allowed a partible inheritance for the widow. A widow was assured of a dower at least for lifetime use. In several colonies, when a husband died testate, the widow could choose between property willed her or the dower. A widow's dower right was defined as a claim to at least one-third of the estate. In the South, for a husband dying without a will and with no more than two children, the widow received one-third of the estate, and if more than two children a share equal to that of any one of the children. In Massachusetts the widow's dower was free from her husband's creditors. In some colonies a widow might lose her inheritance if she remarried. The legacies given to daughters were usually about half those granted to brothers, most likely in personal rather than real property, such as household goods, livestock, or slaves. The main reason for this practice was that daughters were expected to marry and therefore had less need for property than male heirs.

WOMEN'S ECONOMIC LIFE

For most colonial women, who were not wealthy, life consisted of unrelenting toil. Besides child rearing, the average housewife went about her household duties amid the smells of grease, tallow, and smoke (light was often provided by the burning of grease-soaked wicks). She cooked on cast-iron stoves or in fireplaces, toting heavy iron pots and brass or copper kettles. The colonial housewife also doubled as a producer of goods—

soapmaker, distiller, miller, baker, gardener, weaver, spinner, knitter, butcher, and food, dairy, and meat processor. The cellar served as a refrigerator. For water, the housewife had to carry buckets from outdoor wells or nearby streams. As the physician of the household, she gathered and dried herbs. Women also shared in the shop and farm work with their husbands, meeting with customers or engaging in business transactions. Some husbands even had their wives attending to the family's financial affairs. Judge Samuel Sewall of Boston noted in his diary that he gave his wife, Judith, all his cash, and "if I want I will borrow of her. She has a better faculty than I at managing Affairs."

Thus for many colonial Americans, male and female space intersected and overlapped. There was little distinction between the workplace and the home. Servants and apprentices joined the family for meals and other activities. During the eighteenth century, however, the workplace became increasingly separate from the home, particularly with the rise in affluence and, in the South, greater reliance on slave labor. The housewife's role became even more segregated as the guardian of the household and the family.

Married women entered directly into the economic life of a community in any of three ways: acting as agents for their husbands, managing the family business, or pursuing occupations of their own. The colonies followed English equity principles in allowing a feme covert to act as a feme sole trader. Although a married woman was required to obtain court approval of this status, many married women pursued economic endeavors without bothering to petition a court, and colonial authorities usually ignored the situation. It was expected, however, that a married woman as a feme sole trader had to have the consent of her husband. In South Carolina (laws of 1712 and 1744) feme sole traders were responsible for their own debts.

Married, single, and widowed women worked as craftsmen. Newspaper advertisements give testimony to the wide variety of trades in which women were employed, including positions as blacksmiths, farriers, silversmiths, gunsmiths, shoemakers, glaziers, tanners, bakers, printers, butchers, tailors, and shipwrights. Women also operated small-scale businesses, such as coffee or food shops and retail stores, especially millinery and dry goods outlets. Several iron forges were run by women, such as that of Jane Burgess in Maryland.

Widows operated printing establishments that had belonged to their husbands, notably Dinah Nuthead at St. Mary's, Maryland (1694), and some of them published newspapers—Elizabeth Timothy (*South Carolina Gazette*), Clementine Rind (*Virginia Gazette*), and Anne Catherine Greene (*Maryland Gazette*).

A major female enterprise was innkeeping. Between 1643 and 1689, five percent of inns in New England and 18.9 percent in Boston were operated by women. Boston in 1714, with a population of ten thousand, had thirty-four taverns (or inns), twelve of which were run by women; at the same time, seventeen of forty-one liquor dealers in Boston were women. In Pennsylvania between 1762 and 1776, fifty women advertised taverns in newspapers (twenty percent of the total). Among famous colonial taverns with women as proprietors were the King's Tavern (Jane Vobe) and an inn operated by Elizabeth Dawson (widow of the former president of William and Mary College) in Williamsburg, Virginia, and the Sign of the Ship (Elizabeth Marriott) in Annapolis. A well-known establishment was Peg Mullen's Beefsteak House in Philadelphia. Perhaps one of the earliest "fast food" retailers was Nancy Rumsey, "fat, square, and forty," who in Georgia peddled cider, gingerbread, and nuts from an oxcart at a town square. Women could be found even in occupations outside the law. Anne Bonny, the illegitimate daughter of an Irish lawyer in Charleston, had eloped with a pirate, James Bonny. Captured and tried herself for piracy, Anne escaped the gallows and won a pardon by pleading pregnancy.

Widows took over the management of businesses and plantations from their deceased husbands. Eliza Lucas Pinckney, who had administered her father's plantation near Charleston, also later managed the nearby Belmont plantation after her husband's death in 1758 and became well known for successful production of indigo, flax, hemp, and silk. When she died in Philadelphia in 1793, President Washington was one of the pallbearers. Among other successful widows in business management were Temperance Grant, who ran a shipping firm in Rhode Island, and Martha Turnstall, who took over her husband's whaling business on Long Island.

Women had the role of "deputy husbands" during the absence of their spouses. For example, Deborah Read Franklin handled the family's financial affairs while Benjamin Franklin was in France. Sara Bland went to Virginia in 1678 to supervise the estates there owned by her husband, John Bland, a London merchant. When Jeremias Van Rensselaer died in 1674 without a direct heir, family members appointed Maria Van Cortlandt Van Rensselaer administrator (treasurer) for Rensselaerwyck, the million-acre estate running twenty-four miles along both sides of the Hudson River and "stretching two days into the interior," a post she held for fifteen years.

Many colonial women received land grants. In Georgia, for example, between 1755 and 1775, thirty-one women acquired fifty-three patents for land ranging in size from 500 to 999 acres, and sixteen others were granted parcels of one thousand acres or more. Mary Musgrove Matthews Bosomworth was awarded 6,200 acres on St. Catherine's Island for her services as Indian negotiator and interpreter. Lady Deborah Moody, widow of a baronet, was granted land in Massachusetts, but getting into trouble with the authorities because of her religious beliefs, she moved to New Netherland, where she also received a land grant and founded the town of Gravesand.

Nurturant occupations provided economic opportunity. Women held positions as teachers in small private schools for girls, tutors, music and dancing instructors, and governesses. Especially during the early colonial period, women worked as medical professionals—physicians, surgeons, nurses, and midwives. In seventeenth-century New England, twenty-four percent of medical practitioners were women. Women served as nurses and surgeons with military forces. Charlotte Brown, matron of the Nursing Service for the British army, left a diary of her experiences in Pennsylvania from 1754 to 1757.

The minimal schooling and general exclusion from job training outside the home nevertheless limited opportunities for women. The insufficiency of women's education is perhaps reflected in the scantiness of their literary output; of 911 works published in seventeenth-century New England, only four were by women—Anne Bradstreet (poetry), Mary Rowlandson (narrative), M. Hooper ("lamentations" on the death of her sons), and Sarah Goodhue (journal).

COURTSHIP, MARRIAGE, AND SEPARATION

Most colonists married, and indeed, as William Byrd II said, "an Old Maid or an Old Bachelor are as scarce among us and reckoned as ominous as a Blazing Star." Bachelors were suspect, and colonial legislation tried to coax them into matrimony, such as requiring single males to live with families or taxing them. Unusual was one of the Pilgrim fathers, Robert Cushman, who did not marry until age eighty. In early New England bachelors came under the surveillance of town officials and tithingmen. A Maryland law levied a five-shilling tax on bachelors' estates under three hundred pounds and twenty shillings over that amount. Unattached women past their mid-twenties merely faced community reproach, enduring epithets such as "spinster," "thornback," or "old" or "ancient maid." William Byrd II referred to his daughter Evelyn, age twenty, as an "antique virgin." An unmarried woman of independent means, however, was treated with respect. Mary Carpenter, sister of Alice Bradford, wife of William Bradford, died in 1667 at age ninety-one: "She was a godly old maid never married."

Contrary to what one might expect, teenage marriages were rare in New England. Generally, from the analyses of the demography of Plymouth, Dedham, Andover, and Woburn, age of first marriage in the seventeenth century for women averaged at about twenty-two years old and for men, twenty-seven; by the next century, the age at marriage for women remained the same but that for men had dropped to around twenty-five. The Chesapeake society showed marked differences. Immigrant women in Maryland in the seventeenth century tended to marry in their mid-twenties, but with men greatly outnumbering women, native-born women married early, the mean being sixteen and one-half years; there were instances of girls marrying as early as age twelve. Early marriage in Virginia was also common for the same time period. William Byrd's sister, Ursula, married Robert Beverley at age sixteen and died in childbirth several days before her seventeenth birthday. After about 1720, when sex ratios had evened out, women in the Chesapeake society tended to marry around age twenty-two and men around twenty-four.

It was the custom and even a requirement in several northern colonies that a suitor receive consent from the parents of his prospective bride in order to marry. Parents on both sides often negotiated for the amount of a dowry. Among the small farmers and the poor, however, a formal contract among parents was not a common practice. If males were over age twenty-one and females at least sixteen years old, there was little that parents could do to prevent a marriage except to withhold a patrimony. A Massachusetts law of 1641 stated that parents might be prosecuted for "unreasonably denying any child timely or convenient marriage." But obtaining parental consent caused few problems. As Fitz John Winthrop said in 1707, "It has been the way and custome of the country for young folkes to choose, and where there is noe visible exception everybody approves it." One prominent colonial figure almost resorted to violence when his marriage suit was rejected by the parents of his intended bride and even, it seems, by the young lady herself. Francis Nicholson, governor of Virginia, at age forty-three attempted to woo the teenaged Lucy Burwell. When Lucy accepted another suitor, Colonel Lewis Burwell, her father, barred Nicholson from the Burwell family home, whereupon Nicholson threatened to slit the throats of the minister who would perform the wedding, the justice of the peace who would license it, and the bridegroom.

Despite the businesslike arrangements of many marriages, young people did "play the field." Robert Carter's son Bob, in Virginia, kept a list of local girls whom he classified on a scale of 1 to 4: ugly and with freckles, pretty, beautiful, and "nymphs" (beautiful and graceful). One problem for a young man among the southern gentry in seeking a marriage partner was a segregation of the sexes, but this was largely overcome by attending barbecues, dances, and the like or simply visiting neighboring plantations.

Colonial parents advised their daughters to avoid rushing into marriage and to get to know their suitors well. Such concerns did not need to be expressed, as young couples even frequently experienced sexual intimacy before marriage. Robert V. Wells (1982) has estimated that around 1680 some eight percent of brides were pregnant at the time of marriage, one-third by 1800. Other studies have shown that in Somerset County, Maryland, during the seventeenth century, twenty percent of brides bore children within eight and a half months of marriage and that in Kingston Parish, Gloucester County, Virginia, between 1749 and 1780, one-fourth to one-third of the women were pregnant at the time of legal engagement. Sixty-three of two hundred persons owning the baptismal covenant at the Braintree church in Massachusetts between 1761 and 1775 confessed to premarital sexual relations. John Harrower, tutor at the Daingerfield plantation in Virginia, noted that male and female servants often bedded together. Having sexual relations after betrothal, however, was not regarded as serious an offense as before. In the Plymouth colony, sexual misconduct between engaged persons merited only one-fourth the punishment reserved for other single people committing similar offenses. Civil punishment for premarital pregnancy gradually declined in the colonies after 1700.

One courtship custom, regarded by some as "wicked and base," was bundling, whereby a consenting couple slept in the same bed at the house of the parents, fully clothed and sometimes with a "bundling board" set on edge between them. Bundling did not imply an improper relationship any more than an unchaperoned automobile ride in later generations. Although no colonial court cases explicitly refer to bundling, numerous other commentaries attest to its prevalence. Travelers in western Massachusetts, Connecticut, and New York and among the Pennsylvania Germans in the eighteenth century frequently mentioned the custom. During the Great Awakening, preachers, including Jonathan Edwards, condemned bundling. Yet it had its defenders. John Adams, who thought that engaged couples should try to get to know each other, remarked in a 1761 essay, "I cannot wholly disapprove of Bundling." Marriage, of course, would atone for all guilt. By the late eighteenth century, bundling was suppressed, owing largely to the building of larger houses and therefore less crowded conditions, abuse of the custom, and religious and public denunciations that bundling led to fornication.

After formal engagement and agreement on a dowry, a betrothed couple announced the intent to marry. Throughout the colonies it was customary to issue banns, a practice required through the Anglican church in Virginia and South Carolina. Typically in New England, notice of impending marriage was given by declaration at a public meeting three weeks in a row or by placement of a written statement on a meetinghouse door for fourteen days (eight days in Connecticut). Banns eventually gave way to the issuance of marriage licenses by county clerks.

Marriage in New England was originally a strictly civil observance. Any official, including militia captains, could perform this duty. Governor Richard Bellingham of Massachusetts in 1641 even presided over his own marriage. Times would change, and in 1686 the first president of the Dominion of New England published an "order of council" empowering ministers and justices of the peace "to consummate marriage." Thereafter New England ministers often conducted weddings. North and South, marriage ceremonies were typically held at the home of the bride, followed by festivities. Sometimes the celebrations were prolonged. For instance, in Philadelphia it was customary for the groom's friends to call for two days, dipping incessantly into the punch bowls, and for the bride to sponsor tea parties for members of the wedding ensemble every evening for a week.

Absolute divorce was either rare or nonexistent in the colonies. In the Puritan colonies during the seventeenth century, divorce (or separation) was sparingly granted on grounds of adultery, impotence, bigamy, incest, refusal to consummate the marriage, and desertion. In Puritan Massachusetts the court of assistants had full authority to decide on "all causes of divorce," while in Connecticut a divorce was granted by the General Court as a whole. After the royal charter of 1691, Massachusetts divorces were granted by the governor and council. In Massachusetts between 1639 and 1692, only twenty-seven divorces and thirteen annulments were granted; between 1692 and 1786, more than sixty percent of the 299 petitions for divorce were granted. A divorced wife, as the innocent party, could claim a right of dower for life equal to one-third of the husband's real property. In the southern colonies and New York, a marriage could be dissolved only by the governor and council. Legal separations were allowed in the southern colonies but did not confer upon the parties the right to remarry, though sometimes they did so anyway. With the dissolution of the Anglican establishment at the time of the American Revolution, a divorce could be obtained in the southern colonies, upon petitioning, by an enactment of the lower house of the legislature.

CHILDREN

Childbirth was perilous. In the Plymouth colony one of every thirty births resulted in the mother's death. Since a woman could expect to give birth six or more times, her likelihood of dying in childbirth was at least one out of five. One concoction to ease childbirth, the "curse of Eve," consisted of beaver testicles, basil, dittany, powdered hair from the head of a virgin, dried ant eggs, and one-fourth pint of milk. Women in New England had a long lying-in period of three weeks, with only female visitors permitted during the first two weeks. The new mother remained in bed for a week. Giving birth was considered by the Puritans a purifying event, and the "holiday" for the mother celebrated her role in the miracle of birth.

New England mothers breast-fed infants for about a year. Babies arrived about two years apart. In the Chesapeake society, women nursed their infants for eighteen months, and birth intervals were twenty-four to thirty months. Wet nurses were sometimes retained to suckle infants; it was not uncommon in the South for slave women to nurse white infants.

Women monopolized midwifery until after the mid-eighteenth century, when they were gradually replaced by trained male physicians.

Infant mortality in colonial times varied between ten and thirty percent, depending on time, place, and epidemics. The rate of early childhood deaths also remained high. Not infrequently, of six to eight children in a family, only two lived to be adults. Of Cotton Mather's fifteen children, only two survived him; of Samuel Sewall's fourteen, only three. Many colonists engaged in child-rearing practices that would be considered dangerous today. John Locke's book *Some Thoughts concerning Education* (1693) was widely popular in the colonies, and extracts were published in almanacs. Locke advised parents to wet regularly "children's feet in cold water to toughen them; and also have children wear thin-soled shoes that the wet may come freely in." Josiah Quincy (who lived to be ninety-two years old), at age three, was frequently taken from bed to the kitchen cellar, where he was dipped three times in the cold water from the pump. Baptisms were conducted in cold churches, and boys went hatless.

Colonial infants were dressed in clouts (diapers) and long smocks extending below the feet. When able to walk, children were "short-coated" in petticoats reaching to the ankles; nothing was worn underneath so that they could urinate freely out of doors. At age five or six, segregation by sex began, with boys dressed in breeches and girls in bodices laced up the back. Girls now began to learn household duties. As William Byrd II wrote of his daughters: "They are every Day up to their Elbows in Housewifery, which will qualify them effectually for useful Wives and if they live long enough, for Notable Women."

Despite different patterns of child rearing, most colonial parents, South and North, adhered to the Lockean ideal that it was better to "rule" by "reason and experience" than by brutal enforcement. Most parents agreed with the Lockean sensational psychology that children entered the world with minds blank, and therefore "the little, and almost insensible Impressions on our tender Infancies have very important and lasting Consequences." Parents, rather than relying on coercion, should set examples in learning for their children. Spiritual training, however, required close instruction.

Puritan parents constantly reminded their children of their sinful nature and the closeness of death, yet they sought to gain their children's confidence. Samuel Mather said of his father, Cotton Mather:

> He would not say much to them of the evil angels; because he would not have them entertain any frightful fancies about the apparitions of devils. But yet he would briefly let them know that there are devils to tempt to wickedness.

Sinful ways nevertheless had to be punished. Samuel Sewall, writing of his own children in his diary in 1692, observed:

Joseph threw a knop of Brass and hit his Sister Betty on the forhead so as to make it bleed and swell; upon which, and for playing at Prayer-time, and eating when Return Thanks, I whipd him pretty smartly. When I first went in (call'd by his Grandmother) he sought to shadow and hide himself from me behind the head of the cradle: which gave me the sorrowful remembrance of Adam's carriage.

One southern mother, who raised her four sons alone after her husband's death, set down a goal for child rearing much like that of other colonial parents. In one of the daily resolutions she put in writing, Eliza Lucas Pinckney of South Carolina, though more gentle-minded and less attuned to warring with Satan, expressed an ideal not too far from that of the Puritans. "I am resolved to be a good Mother to my children," she said,

> to pray for them, to set them good examples, to give them good advice, to be careful both of their souls and bodys, to watch over their tender minds; to carefully root out the first appearing and budings of vice, and to instill piety, Virtue and true religion into them.

One modern historian has discerned themes of colonial child rearing: evangelical (New England), moderate (middle colonies), and genteel (southern colonies). Evangelicals, according to Philip Greven (1977), sought to break the child's will and to instill a sense of denial of self and surrender to God. They believed that too much affection interfered with thoughts of God. Evangelicals also emphasized the dangers of idleness in youth. Moderates stressed self-control rather than self-repression—bending instead of breaking the will. They also encouraged a greater social awareness among their children than the evangelicals did. Genteel parents took for granted the state of grace and emphasized individual self-assertion rather than self-control. Discipline was lax. Landon Carter of Sabine Hall complained that too many of his fellow Virginians believed that "to curb their children is to spoil their genius." Southern children, of course, witnessed the breaking of wills other than their own—those of the slaves. Genteel families were more at ease with sensuality and sexual experience. There was more intimacy among family members, and children, often kept at a distance under the guidance of nurses and tutors, showed warm affection when they were in the presence of their parents.

THE FAMILY

Filial loyalty and a degree of patriarchal control characterized most colonial families. Households, North and South, tended to be moderately extended rather than nuclear or elaborately extended.

Colonial families averaged three to five surviving children. In the Puritan colonies legislation reinforced parental authority. The Massachusetts General Court in the 1670s authorized localities to appoint tithingmen each to inspect ten to twelve households for any breach in family relations or in discipline of children. If parents were negligent in giving care or governance, children could be removed from the home by the authorities. Massachusetts, Connecticut, and New Hampshire, following the precedent of Calvin's Geneva, enacted the death penalty for children chronically abusing or striking their parents. No children were actually put to death under this law but some interesting cases were heard. For instance, John Parker, Jr., age forty, was tried in 1664 for tormenting his parents by attempting to destroy family property and calling his father a "theife, lyar, & simple ape, shittabed" and his mother a "Rambeggur, Gammar Shithouse, Gammar Pissehouse, Gammar Two Shoes, & told hir her tongue went like a peare monger, & sayd she was the rankest sow in the towne." Parker was sentenced to stand on the gallows for an hour with a rope around his neck, be "severely whipt," pay a fine of two hundred pounds, and be confined in the "house of correction."

Most children sought to comfort their parents in old age, like William Fitzhugh of Virginia, who remarked that he thought it his duty "not to suffer one to want, who gave us being, nor suffer her to struggle to live. . . . Nature, duty, the Laws of God . . . command . . . to give the utmost help to a distressed parent." Children were also expected to give deference to their parents throughout life. But this ideal was not always achieved. Landon Carter of Virginia frequently noted in his diary the stubbornness and the filial disrespect shown by his eldest son, Robert Wormeley Carter, who lived in his father's home. Localities provided maintenance for the indigent elderly without children for support. Most aged parents, if they were able, insisted on self-sufficiency and continued to live in their own houses; "retirement" was almost unheard of. Grandparents sometimes raised grandchildren, and it was not unusual for grandchildren to contribute to the life support of their grandparents. In New England, where the number of persons over sixty averaged about six percent throughout the colonial period, at least ninety percent of youths under age nineteen had at least one living grandparent.

A stem family, consisting of parents and a son and his wife under one roof, was rare in New England, although there were exceptions, such as in East Guilford, where fifty-three percent of households were multigenerational. More typical, as Philip Greven (1966) has shown for Andover, was the settlement of sons on plots near the parental household, with the lands being acquired by purchase or by conditional deeds whereby offspring could not secure full title as long as the father lived. Frequently written into the contracts was provision that the sons provide support for the parents if the need arose. Only about one-fourth of sons in Andover owned land before their fathers died. Although individual households were nuclear, with offspring close by, a kinship network was maintained. As Greven explains for Andover in the late seventeenth century:

> This distinctive form of family structure is best described as a *modified extended family*—defined as a kinship group of two or more generations living within a single community in which the dependence of the children upon their parents continues after the children have married and are living under a separate roof. . . . But it is still an *extended* family because the newly created conjugal unit of husband and wife live in separate households in close proximity to their parents and siblings and continue to be economically dependent in some respects upon their parents. And because of the continuing dependence of the second generation upon their first-generation fathers, who continued to own most of the family land throughout the better part of their lives, the family in seventeenth-century Andover was *patriarchal* as well. (p. 255)

In the Chesapeake society, extended families were rare. Sons of the poorer farmers moved further toward the frontier. Among the Virginia gentry, who controlled an abundance of land and held many tracts, sons received full possession of estates early. Thus unlike the many town areas in New England, sons were not dependent on a powerful patriarch. Nevertheless, there was something of a modified extended family, to borrow Greven's phrase, in a neighborhood network of kinsmen and friends. Landon Carter, over a 22-year period, had visits from sixty-eight relatives; George Washington would provide another example of frequent mingling with a host of relatives.

At the end of the colonial period, families in New England experienced tension because of increasing population and the diminishing availability of land and economic opportunity. This was less the case in the South, in part due to expansive landholdings and the profitability of a slave-based agriculture. Despite the population squeeze in New England, sons were reluctant to seek out an unfamiliar environment. Kenneth A. Lockridge estimates that only ten percent of the population moved out of Dedham, Massachusetts, in the eighteenth century. A son aspired merely to improve himself slightly above the economic level of his father. Senior family lines stayed in or close to the village, while junior family branches took up marginal land beyond the town and seldom rose above poverty. Another trend was the decline of patriarchal authority in northern households. Larger houses made for greater specialization of space and privacy. Kitchens were set apart from the rest of the house, and children had their own place to sleep. More attention was given to child care and nurture.

12

Social Structure and Leisure

Early American society was both fluid and structured. Anyone could attain prominence by wealth or position and having done so could expect certain privileges. The colonists, in accepting social gradation, recognized the inequality of abilities and the necessity of a deferential relationship among constituent members of society, believing that such conditions were ordained by Providence or in the natural scheme of things.

To the Puritans, God had ordained social inequality. John Winthrop's *Modell of Christian Charity* (1629) contended that God "hath so disposed of the Condicion of mankine, as in all times some must be rich, some poore, some highe and eminent in power and dignitie, others meane and in subjection." Rev. William Hubbard, in an election sermon in 1676, expressed the view that social cohesion was strengthened by the existence of a hierarchy of classes. "It suited the wisdom of the infinite and omnipotent creator to make the world of differing parts," Hubbard said, and "persons of differing endowments and qualifications need differing stations to be disposed" into "the rational and political world," the "keeping of which is both the beauty and strength of society." Puritans believed in a general and particular calling. Not everyone received the general call of grace, but all persons had been destined by God to perform a certain role that fit into the common good. Thus Cotton Mather noted in a 1716 sermon: "If a man cannot keep out of a *Low and Mean Condition*, without a plain *wrong to the Estates of other Men*, he is then most Evidently called of GOD into a *Low and Mean Condition*." Hardly anyone believed in the perfectibility of mankind on earth, though a few could argue, like Quaker John Woolman, that the earth belonged to God and hence all persons had an equal claim to rights and property.

The colonists did not disparage the accumulation of wealth. James Logan, a Pennsylvania official and a Quaker, observed that the acquisition of individual wealth, though not essential for personal happiness, was necessary to the welfare of the community. Without a number of well-to-do persons, the economy and thus also society as a whole would suffer; moreover, by increasing wealth there is "the greater Support and Encouragement" for the poor. In the Protestant ethic, seeking wealth was regarded as more conducive to virtue than being content to remain in poverty. Moderating influences, however, such as Christianity, knowledge of English aristocratic paternalism, and a belief that obsessive attention to prosperity thwarted improvement of virtue, helped to instill a sense of moral obligation to the community among upper-class colonial Americans.

WEALTH AND STATUS

Few progenitors of the wealthy and powerful eighteenth-century families had started life in America with immense resources. But in most instances there had been enough means to get a firm footing in the New World. Very few of the founders of the great families had to initiate settlement. Fortunes were acquired and enhanced through efforts of members of succeeding generations, who availed themselves of opportunities for land acquisition and industrial and trade pursuits. Many of those who became prosperous benefited from marriage into wealth and favors bestowed by colonial governments. The increases in great wealthholding and increased wealth disparity were most evident in the large urban commercial centers and in regions with slave-based economies.

Mercantile involvement, even in the southern colonies, accounted for a large part of the rise to great wealth. Success in business or agriculture allowed for investment in new enterprises. Thomas Hancock is a good example of the rise to immense wealth in New England. Son of a Congregational minister, he was apprenticed to a bookseller, subsequently opened his own shop, expanded into overseas trade, and then acquired his own merchant fleet. With money came power. As one of Boston's most influential citizens, he was elected a selectman and a member of the governor's council. His nephew, John Hancock, his business partner and chief heir, matched a political career with great wealth; among John Hancock's public services were the governorship for nine terms and the presidency of the Second Continental Congress. As a Rhode Island sea captain noted in 1748, "Money is here the true fuller's earth for reputation, there is not a spot or stain but it will take out."

In New York, four landed families—the Philipses, Van Cortlandts, De Lanceys, and Schuylers—from 1675 to 1725 came to dominate the New York commercial community, while the Livingstons and Morrises sought wealth chiefly through land speculation and engrossment of the inland Indian trade. Great fortunes were made in Philadelphia through commerce, privateering, land speculation, and the fur trade. With the increasing complexity of trade operations, professionals, such as lawyers, reaped huge profits. Typical of men of wealth in Philadelphia was William Allen, who made his fortune in mining, real estate speculation, local rentals, mercantile enterprises, and lotteries. He also became a financier. Much like others who had achieved wealth in the cities, Allen also aspired to being a country squire, moving out of the city to a large country estate. Men such as Allen dominated political life in the middle colonies, yet they were not given the deference that was characteristic of southern society. As the *Pennsylvania Journal* observed in 1756, the people of Pennsylvania "are generally of the middling sort.... They are chiefly industrious farmers, artificers or men of trade; they enjoy and are fond of freedom, and the *meanest among them* thinks he has a right to civility from the greatest."

Most of the founders of the great eighteenth-century families in the Chesapeake colonies, who came over around the mid-seventeenth century, were from established English merchant families or, as in the case of Richard Lee I, from landed aristocracy who were royalists. There were exceptions; the founder of one prominent and wealthy dynasty started at the bottom rung of society. Daniel Dulany, who came to Maryland from Ireland in 1704 at age eighteen as an indentured servant, struck out in a multiple career of law, trade, farming, and real estate speculation. Eventually he owned 55,000 acres of land. Like Dulany, the great planters of Virginia and Maryland typically mixed business and industrial pursuits with agriculture. The middle-class origin of the Virginia great families is apparent, for example, in Thomas and Philip Ludwell, sons of a cloth merchant; William Fitzhugh, whose father was a woolen draper; William Byrd I, son of a goldsmith, who came to Virginia to administer his uncle's lands; and John Washington, mate and voyage partner of a ship.

Grantees of proprietary lands and immigrant Barbados planters formed the basis of aristocratic families in South Carolina. Though large land grants in North Carolina contributed to the rise of a few wealthy families, the checkered economic patterns, the lack of large commercial ports, and the invasion of a horde of settlers from the north hindered opportunity for the accumulation of great wealth in the colony. Georgia's first years, not too different from those of other southern colonies, were beset with the difficulties of pioneering and a disordered society; a great planter society did not take hold until the 1750s and 1760s.

Ratios of wealth distribution varied in relationship to age, occupation, place of residence, and population trends. Jackson T. Main (1985) and other historians have noted that at least in parts of New England, raw data naming persons with scant or no property is misleading because of quasi-dependency in many families. Most of the persons who appear to be deprived were actually single persons under age thirty biding their time before receiving their full inheritance and elderly parents who had transmitted much of their estates to their offspring. It may also be observed that generally throughout the colonies, the availability of lands on the frontier also mitigated the increased disparity in wealth.

In certain areas, primarily urban centers and the tidewater South, wealth tended to be concentrated in the hands of a minority. A sampling from quantitative studies supports this assertion. For instance, it is estimated that overall for the colonies the top twenty percent of wealthholders controlled sixty-six percent of the wealth in New England, fifty-three percent in the middle colonies, and seventy percent in the South. At the mid-eighteenth century, the real poor amounted to ten to twenty percent of the population of Boston, New York City, and Philadelphia. In Boston in 1687, twenty-five percent of male adults controlled sixty-six percent of the assessed wealth in the city, and by 1771 their share had increased to seventy-eight percent. In Maryland around 1750, ninety percent of plantation families owned estates worth less than five hundred pounds, and in Virginia two-thirds of the farms covered two hundred acres or less. South Carolina's large wealthy class controlled sixty percent of personal property in the colony.

Most conspicuous in the South, wealthholding led to conscious efforts to develop an aristocracy. The great planters set themselves up as the political, economic, and social leaders. Like the country gentry of England, they dominated officeholding—sheriffs, justices of the peace, legislators, and councilors. Most of the landed proprietors adopted coats of arms. They cultivated gentility and an upper-class lifestyle. A true aristocracy, however, could only be made over generations. The American progenitors of the great families of the Chesapeake area, as Warren M. Billings (1986) has observed, merely

> elbowed themselves to the head of colonial society, amassing as they did fortunes in land, servants, and offices as well as complex ties to each others' families. But their pretension to rule lacked the imprimatur of immemorial custom, for it rested on nothing more than their considerable ability to outdistance their competitors. (p. 59)

Eventually inherited wealth and ancestral ties became the major criteria for full acceptance among the ruling elite.

CLASS DISTINCTIONS

Despite familiarity in colonial society and the absence of a sanctioned aristocracy, colonists were expected to know their place, according to their standing in the community. In all the colonies distinctions were made on the bases of wealth, professional achievement, and public officeholding. In early New England, ministers, magistrates, and a few landed gentlemen (such as the Saltonstalls, Dudleys, Bradstreets, and Pynchons) held sway at the apex of society; later the wealthy traders and speculators joined the ranks of the elite. Next below in the social hierarchy came the freeholders, then the artisans, the farm laborers, and finally the indentured servants and slaves. In the Puritan villages, comportment and age in addition to one's economic position were also measures of esteem, and status was recognized through the assignment of pews in church.

Elsewhere in the colonies, a preferential position in society corresponded more with wealth per se than in New England. Lieutenant Governor Cadwallader Colden of New York in the mid-eighteenth century placed that colony's residents into four broad categories: proprietors of large tracts of land, lawyers and other professionals, merchants, and, at the bottom, farmers and mechanics. Increasingly, the merchant gentleman represented a superiority over the "inferior sort." Middle-class values found general acceptance in the northern colonies. Benjamin Franklin, who himself was never fully admitted into Philadelphia's high society, hoped that his son, William, would not become "what is commonly called a gentleman." Rather, "I want to put him to some business by which he may, with care and industry, get a temperate and reasonable living."

From Maryland southward the social hierarchy, from top to bottom, consisted of the large planters, a broad category of merchants and professionals (such as lawyers and clergymen), small planters and yeomen, merchants and factors, artisans along with schoolteachers and tavernkeepers, maritime workers (fisherman, store clerks, sailmakers, and sailors), overseers of plantations, servants and laborers, slaves, and that small group found everywhere, even in the North, the indolent "cottagers," who in South Carolina were dubbed by slaves as "po' buckra" (poor buccaneers).

The titles by which one was addressed suggested social rank. In the Chesapeake society, *esquire* referred to a member of the council; *gentleman*, a large planter; *mister*, a person just above the status of yeoman; and *yeoman*, the more humble farmer. In New England anyone who did not perform manual labor could be called *gentleman*. High government officials, especially justices of the peace, could be greeted with *esquire*. Those regarded to be in the upper middle class could be referred to as *mister* or *master*. Artisans and yeomen might be addressed as *goodman* or *goodwife*.

Last names alone, such as *Jones* or *Smith*, were sufficient for common laborers.

Apparel also reflected rank. In all the colonies persons were expected to dress according to their status in life. Laws prohibited common people from attiring themselves in clothes suggestive of a higher position in society than their own. For example, the Massachusetts General Court in 1651 ordered that ladies and gentlemen might wear lace, slashed sleeves, hatbands, and elaborate girdles, but a goodman or goodwife could not. Men of the lower classes were expected to wear leather breeches, wooden buttons, and none of the high-quality fabric or ornamentation reserved for gentlemen. A wardrobe of a "complete" gentleman most likely included silk stockings (usually red); boots with wide-spreading tops; breeches made of broadcloth, velvet, or silk; shoe and knee buckles; a dark blue or black broadcloth coat that extended to the knees and flared at the waist; a vest of colored silk (usually green or scarlet, long in front and tight-fitting); white linen shirts with lace ruffles on the bosom and wrists; silver or brass buttons; a large, wide-brimmed hat; and, in cold weather, a cloak. Wigs were not as popular in the South as in New England, where most men wore them from 1710 to 1770. In the South wigs signified persons of high station or authority. The silk or satin bay wig eventually became the favorite.

Reminders of class distinctions were everywhere. A gentleman was exempt from corporal punishment—whipping, the pillory, and the stocks. Certain sports were the province of the gentry, not the least horse racing and foxhunting. Even in Virginia it was a punishable offense for a poor man to attempt to race a horse against one belonging to a gentleman or to bet on the races. Everywhere the landscape gave evidence of social disparity, for example, in the size and architectural style of dwellings, ownership of coaches or carriages, and the assistance of slaves or servants. Belonging to certain religious bodies carried class distinctions, with the poorer sort, at least in the late colonial period, more likely to be members of dissenting congregations.

The southern gentry, more so than their northern counterparts, established a tone of gentility that set them above the rest of society. The isolation of the great plantations heightened a sense of sociability among Chesapeake planters, who were known for their hospitality. South Carolina grandees, escaping "country fever," fled to Charleston for a season that extended from about May 10 to November 1. In January they again returned to the city for a round of concerts, balls, and races. Chesapeake planters were inclined to be freethinking in religion and were imbued of a Renaissance spirit. It was a world that they themselves had made, one that they, not institutions, would dominate. The Chesapeake gentry loved the outdoors and delighted in horsemanship and hunting. While Carolina planters relied on Charleston as the scene for recreation, the Chesapeake gentry found entertainment at their own plantation houses. They seldom traveled widely, except to assume public duties at courthouse or capital or occasionally visit the baths at Warm (Berkeley) Springs or elsewhere in the valley. High-ranking South Carolinians, most of whom came by their wealth from business rather than by genteel birth, more recklessly engaged in the pursuit of luxury than the Virginians did. There were, however, wastrels among third-generation Virginia gentlemen, who squandered their inheritance on gambling or drink; William Byrd III, Robert Wormeley Carter ("Wild Bob," Landon Carter's eldest son), and Robert Burwell were such heirs.

Chesapeake planters were a working gentry. They kept daily contact with the management of the plantation and its personnel. They also studied to improve their breadth (if not depth) of knowledge in things practical and intellectual. Men like William Byrd II and Landon Carter took a paternal interest in their slaves' lives and performances. The proximity to the slaves and thus the familiarity was a factor in giving Virginia gentlemen a bit of arrogance. Philip Fithian wrote in 1774 that "you will find the tables turned the minute you enter" Virginia. "Such amazing property" in slaves "blows up the owners to an imagination which is visible in all." A combination of noblesse oblige and a certain haughtiness characterized the Virginia gentleman. Recognition of the special station of a gentleman was expected in Virginia life. As Rev. Devereux Jarratt (1733–1801), the son of a small farmer and carpenter, once recalled:

> We were accustomed to look upon, what were called *gentle folks*, as beings of a superior order. For my part, I was quite shy of *them*, and kept off at a humble distance. A *periwig* . . . was a distinguishing badge of *gentle folk*—and when I saw a man riding the road, near our house, with a wig on, it would so alarm my fears, and give me such a disagreeable feeling, that I dare say, I would run off, as for my life.

Such deference, however, was not prevalent in North Carolina, where, as William Byrd II commented, the people "are rarely guilty of flattering or making any court to their governors but treat them with all the excesses of freedom and familiarity."

To be a true gentleman required adherence to a special code of behavior. Most Virginia planters had in their libraries copies of Henry Peacham's *Compleat Gentleman*, Castiglione's *Book of the Courtier*, and Richard Allestree's *Whole Duty of Man*. A staple in the education of a young gentleman in Virginia's Northern Neck was a published abridgment of the sixteenth-century French work *Rules of Civility and Decent Behavior in Company*, which George Washington copied down as a boy. A gentleman, as Landon Carter told Washington in 1755, should "regard the inward man." A gentleman cultivated his manners and exhibited a dignity of bearing and polished speech. He was at all times expected to be honorable and truthful; cowardice and cheating were regarded as the worst transgressions. Courtesy should be instinctive and not ostentatious. Sins of the flesh, however, could be forgiven if they were not flagrant or seductive of the innocent. As Louis B. Wright (1964) has noted, the Virginia gentry were expected to live by six virtues, four of then Aristotelian (fortitude, temperance, prudence, and justice) and two from the Renaissance heritage (liberality and courtesy).

One might expect that a pure aristocracy would have emerged in New York. Like the Virginia gentry, New York's prominent landed families sought to imitate styles of the English upper class and also progressed over generations to the acquisition of wealth and power. Like those in Virginia, as Patricia U. Bonomi writes (1971), the great New York families were founded by men who were not born into wealth but had to make their own fortunes. For example, William Smith was the son of a tallow chandler; the first Livingston was the son of a Scottish Presbyterian minister; the first Schuyler was the son of an Amsterdam baker; the first Philipse was a carpenter; the first Van Cortlandt was a Dutch soldier; and the first De Lancey was a Huguenot refugee with little means. As in Virginia, the great New York landlords and "merchant princes" exerted powerful influence in the colony's political affairs. A sort of aristocracy did appear, Bonomi notes, "but compared with the true upper level of English society the colonial elite was a world apart, largely *nouveau riche* in composition, insecure in its pretensions, and infinitely less exclusive than its model" (p. 8). Unlike Virginia, in New York a large number of middle-class persons (substantial yeomen, shopkeepers, and country merchants) shared power in the legislature with the colony's elite.

RECREATION

Notwithstanding efforts to have a society devoted wholly to work, colonial Americans found ample and diverse ways for amusement. Colonial authorities banned many games and sports in order to discourage gambling and distraction from one's occupational calling. Sabbath laws further curtailed recreational use of leisure time. But laws regulating amusements were more often than not honored in the breach, even in Puritan New England.

The colonial governments promoted festivities associated with public events. Thanksgiving was a regular annual holiday in Connecticut and Massachusetts, the celebration lasting a week. New Year's Day, May Day, and Shrovetide were special holidays in New York. Though prohibited in Puritan New England, Christmas was universally celebrated in the eighteenth century. College commencement days (Harvard, Yale, and Princeton) drew crowds of country folk, attracted by horse racing, games, dancing, and drinking. There were other public rejoicings, such as celebrating the sovereign's birthday or coronation or the governor's birthday. A raucous annual holiday in New England and New York was Pope's Day (also Guy Fawkes Day), on November 5, which commemorated the crushing of the Gunpowder Plot (a failed attempt to blow up Parliament) in 1605 and also the landing of William III in England in 1688. The occasion brought parades and rival gang fights to see who could capture the other side's "guys" or popes (straw effigies). The Thursday lecture day in Puritan Massachusetts led to suppression of most work, and after the morning lecture sermon, the congregation gathered on the village green for games and sports.

Militia training days were occasions for festivity. When the drills and tests for marksmanship had ceased, the troops headed for the nearest tavern or a private home for liquid refreshment, and thereafter there would be sports and in the evening often a ball. Cotton Mather once remarked that training days had "become little other than Drinking Dayes." Court days and election days, throughout the colonies, brought together all segments of the local population, resulting in a great deal of ribaldry. Ebenezer Cooke described Marylanders at a court day as follows: "A Herd of Planters on the ground, /O'er-whelmed with Punch dead drunk we found." Local fairs, governmentally and privately sponsored, especially in the South, provided games for persons of all ages and also often horse racing.

Not the least of public entertainments were hangings. Large crowds gathered to watch a culprit turned off and slowly strangled. Such events were frequently hyped by parading the condemned person to public meetings before the time of execution. At the execution a prominent minister preached a lengthy sermon. Samuel Sewall tells of a great throng witnessing the hanging of six pirates. Not only was there a large crowd at the riverfront but also many spectators among 100 boats and 150 canoes. "When the Scaffold was let sink, there was a Screech of the Women" heard by Sewall's wife at their house a mile away.

Taverns (inns and ordinaries) were popular watering holes for men of all ranks, although some establishments catered to certain levels of society. Roadside inns were notorious for bad food and scant accommodations. Often a guest had to sleep in a bed with strangers. William Byrd II once complained that at Manakin Town, Virginia, he had to put up with a "no very clean bedfellow." Most taverns in or near towns were two- or three-bedroom houses, with a main room and parlor. One could find a variety of alcoholic beverages at the taverns, including beer, cider, ale, sack (wine), rum, whiskey, beverige (mild watery drinks, such as cider and water or vinegar and water), perry (pear cider), and even such concoctions as flip (beer, wine, or rum mixed with sugar and molasses with a red hot poker placed in the liquid to give a burnt or bitter flavor) or "whip-belly vengeance," sour beer simmered in a kettle and mixed with molasses. But among the Chesapeake elite, bumbo (rum punch with lime or lemon juice) was the great favorite. George Washington ran up a tab for bumbo and meals at George Weedon's Fredericksburg tavern. Of course, the colonists were heavy drinkers, in or out of taverns. Almost any occasion could be used for drinking. For Rev. Edwin Jackson's ordination at Woburn, Massachusetts, the itemized fare showed that the congregation drank sixty-two barrels of cider, twenty-five gallons of wine, two gallons of brandy, and four gallons of rum.

Increasingly, taverns in New England were required to be near the meetinghouses. Most taverns served as post offices. A favorite tavern game was billiards. The colonial billiard table was oblong, with a sort of wicket made of ivory at one end, called the port, an ivory peg at the other end, called the king, and six "hazards" or pockets as in the modern pool table. Each of two players had a ball. Points were scored by a player sending his ball first through the port, hitting the king without pushing it over, or knocking an opponent's ball into a hazard. The billiard cues looked like hockey sticks, with one end curved and flat. Many of the Virginia gentry had their own billiard tables. William Byrd II one day played thirty games, and once he gave an opponent "three and a go to beat him." In his youth, George Washington enjoyed the game; in one billiard session in 1748, he won 1 shilling 3 pence from Thomas Turner.

The Puritans condemned tavern dancing but otherwise did not attempt to abolish this recreation. Puritan ministers Cotton Mather and Increase Mather held mixed dancing, with the "unchast Touches and Gesticulations," in disfavor, but John Cotton was of a more liberal mind. In 1625 he wrote, "Dancing (yea though mixt) I would not simply condemn—Only lascivious dancing to wanton ditties and in amourous gestures and wanton dalliances, especially after great feasts, I would bear witness against." Dancing schools advertised in all the colonial newspapers. Dancing assemblies became popular, such as the "Fishing Company," organized in Philadelphia in 1759, consisting of sixteen men and sixteen women who met twice a month. Virginians were especially fond of dancing, and most great houses had a ballroom. Dancing masters made the rounds of the plantations. Virginians liked the minuet and the French quadrilles but were known, as the evening wore on, to engage in country (Scottish and Irish) reels and even African dances. Nicholas Cresswell noted that at a Twelfth Night ball in Alexandria in 1775:

> Betwixt the Country dances they have what I call everlasting jigs. A couple gets up and begins to dance a jig [to some Negro tune], . . . others comes and cuts them out, and these dances always last as long as the Fiddler can play. This is sociable, but I think looks more like a Bacchanalian dance than one in a polite assembly.

Numerous indoor games were played in tavern and parlor. Cards, backgammon, chess, dominoes, and dice were the most popular. Most localities had laws imposing a fine on any tavern allowing persons under twenty-one or journeymen or apprentices to gamble at cards or dice. Bowling and shuffleboard were both outdoor and indoor sports; some taverns had skittle (ninepin) alleys. Favorite card games were whist (similar to bridge), piquet (like rummy), all fours or pitch (like today's seven-up), put (akin to modern poker), cribbage, and loo. Many later colonists kept close at hand a copy of Edmond Hoyle's *Short Treatise on the Game of Whist* (1748).

The colonists were great enthusiasts for outdoor sports. Benjamin Franklin, who almost stayed in England to open a swimming school, in his *Proposals Relating to the Education of Youth in Pensilvania*, advocated that students should "be frequently exercis'd in Running, Leaping, Wrestling, and Swimming." Among favorite outdoor amusements were hunting, fishing, tennis, cricket, fives, backsword (fencing), stool ball (like cricket), quoits, foot ball (barefooted and like soccer), and golf. An inventory of Governor William Burnet of New York in 1729 showed "nine gouff clubs, one iron ditto and seven dozen balls." Bowling was conducted on greens or even in the streets, as in early Jamestown. Lawn bowling, unlike ninepin or tenpin bowling, involved a 120-square-foot open area, divided into rinks. Round wooden balls (unevenly weighted with a bias toward one side) were rolled toward a small white ball at the end of the green, with points scored as to which player came closest to it.

Colonists enjoyed being spectators to cruel animal fights, reflecting the taste for violence prevalent in England in the eighteenth century. Bear baiting (with dogs) was common, even in New England. Upper and lower classes alike, even slaves, thrilled at cockfights. George Washington was known to attend such events. Silver and steel spurs were on the shelves of many stores. High bets were placed on fighting cocks, but beware the person who tried to cheat by such tricks as putting garlic on a beak or giving a bird a shot of brandy. Pulling the goose was popular in frontier communities, whereby horsemen had to wring the neck of a greased gander suspended upside down from a pole.

English bareknuckle boxing reached the colonies, but aficionados of the sport in America preferred a more barbarous version, cudgels, which had few rules. Philip Fithian witnessed one such contest:

> Every diabolical strategem for Mastery is allowed and practised, of bruising, kicking, scratching, pinching, biting, butting, tripping, throttling, gouging, cursing, dismembring, howling, etc. This spectacle (so loathsome and horrible!) generally is attended with a crowd of people!

The closer to the frontier, the greater the barbarity, particularly in the southern upcountry. Much of the fighting involved a primitive code of honor. Wrestling was no holds barred, with biting off of ears and noses and gouging of eyes. Any free-for-all among the hunters, trappers, herdsmen, or even rugged pioneer farmers might end up with a bushel basket of assorted appendages. Most repulsive were "to feel for a feller's eyestrings and make him tell the news" (eye gouging) and "balloching" (emasculation).

Horseback riding was an important exercise, for pleasure, transportation, or hunting. George Washington loved the foxhunt; during one six-year period he went on 155 such excursions, returning 65 times unsuccessfully. An entry in John Adams's diary in 1760 noted:

> Take my Advice, rise and mount your Horse, by the Mornings dawn, and shake away amidst the great and beautiful Scenes of Nature, that appear at that Time of the day, all the Crudities that are left in your stomach, and all the obstructions that are left in your Brains.

Horse racing was popular throughout the colonies, especially in New York and the South. In Virginia during the seventeenth century, races were usually over a quarter-mile narrow path, one on one. By the 1730s, course racing appeared. Subscription races, conducted by members of a jockey club, became the order of the day, with races most likely in four heats, each of which might be as much as four times around a mile course. Gambling was rife among the gentry, some of whom lost substantially. William Byrd III in 1752 lost five hundred pistoles (Spanish coins). Races in Virginia were held in conjunction with semiannual fairs. Many planters also had their own tracks, with April and August as the favorite racing months. Horse racing might also be included in a day of planned frolicking and picnicking. The inauguration of one such annual occasion, sponsored by Scottish residents, was announced in the *Virginia Gazette* in the September 30–October 7 issue:

> We have advice from Hanover County that on St. Andrews Day [November 30] . . . there are to be Horse Races, and several other Diversions for the entertainment of the Gentlemen and Ladies, at the Old Field, near Capt. John Bickerton's . . . The Substance of which are as follows, viz:
> 1. It is propos'd That 20 Horses or Mares do run around a Three Miles Course, for a Prize of the Value of Five Pounds. . . .
> 2. That a Hat of the value of 20*s*. be cudgell'd for, and that after the first Challenge made, the Drums are to beat every Quarter of an Hour for Three Challenges, round the Ring . . . and none to play with their Left Hand.
> 3. That a Violin be played for by 20 Fiddlers . . . no Person to have the Liberty of playing, unless he bring a Fiddle with him. After the Prize is won they are all to play together, and each a different Tune, and to be treated by the Company.

4. That 12 Boys of 12 Years of Age, do run 112 Yards, for a Hat of the Value of 12 Shillings.

5. That a Flag be flying on said Day, 30 Feet high.

6. That a handsome Entertainment be provided for the Subscribers, and their Wives; and such of them who are not so happy as to have Wives, may treat any other Lady.

7. That Drums, Trumpets, Hautboys, &c. be provided, to play at the said Entertainment.

8. That after Dinner, the Royal Healths, his Honor the Governor's, &c. are to be drunk.

9. That a Quire of Ballads be sung for by a Number of Songsters; the best Songster to have the Prize, and all of them to have Liquor sufficient to clear their Wind-Pipes.

10. That a Pair of Silver Buckles be Wrestled for, by a Number of brisk young Men.

11. That a Pair of handsome Shoes be danced for.

12. That a pair of handsome Silk Stockings of One Pistole Value be given to the handsomest young Country Maid that appears in the Field; With many other Whimsical and Comical Diversions, too numerous to mention here.

Government-sanctioned racing began in New York in 1665, under the auspices of Governor Richard Nicolls. Subscription races were held twice a year on Hempstead Plains, beginning in 1669 and continuing each year until the Revolution. There were other important racetracks on Long Island, on Manhattan Island, and along the New Jersey coast. Ladies were permitted as spectators in the grandstands. After about 1740 horses were bred systematically in the colonies from imported English Thoroughbreds. Colonial newspaper advertisements announced Thoroughbreds put out to stud.

Theater- and concertgoing provided diversions for upper-class patrons in the major towns. Many private societies sponsored recreational activities. Philadelphia had the first sporting club in 1732. Small groups united by ethnic or professional bonds, such as the St. Andrew's Society in Philadelphia and the French Club in Charleston and New York, mixed entertainment with fraternal and charitable activities. The Masonic lodges held balls and dinners. Other loosely formed groups—for example, Charleston had the Meddlers, Laughing Club, Fancy Society, and Beefsteak Club; Savannah, the Ugly Club and Amicable Club—provided amusements and conviviality for members.

13

The Urban Challenge

Ten percent of colonial Americans lived in towns and cities. Urban centers were often planned communities, though they eventually had to make adjustments in the physical layout and in municipal regulations and services. Colonial cities and towns faced many problems similar to those encountered in today's urban development.

By 1760, Philadelphia was the largest city, with a population of 23,750, followed by New York City, 18,000; Boston, 15,630; Charleston, 8,000; and Newport, 7,500. Other seaport towns of regional importance at the end of the colonial period included Salem, New Haven, Perth Amboy, Providence, Baltimore, Norfolk, Wilmington (North Carolina), and Savannah. Upriver towns, such as Richmond, Fredericksburg, and Albany, were important social and economic centers. Moreover, the colonial landscape was dotted with country towns (often county seats), secondary centers in rural counties, farming villages, and frontier communities. Many towns and other urban centers resulted from promotion by a person seeking to attract residents and businesses to land staked out as a townsite. Of course, not all would-be town developers succeeded. Town proprietor-planners not only sought means to dispose of lots but also saw to it that there was a basic arrangement for establishment of common facilities, neatly laid-out streets, open spaces, and a central area for government, church, and market buildings.

TOWN AND CITY PLANNING

New England town planning followed one of two patterns known in England, rectangular or linear, the latter determined by population growth and topography. Boston simply fitted into the configuration of footpaths and cowlanes, although minimal planning called for two wide intersecting thoroughfares—Great (now State) and High (now Washington) streets; an open space was also reserved at the center of the town for a market and public buildings. New Haven, established in 1638, showed more consistency in planning, with nine squares and garden lots in each of the peripheral squares. New England towns had a village green or common, and most buildings were set back from the street.

Throughout the colonies, function was the main determinant in the success of town building. As James T. Lemon (1967) has noted, in the "preindustrial time commerce was the most universal and obvious characteristic of all urban places"; hence most colonial towns "can be classified as service centers, or 'central places' within their tributary trade areas. Successful central places were points of maximum accessibility for buyers and sellers" (pp. 502–3). For the Pennsylvania and Delaware region, Lemon observes, this criterion held true for county seats as well as other

A South View of the Great Town of Boston, drawn by William Burgis (1725), revised by William Price, 1743. Engraving by John Harris. Courtesy of the American Antiquarian Society, Worcester, Massachusetts

towns and hamlets—often located for centrality and accessibility. Numerous unplanned small communities evolved around an industrial site such as a forge.

In the South urbanization proceeded slowly. The self-contained plantation units and direct marketing with British merchants impeded the growth of towns. By the mid-eighteenth century, however, the need for distribution centers and concentrated marketing led to the rise of a number of medium-sized towns, particularly those that served the piedmont and the further backcountry. In Virginia, Richmond, Fredericksburg, and Alexandria are good examples of such new commercial towns. Camden, South Carolina, 125 miles northwest of Charleston, is typical of new towns in the Deep South. Located one mile from the Wateree River, it was astride trading paths of the Catawba Indians. The town was on an axis for trade, reaching from Charleston to Philadelphia. Cross Creek, North Carolina, was also a trading town, a forwarding center for wheat and flour from the backcountry. Besides springing up as trading centers, some South Carolina towns were initially laid out as townships to accommodate immigrant groups.

Despite factors deterring town planning in the Chesapeake colonies, both Maryland and Virginia made efforts to create urban centers. The governments of both colonies, prompted by royal instructions, from time to time passed laws designating townsites, stipulating methods for land acquisition for town lots, and providing for the layout and disposition of town lots. The main incentive was for the government to have better control over trade and to collect customs duties. A Virginia law of 1662, for instance, called for building towns on every major river. Each town was to consist of thirty-two brick houses (forty feet long, and twenty feet wide, eighteen feet high), with a pitched roof covered with slate or tile. An act of 1680 named twenty sites for new towns, each to be fifty acres in size and the houses to be arranged in a square or as the government otherwise should decide. Maryland statutes of 1684 and 1686 sought the establishment of fifty-seven towns. But these plans met with little success. A common feature in the Chesapeake landscape was county seats, consisting of a courthouse, a tavern, and little else. Yet planned towns materialized, largely because of their situation as river ports. William Byrd II had Major William Mayo, who had been a surveyor on the island of Barbados, lay out a proposed town on Byrd's lands at the falls of the James River in 1721. Byrd also did the same for what became Petersburg, Virginia. He commented, "Thus we did not build castles only, but also cities in the air!" For Richmond, which had its main streets parallel to the river, Mayo laid out thirty-two squares (four horizontal and eight vertical), with four lots in each square; streets were sixty-five feet wide. Every purchaser of a lot had three years in which to build a house measuring sixteen by twenty-four feet facing the street. Alexandria, Fredericksburg, and Tappahannock are examples of other eighteenth-century Virginia towns laid out in a gridiron pattern.

Colonial urban design, reflecting trends in England and elsewhere in Europe, emphasized harmony in layout, broad straight avenues, large open spaces, regulated façades, and public squares. The rebuilding of London after the great fire of 1666 (370 acres burned and 13,200 houses were destroyed) served as a model. Following plans submitted by John Evelyn, Christopher Wren, and others, London was recast with wide streets in order to prevent the spread of a fire; all new houses were required to be of brick or stone. William Penn had surveyor Thomas Holme lay out Philadelphia with London in mind. As Margaret B. Tinkcom (1976) states, "Philadelphia became in many ways a trans-Atlantic mirror of post-Fire London reflecting that English city in its architecture and in its design for urban living" (p. 287). Though Philadelphia was located between two rivers, the intent of the city's design was to draw attention into its interior. In a map and description published by Holme in 1683, Philadelphia consisted

> of a large Front-street to each River, and a High-street (near the middle) from Front (or River) to Front, of one hundred Foot broad, and a Broad-street in the middle of the City, from side to side, of the like breadth. In the Center of the City is a Square of ten Acres; at each Angle are to be Houses for Publick Affairs, as a Meeting-House, Assembly or State-House, Market-House, School-House, and several other Buildings for Publick Concerns. There are also in each Quarter of the City a Square of eight Acres, to be for the like Uses, as the Moore-fields in London; and eight Streets (besides the High-street), that run from Front to Front, and twenty Streets, (besides the Broad-street) that run cross the City, from side to side; all these Streets are of Fifty Foot breadth.

But by the mid-eighteenth century, the design of Penn's city beautiful had undergone considerable tampering. City blocks were cut up, resulting in narrow streets and alley dwellings; tightly packed row houses lined many of the streets. Penn himself had anticipated suburban development, and he had arranged for 500-acre plots, "liberty lands," outside the city. But what he did not envision was the flight of Philadelphia's well-to-do merchants, who settled in "country homes" outside the city; in the mid-eighteenth century there were some 150 such estates within a twelve-mile radius of Philadelphia.

New York City, not having the benefit of a grand design, became the most crowded and compact city. Many houses were closely placed. Streets, as a visitor from Maryland, Dr. Alexander Hamilton, noted, were "not regularly disposed" and wharves "were mostly built of logs with stone foundation." The condition of buildings in the inner city had already begun to deteriorate. The fort and battery were in ruins, and the Exchange,

Charleston Harbor by Bishop Roberts. Courtesy of the Colonial Williamsburg Foundation

which "stands near the water and is a wooden structure," was "going to decay." After 1766 new houses and buildings could be only of brick or stone. Yet New York City residents could take pride in several large government structures and spacious churches.

Charleston, following the "grand model" of the proprietors, was laid out in gridiron fashion, with sixty-foot-wide streets and an open square in the center. Little care, however, was taken to preserve an open plaza, and by the end of the colonial period this area had at its corners a church, a market, an arsenal, and a courthouse. Savannah's rectangular design provided for six wards, each of which had forty house lots, sixty feet by ninety feet. Garden lots of five acres each were interspersed in the town plat, and small farms were placed adjacent to the city.

Each urban center, by the late colonial period, usually had the same kinds of public buildings: town hall, jail, almshouse, warehouses, schools, watchhouse, exchange, customs house, and hospital or pesthouse. The market served as a place where perishable goods could be brought by country people for sale in the town. Faneuil Hall, in Boston, provided a centralized market; New York City had five markets. Warehouses and lofts lined the waterfront. Real estate values were usually highest in the heart of a city.

Francis Nicholson, who governed six American colonies during his career, might well earn the distinction of colonial America's most innovative urban designer. As governor of Maryland in 1695 he platted the town that was to be the colony's capital, Annapolis (originally named Anne Arundel). The Annapolis plan featured two great circles—a Public Circle, five hundred feet in diameter, and a Church Circle, three hundred feet wide; a "Bloomsbury Square," 350 feet from each side; several radiating terminal diagonal streets; a market square, one hundred feet from each side; an open area; a school site; public landings; and common lands beyond the town. Nicholson, as governor of Virginia, planned that colony's second capital at Williamsburg. The General Assembly followed Nicholson's suggestions in 1699. The axis of Williamsburg was Duke of Gloucester Street, ninety-nine feet wide, with the College of William and Mary at one end and the capitol at the other. Midway in the three-fourths-mile thoroughfare were a market square, courthouse, magazine, and church.

STREETS

To venture out into the streets of a colonial town or city, to say the least, was hazardous to one's health. Only important thoroughfares were adequately paved with stones or gravel. One had to keep an eye out for bolting horses. Streets were laden with rubbish and horse offal. A growing and heterogeneous population made it more difficult to get inhabitants to cooperate in keeping the streets clean. In the early days, hogs, goats, and turkey buzzards provided the garbage collection service. But animal scavenging had to be brought to bay, and it became lawful to kill any stray swine. Municipalities began to hire public scavengers, as Boston and New York City did in the 1680s, or arrange for garbage disposal by contract, as Philadelphia did in 1762. New York City had the first commission for street cleaning in 1691.

Street lighting at public expense came late in the colonial period. Householders were initially expected to provide light from their houses. New York City required every seventh house to be lighted at night. There was no attempt to establish general street lighting in New York City until 1761, when the assembly voted for a tax to pay for lamps, posts, barreled whale oil, and hiring of lamplighters. As in London, lamps were ten feet high and at intervals of fifty feet. Boston and Philadelphia soon followed suit. The lamps were not lit when there was moonlight.

Compulsory citizen service for street repair and paving continued well into the eighteenth century. If a householder refused to perform the labor himself, he was assessed the cost of having someone else do it for him. Because of the difficulty of enforcing this obligation, municipalities then opted for maintenance workers paid from the public revenue. The workers were under the supervision of street commissioners, who usually also had responsibility for the upkeep of ferries and bridges.

FIRE PROTECTION

City residents were aware of the dangers of the spread of fire, and most urban areas experienced at least one major conflagration. Municipalities sought to provide fire protection through three means: chimney regulation, requiring new buildings to be of brick or stone, and establishing a firefighting system. It usually took a great fire, however, before regulations were passed against erecting wooden structures. After the Boston fire of 1652, the town required households to have handy a ladder and a pole with a swab for quenching roof blazes. Typical of ordinances passed in the municipalities were prohibition of wooden chimneys and requirements for keeping outside a house a ground-to-roof ladder, buckets, and a hogshead of water. After the Charleston fire of 1704, houses not complying with the chimney law could be destroyed.

By 1700 fire engines had been introduced. New York City eventually had twenty-four firemen and two fire engines, each worked by twelve men. Water was poured into a wooden trough, which could send a jet as high as seventy feet. Benjamin Franklin in the 1730s campaigned for fire protection in Philadelphia and founded the Union Fire Company. By 1764 there were five companies, which cooperated with one another and had a joint president.

SANITATION AND HEALTH

Though ignorant of the specifics of etiology, colonists suspected a relationship between putrid conditions and disease. Numerous regulations were passed to provide for a more sanitary environment, though often the intention was merely to remove malodors. For drainage of streets, pavements were slanted to form a crown in the middle, and gutters were placed by the sides of the roadbeds. Some communities experimented with underdrains, about ten feet deep. The "common shewer" under Broad Street in New York City in 1747 was arched with stone. There were penalties for leaving a "dead beast or stinking thing" in the streets. Many localities regulated against having privies within a certain distance of a street. Slaughterhouses were confined to certain sections of a town.

Diseases spread quickly in urban areas. Immigrants and sailors especially were sources of new infections. Smallpox was the one virulent disease that was a regular visitor. To a lesser extent there were epidemics of malaria (but not in New England), dysentery, typhoid fever, typhus, measles, influenza, diphtheria, scarlet fever, and venereal diseases. To combat smallpox, variolation (inoculation with puss from pustules of a smallpox victim) began about 1720. With the disease raging in Boston in 1721, Dr. Zabdiel Boylston, supported by Rev. Cotton Mather, inoculated some three hundred residents, of whom only six died, compared with 145 of those with smallpox; in the 1730 Boston smallpox epidemic, three percent of those inoculated died, while the mortality was twelve and one-half percent among those with the disease. The epidemic was so great in Boston in 1752 that the government fled to Dorchester and thirteen hundred citizens left the city; at that time, of 2,109 inoculated, 31 died, compared with 514 of the 5,544 persons with smallpox. Benjamin Franklin was an ardent supporter of variolation, and by the mid-eighteenth century the practice had been accepted in varying degrees throughout the colonies. To prevent the spread of disease, quarantine laws were passed, and persons on shipboard could not debark until passing a health inspection. The cities had quarantine policies, with most providing pesthouses; for example, Boston put smallpox victims and the like on Rainsford Island in the harbor, and the Charleston authorities did the same on Sullivan's Island.

About the only regulation of the water supply consisted of provisions for depth of wells and distance of privies from water sources. Water purification in any form would have to wait until the late nineteenth century.

ORDER AND DISORDER

In urban areas, constables or marshals, responsible to justices of the peace or to the mayor and aldermen, provided police protection during daytime hours, and watchmen took over at night. During the early colonial period, citizens were expected to serve in the watch on a rotating basis. Though Albany had the earliest paid watch, in 1659, most municipalities did not allow for this service until well into the eighteenth century. Usually each section or ward had its own watch. In New York City two constables of each ward, elected annually, were in charge of their respective watches, while in Philadelphia wardens supervised the night watch and, along with the tax assessors, levied and collected the watch tax.

A major problem for urban law enforcement was the insufficiency of jail space. What jails there were served mostly as detention centers for persons waiting to be tried or sentenced. Thus most culprits were punished with fines, whipping, stocks, pillories, or, for women in rare instances, ducking stools. Disturbers of the peace and drunkards could expect to undergo the humiliation of several hours in the stocks or pillories. New York City, however, had no ducking stool, and after 1740 there is no mention in the records of the stocks. New York City officials in 1764 could boast of "a New Pillory" with a "large Wooden Cage behind it. The Cage is said to be designed for disorderly Boys, Negroes, &c. who publickly break the Sabbath." Philadelphia, which had a cage for prisoners in 1683, at last obtained a jail surrounded by a high wall in 1722. In New York City, prison quarters were located in the City Hall until 1759, when a new jail was built.

John Winthrop once rightly said, "As people increased so sin abounded." Urban areas witnessed the rise of theft, assaults, excessive drinking, and vice in general. Not the least of urban problems was commercialized vice, which often went hand in hand with pickpocketing and thievery.

In 1672, Massachusetts passed a law prohibiting the operation of "a stews, whore house or brothel house." Yet prostitution and bawdyhouses thrived in Boston throughout the colonial period, owing in large part to the regular influx of sailors. Lecture days and fairs also brought in patrons for the houses of ill repute. Scollay Square was known for its large number of harlots. Cotton Mather formed the Society for the Suppression of Disorder, America's first watch and ward society, which obtained names of prostitutes and sent admonitions to young men.

British and provincial soldiers during the colonial wars patronized prostitutes in the cities. The Battery area in New York City became a popular place to pick up strumpets, and by 1770 some five hundred of them had settled there, about two percent of the city's population. The "Holy Ground," on land owned by Trinity Church, gained notoriety. The city's best-known whores lived on a street near the entrance to King's College. Philadelphia's "Hell Town," along the riverbank, an area that contained most of the city's taverns, was known for its "half cellars" (brothels), which catered to sailors, fur traders, and other transients. Even the small urban centers, such as Fredericksburg, Virginia, had bawdy-houses on the outskirts of town. Virginia citizens, such as William Byrd II, were proud that there were few whores in Williamsburg, overlooking the fact that women of ill repute flourished elsewhere in the colony, particularly Warm (Berkeley) Springs, where some patrons suspected they had contracted venereal diseases.

From time to time authorities cracked down on prostitution, resulting in mild to stern punishments. For example, in Boston in 1753, Hannah Silkey was convicted of running a bawdyhouse and was sentenced to one hour in the stocks while wearing a placard. Prostitutes in early Massachu-setts, however, could face the penalty of being stripped to the waist, tied to the tail end of a cart, and whipped as the cart moved slowly through the town. In Boston in July 1753, twenty-two prostitutes received five to fifteen lashes at the workhouse and were compelled to leave the city within forty-eight hours.

Municipal authorities were usually tolerant of the poorer sort of people forming into disorderly crowds in order to vent frustrations and anxieties. Paul A. Gilje (1987) has observed four overlapping types of ritualized popular disorder in New York City: the charivaris (the shivaree, skimmington, or "rough music"), wherein crowds serenaded and ridiculed a miscreant; a ritual of misrule—a carnival atmosphere exhibited by a crowd on a popular holiday, such as Pope's Day, New Year's Eve, or Pinkster Day; a ritual of role reversal, when crowds assumed attributes of the upper class, making fun of patricians and reminding them of their obligations; and a rite of passage, the "disorderly riotous Frolicks" of young people. Invariably the main participants in colonial urban mobs were youths, seamen, mechanics, laborers, and slaves.

But there were times when disorderly gatherings became full-fledged riots. More often than not, such occurrences aimed at singular objectives, which were condoned by the majority of a community. Hence urban riots were seldom countered by the authorities. Such instances include Boston mobs attacking brothels in 1734, 1737, and 1771. In Philadelphia lower classes attacked the pillories and stocks (1726), demonstrated against laws prohibiting fish weirs and racks in the Schuylkill River (1738), and interrupted an election (October 1742). In several cities rioters protested against exporting grain in times of scarcity. Poor people in New York City (January 1754) rioted against the merchants who conspired to devaluate copper pennies, which had the effect of raising the price of bread and lowering wages.

One kind of urban rioting, however, led to bloodshed and had serious overtones, even to the detriment of Anglo-American relations—protests against the visitation of naval press gangs, which affected the plebeian but not the patrician segments of urban society. Such riots in New York City in 1758 and 1760 each resulted in one person killed and several wounded. Press gangs forcibly entered private houses as well as public establishments. When Commodore Charles Knowles sent out a press gang in November 1747, a mob assaulted the sheriff and seized hostages for the return of impressed Bostonians. Bricks were thrown through windows of the state-house, and Governor Shirley had to flee to Castle William. The British ship came close to bombarding the city.

POOR RELIEF

The challenge to meet demands for aid to indigents was much greater for cities than for smaller communities. Cities had their own impotent poor: orphans, often of families who lost a father at sea; disabled war veterans; the unemployed, whose numbers rose during economic depressions; victims of fire, accidents, or disease; and the aged. Cities also had to contend with immigrants, persons who had been warned out of the small towns or who were escaping economic adversity, and, of course, an assortment of vagrants and vagabonds.

To prevent excessive tax burdens in the care of the needy, localities tightened the rules of eligibility for assistance. Several methods were used to deter indigent persons from settling in a community and thereby becoming public charges. Warning out was effective, especially among smaller communities in the northern colonies. A pauper who entered a town would be told to leave; returning to the same community, the person might face a court-ordered whipping and then be expelled again. Of course, there were problems when no town would claim an indigent as an inhabitant, and heated squabbles resulted, sometimes with a third town arbitrating the dispute. In the 1692 Massachusetts settlement law, however, persons not legally warned out within three months were entitled to become inhabitants and to receive poor relief. Eventually warning out meant only the denial of public assistance, not eviction. The numbers of those warned out in Boston steadily increased in the eighteenth century (the practice ended in 1793): As Gary Nash (1979) has shown, the *Warning Out Book* of the Boston Overseers for the Poor indicates that from 1721 to 1742, an average of twenty-five persons were warned out each year; from 1745 to 1752, sixty-five; from 1753 to 1764, two hundred; and during the decade before the Revolution, four hundred fifty.

To keep out "Vagabonds and Idle Persons" disembarking in seaport communities, ship captains had to reveal all names and occupations of passengers, and those who were listed as having no vocation or property had to be transported back. Communities also sought to prevent the influx of indigents by placing responsibility on individual inhabitants. Householders allowing strangers to stay with them had to put up security that they would not be a burden on society. New York City required that no stranger could remain in a private home or tavern for more than a week without first registering with the city recorder. Failure to inform authorities of the presence of a stranger residing in one's home was punishable by a fine. As early as 1636 the Boston selectmen prohibited inhabitants from "entertaining" an outsider for more than two weeks without permission. In the various urban centers, constables or other officials were empowered to search out strangers and present them to the mayor or other city authorities. Most transients, as Douglas L. Jones (1981) has shown for the seaport towns of Essex County, Massachusetts, were young single men and women, with the elderly accounting for only fifteen percent of the newcomers. Many of the indigent strangers were ex-servants seeking jobs. For Salem and Boston, the majority of new poor persons came from within ten miles of the two towns; foreign immigrants accounted for one-third of the poor strangers.

Colonial legislation concerning the poor used as guidelines the English labor statutes, the Elizabethan Poor Law of 1601, and the Settlement Act of 1662. Local taxation supported care for the poor, and legal settlement status had to be established as eligibility for relief. Colonial assemblies made localities responsible for their own poor relief; for example, Plymouth did so in 1642, Virginia in 1646, Connecticut in 1673, and Massachusetts in 1659 and also under the new charter in 1692. The Duke's Laws for New York (1665) divided the colony into parishes, with eight overseers for the poor and two church wardens in each parish to administer relief from local taxation. The first New York Assembly of 1683, however, made the counties responsible for poor relief. In New

York City, elected aldermen of each ward acted as overseers of the poor relief; in 1691, however, vestrymen and church wardens took over this duty. In the South the parish vestry, as an administrative unit, had charge of aid to the poor, while in New England this responsibility was exercised by town selectmen, tithingmen, or overseers of the poor. In the northern colonies outside New England, poor relief was generally the province of the counties.

During the early colonial period, poor relief was essentially nonspecialized and noninstitutional. Much of the aid was outdoor relief, whereby direct grants were made to individuals in the form of money, firewood, clothing, food, and medical or nursing care. Several cities retained a physician for the poor. A common practice, North and South, was to put destitute aged and infirm persons up with a family, often on a rotating basis, with the government paying for the room and board. Usually poor children and orphans were apprenticed, and adult indigents were bound out as indentured servants.

Besides direct relief there were various kinds of supplementary aid. For example, town cows were reserved for the use of the poor. Tax abatements were granted. Poor persons were allowed discounts on purchases. Thus Boston in 1740 converted an old church into a granary where the poor could purchase grain at only ten percent above cost (this amount reckoned to cover waste and expenses).

Significantly, the poor during the early colonial period were not invisible. As time went on, with public assistance becoming a greater burden, there were efforts to confer a stigma on pauperism. In New York City indigents were required to wear blue or red badges with the letters *NY* sewn on them.

Gradually localities began to show more sensitivity, if not greater compassion, toward the poor. The indigent were placed in categories, and there was greater specialization in the granting of aid. While diversity in kinds of care continued, indoor and institutional relief became a common mode for public welfare, largely prompted by the increase of what were considered undesirable elements. As a means primarily for cost effectiveness, the almshouse (or poorhouse), intended originally to house the worthy destitute (the blind, lame, sick, and aged), found general acceptance in the northern colonies but rarely in the South. Virginia, for example, never had an almshouse or even a workhouse. Among the larger urban centers that built almshouses were Boston (1664), New York City (1700, 1736), Portsmouth, New Hampshire (1716), Salem (1719), Newport (1723), Philadelphia (1732), Charleston (1736), Providence (1753), and Baltimore (1773). Overcrowding became a grave problem. During the French and Indian War, refugees and sick soldiers added to the distress. During the 1760s the Boston almshouse, with thirty-three rooms, took in 250 indigents, one-fourth of them children. During the same period Boston provided annual outdoor relief to about a thousand persons.

Unfortunately, some communities placed incorrigibles along with the impotent poor in the almshouses. Thus New York City had a threefold purpose when it opened its "Poor House, Work House, and House of Correction," a two-story brick building, in 1736: to provide a home for young and old paupers; to serve as a house of correction, where for a fee, a master could have a slave or servant whipped; and to function as a workhouse for "Beggars, Servants running away or otherwise misbehaving themselves, Trespassers, Rogues, and Vagabonds." But the New York workhouse did permit some separation of the inmates: an infirmary, a cellar for the "unruly and obstinate," and a room for "Carrying on Trades, Occupation and Manufactures," such as spinning, weaving, and shoemaking. Inmates also tended a garden on the grounds.

Elsewhere, a few localities had separate structures for the worthy poor and for those who could but would not work. Boston led the way in 1699, when the Massachusetts legislature passed an "Act for Suppressing and Punishing Rogues, Vagabonds, Common Beggars . . . and also for Setting the Poor to Work." The Boston workhouse, next to the prison, was the receptacle for petty offenders and various "idle and stubborn" persons; numbering among the inmates were "Common Drunkards," "Common nightwalkers," "Wanton persons, as tending to uncleanliness in speech and actions," "Whores or vile Persons," disorderly youth, and even Indians who did not stay at assigned places of residence. Workhouses were considered cost-efficient, since one elected or appointed official could take charge of the whole operation. A keeper had virtually dictatorial power and could have punishment administered as he saw fit. Persons were committed to workhouses for no specific terms, and inmates left only when they were deemed capable of self-sufficiency, proved to be unable to work and were therefore sent to the almshouse, or died. The workhouse prisoners had to wear distinctive clothing. Despite the intention of making workhouses self-supporting, financial aid came chiefly from public revenues. It can be assumed that another goal—discouraging needy strangers from entering the community—was scarcely achieved.

By the mid-eighteenth century, awareness was growing that many indigents were mentally ill. Insane poor were put into the cellars or attics of almshouses. The Friends Alms House in Philadelphia (1732) contained both an infirmary and rooms for persons with mental disorders. The Pennsylvania Hospital (opening in 1752), which had the declared purpose of "restoring useful and laborious Members to a Community," had a separate mental section. Elsewhere, mental patients were kept in shacks or jails. The first true hospital for the insane was established at Williamsburg in 1769.

Private charity substantially complemented public poor relief. Religious, ethnic, and occupational charitable groups proliferated after the mid-eighteenth century, owing in part to Enlightenment views on the betterment of humanity and the stirring of conscience by the religious Great Awakening. The Quaker "Contributors to the Relief and Employment of the Poor of the City of Philadelphia," founded in 1766, at first gave funds for public poor relief but eventually established its own "bettering house," which functioned as a home for invalids, a hospital, and a vocational training school for orphans. Looking after the needy within their own ranks were such organizations as the St. Andrew's Society in Charleston (1729), Philadelphia (1749), and New York (1756), and, in Boston, the Scot's Charitable Society (1657–1667, revived 1689), the Marine Society (1754), the Episcopal Charitable Society (1754), and the Charitable Irish Society (1767).

Factors in limiting municipal expenditures on poor relief and other services were the heavy tax burdens of urban inhabitants and the constraints on the taxing powers of municipalities imposed by the colonial legislatures. It is estimated that in the 1760s, citizens of Philadelphia supplied one-fourth of the colony revenue; in New York City, one-third; in Charleston, one-fourth; and in Newport, one-fifth. Municipalities were constantly in financial straits and had to resort to borrowing. In all the colonies, towns and cities were incorporated by the legislature, on conditions stipulated by that body. Most often rural interests prevailed over the concerns of urban areas. In New York the governor and council had to approve all municipal ordinances and bylaws. William Smith of New York in 1706 voiced the resentment of city dwellers toward rural-dominated legislatures: "The members for the metropolis always complain of the intrigues of the country gentlemen, in loading their city with a third part of the public burdens, for the ease of their own counties."

Legislatures preempted most forms of direct taxation. Municipal councils had to rely chiefly on indirect revenues, such as license and marketing fees, rentals of property, lotteries, and single-item levies, authorized by a legislature, such as for the purpose of paving streets or building a new dock. Much of Philadelphia's revenue came from ferry fees and vendor stall rents. New York City, however, had its own property tax, and Williamsburg had a poll tax. Adding to problems of urban revenue raising, legislatures placed limitations on the taxing power of municipalities, set deadlines for collection, and insisted on exercising authority in determining the kinds of levies.

14

Government and Politics

By the middle of the eighteenth century, the colonists claimed three political tenets: a fixed constitution, popular sovereignty, and the enjoyment of the rights of "freeborn" Englishmen. They favored both a mixture of powers and separation of powers within a government. While the people should rule, there must be checks on the excesses of democracy, chiefly through lawmaking by the people's representatives. Power must be kept under control. Yet, as Roy N. Lokken (1959) has observed, "the colonists did not consider democracy or any other form of government practicable or desirable in its unadulterated state" (p. 573). The colonists nevertheless insisted on a large measure of democracy, as evident in voting directly for representatives, frequent elections, competition for office, and accountability for official conduct.

New England clergy in the eighteenth century, like their predecessors, addressed the idea of the social covenant but expanded on its meaning by noting the right of the people to dissolve a political compact. Reverend John Wise of Ipswich, Massachusetts, in his *Vindication of the Government of New-England Churches* (1717), argued that there were three covenants: agreement for majority rule, acceptance of rule by law, and agreement by "those upon whom Sovereignty is conferred" to guard "the Common Peace and Welfare; and the Subjects, on the other hand, to yield them faithful Obedience." A people could withdraw powers "when a Government so settled shall throw it self from its Foundations . . . or shall subvert or confound the Constitution." Neither Wise nor others defined a right to resistance. But the idea of popular sovereignty persisted. Thus Jonathan Mayhew, minister of the West Church in Boston, stated in a sermon in 1750 on the anniversary of the execution of Charles I, "A Discourse concerning Unlimited Submission and Non-resistance to the Higher Powers," that the people had a right to revolt against arbitrary authority: "No government is to be submitted to at the expense of that which is the sole end of all government—the common good and safety of society."

Colonists reflecting on the rights of the people during the eighteenth century acknowledged their indebtedness to writers during the preceding century—John Milton, James Harrington, Algernon Sidney, John Locke, and others. But as Bernard Bailyn (1965) argues, the colonists identified even more closely with "the early eighteenth-century transmitters" of the "tradition of seventeenth-century radicalism" (p. 29). The later colonists were influenced by John Trenchard and Thomas Gordon's *Cato's Letters* and generally by the thought expressed by English "coffeehouse radicals" and opposition politicians. The English political malcontents did not consider individual liberty safe under the tutelage of a sovereign Parliament. They continually argued for the necessity of vigilance against expansive governmental power and of reforms such as a democratic voting franchise, equal representative districts, and complete freedom of the press and religion. Jack P. Greene (1966), however, takes issue with Bailyn in that the colonists championing popular sovereignty and individual freedoms relied more on the colonial experience itself. Constitutional development in America molded colonial political ideology. At the "peripheries" of empire, the colonists enjoyed certain independence and freedoms from the start; in time the colonists became defensive of their own political tradition and sought to redefine their constitutional liberties in the context of the empire.

THE IMPERIAL CONNECTION

The British crown and its administrative agencies had the primary responsibility for supervision and direction of imperial relations. The growing authority of Parliament in the realm did not alarm the Americans. Parliament itself showed little inclination for encroaching on colonial legislative powers. Not until the 1760s did Parliament pass any acts affecting the internal political affairs of the colonies. It also became the practice that parliamentary statutes had no effect within the colonies unless reenacted by the local assemblies.

Lacking in imperial colonial administration were clear lines of responsibility and effective mechanisms for enforcement. In 1634 a standing committee of the Privy Council, presided over by the archbishop of Canterbury, William Laud, oversaw colonial affairs, but its decisions had to be confirmed by the whole council. During the period of the English Civil War and the Commonwealth, first a Parliamentary Commission for Plantations, consisting of eighteen members, and then an executive Council of State (1649), whose members were appointed by Parliament, supervised English-colonial relations. With the Restoration, two Privy Council committees, the Council of Trade and the Council for Foreign Plantations, assumed responsibility for colonial administration, and in 1676 these committees were replaced by the Committee of Trade and Plantations (the Lords of Trade). In May 1696 the Board of Trade took over from the Lords of Trade. The board had eight salaried and seven unpaid members, all of whom either served on the Privy Council or sat in the House of Commons. The Board of Trade's duties included overseeing poor relief at home and serving as an agency for information and advice for the king in council. With jurisdiction over all the English plantations, not just the mainland colonies, it was incumbent on the board to issue governors' instructions, correspond with colonial officials, examine colonial legislation, hear complaints, recommend persons for royal appointments, and send reports to the king. The board also made recommendations on disallowing colonial legislation.

Other departments and officials shared responsibility in imperial-colonial relations with the Board of Trade, but there was no central authority for coordinating their work. The secretary of state for the Southern Department was concerned with all southern European and colonial affairs, and technically the Board of Trade was part of this department. The secretary was an ex officio member of the Board of Trade and also of the Privy Council committee on colonial affairs, but he usually ignored both groups. The Treasury Board (consisting of the first lord of the Treasury, the chancellor of the exchequer, and three junior Treasury lords), with its subdepartment of Commissioners of the Customs, had charge of the collection and accountability of revenues raised from the colonies. Imperial colonial administration was also conducted by the Admiralty (Royal Navy), War Office, bishop of London (in ecclesiastical affairs), High Court of Admiralty, and, at the end of the colonial period, commander in chief of British forces in America and Indian superintendents.

The Board of Trade languished in effectiveness before 1748. It ceased to be a forum for discussion of colonial affairs and forfeited its role as the sole information gatherer pertaining to the colonies. The quality of its personnel deteriorated, with membership being regarded as a sinecure. The duke of Newcastle (Thomas Pelham-Holles), as secretary for the Southern Department, took over much of the board's business. The earl of Halifax (Charles Montague-Dunk), as president of the Board of Trade, once again made the Board of Trade an active agency, but after his resignation in 1761 the board again slipped back into lethargy. Between 1696 and 1765, the ninety-five appointees to the board and its eighteen presidents had an average tenure of only about five years. A major reform in 1768 was the creation of a position of secretary of state for the colonies only and having that official also serve as president of the Board of Trade.

There was little judicial connection between England and the colonies. Though the Privy Council could review decisions by colonial courts, in practice this recourse was limited chiefly to civil cases involving large sums of money and those concerning governments, such as boundary disputes. The crown, of course, shared in the appointment of colony-level judges, since these were councilors, and also chief justices in the colonies that had them.

The crown, however, exercised important judicial power in its right to disallow colonial legislation. All laws had to be sent to the king in council for review, although this was never fully insisted on for the charter colonies of Rhode Island and Connecticut. There were several options for the king in council: The law could be sent back for modification of offensive features, the governor could be ordered to press for repeal, the governor could be instructed to veto the law, and ultimately the king in council could declare the law either in force or null and void. Mostly the Privy Council permitted colonial laws to "lye by probationary"—that is, to have the laws remain on the books indefinitely, with no action taken, but still subject to disallowance. About three-fourths of colonial laws considered by the Privy Council resulted in no recommendation or action. Once a law was confirmed, however, it could not be disallowed. An act was in full force in a colony if signed by the governor and not disallowed. In the eighteenth century, however, certain types of colonial legislation were required to contain a suspending clause, preventing the legislation from being operable until approved by the king in council. Colonial legislatures at times ignored the requirement for a suspending clause and also made laws for a short duration and repassed them in slightly different form, thereby making any eventual disallowance ineffective. Generally, three main reasons were given for disallowance of colonial laws: a threat to decrease royal revenues, incompatibility with English laws, and violation of the royal prerogative. In Virginia between 1700 and 1759, twenty-six laws were disallowed and seventy-four were confirmed out of a total of 697. Overall, it is estimated that for the colonies as a whole until the Revolution, five percent of colonial laws were disallowed—469 of 8,563 acts.

THE GOVERNOR

In the eight royal colonies (New Hampshire, Massachusetts, New York, New Jersey, Virginia, North Carolina, South Carolina, and Georgia), the crown appointed the governors, usually upon nomination by the Board of Trade. Proprietors named the governors for Pennsylvania, Delaware, and Maryland, subject to royal approval. Connecticut and Rhode Island, self-governing under their original charters, annually elected their chief executives. To secure a royal or proprietary governorship, one had to have the right patrons in England. Many who successfully sought the office were in dire financial straits and saw an opportunity in America to gain wealth. A few were scapegraces, who were related to the sovereign or were once powerful politicians; British authorities were only too glad to send them to America. Not the least in this category was New York's governor, Lord Cornbury, who, fancying himself as resembling his cousin, Queen Anne, put on woman's apparel for public appearances. Some governors, preferring to stay in England, farmed out the actual office to deputy or lieutenant governors, splitting the salary; this was especially true in Virginia during the eighteenth century. Of the three hundred governors, lieutenant governors, and deputy governors appointed by the crown between 1624 and 1783, one-fourth were peers or sons of titled nobility, forty-five had served in Parliament, fifteen were members of the Royal Society, and twenty had studied at the Inns of Court. A few had had military careers, among these Francis Nicholson, Edward Cranfield, Alexander Spotswood, George Clinton, William Denny, Robert Hunter, Benning Wentworth, and Samuel Ogle. Several royal governors had won fame as wealthy merchants, such as Robert Dinwiddie. Because of the politics and patronage involved in England in order to obtain a governorship, it is not surprising that only a few native-born Americans received such an appointment, among them being William Phips (Massachusetts), Jonathan Belcher (Massachusetts and New Jersey), Lewis Morris (New Jersey), James Hamilton (lieutenant governor of Pennsylvania), and William Bull, Jr. (South Carolina).

The royal governor had viceregal powers. He exercised authority on behalf of the king. Indeed, on the surface the royal governor had more powers locally than the king himself had in England. In actuality, however, much of the power conveyed to the governor by his commission and his instructions, both given by the crown, was illusory and shared. In the royal colonies, except for Massachusetts, the governor's commission, which authorized the form of government, served as the colony's constitution. Colonists, however, denied that the governor's instructions, often kept secret from the public, were anything more than advisory.

Governors in the royal colonies had a broad range of authority: to enforce the laws; to convene assemblies of representatives of the free-

Edward Hyde, Lord Cornbury. Courtesy of The New-York Historical Society, New York City

holders; with the consent of the legislature, "to make, constitute, and ordain Laws, Statutes and Ordinances"; to exercise an absolute veto over legislative enactments considered to be contrary to the interests or policy of the crown; in most colonies, to preside over the council as the highest court of justice; to erect courts for hearing cases, civil and criminal; to appoint judges, justices of the peace, and commissions of oyer and terminer; to adjourn, suspend, or dissolve assemblies when deemed necessary; to grant pardons for most criminal offenses and temporary reprieves to traitors and willful murderers; to serve as "Captain General and Commander in Chief" of all of the colony's military and naval forces, and, if necessary, declare martial law; to issue warrants on the public moneys; to grant lands; to determine fees; to remit fines and forfeitures; to enforce English navigation and trade laws; to appoint high officials, upon final approval by the crown, and certain county officeholders, such as the coroner, escheator, and county attorney; to create fairs, markets, ports, and harbors; and to serve as the head of the church, including the collation of ministers to ecclesiastical benefices (though actually such authority was severely limited by the vestries).

The royal governor vis-à-vis the assembly raised constitutional issues, not the least being questions over control of expenditures, adjournment of the assembly, appropriations of funds, and the governor's salary. The crown unsuccessfully pressed for a fixed and permanent annual stipend for the royal governors. Only in Virginia was this obtained, dating back to Governor Lord Culpeper's instructions in 1679 to take two thousand pounds a year (incidentally, the highest base salary of a colonial governor) from local revenues—two shillings per hogshead of tobacco exported and one-half of all escheats, fines, and forfeitures (although fines were soon dropped). Other royal governors received salary supplements from revenue derived from an assortment of fees and licenses.

THE COUNCIL

The colonists viewed their governments as replications of that of the mother country. If the royal governor was a viceroy, the council was a miniature House of Lords, minus the legal hereditary and noble trappings. The council had a threefold role: advisory board to the governor, upper house of the assembly, and highest court in the colony, as a court of appeals (though limiting civil cases to those involving three hundred pounds or more) and in the trial of certain felonies. The council had an equal vote on legislative bills. As a council of state, it shared powers with the governor in summoning assemblies, appointing officials, issuing money from the treasury, and creating courts of justice, but otherwise in this capacity its functions were simply advisory.

Members of the royal and proprietary councils, normally about twelve in number, were nominated by the Board of Trade from lists submitted by the governor. In Massachusetts the House of Representatives and the outgoing councilors selected new councilors, subject to the governor's veto. The councils in Connecticut (the assistants) and Rhode Island (the magistrates) were elected by the freeholders at large.

Councilors could serve for life, although governors could suspend or dismiss them, subject to approval by the crown. Although unsalaried, councilors usually monopolized high-paying posts in a colony, namely collectorships and the offices of attorney general, receiver general, auditor general, and secretary. There were two types of councilors—the placemen, mainly English by birth, who depended on official positions other than councilor for their livelihood, and the native colonists, who comprised the vast majority of councilors.

Invariably councilmen came from the wealthiest and oldest families, chiefly from the seaboard region of a colony. Kinship was common among them. In Massachusetts between 1680 and 1775, of ninety-one councilors, one-third bore only nine family names. In Virginia during the same period, sixty percent of councilors came from twenty-three families, and one-sixth of them were descended from "Grandmother Lucy" Higginson, who in the mid-seventeenth century had married Philip Ludwell.

For political expediency, governors found it wise not to alienate their councilors—they were too powerful a force in a colony. Lieutenant Governor Alexander Spotswood in 1717 nevertheless reviled the Virginia council as a "hereditary faction of designing men" who exhibited

> the haughtiness of a [Robert] Carter, the hypocrisy of a [James] Blair, the inveteracy of a [Philip] Ludwell, [Jr.] the brutishness of a [John] Smith, the malice of a [William] Byrd, the conceitedness of a [John] Grymes, and the scurrility of a [Gawin] Corbin, with about a score of base disloyalists and ungrateful Creolians for their adherents.

Spotswood successfully deposed Philip Ludwell Jr. as auditor general but was unable to persuade the earl of Orkney, the actual governor of the colony who resided in England, to purge the council of four members. Even then, Ludwell was replaced as auditor general by his son-in-law, John Grymes. Spotswood complained to Orkney in July 1718, why should "a Juncto of relations" be permitted to "grow to that height of power as to bear Uncontroulable Sway over both Govr and People?" Spotswood, largely because he wanted to increase his own landholdings, soon found it best to join interests with recalcitrant councilors rather than fight them.

THE LOWER HOUSES OF ASSEMBLY

In all the colonies, the lower houses of assembly secured dominance in the colony governments by obtaining exclusive power of the purse, though in the royal and proprietary colonies this was accomplished gradually. The lower houses initiated and amended money bills, conducted audits, controlled expenditures through the making of appropriations and the appointment of officers for the disbursement of funds, voted on the salaries for the governor and other officials, and issued paper money. They also staked out a role in executive functions, encroaching on the governor in the making of public policy, nominating and appointing officials, conducting military and Indian affairs, and serving as head of the church. The legislatures had their own standing committees, usually two that dealt with their own business, on "propositions and grievances" and elections, and three that infringed on the powers of the governor— trade, courts of justice, and religion.

An important distinction between the colonies and the mother country was the insistence on actual rather than virtual representation. The colonies made strides toward fair apportionment and a one-man, one-vote system, but in many areas much remained to be accomplished by the end of the colonial period. In New England representatives were chosen at town elections, resulting, as Michael Zuckerman (1970) has put it, in a "congress of constituencies." In Rhode Island the original four towns had four delegates, the other communities only two each. In the Massachusetts House of Representatives, Boston had four delegates, each town over 120 freeholders had two, and towns with less than this number had one. Representation was weighted in favor of coastal regions. In Pennsylvania, for example, the three eastern Quaker counties—Philadelphia, Chester, and Bucks—each had eight representatives plus two for the city of Philadelphia, for a total of twenty-six. The next county created, Lancaster (1729), returned four delegates; then York (1749), two; Cumberland (1750), two; and Berks and Northampton (both created in 1752), one each. Each county in Virginia elected two burgesses, but the members of the assembly from smaller Tidewater counties greatly outnumbered those from the larger western counties. In the 1760s the crown sought to deter the establishment of new counties in the Carolinas.

Colonial assemblymen were expected to possess some wealth, whether required by statute or not. Pennsylvania, New York, and Massachusetts set no minimum estate requirements, and Virginia had the same property requirement for burgesses as it did for voters. Among other colonies, a person sitting in the Commons House of Assembly in South Carolina had to own three hundred acres of land, ten slaves, or real estate valued at 150 pounds; in North Carolina, one hundred acres; in Georgia, five hundred acres; in New Jersey, one thousand acres or fifteen hundred pounds in land and personal property; and in New Hampshire, real estate worth three hundred pounds. There were also requirements for residence in the districts represented. In some instances, persons could be disbarred from sitting in a legislature because of religion, for example, Catholics in the royal colonies and Quakers in the Carolinas during the early eighteenth century. Similar to councilors, legislators to a large degree formed a kinship network. In New Jersey, for example, between 1737 and 1776, eighty-three percent of the representatives elected were related to another representative or a councilor.

The assemblies claimed the same privileges and immunities as

Parliament. Absent members could be suspended, fined, expelled, or jailed. It was usual for the sergeant at arms to be ordered to take an absent member into custody. Breach of discipline also brought similar punishment. One reason that few men of limited means served in the colonial assemblies was that the posts were unsalaried. Per diem allowances were granted but ordinarily undercompensated expenses by about fifty percent. Virginia burgesses, though, were doing rather well by 1752, when compensation was figured at ten shillings a day and reimbursement of travel expenses.

Two views on the role of the Virginia burgesses, nearly twenty years apart, indicate a shift in colonial opinion with respect to the fundamental obligations of a legislator. Sir John Randolph, speaker of the House of Burgesses, in 1736 called on his colleagues to refrain from trying to appease particular interests and instead to pursue what they perceived "to be the true Interest of the People: Tho' it may be often impossible to conform to their Sentiments, since, when we come to consider and compare them, we shall find them so various and irreconcileable." Landon Carter, in his diary of 1754, commented on a House of Burgesses debate on the question of "Whether a Representative was obliged to follow the directions of his Constituents against his own Reason and Conscience or to be Governed by his Conscience." The argument "for implicit obedience" was

> that the first institution of a Representative was for the avoiding the Confusion of a Multitude in assembly. He, therefore, was to Collect the sentiments of his Constituents and whatever that Majority willed ought to be the rule of his Vote. . . . [But] the Admirers of Reason and Liberty of Conscience distinguished upon it and said, where the matter related particularly to the interest of the Constituents alone, there implicit obedience ought to Govern, but, where it was to affect the whole Community, Reason and Good Conscience should direct.

Combining both views, it may be stated that a legislator in the late colonial period was considered an agent of the people and also of his own conscience.

LOCAL GOVERNMENT

Uniquely, the most pervasive democratic government at the local level was that of the New England town. In all 550 towns in mid-eighteenth-century New England, all town officials were elected. At an annual election in March, presided over by the moderator, freemen who met age and resident requirements (generally with little or no concern for property qualification as stipulated for provincial elections) voted for the town officials. Cottagers and other nonfreeholders attended and participated in the town meetings and presumably often were allowed to vote. The first order of business for an election town meeting was to choose a moderator, either by paper ballots or by nomination and acclamation. Then the major officials were chosen by ballot—selectmen, clerk, treasurer, and constable. The most important officeholders were the selectmen (three to nine, depending on individual towns; in Rhode Island they were called councilmen, six to a town). Selectmen had executive, ordinance-making, and limited judicial authority. They administered the fiscal affairs, sold or allotted lands, settled land claims, admitted new inhabitants, and issued fines and injunctions. In Rhode Island town councilmen acted as a court of probate, whereas selectmen did not.

Selection of some forty minor New England town officials was by "nomination and vote" or by show of hands. One group of the lesser officials was largely supervisory, including the highway surveyors, fence viewers, tithingmen (who checked for sabbath and license violations and reported to the county court), inspectors and "sealers" (who determined the quality and quantity of commodities), and clerks of the market. Others were those who performed chiefly menial tasks, such as catching and herding stray livestock. A third category consisted of those who primarily "ran errands," such as tax collectors.

The full participation in town meetings made for inclusiveness and consensus in town government. Nevertheless, leading families dominated town affairs. Serving in major town offices was a springboard to provincial positions. For the seventy-three towns studied by Edward M. Cook, Jr. (1976), three-fourths of the provincial representatives from these towns had served as clerks, treasurers, moderators, or, overwhelmingly, selectmen.

Pennsylvania had four units of local government—borough, township, city, and county. The county was the main unit of government to which the others were connected. The borough was a village, incorporated with nearly the same governmental functions as a city. A township covered a wider geographic area than that of any municipality and was usually rural. The boroughs (Chester, established in 1701; Bristol, 1720; and Lancaster, 1742) had greater independence than the townships from county jurisdiction. In the boroughs, burgesses, assisted by councilmen or assistants, conducted town meetings and presided over government much as in New England towns. Pennsylvania townships had no local governing board; the constable and overseers of the poor were selected by the court of quarter sessions, and the few other officials were elected. Philadelphia, the only city, was under both municipal and county government. County government in Pennsylvania was similar to that of the other colonies, but more democratic than in the royal colonies. County commissioners and assessors were elected. Also, the electorate voted annually for two candidates each for sheriff and coroner, with the governor making the selection from one of the two highest vote getters. Justices of the peace, appointed by the governor, sat as a court of quarter sessions (criminal and breach-of-the-peace jurisdiction and also administrative duties), court of common pleas, and orphan's court. Other county officers were appointed either by the governor or other provincial officials or by the local commissioners and assessors.

New York, like the other northern colonies, had a hybrid local government. Within the counties were townships and precincts (areas of scattered population), each of which elected annually one person to serve on the county board of supervisors. The board attended only to administrative affairs, leaving the commission of the peace (justices of the peace) to function solely in a judicial capacity. Most of the supervisors were of the "middling sort." New York county sheriffs, justices of the peace, and judges were appointed by the governor. Two or three specially appointed judges formed a court of common pleas and, when joined by justices of the peace, a court of general sessions of the peace.

Incorporation of cities in the colonies followed English patterns for municipal government. The government of New York City, under a charter of 1686 conferred by Governor Thomas Dongan, was typical of that of other cities, North and South. Annually, each ward elected an alderman, an assistant, and a constable. The aldermen and assistants formed a common council, which enacted local ordinances and oversaw various municipal functions. The governor annually appointed a mayor, sheriff, and recorder (in other colonial municipalities, however, the mayor was usually elected from within the common council). The mayor's court consisted of the aldermen, who individually also served as justices of the peace. Some municipalities, such as Williamsburg, Virginia, had a Hustings court (so named from the court held in Guild Hall in London by the Lord Mayor and aldermen), which, like the New York mayor's court, had essentially the same functions as a county court.

In the Chesapeake colonies, except for the few municipal (or borough) corporations, all local government revolved around the county court and vestry. The justices of the peace, sheriffs, and coroners, nominated by the existing justices of the peace, were appointed annually by the governor. The county court had judicial and administrative functions. It consisted of the justices of the peace, usually ten to fifteen per county, four of whom made a quorum. A justice of the peace could serve for life. The county court, as a court of quarter sessions, could try misdemeanors and noncapital cases. Vestries, unlike England, were autonomous and had local duties, such as supervising poor relief. In eighteenth-century Virginia they were self-perpetuating, electing new vestrymen as vacancies occurred. The offices of sheriff and justice of the peace were dominated by the gentry, while lesser county positions, usually salaried, were held by persons of moderate wealth. Jurors, though selected from the small planter class, had to possess ratable estates in the value of fifty pounds for service in the county courts and one hundred pounds for the General Court. Service as a justice of the peace or as sheriff was a means for acquiring a political following that would be advantageous in running for a seat in the House of Burgesses. The division of officeholding was an important compromise. The well-to-do gentlemen could afford the time and expenses of being a justice of the peace or a burgess, whereas the small planter could not. The office of sheriff was also very time-consuming, though remunerated out of the fees collected. Reserving lesser offices for the nongentry was a factor in itself for the deference given to those who held the higher county offices and served as burgesses.

Of the colonies, South Carolina was the slowest in developing a strong county system. The most important form of local government there, outside of Charleston, was the parish vestry (or precinct), twenty-three of which were established between 1706 and 1770. Seven vestrymen in each parish were elected annually by freeholders with ratable estates. Vestrymen, besides caring for the poor, had police and executive authority and performed such duties as acting as road and creek commissioners. The county court system was not fully established before 1769. Justices of the peace had only minor administrative and legal responsibilities, and, unlike the Chesapeake society, men of wealth were reluctant to serve on a commission of the peace. One reason for the hesitance in creating a viable county court system during the colony's early history was the easy access to courts of common pleas and of general sessions in Charleston.

VOTING

If elitism was a dominant factor in colonial political life, there was nevertheless a broad electorate. Of course, the great majority of the population was excluded from the franchise—women, servants (in most colonies), slaves, minors, and all others who failed to meet voting requirements. Historians, however, have been divided on estimates of voter eligibility and participation. Among early twentieth-century historians, Albert E. McKinley (1905) and J. Franklin Jameson (1926) agreed that the franchise was widespread, while Carl Becker (1909) estimated that in New York only about half of the white male adults could vote. Clinton Rossiter (1953) considered that no more than one-fourth of white male adults were enfranchised. Other historians, probing more deeply and quantitatively, have found that most white male adults could vote. Although their figures have been accused of being inflated, Robert E. Brown (1955) found that ninety-five percent of white male adults could vote in Massachusetts, and Brown and coauthor Katherine B. Brown (1964) estimated that figure at eighty-five percent in Virginia. Among other historians who agree roughly with the Browns' high percentages are Richard P. Mc-

Cormick for New Jersey (1953), David S. Lovejoy for Rhode Island (1958), and Milton M. Klein for New York (1974).

Royal instructions insisted on property qualifications for voting, and except during the early period of a colony's founding, this criterion was met. Generally the colonists followed the forty-shilling freehold requirement for elections in England. A sampling of voting qualifications in the colonies, though they underwent slight changes from time to time, shows a pattern of requiring "a stake in society" in order to enjoy the franchise. Massachusetts, Connecticut, and Rhode Island required a forty-shilling annual income from a freehold estate or real or personal property worth fifty pounds (Massachusetts), twenty pounds (Connecticut), or one hundred pounds (Rhode Island); New York required a freehold valued at forty pounds; New Hampshire, a freehold of fifty pounds; New Jersey, one hundred acres if no personal property; Pennsylvania, fifty acres or fifty pounds in property; Maryland, fifty acres; Virginia (1736), one hundred acres (reduced to fifty acres in 1762) or twenty-five improved acres or a house in town measuring twelve feet square; Georgia and North Carolina, fifty acres; and South Carolina, one hundred acres. Six colonies provided alternatives to real estate qualification: personal property or payment of taxes. South Carolina, for example, gave the franchise to all paying taxes of twenty shillings (1721), reduced to ten shillings in 1759.

The franchise was also broadened in other ways for those without sufficient real or personal property. For example, New York and Virginia allowed the vote to tenants with a lifetime lease on a forty-shilling freehold. Similar to the English borough franchise, householders could vote in some urban areas—for example, in Williamsburg; Norfolk; Burlington and Perth Amboy, New Jersey; Annapolis; and towns in North Carolina. In large cities, to encourage the residency of skilled craftsmen, provision was made for the franchise upon obtaining the "freedom of the city." Thus probably most artisans voted in Philadelphia without the requisite property. In New York City one could purchase the freedom of the city for amounts ranging from five pounds for a merchant or shopkeeper down to twenty shillings for an artisan; apprentices were eligible to vote upon completion of seven years' service. Albany also allowed for voting upon admittance to the freedom of the city.

Residency requirements varied; for example, in New England one had only to be admitted as a freeman; in New York one had to be a resident for three months; in New Jersey and South Carolina, one year; in Pennsylvania and Delaware, two years; in Virginia, twelve months (reduced to six in 1770); and in Georgia and North Carolina, six months. Age requirements ranged from twenty-one to twenty-four years old (the latter in Massachusetts). It can be presumed that suffrage restrictions were occasionally ignored if a person was in good standing with his neighbors. In most colonies Catholics and non-Christians (Jews) were disqualified, but probably many of them voted anyway. In hotly contested elections votes were at a premium. In Virginia candidates were known to confer small parcels of land on would-be supporters. During a 1762 Virginia burgess election, one Thomas Payne purchased a milkpan shed from a woman and carted it off to a lot "to qualify himself to vote."

Frequent provincial elections were ensured by colonial laws or charters, which imposed maximum lengths of time between elections. In Connecticut the elections were semiannual; in Massachusetts, Rhode Island, and Pennsylvania, annual; in North Carolina and South Carolina, biennial; in New Hampshire, Maryland, and Virginia, triennial; and in New Jersey and New York, following the English practice, every seven years. Governors of the royal colonies could and did call elections at less than the maximum intervals as they saw fit.

Typically, in Virginia, under an election law of 1705, forty days before the governor proposed a meeting of an assembly, he signed election writs (returnable in six to eight weeks with voting tallies). The secretary then delivered the documents to the sheriffs, who in three days had to post notices of the time of the elections, which were usually scheduled several weeks in advance and on a court day. Most provincial elections were conducted similarly to that held in a Virginia county courthouse. There poll sheets were placed on a long table, and voters declared their choices to the sheriff vocally; the candidates' own "clerks" then recorded votes on the poll sheet. Elections were conducted by voice vote in all the colonies except for Massachusetts, Connecticut, Pennsylvania, North Carolina (1715–1760), and South Carolina. Although voters might have felt intimidated by voice voting at least the practice left little chance for fraud.

There was not much electioneering until the eighteenth century, and even then gentlemen were not expected to court favor. Many election contests were raucous, especially in Philadelphia and New York City. In Virginia alone, there were election riots at the county courthouses of Northumberland (1728), Hanover (1736), Prince William (1750), and Augusta (1754). George Washington got involved with some tough politicking at election time. In 1755, while avidly supporting a candidate for burgess, he was knocked down with a stick by William Payne, to whom Washington apologized the next day. In 1758, Washington, now himself a burgess candidate for Frederick County, could not get away from his military duties and therefore had his political lieutenant supply prospective supporters with twenty-eight gallons of rum, fifty of rum punch, thirty-four of wine, forty-six of beer, and two of cider. Not too certain of his reelection in 1761, Washington accused one of his leading opponents, Adam Stephen, who also happened to be second in command of the Virginia regiment, of dirty tactics, namely being too solicitous of votes, while Washington himself tried to persuade the sheriff to let his followers vote first and also made the rounds, including attendance at a cockfight.

"Treating" the electorate with food and drink was illegal in Virginia but was done anyway under different pretenses.

Robert Munford of Mecklenburg County has left a delightful contemporary description of the "humours" of a Virginia colonial election in his play *The Candidates* (ca. 1770). Wou'dbe, an incumbent burgess in the play, is the favorite, but the other burgess, Worthy, refuses to stand for election again. Other candidates, appropriately characterized by their names, were Smallhopes, Strutabout, and Sir John Toddy. After these three have further revealed their rascality or incompetence, Worthy is persuaded to run again for burgess, "joining interests" with Wou'dbe. The outcome of the election is then never in doubt—Virginians deferred to their purported betters in politics.

POLITICAL RIVALRIES AND ISSUES

Most colonial Americans believed that factions and parties did not belong in constitutional government. Consensus, coherence of the governmental system, and order were desired objectives. Yet the colonial period was beset with a variety of factional conflicts—primarily the struggle between the crown or proprietary supporters and the assembly but also personal, ethnic, religious, sectional, economic, and social disputes. As Bernard Bailyn (1965) has noted, colonial politics often became unstable in the "aggressive pursuit of power." Political rivalries in the colonies during the eighteenth century more often than not paralleled the factionalism of Georgian England, Whig versus Tory, and simply ins versus outs. In England the Whigs traditionally favored the enhancement of parliamentary supremacy and having the king's ministers representative of the majority in Parliament; they also tended to back mercantile and industrial interests. The Tories supported the powers of the king and also agricultural interests. Actually, as in America, English politics came down mainly to who should receive the spoils. In the colonies the designations of court party and country party were used in place of Tories and Whigs. The court party supported the royal governor, while the country party was supposedly more concerned with legislative right and the interests of the colony as a whole. At the end of the colonial period, a young generation of politicians was challenging the entrenched power of the older leaders.

During the eighteenth century, political factionalism was most pronounced and persistent in New York, the New England colonies, and Pennsylvania. The repercussions of the revolution of 1689 in New York, which uprising had culminated with the execution of its leader, Jacob Leisler, led to a power struggle between the Leislerians and the anti-Leislerians. As Patricia U. Bonomi (1971) has written:

> The political history of New York from 1692 until 1710 is a rapid series of
> policy and party reversals which pitted "ins" against "outs" and interest
> against interest, making factional strife an almost endemic condition of the
> colony's public life. (p. 78)

Afterward, the Morris-Livingston faction, associated with the upriver
landed gentry, vied for political control of the colony with the commercially
oriented De Lancey party.

By 1700 in Massachusetts there was growing concern for reducing
the powers of the royal governor. For this purpose, in 1720, Bostonians
created a political organization, the Boston Caucus, that backed candidates
for the House of Representatives. In the legislature a group led by Elisha
Cooke, Jr., fought with Governor Samuel Shute over such issues as
appointment of the speaker, adjournments of the assembly, the auditing
of expenditures, and a permanent salary for the governor. The most
intense political issue, however, was the question whether to find means
for currency expansion. During the 1730s, Governor Jonathan Belcher
battled inflationists in the House of Representatives. The land bank
scheme of 1740 and 1741, whereby land mortgages could be used to
secure circulating notes, generated heated political controversy. Belcher
attempted to outlaw the bank by proclamation, but land bankers won the
provincial elections. The House of Representatives, which had a final say
in choosing the councilors, ousted sixteen antibank councilors, whereupon
the governor dissolved the assembly. He also jailed the ringleaders of
poor debtor farmers who marched on Boston. But the issue of a land
bank became moot when Parliament outlawed all such private banks. The
land bank contention was significant not only for pitting court versus
country party and merchant against farmer but also because it politicized
the electorate. Seventy percent of the deputies from the towns to the
House of Representatives failed to be reelected.

William Shirley seized opportunity from the dissensions in Massachusetts and built up a political machine from old country families and
newly arrived Bostonians; through connections in England, he secured
the removal of Belcher and was himself appointed governor. At the end
of the colonial period, Massachusetts politics became enmeshed in the
personal feud between the Otises, originally outsiders from Cape Cod,
and Thomas Hutchinson, a leader of the urban mercantile families.
Governor Thomas Pownall's appointment of Thomas Hutchinson, already
the lieutenant governor, as chief justice instead of James Otis, Sr., created
a rancor that influenced the coming of the revolutionary movement in
Massachusetts. The Great Awakening, as Richard L. Bushman (1967)
states, also served to break the "seal on political controversy." This was
particularly true in Connecticut, where the New Lights in the western
part of the colony, advocating paper money, less state control of the

church, and the interests of small farmers, formed political opposition to the Old Lights.

Pennsylvania came the closest of all the colonies to having organized political parties. The Quaker party, championing low taxes, good government, and paper money, enjoyed a long success in controlling the legislature. Presbyterians, Anglicans, non-Quaker Philadelphia merchants, and backcountry farmers supported the Proprietary party. The withdrawal of Quaker members from the assembly in 1756 because of the hostility toward their pacificist position regarding the war effort and defense against the Indians left the Quaker party in disarray. Benjamin Franklin tried to form a new political coalition from the remnants, with the main objective to make Pennsylvania a royal colony.

There was little factional strife in the southern colonies. The paper money controversy did not prove divisive in the long run as it did in the northern colonies. But there were constitutional issues and regional discontent. The pistole fee affair in Virginia in 1753 and 1754, whereby Governor Dinwiddie sought to levy the fee of one pistole (fifteen shillings) on new land patents on his own authority, angered the burgesses and their constituents alike, alerting Virginians to the issue of "no taxation without representation." North Carolina, South Carolina, and Georgia faced the same contention over governor and assembly power struggles as elsewhere. Moreover, sectionalism, as in Pennsylvania, was becoming a volatile force in the South. Settlers of the Albemarle and Cape Fear regions in North Carolina were bitterly divided over the governor's land dealings, which favored the Cape Fear region. The question of collection of quitrents in the remaining proprietary lands was also a political issue. Underrepresentation and lack of courts in the southern backcountry aroused hostility toward the coast-dominated governments.

At the end of the colonial period, the growing restlessness of the backcountry as well as that of urban artisans and mechanics was reason enough for colonial leaders, granting some validity to Carl Becker's thesis, to stake out external issues to obscure real and potential internal dissension.

15

Criminality and Radical Counterculture

Criminals were always present in colonial society. Some malefactors, as professionals and members of gangs, fit a countercultural mold. In sharp contrast, Christian perfectionists and enthusiasts, sharing feelings of alienation, formed alternative communities and distanced themselves from the confining dictates of mainstream colonial society.

FELONS

The most unusual of the colonial criminal codes, which also departed most from English law, were those of the New England colonies and East Jersey during the seventeenth century. The criminal provisions emphasized moral offenses, and crimes against property were excluded from capital punishment. The early criminal code of Massachusetts, first in the "Body of Liberties" in 1641 and in its reenactment in 1648, nevertheless contained twelve capital crimes: idolatry; witchcraft; blasphemy; willful murder; manslaughter, if out of "anger or cruelty" of passion; poisoning that resulted in death; bestiality; sodomy, involving a man that "lyeth with mankinde as he lyeth with a woman," unless the accused was forced or under the age of fourteen; adultery (added in 1648); manstealing; bearing false witness in a capital case; and conspiracy and rebellion. By the time Massachusetts became a royal colony in 1692, many more capital crimes had been added—rape; cursing or smiting a parent; stubborn or rebellious behavior of a son toward his parents; burglary; robbery; defiance by Jesuits; heresy; arson; defiance by Quakers; military insubordination, mutiny, and the like; piracy and mutiny on the high seas; treason against the king; and militarily aiding an enemy; other crimes were no longer capital—idolatry; blasphemy; manslaughter; witchcraft; incest; cursing parents; false witness in capital cases; adultery; and manstealing. The Privy Council, however, approved fourteen capital crimes for Massachusetts: burglary (third offense); robbery on a field or highway (second offense); polygamy; piracy; concealing the death of a bastard child; treason; willful murder; rape; sodomy and bestiality; defiance by Jesuits; counterfeiting; arson; dueling; and stealing (third offense of three pounds or more value). In Puritan Massachusetts before 1692, it is interesting to note, as Edwin Powers (1966) does, that fifty-six or fifty-seven persons were executed: twenty-three for witchcraft; thirteen for murder; five or six for piracy; four for rape and for Quakerism; and two for bestiality, for adultery, for arson, and for treason.

Of the early northern colonies, the criminal codes of West Jersey and Pennsylvania were the most lenient, with murder and treason the only capital offenses. At the end of the seventeenth century, however, West Jersey adopted much of the Puritan East Jersey code, and for New Jersey as a royal colony (1702–1776) there were few changes. Pennsylvania also went from leniency to severity. In 1718 the colony adopted the English criminal code, which had over three hundred capital felonies.

A look southward also reveals that Virginia made nearly every felony punishable by death, though, as in Pennsylvania and New Jersey, the death penalty for crimes against property was almost never meted out if the defendant was white. Treason in Virginia, paralleling laws of other colonies and England, was of two kinds: high treason (rebellion, speaking derogatorily of the king or the government, counterfeiting, and slave rebellion) and petit treason, which also involved obedience and allegiance (a servant killing a master, a wife murdering a husband, an ecclesiastical person killing a superior). The supreme penalties for all treason were hanging, drawing, and quartering for men and strangulation and burning at the stake for women. In eighteenth-century Virginia, petit treason was confined solely to slave crimes. Convicted capital felons had several recourses for avoiding execution: petitioning the court for clemency; a female pleading pregnancy, at least securing a reprieve until after birth; proving a technical error and gaining a new trial; suing for a "pardon of grace" from the governor; seeking amnesty (a new governor usually pardoned the first felon convicted during his term in office, and persons were also amnestied to celebrate the accession of a new sovereign); and, for certain crimes, pleading benefit of clergy, which could lead to remission of the sentence altogether, except for branding of the left thumb. Benefit of clergy, however, did not apply if a prisoner was convicted of willful murder, rape, treason, arson, horse stealing, or robbery. Initially, to gain benefit of clergy, the malefactor had to read a passage from the Bible, usually the Fifty-first Psalm: "Have mercy upon me, O God . . ."; in 1732 in Virginia the reading requirement was eliminated, and women were also allowed to plead benefit of clergy. The plea of benefit of clergy could be used only once.

Indeed, the avenues available for convicted capital felons as well as mitigating factors presented in trials kept the infliction of death penalties at a minimum. Of 336 felony trials in Virginia, from a spot newspaper check by historian Hugh Rankin (1965), involving forty-seven court sessions from 1737 to 1772, one-half of the defendants were acquitted or were allowed benefit of clergy, five were pardoned in court by the governor, twenty-nine were imprisoned or received other punishment short of death, and 125 were given the death penalty, of whom, it is estimated, about one-fourth were pardoned. Rankin also finds that of fifty-nine murder trials listed in the *Virginia Gazette*, twenty-five persons were acquitted and two were found guilty of manslaughter (both receiving benefit of clergy). Conviction rates were also low in other colonies. For example, as Douglas Greenberg (1982) has noted, in New York for the period of 1691–1776, the conviction rate for all crimes was less than forty-five percent, with more than one-third of all defendants failing to appear for trial or escaping. Also in New York, fifty-two percent of capitally convicted defendants were pardoned.

One of the easiest major crimes to commit was horse stealing. The seventeenth century witnessed few prosecutions for this felony, but as population expanded and became more dispersed, horse stealing plagued many communities. By the mid-eighteenth century the colonies were taking strict measures to discourage this crime. A Virginia law of 1748 required certificates of sale for horses brought into the colony and also made horse thievery a capital crime. Gangs of horse thieves operated almost with impunity in the back counties of Virginia and Maryland. Executions did not offer much of a deterrent. Networks of criminals made it possible to dispose of stolen animals. "The Villains had their Confederates in ev'ry Colony," wrote Rev. Charles Woodmason, in reference to the Carolina backcountry.

> What Negroes, Horses, and Goods was stolen Southwardly, was carried Northerly, and the Now'd Southward. The Southward shipp'd off at New York and Rhode Island, for the French and Dutch Islands, the Now'd carried

to Georgia and Florida, where smuggling Sloops would bargain with the Rogues and buy great Bargains.

Horse stealing was rife in New Jersey, which also had the death penalty for the crime. From 1706 to 1779, more than four hundred notices in colonial newspapers mentioned horses stolen in that colony. Usually the thieves took horses westward, selling the animals to frontiersmen and Indians. Of persons in New Jersey indicted for horse stealing between 1751 and 1766, three were not tried, two were acquitted, two were pardoned, and eight were hanged.

Similar to horse thievery, outlaw gangs frequently shifted locales in robbing and disposing of stolen goods. Individual robbers also escaped detection and arrest by traveling and using assumed identities. Flimflammers, keeping on the move, readily found unsuspecting prey. Such was Robert Jamieson, who journeyed through Massachusetts, Rhode Island, New York, and Pennsylvania, posing as a parliamentary commissioner. The most talented and famed of this breed was Tom Bell. The Harvard-educated Bell mastered impersonation. Thief, confidence man, and counterfeiter, he passed himself off in such guises as gentleman, soldier, and sailor. Sentenced to death at Charlestown, Massachusetts, in 1759, he escaped. Eventually Bell "retired" and wound up teaching school in Hanover County, Virginia.

Counterfeiting caused havoc to the economic well-being of society as a whole. This crime was easily accomplished, due to the illiteracy of so many colonial Americans, the numerous types of coins, the naiveté of the Indians, and the uncomplicated engraving of paper money. Although counterfeiting became a treasonable offense in most colonies, as in England, and thereby punishable by death, a wide variety of sentences were handed down for the crime, and colonial juries were reluctant to mete out the extreme penalty.

Colonists learned early how to tamper with English, foreign, and Massachusetts coins, even making replicas using gold or silver plating over inferior metals. Churning out paper money, however, afforded the greater reward. Some skilled craftsmen tried counterfeiting, and intercolonial gangs facilitated the circulation of fraudulent money. Occasionally the illegal moneymakers ended up on the gallows; for example, four were hanged in North Carolina in 1752, including a tailor from Virginia, and at Williamsburg, Virginia, in 1739 seven were executed, including one woman. One notorious head of a gang of counterfeiters, John Potter, a Rhode Island Quaker, had an advantage over competitors in that in 1740 he was appointed to the committee for signing the Rhode Island bills of credit.

SEXUAL TRANSGRESSORS

Sexual offenses were abundant in the seventeenth century because of the large number of unmarried immigrants, especially servants, and persons who had left their spouses behind in England and also because of close observance by neighbors in the small or rural communities. As areas became more urbanized, prosecutions for sex offenses declined.

Varieties of sexual misconduct generally merited fines, the stocks, the pillory, different forms of humiliation such as standing on the gallows with a rope around the neck, banishment, and, most frequently, whipping. Accused persons also faced rebuke from the churches, resulting in the extreme in excommunication; often culprits, however, upon remorsefully confessing their sins, would be forgiven by a congregation. Penalties for felonious sex crimes were most severe in the seventeenth century.

Sex crimes were difficult to prove (unless, in rare instances, when there were witnesses), a major factor in not meting out the extreme penalties. Defendants in a capital sex case were usually found guilty of lesser charges. For example, in early Massachusetts, a jury found a person accused of adultery "not guilty according to Indictment but found him Guilty of vile filthy and abominably libidinous Actions." Adultery was a capital offense in all the New England colonies, the Jerseys, and briefly in Virginia (under the Dale Code) during the seventeenth century. Only two adulterers were executed in the colonies: Massachusetts in 1644 put to death Mary Latham and her paramour, James Britton. For men and women alike, following the removal of the death penalty for adultery in Massachusetts in 1694, persons convicted of this crime faced a threefold sentence: standing an hour on the gallows, receiving up to forty lashes, and wearing a capital letter *A*, two inches high, on the upper garment (Plymouth colony had already had a similar punishment, wearing *AD* on the left sleeve). Elsewhere in the colonies, fines and whipping were the usual penalties for adultery. With acquittals running high (for example, at a rate of more than three-fourths of cases in New Jersey between 1702 and 1776), adultery laws were increasingly nonenforced. Similarly, outside of early New England, prosecutions for fornication were all but nil; for example, in seventeenth-century Maryland, there was only one fornication case despite one-third of the brides being pregnant.

Bigamy, though a capital crime in most colonies, resulted in no executions; in Virginia and Maryland persons convicted of this crime could plead benefit of clergy. Bigamy was considered justifiable if a mate had been absent seven years "beyond the Seas." Incest troubled the colonists, but, like most sex crimes, it was difficult to prove, and persons suspected of the crime were often indicted for a lesser offense involving loose morals.

Rape was a different matter, as a person wronged was likely to come forward, but still, if no confession was made, there was a lack of a corroborating witness. Despite the many acquittals and reduction in charges of rape, executions for the crime were carried out in the colonies. Of only eight rape cases involving whites decided by the Virginia General Court in the eighteenth century, five persons were acquitted, two were hanged, and one was pardoned. Juries considered mitigating circumstances; one of the most unlikely verdicts was the one rendered by a jury in Plymouth colony in 1682 ordering that an Indian named Sam, who had raped a young white girl, be severely whipped and banished, "considering hee was but an Indian, and therefore in an incapasity to know the horiblenes of the wickednes of this abominable act, with other cercomstances considered."

The infliction of death penalties for sodomy and bestiality was relegated chiefly to the early seventeenth century, and even then prosecution of such crimes was extremely rare. After 1625 in Virginia there were no trials for these crimes, although the justices of the peace held examining courts in a few instances to consider charges. Only two persons were executed for sodomy: one in New Haven Colony and one in Virginia. There is a void regarding lesbianism, although a person so accused in Plymouth colony was ordered to make "public acknowlidgment and to take heed for future otherwise greater punishment." At least three persons were executed for bestiality in the New Haven colony, one (a sixteen-year-old) in Plymouth colony in 1642, and, strangely not again until 1757 and 1774, two persons in New Jersey (not including one Negro servant who was convicted of bestiality in East Jersey in 1692 but escaped).

WITCHES

Early Americans carried with them from Europe fears of the supernatural. Phenomena, the work of God or the Devil, in the form of phantom ships, ghosts, strange lights, and other inexplicable scenes were constantly reported. Like Englishmen and other Europeans, most colonial Americans dreaded the Devil's powers of *maleficium* (the supernatural means to injure humans and property). It was the belief of Protestants and Catholics that Satan, in fighting against God, recruited his minions on earth. To believe in the Devil, one had to believe in witches. Witches gave their allegiance to the Devil versus God. Accepting a view prevalent in Christianity since the late medieval period, the American Puritans considered that a person possessed of demonic spirits had voluntarily entered into a compact with the Devil. A witch exhibited certain symptoms, especially transmogrification in personality and behavior and, if a woman, witch's teats (unusual marks on the body).

In New England between 1638 and 1691, Lyle Koehler (1980) notes, there were at least 101 accusations of witchcraft: in Massachusetts, forty-eight, including eight Quakers; in Connecticut, thirty-two; in New Hampshire, sixteen; in Maine, two; in Plymouth, two; and in Rhode Island, one (which never came to trial). According to Carol F. Karlsen (1987), at least 344 persons were accused of witchcraft in New England between 1620 and 1725, of whom 267 were clearly identifiable as women. The first execution for witchcraft was that of Alse Young in Connecticut, May 26, 1647; later the colony was to hang three more convicted witches. Margaret Jones was the first to be hanged for witchcraft in Massachusetts, executed in Boston on June 15, 1648. The execution of Anne Hibbins in Boston in 1656 was unusual in that she was the widow of William Hibbins, who had been a wealthy merchant and an assistant in the General Court; Anne, however, had a reputation for contentiousness and had been excommunicated from the Boston church.

The witchcraft scare never caught on outside of New England. In New York, which had a sorcery law rather than a witchcraft law, several persons were brought up on charges tantamount to witchcraft: a rich widow of Westchester County in 1670, who was not indicted, and Ralph Hall and his wife, Mary, in Suffolk County, on Long Island, in 1665; the Halls received a jury verdict to post bond for their good behavior. Pennsylvania, which did not have a witchcraft statute until 1718, had only two witch trials, dating back to 1684; in these instances the governor directed a not-guilty verdict. In Maryland, Rebecca Fowler, one of five persons accused of witchcraft in the colony's history, was the only one hanged for it (1685). Two women were hanged on shipboard as "sea witches" on their way to Maryland: Mary Lee in 1654 and Elizabeth Richardson in 1659. Colonel John Washington, great-grandfather of George Washington, brought charges of murder against the sea captain, Edward Prescott, in the Richardson case, but because he had to attend to a son's baptism, he missed the trial, and Prescott was acquitted. There were several other instances in Virginia of persons being accused of witchcraft, but the threat of an accused person to bring a defamation suit against the accuser was usually enough to deter witch hunting. In 1709, South Carolina meted out minor punishment for several persons accused of witchcraft.

There was, however, one unusual case in Virginia. Grace Sherwood, a widow who did not get along with her neighbors, was "tried by water," in Princess Anne County in July 1706. With her left thumb tied to her right toe and vice versa and a Bible secured on her neck to weight her down, she was tossed into Lynnhaven Bay. Unfortunately, she floated, thereby giving proof that pure water rejected her unclean spirit. Subsequently she was bound over for trial as a witch in the General Court. Because the records of this court for this period are no longer extant, the outcome is unknown; whatever it was, though, Grace Sherwood lived to an advanced old age, dying in 1740.

During the Salem witchcraft delusion, two hundred persons were accused of witchcraft (three-fourths of them women). Twenty-two women and five men were tried and convicted, and hangings from June 10 to August 19, 1692, took the lives of fourteen women and five men (including Rev. George Burroughs). Seventy-five-year-old Giles Corey, apparently hoping to preserve his estate for his heirs, refused to respond to his indictment and was submitted to the English torture known as *peine forte et dure*, whereby stones were progressively heaped upon his body in order to force him to enter a plea; Corey refused to make the desired utterance and was pressed to death.

The Salem witchcraft hysteria began when Elizabeth Parris, age nine, and her cousin, Abigail Williams, age eleven, threw fits, supposedly under the spell of a West Indian servant, Tituba, in the Parris home. Soon other youngsters in the community behaved erratically as well, and they accused persons of putting them under evil incantations.

Massachusetts's new royal governor, William Phips, on June 2, 1692, created a court of oyer and terminer solely for the trial of persons accused of witchcraft. Many people saw this special court as an opportunity to address grievances against neighbors. Indictments were drawn up blank, with names, residences, and dates entered afterward.

Since the Devil himself could not be subpoenaed, spectral evidence played an all-important role in the Salem witch trials. Spectral evidence, allowed under English law since 1593, involved testimony of the victim that he or she had been with the accused in the presence of the Devil or had been tormented by the spirit, specter, or shape of the accused. Increase Mather and thirteen other ministers, however, protested against using such testimony of the supernatural in court. Mather, who wrote an essay on the subject, argued that the workings of Satan were beyond comprehension.

Like scapegoating at other times and places in history, to sustain the hysteria there was need for fresh names and faces, eventually to reach out among the elite of society. Prominent persons, including the governor's wife, Lady Mary Phips, were accused. Governor Phips, now recognizing the excess as well as the error of the witch hunt, on October 12 ordered no further imprisonment of accused witches and on October 29 dissolved the court. A special court of judicature, with spectral evidence prohibited, heard the remaining cases in early 1693, acquitting all those still accused of witchcraft; the governor pardoned three persons who were under sentence of death.

The Salem witchcraft delusion has not wanted for explanations. Certainly there were anxieties and frustrations over the loss of the colony's charter, the rule under the Dominion of New England, an increase of immoral and disruptive behavior pointing to the work of the Devil, a rebellious sense among the young toward Puritan strictures and parental authority (most of the accused were middle-aged married women or widows), and most important, a rise of tension in personal relationships. It is true that a common factor among the accused was that they were misfits of some sort—eccentrics, slanderers, and troublemakers, some of whom had been law violators. But particularly, as John Demos (1970) has noted,

> the dynamic core of belief in witchcraft in early New England was the difficulty experienced by many individuals in finding ways to handle their own aggressive impulses. Witchcraft accusations provided one of the few approved outlets for such impulses in Puritan culture. Aggression was thus denied in the self and attributed directly to others. (p. 1322)

Still to be answered is why the delusion of 1692 was confined to Salem. One daring interpretation is intriguing, if unlikely. Linnda R. Caporael (1976) argues that a disease contracted from contaminated grain, convulsive ergotism, may well have been the cause of the witchcraft scare in Salem. Ergot is a fungus that grows on cereal grains, especially rye. There are two kinds of ergot, gangrenous and convulsive. The latter produces deposits on plants that contain isoergine (lysergic acid amide), which like the modern LSD can produce a range of disoriented behavior. Caporael notes that of the thirty-two adult accusers, thirty lived in the western section of Salem Village, where rye was grown on the marshy lands, a kind of environment especially favorable for the fungus.

Historians, in particular Paul Boyer and Stephen Nissenbaum (1974), emphasize that the Salem witch hysteria probably had to do with the bitter factional rivalry between those who rallied around the preacher at Salem Village, Rev. Samuel Parris, and an anti-Parris group that had just won elections for selectmen. Most of the accusers came from the Parris group in Salem Village, while the accused sided with the anti-Parris faction and were also from across the Ipswich Road in neighboring Salem Town. Residents of Salem Village were mainly agrarian and devout, and they resented the prosperity, commercialism, and secularism of Salem Town.

PIRATES

Like witches, men who spent their lives at sea also bargained with the Devil and got the worst of it in this world. At least such could be said of the pirates.

Yet the sea held a fascination for many young colonial Americans; even George Washington and Benjamin Franklin contemplated a naval career. New England farm youths enlisted for short service aboard merchantmen. But many of the jack tars (seamen on merchant ships) and sailors in the Royal Navy were persons who had known economic adversity and were of foreign birth and background. Some recruits were runaway servants and slaves, fugitives from the law, army deserters, and unemployed laborers. Those impressed into the Royal Navy also came from the lower reaches of society. Service aboard deep-sea vessels meant unrelenting hardship and deprivation—disease, high mortality, shortage of food, low wages, separation from civil society and family, and treatment as a child under the most abject conditions.

Everything about the life of a seaman contrasted to that of regular society—segregation by sex, rowdy and outlandish behavior, submission to the absolute authority of the captain, a fraternal and collectivist bonding among the men, and even the rapid speech, profusely mixed with profanity and jargon. Despite the ever present threat of severe punishment, seamen nourished egalitarianism and a spirit of rebelliousness. Many a captain acted contrary to his will when confronted with the potential for a wide mutiny. One characteristic of the "seaman's oppositional culture, closely related to collectivism," writes Marcus Rediker (1987), "was the value of antiauthoritarianism" (p. 244). Seamen had little use for the established rules of society or its institutions, especially courts, judges, and churches. Rediker also recounts a story of a priest aboard a colonial ship, who inquired of the captain the dangers of an ensuing storm.

> The captain puzzled the priest when he told him to go on deck and listen to the sailors as they worked the masts and sails. The priest complied, only to find that the fury of the seamen's language matched that of the elements. Bursting back into the captain's quarters, he reported that the sailors were cursing and swearing like madmen, to which the captain nonchalantly responded that there was no great danger. Still later, the priest returned with news that the seamen cursed no longer, but now occupied themselves with prayer. The captain gravely replied, "Oh, I am afraid that if they have stopped swearing and started praying there is no hope for us." (p. 169)

Some dejected seamen turned to pirating, seeking greater freedom, adventure, and a chance to get rich quick in sharing in captured booty. Most pirates had experience on merchant ships. Buccaneers, who preyed on Spanish ships and settlements in the West Indies in the mid-seventeenth century, expanded their freebooting indiscriminately, and privateers, who were commissioned to attack enemy commerce in wartime, kept to their ways in peacetime as pirates. Seamen aboard captured merchantmen often voluntarily chose to join pirate crews. Besides gaining material rewards, a rationale for becoming a pirate was to take revenge on the rich and powerful, even in the redistribution of wealth at the expense of merchant "knaves." As Rediker observes:

The social organization of piracy, even though based upon a relatively new form of collectivism, was part of that tenacious tradition that linked medieval peasants, seventeenth-century radicals such as the Ranters and Levellers, and the free wage laborers of the eighteenth century. (p. 108)

Colonial merchants, who engaged in smuggling during wartime and who evaded the Navigation Acts, were quite willing to trade for pirate goods with no questions asked. As long as vessels belonging to colonial merchants were not attacked, piracy was tolerated. William Markham, lieutenant governor of Pennsylvania, 1693–1699, was regarded as a "steddy freind" of pirates, and allegedly sold protection for one hundred pounds to each pirate. Governor Charles Eden of North Carolina performed the marriage of Blackbeard to his fourteenth wife after this pirate had accepted the king's amnesty in 1718 and had settled, albeit briefly, in the colony. Attitudes toward pirates, however, changed in the early eighteenth century as increasing depredations were made on American shipping. The periods just after King William's and Queen Anne's War witnessed sharp rises in piratical activity. With their fast fore-and-aft-rigged sloops, pirates found refuge and concealment within the Outer Banks and sandbars along the inlets of the Carolina coast.

Francis Nicholson was one of the first governors to crack down on piracy. In early 1700, with shipping at a standstill within the Virginia capes, he was determined to take forceful action. Upon learning that a pirate vessel, the *La Paiz*, was anchored in Lynnhaven Bay, he called out the militia to defend the shores and put the HMS *Shoreham* into service against the pirates. In the close-range firing between the two ships, Nicholson's force gained victory; thirty-three pirates were killed or later died of wounds, while the *Shoreham* lost but four sailors. Nicholson sent 111 pirates to England for trial, and three of the crew were hanged in Princess Anne County.

The most celebrated of American pirates, William Kidd, had lived a life of respectability as a New York shipowner and sea captain. In England in 1695, Kidd received a commission from the king to lead an expedition against Red Sea pirates who had been preying on commerce of the East India Company. Well-placed Whigs in England as well as several New York merchants invested in the enterprise. In January 1698, Kidd captured an Armenian ship, the *Quedah Merchant*, flying French colors but probably in the service of the East India Company. Kidd scuttled his own ship, the *Adventure Galley*, and sailed home in the captured vessel. During the voyage in the East, Kidd, in a fit of rage, slew his gunner, William Moore, crushing his skull with a wooden bucket. On Kidd's return in 1699, Governor Bellomont of New York and Massachusetts had him arrested for murder and piracy and sent him to England in chains. Executed on May 23, 1701, Kidd was as much a victim of political strife between Whigs and Tories as he was of what he considered trumped-up charges.

After Queen Anne's War, pirating thrived off American coasts. Between 1716 and 1726 some five thousand Anglo-Americans sailed under the Jolly Roger. The king's general amnesty, extended to persons who had committed acts of piracy before January 5, 1718, if they surrendered by September 5, 1718, produced only a temporary reduction in piracy.

Pirates since 1714 had made their headquarters at the town of New Providence, on Nassau, in the Bahamas, and also at Port Royal, Jamaica. At New Providence in 1718, Woodes Rogers, governor of the Bahamas, succeeded in ousting the pirates, who then established bases in Africa and on the Carolina coast. Blackbeard (Edward Teach or Thach) returned to pirating, and with the harbor at New Providence denied him, he clung to the Carolina shores. A native of Bristol, England, Blackbeard could have been the Devil incarnate; his coal black beard reached from his eyes to his waist, and his hair was snarled in tails. Surprised at Ocracoke Inlet by a small force sent out by Governor Spotswood of Virginia and commanded by Lieutenant Robert Maynard, Blackbeard met his end in hand-to-hand fighting. Nine other pirates were killed, and fourteen were later hanged.

Elsewhere authorities pursued a war on pirates. Eight were executed at Boston in 1717. Spotswood hanged six more in Virginia in 1720. One of the most tragic cases was that of Stede Bonnet, who, at middle age and possessing a profitable sugar plantation in Barbados, decided to turn pirate. After sailing for a while with Blackbeard, he made his headquarters at Lower Cape Fear and preyed on South Carolina shipping. Captured by Colonel William Rhett off Charleston, Bonnet was hanged on December 10, 1718. In all, during November and December, forty-nine pirates were executed at Charleston.

The mass hangings effectively cleared out pirates from the South Atlantic coastal areas. Pirates still operated, however, in the sea lanes off Newfoundland in the summer and transferred their plundering to the West Indies during the winter. Before the wholesale hangings, pirates had a reputation for fair treatment of their prisoners, often giving them their own abandoned vessels. But with the executions, pirates subjected prisoners to hideous tortures. The most notorious of the later pirates were Edward Low and George Lowther, whose wide range of looting extended from New England and the capes of Virginia to the West Indies. Once Low sliced off the ears of a mariner captured off Block Island and forced the victim to eat them, salted and peppered. Twenty-seven of Low's men were captured and hanged in Rhode Island. Low himself escaped—and disappeared from history. Lowther, in summer 1723, during an encounter with a South Seas ship near Tortuga, was killed or committed suicide. Besides the campaigns against the pirates, a major factor in spelling an end to widespread piracy in American waters was the Piracy Act of

Parliament in 1721, which made anyone who traded with pirates an accessory.

MAROONS

Some colonists lived like maroons—persons stranded in a remote area and cut off from civilization. "Hidden Americans" inhabited isolated pockets of land, swamplands, and forests of the frontier. Settlements in North Carolina, north of Albemarle Sound and east of the Chowan River (the original Albemarle County, divided in 1670 into the counties of Currituck, Pasquotank, Perquimans, and Chowan), had many of the characteristics of a maroon society until the early eighteenth century. Although having their own assembly and government, the people of the region were isolated from the rest of the world and acquired the reputation of providing sanctuary for refugees from other colonies. The Albemarle assembly in 1670 passed a law that fugitive debtors coming from other colonies could not be sued for debt within five years. Governor Lord Culpeper of Virginia in 1681 informed the Lords of Trade and Plantations that "as regards our neighbours, North Carolina is and always was the sink of America, the refuge of our renegades: and till in better order it is a danger to us." The crown's surveyor general, Edward Randolph, in 1700 commented that the Albemarle area was "a place which receives Pirates, Runaways, and Illegal Traders." There was an absence of churches and church members, except for Quakers, and persons of different races mixed freely and on equal terms. As Hugo P. Leaming (1979) notes, the Albemarle community "was a deviant from the American social norm in race relations in respect to African-Americans as well as Native Americans" (p. 166). Lacking a harbor and cut off northward by the Dismal Swamp, survival depended on subsistence production.

William Byrd II and his companions running the boundary line between North Carolina and Virginia, even as late as 1728, found the Albemarle inhabitants shiftless and depraved. On the south shore of Currituck Inlet, he said,

> dwelt a marooner that modestly called himself a hermit, though he forfeited that name by suffering a wanton female to cohabit with him. His habitation was a bower covered with bark. . . . Like the ravens, he neither plowed nor sowed but subsisted chiefly upon oysters, which his handmaid made a shift to gather from the adjacent rocks. Sometimes, too, for change of diet, he sent her to drive up the neighbor's cows, to moisten their mouths with a little milk. But as for raiment, he depended mostly upon his length of beard and she upon her length of hair, part of which she brought decently forward and the rest dangled behind quite down to her rump, like one of Herodotus's

East Indian Pygmies. Thus did these wretches live in a dirty state of nature and were mere Adamites, innocence only excepted.

The northern part of the Albemarle region contained the Dismal Swamp, which also extended into Virginia. Here was a maroon community that would be of longest duration in American history. White fugitives, escaped slaves, and Indians lived in the inner swamp, which was inaccessible unless the way was known. They subsisted by harvesting corn and other crops on the small patches of land and by hunting, venturing out of the tangled morass only to trade with people living on the border of the swamp.

There were maroon settlements elsewhere in the South. Outliers lived in small groups in the swamps and in the mountains. Frequently members of such bands degenerated into desperadoes. Maroon camps, consisting of hunters, squatters, fugitives, deserters from military service, escaped slaves, and assorted ruffians, appeared in the backcountry of Georgia, the Carolinas, and Virginia, as well as in Florida and the Far Southwest. Bands of runaway slaves, though eventually uprooted, inhabited swamps north and northeast of Savannah and raided plantations. South Carolina vigilantes, known as the Regulators, raided the backcountry from Georgia to Virginia in 1766–1768, dispensing justice to outlaw gangs. Near Mount Airy, North Carolina, the Regulators killed several of the renegades in skirmishes and hanged sixteen prisoners. Thirty more were hanged on the spot or in Charleston. The Regulators recovered more than one hundred stolen horses and thirty-five young girls who had been abducted.

COMMUNITARIANS

Non-English immigrants contributed to the counterculture in early America. Religious groups, such as the early Quakers, European pietists, and separatist Baptists sought new social and moral imperatives. Further on the religious fringe, enthusiasts formed cohesive brotherhoods in search of purification and perfection of faith.

Communitarian utopianism began in North America in 1664 when Pieter Corneliszoon Plockhoy and Dutch Mennonites settled at what is now Lewes, near the mouth of the Delaware River. The commune ended the next year when the British plundered the settlement during the conquest of New Netherland.

The Labadists, disciples of Jean de Labadie (d. 1674), an ex-Jesuit and mystic, in 1684 settled on 3,750 acres of land donated by Augustine Herrman, a Maryland convert. These immigrants from Friesland, the Netherlands, were led by Peter Sluyter and Jasper Dankarts. The new community, at the junction of the Bohemia and Elk rivers where they empty into the Chesapeake, was named Bohemia Manor. Sluyter was the superintendent, though Bohemia Manor, as a mission, was under the direction of the mother church in the Netherlands. The Labadists sought to live hidden in Christ; they held all property in common, kept the sexes segregated, practiced celibacy, took meals in silence, and lived in unheated cells. Agriculture, milling, and trade provided economic support. The colony never numbered more than one hundred men, women, and children. With only eight families remaining in 1698, property was divided among the survivors. Sluyter became a wealthy tobacco planter and slaver and lived until 1722.

In 1691, Johannes Kelpius and Heinrich Bernard Koster brought over from Germany forty followers of Rev. John Jacob Zimmerman, a mystic and Rosicrucian. Kelpius and this group, finding Germantown too worldly, obtained a 175-acre tract from a Philadelphia citizen in a forested area, called the Ridge, along the Wissahickon River, three miles from Germantown. The little band called themselves the Contented of the God-loving Soul but was mainly known as the Woman in the Wilderness, after imagery in the Book of Revelations. The all-male group lived celibate and as hermits. The order gradually disintegrated. Kelpius, who lived in a man-made cave, died in 1708; the last survivor, Conrad Mattai, lived until 1748.

Other German pietist groups experimented more successfully with communitarian living. In 1732, Johann Conrad Beissel, with defectors from the Dunkards (German Baptist Brethren), founded Ephrata, along Cocalico Creek in Lancaster County, Pennsylvania. Soon the group was joined by Mennonites and Brethren. Part of the community was monastic (women and men), and the other was the "outdoor membership." Property was held in common only by the monastic order. A Sister House was built in 1735, and a Brother House three years later. At its height around 1750, Ephrata had about three hundred members (eighty of whom were monks or nuns). The Ephratists operated paper and flour mills, a tannery, and a print shop. The society became famous for its singing schools, music manuscripts, and hymnbooks. Communal life lasted until 1814, when the Pennsylvania General Assembly incorporated the community as the "Society of Seventh Day Baptists of Ephrata" and appointed trustees for the administration of the buildings and lands. Today Ephrata is restored as the Ephrata Cloisters Park.

The Moravians also experimented with communal society. Officially known as the Church of the Brethren (*Unitas Fratrum*), they dated back to the followers of John Huss in the mid-1400s. Forced to flee Bohemia and Moravia, they were successively hounded elsewhere in central Europe. In 1722 a group of Moravians found refuge on the Saxony estate of Count Nicholaus Ludwig von Zinzendorf. In 1734 a small group of these

Moravians settled in Georgia, followed by another band the next year, led by August Gottlieb Spangenberg. With war ensuing between Britain and Spain, the Georgia Moravians in 1740 moved to Pennsylvania, founding the towns of Bethlehem and Nazareth. In 1753, Spangenberg also brought Moravians to North Carolina, establishing Wachovia, which then spread out to Bethany (1754) and Salem (1766). The General Economy was put into effect in Bethlehem in 1744. All lands and property were held in common; there were no wages, and everyone shared in the fruits of the labor. Three buildings housed the flock, one in Nazareth and the other two in Bethlehem, on a sex-segregated basis, even if married. Work and activities were organized in a choir system, according to age, sex, and marital status. All males and female "workers" participated in the Communal Conference, though Zinzendorf, as the "Chief Elder Jesus," maintained almost dictatorial control. The General Economy was dissolved in 1762, and the thirteen hundred members divided the wealth, which amounted to nearly three pounds per person.

Colonial America had at least one dreamer of a secular communitarian utopia. William Gottlieb Priber, a scholar from Saxony, emigrated to South Carolina in 1734. Three years later he went to live among the Cherokees, becoming, by his own words, the Cherokee "secretary of state." Priber dressed in Indian fashion and painted his face. The South Carolina and Georgia governments and white traders thought Priber was interfering too much in the Indian trade, and on grounds of his being a French agent, a military officer at Fort Frederica had him captured. At his confinement at the fort's barracks, as the *South Carolina Gazette* announced in August 1743, Priber was found to be in possession of

> a Book . . . of his own Writing ready for the Press. . . . It demonstrates the Manner in which the Fugitives are to be subsisted, and lays down the Rules of Government which the town is to be governed by; to which he gives the Title of Paradise; He enumerates many whimsical Privileges and natural Rights. . . . The Book is drawn up very methodically, and full of learned Quotations; it is extreamly wicked, yet has several Flights full of Invention; and it is a Pity so much Wit is applied to so bad Purposes.

Although the manuscript on the "Kingdom of Paradise" has never been discovered, other details have been learned of the proposed utopia from French prisoners who had been conversant with Priber. In Paradise there would be no marriage contracts, and children would be raised by the community. There were two fundamentals to be observed: liberty and equality (including economic communism). Priber's Paradise was to be located at the foot of the mountains between Cherokee and Creek territory and would be a receptacle for persons from all nations and Indian tribes. Of course, from the view of the British colonial authorities, Paradise would be no more than a "City of Refuge for all Criminals, Debtors, and Slaves, who would fly thither from Justice or their Masters." Priber, still held at Fort Frederica, died in 1744.

DERANGED CULTISTS

While outlawry and religious communitarianism represented opposite poles in colonial American counterculture, there were also episodes of derangement, suggestive of the "Manson family"–type cult of the 1960s. In South Carolina during the 1720s, the Dutarte family members, descendants of French refugees, thought of themselves as the only people on earth through whom God communicated. Peter Rembert, husband of Peter Dutarte's eldest daughter, declared himself a prophet, commissioned by God to destroy evil mankind and reestablish from the Dutarte seed a new human race. Rembert had a visitation from God in which he was commanded to "put away" his wife and make her sister, Judith, the mother of the new world family. The Dutartes offended the authorities not only by their immorality but also because they would not bear arms as militiamen or do their share of road duty. Yet the Dutartes had no qualms about taking up arms in defense of their family. A shootout between the Dutartes and an arresting party resulted in the death of a justice of the peace and the wounding of several others. Rembert and Peter Dutarte were convicted of murder and hanged. Two young Dutartes, aged eighteen and twenty, showing repentance, were pardoned.

Even more bizarre was the "Weber heresy" that occurred among the Swiss and German settlers of the South Carolina backcountry between 1756 and 1761. Jacob Weber, a Swiss immigrant, had been a successful planter. Distraught by the death of his brother, Weber underwent a religious experience and began preaching to his neighbors. Mesmerized, Weber's followers declared him God; then, to fill out the Trinity, they proclaimed John Smithpeter the Son and a black named Dauber the Holy Ghost. Devastating Indian raids during the Cherokee War provoked frenzy among the cult. The three members of the Trinity quarreled, resulting in the Weberites' smothering Smithpeter in a pit filled with mattresses and killing Dauber by beating him and stomping on his neck. For these crimes Weber was hanged in April 1761; the accessories, however, were pardoned. The Dutarte and Weberite delusions may have stemmed in part from knowledge of Old World fanatic cults, particularly the extreme Anabaptists and, during the late seventeenth century, the Camisards (the French Prophets).

16

Toward the Bill of Rights

The colonial experience reinforced and expanded upon British constitutional guarantees of basic rights and privileges of the individual. Since they emigrated voluntarily as Englishmen and lived under charters granted to them by the king, the colonists regarded themselves as possessing all the liberties of Englishmen. Parliamentary statutes in 1351 and 1708 confirmed that English subjects abroad had all the rights and privileges of Englishmen at home. Americans claimed the full benefit of the Magna Carta (1215), the Petition of Right (1628), and the English Bill of Rights (1689), and they repudiated, as did Englishmen in 1641, justice through special royal courts such as the Star Chamber and the High Commission.

The colonists drew not only on the liberties of Englishmen in establishing constitutional guarantees for the protection of the rights and privileges of citizens but also from what they regarded as their own fundamental law—the royal, corporate, and proprietary charters and the code enactments of their own legislatures. The colonial charters, as Zechariah Chafee, Jr. (1947) has noted, had two types of clauses guaranteeing the colonists the liberties of Englishmen: (1) those granting the customary rights of Englishmen and (2) those requiring that laws enacted conform to the laws of England (statute and common law).

Planting their communities afresh in the New World, the colonists had more affinity for the idea of a fixed constitution than Englishmen of the realm. They also claimed the exclusive right to make their own statute law and the right to determine principles of due process not in conflict with parliamentary law or English common law. Thus Massachusetts's Declaration of 1646, issued by the General Court in reply to the petition of Dr. Robert Child and others advocating limitations on legislative power in the colony, stated: "Our allegiance binds us not to the laws of England any longer than while we live in England . . . nor do the king's writs under the great seal go any further," but English authorities "have no cause to complain, for we have no laws . . . contrary to the law of God and of right reason." Another point of departure in constitutionalism between England and America was the growing conception of natural law, owing to the condition of humankind and not to conferral by crown, legislature, or judiciary.

As colonists became more familiar with the legal technicalities of English jurisprudence, with greater access to English lawbooks and the rise of the legal profession in America, there was a more conscious adoption of English common law (law common to all of England as applied in the courts of King's Bench, Exchequer, and Common Pleas, distinct from legislation and equity law). Legal historians have debated whether or not English common law was substantially in force in the colonies from the beginning. Paul S. Reinsch (1899/1970) and Charles J. Hilkey (1910) have argued that the colonists originally constructed their own primitive and innovative law, improvising rather than following directly English common law. Julius Goebel, Jr. (1931) pointed out that early colonial law was a carry-over of English customary law (administered in the local courts in the counties, towns, boroughs, and manors), with which the colonists had been most familiar in England. The emigrants to America had never had much involvement with litigation or serious crimes tried in the king's courts. Zechariah Chafee, Jr. (1947), however, argues that the colonists were influenced by the "ideas they carried across the Atlantic" (p. 147), and in their lawmaking drew from their general impressions of common law principles, English local law, and knowledge of legal reforms during the Cromwellian period, meanwhile making "homemade law" in response to colonial conditions.

The Plymouth and Massachusetts colonies led the way in the inclusion of statements of rights in their legal codes. The Plymouth Code of 1636, according to George L. Haskins (1969), "contains a rudimentary bill of rights, certainly the first in America" (p. 123). The preamble declared that the settlers, "as freeborne subjects of the State of Engl.," arrived "indewed with all & singular the priviledges belonging to such." Significantly, as to due process, the code guarantees trial by jury in capital cases. The *Lawes and Libertyes* of Massachusetts (1647, published in 1648) and its revision (1671) contain many provisions relating to guarantees of due process of law, including some of the protections listed in the United States Bill of Rights of 1791. The Connecticut Code of 1650 is almost identical to its Massachusetts counterpart.

The study of civil liberty in the colonial period has been neglected. It is important, however, to appraise the breadth of individual freedom in the colonies in the context of the rights and privileges guaranteed in the U.S. Constitution. Protections of due process of law in America at the end of the colonial period paralleled those of English common law. Freedom of expression, however, achieved broader latitude than in England.

FREEDOM OF RELIGION

The status of religious freedom in the colonies can be described as one that tolerated religious beliefs but also allowed, in some areas, church establishment (mainly characterized by tax support of preferred religions) and political disabilities, at least officially, for Catholics, Jews, and certain dissenters. Severe persecution on behalf of religious conformity was almost entirely limited to the early history of the Massachusetts Bay colony, with the banishment of Roger Williams, Anne Hutchinson, and others in the 1630s and 1640s and the brutality (including imprisonment and whipping) visited chiefly on Baptists and Quakers. The Quakers briefly underwent some repression in Virginia, including imprisonment, and in that colony, on the eve of the Revolution, thirty-four Baptist preachers were jailed for not securing licenses to hold services. In Connecticut during the early 1700s, Baptists on several occasions were imprisoned for violating a law prohibiting any baptismal service not presided over by a licensed minister. In New York in 1707, Governor Lord Cornbury jailed two Presbyterian ministers for preaching without a license; the trial of one of whom, Francis Makemie, ending in acquittal, proved to be a landmark case for religious toleration in New York. The Quakers stand alone as martyrs for the cause of religious liberty in English mainland North America. Quakers were banished upon pain of death from Puritan Massachusetts. They were imprisoned in unheated shelters during wintertime. Four who violated their sentences of banishment were hanged. The harshness of penalties against Quakers in Massachusetts, however, was short-lived; in 1661, Charles II ordered the suspension of the death penalty on religious grounds. The witchcraft executions in seventeenth-century New England, however, may be viewed in the context of punishing the ultimate heresy— allegiance to the Devil.

Important to the development of religious freedom was the absence of church punitive jurisdiction over citizens (other than sanctions of churches on their own members). Unlike in England, ecclesiastical law and courts did not exist in any of the colonies. Also, American clergymen enjoyed no exemptions from application of the laws. Even in Puritan New England, though churches were approved by the state and in early Massachusetts freemen had to be church members, each congregation determined its own membership, doctrine, worship, and discipline. New England ministers were by custom generally excluded from holding public office, and this was much the same elsewhere, though in Virginia prominent clergymen, namely the Anglican commissary, sat on the council.

The founding of Rhode Island, New Hampshire, Pennsylvania-Delaware, and Maryland had as the leitmotif the offering of sanctuary to persons distressed on account of religion. From the Restoration period onward, colonial governments and proprietors invited and welcomed as immigrants disparate groups of ethnic Protestants, which made for a religious pluralism that enhanced toleration. Roger Williams's Rhode Island had led the way in providing for religious freedom, a policy confirmed by the 1663 charter: "No person within the said colony . . . shall be in any wise molested, punished, disquieted or called in question, for any differences in opinion in matters of religion, and do not actually disturb the civil peace of our said society." In the eighteenth century, however, even Rhode Island succumbed to denying citizenship and eligibility to public office to Jews and Catholics.

The charters of Carolina, West Jersey, Pennsylvania, Maryland, and Georgia carried provisions for granting liberty of conscience, though in Georgia "Papists" were excepted. Subsequent documents issued by the proprietors of Carolina, East Jersey, West Jersey, and Pennsylvania reaffirmed religious freedom. The Maryland Toleration Act of 1649, though in force briefly, underscored freedom for all Christians, if not for others. Ironically, in Maryland, where most of the Catholics resided, Catholics were forbidden to hold office. In 1692 in that colony they could not act as attorneys, and in 1718 they were disfranchised. The Maryland Act to Prevent the Growth of Popery (1764) prohibited Catholic worship and priests from making converts or baptizing children except of Catholic parents.

Most colonies where the Anglican church was established abided by Parliament's Act of Toleration of 1689, though not reenacting it (Virginia did, however, in 1748). Under the Toleration Act, Christians were to be unmolested in attending their own services, on condition that preaching be conducted at registered places and that tithes be paid for the support of the established church. Various other factors contributed toward the reality of religious toleration, if not full religious freedom: the plentifulness of open country; the proliferation of religious denominations; the material and secular emphasis in society, aided by commercial pursuit; ecumenical and democratic attitudes and a social consciousness engendered by the Great Awakening; the influence of writers such as John Locke and

Enlightenment figures versus coerced belief; and the lack of a central disciplining means for the Anglican church in the colonies. A people on the move made for scarcity of churches and clergy.

Rhode Island, New Jersey, and Pennsylvania-Delaware had no church-state ties, and elsewhere the religious establishments were frail. Religious establishment in the colonies had its beginnings in Virginia under the first charter (1606), which stipulated that ministers must preach according to the "doctrine, rites, and religion now professed and established within the realm of England." Subsequent laws provided for maintenance of every Anglican minister from tithes collected from the public, and special taxes were raised for erecting and repairing of churches; only Anglican clergymen could perform marriages. The eventual trend in the New England colonies was the multiple establishment of religion, namely, leaving to local option which minister and denomination were to be supported by public revenue. The Duke's Laws (1665) and the Charter of Liberties (1683) in New York allowed for this arrangement. In 1693 the New York Ministry Act established the Church of England in four counties: New York, Westchester, Kings, and Queens. In Georgia the Anglican church was not established until 1758.

In the multiple establishment of New Hampshire, public funds were divided among sixty-six churches by 1765. Even though Congregationalism enjoyed the preference in the church establishments of Massachusetts and Connecticut, the practice there too was to allow communities to decide which church to support; of course, when Congregationalists were in the minority, allowance was made for a dual establishment, including the Congregational church. When Quakers and Baptists were in the majority at a Massachusetts locality, they refused to pay tax assessments for support of religion. Interestingly, the Boston churches received no support from tax funds, being amply supplied with voluntary contributions. Though the Revolutionary War ended Anglican-state ties, multiple establishments continued in Massachusetts, Connecticut, and New Hampshire. The Virginia General Assembly in the 1780s only narrowly defeated a general assessment law in support of a multiple establishment.

SPEECH

Colonists wagging their tongues could get into trouble for inappropriate and malicious speech. Three types of civil offenses for slander were recognized under English common law: "theft" of reputation; lying, thereby robbing a situation of its truth; and engaging in an abusive verbal style. The colonies meted out such punishment for defamation as fines, public humiliation (for example, wearing a "Clefte stick" on one's tongue or wearing a placard noting the slander), and corporal punishment—

stocks, whipping, and, in the case of women who were adjudged "common scolds," ducking. At Jamestown in 1624, Richard Barnes, convicted of slandering the governor, had his weapons taken away and broken; had his tongue bored through with an awl; was forced to run a gauntlet of forty men, at the head of which he was "kicked downe and footed out of the fort"; was banished from Jamestown; was stripped of citizenship rights; and had to post bond of two hundred pounds for good behavior.

Eventually in the colonies the authorities took a less active role in regard to private slander and left judgment to civil suits for damages. The history of defamation suits in the colonies is intriguing and sheds light on personal and community relations. Although plaintiffs usually won their cases, little material recovery for damages resulted—the restoration of reputation was considered sufficient reward. Defamation suits frequently involved women. As Mary Beth Norton (1987) notes in a study of two thousand cases in seventeenth-century Maryland, since women could not vote, hold office, serve as jurors, or engage in other such civic activity, gossip for them was "an essential tool, perhaps the most valuable and reliable means of advancing or protecting their own interests" (p. 6). Norton finds that women appeared as litigants or witnesses in 54.5 percent of the defamation suits, though they made up less than one-third of Maryland's population. Defamation suits declined in the colonies because courts were reluctant to award full court costs to successful plaintiffs and, with the adoption of complex English defamation law, cases required lengthy preparation by lawyers.

Except for Rhode Island, all the colonies had laws against blasphemy. Such restriction first appeared in Virginia's early Dale Code, which prescribed the death penalty for anyone who spoke against the Trinity or "the Knowne Articles of the Christian Faith." Though the death penalty was removed in Virginia, other colonies (Massachusetts, Maryland, and New Haven) made blasphemy a capital crime. A 1782 Massachusetts statute, which omitted the death penalty, declared that a blasphemer be punished "by Imprisonment not exceeding Twelve Months, by sitting in the Pillory, by Whipping, or sitting on the Gallows with a Rope about the Neck, or binding to the good Behaviour, at the discretion of the Supreme Judicial Court." As late as 1977 the Massachusetts state legislature refused to remove blasphemy as a punishable offense.

Swearing or cursing was considered such a serious crime because, as Robert St. George (1984) observes, "the speaker was promising to control the will of God in attempting to execute against other men judgments reserved in the Old Testament (Deuteronomy 28:15–20) for His wisdom alone" (p. 287). No one was executed for blasphemy in the colonies, but Samuel Gorton in Puritan Massachusetts barely escaped the penalty; he was imprisoned and banished.

As society became less religiously based, efforts were made to define blasphemy as a secular offense, which, however, still posed the problem of fusing Christianity with the common law. Blasphemy prosecutions declined in the eighteenth century, with only about a half dozen convictions in all the colonies. As Leonard W. Levy (1981) notes, the worst case of that time was that of a Maryland sea captain who committed blasphemy when hot pitch was poured on his foot; his sentence was a twenty-pound fine, having his tongue bored through three times, and one year in prison.

The last conviction for blasphemy in Massachusetts was that of Abner Kneeland (1833–1838), whose sentence was upheld on appeal; prosecutions for this offense, however, occurred until the 1920s. There have been several blasphemy cases in recent times: A Maryland conviction in 1968 was reversed on appeal, and prosecutions for a case in Delaware (1968) and one in Pennsylvania (1971) were eventually dropped.

Passing and heated remarks disparaging officials, judges, and the assemblies were only a fine line away from seditious libel. Early records of the colonies are filled with persons held to account for uttering scandalous speech against persons in authority. Some offenders were punished severely; for example, Phillip Ratliffe in Massachusetts in 1631 was whipped, had his ears cut, and was branded "for mallitious and scandalous speeches" against the government and the Salem church. In Virginia after Bacon's Rebellion, the law prescribed the maximum penalty of one year in prison and a fine of not more than five hundred pounds for defamation of the governor; for slander of councilors, judges, and other "principal officers," imprisonment of three months and a fine of not more than one hundred pounds. Legislatures frequently conducted their own proceedings against persons who impugned the integrity of individual members or the legislature as a whole. Offenders were brought into the lower house of assembly to seek forgiveness on bended knee and were assessed all costs. Contempt of court usually brought any combination of a public apology, fine, imprisonment, or standing one or two hours in the stocks.

The more serious kind of disparagement of authority was seditious libel. As defined by Zechariah Chafee, Jr. (1967), sedition "applied to practices which tend to disturb internal public tranquility by deed, word, or writing, but which do not amount to treason and are not accompanied by or conducive to open violence" (p. 497). Under English common law any words that maligned a government official, irrespective of truth or falsity, could be construed as seditious libel. Indeed, if the words uttered were true, it was considered that there was the greater danger of breach of the peace. Thus John Wheelwright was convicted for the seditious intent of his fast-day sermon in March 1637, as was Anne Hutchinson for her remarks, though she criticized the ministers rather than the magistrates. Most prosecutions for oral expressions against authority in the colonies were considered contempt and slander rather than seditious libel.

It is important to note that falsehood had to be proved for conviction of slander, but not seditious libel.

PRESS

The issues colonists faced pertaining to written and published seditious libel were whether government could exercise prior restraint through licensing and other advance censure and, if allowing no prior restraint, whether there was any latitude for criticizing constituted authority. The common law followed the no-prior-restraint doctrine but provided criminal liability for any written blame of government, public officials, laws, or any institution established by law.

In 1543, Parliament acknowledged the right of the crown to regulate the press and other means of public communication. The Star Chamber passed its first ordinance for regulating printing by licensing in 1586. A Star Chamber decree in 1637 ordered that licensed books had to bear the imprimatur of chief justices (law), a secretary of state (history and the like), or the archbishop of Canterbury, the bishop of London, or chancellors of universities (most other publications). No book in English could be imported. The severe penalties imposed upon John Lilburne for publishing and importing heretical and seditious books during the 1630s influenced Parliament to abolish the Star Chamber in 1641. John Milton, in his *Areopagitica* (1644), gave a ringing defense of the complete freedom of the press. It was "as good almost to kill a man," Milton declared, "as kill a good book; who kills a man kills a reasonable creature, God's image; but he who destroys a good book kills reason itself." The Cromwellian government nevertheless continued restrictions on publishing. After the Restoration, Parliament passed the Licensing Act (1662) "for preventing abuses in printing seditious, treasonable, and unlicensed books and pamphlets, and for regulating of printing and printing presses." Though the Licensing Act expired in 1695, publication still came under the strict constraints of common law provisions against seditious libel. Sir William Blackstone, in his *Commentaries on the Laws of England* (1765–1769), stated the position held by the courts: that, although there might be no prior restraint, there was

> no freedom from censure for criminal matter when published. . . . To punish (as the law does at present) any dangerous or offensive writings, which, when published, shall on a fair and impartial trial be adjudged of a pernicious tendency, is necessary for the preservation of peace and good order, of government and religion, the only solid foundations of civil liberty.

Truth was not a defense in any way against a charge of seditious libel.

Except in Massachusetts, during the seventeenth century not much thought was given to printed seditious libel. By the 1690s there were only two or three printing presses in Boston and one each in Cambridge, Massachusetts, Philadelphia, New York, and St. Mary's, Maryland. Printing was forbidden in Virginia as late as 1693, and that colony did not have an established press until 1730. Governor William Berkeley in 1671 had prophetically said

> I thank God, there are no free schools nor *printing*, and I hope we shall not have these hundred years, for learning has brought disobedience, and heresy, and sects into the world, and *printing* has divulged them, and libels against the best government. God help us from both.

Massachusetts, which had its first press in 1639 at Cambridge, witnessed censorship of materials imported from England as well as those printed in the colony. In 1652 a resident of Springfield, William Pynchon, had his book, *The Meritorious Price of Our Redemption* (published in England), burned by the executioner, and books owned by Quakers later met the same fate. Rev. John Eliot in 1661 was forced to retract his book, *The Christian Commonwealth* (1659). Massachusetts had its first censorship law in 1662; it stated that nothing could be printed unless approved by a special committee and the council. In 1667 licenses were required for books, and printer Samuel Green was convicted for neglecting this condition. Edmund Andros, governor of the Dominion of New England, also established a censorship committee. Benjamin Harris's news sheet, *Publick Occurrences, Both Forreign and Domestick*, September 15, 1690, printed by Richard Pierce in Boston, startled citizens by its criticism of the governor's policy toward the Indians. The governor and council issued a broadside declaring their "high resentment and disallowance" and prohibiting any further publication unless with a license. Royal instructions to Governor William Phips in 1692 ordered the governor to control the press. Afterward, into the eighteenth century, Massachusetts had several prosecutions for printed seditious libel.

Newspapers, published on a regular basis and reaching a wider audience than books or pamphlets, posed a graver threat of criticism of government and officials. It is no wonder that most printing presses publishing newspapers were located in the colonial capitals and depended on financial support from printing government records. The first continuing newspaper, the *Boston News-Letter*, beginning in 1704, was "published by authority." William Bradford, who was jailed for seditious libel in Philadelphia, moved to New York, where he served as the king's printer from 1693 to 1744; he began publishing the *New-York Gazette* in 1725 as an organ for government views. James Franklin was one who offended government in Massachusetts when his *New England Courant* in 1722 accused the governor of not going after pirates off the coast of New England. Franklin was jailed for several weeks, but when tried for seditious libel, he was acquitted.

The Zenger case in New York paved a narrow path for the use of newspapers to wage political warfare. During the delay in the arrival of William Cosby (appointed governor in 1731) for more than a year, Rip Van Dam, senior councilor and acting governor, kept for himself one-half of the governor's salary. Cosby brought suit for the whole salary, but Chief Justice Lewis Morris threw the case out of court. Dismissed by Cosby, Morris ran for a seat in the assembly, only to find that the governor had rigged the election. Morris and other opponents of the governor hired John Peter Zenger, an assistant to William Bradford, to establish the *New-York Weekly Journal,* which began publication in November 1733 as a competitor to the government's *New-York Gazette.* Lewis meanwhile went to London to try to get Cosby recalled. Zenger's newspaper attacked the malfeasance and corruption of the Cosby administration and the governor's allies, the De Lancey–led political faction. For example, one item stated:

> A Governor turns rogue, does a thousand things for which a small rogue would have deserved a halter, and because it is difficult if not impracticable to obtain relief against him, therefore it is prudent to keep in with him and join in the roguery.

Zenger was arrested and imprisoned awaiting trial for a charge of seditious libel. Under English common law, the printer and not the author was held responsible for a libelous offense. James Alexander, William Smith, and a noted Philadelphia lawyer, Andrew Hamilton, acted as Zenger's defense counsel. The unsung hero is Alexander, who wrote most of the essays critical of Cosby in the newspaper and who also wrote the brief in the case. The jury returned a verdict of not guilty on grounds, departing from the common law, that truth was a defense against a charge of seditious libel. Significantly, however, defense counsel during the trial did not attack seditious libel as a criminal offense, and the acquittal came only to be an important precedent in allowing founded criticism of the governor, not the colonial assembly.

The limited effect of the Zenger trial on gaining freedom of the press is seen in the arrest of Alexander McDougall, a New York merchant and leader of the Sons of Liberty, in 1770 for seditious libel. The previous year McDougall had written a handbill, "To the Betrayed Inhabitants of New York," criticizing the legislature for having voted provisions for the king's troops. James Parker, the printer, fearing loss of his post office position, identified McDougall as the author. McDougall refused to go bail and was held in jail incommunicado for two and one-half months by order of the assembly; though he was eventually indicted by a grand jury, the death of the leading prosecution witness, Parker, forced his release. Still, a full freedom of the press to question the actions of all branches of government had to await later times.

ASSEMBLING

The colonists paid little heed to persons peaceably assembling except in regard to slaves. They also recognized the freedom of association, though attempting some restrictions as to religion and personal behavior. For unlawful assembly, the colonists accepted the threefold English common law definition: illegal assembly for an illegal purpose against the peace even if nothing is accomplished in pursuance of that purpose; rout, an assembly proceeding on that purpose; and riot, executing that purpose.

Spontaneous riots, usually sanctioned by a community as a whole, were not uncommon in urban areas. Officials had difficulty quieting riots because they lacked an adequate police body. When a mob was assembled from the general population, the militia could not be relied on, and actions by sheriffs, deputy sheriffs, and constables could be effective only when communities were willing to have order restored.

Riots that caused destruction of property and aimed at nullifying a colonial law or policy, however, were a different matter and were usually viewed as having insurrectionary overtones. The Virginia tobacco-cutting riots of 1682, which began in Gloucester County and spread to neighboring counties, destroyed crops on more than two hundred plantations. The purpose was to produce through scarcity a rise in tobacco prices. After three months militia patrols brought an end to the spree; two of the tobacco cutters were hanged. Rioting continued intermittently in New Jersey from 1745 to 1755 over settlers disputing proprietary claims to ownership of land in the Elizabethtown Purchase and Monmouth Purchase tracts. Mobs freed prisoners from jail, grand juries refused to indict, and trial juries refused to convict. In 1748 the New Jersey legislature reenacted the English Riot Act (1714), which provided that anyone in a group of twelve or more persons unlawfully assembled for the purpose of disturbing the peace, who refused to disperse after being "read the Riot Act" by a local official and continued to assemble for an hour afterward, was guilty of capital felony. Tensions in New Jersey finally eased when proprietors lessened efforts to have persons arraigned for trespassing. Land disputes along the New York–Massachusetts border during the 1750s and 1760s brought violence. Robert Livingston claimed much of the contested territory as part of his manorial estate, while Massachusetts gave land titles to settlers in the same area. Tenants refused to pay rents to Livingston, and bands for both sides sought to take the law into their own hands.

Elsewhere, in Dutchess County, New York, tenants on the estates of the large landlords rioted, seeking to remove themselves from tenant status and gain full title to their farms. In June 1766 "levelers" appeared with firearms at Poughkeepsie, led by William Prendergast. The uprising was quelled, and about seventy rioters were punished by fines, the pillory, and imprisonment. Prendergast was convicted of high treason in Albany, but the governor, in response to a plea by Prendergast's wife, granted him clemency.

PETITION FOR REDRESS

The right to petition government for the redress of grievances is integral to that of representation. For a people to be truly represented, channels for communication at all levels of government need to be kept open between constituents and the elected and appointed officials. In early Massachusetts, Governor John Winthrop, however, did not have much respect for freemen airing grievances against the magistrates. All eighty-one persons from the town of Hingham who petitioned the General Court in protest of the governor's interference with a militia election were fined for making "false and scandalous" challenges to political authority. But this action notwithstanding, citizens and even nonfreemen were guaranteed the right to be heard by the Massachusetts *Lawes and Liberties* of 1648:

> Everie man whether Inhabitant or Forreiner, Free or not Free shall have libertie to come to any publick Court, Counsell, or Town-meeting; and either by speech or writing, to move any lawfull, seasonable, or material question; or to present any necessarie motion, complaint, petition, bill or information.

Most colonies had legislative standing committees to receive petitions. By 1663 in Virginia it was the custom for persons to submit petitions to the House of Burgesses through the burgesses who represented them. Because of the large number of petitions, however, the General Assembly in 1680 ordered that a county sheriff appoint a time and place to receive petitions, which then had to be signed by the clerk or presiding judge of the county court. To withhold petitions was cause for contempt of the General Assembly. Infrequently, petitions were addressed to colonial councils in legislative matters; petitions to governors mainly concerned requests for the reduction of court sentences.

Petitions, memorials, and remonstrances could be sent to the king in council, a privilege exercised mainly by colonial legislatures. Chapter 5 of the English Bill of Rights of 1689 reaffirmed "That it is the right of the Subjects to petition the king and all Committments and prosecutions for such petitioning are illegal." Documents for the attention of the king in council had to be sent through the secretary of state for the Southern Department. One petition to the king, which contained 309 signatures of the Elizabethtown, New Jersey, "Associates," was read in the Privy Council in 1744, but no action was taken. Typically, a reply from the king came to the governor, who then transmitted it to the assembly.

The colonists could also petition Parliament, but only a member of that body could turn over a petition to the House of Commons. Because of distance and the need to have persons in direct contact with members of Parliament, by the end of the seventeenth century it was becoming a common practice for colonies to have their own agents residing in London. These agents channeled petitions from the colonies to the House of Commons, where a clerk read a summary of the document and, if the Commons agreed, then presented it in its entirety. In the House of Lords, an agent could either be heard personally or be represented by counsel.

MILITIA AND THE BEARING OF ARMS

The insistence on the right to bear arms and the necessity of a citizen army had deep roots in English history. As Helen H. Miller (1965) writes:

> Down the centuries, a conviction that for the defense of liberty a militia was far sounder than a professional force had been ingrained in the English yeoman. He was sturdily opposed to standing armies in peacetime; he had observed that the military all too easily became makers of kings, initiators of policy, independent repositories of power. He was proud that the eyes and arms of the longbowmen of Agincourt were trained in the butts of England's villages, proving that a citizen army was not only a constitutionally sound defense but a militarily effective one as well. Conviction that the common man had a right to keep and bear arms came to the New World with its English settlers. (p. 68)

The right to bear arms was even more essential to the early Americans, who needed weapons for sustenance and for defense against danger from Indians and foreign enemies.

The American colonists also carried with them from England the idea of compulsory military training of a citizen militia. Before the Revolutionary War, all the colonies except Pennsylvania required collective exercise in arms. Males between the ages of sixteen and sixty were required to enroll in militia units and to attend musters and training. In early Massachusetts militiamen had to drill every Saturday, but generally throughout the colonies it became the practice to have only annual militia training days.

Lessons from the efforts of the Stuart kings to keep standing armies in peacetime were not lost on the colonists, and they agreed with the injunction in the English Bill of Rights prohibiting the king from raising an army in peacetime without the consent of Parliament. The militia in America, as Lawrence D. Cress (1982) observes, had an important constitutional role:

> [It] had the dual function of maintaining civil order while ensuring that the demand for domestic order did not become a disguise for tyranny. As long as the local militia held the power to prevent the colonial authorities from pursuing a policy contrary to the public interest, the exercise of civil and military authority at the provincial level could not be abused. (p. 9)

QUARTERING OF TROOPS

Provision for lodging and board of the king's troops without legislative consent and the requiring of citizens against their will to supply these amenities were denied in England and America. The Petition of Right of 1628 stated "That no man hereafter be compelled to make or yield any gift, loan, benevolence, tax, or such-like charge, without common consent by act of parliament." The Anti-Quartering Act of 1679 stipulated that no civil or military official "nor any other person" could "quarter or billet" any soldiers "upon any subject of this realm" without "his consent" and that it was "lawful for every such subject and inhabitant to refuse to sojourne or quarter any souldier or souldiers." The Bill of Rights of 1689 also prohibited quartering troops "contrary to law." The Mutiny Act of 1689 stated that soldiers on the move or in areas without barracks could be put up in inns and public houses. This act, however, did not extend to the American colonies. The first legal declaration on the subject in the colonies was in the New York Charter of Liberties (1683), which said that in peacetime no citizen could be forced against his will to billet troops in his home. Similar measures passed by other colonial legislatures did permit quartering in inns and public houses. What is important is that colonial assemblies, and not Parliament, were making the decisions as to the support of the king's troops.

Not until the French and Indian War, when there were large numbers of British troops in the colonies, was there any major controversy over quartering. The English secretary of state for the Southern Department ordered that for the Braddock expedition "quarters must be taken in the plantations as they are in England in the time of war." Problems that beset quartering of English troops in America were the insufficiency in number of barracks, inns, and other public houses and the reluctance of city corporations and legislatures to act quickly enough to authorize the securing of provisions and lodging. The crown offered reimbursement for supplies voted by a legislature and per diem allowances for innkeepers and the like (usually one shilling per officer and four pence per common soldier). General Lord Loudoun, the British commander in chief in America, intimidated Pennsylvanians by indicating that he would send Major General Daniel Webb into Philadelphia to commandeer quarters by force if necessary. He used the same tactic in New York City and Albany. In the latter city, from where Loudoun intended to stage operations against Canada, he forced billeting in private homes on a temporary basis until he completed construction of barracks. After the war, Parliament's extension of the Mutiny Act to the colonies (1765) had the effect of turning what had been largely a fiscal issue into a question of encroachment on colonial legislative autonomy.

SEARCH AND SEIZURE

The right to privacy, including the security of one's own home, was recognized in America as it was in England. During the early colonial period, when intimacy among neighbors prevailed, settlers were more apprehensive about intrusion into their communities than into their individual privacy. Yet the colonists believed in the ancient maxim that "a man's house is his castle." Everywhere there were stiff penalties for breaking and entering upon property belonging to other persons. Eavesdroppers and peeping Toms were punished usually by posting bond for good behavior or by church discipline.

The colonies did allow for forcible entry of houses and buildings by officials in search of contraband, but only under strict conditions. Increasingly, warrants were required for search and seizure, based on probable cause as to what goods might be illicitly possessed. English common law allowed entry and seizure almost exclusively in quest of stolen goods. But statute law, like earlier royal court decrees, modified traditional common law prescriptions governing search and seizure. The English Act of Frauds of 1662 stated that it was lawful for anyone,

> authorized by Writ of Assistance under the Seal of his Majesty's Court of Exchequer, to take a Constable, Headborough or other Public Officer inhabiting near unto the Place, and in the Daytime to enter, and go into any House, Shop, Cellar, Warehouse or Room, or other Place, and in Case of Resistance, to break open Doors, Chests, Trunks and other Package, there to seize . . . any Kind of Goods or Merchandize whatsoever, prohibited and uncustomed, and to put and secure the same in his Majesty's Store-house, in the Port next to the Place where such Seizure shall be made.

The Act of Frauds of 1696 extended these powers to America, but in actuality it was not until the 1750s that such customs enforcement through general warrants and writs of assistance was used in the colonies. With the colonies lacking special courts of exchequer, it was assumed that the highest court of a colony could exercise the authority in permitting customs officials to employ general warrants and writs of assistance. In 1755 the British government gave instructions for the use of writs of assistance in Massachusetts, which the Superior Court of Judicature approved. Thus customs officials could compel constables and other local or colony officers to assist in entering private warehouses and homes in search of uncustomed goods. Bostonians complained primarily because these sanctions against smuggling did not apply in Rhode Island at the time.

Court approval of the use of writs of assistance had to be renewed within six months after the death of a sovereign. Thus when George II died on October 25, 1760, merchants saw the opportunity to prevent further use of writs of assistance. Sixty-three merchants petitioned the Superior Court to deny the authorization. What followed was the famous "writs of assistance" case. James Otis, Jr., the leading counsel for the merchants, was perhaps partly motivated by a desire to even the score with Thomas Hutchinson, who had been appointed chief justice over his father, who had been promised the position. Jeremiah Gridley, the crown's counsel, pointed out that a nation had the right to protect itself and that it was necessary to have speedy collection of taxes. Otis argued that a law of Parliament, such as the Acts of Fraud, could not transcend fundamental and natural liberties guaranteed by the English constitution—"inherent, unalienable, and indefeasible" rights of men who had been "drawn together in society" for "the mutual defence and security of each individual's right to life, liberty, and property." Thus "no acts of Parliament can establish such a writ . . . An act against the constitution is void." Though Otis did not win his case, the theory that natural rights were above Parliament or other man-made law became seeded in the American political consciousness.

JURY TRIALS

The colonists sought to follow English common law for fair treatment and trial in the courts of justice, what has come to be known as the "due process of law." The phrase first appeared in a parliamentary statute of 1354, and after several centuries it became generally associated with Chapter 39 of the Magna Carta (signed by King John in 1215), which said that no one would be deprived of life, liberty, or property except by judgment of one's peers or by law of the land. Due process has been categorized as being of two kinds: procedural (right to trial by one's peers) and substantive (protection in the judicial process of one's right to life, liberty, and property). The Virginia governor and council in the 1620s recognized that due process affected arrest, examination, indictment or presentment, bail, trial, judgment, and execution of a sentence.

The colonies adopted in varied form, mainly with respect to size, the use of grand and petit juries as known in England. By Tudor times petit juries in England had evolved from bodies for the discovery of local events to panels passively receiving and evaluating evidence. In the early American colonies the practice of using juries varied. New Haven colony had no juries, even for capital crimes, nor did New Netherland, which functioned under Roman law. Several colonies used juries only for capital cases.

The first law recorded in New England (Plymouth, December 1623) ordered that "all Criminall facts, and also all [matters] of trespasses and debts between man and man should [be tried] by the verdict of twelve Honest men to be Impanelled by Authority in forme of a Jury upon their oaths." The Virginia General Assembly in 1642 resolved that there should be a jury trial "in all criminal and civil causes where it shall be demanded." For capital trials held at Jamestown (and later at Williamsburg), it was provided that six jurors should be summoned from the neighborhood where the crime was committed and the remaining jurors from bystanders at the court. Colonial juries generally had more leeway than in England or even in subsequent American history; if evidence was obscure, juries could direct a special verdict, with judgment left to the bench. Colonial juries could also decide on law as well as fact.

The most volatile judicial controversy regarding trial by jury in colonial America centered on the case of *Forsey* v. *Cunningham* in 1764, which affirmed that in a case tried by a jury, the facts could not be retried by a higher tribunal. It was the accepted practice, in the colonies as well as in England, that jury verdicts in civil cases could be appealed only on grounds of possible error in the proceedings. In the New York case, Thomas Forsey brought a suit for damages for assault committed upon him by Waddell Cunningham. A jury awarded Forsey fifteen hundred pounds. Cunningham sought to get a review of the facts in the case from the New York supreme court (governor and councilors). Lieutenant Governor Cadwallader Colden, serving as governor, ordered that the appeal should be heard—an action resisted by Chief Justice Daniel Horsmanden and the other councilors. Colden tried to get Horsmanden and the other judges removed. The supreme court denied Cunningham's appeal as well as permission for him to carry his cause to the king in council. Colden himself forwarded Cunningham's petition to the Board of Trade. Meanwhile the controversy became a heated issue among the people of New York, and the legal communities of New York, New Jersey, and Pennsylvania rallied against any appeal. The New York assembly censured Colden. Finally, the Board of Trade found against an appeal and upheld the view that only on the basis of error could there be an inquiry into a jury's verdict in a civil suit.

COUNSEL

Although scant attention was paid to the right to counsel in the seventeenth century, the colonies permitted it to a limited extent while also expanding on English common law procedure. Common law permitted defense counsel only for civil and misdemeanor cases and not for felony trials; on appeal, however, it was allowed for all cases. The English Treason Act of 1695 provided for counsel in treason cases.

Several colonial legislatures established guarantees for the right of counsel. The Massachusetts Body of Liberties of 1641 stated:

> Every man that findeth himselfe unfit to plead his owne cause in any Court shall have Libertie to imploy any man against whom the Court doth not except, to helpe him, Provided he give him noe fee or reward for his paines. This shall not exempt the partie him selfe from Answering such Questions in person as the Court shall thinke meete to demand of him.

The Pennsylvania Charter of Liberties of 1701 declared that "all criminals shall have the same Privileges of Witnesses and Council as their Prosecutors." By the Revolution, some colonies permitted counsel in felony cases—a shift from English practice, which did not recognize counsel in felony trials until 1836. In most colonies, counsel could only intercede on points of law. In Virginia, defense counsel in capital cases could not conduct a cross-examination or address the jury.

The rise of a law profession made use of counsel more prevalent. Throughout the seventeenth century, however, there were only a few trained lawyers, and these were looked on as undesirable persons. Of the sixty-five men who landed at Plymouth in 1620, none was an attorney, and there were no practicing lawyers among the early settlers of Massachusetts. The law profession was held in low repute until well into the eighteenth century. Merchants considered attorneys rivals for political power, and small landholders and proprietors alike feared that lawyers would find flaws in property claims. The denial of fees to counsel in the early colonial period also deterred representation by trained lawyers. But there were breakthroughs encouraging the use of legal counsel. Massachusetts in 1673 permitted lawyers to sue in the name of their clients instead of in their own names—a departure from English practice; in 1683 the colony recognized a professional bar by admitting attorneys to practice in the courts upon taking an attorney's oath. Other colonies followed suit in licensing attorneys; Virginia's licensing act of 1680, however, was repealed ten years later and not reinstated until 1732. A number of well-to-do Americans, especially in the Chesapeake colonies, studied at the Inns of Court in London, but rather than becoming barristers they simply applied knowledge of the law on their own behalf in suits before the courts.

INCRIMINATION, RECOGNIZANCE, AND PUNISHMENT

In the colonies, conviction for a felony relied, in accordance with biblical as well as English law, on the testimony of two or more witnesses or the confession of the accused. Generally, the right to confront witnesses was recognized, at least in capital cases. Witnesses in noncapital cases who lived at a distance or were in some way incapacitated could send in depositions rather than appear in court.

The privilege against self-incrimination had gained acceptance in seventeenth-century England. A clerk of the Privy Council in 1590 noted, "For a man to accuse himself was and is utterlie inhibited by Magna Carta." When Parliament abolished the Star Chamber and High Commission courts, it also outlawed the use of the oath ex officio, whereby an accused person had to take an oath to answer all questions truthfully without learning the identity of his accusers or the nature of the allegation; anyone who refused the oath was presumed guilty.

Even though Virginia, Maryland, and New England were founded before the dismantling of the Star Chamber and the High Commission, the colonists never seemed to have adopted the use of oaths ex officio. Some colonial codes were silent regarding immunity against self-incrimination. The general assembly of Virginia in 1677 declared that no law could force a person to testify against himself in cases where convictions could result in corporal punishment. Generally, in the colonies the accused could be questioned during preliminary examinations but not under oath. A form of forced incrimination of others, however, was the threatening of an accused with a harsher penalty if he did not testify against persons involved in the same crime; the New York slave conspiracy trials of 1741 are good examples. Torture could not be used to compel a person to confess, though it was allowable in Massachusetts after conviction, as stated in the Body of Liberties of 1641:

> No man shall be forced by Torture to confesse any Crime against himselfe nor any other unlesse it be in some Capitall case where he is first fullie convicted . . . After which if the cause be of that nature, That it is very apparent that there be other conspirators, or confederates with him, then he may be tortured, yet not with such Torture as be Barbarous and inhumane.

Massachusetts seems not to have implemented the provision concerning the coercion of a convicted person to testify against confederates except during the Salem witch trials. At that time John Proctor, one of the accused witches, reported cases where there were "young men who would not confess anything till they tied their neck and heels till the blood was ready to come out of them."

It was a rare occasion, however, for colonial courts in criminal trials to stretch the law of evidence involving testimony from witnesses. Such an instance was the admission of spectral evidence during the Salem witch trials. Several cases in the New Haven colony even pushed the kind of testimony used beyond credulity. Regarding the case of George Spencer, writes John M. Murrin (1984):

> One foul day a local sow inconsiderately gave birth to a deformed piglet whose single eye and awkward protrusion from its head like unto "a mans instrument of generation" oddly reminded the good people of New Haven of George Spencer.

The piglet as a witness and the confession of the accused led to Spencer's conviction and execution for bestiality. Shortly afterward, Murrin notes:

> The next abominable piglet resembled a fellow named (what else?) Thomas Hogg, an unfortunate man bent over with his hernia, his genitals sometimes hanging out where his steel truss had worn through his britches. . . . His neighbors thought him guilty because the piglet's misshapen eyes seemed to resemble his scrotum, which apparently had been seen by too many people. But because he firmly and consistently denied all erotic contact with the sow, the court could not hang him without a second witness.

But for good measure they kept him in jail for several months.

Suretyship, a practice of English local government whereby persons pledged a monetary amount or its equivalent to guarantee their appearance in court, keeping the peace, or fulfilling a contract or debt obligation, was widely used in the colonies. Granting bail followed English law practice, with factors such as the nature and quality of the offense and the reputation of the person accused taken into account. Colonial laws usually made capital crimes unbailable and sometimes, as in Massachusetts, "Contempts in open Court." Colonial practice also coincided with the common law in regard to double jeopardy. The Massachusetts Body of Liberties of 1641 stated that "No man shall be twice sentenced by Civill Justice for one and the same Crime, offence, or Trespasse."

Mindful of persecutions in England and elsewhere in Europe, the colonists were careful to avoid cruel and unusual punishment. The prohibition in the Massachusetts code against "inhumane, barbarous or cruel" punishment was owing primarily to biblical sanctions. Colonial punishment was moderate by comparison with English practice, and the

Puritans excluded such biblical punishments as stoning or burning to death. Whipping in Puritan New England was limited to forty stripes, as prescribed in the Bible. Hanging, drawing, and quartering did not appear in the colonies (other than in rare instances for crimes committed by slaves). One William Matthewes was convicted of petit treason in Virginia in 1630 and sentenced "to be drawn and hanged," and a renegade white man named Joshua Tefft was hanged and quartered after conviction by a military court for treason during King Philip's War. Of course, slave punishments were excessively cruel, including dismembering and burnings; quartering, however, came after execution. One factor for mitigating the harshness of penalties in the colonies was the heavy reliance on such punishments as fines, public humiliation, and giving sureties for good behavior.

17

Colonial Rebellions

Colonial revolts erupted out of widespread discontent with the established order. Political, economic, and social factors fueled restlessness. Overriding all was the feeling on the part of a large segment of society of exclusion from government access. Rebellion served as an aggressive way for powerful groups who felt unfairly excluded from both governance and economic pursuits to demand redress. The Glorious Revolution in England sparked the overthrow of consolidated rule in New England and in New York. Economic grievances affected decisions to rebel. However, among the underclass, discontent never surfaced to the extent of fomenting a social revolution. Yet in several instances the threat was recognized. Each revolt had democratic implications—to make the government more amenable to a broader constituency and to modify or change access to power. In most situations, too, concerns and fears involved religion, not the least being apprehension of a Catholic-French conspiracy.

Colonial uprisings to overthrow governments occurred during a period of transition when political factions struggled to gain dominance or there was a vacuum of power owing largely to indecision or upheavals in the mother country. In each instance rebelliousness was confined to a single colony, with the insurgents claiming that they acted legitimately in the name of the crown. They stated as their objectives the prevention of local arbitrary rule over the people and the preservation of law and order. Taking their cue from the army and Parliament of the English Civil War, rebellious colonists usually followed the course of creating an association, then a convention, and finally a restoration of the colonial assembly; in some instances, for an interim executive and administrative body there was recourse to a committee or council of safety. Only in Maryland's early civil wars, Bacon's Rebellion of 1676, and Leisler's Rebellion of 1689–1691 was there bloodshed.

VIRGINIA

Before 1676, Virginians faced only a scant possibility of any kind of revolt. In 1635 the council, backed by armed men, had little difficulty in "thrusting out" Governor John Harvey and sending him back to England. Governor William Berkeley in 1652 gathered a thousand armed men to challenge an English fleet that bore Cromwell's commissioners who had been ordered to compel the submission of Virginia to the Commonwealth of England. To avoid bloodshed, however, the Virginia government accepted the generous terms of the commissioners, which required no indemnity and recognized the supremacy of the general assembly in the colony; of course, Berkeley, a staunch royalist, was removed as governor.

During the 1660s and early 1670s fears arose from the restlessness of the "giddy multitude"—laborers, servants, black slaves, and even small farmers. Abortive servant plots in York County in 1661 and Gloucester County in 1663 fed anxiety over the potential of an underclass uprising. Indeed, when Bacon's Rebellion did come in 1676, it was acknowledged that many of the participants were "free men that had but lately crept out of the condition of Servants." The House of Burgesses in 1677 recognized that "false Rumors, Infused by ill affected provoking an itching desire" had stirred up the lower class of people. Governor Berkeley viewed the uprising as one of the "rabble" versus the "better sort people."

Many factors combined to spread discontent among Virginians against the government under William Berkeley, who had been reinstated as governor upon Charles II's ascension to the throne. While the people were undergoing hard times and tobacco prices were depressed in the 1660s and 1670s, the governor and his cronies were getting richer. As governor, Berkeley was the recipient of many fees and gifts, including the beaver tributes of the Indians, the charges collected for marriage, tavern, and other licenses, and tonnage duties, to name but a few sources. There was resentment of the council, whose members came from only three counties (Charles City, James City, and York) and held offices of profit, such as collectors, secretary, and escheators of land. Citizens complained that there had been no election of burgesses since 1661 and

Sir William Berkeley. Courtesy of the Virginia Historical Society

that the offices of sheriff, justice of the peace, and vestryman were no longer elective. The poll tax and the levy to pay for frontier forts formed a heavy burden on the small farmers. The assembly had also enacted a special tax to cover the expenses of agents sent to England to lobby for the disallowal of the king's grant in 1673 of all land in Virginia south of the Rappahannock River to the earl of Arlington and Thomas Lord Culpeper (the mission did succeed in 1681 in gaining an annulment).

Berkeley's policy of protecting friendly Indians, intended to create a buffer zone, left the colony defenseless against marauding tribes from western Pennsylvania and Maryland. The governor and his "Green Spring" faction were accused of attempting to monopolize the Indian fur trade. The colony was almost totally defenseless during the third Anglo-Dutch War; eleven Virginia merchantmen were sunk by the enemy in July 1673. Due to recurring crop blights and bad weather, some three-fourths of Virginians had hardly enough to live on. The cattle plague of 1672 and 1673 killed off more than one-half of the colony's cattle, and the drought of 1675 destroyed most of the corn crops.

Indian-white conflict triggered Bacon's Rebellion. Doeg Indians of the Potomac River valley, smarting over not being paid in dealings with

Thomas Mathew, sent a war party to Mathew's Maryland plantation; attempting to steal hogs, they were intercepted, and several Indians were killed. For revenge, the Doegs murdered Mathew's herdsman. Colonel George Mason and Major George Brent crossed the Potomac in search of the culprit Indians; at a parley, Brent and his men killed a Doeg chief and ten other Indians, and shortly thereafter, Mason and some of the troops, not distinguishing one Indian from another, murdered fourteen Susquehannocks. The Susquehannocks, whom John Smith had described as "giantlike," had been pressed by the Senecas and had moved into Maryland. Subsequently, Colonel John Washington and Major Isaac Allerton led a thousand militia into the field and killed six Susquehannock chiefs during a parley. The Susquehannocks then struck terror as far south as the falls of the James River, killing in all some three hundred Virginians, including an overseer at Nathaniel Bacon's outer plantation. Governor Berkeley sent Sir Henry Chicheley against the Susquehannocks, but then all of the sudden had the force disbanded.

Planters along the frontier of the upper James decided themselves to bring war to the Indians and elected Nathaniel Bacon, Jr., to take the command. Bacon had arrived in Virginia in 1674 at age twenty-seven and had bought two plantations, one at Curles Neck and the other twenty miles up the James at the falls. Having been in trouble in England as a confidence man, Bacon received eighteen hundred pounds from his father to go to Virginia. His wealthy cousin, Nathaniel Bacon, Sr., a Virginia councilor, helped Bacon also to secure a seat in the council. Arrogant and pensive, Nathaniel Bacon, Jr., was ambitious for economic and political power.

Governor Berkeley denied Bacon a military commission. On May 10, 1676, the governor issued two proclamations, one declaring Bacon a rebel and the other dissolving the long-sitting assembly and ordering an election. Meanwhile Bacon led a force southward to a stronghold of the Occaneechee Indians on an island in the Roanoke River. The Susquehannocks found there were tortured and killed. On the pretense that the Occaneechees had aided the Susquehannocks, Bacon provoked a fight with them, slaughtering most of the Indians and plundering their furs. On his return Bacon found that he was elected to the House of Burgesses, even though he was ineligible as a councilor. Still outlawed as a rebel by Berkeley, Bacon, with a band of fifty men, headed for Jamestown, but he was captured by a small force that the governor had sent out. Bacon did penance by asking forgiveness before the assembly. Since Bacon had many supporters in the town and in the assembly, Berkeley removed the outlawry and restored Bacon to the council. Bacon again demanded a military commission, but the governor demurred. On June 7, Bacon fled, only to collect another armed force and march on the capital. Confronted with Bacon's troops in Jamestown, Governor Berkeley granted the commission, and the assembly declared war on the Indians, naming Bacon commander in chief.

In June, while Bacon gathered recruits in Gloucester County, the assembly passed "Bacon's laws," which included certain reforms: A person could hold only one office at a time; vestries were to be elected rather than self-perpetuating; all freemen could vote, even without property; only prescribed fees could be collected; sheriffs were to serve only one year at a time; councilors were no longer exempt from taxation; and no council member could sit in court with the justices of the peace. Most of this legislation was later accepted by the Berkeley assembly in 1677, indicating that it had little bearing on the rebellion itself.

Governor Berkeley went to the eastern shore to raise troops and enlist naval support. Bacon rallied his force at Middle Plantation, a few miles from Jamestown, and in July issued the "Declaration of the People," signing it "General, by consent of the People." The declaration emphasized Berkeley's favoritism, "unjust Taxes," failure of defense of the frontiers, and monopolization of the Indian trade ("By having in that unjust gaine Bartered and sould his Majesties Country and the lives of his Loyal Subjects to the Barbarous Heathen"). It was ordered that Berkeley and nineteen of his "pernitious Councellors, Aiders and Assisters" should surrender within four days or otherwise be deemed "Traytors to the King and Countrey," whose estates would be seized. About the same time, Bacon issued his "Manifesto concerning the Troubles in Virginia," more specifically outlining grievances and reiterating that it was Berkeley who was the traitor and not Bacon. This document closed with the following entreaty:

> May all the world know that we doe unanimously desire to represent our sad and heavy grievances to his most sacred Majestie as our Refuge and Sanctuary, where wee doe well know that all our Causes will be impartially heard and Equall Justice administered to all men.

Bacon also called for an assembly elected by all "the housekeepers and freemen" to meet at Jamestown on September 4 to legislate concerning Virginia's "Blood & Confusion"; this assembly, however, did not convene.

It is not known whether Bacon ever really intended to broaden the rebellion to win support of insurgents in other colonies and, if necessary, to confront any troops that the king might send against him. A reported dialogue between Bacon and John Goode, one of his prisoners, is only suggestive. Supposedly in Henrico County, on September 2, Bacon asked Goode about rumors of two thousand English troops on their way to Virginia. Bacon allegedly pointed out that five hundred Virginians could beat the king's troops. Goode replied, "You speak as though you designed a total defection from His Majesty and our country," and he reminded

Bacon that Bacon's followers considered themselves enemies of the Indians and not of the king. Bacon was said to have then declared:

> I think otherwise, and I am confident that it is the mind of this colony and of Maryland as well as Carolina, to cast off their governors. And if we cannot prevail by arms to make our conditions of peace, or obtain the privilege to elect our own governor, we may retire to the Roanoke and establish our own government there.

At a revolutionary convention called by Bacon at Middle Plantation in early August, consisting mainly of company grade officers, it was proclaimed that Berkeley had vacated his office and that now Bacon headed the government; as had been done before, citizens were required to take an oath of allegiance to Bacon. Bacon's men plundered loyalist estates, and Bacon himself led troops into the Great Danger Swamp (chiefly in New Kent County) in search of Pamunkey Indians. Though killing about a hundred Indian men, women, and children and capturing booty, the excursion wasted strength and resources. In September a battle almost occurred between forces under Bacon and Berkeley at Jamestown. Bacon paraded seized wives of local loyalists (the "white aprons") on the ramparts, defying the governor's ships to use their artillery. On September 19, Bacon burned Jamestown. He issued another declaration, perhaps the first emancipation proclamation in American history, that servants and black slaves belonging to loyalists who joined his cause would be freed. The governor's force dropped back to the eastern shore, while Bacon's men plundered in Gloucester County. Bacon had hoped to create a naval force, but this expectation was diminished when Giles Bland and William Carver and three hundred men shipboard were captured by the governor's own navy. A thunderclap struck the rebel force when Nathaniel Bacon died of dysentery on October 26, 1676. Joseph Ingram succeeded to the rebel command. During the winter the rebels put up at fortified houses. Prominent persons who had sided with Bacon now joined with Berkeley. The governor waged a campaign along the York and James rivers, beating rebel bands in skirmishes. By mid-January 1677 the rebellion was over.

Berkeley took a terrible retribution. Twenty-three of Bacon's supporters were hanged, fourteen of whom were convicted by court martial, and estates of insurgents were seized. On January 29, 1677, six English men-of-war, a flagship, and eight transports, carrying a thousand troops, arrived at Jamestown. On board also were three royal commissioners, one of whom, Herbert Jeffreys, had been named by the king to succeed Berkeley. Though the commissioners had a pardon from Charles II for all insurgents except Bacon, Berkeley, who delayed in turning over the reins of government, continued to make arrests and plunder rebel estates. Finally he relinquished the governorship to Jeffreys and departed for

England, where Charles II refused to meet with him. Berkeley died in England on July 9 of that year.

Bacon's Rebellion may be considered essentially a sectional conflict that sought more open government, though the chief beneficiaries would be the gentry "outsiders" rather than the people as a whole. It also demonstrated that the crown could readily dispatch soldiers to an American colony to enforce imperial policy. In the long run, most of the political reforms survived, factional identity diminished, and a new cohesiveness emerged in the power structure in the colony as great families consolidated their power.

NEW ENGLAND

Puritan New England remained relatively free from acute internal dissension. The hivings-out to form new plantations provided a safety valve. Founded early, the self-made governments had achieved maturity and represented a consensus of the majority. During the disruptions of the English Civil War and subsequent dominance of the English government by Puritans, the New England colonies were allowed to go their own way. After the Restoration, tension did begin to mount over Stuart policies for firmer imperial administration. Before 1689 the only rebellion, of minor importance, was the one attempted by Edward Gove in New Hampshire in 1683. The royal governor, Edward Cranfield, alienated citizens by leasing the Mason proprietary grant and then charging quitrents. He also dismissed several popular councilors, dissolved the assembly when it refused to vote appropriations, and informed the crown that New Englanders were on the point of revolution. Gove, an assemblyman, went about the countryside using the rallying cry "liberty and reformation," attempting to enlist a military force to drive Cranfield out of office. But he had little success, and when Gove and eight of his recruits marched into Hampton, they were disarmed and arrested by militia under orders of a justice of the peace, Nathaniel Weare. Gove was tried in a court of oyer and terminer for high treason and was convicted and sentenced to be hanged, drawn, and quartered. But since the governor's commission did not permit the sentence to be carried out and Gove himself appealed for clemency to the crown, he was transported to England in chains. After three years of extreme deprivation in the Tower of London, Gove received a royal pardon.

The Massachusetts Puritans had watched the Gove affair very closely and even insisted that Gove was demented. They feared that Gove's actions might be taken as evidence of a growing mutiny against the crown in New England. Indeed, under the Stuart monarchy, the Massachusetts Bay colony did fall under that suspicion. Reports of the king's commissioners, who visited the colony in 1664, and of Edward Randolph, collector of customs and agent for the Lords of Trade, in 1676 charged the colony with distancing itself from England and violating English laws and liberties. The colony was considered to have been amiss in the persecution of the Quakers; unlawful annexation of New Hampshire and Maine; restriction of voting to Congregationalists; denial of the power of the crown in the colony by refusing to mention the king in public documents, preventing the taking of an oath of allegiance to the king, stopping appeals to England, spending funds owed the king from fines and forfeitures, and coining money; disobedience of the Navigation Acts, compounded by local juries not convicting violators; and placement of import duties on English goods. The government of Massachusetts still rested on a trading company charter. When requested to send agents to England to answer the charges before the Lords of Trade, the colony at first balked; when it finally acceded, its agents refused to answer the pertinent questions. Proceedings of quo warranto were brought against the governor and company of Massachusetts in the English Court of Chancery, but the attorneys representing them would not enter a plea. Thus on October 23, 1684, judgment was rendered by default, declaring the Massachusetts charter null and void.

The vacating of the Massachusetts charter coincided with the crown's plans to consolidate government in the northern colonies, largely with the view of strengthening military defense against the French. In May 1686 a provisional government, uniting Massachusetts, New Hampshire, Maine, and the King's Province (Narragansett Country), went into effect. Joseph Dudley served as the president of an appointed Council of New England, which group supplanted the legislatures. Within ten days of installation of the council, local government was reorganized; most of the existing officeholders, however, were retained. Surprisingly, New Englanders expressed little concern, though there were protests on religious grounds against the flying of the English flag with its cross of St. George and the use of the Town House for Anglican services. The provisional government accomplished almost nothing as a governing body. A quorum was rarely attained, and no attempt was made to impose taxes. In summer 1686 the final structure for the Dominion of New England was approved, and Dudley's replacement, Sir Edmund Andros, arrived amid pomp and circumstance at Boston on December 19, 1686. The next year Plymouth, Rhode Island, and Connecticut were added to the Dominion of New England, and in 1688 also New York and East and West Jersey. Andros and the council held full legislative and executive authority for the whole dominion; councilors were selected from former colonial officeholders: seven for Massachusetts; one for New Hampshire; two for Maine; six for Plymouth; one for the King's Province; seven for Rhode Island; eight for New York; and none for the Jerseys. Francis Nicholson, who came over with Andros as captain of grenadiers, was made lieutenant governor. Nicholson took up residence in New York.

It was a mistake to carve out such a vast territory for the Dominion of New England. New York and Jersey leaders resented the gravitation of power to Boston, where the council sat and the colonial and dominion records were kept. Andros himself moved too precipitately in matters certain to offend citizens. New Englanders protested the requirement that royal patents had to be secured for land titles; many persons who lacked clear titles feared that they might lose their lands. Moreover, the imposition of quitrents and the threat of taking over common lands belonging to the towns provoked anger. New Englanders also objected to the appointment of sheriffs and jurors, the use of one of the three Boston meetinghouses for Anglican worship, censorship of the printing presses, enforcement of the Navigation Acts, increases in import duties, prohibition of taxes for church support, limitation of town meetings to only one a year, and, not the least, Andros's permitting the outlawed celebration of Christmas and laxity in observing the Sabbath.

As opposition grew against Andros and the Dominion of New England, Massachusetts leaders sent to England agents (Eliakim Hutchinson, Increase Nowell, and Increase Mather) whose main objectives were to obtain a representative assembly, confirmation of old land titles, and protection of town ownership of common lands. Added to dissension against Andros's policies were fears of a French and Indian invasion. French settlement had extended from French Acadia as far westward as the Penobscot River in territory claimed by Massachusetts. Andros led a military force to the frontier, where fighting broke out with the French and their Indian allies. Andros's absence from the seat of government encouraged plotting for his overthrow. Rumors circulated that Andros favored Catholicism (several of Andros's British army officers were of this faith) and that the dominion governor might be prone to seek a rapprochement with the French.

News arrived in early April 1689 of William of Orange's seizure of the throne of England and the flight of James II. Troops on the Maine frontier mutinied and returned to Boston. On April 18, lecture day, mobs and militia swarmed into the streets. To forestall bloodshed, former Massachusetts magistrates, several dominion councilors, and merchants assembled at the Town House. At noon, from the balcony, Cotton Mather announced "The Declaration of the Gentlemen, Merchants, and Inhabitants of Boston and the Country Adjacent," which stated grievances against the Andros regime. An open letter to Andros, signed by fifteen persons, with dominion councilor Wait Winthrop at the head of the list, was also made public. Part of it read:

Being surprized with the People sudden taking of Arms ... [and] for the quieting and securing of the People . . . and tendring your own Safety, We judge it necessary you forthwith surrender and deliver up the Government and Fortification, to be preserved and disposed according to Order and Direction from the Crown of England.

Two days later a "Council for the Safety and the Conservation of the Peace" was formed, consisting of five dominion councilors, five churchmen, and five merchants; other leaders soon joined, raising the number of members to thirty-seven. The council of safety appointed eighty-seven-year-old Simon Bradstreet, the last governor under the company charter, president of the council and Wait Winthrop commander of the militia. Andros surrendered the Fort Hill garrison, and British troops at Castle William also yielded. Andros, Joseph Dudley, and Edward Randolph were imprisoned. In August, Andros broke jail; disguised in woman's dress but still wearing his boots, he was apprehended in Rhode Island. Eventually all three captives were sent to England.

The council of safety lasted only five weeks. In imitation of William of Orange's convention of January 1689, the members of the council called for an assembly of delegates from sixty-six towns to meet at Boston on May 9 to decide on a course of interim government. This meeting led to a second convention on May 22–24, when it was resolved by representatives of forty-four of fifty-three towns (nine preferred to continue the council of safety) that "Government in this present Juncture lieth wholly in the Voice of the People" and until "Order shall come from the higher powers," government as it was under the old charter should be reestablished. Bradstreet and the former magistrates immediately took up the offices they had held in 1686. A convention of the four towns in New Hampshire in February 1690 voted for annexation with Massachusetts, which was accepted. In 1691 the crown granted a royal charter to Massachusetts (combining Massachusetts and Plymouth), which differed from the old system chiefly in the appointment of a royal governor, a property instead of a religious basis for the suffrage, review of laws by the king in council, veto power for the governor, and a guarantee of appeals to the crown. New Hampshire again became a separate royal colony. Connecticut and Rhode Island were allowed to resume the governments under their charters of 1662 and 1663, respectively. The Glorious Revolution in Massachusetts diminished the influence of Puritanism in political affairs, provided a more fixed and more liberal constitution, and strengthened royal ties in government.

NEW YORK

The Glorious Revolution in New England touched off a New York rebellion, which also happened at a time of discontent and feelings of frustration among the populace. New York did not have a representative assembly until 1683, and, even then, James II, three years later, ordered its "Charter of Liberties" repealed and declared that although the legislature should continue, only the governor and council could levy taxes. The assembly was dissolved altogether when the colony entered the Dominion of New England. Many New Yorkers resented the power of New York City merchants, who made up a majority of the colony's council (before dominion status). In 1670 the governor and council gave New York City merchants a monopoly of the Hudson River carrying trade and eight years later also of the colony's export-import business. Farmers could only buy and sell commodities in the external market through New York City merchants, paying high prices for goods they received. In 1684, Long Islanders, many of whom were displaced New Englanders and had resented annexation of Long Island by New York in 1664, were required to pay a ten percent tax on any goods not shipped directly from England or places of production and also on European imports not coming from England. Declining prices for wheat and bread worked a hardship for farmers. The tobacco trade was being siphoned off to Philadelphia. Additional taxes were levied for support of frontier defense. Governor Thomas Dongan (in office from 1683 to 1688) lined his pockets with fees that were required for new charters and land patents. That Dongan was a Catholic did not help to stay a growing anti-Catholicism in the colony. The French and their Indians, now making war with New York's allies, the Iroquois, posed a threat of invasion of the colony.

In March 1689, Lieutenant Governor Francis Nicholson of the dominion government received dispatches telling of William of Orange's victory in England but kept them secret. On April 26, 1689, New York received news of the Boston uprising. Seeing the collapse of the Dominion of New England, Long Island merchants refused to pay customs. In Suffolk, Queens, and Westchester counties, magistrates were forced out of office and new ones were elected in their stead. With rebellion spreading, Nicholson called on aldermen and militia officers to fortify the city. Militia, however, defected and seized the city's fort. Nicholson fled to England.

To fill the void in government, militia captains formed a committee of safety, electing Captain Jacob Leisler as its head. Leisler had arrived in the city in 1660 from Frankfurt, Germany, as a soldier of the Dutch West India Company; he subsequently married the widow of a wealthy merchant. On June 22, 1689, Leisler recognized William and Mary as the English sovereigns. The committee of safety called for a convention of two representatives from each county—upper New York and eastern Long Island did not respond; only New York, Kings, Queens, Richmond, and Westchester counties did, along with several jurisdictions in East Jersey. The convention, meeting from late June to mid-August 1689, merely confirmed the committee of safety and made Leisler commander in chief. Leisler dispatched letters to the king and the bishop of Salisbury justifying the rebellion and also sent Joist Stoll to England to present the English government with a firsthand account of the happenings. Stoll, however, was ignored in England. In December 1689 a letter arrived in New York, signed by the king in July, addressed to Nicholson or "to such as for the time being" might be taking charge of "Preserving the Peace and administring the Lawes" in New York. Leisler interpreted the letter as recognizing him as interim lieutenant governor in the place of Nicholson, and he even occupied Nicholson's pew in church, placing a red carpet in front of it.

Leisler could count only on hard-core support from lower-middle-class Dutchmen from New York City and its immediate environs. In February 1690, Leisler called for election of an assembly. Before Leisler dismissed it, this legislature further alienated many New Yorkers from the Leisler regime. It increased real and property taxes, exacted fines for refusing civil and military employment, gave all towns equal privileges in trade (thus displeasing New York City merchants), and prohibited anyone from Albany or Ulster County from departing the province without permission from Leisler himself. Leisler had provisions impressed from citizens, and bands of militia roamed the streets, often pillaging. Leisler jailed forty civil officials on charges of treason. Albany resisted submitting to the Leisler government until forced to do so by troops sent there under Leisler's son-in-law, Jacob Milborne.

To many New Yorkers, Leisler's dictatorial rule reminded them of a 1640s uprising in Naples by one Tommaso Aniello ("Masaniello"), a fishmonger, who led his followers on a brief rampage of terror, only to be assassinated himself; as David S. Lovejoy (1972) has shown, Americans had learned of the episode and equated it with the consequences of anarchy. Indeed, a number of prominent New Yorkers petitioned William and Mary for protection against Leisler's rule "by the sword."

The French-Indian attack and massacre at Schenectady on February 8, 1690, shocked New Yorkers. Leisler, to his credit, attempted to mobilize an intercolonial army to invade Canada, but because of quibbling between New York and New England troops and other problems, the expedition soon disbanded. Leisler also outfitted a small fleet to be sent against the French. Ironically, Leisler, the usurper, was living up to a governor's responsibility in fighting England's enemies in the New World.

In May 1690, Stoll returned with word that the crown had appointed a new governor, Colonel Henry Sloughter, who would soon be on his way with two companies of British soldiers. But their arrival was delayed. Meanwhile, every day hostility toward Leisler grew. In October 1690, Milborne put down an incipient uprising in Queens County, arresting the leaders as traitors.

At last, on January 23, 1691, Major Richard Ingoldesby and the British companies, accompanied by officials and councilors appointed by the king, set foot in New York City. Leisler refused to surrender the fort to Ingoldesby on grounds that he had not been shown orders to that effect from either the new governor or the king. Sloughter finally arrived offshore on March 16, 1691, but did not debark until three days later. On March 18, when Ingoldesby and a body of troops demanded that Leisler surrender the fort, they were fired on; one civilian laborer and seven New York citizens were killed, and one of the king's soldiers was wounded. Leisler's own militia then dropped their arms and marched out of the fort.

Arrested, Leisler was charged with high treason and the murder of the laborer, Josias Brown. On March 26, Sloughter commissioned a court of oyer and terminer, composed entirely of Englishmen. Milborne stood trial on the same charges, and thirty others were also arraigned. Only Leisler and Milborne refused to enter a plea, denying the right of a colonial court to try persons for high treason. Leisler, Milborne, and six others were sentenced to death. Sloughter, however, reprieved all but Leisler and Milborne. The New York assembly also voted a bill of attainder condemning both men. Though sentenced to be hanged, drawn, and quartered, the governor permitted only hanging, followed by decapitation. The two men were executed May 16, 1691.

A campaign in England by Jacob Leisler, Jr., and Abraham Gouverneur to get Parliament to remove the legislative attainder succeeded in April 1695, with the additional recognition by Parliament that Leisler had been the legal acting governor of New York and Ingoldesby had exceeded his authority. Thus, in effect, both Leisler and Milborne were posthumously cleared, and their property could not be forfeited. Both men were ceremoniously reburied in the Dutch church in New York City in 1698. Had Leisler been less the foreigner and had he cast the revolution in terms of basic rights, avoided his dictatorial style and rough tactics, and recognized the need to appease a variety of interest groups, the rebellion might not have ended in bloodshed.

MARYLAND

Maryland had more brushes with conspiracy for overthrowing government and revolts than any other colony. As early as the 1630s, William Claiborne, a member of the Virginia council, unsuccessfully attempted to keep Kent Island, in Chesapeake Bay, from coming under the jurisdiction of Maryland. The English Civil War had affected Maryland, where a large number of Puritans and other Protestants had settled. One Maryland rebel on behalf of Parliament was Captain Richard Ingle, a tobacco trader representing English merchants. In 1643 he secured from Parliament letters of marque empowering him to capture the king's ships in the Chesapeake.

Arrested and released by Maryland authorities, he made his way to England. Two years later he returned in a heavily armed ship and proceeded to seize the capital, St. Mary's. Ingle compelled inhabitants to take "an oath of submission"; those who refused had their estates plundered by his men. William Claiborne joined with Ingle and reclaimed Kent Island. Governor Leonard Calvert fled the colony. The "plundering time" ended when Calvert returned and raised an armed force, dispersing the rebels at a time when Ingle was in England. The Maryland governor also reestablished proprietary control over Kent Island.

Civil war again erupted in 1654. A military band, commanded by Richard Bennett, one of the parliamentary commissioners sent over to accept submission of the Chesapeake colonies to Cromwell's rule, marched on St. Mary's. Governor William Stone resigned, being replaced by a board of ten persons, including William Fuller as governor. The proprietor, Cecilius Calvert (second Lord Baltimore), however, prevailed upon Stone to try to restore the former government. Stone and 130 armed men raided Puritan settlements and then moved down the Severn River, where they were met by a force of 175 militia under Fuller and a group of sailors from New England merchantmen. The New England ships provided a protective cover at Fuller's rear. Stone, outmaneuvered and outnumbered, surrendered on condition of receiving quarter. Fuller nevertheless held a court-martial, which condemned Stone and nine others to death; Stone and four men were spared by intercession of women and some of Fuller's soldiers. Puritan supremacy was thus established in the colony, but in 1657 negotiations between Lord Baltimore and Richard Bennett led to restoration of proprietary rule in Maryland.

The new governor, Josias Fendall, soon sided with the antiproprietary faction. On February 28, 1660, he joined with the assembly in proclaiming that body supreme in the colony; the governor and council would no longer act as an upper house but would sit in the assembly as a whole. Fendall accepted a new commission as governor from the assembly. This arrangement, however, sustained little popular backing. With the Restoration in England, the proprietor removed Fendall and named his brother Philip governor, who upon his death in 1661 was succeeded by Charles Calvert. Though there was relative calm during the governorship of Charles Calvert (1661–1684), there still was a spirit of rebelliousness in the colony. In 1676 an incipient uprising of sixty armed men assembled along the Patuxent River was suppressed; two leaders were hanged. Josias Fendall and John Coode were tried in 1681 for attempting to stir up rebellion; both men were heavily fined, and Fendall was banished from the colony.

In the 1680s opposers of the proprietary government cited many grievances. Not the least was favoritism: Lord Baltimore's relatives held offices at all levels; of the nine councilors who served between 1685 and

Charles Calvert by John Hesselius. The Baltimore Museum of Art: Gift of
Alfred R. and Henry G. Riggs, in Memory of General Lawrason Riggs.
BMA 1941.4

1687, seven were kinsmen; and most public servants were Catholic even
though the great majority of the population was Protestant. Other political
complaints included proprietary appointment of sheriffs; excessive fees
and taxes; since 1670, a property requirement for voting set by the
proprietor and not by the legislature; issuance of writs to return two
instead of the four delegates prescribed by law from each county to the
assembly; and the overuse of the veto—in 1684 the proprietor nullified
all eighteen acts of the 1678 legislative session. Protestant colonists resented
favoring Catholics in receiving arms and ammunition for frontier defense.
Economic distress added to the discontent: overproduction of tobacco and
depression in its price, a doubling of quitrents in 1671, and collection of
port duties on Maryland ships. The 1680s was a time of the "Great Fear,"
with anti-Catholicism reaching a high pitch. Rumors spread of a Catholic-
Indian plot to murder Protestants. The policy of raising orphans as

Catholics provoked anger. Fueling religious animosity was the belief that the proprietary government had a double standard of justice. In 1684, Christopher Rousby, collector of customs, was stabbed to death by Lord Baltimore's nephew, George Talbot, a councilor and deputy governor for the proprietor's minor son, Benedict; Talbot was never brought to justice.

In spring 1689, Marylanders wondered why the proprietary government did not recognize William and Mary. Actually, Lord Baltimore's orders to this effect were not delivered in the colony because of the death of the messenger en route. To ensure the recognition of William and Mary and also in hopes of overthrowing the proprietorship, a group mostly from the lower house of assembly formed "an Association in Arms for the Defense of the Protestant Religion and for Asserting the right of King William and Queen Mary to the Province of Maryland and all the English Dominions." Colonel John Coode emerged as the leader of the Protestant Association. A resident of St. Mary's, Coode owned a plantation in Charles County. An Anglican, though supposedly having trained for both the Anglican and Catholic priesthoods, Coode had held various local political offices and a seat in the assembly. He had a reputation for heavy drinking and swearing. On July 25, 1689, the Protestant Association issued the "Declaration of the Protestant Association," which expounded on grievances and asked that all residents "tender their Allegiance, the Protestant Religion, their Lives, fortunes and Families to ayd and assist us in this our undertaking." Coode, at the head of several hundred armed men, marched on St. Mary's. Henry Darnall and Nicholas Sewall failed to rally enough troops to support the loyalist cause. Their few followers surrendered at Lord Baltimore's manor house, eight miles from St. Mary's, and at the fort in the capital.

The assembly, meeting as a convention from August 22 to September 4, 1689, with four delegates from each county except Anne Arundel, petitioned the English government to nullify the proprietary rights and to make Maryland a royal colony. A second convention in April 1690 sent Coode and Kenelm Cheseldyne as agents to England. Administrative responsibility during the convention's adjournments was carried on by a committee headed by Nehemiah Blakiston.

In February 1690 the crown sent a letter to Maryland expressing approval of the actions of the associates and asking them to continue their government for the time being. Maryland was made a royal colony in June 1691, although Lord Baltimore retained his property rights in the colony and also the revenues previously accorded him. Lionel Copley arrived in Maryland in April 1692 as the first royal governor. When the third Lord Baltimore, Cecilius Calvert, died in February 1715, he was succeeded by Benedict Calvert, who had earlier converted to the Anglican religion. With Maryland now having achieved political stability and the religious issues settled, the colony reverted to proprietary government.

NORTH CAROLINA

In the Albemarle section of North Carolina (which had its own governor and assembly), John Culpeper, aided by New England ship captains, in 1677 led armed protesters in seeking to prevent payment of customs duties to the crown on exported tobacco. The insurgents seized customs records, deposed Thomas Miller as deputy governor and customs collector, cleared ships without payment of duties, and took over funds belonging to the English government. Miller and his supporters were imprisoned, awaiting trial by a special court created by a new rebel-controlled assembly. Meanwhile, the governor of Albemarle, Thomas Eastchurch, upon arriving in Virginia, issued a proclamation calling for an end to the insurgency. The rebels sent armed men to prevent Eastchurch from entering the colony. Eastchurch died in February 1678, and Miller escaped to England. Later when Culpeper visited England, he was tried for high treason but was acquitted.

To restore order, the Carolina proprietors appointed one of their own as governor of Albemarle. Delayed because of his being captured by Turks and taken to Algiers, from where he escaped, Seth Sothel assumed the governorship in 1683. He quickly alienated settlers by the corruption of his administration and his jailing of opponents. In 1689 an armed band, led by Thomas Pollock, surprised Sothel at his home and forced him to relinquish the governorship. The assembly put him on trial and banished him, whereby Sothel made his way to South Carolina.

Between 1689 and 1712 the Carolina proprietors appointed a deputy governor of North Carolina. Cary's Rebellion, a contest over this office, resulted chiefly from religious causes. In 1704, Deputy Governor Robert Daniel began enforcing the Vestry Act, which required officeholders to take an oath of allegiance to the queen as well as the Thirty-nine Articles of the Anglican church. Quakers were excluded from the legislature and other offices. The following year Thomas Cary was appointed to succeed Daniel. Although initially siding with the Quakers, he also enforced the oath-taking. When he was removed by the proprietors and William Glover, president of the council, became acting deputy governor, Cary again threw in with the Quakers and other non-Anglicans, forming what was called the Popular party. The dissidents recognized Cary as deputy governor, and thus the colony had two claimants to this office. Both Cary and Glover agreed to let the legislature decide the dispute; Glover, however, refused to abide by the decision in favor of Cary.

In the midst of the crisis, Edward Hyde arrived as deputy governor, appointed by the governor of South Carolina, Edward Tynte, who, however, died before giving a commission to Hyde. The council nevertheless installed Hyde as deputy governor. The Anglican majority in the assembly reestablished the Church of England (this was originally done in 1701 but was disallowed by the proprietors two years later). The test oath for officeholding was again applied. Cary, who denied that both Hyde and the assembly had any right to govern, accepted leadership of the dissenters and declared himself president of the council and acting deputy governor. Preparing to seize control of the government, Cary and sixty followers took up arms and also sought to enlist support from the Tuscarora Indians. Hyde appealed to Governor Alexander Spotswood of Virginia for help in crushing the rebellion. Spotswood, remembering Bacon's Rebellion and fearful that the North Carolina situation might incite a slave revolt, ordered militia and a guardship to North Carolina. Cary's Rebellion collapsed. The rebel leader fled to Virginia, where he was arrested and then sent to England for trial; he was released because Spotswood had neglected to forward documentary evidence. The appointment of Edward Hyde as full governor in 1712 eased tension, and the Tuscarora War of 1711–1712 was a unifying factor among North Carolinians.

SOUTH CAROLINA

South Carolina's political instability had much the same roots as North Carolina's, but more related to neglect on the part of the proprietors. In 1690, Seth Sothel, exiled from North Carolina, himself conducted a coup in South Carolina. Claiming the governorship as a resident proprietor, Sothel, backed by nearly five hundred persons who signed a petition in his favor, persuaded the colony's Commons House of Assembly to remove and banish Governor James Colleton. The next year the proprietors in England dismissed Sothel, replacing him with Philip Ludwell, a decision that Sothel accepted.

After the turn of the century, an antiproprietary party, based among Anglicans and the planters who lived along Goose Creek, gained strength. The pirate situation of the time and fear of impending attacks by Spaniards hastened the decision to seek an overthrow of the proprietary government and to ask the crown to take over the colony. The antiproprietary party voiced many complaints, chief among which were that the proprietors had provided no assistance during the Yamasee Indian War of 1715 and continued to avoid responsibility for frontier defense, had assigned all ungranted lands to themselves and had charged high prices for their purchase, and had frequently repealed laws passed by the assembly.

The Revolution of 1719 was sparked by a letter on November 28 of that year to Governor Robert Johnson from assemblyman Alexander Skeene, Colonel George Logan, and Major William Blakeway, telling the governor that an association had been formed for the purpose of ridding the colony of proprietary rule. Johnson called a meeting of the council, which advised him to wait until the assembly convened before taking any action. Twenty-three members of the assembly visited the governor, informing him that ties were being severed with the proprietary government, but if he wished he could stay on as governor, subject to the king's approval. The governor responded by dissolving the assembly, which then met on its own on December 10, declaring itself "a Convention delegated by the People, to prevent the utter Ruin of the Government, if not the Loss of the Province until His Majesty's Pleasure be known." The convention selected a new governor, Colonel James Moore, and sent a petition to the Board of Trade requesting that South Carolina become a royal colony. The militia refused to back Johnson. On December 21, 1719, members of the convention proclaimed Moore governor before a large crowd at the fort and then, returning to the legislative chamber, elected twelve councilors. The convention voted itself back into an assembly. Francis Nicholson, appointed by the crown, succeeded Moore as provincial governor in 1721. When the proprietary charter was surrendered in 1729, as an indication of the conservativeness of the Revolution of 1719, Johnson (the last proprietary governor) became the first governor of South Carolina officially as a royal colony.

By 1720 colonial relations with the mother country had been more precisely defined. Though plans were proposed for tightening further imperial administration of the colonies, no sustained effort was made for this end, and no real external provocation unsettled the colonial political systems. Nor did serious internal political upheavals occur during the remainder of the colonial period (to 1763) that can be considered rebellions against colonial governments. Of course, during the decade before the American Revolution there were the Stamp Act crisis, urban riots, and some backcountry uneasiness, such as the march on Philadelphia by the Paxton Boys in early 1764. The single major uprising before the Revolution was that of the Regulators of western North Carolina, which ended with an army under the command of the North Carolina governor crushing the insurgents at the battle of Alamance in 1771.

PART SIX
CULTURAL ENLIGHTENMENT

18

Religion

Ethnic immigration and schisms within denominations contributed to a proliferation of religious bodies in early America. By the end of the Revolutionary War era, there were twenty-eight denominations. Churches under state establishment held their own during the colonial period, but they had to meet the challenges of the openness of American society, competition in winning adherents, and satisfying emotional needs. There was a rebirth of the sense of being on an errand in America to advance the reformation of Christianity. Evangelism led to greater soul-searching. Some Americans expected to restore primitive Christianity, others sought to strengthen orthodoxy in theology and polity, and some preferred religion on a more rational basis.

CONGREGATIONALISTS

Puritans had only wanted to purify the Anglican church, not to withdraw from it. But in America such a distinction was lost. Puritans acted similarly to the separatists in establishing autonomous congregations, who ordained their own ministers. The Scriptures were the sole and final authority.

Fittingly, the American Puritans and separatists were called Congregationalists, though this designation was not officially adopted during the
colonial period. In religion, Congregationalists believed that they were
joined by a covenant of grace (faith meriting salvation) and, by their own
doing, a covenant for God's church on earth.

Though each congregation was supreme unto itself in church polity
and doctrine, elected officials had charge of church affairs. The pastor,
according to the Cambridge Platform of 1648, specially attended

> to exhortation: & therein to Administer a word of Wisdom: the Teacher is
> to attend to Doctrine, & therein to Administer a word of Knowledge: &
> either of them to administer the Seales of that Covenant [such as the
> sacraments], unto the dispensation wherof they are alike called: as also to
> execute the Censures.

Actually the teacher was an associate pastor. The elders had the power
"to feed & rule the Church of God," more especially to watch over the
behavior of members. Deacons and deaconesses ("widows") aided in the
"care of the temporall good things of the church." Deaconesses were rarely
appointed, however.

For a typical Congregational service, the nonliturgical worship began
with a long prayer by the pastor, followed by supplications on behalf of
the ill, a "dumb-reading" of the Scriptures by the teacher, the singing of
a psalm led by an elder or "brother," the sermon by the pastor, and a
concluding prayer by the teacher or other official. The congregation met
for a Sunday afternoon service, during which baptisms were conducted
and collections taken, and also for a weekly lecture, usually on Thursdays.
Ministers delivered sermons in the "plain style": They "opened" a biblical
text and related it to relevant axioms; from an ensuing discourse they
then arrived at a clear and valid exegesis. The Lord's Supper, held once
a month, was administered by elders to the parishioners passing in front
of the communion table.

Despite their autonomy, New England churches sent delegates to
synods or associations for the purpose of seeking guidance and interpretation in matters of doctrine and polity. The synod, which met on call by
the Massachusetts General Court at Cambridge three times (September
1646, June 1647, and August 1648), approved the main parts of the
Westminster Confession of Faith. The Cambridge Platform, which issued
from the meetings, declared that

> a Congregational church is by the institution of Christ a part of the militant
> visible church, consisting of a company of saints by calling, united into one
> body by an holy covenant, for the public worship of God and the mutual
> edification of one another in the fellowship of the Lord Jesus.

Though stating that the Scriptures were the only final authority for the churches, the Cambridge Platform recognized the power of the state to punish such offenses as idolatry, blasphemy, heresy, contempt of religion, profanation of the Lord's Day, and the disturbance of worship.

Second- and third-generation Puritan ministers decried the loss of a sense of regeneration among their flocks. Their frequent "jeremiads" bemoaned the increase of sinfulness and lack of calling. It was felt that even the very survival of the churches would be in jeopardy. The New England church covenants had always been restrictive; membership was available only to those who gave proof of a blameless life and, importantly, also testified to a personal religious experience before the congregation or to the elders. The Puritan Congregationalists, of course, did not believe that man was an agent in securing his salvation—grace was bestowed only by an omniscient and omnipotent God, whose divine attributes allowed Him to predestine the outcome of any event. But to the Puritans, one could experience a calling into the church of the visible saints. The problem for the later Puritans was that fewer young people could attest openly to evidence of saving grace in their lives. Though baptized as infants, they could not become full members of the church without giving proof of such an experience. The synod, called by the Massachusetts General Court in 1662, settled on a compromise for church membership— the Half-Way Covenant, whereby baptized persons not giving proof of a conversion experience could be accepted into a congregation but could not be full members or admitted to the Lord's Supper. "Halfway" members, however, could still have their own children baptized. Though most New England churches accepted the compromise, the Half-Way Covenant created some internal and external discord among churches.

A wedge into the New England way was further provided by Solomon Stoddard (1643–1729), grandfather of Jonathan Edwards and minister of the church in Northampton for fifty-nine years. Although the practices did not originate with him, Stoddard baptized all children in his congregation and admitted all adults "who are not scandalous" to the Lord's Supper. The sacraments of baptism and communion were not regarded as seals but as instruments of conversion, along with prayer, Scripture reading, and exposure to preaching.

Stoddard's idea of preaching as a means of aiding in the dispensation of God's grace led him, during his last fifteen years, to engage in evangelism. He also contributed (until 1708) to divisiveness in the New England churches by championing a Presbyterian model for an "instituted church." The ideal was to have synods of elders from the churches on both provincial and national levels. The Saybrook Platform of 1708, accepted by many churches, was a compromise between Presbyterianism and Congregationalism; it called for a general council or synod of churches to meet annually for discussion but not to have enforcement powers and "consociations" of one or more delegates from each county to decide on all cases of discipline brought before them.

New England Congregational clergy continued to despair of the decline of the pure covenanted church. Distinctions between the elect and others diminished. As New England churches struggled over doctrine and polity, the way was open for dissidents to break away in search of "true" congregationalism and vital principles of faith. Yet Congregational churches held their own, numbering 658 by the time of the American Revolution.

ANGLICANS

During the seventeenth century the Church of England neglected its American establishment. The English government, with a policy of attracting immigrants to America regardless of religious persuasion, was reluctant to promote expansion of the Anglican church in America. The Cromwellian regime had no intention of doing so, and the later Stuarts also showed little enthusiasm, James II himself being a convert to Catholicism. Except in New Hampshire, the Anglican church was all but excluded from seventeenth-century New England. By 1720 the only organized Anglican church in Connecticut was that at Stafford, where communicants were of the "poorer sort of people." Where the church was established it was in a weak position compared to its status in England. Although the colonial Anglican church was under the jurisdiction of the bishop of London, it was largely under lay control. For example, in South Carolina, twenty-four lay commissioners had charge of the colony's ten parishes, and the legislature denied the church of all patronage; appointment of ministers was conducted by election in open meetings of parishioners and freeholders. The absence of a resident episcopacy (and therefore no clergymen could be ordained in America), low salaries, and oversized parishes also impeded the effectiveness and expansion of the church. In Virginia in 1662 there were only ten clergymen serving forty-eight parishes; by 1700 a mere sixty Anglican priests served all the colonies. Lay leaders, substituting for absent ministers, could only give lessons and a homily.

At the turn of the eighteenth century, the Church of England began to adopt vigorous policies overseas, and by midcentury the Church had become well seated in all the colonies, even in New England. In 1742, Connecticut had fourteen Anglican churches, attended by seven clergymen. Between 1701 and 1783, three hundred Anglican churches were founded. The instruments for more effective administration and expansion of the Anglican church in the colonies were the commissaries, as representatives of the bishop of London, and the missionaries of the Society for the Propagation of the Gospel in Foreign Parts (SPG, founded in 1701 by the Reverend Thomas Bray). The commissary had the responsibility of watching and investigating the conduct of ministers, calling conventions of clergy, and generally promoting the interests of the church. Much of the work of the commissary was political. Scotsman James Blair (1654–1743), as commissary for all of Virginia (for fifty-three years), had an extraordinary and powerful role in the colony's affairs, as commissary, rector of the church at Jamestown and then at Williamsburg, member of the council, and president of the College of William and Mary.

The SPG (which Thomas Jefferson referred to as "Anglican Jesuits"), supported mainly by private funds with the archbishop of Canterbury as president, sent some 309 missionaries throughout the thirteen colonies from 1702 to 1783. The proportion of missionaries indicates that the response of the Anglican church was to areas of greatest need: eighty-four missionaries to New England, fifty-eight to New York, forty-four to New Jersey, forty-seven to Pennsylvania and Delaware, five to Maryland, two to Virginia, thirty-three to North Carolina, fifty-four to South Carolina, and thirteen to Georgia; some of the missionaries worked in several colonies. The SPG missionaries were the proselytizing arm of the church, even charged with instructing "Heathens and Infidels" in the "Principles of Natural Religion" and the "Necessity of Revelation." They also advised persons on doctrine and use of the sacraments and assisted in catechizing children.

Still the greatest hindrance to strengthening the national church in America was the failure to appoint a resident bishop. Attempts were made several times. In 1672 a charter was drawn up for establishing a diocese of Virginia, with Rev. Alexander Moray being named bishop-designate; but hearings on the prospective appointment, for whatever reason, were suddenly ended. The SPG labored for an American bishop and in 1712 provided a house in Burlington, West Jersey, for the episcopal see. Proposals for an American episcopacy advanced in the 1760s were vehemently denounced by many colonists; not until 1784 did the Episcopal church in America have its own bishop. The opposition against an episcopacy during the colonial period came from dissenters (the majority of the colonial religious population), merchants and land speculators who feared that an episcopacy would adversely affect immigration, London dissenters (many of whom were part of the ruling Whig coalition in England), and American Anglican clergy who were afraid that they might lose their jobs or that they might be placed under the jurisdiction of ecclesiastical courts.

PRESBYTERIANS

Scotch-Irish and Scottish immigration and a commingling of Congregationalists and Presbyterians outside of New England aided in the growth of the Presbyterian church in America. Puritans from New England frequently turned Presbyterian when taking up residence in other colonies. Like Congregationalists, Presbyterians were Calvinists in the Reformed tradition. Both deemphasized creed and dogma, practiced congregational autonomy, stressed personal piety, and considered the sacraments as not essential for obtaining grace. They differed primarily in that Congregationalists ordained ministers only for a local church, while Presbyterians did so for the whole Church Universal; this difference also applied to the elders.

By the beginning of the eighteenth century, the colonial Presbyterian church consisted of twelve churches—five in Maryland, two each in Delaware and Virginia, and one each in New York, Pennsylvania, and South Carolina. In 1758 there were two hundred congregations and ninety-eight ministers. Francis Makemie (1658–1708), trained at the University of Glasgow, became the great leader and organizer of Presbyterians, traversing the colonies from Maine to the Carolinas. For a while he resided on the eastern shore of Maryland, where he founded five churches. Makemie and six others organized the first American presbytery (for Maryland, Pennsylvania, and Delaware) in Philadelphia in 1706. The presbytery assumed the authority to ordain ministers and adjudicate disciplinary cases of the churches. By 1745, six presbyteries had been created for the middle colonies, two for New England, and one for South Carolina; the number had doubled by 1775. Significantly, the presbyteries were voluntary and not summoned by outside authority. In 1716 the synod of Philadelphia was formed, representing four presbyteries—Snow Hill (Maryland), Newcastle (Delaware), Long Island (New York), and Philadelphia. Lacking in the colonial Presbyterian experience, however, was a national convention (one step above the synod), which was not created until after the Revolution.

Colonial Presbyterianism faced two divisive issues: whether or not to subscribe to the Westminster Confession of Faith and the schism between New Sides and Old Sides during the Great Awakening. Both problems were healed in time. In 1729 a general synod agreed to the Westminister Confession of Faith and Catechisms, and the divided church (New Sides splitting off from the Philadelphia synod in 1745 to form their own synod in New York) was reunited in 1758. The American Presbyterian church reflected a strong Scotch-Irish influence, with emphasis on voluntary actions, a flexible hierarchy, local autonomy, an educated ministry, tolerance of nonessential differences, and reluctance to accept the creeds and instructions of the Church of Scotland.

With the great movement of the Scotch-Irish into western Pennsylvania and Maryland, the Great Valley of Virginia, and the North Carolina piedmont, Presbyterianism was firmly planted in the backcountry. Colonial Presbyterianism had a dichotomous success: appealing to the western pioneers while at the same time gaining support from the middle and upper classes.

OTHER DENOMINATIONS

Lutherans First established at New Sweden and New Netherland (the first church erected at Tinicium Island in the Delaware River about 1644), Lutheranism spread rapidly during the eighteenth century due largely to the influx of German exiles and redemptioners. Henry Melchior Mühlenberg (1711–1787), a professor and pastor in Germany, dedicated himself to the "planting of the church" in the colonies. Mühlenberg organized a synod (the Ministerium of Pennsylvania) in Philadelphia in 1748, consisting of six pastors from Pennsylvania, New Jersey, and New York, twenty-four lay delegates, and the church council of St. Michael's Church in Philadelphia; the next synod would not be held until 1786 in New York. The Lutheran church service in America usually avoided liturgy and consisted simply of a sermon, free prayer, singing of hymns, Scripture reading, and a benediction. A major problem in the founding of Lutheran churches was the absence of clergy; no seminary for the education of ministers was established until after the Revolution. By 1765 there were 133 congregations and thirty-three pastors.

Reformed churches The Dutch Reformed church, located primarily in New York City, in Albany, along the Hudson River, and on Long Island and Staten Island, grew steadily out of the natural increase in population. By 1776 there were one hundred congregations. The church received non-Dutch immigrants—Huguenots and especially Germans, most of whom were from the Palatinate. The similarities between the Dutch and German Reformed churches—both adhered to the Heidelberg Catechism and were followers of Zwingli and Calvin—led to easy fusion between the two. Dutch pastors often filled the pulpit for German Reformed congregations. Intermarriage was a factor in Germans joining the Dutch Reformed church. John Philip Boehm, a Pennsylvania farmer who was eventually ordained by Dutch ministers in New York, founded German Reformed churches in the Perkiomen Creek valley in Pennsylvania.

Other German churches Anabaptist pietists from Germany and Switzerland, fleeing religious persecution, settled primarily in Pennsylvania. Most pronounced of these arrivals were the Moravians (see Chapter 15), Mennonites, German Baptist Brethren (Dunkards or Dunkers), and Schwenkfelders. All these groups had worship that included a "love feast," washing of feet before partaking of the Lord's Supper, and a concluding "holy kiss of charity." The Mennonites (see Chapter 8) settled chiefly in

and around Lancaster County, Pennsylvania; their churches were autonomous, with each congregation electing a bishop, elders, and deacons.
The Dunkards (existing today as several different Churches of the
Brethren), led by Alexander Mack, arrived in Pennsylvania in 1719 and
four years later established their first church at Germantown. Similar to
the Mennonites, the Dunkards differed in administering baptism: Whereas
the Mennonites used pouring, the Dunkards practiced trine immersion
(submerging the baptismal candidate three times, to symbolize the Trinity).
By 1770 the Dunkards had fourteen congregations in Pennsylvania and
one in New Jersey. The Schwenkfelders, followers of Caspar Schwenk-
felder in southern Germany (of whom there are about two thousand
members today in a half dozen congregations in the Philadelphia area),
differed mainly from other Anabaptist groups by placing the Holy Spirit
above the Scriptures as a source of guidance. The Schwenkfelders had no
formal organization until 1782.

Quakers   The Quakers, probably so called because of their trembling
with emotion at religious meetings, first appeared in England in the mid-
seventeenth century under the leadership of George Fox. They referred
to themselves originally as Children of Light, then as Friends in the Truth,
Friends, and eventually the Society of Friends. The first Quakers in
mainland North America came to Boston in 1656, and more came the
following year to New Amsterdam and Virginia. Denying all outward rites
of worship, Quakers claimed that an "inward light" within each person
revealed divine truths. The early Quakers had a strong missionary zeal,
engaging in such activity as disrupting church services, with even a few
of the most radical (such as those called Ranters) demonstrating in public
naked. Viewed as subversive, they met stiff penalties in all early colonies
except Rhode Island. With the growth of toleration in the late seventeenth
century and the adoption by Quaker leaders in London of a policy of
coordination rather than individual activity, excessive behavior diminished.
By 1700 the Friends had entered into a period of "quietism." The rise to
prosperity and power, particularly in Pennsylvania, made American Quakers increasingly conservative, though they became known for their social
conscience and community benevolence. Quaker immigration was spurred
by Quaker proprietors gaining control of West Jersey in 1674 and by the
founding of Pennsylvania. At the time of the Revolution, the Society of
Friends, with nearly fifty thousand members, ranked fifth in numbers
among colonial Protestant denominations (after the Anglican, Congregational, Presbyterian, and Dutch Reformed churches).

The Quakers lacked a settled ministry, and during the early days of
the movement, in worship everyone sat silent until God "prepared a
mouthpiece for his Word." Eventually, however, "public Friends," those
who were more visibly called to preach, acted as elders or ministers. To

avoid obnoxious speakers, it became a requirement for the public Friends to be certified by the monthly meetings. Between 1683 and 1776 some one hundred persons served in the "traveling ministry." The Quakers governed themselves through local meetings, the monthly meetings, and through quarterly and yearly meetings (both of which represented regional groups of congregations). "Overseers," or "internal Friends," looked after membership and other business between the monthly meetings. In 1737 the Friends recognized birthright membership, with wives and children accepted if their husband or father was a member.

Baptists   Baptists practiced baptism of believers rather than infant baptism and followed a congregational polity. There would be a variety of Baptist sects in America, some more Anabaptist, Calvinist, or Arminian than others. Early American Baptists either originated in Europe or split off from other religious bodies in America. The leading Baptist groups in the colonial period were the General Baptists, Particular Baptists, Free Will Baptists, Six Principle Baptists, Seventh Day Baptists (German Dunkards), and the Separate Baptists, a product of the Great Awakening. The General Baptists originated in Holland about 1608 when John Smyth and other English separatists rebaptized themselves. These Baptists, unlike their separatist brethren, believed in general atonement—that saving grace could reach all persons. Particular (Calvinist) Baptists originated in England in the 1630s, during which time a group of them came to New England. The first Baptist churches established in America, at Newport (led by John Clarke) about 1638 and at Providence (including Roger Williams briefly) in 1639, were of the Particular persuasion. The Providence church in 1652 split into two factions: Six Principle (Arminian) and Calvinist groups. Free Will (Arminian) Baptists were organized in North Carolina and Virginia in the 1720s. The Six Principle Baptists founded their own church in Providence in 1653; they were called by this name because they followed principles expressed in Hebrews 6:1–2: repentance, faith, baptism, laying on of hands, resurrection of the dead, and eternal judgment. Welsh Baptists, mainly Calvinist, came to Plymouth colony and Massachusetts in 1663 and to Pennsylvania in the 1680s. The Welsh also founded Baptist congregations in South Carolina. Welsh Free Will Baptists arrived in 1701 and settled on the Welsh Tract in Pennsylvania.

In 1707, nine churches in Pennsylvania and New Jersey formed the Philadelphia Association, which later would draw representatives from most of the other colonies. The Philadelphia Association in 1742 adopted the London Confession (the platform of the Particular Baptists), which Calvinist slant would be a factor in some congregations' withdrawal from the association; by 1762 the Philadelphia Association had a membership of twenty-nine congregations with more than four thousand members. As a result of the Great Awakening, the older Baptists (principally those of

English and Welsh origins opposed to revivalism and emotionalism) became known as Regular Baptists, in contrast to New Light or Separatist Baptists, who stressed a reborn and converted church membership. By the time of the Revolution, there were about one hundred Baptist congregations of one type or another with some twenty-five thousand members.

Catholics and Jews   The story of early American Catholicism belongs mainly to the history of New France, Louisiana, Florida, and the Spanish American West. Maryland, of course, was settled in part as a refuge for Catholics, but few came over. By 1677 there were only three priests and thirteen Jesuits in the colony. During the eighteenth century more progress was made for the church in Pennsylvania than elsewhere, with the immigration of German Catholics. In 1765, Pennsylvania had six thousand Catholics and Maryland about ten thousand. From 1634 to 1773 some 186 Jesuit priests did missionary work in British North America. Like the Anglicans, American Catholics had a similar disadvantage in not having a resident bishop. The vicar apostolic of London had jurisdiction over the church in America; not until 1790 did the American church have a bishop (John Carroll).

Most early American Jews were Sephardic (see Chapter 8), and by the time of the Revolution their population was about twenty-five hundred, living in the major urban areas.

THE GREAT AWAKENING

The surge of emotionalism in the Protestant churches—chiefly Congregational, Presbyterian, and Reformed—left an imprint on American religion and character. The Great Awakening of the 1730s and 1740s was a natural response to problems facing American Christianity as well as a broadening of religious experience.

Since the turn of the eighteenth century, clergy had become ever more mindful of the decline in religion. A vast majority of Americans had no religious affiliation. Ministers denounced sin, contempt for authority, and contentions in church and community. Religion had become too staid, selective, and authoritarian for many Americans. There was a growing awareness of the needs of the common people. New ideas of philosophy and learning influenced ministerial views of doctrine and church discipline. Not the least was that of John Locke's epistemology, which stated that one could know only through sensations received in the mind and that volition itself was a property of the mind. Pietism, stressing personal religious experience and piety, held sway among many of the ethnic churches. The belief in revelation, whereby one could receive the Holy Spirit directly, had been an article of faith of various groups in early times, most notably Anne Hutchinson and her followers and also the Quakers. Americans felt the need for a more personal religion, even one affected by enthusiasm (in the sense of its Greek root enthousiasmos, "inspired or possessed by divine will"). The Great Awakening brought little change to orthodoxy in theology; rather, it offered a "new birth"—a conversion experience following the intense awareness of guilt, a "circumcision of the heart," as Jonathan Edwards called it.

Although there were already evangelical stirrings in New England, the Great Awakening may be said to have begun with the preaching of Theodorus Jacobus Frelinghuysen (1691–ca.1748). Frelinghuysen, a native of Westphalia, Germany, and raised in Holland, arrived in America in 1720 and assumed the pastorate of four small Dutch Reformed churches in the Raritan valley of New Jersey. The older conservative members of these Dutch congregations were hardly ready for Frelinghuysen's exhortations on inward consciousness of sin and repentance and his "howling prayers," but his evangelism did touch the poorer and younger church members. The fanning of revivalist enthusiasm in the middle colonies, however, was owing mostly to the efforts of Gilbert Tennent, who knew and cooperated with Frelinghuysen.

Gilbert Tennent was the eldest son of William Tennent, who arrived with his family in America in 1718 and became the pastor of three Presbyterian congregations along the Neshaminy River. In 1726, William Tennent established the Log Cabin College, where for twenty years he trained revivalist Presbyterian ministers. Gilbert Tennent, himself a recipient of the M.A. degree from Yale and licensed by the Philadelphia presbytery, began his ministry at New Brunswick. Also filling the pulpits of other churches as a visiting preacher, he impressed on his hearers the need for a conversion experience. Gilbert Tennent gave his most famous sermon at Nottingham (at the border of Pennsylvania and Maryland) on March 8, 1740: In "The Danger of the Unconverted Ministry," he declared, "An ungodly Ministry is a great Curse and Judgment: These Caterpillars labour to devour every green Thing." As George Whitefield said of Gilbert Tennent:

> He convinced me more and more that we can preach the Gospel of Christ no further than we have experienced the power of it in our hearts. Being deeply convicted of sin, by God's Holy Spirit, at his first conversion, he has learned experimentally to dissect the heart of a natural man. Hypocrites must either soon be converted or enraged at his preaching. He is a son of thunder, and does not fear the faces of men.

The Great Awakening in the middle colonies created a 23-year division in the Presbyterian church, with the conservative Old Sides pitted against the conversion-minded New Sides.

Gilbert Tennent, probably by Gustavus Hesselius. Collection of Princeton University

The New England Awakening may be dated to the fall of 1734 at Jonathan Edwards's Northampton church. Actually, the first wave of convictions came outside the pulpit, from Edwards's meeting with young people after evening lectures. Soon older members also reported emotional experiences. Edwards preached intensely on justification by faith, even though God had chosen only a few to be saved. He painted lurid pictures of the horrors of damnation. Not a dynamic speaker, Edwards nevertheless entranced his audiences. He preached his most famous sermon while supplying the pulpit of the Enfield church on July 8, 1741—"Sinners in the Hands of an Angry God," based on Deuteronomy 32:35, "Their foot shall slide in due time"; there were so many shrieks and cries that Edwards,

Jonathan Edwards by Joseph Badger. Courtesy of the Yale University Art Gallery. Bequest of Eugene Phelps Edwards

with his eyes fixed on the bellrope, had to pause throughout the sermon. Though always a strict predestinarian, Edwards was amazed at the outpouring of religious "affections," which he described in *A Faithful Narrative of the Surprising Work of God in the Conversion of Many Hundred Souls in Northampton, and the Neighboring Towns and Villages* (1736) and other works.

Revivalism spread throughout New England. As J. M. Bumsted (1971) notes about Norton, Massachusetts, a crisis conversion experience affected mostly the young people, who were distressed with lack of opportunity for economic and social mobility. After twenty-three years in the Northampton pulpit, Jonathan Edwards was dismissed by his congregation, in retaliation for his attempts to restore the full sanctity of the Lord's Supper. Thereafter, he served as a missionary to the Stockbridge Indians and twelve white families on the New England frontier. In 1757, a year before his death, he became president of the College of New Jersey (formerly the Log Cabin College and later Princeton).

The one individual who most gave the Great Awakening an ecumenical as well as an intercolonial thrust was George Whitefield, an Oxford-ordained Anglican priest. Whitefield had witnessed the emotional preaching of John Wesley in England. Of Whitefield's four visits to the colonies, his tours of 1739–1740 (New England to Georgia) and 1741 (Georgia to New Jersey) were the most spectacular. Outdoor services in New York City and Philadelphia drew more than six thousand listeners. During three weeks in September 1740 he spoke seventeen times at Boston churches; some twenty thousand bade him farewell at the Boston Common. Whitefield owed his success to his magnificent voice, histrionics, advance publicity, and rapport with common people. Interestingly, he found almost no reception from Anglicans.

For the Southern Awakening, Samuel Davies (1723–1761), a New Side Presbyterian minister, carried the revival movement to Virginia. Careful not to anger Anglicans and civil authorities, he spoke at licensed meetinghouses and attacked only irreligion, not the Anglican church. Much in the style of later American evangelists, Davies preached "as a dying man to a dying man." Davies accepted the presidency of the College of New Jersey two years before his death. Reverend John Thompson also led the Presbyterian revival in Virginia. Because of the fear of arousing slaves, the Awakening barely took root in South Carolina and Georgia. One controversial figure, however, in the Awakening in South Carolina was Hugh Bryan, a wealthy planter, who in the early 1740s held revival meetings for whites and slaves alike in St. Helena's Parish. His "prophecies," which he recorded in a journal, relating to "the Destruction of Charles-Town and Deliverance of the Negroes from their Servitude," were too much for the South Carolina aristocracy, with the Stono Rebellion a burning memory; Bryan was forced to back down from his revivalist preaching.

The Great Awakening had a negative side. Jonathan Edwards was exceedingly troubled when a mentally unstable parishioner at Northampton, Joseph Hawley, slit his own throat. James Davenport, minister at Southold, Long Island, preached also in New England, always exhibiting some bizarre behavior; he was imprisoned in Boston and sent home. Ministers such as Charles Chauncy of the First Church in Boston and Benjamin Doolittle of the Northfield church criticized the evils of unrestrained emotionalism in religion, emphasizing that evangelical ministers showed contempt for reason, had faith without foundation, blindly followed impulses and "heated imagination," disparaged those not in agreement with them, disrupted churches, and threatened social stability.

Actually, the Great Awakening did little to increase the size of congregations; the number of people professing religious experiences was small and came from the membership rather than the unchurched. It nevertheless influenced religious trends and society as a whole. The Great Awakening contributed to itinerant evangelism, the use of lay exhorters, a renewal of emphasis on conscious conversion experiences in the churches, greater opportunities for individual responsibility in the churches (thus further encouraging church autonomy), missionary activity, a narrower piety reflected in social as well as religious attitudes, the formation of new sects, and religious toleration. Baptists and, later, the Methodists were beneficiaries of the revival, as were Anglicans, for different reasons. As Samuel Johnson, a former Congregational minister and Anglican convert, observed, revivals "occasioned endless divisions and separations, so that many could find no rest to the sole of their feet till they retired into the [Anglican] Church, as their only ark of safety." The Great Awakening divided Congregationalists into conservative and liberal camps. The so-called New Divinity, an orthodox adaptation of Edwards's theology, enunciated by Samuel Hopkins, pastor at Newport, Rhode Island, and others, extolled the absolute sovereignty of God. New Divinity pastors sought to return to the pre–Half-Way Covenant days and refused to baptize children unless parents gave proof of religious experience. The New Divinity held that no person had any means at all to enhance his or her salvation. Contrary to the New Divinity, however, the Great Awakening furthered the idea of general atonement, appealing to all classes of individuals, even the poor and slaves. It also led to the founding of colleges for the training of conversion-conscious ministers—Brown, Dartmouth, the College of New Jersey, and Rutgers.

The Great Awakening stimulated a humanitarian impulse, reflected in the establishment of schools and orphanages; Whitefield himself helped to found a Negro school in Philadelphia. On a broader scale, the Great Awakening encouraged democracy and advanced the idea of freedom as a cause of God, a disposition quite adaptable to the revolutionary movement against Great Britain. But it must also be pointed out that the Great Awakening, by directing persons to spiritual concerns, dampened expectations for social and political reforms. A return to the quest for reformational Christianity, as encouraged by the Great Awakening, comported with a later national psychology of manifest destiny.

RISE OF THE SEPARATE BAPTISTS

As the Presbyterian churches divided into Old Sides and New Sides during the Great Awakening, so did New England Congregational churches into New Lights and Old Lights. New Lights wanted each church completely separatist. They rejected the Half-Way Covenant, holding that to receive the blessings of God, the visible church must be reborn; they believed that the Holy Spirit was an active agent in each person. The Separate congregations consisted largely of the poorer classes. By the mid-eighteenth century many of these congregations had "gone to the Baptists." The Separate Baptists restricted adult baptism to reborn believers.

Isaac Backus (1724–1806), a Congregational pastor in Norwich, Connecticut, was rebaptized and in 1756 founded a Baptist church in Middleboro, Massachusetts, where he remained pastor until his death. Backus helped to organize New England Baptists in the Warren Association at Warren, Rhode Island, separate from the Philadelphia Association, primarily for the purpose of fighting for religious liberty. Backus was active in evangelical preaching and from 1756 traveled fifteen thousand miles, giving 2,412 sermons. He strongly denounced infant baptism, which he felt contributed to a national "territorial" church, undifferentiated from society as a whole.

The greatest expansion of the Separate Baptists occurred in the South, where two Connecticut evangelists led the way. Shubal Stearns (1706–1771), converted during Whitefield's visit in 1741, founded the Baptist church at Tolland, Connecticut, and was ordained its pastor. For a while he attempted to organize Baptist churches in Berkeley and Hampshire counties, Virginia. His brother-in-law, Daniel Marshall (1706–1784), helped to settle a community of Baptists near present-day Winchester, Virginia. Stearns and Marshall in 1755 brought their families and others to Sandy Creek, North Carolina, where they founded a church, with Stearns as its pastor until his death. The Separate Baptists grew rapidly, adapting to the needs of the frontier. The new Baptist churches were strongly democratic; all members had an equal voice in every aspect of church affairs. A call was considered more important than education for those who entered the ministry; Separate Baptist pastors engaged in all kinds of histrionics, such as falling down, jerking, and crying out.

The Separate Baptists were viewed with disdain in Virginia, as subverting established religion and morality and intoxicating poor people and slaves. Equally offensive were Baptist efforts at defying authority by preaching without a license and aggressively proselytizing—considered as disturbing the peace. One Virginian aptly charged that the Separate Baptists "cannot meet a man on the road but they must ram a text of Scripture down [his] throat."

As the Baptist movement slackened about 1775, another religious group gained wide appeal, especially along the frontier. The Methodists, founded by John Wesley and intended as a reform segment of the Anglican church, took on the semblance of a new denomination. Like the Baptists, Methodists operated in a counterculture context. They also engaged in extemporaneous preaching, love feasts, and the like. John Wesley had visited Georgia in 1736. The great success of the Methodists during the Revolutionary War era was owing to such evangelical circuit-riding ministers as Devereux Jarratt (1733–1801), who began preaching in 1763 as an Anglican minister. Methodist preachers from England in the 1760s assisted in getting churches started in the colonies.

ARMINIANISM AND RATIONALISM

Much of the religious awakenings of the eighteenth century, even with the stress on religious conversion experiences, left Calvinist doctrines only bleached, not repudiated. Yet a residue of the evangelical movement was the feeling that an individual could discern his own standing with God and put himself into a condition to receive grace. Some Congregationalists in eastern Massachusetts held this view in its extreme. They were known as Arminians, after the liberal beliefs of a Dutch professor of theology, Jacobus Arminius (1560–1609), who remonstrated against Calvinist doctrines of the Dutch Reformed church. Though not intending to appropriate Arminius's theology as such, these New England Congregationalists essentially agreed that man in rightly exercising his free will could achieve salvation. They also denied that man was tainted with original sin and believed that one could overcome his evil nature through discipline and assistance from God. Arminian Congregationalism placed a premium on education and discovery of the natural laws of God.

The Brattle Street Church in Boston, founded in 1699, was the first New England church to adopt these principles; it admitted all persons of visible sanctity. Two prominent Boston ministers, Jonathan Mayhew (1720–1766) of the West Church and Charles Chauncy (1705–1787) of the First Church, preached almost entirely of God's love and the attainment of salvation through goodness. In their view, God sought the happiness and salvation of all mankind. Thus Chauncy observed that man is "an intelligent moral agent; having within himself an ability and freedom to will, as well as to do, in opposition to necessity from any extraneous cause whatever." God is "the Supreme Being," who "communicates good by general laws, whose operation he does not counteract, but concurs with, in a regular uniform course." Doing evil resulted from misuse of one's reason. Reason, however, was not enough alone but should be used with imagination and faith. The religious liberalism of Mayhew and Chauncy lacked only the anti-Trinitarian component that distinguished Unitarianism in the New England of the next century.

Some Americans went further than the Arminian liberal theology and took their inspiration even more from ideas transmitted from the European Age of Reason and the Enlightenment, adopting essentially a world view blending Newtonian science and Lockean empiricism. Best described as deists, they rejected any form of instituted religion and considered that man needed only to discover laws of nature and live by them. Deistic principles had been set forth in the seventeenth century by Edward Herbert (Baron Herbert of Cherbury, 1583–1648), an English philosopher and diplomat, who expounded on natural religion in such works as *De veritate* (1624) and *De religione gentilium* (1663). Herbert declared five articles of faith: existence of God, His worship, practice of virtue, repentance of sin, and faith in immortality. To deistic thinking, the universe was created by God, but once in motion, it functioned by natural laws, without interference or revelation from God. Deism in eighteenth-century America never developed into any type of religion, though efforts were made to give it a kind of creed, as expressed in a pamphlet by Ethan Allen (1737–1789), *Reason the Only Oracle of Man* (1784), and in Elihu Palmer's "Principles of the Deistical Society of the State of New York" (ca. 1795); Palmer organized deistic societies in New York City and Philadelphia in the 1790s.

Deistic principles appealed to some early American leaders and intellectuals, including Benjamin Franklin, Thomas Paine, and Thomas Jefferson. Benjamin Franklin himself moved from being a radical to a moderate deist. Franklin believed that God shared the blessings of nature with every creature. Though he repudiated traditional religion, he was nevertheless attracted to it. In 1738, Franklin wrote to his father:

> The Scriptures assure me, that at the last day we shall not be examined what we *thought*, but what we *did*; and our recommendation will not be, that we said, *Lord! Lord!* but that we did good to our fellow creatures.

19

Science
and the Arts

Inquiry for the sake of learning and the desire to make worldly existence more comfortable and pleasurable influenced colonial Americans to seek new vistas of knowledge and experience. Most often utilitarianism was a guiding principle. By the time of the Revolution, Americans embraced the idea of progress as a condition for their own destiny. As Henry Steele Commager (1977) has written: "The Old World imagined, invented, and formulated the Enlightenment; the New World—certainly the Anglo-American part of it—realized and fulfilled it" (p. xi).

PHILOSOPHICAL AND SCIENTIFIC INQUIRY

Even the Puritans, though believing that humankind was caught in a vise of circumstances preordained by God, encouraged inquiry into the nature of things and of being. The study of nature more fully revealed God's plan. To John Cotton, nature was but "a mappe and shadow of the spiritual estate of the souls of men." Cotton Mather, in *The Christian Philosopher* (1720), wrote that science "is no Enemy, but a mighty and wondrous incentive to Religion;" the discovery of "a small Part of the

Wisdom that made all things" leads to God himself. John Winthrop IV, a Harvard professor in the mid-eighteenth century, in replying to criticism of religious leaders to his scientific experiments, stated:

> [The] main business of natural Philosophy is, to trace the chain of natural causes from one link to another, till we come to the FIRST CAUSE, who, in Philosophy, is considered as presiding over, and continually actuating this whole chain and every link of it.

A few American intellectuals went beyond the pursuit of knowledge to grapple with the fathoming of the nature of the mind and of human will. Jonathan Edwards, in such works as *A Careful and Strict Enquiry into . . . Freedom of the Will* (1754), *A Treatise concerning Religious Affections* (1746), and *Notes on the Mind* (published in 1830), contended that reality exists only in the mind of God, who instills His own presence in human minds. To Edwards, truth is the consistency and agreement of our ideas with the ideas of God. Samuel Johnson (1696–1772), first president of King's College, in *An Introduction to the Study of Philosophy* (1731) and *Elementa philosophica* (1752), adhered to much of the Platonic and Berkeleian idealism of Edwards. To Johnson, nothing was completely external or independent of the mind, though all things were perceived by God; it was incumbent on man to cultivate his God-given reason and understanding. Other Americans, however, emphasized objective rather than subjective reality. Thus deists sought merely the discovery of natural laws, without admitting any continuing transcendent power of God. Cadwallader Colden (1688–1776) went even further, asserting that intelligence resided in different forms of matter; he held that it was impossible to assign any deeper meaning to things other than the observance of their existence and activity. But to most Americans who pursued scientific inquiry, it was enough just to obtain knowledge rather than to speculate on metaphysical components. Isaac Newton's *Philosophiae naturalis principia mathematica* (1687) had enormous appeal to Americans, with its insistence that all phenomena had mechanical explanations.

Anyone could find enjoyment in the pursuit of science and find ennoblement, through its requirement of patience, accuracy, and diligence. American scientists themselves displayed a wide variety of interests. It is not surprising to find that many physicians were active in scientific endeavors other than their own professional calling.

Scientific research in the colonies received encouragement through the Royal Society for Improving Natural Knowledge (founded in 1662). From 1663 to 1783 the Royal Society admitted fifty-three Americans as fellows, the first being John Winthrop, Jr. The Royal Society furnished its members with books, scientific instruments, and occasionally financial support. It also served as a clearinghouse for information and published the *Philosophical Transactions*, which carried 260 articles by American colonists.

Learned associations also cropped up in America, the first being the short-lived Boston Philosophical Society, organized in 1683. Of greatest importance was the American Philosophical Society, founded in 1743 from a group brought together by Benjamin Franklin in 1727. In 1769 the American Philosophical Society united with the American Society for Promoting and Propagating Useful Knowledge (established in 1750).

Science, not yet reaching the level of specialization, during the early colonial period was simply referred to as natural philosophy; later it was defined usually by two categories: natural philosophy (all the modern physical sciences, including physics, chemistry, astronomy, geology, and meteorology as well as mathematics) and natural history (botany and zoology). Medicine and surgery belonged to both classifications—to natural philosophy, in chemistry, and to natural history, in anatomy and materia medica.

NATURAL PHILOSOPHY

Two of colonial America's most versatile investigators were Cadwallader Colden and Benjamin Franklin. Colden received a M.A. degree at the University of Edinburgh and acquired medical education from private tutors in London. Coming to Philadelphia in 1710, he practiced medicine before moving to New York in 1718, whereupon he entered a political career that included the lieutenant governorship. Never a painstaking researcher, Colden nevertheless came up with curious ideas, much criticized in his time but not altogether far-fetched. He rattled the scientific community most with his attempt to formulate a field theory of gravity. In *An Explication of the First Causes in Matter; and of the Cause of Gravitation* (New York, 1745; London, 1746 and later editions) he cited three substances of the material world: ether (elastic and subtle substance), resisting matter (mass, bodies occupying space), and moving matter (essentially corpuscular particles—light). Significantly, Colden touched on the idea of energy as matter in stating that action was the basis of all matter. Colden theorized that gravity was caused by the exertion of ether on all planets and stars. Similar to Newton, he considered that the force of gravitation "at every distance" toward any body acted inversely "as the squares of the distance."

By the mid-eighteenth century, scientists, in both the Old World and the New, were making electrical experiments. Pieter van Musschenbroek and E. G. von Klienst had developed a rudimentary form of condensor— a Leyden jar, whose negative charges inside were balanced by positive charges outside. Benjamin Franklin was familiar with the electrical dem-

Cadwallader Colden by John Wollaston. The Metropolitan Museum of Art, Bequest of Grace Wilkes, 1922

onstrations of Dr. Archibald Spencer, who lectured widely in the colonies. Franklin's famous kite experiment, directing lightning into a Leyden jar, demonstrated that lightning and electricity were one and the same. Believing that electricity consisted of particles of electrical "fluid," Franklin noted that "electrical fire was not created by friction, but collected, being really an element diffused among, and attracted by, other matter, particularly by water and metal."

Benjamin Franklin also investigated the conductivity of heat, though thinking it was a fluid like electricity; his only contribution was to show differential thermal conductivity (such as by placing broadcloth patches of different colors in the snow and by noting the degree of heat in objects held close to a fire). His Pennsylvania fireplace operated on the principle of forcing heat to descend before escaping through a chimney, thereby warming a room at all levels. Franklin was both a practical scientist and a tinkerer. Among his useful gadgets were bifocals. He perfected an armonica (which name he changed to harmonica), an instrument of thirty-seven revolving glasses (with holes in their middle), mounted on an iron spindle, played by rubbing moistened fingers on the rims of the glasses. There was hardly any area of knowledge that eluded Franklin—among his active interests were astronomy, meteorology, oceanography, optics, botany, medicine, phonetics, and music (he even composed a string quartet). Franklin's breadth of scientific investigations, though mostly dabbling at the surface, effectively popularized science and stimulated its pursuit.

Astronomy held a fascination for many Americans. John Winthrop, Jr., owned the first telescope, which he presented to Harvard in 1673. That institution acquired a second telescope by the end of the seventeenth century. Samuel Danforth described a comet that appeared in 1665, as did Increase Mather on a later occasion in his *Kometographia, or a Discourse concerning Comets* (Boston, 1683). Rev. William Brattle of Cambridge, Massachusetts, published *An Ephemeris of Coelestral Motions, Aspects &c. for the Year of the Christian Aera 1682* (Boston, 1682). John Winthrop IV (1714–1779), Hollins Professor of Mathematics, Natural and Experimental Philosophy at Harvard, described a transit of Mercury and a lunar eclipse. Winthrop, however, was best known for his theory that an earthquake was caused by "an undulatory motion of the earth." Thomas Robie (1689–1729) taught astronomy at Harvard. Thomas Godfrey (1704–1749), a glazier by trade, invented a mariner's quadrant for measuring longitude. David Rittenhouse (1732–1796), a clockmaker, reported on the transit of Venus. Rittenhouse developed the theory of the "plurality of worlds" and calculated the solar parallax. He invented a metallic thermometer and constructed a refracting telescope. Rittenhouse was best known, however, for erecting an orrery (a device for depicting the relations of bodies in the solar system) and the Astronomical Observatory (begun in 1768), a mechanical planetarium, located at Norriton, twenty miles from Philadelphia. Among the many other colonists who pursued an interest in astronomy were Landon Carter and John Page in Virginia, the latter using a telescope from the roof of his Rosewall plantation.

The *Compendium physicae* (1687) by Charles Morton (1627–1698) was long used as a textbook at Harvard; though not a significant scientific work, it did stimulate interest in research in various areas of physics. Yale followed Harvard in the teaching of natural philosophy and astronomy. Thomas Clap (1703–1767), president of the college, weighted the curricula with science, and himself published *Conjectures upon the Nature and Motion of Meteors Which Are Above the Atmosphere* (Boston, 1744).

The study of chemistry, except in a most cursory way, was neglected until the establishment of medical schools at the end of the colonial period. At Harvard, however, there was some interest in chemical experiments, as reflected in the topics of commencement theses and questions. Morton's *Compendium physicae* had a chapter on chemistry: commentary on Aristotle's four elements—fire, water, earth, and air; the "3 matters of Descartes"; the atomic theories of Pierre Gassendi (1592–1655) and others; the "5 Principles (Elements, or Matters)" that by fire "can Separate, and make Sensibly distinct"; and the "two Elements," "Active" and "Passive," that "Other Chymists will have." Until the end of the eighteenth century, in Europe and America, scientists held to the phlogiston theory as advanced by Johann Becher (1635–1682) and Georg Ernst Stahl (1660–1734)—that oxidation results from the burning off of a substance known as phlogiston (modern theory holds that oxidation results from the *absorption* of a substance, oxygen).

NATURAL HISTORY

By the mid-eighteenth century, Americans had achieved recognition as an important part of an international natural history circle, which included collectors of specimens of fauna and flora in England, France, Holland, Sweden, Germany, and Italy. The botanists followed the lead of Carolus (Carl) Linnaeus (1701–1778), a Swedish physician and naturalist whose binomial nomenclature became the standard means of classification—identifying plants and animals by two names, one denoting the genus, or general group, and the other the particular species. Peter Collinson (1694–1768), a wealthy London cloth merchant, corresponded with colonial naturalists and popularized American plants in England.

Colonial naturalist-collectors sent a steady stream of specimens to England and wrote about them in the Royal Society's *Transactions*. William Byrd II was one of many who supplied English and other foreign correspondents with samples of animal and plant life. Once, upon his arrival in England in 1715, Byrd presented the Royal Society with "the bones of the penis of a Bear and of a Raccoon." Byrd's American diaries were filled with naturalist observations; his *Newly Found Eden . . .*, a treatise on the flora and fauna of several colonies where he had traveled, was printed in German, in Bern, Switzerland, in 1737 "at the command of the Helvetian Society."

John Banister (1650–1692) was one of the earliest botanists to receive general praise for fieldwork in America; his catalog of Virginia plants was published in John Ray's *Historia plantarum* (three volumes, 1686–1704). Banister was hard at work on his "Natural History of Virginia" when he was killed by a hunter mistaking him for a deer. Another Virginian, John Clayton (1694–1773), clerk of Gloucester County, traversed the eastern slope of the Blue Ridge Mountains; the *Flora virginica* (1739, 1743, and 1762), published in Leyden by John Frederick Gronovius, was based on

Clayton's "Catalog of Plants, Fruits and Trees Native to Virginia." Mark Catesby (ca. 1680–1749), who has been referred to as "the colonial Audubon," pioneered scientific illustration. From his fieldwork in America and the West Indies (1712–1719 and 1722–1726) he published *The Natural History of Carolina, Florida and the Bahama Islands* (two volumes, 1731 and 1743) in which he covered botany, zoology, ichthyology, and especially ornithology. Some of Catesby's figures, however, were criticized for being composites of species and subspecies. Dr. John Mitchell (1711–1768), a native of Lancaster County, Virginia, and educated at Edinburgh, had a multifaceted career as a physician, medical researcher, and naturalist. His main correspondent was Johann Jacob Dillenius (1687–1747) at Oxford. Mitchell preferred to consider an entire plant in determining genus, rather than just the reproductive system, as Linnaeus did.

Two Charleston, South Carolina, physicians, Alexander Garden (1730–1791) and John Lining (1708–1760), worked extensively in natural history. Garden, for whom the gardenia was named, achieved most fame for his *Corals and Corallines*, which showed that coral organisms are animals.

To the north, James Logan (1674–1751) gained a reputation as a collector of insects, birds, eggs, and fossils and as an experimenter in plant breeding on his farm outside of Philadelphia. Cadwallader Colden collected plants from his estate, Coldengham, and the forests and valleys of New York, earning the praise of Linnaeus, who published Colden's catalog as *Plantae coldenghamiae* in the first part of *Acta upsaliensis*. Jane Colden continued her father's work in natural history. Her "Flora of New York," with 340 illustrations drawn by her, was placed in the British Museum. When it was learned that a London botanist intended to name an American filipendula (a shrub with deep peach flowers growing wild in New York) for her, Jane's aunt exclaimed, "What! Name a weed after a Christian woman!"

John Bartram (1699–1777), from his farm on the Schuylkill River, supplied London merchants with seeds and obtained a fifty-pound annual pension from the king. Bartram also sent seeds and plants to Gronovius in Holland and to Linnaeus in Sweden. Linnaeus called Bartram "the greatest natural botanist in the world." His son, William Bartram (1739–1823), also became a noted botanist. Of three hundred new plants entering England before the American Revolution, forty were credited to John Bartram.

MEDICINE

Colonists were plagued with ill health, not helped by bad sanitation, lack of hospitals, scarcity of doctors, and ignorance as to the cause and cure of ailments. Surgery was seldom performed, due to physicians' insufficient knowledge of and training in anatomy. Colonial medical practitioners held to the Greek speculative pathology that illnesses resulted from impurities in body fluids (humors) or disorders in the vascular or nervous system.

Etiology made some headway in the eighteenth century. Even Cotton Mather, in his *Angel of Bethseda* (1723), came close to a germ theory by stating that minute worms sent by God caused diseases. One breakthrough in Europe was the improvement in microscopes, such as those constructed by Antonie van Leeuwenhoek (1632–1723) in Holland, which made it possible to observe protozoa and bacteria and to analyze the structure of blood cells.

A sick person in the colonies probably had a better chance of survival by staying away from physicians. Dr. William Douglass commented upon his arrival in Boston in 1718:

> I asked a most noted facetious practitioner what was their general method of practice; he told me their practice was very uniform: bleeding, vomiting, blistering, purging, anodynes, &c.; if the illness continued, there was *repetendi*, and finally *murderandi*.

One could well wonder about a physician's diagnosis and prescription. Cotton Mather in 1724 mentioned a doctor who advised a woman patient suffering from "distemper" (a twisting of the gut) to swallow two leaden bullets. A recipe for treating whooping cough consisted of boiled and pounded snakes, mixed into white wine, with a sprinkling of twenty herbs and opium. Among many remedies were oil of turkey buzzard for sciatica, eagle's flesh for gout, its powdered skull for migraine, its brain mixed with wine for jaundice, and its dung for tremors. Purging, sweating, and bleeding were heavily relied on. One classic prescription was General James Wolfe's mother's remedy for consumption:

> Take a peck of green garden snails, wash them in Bear [beer], put them in an oven, and let them stay till they've done crying; then with a knife and fork pick the green from them, and beat the snail shells and all in a stone mortar. Then take a quart of green earth-worms, slice them through the middle, and strow them with salt; then wash them and beat them, the pot being first put into the still with two handfulls of angelica, a quart of rosemary flowers, then the snails and worms, the egrimony, bears' feet, red dock roots, barbery break, bilbony, wormwood, of each two handfulls; one handful of rue rumerick and one ounce of saffron, well dried and beaten. Wait till morning, then put in three ounces of cloves (well beaten), hartshorn, grated. Keep the still covered all night. This done, stir it not. Distil with a moderate fire. The patient must take two spoonfuls at a time.

Colonial physicians used an enormous variety of herbs: native American, West Indian, and South American. Such medicines, many in use today, included ipecac (inducing vomiting), jimson (Jamestown) weed (curing burns), Jerusalem oak (deworming), snakeroot (ending diarrhea and other ailments), alum (treating dropsy), and chinchona or Jesuit's bark as quinine (preventing malaria). Ginseng, a perennial root growing abundantly in American forests, was highly prized as a cure-all and for its alleged invigorating qualities. Colonial physicians often operated apothecary shops, doing a thriving business selling herbal and mineral drugs.

During the seventeenth century, medicine in the colonies was practiced almost entirely by men in other fields, and a medical profession did not emerge until after 1700. Even as late as 1753, William Smith of New York could write that "Quacks abound like locusts." On the eve of the Revolution, of some 3,500 medical practitioners in the colonies, only five hundred had a formal medical education (of whom only about twenty-five held degrees).

A number of colonial "physicians" had served as naval surgeons. Most educated physicians in the colonies received their training at Scottish universities (principally Edinburgh), while a few had attended a continental medical school, such as at Leyden, or had studied with tutors in London. Some of the Scottish trained physicians wound up as career public servants. Adam Stephen, who studied medicine at the University of Edinburgh, forewent medical practice for an army career in the French and Indian and Revolutionary wars; on the side, however, he attended to neighbors' ailments and occasionally performed surgery.

In the seventeenth century, only a scant few Americans took medical degrees abroad, mainly men from Massachusetts—Samuel Bellington at Leyden, John Glover at Aberdeen, Leonard Hoar at Cambridge, Edmund Davie at Padua. The situation, however, was quite different after the mid-eighteenth century. Between 1750 and 1800, for example, 106 Virginians studied medicine at the University of Edinburgh.

A medical profession eventually took shape in the colonies. Societies of physicians appeared in the major cities. New York passed the first medical license law in 1760, requiring the examination of a candidate's fitness to practice. The College of Philadelphia (1765) and King's College (1767) established medical departments. Dr. William Shippen (beginning in 1762 in Philadelphia) offered the first formal course in anatomy in the colonies. The only two hospitals in the colonies before the Revolution, in Philadelphia (1752) and New York (1769), allowed for clinical teaching by the faculties of the two schools.

Some colonial physicians researched particular illnesses, for example, William Douglass, scarlet fever; Cadwallader Colden, cancer and lead poisoning; John Mitchell and John Lining, yellow fever; and Lionel Chalmers, tetanus. Nonphysicians also interested themselves in the investigation of diseases, such as Cotton Mather and smallpox. William Byrd II wrote *A Discourse concerning the Plague with Some Preventions against It* (1721); to ward off this disease, which never came to the colonies, Byrd advocated the placing of tobacco in large quantities in rooms of houses and wearing it on clothes. Tobacco, a "great Antipoison," said Byrd, should be chewed frequently. The most prolific and popular of colonial writers on medicine was Dr. John Tennent (ca. 1700–1748), residing in Virginia and England, whose books included *Every Man His Own Physician; or the Poor Planter's Physician* (second edition, 1734).

John Foster's Footstone. Attributed to the Charlestown stonecutter. Museum of Fine Arts, Boston

Mrs. Elizabeth Freake and Baby Mary. Worcester Art Museum, Worcester, Massachusetts

PAINTING

While colonists pursued discovery and collecting in areas of science, they found avenues for creativity in artistic expression. Craftsmen excelled in the decorative arts, turning out fine furniture, silverware, and pewter. German immigrants especially were known for their glass and earthenware. Though some attempts were made to produce porcelain, most colonists preferred to get their china from abroad. In the graphic arts, the few engravers, who depicted mostly topographical views and events, were not distinguished in their work. Though avoiding large-scale projects such as statues and monuments, colonial sculptors skillfully applied their talents in three-dimensional art: carved trade signs, tombstones, weather vanes, and ship carving—figureheads, ornamental billetheads, and sternpieces. Both native-born Americans and visiting Englishmen produced prodigious numbers of paintings, many of high quality. Colonial painting reflected American society and was characterized by a simple matter-of-factness in styles derived from the European.

Limners in New England dominated colonial painting in the seventeenth century. These artists usually started out as house, carriage, or sign painters. The typical painting was flat, two-dimensional, with a predominance of black and brown. Early limner portraitists sought to show the adult subject as a somber, exemplary figure, often in three-fourths body profile. But children were depicted as full of life and in more cheerful colors—with mortality so high, parents wanted pleasant mementos of their offspring. The most outstanding of the limners' portraits that survive were by the unknown artists who painted Elizabeth Freake and Baby Mary and the Gibbes children—Robert, Henry, and Margaret. By the 1680s the advent of New England merchant princes was evident; portraits featured more cavalierlike personalities, a greater use of colors, and more attention to clothes and objects. Lillian B. Miller (1984) has observed:

> The fact that such a large number of portraits have survived from seventeenth-century New England, and so many of charm and interest, suggests that Puritan New Englanders took as much—if not more—delight in color and form as any other group of people in the same situation, facing similar problems of survival. (pp. 183–84)

A limner painter in South Carolina and Maryland, German-born Justus Engelhardt Kühn (d. 1717), employed backgrounds and accessories and achieved a greater sensitivity in his paintings, such as *Eleanor Darnall*, than his northern counterparts.

American painting in the eighteenth century exhibited greater realism and attention to detail. Two men had a profound influence on art before midcentury: John Smibert (1688–1751) and Robert Feke (ca. 1705–ca. 1750). Smibert, who began his career as a house painter and plasterer in Edinburgh, came to America in 1728. Residing at Newport and then Boston, he is credited with 241 portraits. His most famous painting, *Dean George Berkeley and His Family*, has curved accents, a three-dimensional effect achieved by contrasting light and distance of landscape in the background, and a harmony of color. The realism of most of his portraits is suggestive of the work of the English painter and satirist William Hogarth. Feke, perhaps colonial America's most important native painter, grew up either on Long Island or in New England; except that he painted in Newport, Boston, and Philadelphia, not much is known about his life. In his *Isaac Royall and Family*, he differed from Smibert in stressing linear alignment and isolation of forms. Feke's portraits gave attention to minute detail in accessories and used bright colors in depicting clothes. His figures express sensitivity. Imprecise, like Smibert, with respect to anatomy, Feke seemed to aim at interpretative perception. As James T. Flexner (1947/1969) has written, "Through the use of imagination, he brought to life not reality itself, but symbols of reality" (p. 144).

Samuel Shrimpton. Courtesy of the Massachusetts Historical Society

Gustavus Hesselius (1682–1755), who came to the Delaware valley from Sweden in 1712, though employing baroque flourishes in such paintings as *Bacchanalian Revel* and *The Last Supper*, is best known for his somber portraits of two Delaware Indians, Tishcohan and Lapowinsa— their faces foretelling the death of their tribe. His son, John Hesselius (1728–1778), was probably the most prolific colonial painter after Smibert; his paintings had more color than those by his father but less humanity. John Greenwood (1727–1792), who left the colonies in 1762 to become a London art dealer, is believed to be the first native-born American to execute a genre painting, *Sea Captains Carousing in Surinam* (1757).

Portraiture found ample patronage among the aristocracy by the second quarter of the eighteenth century, and hence many works exhibited a courtly style. Many of the portraitists were Englishmen who visited the colonies for only a spell. Most prominent among portrait painters, other than those already named, were Joseph Blackburn, Charles Bridges,

The Bermuda Group: Dean George Berkeley with his Family and Friends by John Smibert. Yale University Art Gallery. Gift of Isaac Lothrop

William Dering, Joseph Badger, Henrietta Johnston (who introduced pastels), William Williams, and John Wollaston I and II.

Three native-born American painters, two of whom became expatriates, laid the groundwork for the coming of age of American artists at the end of the colonial period: John Singleton Copley (1738–1815), Benjamin West (1738–1820), and Charles Willson Peale (1741–1827). Copley averaged twenty portraits a year from 1762 to 1774, after which time he lived in London. His brushwork yielded a brilliant and harsh chromaticism. West remained in England after 1760; known for his heroic style, he taught many American artists. In 1792, West was named the president of the Royal Academy. Peale, who gained repute for the rich textural quality of his paintings, studied with West in England from 1766 to 1772 and went on to become the most popular portrait painter in America.

ARCHITECTURE

Like their descendants on a farther frontier, the first settlers along the Atlantic coast often resorted to primitive shelters. Temporary dwellings ranged from a dugout covered over by sticks and bark to a kind of sod

Eleanor Darnall (Mrs. Daniel Carroll of Upper Marlboro I) as a Child by
Justus Engelhardt Kühn. Collection of the Maryland Historical Society,
Baltimore

house, which had walls of tree branches daubed with clay and a roof of
turf or thatch. The next step was to build a frame structure of hewn
planks or squared timber, with the sides covered by wattle-and-daub or
clapboards. Contrary to myth, the log cabin, with round logs notched at
the corners, was unknown in the colonies during the seventeenth century
except among the Swedes along the Delaware, who had been accustomed
to log cabins in their home country. In the eighteenth century the log
cabin caught on among backcountry settlers, especially the Scotch-Irish
pioneers. A precursor of the log cabin was the blockhouse, first made of
hewn timber and then of logs, for protection against the Indians.

In settled areas, houses were generally made of wood in New England,
of brick and stone in the middle colonies, and of wood and brick in the
South. The typical frame house of New England and Virginia had walls
of hewn lumber covered by overlapping weatherboards (clapboards). The

Henry Darnall III as a Child by Justus Engelhardt Kühn. Collection of the
Maryland Historical Society, Baltimore

kitchen had a large exterior chimney, which narrowed into a straight flue. Roofs were steeply gabled or hipped. The Cape Cod house, popular throughout New England in the eighteenth century, was a small dwelling in the shape of a saltbox; roofs sloped to the rear, windows were small, and four large fireplaces connected to a central chimney. A lean-to or other addition was often constructed as a kitchen or storage area.

Many Dutch stone and brick houses in New York and also residences in Charleston, South Carolina (where after the fire of 1740 all houses had to be of brick or stone), were narrow, the side facing the street containing a tradesman's entrance. Philadelphia townhouses were usually three-storied, with parlors on the first floor, a ballroom on the second, and living chambers on the third; the kitchen was in a two-story wing. Flemish-style houses could be found on Long Island, in southern New York, and in northern New Jersey; these one-and-a-half-story structures had gambrel

Isaac Royall and His Family by Robert Feke (1741). Harvard Law Art Collection

roofs with eaves projecting two or more feet in the front and back and stone, clay, or sandstone walls.

Renaissance neoclassicism came to England in the seventeenth century, largely owing to the influence of Inigo Jones (1573–1652), an English architect who had studied in Italy and became James I's surveyor of public works. Jones's designs reflected architectural principles in the works of Andrea Palladio (1518–1580), who in 1570 published *Four Books of Architecture*. Christopher Wren (1632–1723), responsible for the architecture in the rebuilding of London after the Great Fire of 1666, was also influenced by Palladianism.

Colonial Americans who designed large residences and public buildings were familiar with works by English architects who favored the Palladian style. Georgian architecture stressed the uniformity and balance of Palladianism, without its grandiose embellishments. Georgian edifices in the colonies were usually rectangular and symmetrical. Features included rows of identical windows with pediments; sash window panes separated by wooden bars; framed pedimental doorways topped with dentils and a cornice; two or more rectangular chimneys at the ends of the house; triangular, gable, gambrel, or hipped roofs; and, in the interior, a great entrance hall and plastered or wallpapered walls.

During the third quarter of the eighteenth century, Georgian archi-

George Booth by William Dering. Courtesy of the Colonial Williamsburg
Foundation

tecture exhibited tighter control. "Drudgeries," such as kitchens, were
placed in separate outbuildings. The Georgian plantation houses seemed
to accentuate a hierarchy of space; the plantation itself bore a centrifugal
relationship to the "great house," which, with its two stages of entry
(doorway and the large hallway), seemed to say, "this far and no further."
Neo-Palladianism made strides in American towns and cities, giving
expression to early Renaissance features, such as Venetian windows,
porticos, a projecting central bay, lower roofs with balustrades, and Greek
columns and entablatures. Peter Harrison (1716–1775), colonial America's
preeminent architect, who as a merchant kept abreast of English architectural trends, brought neo-Palladianism to his designs of such structures
as the Redwood Library, Jewish synagogue, and Freemason's Hall in
Newport, Rhode Island, and King's Chapel in Boston.

Westover Plantation, Virginia. Collections of the Virginia Historical Society

MUSIC

The Pilgrims and Puritans enjoyed music. They only refused to allow instrumental music in the churches and insisted that music in general not express or encourage wanton or lewd behavior. None of the New England colonies passed any antimusic laws.

The Puritans uncharacteristically allowed the New Testament to prevail over the Old in declaring instrumental music unfit for worship. Thus John Cotton, in *Singing of the Psalmes* . . . (1647), stated:

> Singing with Instruments was typicall [in the Old Testament], and so a ceremonial worship and therefore is ceased. But singing with heart and voyce is a morall worship . . . nor is any voyce now to be heard in the Church of Christ, but such as is significant and edifying by signification . . . which the voyce of instruments is not.

Cotton Mather, in *Magnalia Christi Americana*, was of the same mind:

> The Instrumental Music used in the old Church of Israel was an institution of God. . . . Now there is not one word of Institution in the New Testament for Instrumental Music in the Worship of God. And because the holy God rejects all he does not command in his worship, he now therefore in effect says to us, *I will not hear the melody of thy Organs.*

For church worship, the Puritans took to heart the biblical instruction "to sing praise unto the Lord, with the words of David." The Massachusetts Puritans, like the Anglicans, first used Thomas Sternhold and John Hopkins's *Whole Book of Psalms* (1549); the Pilgrims favored a published collection by one of their own, Henry Ainsworth, *The Book of Psalmes Englished Both in Prose and Metre* (1612). The New England churches then adopted their own psalmody: *The Whole Booke of Psalms Faithfully Translated into English Metre* (published in 1640 and referred to as the *Bay Psalm Book*), prepared by Thomas Welde, John Eliot, and Richard Mather. With the words "deaconed" or "lined out" for them, congregations struggled with such lines as:

> The Lord to mee a shepherd is,
>   want therefore shall not I.
>
> Hee in the folds of tender-grasse,
>   doth cause mee down to lie;
>
> To waters calme me gently leads
>   Restore my soule doth hee.

The *Bay Psalm Book* went through seventy American editions (the last in 1773). The ninth edition (1698) for the first time contained thirteen tunes, with diamond-shaped notes and two-part harmony (in later editions a third voice was added).

Indeed, the writings of early New Englanders attest to their love of music. Anne Bradstreet's "Contemplations" has a charming passage:

> I heard the merry grasshopper then sing,
> The black clad Cricket, bear a second part,
> They kept one tune, and plaid on the same string,
> Seeming to glory in their little art.

Samuel Sewall's *Diary* frequently mentioned music. For January 1, 1696, he reported: "One with a Trumpet sounds a Levet [Reveille] at our window just around break of day, bids me good morrow and wishes health and happiness to attend me." For March 16, 1721: "Dr. Mather preaches in the School-House to the young Musicians. . . . House was full, and the singing extraordinarily Excellent, such as had hardly been heard before in Boston."

Organs eventually made their way into the colonial churches in the eighteenth century, even in New England. The first organ in British North America was a little two-stop instrument acquired in 1703 by the hermit group along the Wissahickon River near Germantown (see Chapter 15). Colonial Americans of all rank and file enjoyed singing and playing

A Musical Gathering. A group portrait by unknown artist. Courtesy of the Nassau County Museum, Syosset, N.Y.

musical instruments. Among the most common instruments were drums, winds—trumpets, trombones, post horns, cowhorns, flutes, fifes, curtals (bassoons), hautboys (oboes), and jew's-harps; keyboards—virginals, harpsichords, clavichords, spinets, pianofortes (pianos), and organs; dulcimers (strings struck with hand-held hammers); bowed strings—fiddles, violins, "tenor" or "bass" violins, and viola da gambas; and plucked strings—guitars (gut strings) and citterns (wire strings).

Southern planters considered musical proficiency a mark of gentility. Robert Carter of Nomini Hall, in Virginia, brought family members and certain slaves together frequently for musical sessions; in the household were a harpsichord, a pianoforte, guitars, flutes, violins, a harmonica (the instrument using glasses, not the 'mouth organ', and a two-stop organ. Itinerant music masters made the rounds of plantations, one of the best known being John Gualdo, who gave Landon Carter's daughter, Lucy, lessons two days every three weeks.

Singing schools became popular in the eighteenth century, some of which evolved into choral societies. Reformers sought to convince congregations to engage in "regular singing"—singing by notes. Most common folk preferred the oral tradition not using music. A number of ministers, including Cotton Mather, Nathaniel Chauncey, John Tufts, and Thomas Walter, wrote pamphlets on the desirability of regular singing. Once the battle was won, the way was paved for a more sophisticated publication of church music—collections of psalm tunes, hymns, and anthems. The most important works in this field were *Urania* (1761) by James Lyon (1735–1794), *A Collection of Psalms and Hymns* by John Wesley (published in Charleston, 1737), *A Collection of Psalm Tunes, with a few Anthems and Hymns* (1763) by Francis Hopkinson (1737–1791), and *The New England Psalm Singer, or American Chorister* (1770) by William Billings (1746–1800). The Billings edition contained "Chester," which, when set to patriotic words, became the war hymn of the American Revolution. Billings, a Boston tanner, published other works, perhaps the most significant being *Continental Harmony* (1794), which had both a collection of fugue tunes and instruction in music theory. In all, Billings himself composed more than three hundred musical pieces. Hopkinson's collection had six of his own songs, including "My Days Have Been So Wondrous Free" (composed in 1759), regarded as the first secular composition in the colonies.

The Moravians were noted for their fondness of music, both vocal and instrumental. Benjamin Franklin reported in 1756 that while at Bethlehem he heard "good Music, the organ being accompanied with Violins, Hautboys, Flutes, Clarinets, etc." The Moravians had trombone choirs, which played for festive occasions and announcing a death; once Indians gave up a planned attack on a Moravian settlement upon hearing a trombone dirge. Conrad Beissel, leader of the Brethren at Ephrata, in Lancaster County, Pennsylvania, published hymns, some involving eight voice parts, such as "The Song of the Lonely and Forsaken Turtle Dove, namely the Christian Church" (1747) and "Paradisiacal Wonder Music" (1754).

Colonists attended concerts, usually given to small audiences at residences. By the 1760s subscription concerts were common in the cities. The larger concerts often centered around public events, such as honoring the king's birthday.

Theatrical performances greatly enriched the colonial musical experience. Rarely did a program not have songs and dances. Theatrical fare usually had opening and closing music and also music at intermission and for setting atmosphere and background. Professional actors were expected to sing and play musical instruments. Different kinds of "opera" played the colonies: quasi-opera, such as *The Tempest, or Enchanted Island*; ballad opera, such as *The Beggar's Opera, Flora, The Devil to Pay*, and *The Honest Yorkshireman*; and comic opera or "operetta," such as *Love in a Village*. Full English or Italian operas did not come to the colonies, but theatrical productions often borrowed arias from them. One popular kind of theater piece was the "burletta," a burlesque form of musical comedy.

Common folk in colonial America enjoyed popular Anglo-Scottish-Irish ballads, folk songs, jigs, and reels. Americans often substituted different words for the ballads and folk songs. Some of the popular songs were bawdy; Max Savelle (1948) has given examples of such ballads sung in the colonies—"Kiss Me Quick, My Mother's Coming," "Bonny Lass under a Blanket," "Sweetest When She's Naked," and "Go to the Devil and Shake Yourself." Needless to say, there were those who denounced the tendency of young people to sing "idle, foolish, yea pernicious songs and ballads." America was soon to have its own folk music and ballads. "Springfield Mountain," the earliest known native folk song, lamented the death of Timothy Myrick by snakebite at Springfield Mountain (now Wilbraham, Massachusetts).

THEATER

The colonial theater belongs to the history of the eighteenth century, although, earlier, colloquies had been held at Harvard and William and Mary, and at least one play was presumably performed at Cowle's Tavern on Virginia's eastern shore in 1665—*The Barre and the Cubb*, probably an allegory on the relationship between Virginia and the mother country.

Theater came to Williamsburg in 1718 in a theater that William Levingston, a merchant of New Kent County, constructed near the Palace Green. The theater was a weatherboarded building, 30 feet by $86\frac{1}{2}$ feet. Charles Stagg and his wife, Mary, two indentured servants whom Levingston freed, were the mainstays of the acting group. The last drama was produced at this playhouse in 1737; in 1752 the Virginia capital finally had another theater. New York City, Philadelphia, and Charleston also had playhouses. Most of the actors were members of British traveling companies: at midcentury, troupes led by Lewis Hallam and David Douglass, who married Hallam's widow in 1758. Douglass's American Company, on its first American tour (1758–1761), in a single season staged forty plays, including thirteen Shakespearian works, and a large number of accompanying pieces.

American audiences warmed to the light fare of British farces, such as *The Busy-Body* by Susanna Centlivre, *The Drummer; or the Haunted House* by Joseph Addison, *The Beaux' Stratagem* and *The Recruiting Officer* by George Farquhar, and *The Conscious Lovers* by Richard Steele. Two plays were especially popular during the French and Indian War: Addison's *Tragedy of Cato*, which dramatized Roman republicans standing up for liberty, and Nicholas Rowe's *Tamerlane*, an allegory that suggested the rivalry between William III of England and Louis XIV of France. Soldiers and officers of the Virginia regiment actually produced their own version of *Tamerlane* on the western frontier at Fort Cumberland in December 1755.

Colonial America had its budding playwrights. Governor Robert Hunter of New York wrote *Androboros, a Biographical Farce of Three Acts, viz: The Senate, the Consistory and the Apotheosis* (printed in 1714). A satire, the play ridicules Lieutenant Governor Francis Nicholson and the assembly; Nicholson is Androboros ("Maneater"), who procrastinates in leading an attack on the Mulomachians (the French). It was never produced; Hunter probably intended the play merely as a reply to his critics. *The Prince of Parthia*, written in 1759 by Thomas Godfrey (1736–1763), was printed after his death and was the first play by an American produced professionally, at the Southwark Theater in Philadelphia in April 1767. Having little plot or action, Godfrey's play told of a power struggle over a city-state at the beginning of the Christian era. *The Disappointment; or, the Force of Credulity*, a comic opera by Andrew Barton (supposedly a pseudonym of Colonel Thomas Forrest), published in 1767, was the first comedy accepted for professional production in America. It was scheduled to play a few days before *The Prince of Parthia* at the Southwark Theater, but its story of a search for pirate treasure was too cutting a satire, even featuring southern gentlemen speaking in Negro dialect, and it was therefore withdrawn at the last minute. The first play with both the author and the subject matter American was Robert Rogers's *Ponteach, or the Savages of America*, published in 1766 but not produced. Except for an idealized Pontiac, the drama was an accurate and sympathetic treatment of the Indians and a disparagement of frontiersmen and traders; bigotry shows in the casting the Jesuit priests as villains. Robert Munford (1730–1784), a southside Virginia planter, wrote *The Candidates; or, the Humours of a Virginia Election* (ca. 1770) and *The Patriots* (ca. 1777), the latter satirizing American Revolutionary War Tory hunters as hypocrites. Though the plays were published in 1798 by Munford's son, William, the first performance of record of *The Candidates* was a staging at the College of William and Mary theater in 1949 and of *The Patriots* at Richmond's amphitheater in 1978. The post–Revolutionary War era saw a growing interest in American plays, especially those with the theme of the noble and manly American pitted against the foppish European.

20

Literature and the Diffusion of Knowledge

With the increase and dispersal of population, the need for dissemination of information became more demanding. Once printing presses appeared in the colonies, a wide miscellany of materials was published. Colonial writers experimented with different kinds of literary fare, from the exposition of useful knowledge to belles lettres. Eventually authors discovered they had a usable American past on which they could draw for literary subjects and themes. Yet despite the growing native consciousness, colonial authors and printers often relied on English and European writings for material, whether in a derivative way or in republication; this trend was especially evident in the American periodicals. The colonists also made strides in various areas of education.

PROMOTIONAL LITERATURE

Tracts, books, and letters heralding edenic prospects in America flowed prodigiously and continuously throughout the colonial period. English voyage literature by Richard Hakluyt, Sir Walter Raleigh, Samuel Purchas, and others early popularized the idea of western planting. Thomas Hariot gave a brief glimpse of a new utopia at Roanoke Island. Captain John Smith set the pace for the writing of "pamphlets of news" by persons who visited or resided in America. Smith's *True Relation of Such Occurrances and Accidents of Noate in Virginia* (1608) was followed by William Strachey's *Historie of Travaile into Virginia Britannia* (1618, pub. 1849). The early promotional literature commonly extolled America as a place where a courageous and industrious person could find success and prosperity. Smith's writings, collected in *The Generall Historie of Virginia, New-England, and the Summer Isles* (1624), though autobiographical and self-promoting, form a great epic, combining the themes of discovery and exploitation. Other publicists of the Chesapeake area, offering descriptions of the land and of the people and often portraying the American environment as a curative for the corrupting influences in England, included John Hammond, Andrew White, George Alsop, and Governor William Berkeley of Virginia.

Carolina promotional tracts such as those by Robert Horne (1666), Samuel Wilson (1682), Thomas Ash (1682), and John Archdale (1707) stressed uniqueness of economic opportunity in America and individual liberty under the proprietorship. The best of the works on Carolina was by John Lawson: *A New Voyage to Carolina* (1709) was published in several English and German editions. Its descriptive narrative examines the province's natural history and Indian life, and its humor and earthy language resembles the style of William Byrd II.

The Puritans and Pilgrims tended to be more matter-of-fact than their southern counterparts in describing their New World experiences, emphasizing community affairs and struggles with Indians and those who might subvert the true commonwealths. *Mourt's Relation* (1622), consisting chiefly of materials supplied by William Bradford and Edward Winslow, depicted the Pilgrims as unheroic but also otherworldly. Winslow's *Good News from New England* (1624) praised the bounty of the land and God's protective care over New England. Two works—Francis Higginson's *New-England's Plantation* (1630) and William Wood's *New Englands Prospect* (1634)—gave lively descriptions of the country, ignoring the religious life of the colonists. *The Wonder-working Providence of Sions Saviour in New England* (1654) by Edward Johnson presented an epic view of the redemptive quality of the Puritan experience in New England and triumph over Indian and heretical foes; the Lord, said Johnson, had turned the "most hideous, boundless and unknown Wilderness" into "a well-ordered Commonwealth." Of course, the New England Puritans had their detractors, who portrayed a dystopia, where human dignity and rights were denied; such works include Thomas Morton's *New English Canaan* (1637) and John Clarke's *Ill News from New England* (1652).

In the eighteenth century, promotional literature sought to attract immigrant servants and European refugees, particularly to Pennsylvania and Georgia. Reports by governors and other officials, in England and America, brought attention to the advantages of New World settlement.

RELIGIOUS WRITINGS

Religion was the most prevalent topic for colonial authors. The vast sermon literature was supplemented by meditative pieces, instructional works (such as catechisms), and theological treatises. Both sermon and meditation writing in England and America contributed to the development of the essay form. The sermon, didactic in purpose, discoursed on the doctrinal meaning of a text of Scripture and then proposed a lesson applicable to the lives of individuals. Election, funeral, and other sermons commemorating special occasions gave the opportunity to present a character essay, exemplifying deeds and upright conduct instructive for the living. Sermons were often published in pamphlet or broadside form.

Meditations described personal experience and its meaning; they, too, were frequently composed around a text. Colonial diaries and poems contain meditative segments. Among published meditations were *The Spirit of Man: Some Meditations (by Way of Essay) on the Sense of That Scripture II Thes. 5:23* (1693) by Charles Morton and *Brief Meditations* (1711) by Samuel Willard.

The pulpit, as Howard Mumford Jones (1934) has observed, substantially helped to shape a new kind of expository writing in America. "Between 1700 and 1775, one begins by and by to note an interesting correlation of two facts" in the sermon literature, Jones avers: "avoidance of controversy," or toleration, and "the appeal for a simple, lucid, and direct prose style." Cotton Mather, in his *Manuductio ad ministerium* (1726), advised young ministers on how they could improve their writing. "The reader" should "have something to the purpose in every paragraph," Mather stated, and also "a vigor sensible in every sentence. . . . The writer pretends not unto reading, yet he could not have writ as he does if he had not read very much in his time."

HISTORY

The distinction between promotional works and what passed as history was very slight. Colonial writers who wrote of the past for the most part did so without detachment and clearly had an eye for approval by authorities at home and in England. History written by the colonists was mostly in the form of annals, a chronicle of events, joined with descriptions of flora and fauna and Indian life. If they did not excel in the writing of history, which for English America did not have much of a past, the colonists nevertheless had a great regard for historical works dating back to antiquity. In William Byrd II's library of 2,345 titles (3,513 volumes), there were seven hundred histories. The New England Puritans valued history because they believed that God directed the affairs of man and that lessons could be gained by studying the past.

Uniquely, the early colonial historians were part and parcel of the histories that they wrote. John Winthrop's *Journal* (first published in 1793 and later in two volumes as the *History of New England*, 1825–1826) and William Bradford's *Of Plimmoth Plantation* (first published in 1856) contained a firsthand narration of events in the founding and early years of their respective colonies. Both works, significantly, made an ideological distinction between their colonies and the mother country. Winthrop was more narrowly concerned with political development in justifying Puritan orthodoxy, while Bradford had the greater sense of personal drama. Nathaniel Morton's *New-Englands Memorial* (1669), the first history published in America, borrowed materials from Bradford's manuscript history and the writings of Edward Winslow. Morton's history, which told the story of Plymouth colony to 1668 (Bradford had stopped at 1647), included obituaries of Pilgrim leaders and stressed the theme of New England neglecting its divine errand into the wilderness.

Whereas Indian life had been treated in the early promotional literature and was even romanticized by John Smith, the native American, in all his ferocity, received full attention in two works by Increase Mather— *A Brief History of the War of the Indians in New-England* (1676) and its sequel the following year—and two by William Hubbard—*A Narrative of the Troubles with the Indians of New-England* (1677) and the *General History of New-England from the Discovery to MDCLXXX* (first published in 1815). To Hubbard the New England Algonquian was a "Miscreant with Envy and Malice against the English," a "bloody and deceitful" monster, "very stupid and blockish," a "Murderer from the Beginning," and a "Cannibal." Conversely, Daniel Gookin's *Historical Collection of the Indians in New England* (1792) and *Historical Account of the Doings and Suffering of the Christian Indians* (1836) were written in an attempt to dispel the intense bigotry toward native Americans that came in the wake of King Philip's War.

Hubbard's *General History*, with some critical detachment and dramatic skill, was the first American effort at writing history as history. Hubbard treats with all of New England, and though not repudiating the providential theory of history, he assigns causation to natural and human factors. Thomas Prince's *Chronological History of New England in the Form of Annals* (1736) records, with brevity and exactness, the unfolding events under providential direction from the time of Adam and Eve to the founding of the New England colonies (through 1630). The most ambitious historical project of the colonial period was Cotton Mather's *Magnalia Christi Americana: or, the Ecclesiastical History of New England . . ., 1620–1698* (London,

1702). A conglomeration of bits and pieces, it included seventeen of Mather's previous publications. The work has seven parts: "Antiquities" of New England, lives of New England governors, lives of New England "Divines," Harvard College, "Faith and the Order in the Churches," "Illustrous Wonderful Providences," and disturbances in the churches. An appendix describes the wars with the Indians from 1688 to 1698. Mather accepts religious toleration, even while glorifying New England's past and its heroes. As Kenneth Silverman (1984) pertinently comments:

> What unifies this seven-vault archive of fact, reminiscence, document, verse, and legend is Mather's ever present narrative voice—learned, facetious, emphatic, at once intimate and grand, distinctively showmanlike, as if history were some banquet and he the master of ceremonies. (pp. 158–159)

Virginia shared with Massachusetts a distinction in historiography. *The Present State of Virginia and the College* (1697, published in 1727) by two lawyers, Henry Hartwell and Edward Chilton, and clergyman James Blair, intended as an answer to a questionnaire from the Board of Trade, described uncritically the colony's economic, political, and religious life. Robert Beverley wrote his *History and Present State of Virginia* (1705) during a brief sojourn in London, relying on his memory and notes of his own and others'. Beverley devotes much of his work to the colony's natural history. While admiring the Indians and their customs, Beverley is something of an iconoclast in treating Virginia's history and its gentry, whom he accuses of despoiling the pristine New World garden. In the preface, Beverley explains his own modest pretension to the historian's craft. "I am an *Indian*," he writes,

> but I hope the Plainness of my Dress, will give the kinder Impressions of my Honesty. . . . Truth desires only to be understood. . . . It depends upon its own intrinsick Value, and, like Beauty, is rather conceal'd, than set off, by Ornament.

Beverley's history had an archvillain, Lieutenant Governor Francis Nicholson, whom Beverley was using his influence to get removed from office; Nicholson was opposed "to the Liberties of English Subjects" and "wou'd hang up those that should presume to oppose him with Magna Charta about their Necks."

Hugh Jones, professor of mathematics at William and Mary, published in 1724 *The Present State of Virginia . . . from Whence Is Inferred a Short View of Maryland and North Carolina*. Like Beverley, he included his own observations on the Indians but held a more favorable opinion of the character of southern planters. Similar to the annals written by Thomas Prince, *The History of the First Discovery and Settlement of Virginia* (1747) by William Stith (president of William and Mary, 1752–1755) traced the history of Virginia to 1624; this ponderous volume drew directly from the early promotional literature, often quoting without credit.

By the end of the colonial period, histories began to give attention to America's place within the empire and displaying a greater synthesis in the use of sources. William Smith's *History of the Province of New-York from the First Discovery to the Year MDCCXXXII* (1757) promised readers "only a regular Thread of simple Facts" and not "a Detail of the little Transactions, which concern a Colony scant in its Jurisdiction." *A Review of the Military Operations in North America . . . , 1753–1756* (1759) by the same author brought specialization to early American historiography, as did Cadwallader Colden's *History of the Five Indian Nations* (1727), which, as the first documented study of the Iroquois Confederacy, awakened colonial Americans to the French threat in the West. The first full history in the modern sense, though from the imperial point of view, was Thomas Hutchinson's *History of the Province of Massachusetts Bay* (three volumes, London, 1764–1778). Hutchinson's history, based on his collection of manuscript sources, sympathized with the Indians and dissenters.

JOURNALS AND DIARIES

Personal literature, chiefly journals and diaries, afford intimate and immediate glimpses into colonial life. Most seem to have been intended to be read by others, but few were published during the colonial period. Both journals and diaries had self-contained entries organized day by day.

Many foreign visitors to the colonies wrote journals largely for public consumption on the other side of the Atlantic; yet these writings were also eagerly received in America as valuable to the understanding of a new people and culture. The Huguenot John Fontaine and Scotsman tutor John Harrower are but two of the best journal writers. Fontaine, for example, gave a narrative of the exploring venture of Governor Alexander Spotswood and a party of seventy Virginians to the crest of the Blue Ridge Mountains in 1716. The journals were meant to inform, but in the main the journalists had an eye for human interest items. William Byrd's "Progress to the Mines," "Journey to the Land of Eden," "History of the Dividing Line," and the "Secret History of the Dividing Line" (none of which were published in his lifetime) portrayed real characters stripped of their outer trappings, with exaggeration to the point of burlesque. Dr. Alexander Hamilton's *Itinerarium* (1744), which details his round-trip tour between Annapolis, Maryland, and Maine, provides a witty and urbane survey of early American customs and manners.

Military journals during the colonial and Indian wars were usually kept by the leading participants themselves, writing to justify their actions—for example, colonial commanders John Mason and John Underhill during the Pequot War, John Walley in the expedition against Quebec in 1690, John Barnwell versus the Tuscarora Indians in 1711–1713, and William Pepperrell leading the attack against Louisbourg in 1745.

Stories of Indian adventure tapped a mythic ingredient of the American consciousness, a "regeneration through violence," to borrow the words of Richard Slotkin (1973). Thomas Church's *Entertaining Passages Relating to King Philip's War* (1716) and Cotton Mather's *Decennium luctuosum* (1699) fit into this genre. But it belonged to a Puritan housewife from Lancaster, Massachusetts, to publish the great prose epic on captivity by the Indians. *The Sovereignty & Goodness of God . . . Being a Narrative of the Captivity and Restauration of Mrs. Mary Rowlandson* (1682) tells of Rowlandson's ordeal during King Philip's War, when she was captured and taken deep into the forests. She is separated from her children and witnesses wanton savagery. Through it all, she keeps a passive composure and never doubts the goodness of God. At the end she is ransomed and returned to the loving arms of her husband.

Although there was little difference between diary and journal, the diary was more personally intimate and allowed a wide latitude for expression. Some entries were terse, others introspective and even sometimes melancholic, and others entertaining. But some were merely matter-of-fact, such as the early diaries of George Washington, who avoided any revelation of the inner self, sticking to naming guests, recording his whereabouts, and commenting on climatic and agricultural conditions. Cotton Mather, like most New England clerics, wrote in a psychoanalytic vein, expressing the torment of conscience along with manifestations of Providence. Samuel Sewall recorded the everyday, simple social life of a Puritan merchant while exhibiting a moral point of view and unconscious humor. William Byrd II relished in reporting his rather lecherous behavior while in England and the battle of the sexes between himself and his volatile first wife, Lucy Parke Byrd, at the Westover plantation in Virginia. For the late colonial period, Landon Carter (1710–1778) left a remarkably comprehensive diary revealing details of both intimate family life and plantation management.

POETRY

Puritan and non-Puritan, gentry and common folk alike enjoyed poetry, and most colonial literary publications contained at least quotations from poems. Much of the large quantity of satirical writing was in the form of poetry. Several colonists received acclaim as poets, either in their own lifetimes or afterward.

The poems of Anne Bradstreet (1612–1672), who came to Massachusetts in 1630 with her husband, Simon, who was later the governor of

Cotton Mather (1727). Mezzotint by Peter Pelham. Miriam & Ira D. Wallach Division of Art, Prints and Photographs, The New York Public Library; Astor, Lenox and Tilden Foundation.

the colony, were published as *The Tenth Muse Lately Sprung Up in America* (London, 1650) and posthumously as *Several Poems Compiled with Great Variety of Wit and Learning, Full of Delight* (Boston, 1678). Although most of her poems were labored and filled with elaborate metaphors and neologisms, imitative of the French Huguenot poet Guillaume Du Bartas and others, Anne Bradstreet could also write short poems expressive of inner feelings and intimacy.

Probably the most popular poem ever written in America—at least in the colonial period—was Michael Wigglesworth's *Day of Doom, or a Poetical Description of the Great and Last Judgment* (1662). Wigglesworth (1631–1705) was pastor for fifty years at the church in Malden, Massa-

William Byrd II. Collections of the Virginia Historical Society

chusetts. The poem, as one author has described it, in "dog trot meter," tells of that fatal day when Christ returns to judge the quick and the dead. In effect, the poem sets forth a basic Calvinist theology, which even the humbler people could understand—yet not very comforting doctrines, for even unborn babes would be assigned "the easiest room in hell." One in every thirty-five New Englanders bought the first edition of the poem, and Cotton Mather predicted that it would be read until the Last Judgment itself. Wigglesworth wrote two other major poems: *God's Controversy with New England* (not published until 1873), concerning the drought of 1662, and *Meat Out of the Eater* (1670), also a poem on theology.

Two other New England poets gained critical acclaim. Benjamin Tompson (1642–1714), whose tombstone at Roxbury bears the inscription "The Renowned poet of New England, mortuus sed immortalis," wrote twenty-three elegies and epitaphs; his epic on the degeneracy during the period of King Philip's War was published as *New Englands Crisis* in Boston in 1676 and, with some changes, as *New-Englands Tears* in London during the same year. Edward Taylor (ca. 1644–1729), physician and pastor in the frontier town of Westfield, Massachusetts, though undiscovered and unpublished until the 1930s, is regarded as the best poet of colonial New England. "Preparatory Meditations" consists of 217 poems that Taylor used during his church services. "Gods Determinations Touching His Elect" is a long theological allegory in the style of the "Songs of Solomon" and the "Book of Revelation."

The best known of the southern poets is Ebenezer Cooke, of whom there is not much information, except that he was probably a tobacco merchant who immigrated to Maryland. His hilarious poem *The Sot-weed Factor* (1708), in Hudibrastic couplets, satirizes the Maryland settlers—the men as drunkards and the women as slatterns. Cooke also wrote several elegies and a poem on Bacon's Rebellion. Two other colonial Maryland poets were well known in their day but not later: Richard Lewis (ca. 1700–1734), whose most famous poem was "A Journey from Patapsco to Annapolis," and Rev. James Sterling (1701–1763), who wrote patriotic poems, such as *An Epistle to the Hon. Arthur Dobbs* (1752) and *Zeal against the Enemies of Our Country Pathetically Recommended* (1755). Lewis was the first American to write nature poetry.

NEWSPAPERS

From 1704 to 1775 some seventy-eight different newspapers appeared in the British North American colonies, with thirty-seven functioning at the beginning of the American Revolution. By that time also, circulation for several newspapers had reached to several thousand, with the *Massachusetts Spy* having the highest at 3,500.

Benjamin Harris's *Publick Occurrences, Both Forreign and Domestick* (1690) folded in Boston after a single issue. The next newspaper in the colonies was the *Boston News-Letter*, published by John Campbell, the local postmaster; it was printed until 1776. James Franklin followed with the *Boston Gazette* (1719–1741), but in 1721 he moved on to publish the *New-England Courant* for five years. The *New-England Courant* modeled itself after the *Spectator* and the *Guardian* in London, printing mainly literary essays and humorous letters. A group of contributors to the *New-England Courant*, who were dubbed the "Hell-Fire Club," relished provoking the religious and political establishment; the young Benjamin Franklin supplied the "Silence Dogood" papers, poking fun at Cotton Mather and other clerics. John Campbell said of his competition: "I pity the readers of the new paper; its sheets smell stronger of beer than of midnight oil." Cotton Mather, in the *Boston News-Letter* of August 28, 1721, said of the *Courant*:

We find a Notorious, Scandalous Paper, called the *Courant*, full freighted with Nonsense, Unmannerliness, Railery, Prophaneness, Immorality, Arrogancy, Calumnies, Lyes, Contradictions, and what not, all tending to Quarrels and Divisions, and to Debauch and Corrupt the Minds and Manners of New-England.

Among other major newspapers were the *Pennsylvania Gazette* (1728–1815), started by Samuel Keimer and sold to Benjamin Franklin in 1729; Andrew Bradford's *American Weekly Mercury* (1719–1746), also in Philadelphia; William Bradford's *New-York Gazette* (1725–1744), the first newspaper in New York City; and the *Maryland Gazette*, printed by William Parks from 1727 to 1735 and reestablished in 1745 by Jonas Green. Parks went on to found the *Virginia Gazette* at Williamsburg in 1736, while at the same time being made "printer of the colony" at two hundred pounds per year. After Parks's death in 1750, William Hunter and then Joseph Royle took over the newspaper's publication. The *Virginia Gazette* was heavily doused with literary fare—essays, poetry, and humorous pieces—about half which was original and the rest copied from English periodicals such as the *Gentleman's Magazine, Tatler, Spectator, Guardian,* and *London Magazine.* Similar to other colonial newspapers, the *Virginia Gazette* during the French and Indian War and in the 1760s published letters relating to political controversies. In 1731 in Charleston, South Carolina, Eleazer Phillips established the *South Carolina Weekly Journal,* lasting only a year, and Thomas Whitemarsh began the *South Carolina Gazette* (1731–1775). Lewis Timothy took over the *Gazette* in 1734, and upon his death in 1738 his wife and then her son kept it going. The foreign-language press was represented chiefly by Christopher Sower's Germantown *Zeitung* (1739–1777) and Heinrich Müller's *Wochentliche Philadelphische Staatsbote* (1762–1779).

Published usually weekly or semimonthly, the colonial newspaper at first consisted of a large sheet folded in half making four pages, although sometimes it was enlarged to six or eight pages. Infrequently, a "supplement" was published in addition to a regular issue. Pages originally measured about eight by thirteen inches, with two columns (by the 1750s, three columns); by 1765 most colonial newspapers had been enlarged to ten by fifteen or eleven by seventeen inches with three or four columns. Datelines usually served as headings. Financial support for a newspaper came from subscriptions, advertisements, and fees for inserting unsolicited essays and poems, especially those of a controversial nature. Printers of newspapers also made their living by publishing government documents, selling paper and books, and acting as postmaster and auctioneer.

Foreign and colonial news, including governors' proclamations and legislative enactments, could be found on the first page. One problem was the dearth of foreign news during wintertime, necessitating the inclusion of even more filler material. On the second page could be found local news, unusual incidents reported from neighboring towns, letters addressed to "Sir" or "the Printer," and regular features, such as listings of ships in port and produce exported. Poems or essays could also be found on parts of the second and third pages. The rest of the newspaper consisted of advertisements—a great variety of notices of runaway servants or slaves, sales of imported goods, cultural announcements, real estate for sale, lotteries, services of different kinds, and sports events, such as horse races.

MAGAZINES

Magazines had difficulty making a start in the colonial period. British magazines, shipped over with the consignment of goods from British and Scottish merchants, supplied the limited demand. Americans were eager to imitate British styles and manners, culturally as well as materially. Also magazines, to survive, had to have a subscription base. With the subscribing public so small for the newspapers, magazines did not have much of a chance to succeed. Furthermore, the American mind, with its pragmatic and Puritan bent, did not take to frivolity in large doses. Notably, a full American consciousness did not emerge until the mid-eighteenth century, at which time American magazine journalism also began to take form.

The first true magazine originating in America was *The American Magazine, or a Monthly View of the Political State of the British Colonies*, printed in Philadelphia by Andrew Bradford and edited by John Webbe. Three issues exist—January, February, and March 1741; and presumably the magazine did not continue after the third number. Bradford was involved in a bitter feud with Benjamin Franklin, who had announced in his *Pennsylvania Gazette* that in 1740 he would soon publish *The General Magazine, and Historical Chronicle, for All the British Plantations in America*. Franklin was able to get his magazine out three days after the appearance of Bradford's magazine. *The General Magazine* went through six issues (the last being June 1741). Both magazines borrowed a great deal from English publications and also included subjects of general local interest—for example, on government, agriculture, trade, war preparation, manufacturing, and money. Franklin featured articles on the Great Awakening. The literary fare included poetry and witty and satirical pieces.

These short-lived magazines showed the way. Jeremiah Gridley, a Boston lawyer, published *The American Magazine and Historical Chronicle* from 1743 to 1746, which was distinguished mainly by humorous articles modeled after those in the *London Magazine*. Two other magazines, less successful, were also published in Boston in 1743: *The Christian History* (mostly a chronicle of the Great Awakening) and the *Boston Weekly Magazine* (lasting only three issues). In Philadelphia, the *American Magazine and Monthly Chronicle*, published by William Bradford and edited by Reverend William Smith, featured a series of humorous essays.

In 1752 *The Independent Reflector* began in New York and achieved distinction for its political prose and verse contributed chiefly by its editor-collaborators: lawyers William Livingston, John Morin Scott, and William Smith, Jr. (also the historian). In contrast to other eighteenth-century magazines, which sought primarily to entertain, *The Independent Reflector* had the purpose of exposure and reform, especially promoting Whig political principles in New York. Unlike other magazines, it sought a local rather than a universal appeal. *The Independent Reflector* was radical in its assertions for civil and religious liberty and its attacks on British officialdom. It waged relentless war against the proposal to establish an Anglican college in New York City. After fifty-two issues, yielding to financial and political pressure, *The Independent Reflector* came to an end in 1754, and New York would not have another magazine for thirty-three years. Several other attempts were made to establish magazines in the colonies before the Revolution, but all proved futile; during the war itself, from the end of 1776 to 1783, only one magazine was attempted (the *United States Magazine*, lasting only from January to December 1779).

BROADSIDES

Broadsides, single sheets printed on one side (if on both sides they were called broadsheets, and if folded to form four pages they were newspapers or pamphlets), had a long history in both Europe and America in disseminating information quickly. In the New World the first broadside was *The Freeman's Oath*, issued from Stephen Daye's press at Cambridge, Massachusetts, in 1639. Broadsides were often used for informing the public of government actions, such as new laws, proclamations by the governor, and declarations of special occasions and thanksgiving and fast days. Merchants and tradesmen had broadside advertisements printed. Other uses included thesis sheets (for graduation) in the colleges, obituaries, ballads, notices of criminals and runaway servants and slaves, accounts of strange phenomena, and religious announcements, such as special services. Budding authors and poets found that broadsides allowed the public to sample their talents.

Broadsides reveal social history, as, for example, one in Boston arguing against a bill to ban theater. Sometimes a morbid streak of the colonial mind shows through, as in a broadside announcing or describing an execution or the one circulated by a Virginia tavernkeeper inviting gentlemen to attend a geese-beheading bee in his tavern yard.

Very few broadsides have survived. When their news became stale, sometimes they were used on the blank side for notes or a letter, whereby then they might be preserved, but more often broadsides wound up as kindling or wrapping paper.

ALMANACS

"For all but a few American colonists," writes Marion B. Stowell (1977), "the almanac was the only secular source of useful information and literature." The almanac was "a miscellany: it was clock, calendar, weatherman, reporter, textbook, preacher, guidebook, atlas, navigational aid, doctor, bulletin board, agricultural advisor, and entertainer." The whole colonial family "consulted its almanacs freely and regularly; these served the various family members not only as their general handy helper but even as their diary, memorandum book, and early-day *Reader's Digest*" (p. ix). The second publication to be printed in America, after *The Freeman's Oath*, also in 1639, was *An Almanac Calculated for New England, by Mr. Peirce*, from Stephen Daye's press in Cambridge. Some two hundred almanacs were published in America before 1800, and several had phenomenal circulation—for example, Nathaniel Ames's *Astronomical Diary and Almanack* (1725–1764) sold between fifty and sixty thousand copies annually, and Benjamin Franklin's *Poor Richard's Almanack* (1733–1758 under Franklin's editorship, then lasting until 1796 as *Poor Richard Improved*), ten thousand. It was Ames, a physician and tavernkeeper in Dedham, Massachusetts, rather than Franklin who first made the almanac a witty masterpiece.

Literary material in the later almanacs included poems, moralistic and humorous essays, proverbs, maxims, tall tales, jokes, anecdotes, adventure narratives (particularly relating to Indians), and various kinds of instruction. The almanacs were popularizers of science and had information such as a calendar, astrological signs, tidal charts, phases of the moon, and weather predictions for a whole year. Sometimes there was a serious scientific essay, such as one by John Bartram in the 1749 *Poor Richard's Almanack* on the red cedar, which helped convince Americans of the usefulness of the tree. The almanacs also provided a means for exchanging "recipes" for curing various maladies and recommended healthy diets. Since most readers were farmers, it is not surprising that much of the humor had a rural populist bias, at the expense of tradesmen, lawyers, clergymen, and persons of foppish habits. It is estimated that half of the jokes printed in almanacs in the New York colony were sexually suggestive.

Originally almanacs were printed on one sheet, eight panels to a side. Eventually the "sheet almanacs" were cut up and put into pocket-sized book form, averaging sixteen to twenty-four pages. Each of the first twelve pages normally had a calendar, accompanied by poetry and observations relating to the particular month. Besides the literary fare, the rest of the almanac might contain charts, especially astrological, scientific diagrams, and lists of events, perhaps even dates for fairs and court sessions. A number of women whose husbands had died ran print shops and published almanacs, among them Elizabeth and Ann Timothy in South Carolina, Cornelia Bradford in Pennsylvania, Catherine Zenger and Ann Holt in New York, and Clementine Rind in Virginia.

SCHOOLS

Many Americans found education readily available, though opportunity differed according to geographic residence and social status. Kenneth A. Lockridge (1974) has shown that the level of literacy of white adult males was about seventy-five percent for all the colonies by the Revolutionary period, greater even than the sixty percent rate in England. But regional differences were wide—for example, eighty-five percent of white adult males in New England could read and write, but only sixty percent of those in Pennsylvania and Virginia (German immigrants to Pennsylvania, however, had a literacy rate of seventy-five to eighty-five percent). Generally, most of the wealthy, half of the farmers, and one-third of the poor were literate. Lockridge finds that the near universality of literacy in New England was owing to the "intense Protestantism" among the early settlers rather than to any cohesive social factors. Illiteracy among women ran higher than among men. At the end of the seventeenth century, thirty-eight percent of women could not write their names. This compares favorably with women in England, of whom, David Cressy (1980) has estimated, seventy-five percent were illiterate in the early eighteenth century. Women's illiteracy was much higher in the southern colonies. Women of the small-planter, yeoman, or servant classes had few opportunities for education. Of 3,066 deeds signed by women in Virginia during the colonial period, seventy-five percent bear a mark instead of a signature.

The Puritans believed that to maintain an ordered community and to fulfill their mission in the New World, all persons should have the rudiments of an education. As Edmund S. Morgan (1966) has stated, the Puritans had three presumptions concerning learning: children were born without knowledge; they had the capacity to attain it; and they were born evil as well as ignorant. Education, by removing ignorance, was a means to restrain evil. Furthermore, as James Axtell (1974) has mentioned, the Puritans believed in a hierarchal social structure ordained by God. "One of the chief goals in educating the New English child," writes Axtell, "was, therefore, to show him his proper place in his society, to help him understand the necessity of his placement there, and to give him appropriate manners and means of expressing his relationship with others" (pp. 135–136).

Only the New England colonies developed a public system for basic education. In 1635 the Boston Latin School was established partly with public funds. Philemon Pormont was the schoolmaster. In the 1640s, Massachusetts legislation provided compulsory education. The 1642 law required all parents and masters, upon penalty of fines, to teach children in their care "to read & understand the principles of religion and the capital lawes of the country." In 1647 the General Court passed America's first public school law. Such action was deemed necessary because it was a "cheife project of the ould deluder, Satan, to keepe men from the knowledge of the Scriptures" and there was need to ensure "that learning may not be buried in the grave of our fathers in the church & commonwealth." The law stipulated that each town with fifty families had to establish an elementary school and towns of one hundred families, a grammar school, "the master thereof being able to instruct youth so farr as they may be fited for the university." Towns not abiding by this law were to be fined five pounds annually. In time the localities opted to pay for the schools by general tax assessment. Connecticut (in 1650) and Plymouth colony (in 1658 and 1671) adopted legislation similar to the Massachusetts act of 1647. New Hampshire, until 1680 part of Massachusetts, in 1693 required all towns to have grammar schools but had no compulsory education act until 1766. Rhode Island, though some of its localities provided for public schools, had no colonywide compulsory school law. The Massachusetts education laws of the 1640s were important for introducing in America the ideas of universal education, the right of the state to be responsible for education at the local level, the welfare of the state as related to the education of its citizens, establishment of a minimum standard, and general taxation for support of education.

Elementary education in New England at first followed two lines. "Petty schools," sometimes called dame schools, as in England taught children ages five to seven the basics of reading and writing; girls were admitted to these schools but usually did not go beyond this level. Beginning at age seven, boys attended grammar schools for seven years. Many of the grammar schools, originally intended as college-preparatory, soon became "general schools," with a broader curriculum. Eventually all colonies except Georgia had Latin schools—some with mixed tuition and public financial support. By the end of the colonial period, the academy had begun to displace the Latin school. Also, schools designated as writing schools (entrance at age seven or eight) appeared. The Boston public school system, unchanged from 1720 to 1789, consisted of the South Grammar School, North Grammar School, Writing School in Queen Street, North Writing School, and South Writing School. In sparsely settled areas in New England, for a while until schools could be established, a schoolmaster divided his time, conducting a "moving school" for several months of a year in private homes.

Education in the middle colonies remained almost entirely in private hands (New Jersey passed school laws similar to those in New England but did not enforce them). The Quaker schools were on a tuition basis, except for poor children. German immigrants preferred to have their own church-related schools or to teach their children at home. The Public Grammar School in Philadelphia (chartered in 1697 and existing today as the William Penn Charter School) only admitted poor children free. New Netherland had a church-related public school in every town and a Latin school in New Amsterdam (1638; today it is the Collegiate School). Though Pennsylvania had a law requiring parents to teach their children reading and writing (not enforced), the colony had no publicly supported free schools. Special charity schools for the poor, however, were found in some of the colonial cities. The Anglican Society for the Propagation of the Gospel established and supported schools in New York and in the South.

One important development, dating as early as the 1660s in New Netherland, was the night school, which offered basic learning but also specialized in practical subjects that were useful in one's vocation, such as business, a seafaring occupation, engineering, and surveying. Most students were employed in the daytime independently or as apprentices. Receiving no public funds, the evening school charged about a shilling a week for each student. School sessions, usually held in a rented loft, home, or privately constructed schoolhouse, were advertised in the local papers. For example, Thomas Carroll announced the curriculum of his Mathematical School in the *New York Mercury* in May 1765:

> Writing, Vulgar and Decimal Arithmetic; the Extraction of the Roots, Simple and Compound Interest; how to purchase or sell Annuities, Leases for Lives, or in Reversion, Freehold Estates, &c. at Simple or Compound Interest: The Italian Method of Book-keeping; Euclid's Elements of Geometry; Algebra and Conic Sections; Mensuration of Superfices and Solids, Surveying in Theory . . . Also Gauging, Dialling, Plain and Spheric Trigonometry, Navigation; the Construction and Use of the Charts, and Instruments necessary for keeping a Sea-Journal . . . the Projection of the Sphere, according to the Orthographic and Stereographic Principles; Fortification, Gunnery, and Astronomy; Sir Isaac Newton's Laws of Motion; the Mechanical Powers viz. The Balance, Lever, Wedge, Screw and Axes in Peritrochio explained, being not only an Introduction necessary to the more abstruse Parts of Natural and Experimental Philosophy, but also to every Gentleman in Business.

Carroll gave notice that during the summer he would conduct a Morning School for "young Ladies" from 9 A.M. to 12 noon and a Night School for "young Gentlemen" from 6 to 9 P.M. Also, his wife "proposes teaching young Ladies plain Work, Samplars, French Quilting, Knoting for Bed

Quilts or Toilets, Dresden, flowering on Cat-Gut, Shading (with Silk, or Worsted on Cambrick, Lawn, or Holland."

In the southern colonies the ruling elite was hesitant to provide for general education. Southern planters, however, did see to it that their offspring were well educated, more so in Chesapeake than in Carolina society. Some planters sent their children to England for schooling. Thus William Byrd I's daughter, Ursula, began her education in England at age four (1685). But most planters preferred hiring a tutor, who taught their children individually or sometimes along with those of neighbors. Daughters of the gentry were educated along with the boys to age ten; then for two or three years they were instructed chiefly in music, dancing, and the social graces. Most parishes in the Chesapeake region had a school conducted by a clergyman or lay associate; indeed, the bishop of London prodded the Anglo-American church establishment to have parish schools. In the Chesapeake area the old field school became rather commonplace; church-sponsored or subscription-based, with tuition required, such schools resembled private academies but were located in abandoned barns or sheds on worn-out tobacco land.

In Virginia two charity schools were established in Elizabeth City County in the seventeenth century: the Syms Free School (which became Hampton Academy in 1805), from an endowment bequeathed by Benjamin Syms in 1635, and the Eaton Free School, similarly endowed by Dr. Thomas Eaton (1659). In 1753 and 1759, respectively, the two schools were incorporated by the legislature, the former open to all students and the latter taking in only the poor.

Textbooks and educational materials were scarce during the colonial period. In seventeenth-century New England the hornbook was used. It was a flat piece of wood with a handle, with a sheet of paper or parchment placed on top; on the board were letters, numbers, vowels, syllables, and the Lord's Prayer. The *New-England Primer* became America's first successful general textbook. Averaging about eighty pages (measuring $3\frac{1}{2}$ by $4\frac{1}{2}$ inches), the *Primer* was published by Benjamin Harris in Boston about 1683 and went through many editions, selling three million copies by 1806. The book was a compilation of the information from the hornbook in addition to the religious creed, Decalogue, catechism, pieces of moral instruction, and couplets for learning the alphabet—for example, for *A*, "In Adam's Fall/We Sinned All," and for *Z*, "Zaccheus he/Did climb a tree/ Our Lord to see." The catechism that usually appeared in the *Primer* was an edition of John Cotton's *Spiritual Milk for American Babes Drawn out of the Breasts of Both Testaments, for Their Souls Nourishment* (first published in 1646) or the Shorter Catechism of the *Assembly of Divines at Westminster*. Among popular special textbooks in the eighteenth century were Isaac Greenwood's *Arithmetick, Vulgar and Decimal* (1729), Exekiel Cheever's

Accidence: A Short Introduction to the Latin Tongue (1724), and Thomas Dilworth's *New Guide to the English Tongue* (1740).

Educational reformers advocated that schools in general have a less academic and more utilitarian curriculum. Benjamin Franklin in *Proposals Relating to the Education of Youth in Pensilvania* (1749) and *Idea of the English School* (1751), written in anticipation of founding a new academy in Philadelphia, contended that students should be better prepared for civic and business life. Students should not be compelled to take courses in Latin, Greek, or foreign languages. Franklin's ideas were partly adopted in the founding of the Academy of Philadelphia (1751), with its separate English and Latin schools.

COLLEGES

Until the Revolutionary period, few Americans saw the need to attend a colonial college. Some sons of the southern gentry were sent to London for study in one of the four major Inns of Court—more for the purpose of acquiring social polish and making connections than in anticipation of pursuing a legal career; a very few also studied medicine at Scottish universities. With the colonial colleges so attached to traditional classical education, higher education was viewed as superfluous to everyday life. Only 750 persons were enrolled in the colleges on the eve of the Revolution; about 4,400 graduated between 1715 and 1775. Of the nine colleges founded before the Revolution, all but one had at least a nominal religious affiliation: Harvard (1636, Congregational), College of William and Mary (1693, Anglican), Yale (1701, Congregational; founded as the Collegiate School, moved from Saybrook in 1716 and renamed Yale), College of New Jersey (1746, Presbyterian; formerly the Log Cabin College, later renamed Princeton), King's College (1754, Anglican; later Columbia), College and Academy of Philadelphia (1755, nonsectarian; later the University of Pennsylvania), College of Rhode Island (1764, Baptist; later Brown), Queen's College (1766, Dutch Reformed; later Rutgers), and Dartmouth (1769, Congregational; originally Eleazar Wheelock's Indian School).

Indeed, the primary reason for founding most of the colonial colleges was to provide training for the ministry. A promotional tract describing Harvard, *New England's First Fruits* (London, 1643, reputedly by Thomas Welde and Hugh Peter), declared that "One of the next things we longed for, and looked after was to advance Learning, and perpetuate it to Posterity, dreading to leave an illiterate Ministry to the Churches, when our present Ministers shall be in the Dust." Even in the eighteenth century a college education was viewed largely as irrelevant to real life. Benjamin Franklin, at age sixteen, commented that at Harvard the students learned little more than how to carry themselves handsomely, and enter a room genteely, (which might as well be acquir'd at a Dancing-School,) and from whence they return, after Abundance of Trouble and Charge, as great Blockheads as ever, only more proud and self-conceited.

The colleges essentially adhered to a medieval curriculum—the trivium (grammar, logic, and rhetoric) for freshmen and sophomores and then the quadrivium (arithmetic, geometry, astronomy, and music). The sciences and higher mathematics, however, played an increasingly important role. Students kept a commonplace book for jotting down notes taken from reading, listening to sermons in the chapel, and participating in disputations (debates). In classes, besides hearing lectures, students gave declamations (oral presentations) and wrote essays.

Discipline varied. For students under eighteen years of age, whipping lasted at Harvard until about 1718 and boxing the ears until the 1750s. At Yale there were four levels of punishment: a fine, curtailment of privileges and adding extra duties, demotion in class rank, and expulsion. But the college students could be mischievous and unruly. Jonathan Edwards, while at Yale in 1721, wrote his father of the "Discovery of some Monstrous impieties, and acts of Immorality . . . Particularly stealing of Hens, Gees, turkies, piggs, Meat, Wood, &c—Unseasonable Nightwalking, Breaking People's windows, playing at Cards, Cursing, Swearing, and Damning, and Using all manner of Ill Language." Of course the colonial college student was quite young, usually admitted between the ages of fifteen and seventeen, though some were as young as twelve; Cotton Mather entered Harvard at age eleven, and Jonathan Edwards was a freshman just before his thirteenth birthday.

For admission to a college, a candidate had to demonstrate an ability to translate elementary Latin and Greek and some knowledge of arithmetic. It is doubtful that anyone was denied admission; if an applicant was deficient, he was probably given remedial work. A student could well expect to graduate if he attended classes, paid his fees, and behaved.

A bachelor of arts degree required four years of study in residence; only the College of Philadelphia had a three-year curriculum. At commencement a graduating student was expected to defend a thesis proposition against interrogation by his teachers and the audience. A master of arts degree could be obtained by two years of additional study, during which time residence was not mandatory.

21

The Frontier and Indians

By the beginning of the eighteenth century, pioneers were staking out homesteads in the piedmont regions and were soon to swarm into the valleys of the Blue Ridge and penetrate into the Appalachian plateaus. Activities of traders and speculators spurred the advance to the distant frontier. Frenchmen and Indians readied to resist the Anglo-American expansion.

The charters of half the colonies had set the western borders at the "South Sea," which was thought to be not too distant. Even the myth of such a body of water persisted into the eighteenth century. The far-ranging journeys of French missionaries, explorers, and *coureurs de bois*, however, brought the realization of a vast westward expanse of land—a great continent that stretched perhaps all the way to the Pacific. Father Jacques Marquette and Louis Jolliet traveled down the Mississippi River as far as the mouth of the Arkansas River in 1673. René-Robert Cavelier, Sieur de La Salle, journeyed overland from the Great Lakes to the Illinois River and then down the Mississippi, reaching the mouth of that river in 1682. Médard Chouart, Sieur des Groseilliers, and Pierre-Esprit Radisson explored as far west as Wisconsin. Jesuits established posts along the Mississippi at Cahokia (1699) and Kaskaskia (1703). The founding of Fort

Detroit (1701) and New Orleans (1718) gave the French an axis for maintaining a trade empire in the West.

WESTWARD EXPLORATION

Virginians early probed into the western mountain barriers. Abraham Wood, who built Fort Henry on the Appomattox River, some thirty miles above Jamestown, sought out possibilities for trade with the western Indians. In 1650, Wood, accompanied by Edward Bland (an English merchant), Sackford Brewster, Elias Pennant, and two servants, rode horseback southwest 120 miles to the falls of the Roanoke River. Bland published an account of the expedition, *The Discovery of New Brittaine* (London, 1651). Two other of Wood's assistants, James Needham and Gabriel Arthur, with eight Indian guides, entered the Cherokee country in the Great Smoky Mountains, perhaps reaching the French Broad River. Needham turned back, but Arthur roamed with Indian war parties, ranging from Florida to the Ohio valley. By 1675, Wood's men, using the Occaneechee Indian Path along the Virginia and Carolina piedmont, had blazed a trail from Fort Henry (Petersburg, Virginia) to the Savannah River (at Augusta).

Governor William Berkeley of Virginia, hoping to open up trade connections with Indians of the Blue Ridge and beyond, dispatched John Lederer, a German physician, on three expeditions in 1669–1670, two of which reached the summit of the Blue Ridge Mountains. These jaunts were described in *The Discoveries of John Lederer* . . . (London, 1672).

By 1690, South Carolinians had begun to trade with the Cherokees in the mountains. James Moore, a South Carolina planter and slave trader, noted in that year that he journeyed "over the Apalathean Mountains." In 1700, Jean Couture, a *coureur de bois*, who had defected from service with the French, led a party of Carolinians down the Tennessee and Ohio rivers for the purpose of enlisting Indians in the Charleston trade.

Several decades passed before there were further explorations beyond the Alleghenies. Two Virginians, John Marlin and John Peter Salley, in 1726 set out to inspect Virginia's southwestern frontier. They were captured by Cherokees at the Roanoke River. Marlin escaped, but Salley was taken to Indian villages on the upper Tennessee River. After living with the Cherokees for three years, he was captured on a hunting foray by northern Indians. He was carried as far as Kaskaskia on the Mississippi, and for three years he traveled the western region from Canada to the Gulf of Mexico before making his way back to Virginia. In 1742, Salley and John Howard, commissioned by the Virginia government to visit the upper Mississippi region, were captured by the French while journeying down the Mississippi. Imprisoned, Salley and one of his companions escaped and made their way to Virginia in 1745. Howard and three other Virginians on the mission were sent to France and then released. The Salley and Howard expeditions bolstered English claims to the trans-Allegheny country.

Christopher Gist, a Maryland native, in 1745 settled with his family along the Yadkin River on North Carolina's northwestern frontier. Having achieved a reputation as an explorer, he was hired by the Ohio Company to view lands for prospective settlement in the Ohio valley. In 1750, Gist journeyed along the Ohio to the mouth of the Muskingum River and then to central Ohio and down to the falls of the Ohio River (Louisville). Gist's second expedition, during the winter of 1751–1752, took him through Kentucky, returning eastward, and then he crossed the divide through the Powell, Clinch, and New river valleys. Also searching out western lands for speculation, Dr. Thomas Walker, member and agent of the Loyal Company of Virginia, in 1750 traversed the Roanoke, New, Holston, and Powell river valleys and went through the Cumberland Gap before heading eastward to the Big Sandy River and across the Cumberland Mountains to Staunton, Virginia. John Finley, a Pennsylvania Indian trader, in 1752 descended the Ohio River to near the falls of the river, where he was captured by the Shawnee Indians. Upon his release, Finley revealed that the rich grasslands of central Kentucky could be reached by following the tributaries of the Warrior's Path that connected with the Cumberland Gap. Finley would strike out again for Kentucky with Daniel Boone in 1769.

THE FRONTIER PERIMETER

The parallelism of the western mountain ridges hindered the advance of the colonial frontier. The Blue Ridge Mountains (eastern Appalachians), stretching five hundred miles from Georgia to southwestern Pennsylvania, was broken only by the Potomac, James, and Roanoke rivers and several gaps (or passes) that had once been the location of streams. West of the Blue Ridge Mountains were a series of valleys and low ridges, an area fifty to one hundred miles wide. Beyond this region the colonists met their greatest obstacle to westward expansion, the Appalachian plateaus, a belt of sharply and deeply dissected terrain. This barrier, fifty to two hundred miles wide, consisted of the Catskills overlooking the Hudson river valley in the north; the Poconos of northeastern Pennsylvania; the Allegheny Mountains proper of western Virginia (West Virginia), Maryland, and Pennsylvania; and the Cumberland Mountains, stretching from southwestern Virginia to northeastern Alabama.

At the northern tip of the colonial frontier, New England was blocked by the borders of New York and by the French and Indians to the northeast. The fall of New France, however, opened northeastward expansion, chiefly in the area between the Penobscot and St. Croix rivers. Between 1759 and 1776, some ninety-four towns were founded in Maine. New Englanders also moved westward of the Connecticut River into the region of Lake Champlain.

Little effort was made at westward expansion in New York before 1700. The Albany-Iroquois trade, however, was flourishing during the last half of the seventeenth century. Governor Dongan in 1686 began issuing licenses "for trading, hunting, and making discoveries to the southwest." The granting of huge landed domains in central New York deterred western settlement, deflecting migration southward along the Delaware and Susquehanna rivers. Of the privileged New York grantees, for example, Colonel Nicholas Bayard received a tract, twenty-four to thirty miles in length, along the Mohawk and Schoharie rivers. Scotch-Irish settlers, however, did manage to settle in the Cherry valley, fifteen miles west of the Schoharie. Otherwise, most of New York's frontier lands were open for settlement by tenants only. A main route for pioneers moving from New York southward was the Indian Road near the Susquehanna River; at Harrisburg, Pennsylvania, the trail veered westward into the Cumberland valley and then across the Potomac into the Shenandoah valley of Virginia. By the 1740s the line of settlement in New York reached from Saratoga on the Hudson west along the Mohawk and south to the Cherry valley—a radius of twenty-five to seventy-five miles from Albany. Not until after the Revolution, through vast land speculation schemes, was western New York effectively settled.

Because of the rough terrain, the Indian threat, and the easy access to lands southward in the valleys west of the Blue Ridge, settlement was delayed in western Pennsylvania, except for the very few hardy frontiersmen. Although the Pennsylvania Indian trade had reached the Allegheny River and beyond by 1725, organized western settlement in the colony by the mid-eighteenth century had gone only a short distance from the Susquehanna; the only two counties west of that river were York (1749) and Cumberland (1750).

By the 1740s, English traders were ranging as far as the Illinois country. George Croghan, who immigrated to Pennsylvania from Ireland in 1741, created an Indian trade network throughout the Ohio region, with his northernmost station on the Cuyahoga River at Lake Erie. The building of Braddock's Road (1755) and Forbes's Road (1758) and the defeat of the French and Indians contributed to settlement of the trans-Allegheny region of western Pennsylvania, with pressure mounting for colonial and British authorities to make available lands west and north of the Ohio River.

In the South, with good land in the tidewater regions becoming scarce by the 1720s, settlers began to move into the backcountry. Governor

Alexander Spotswood of Virginia brought over German-Swiss immigrants to work his iron foundries along the Rapidan River in the piedmont in 1714 and 1717. The first German settlers in the Shenandoah valley were a half dozen families led by Adam Müller, who established homesteads at Massanutten on the South Branch of the Shenandoah River in 1727. Joist Hite and eleven families, receiving grants from the Virginia government, in 1731 founded the town of Winchester. To attract settlers to the frontier, Virginia awarded free land grants of one thousand acres per family, with quitrents not due for two years. Germans and Scotch-Irish quickly poured into the valley, the stream of migration reaching to the Holston and Clinch rivers and then eventually down the Carolina piedmont.

In 1748, George Draper and others founded the first trans-Allegheny settlement in western Virginia, at Draper's Meadows (present Blacksburg) on the New River. Moravians, in 1752, were the first white people to move from North Carolina beyond the Blue Ridge. The North Carolina–Virginia boundary line was extended in 1749 when Joshua Fry, a mathematics professor at William and Mary College, and Peter Jefferson surveyed the line to Laurel Fork of the Holston River (Washington County, Virginia); the Fry-Jefferson map was published in London two years later. By 1760 pioneers could travel the Great Wagon Road from Philadelphia nearly five hundred miles to settlements on the Yadkin River in North Carolina or, taking a westward branch of the road, to Fort Loudoun on the Little Tennessee River. In 1765 this road alone carried one thousand wagons through Salisbury, North Carolina.

Indian problems and the pine barren region retarded agricultural settlement in the South Carolina piedmont, but after 1730 the southward migration coming through Virginia and North Carolina reached the South Carolina backcountry. Until about 1760 the Georgia population was confined to a narrow strip along the Atlantic coast. With the removal of the Spanish threat in 1763 and the Georgia-Creek treaty of 1768 defining the Indian boundary, westward expansion in the colony proceeded rapidly.

Gaining sole possession of the trans-Appalachian west at the conclusion of the French and Indian War, the British government entered upon a policy of controlling westward population expansion. The Proclamation of 1763, issued by the crown, forbade settlements beyond "the sources of the rivers which fall into the sea." Besides providing government in Quebec and East and West Florida, this order prohibited private purchase of lands from the Indians and also required imperial supervision of Indian affairs and trade. It was hoped that the proclamation would stimulate the drawing of population to the south and keep western lands open for British investors. The frontier line was intended to be temporary, and as the need might arise, it would be moved westward in stages (as indeed it was, beginning in 1768). A priority was the prevention of Anglo-Indian warfare.

The Proclamation of 1763 had its flaws, both as to misjudging the ability to deter western migration and the ability to define a uniform frontier line along the divide. Because of the zigzag crests of the Alleghenies, it would have been more realistic to have fixed the demarcation at the eastern front of these mountains. Except for maintenance of forts surrendered by the French and a few other outposts in the western country, no attempt was made to establish a military presence along the proclamation line, thus making restriction on trans-Allegheny settlement unenforceable.

LAND SPECULATION

Some enterprising colonists grasped the opportunities for staking out large tracts of western lands in the expectation of luring purchasers. Virginia, with claims of east-west territory from sea to sea dating back to the 1609 charter, led the way in arranging for large-scale land speculation. The Virginia council in 1736 granted John Tayloe and William Beverley 60,000 acres west of the Blue Ridge in the Shenandoah valley; three years later Benjamin Borden was awarded 92,000 acres. By 1740 fully 519,000 acres in the Shenandoah valley had been given to eight individuals or partnerships. In 1745, James Patton and associates received 100,000 acres in the Ohio country, and if they brought in a hundred families, another 100,000 acres would be awarded. At the same time, the Greenbrier Company, headed by John Robinson, speaker of the Virginia House of Burgesses, obtained a similar grant along the Greenbrier River (in West Virginia), and John Blair and associates received 100,000 acres on the Youghiogheny River (northeastern West Virginia to southwestern Pennsylvania). Of other large grants made by the Virginia government, the most spectacular was that given to the Loyal Land Company, founded in 1748 by Peter Jefferson, Joshua Fry, and others: 800,000 acres in the Clinch and Holston river valleys, north of the North Carolina boundary and west of the Alleghenies. The Loyal Land Company had four years to make surveys, a period ultimately extended until 1757. The company, however, was negligent in conducting surveys.

The Virginia land companies were beset with problems. In 1761 colonial governors were ordered not to confer any grants conflicting with Indian rights. The Proclamation of 1763 also nullified such grants, at least until the demarcation line could be moved westward. During the French and Indian War, settlement was almost nil in the western territory because of fear of attack from the French and the Indians. Actually, for the Loyal Land Company's grant, only thirty families had been settled on the company's tract, and only 250 purchasers in all by 1773. The Loyal Land Company and the Greenbrier Company surrendered their tracts before the outbreak of the Revolution, and in 1778 the Virginia legislature invalidated most of the remaining grants belonging to land companies.

The Ohio Company, founded in 1748, secured permission from the Board of Trade to settle a half million acres—initially 200,000 acres, free of quitrents for ten years, and if one hundred families were seated on the land within seven years, the company would receive an additional 300,000 acres. The tract was to be bounded by the Ohio and Kanawha rivers and the Allegheny Mountains. The original membership consisted of twenty-five Virginians, four London merchants, five Marylanders, and Governors Dobbs of North Carolina and Dinwiddie of Virginia. In a reorganization in 1751, George Washington became one of the new members. The government of Virginia determinedly opposed the Ohio Company. Though 200,000 acres were eventually surveyed, the company faced competition from other land company grants, Virginia military land bounties, and, after the Revolutionary War, the creation of a national domain. After many years of litigation, the company's books were closed in 1792.

The Indiana Company, organized in 1765 mainly by the "Suffering Traders," sought land as compensation for losses during the French and Indian War and Pontiac's Rebellion. Enlarged as the Grand Ohio Company in 1769, this group of speculators applied to the British government for twenty million acres (from the forks of the Ohio westward to the Scioto River and southward to the Greenbrier River); the company pledged to pay 10,460 pounds, the amount dispensed for Indian presents at the Treaty of Fort Stanwix in 1768. The Board of Trade and the Privy Council both decided against the project, and the colony (Vandalia) proposed to be settled on the tract never became a reality.

The Mississippi Company, founded in 1763 by George Washington and seventeen other Potomac valley men, sought a 2.5-million-acre grant from the crown that would be bordered by the Wabash and Tennessee rivers on the east and the Mississippi River on the west. Like the Vandalia scheme, the Mississippi Company project, after much lobbying in England, was disapproved by the Board of Trade and the Privy Council.

One Yankee land scheme provoked prolonged controversy and even bloodshed. In 1753, Connecticut promoters formed the Susquehanna Company and brought in shareholders, six hundred in all, from Connecticut, Massachusetts, Rhode Island, New York, and Pennsylvania. The next year the company purchased from the Iroquois the Wyoming Indian District, along the upper Susquehanna River and including the Juniata valley. To complicate matters, Pennsylvania proprietary agents also bought the same tract from the Iroquois. Moreover, the Connecticut government claimed the Susquehanna Purchase area on grounds that it had jurisdiction by virtue of a patent of the Plymouth Company of 1606, which conferred lands between 41 and 45 degrees north latitude from sea to sea, and subgrants given out by the Plymouth Company. In 1762 the Susquehanna Company received a charter from Connecticut for settlement within the Susquehanna Purchase. People from Connecticut took up homesteads in the area, but the Indian War of 1763 and the massacre of Connecticut farmers near present-day Wilkes-Barre delayed further migration into the area for several years. Subsequently Pennsylvania and Yankee settlers in the Wyoming District fought each other in what is known as the Pennamite Wars (1769–1775). Eventually, heavy migration from New York, New England, New Jersey, and Pennsylvania into the disputed area obscured the rivalries. Connecticut in 1786 ceded its Pennsylvania claims, and in 1799 the government of Pennsylvania finally confirmed land titles that had been secured under Connecticut authority.

INDIANS IN THE EIGHTEENTH CENTURY

The Iroquois, living in New York south of Lake Ontario, once exercised dominion over western tribes as far west as the Mississippi. By the end of the seventeenth century, however, epidemics and wars with the French had taken their toll, and Iroquois power and prestige had dwindled considerably. Eastern tribes forced out of their homelands by the Iroquois now added their strength to that of the Ohio country Indians. Smallpox epidemics and economic disasters in the 1740s further drained the vitality of the Iroquois. The Five Nations became the Six Nations when the Tuscarora joined their Iroquoian brethren in the north after 1712. By 1763 the Iroquois Confederacy had a population of about twelve thousand (including two thousand warriors) in fifty villages spaced over a distance of 240 miles west of Albany. The Mohawks lived forty miles beyond Albany; the Oneida, sixty miles farther west, around Lake Oneida; the Onondaga, another thirty miles westward; the Tuscarora, between the Oneida and the Onondaga; the Cayuga, thirty miles beyond the Onondagas, along the eastern shore of Lake Cayuga; and the Senecas another eighty miles westward. The once mighty Susquehannocks along the Susquehanna River had by the end of the seventeenth century been destroyed by epidemics and Iroquois attacks.

At the mid-eighteenth century the Ohio country Indians, boasting six to eight thousand warriors, posed the greatest native threat to the northern colonists. The most important groups of these Indians were the Mingos, an offshoot Iroquois band who had mixed with other Ohio Indians living between the Allegheny and Ohio rivers; the Delawares (originally called the Lenni-Lenape) of the eastern Ohio country; the Shawnees, a tribe that had often been on the move, located along the Scioto River and in western Pennsylvania; the Hurons and Wyandots, along the Sandusky River; the Chippewas, Ottawas, and Potawatomis on

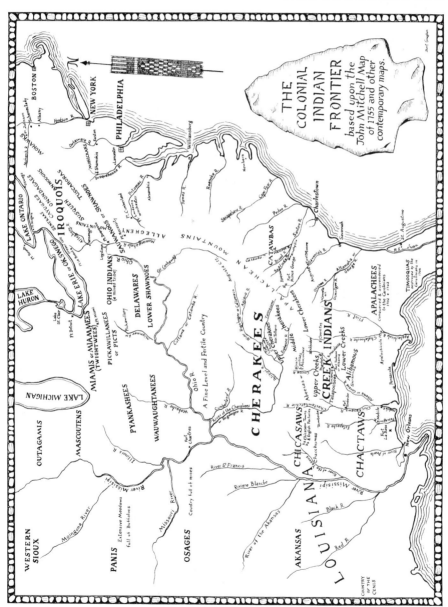

The Colonial Indian Frontier. Based upon the John Mitchell Map of 1755 and other contemporary maps. Reprinted from *The Appalachian Indian Frontier: The Edmond Atkin Report of 1755*, Wilbur R. Jacobs, ed. By permission of the University of Nebraska Press. Copyright © 1967 by Wilbur R. Jacobs.

THE COLONIAL INDIAN FRONTIER based upon the John Mitchell Map of 1755 and other contemporary maps.

Chief Hendrick, or Tee Yee Nee Ho Ga Row, a Mohawk chief and one of the "Four Indian Kings" who visited London in 1710 by I. Verelot, engraved in London. Library of Congress

the southern shores of the Great Lakes; and the Miamis (also called Twightwees by the English) along the Miami River in Ohio. The Miamis after 1763 moved back to their earlier homeland in present Indiana, just south of Lake Michigan.

By the early eighteenth century the southern colonies were free of any Indian problem east of the Blue Ridge Mountains. Virginia had its tributary Indians, the few remnants of the once powerful Powhatan Confederacy and Siouan tribes. Many small coastal tribes in the Carolinas had disintegrated or were absorbed by other Indian groups farther to the south and to the west. The Catawbas along the upper Wateree River lost half their population in the great epidemic of 1738; thereafter they agreed to live on a reservation along the Catawba River between North and South Carolina. The Tuscarora, before their northward migration, resided between the Roanoke and Cape Fear rivers, and the Yamassees, until their disastrous encounter with the English, lived for a while along the Oconee and Ocmulgee rivers in Georgia and in northern Florida and then in lower South Carolina. The Florida mission Indians—Apalachee, Guale, Timuca—were all but annihilated, being carried off as slaves or killed as a consequence of Carolina Indian raids. As R. S. Cotterill (1954) writes:

> The incorporation, expulsion, and destruction of the Siouan and Algonquian families left the Indian South in the stronger hands of Cherokees, Creeks, Choctaws, and Chickasaws, the first belonging to the Iroquoian, the last three comprising the Muskhogean family. (p. 5)

The Cherokees, the strongest of the southern tribes, held sway in a mountainous stretch, 140 miles from north to south and 40 to 50 miles wide, in western Georgia, South Carolina, and North Carolina. With a total population of nearly 14,000 (including 2,800 warriors) during the 1760s and 1770s, four groups resided in forty towns: the Lower Towns, along the rivers and valleys of the upper Savannah, Keowee, and Tugaloo rivers; the Middle Towns, on the upper Tennessee, Tuckasegee, and upper Little Tennessee rivers; the Valley Towns, north of the Hiwassee River and its tributaries and valleys west of the first Appalachian peaks; and the Overhill Towns, along the Little Tennessee and Tennessee rivers, south of the Cumberland ranges and across the Great Smokies. The Overhill Cherokees were the most warlike, with their seven towns astride the warrior path used by hunting and war parties, including those of the Shawnees and Iroquois from the north.

The Creeks lived in the area from the Alabama to the Ogeechee rivers and on the Florida peninsula; the lower Creeks, including the Seminoles, could be found between the Chattahoochee and Flint rivers, and the upper Creeks, along the Coosa, Tallapoosa, and Alabama rivers. The Choctaws were located in northern Mississippi and southwestern Alabama, west of the Big Tombigbee River, while the Chickasaws inhabited the Yazoo country, west of the Tennessee River.

INDIAN RELATIONS

Although the colonists thought of the American aborigines as childlike and even subhuman and having a propensity toward treachery and savagery, interestingly little was made of race distinctions. As Alden T. Vaughan (1982) has shown, the shift from viewing Indians as whites to a tawny or "redskin" race was gradual. Even James Adair, an Indian trader among the Cherokees and Chickasaws for forty years, in his *History of the American Indians* (1775) expressed the belief that the Indian complexion resulted from climate and steady application of ointment. Despite encroachment on Indian lands and hunting preserves, the Indian tribes, until conquered, were treated as foreign nations, with diplomacy conducted between them and the English governments.

The colonial authorities sponsored many Indian conferences, both on the frontiers and at the colonial capitals. These gatherings usually produced concessions agreed to by both the whites and the Indians and vows of friendship. Gifts, doled out in great profusion by both colonial and British governments during the later colonial period, became the necessary lubricant of diplomacy. Besides indicating a willingness to confer in good faith, the kind and quality of presents, to the Indian mind, connoted actual words and wishes. All too often, however, what the Indians regarded merely as agreements for neighborliness, trade intercourse, or specific privileges were construed by the whites as invitations to dispossess Indian lands.

Several Indian treaties before 1763, other than those concluding Indian wars, have a large significance. In 1701, Lieutenant Governor John Nanfan of New York met with representatives of the Five Nations, who recognized the king's sovereignty over (but not ownership of) their hunting grounds in the Ohio country; expecting help from the English to keep the western Indians as tributaries of the Iroquois, the agents of the Five Nations also pledged their people to side with the English in the event of war with France. The treaty at Albany in 1722 between Virginia commissioners and the Iroquois declared that the Iroquois and the Indians under their protection would not journey into Virginia south of the Potomac River or east of the mountains; Virginia would restrict its citizens and tributary Indians from travel north of the Potomac and west of the Blue Ridge. But the opening up of the valley in Virginia and the Indian trade in the Ohio country made further accommodation necessary.

At Lancaster, Pennsylvania, in July 1744, representatives of Maryland, Pennsylvania, and Virginia renewed the "chain of friendship" with the Iroquois, who agreed to be allied with the English against the French and to release claim to the Ohio valley to Great Britain; in return, the Iroquois would have limited free passage through the Virginia backcountry. The treaty now gave further grounds for challenging French dominance in the Ohio country. In 1752 the Treaty of Logstown (located eighteen miles south of the confluence of the Allegheny and Monongahela rivers), between Virginia commissioners and the Iroquois, confirmed the Lancaster deed and allowed the English to build two forts on the Ohio River and to settle southeast of the river; the Iroquois also pledged that the Mingos, Delawares, Shawnees, and Wyandots would recognize English sovereignty. A condition in the treaty that it would not take effect unless ratified by the Onondaga Council of the Six Nations was not met; even if such had been the case, it was presumptuous now for the Iroquois to speak for the Ohio country Indians. Indeed, with the French and Indian War ensuing, the colonial governments had to make substantive concessions. The Treaty of Easton (1758), attended by the governors of Pennsylvania and New Jersey, the Pennsylvania Council, and certain assemblymen, pledged that settlers would be kept east of the mountains.

On the southern frontier, upon the conclusion of the French and Indian War and the withdrawal of the Spaniards from Florida and the French from the Southwest, a general Indian war against the British was feared. But this prospect was put to rest by the Treaty of Augusta in November 1763. Under the auspices of the English secretary of state and the southern Indian superintendent, the Congress of Augusta was attended by representatives of all the principal southern tribes, the governors of North Carolina, South Carolina, and Georgia, and John Stuart, the southern Indian superintendent. The Indian boundaries relating to the other tribes were defined. Provisions were also made for the exchange of murderers and rules of trade. The Treaty of Augusta brought stability to the southern frontier until the Revolution.

Problems of Indian relations, especially involving trade and land settlement, could not be solved by individual colonies pursuing their own policies, often in competition with each other. Traders, merchants, speculators, humanitarians, and pioneer farmers all had different expectations. Although the Proclamation of 1763 in effect declared a national domain beyond the mountains, for a well-ordered development of the West it was essential to have a uniform and fair treatment of the Indians.

The colonies appointed their own Indian commissioners and agents, usually only for specific assignments. For example, South Carolina had a board of Indian commissioners in 1707 and after 1721 a single commissioner; the colony also named agents to reside among the Indians. New York had its board of Indian commissioners, whose members, such as secretary Robert Livingston, used their position to obtain preferment in the fur trade and land acquisition.

William Johnson, an immigrant from Ireland in 1738, built up his own private barony among the Mohawks. Governor George Clinton appointed Johnson "colonel of the Six Nations" in 1746. He resigned in 1750 but was reinstated at the insistence of the Mohawks. In 1755, General Edward Braddock gave Johnson the "sole Management & direction of the Affairs of the Six Nations of Indians & their Allies"; the next year the king made Johnson a baronet and commissioned him the "Sole Agent and Superintendent" among the northern Indians. Johnson learned the Indian language and mingled freely with squaws and warriors, earning the friendship and even alliance of the Indians in wartime. Called Warraghi-

Johnson Hall by E. L. Henry. Courtesy of the Knox Family and the Albany Institute of History and Art

yagey ("He Who Does Much") by the Mohawks, Johnson used his estate, Johnson Hall (thirty miles west of Albany), as the site for tribal councils.

At the same time that Johnson was appointed superintendent for Indian affairs in the north, Edmund Atkin gained a similar office for the southern department; the two districts were separated by the Ohio River. John Stuart succeeded to the southern superintendency upon Atkin's death in 1762, holding that post until 1779. Following recommendations of Johnson, Stuart, and General Thomas Gage, the Board of Trade put into effect the Plan of 1764. Under this new policy, all colonial laws relating to the Indian trade were nullified. Indian commerce fell under the supervision of commissaries, who were appointed by the superintendents. These officials were to reside in the Indian villages and could exercise the powers of justices of the peace. Also, traders had to be licensed for a one-year period and had to confine themselves to the use of specific truckhouses. The plan was impracticable from the start: The area to be administered was too vast, there was insufficient personnel to serve in the Indian towns, and the colonial governors opposed it—Governor Dinwiddie of Virginia professed that he had never heard of the program.

INDIAN WARS, 1689–1763

Sporadic Anglo-Indian warfare erupted over territorial rights, abuse of the natives in trade, and depredations and enslavement by the whites. The Indians were also pawns for military purposes in the European contest for New World empire. Unlike the French, whose missionaries worked with the Indians in a native cultural context, Anglo-Americans generally exhibited contempt for Indian religion and ways of living.

The French used Indian allies in their invasion of New York and New Hampshire in 1689 and 1690. The Abenakis, traditionally enemies of the Iroquois, fought against the British during King William's War (1689–1697). The French and these eastern Indians attacked Dover, Exeter, and Salmon Falls, New Hampshire; between 1692 and 1696 they raided Portsmouth four times. The Indian hostility, however, ceased when the war ended.

During Queen Anne's War (1702–1713) the Abenakis and Pennacooks went on the warpath but were thwarted to a large degree from attacking settlements because of a system of garrison houses installed along the eastern New England frontier. French-led Indians nevertheless attacked Wells, Maine, in 1703, and Deerfield in western Massachusetts the following year. The Indian menace was reduced when Colonel Benjamin Church attacked Minas and Beaubassin in Acadia (Nova Scotia) in July 1704, thus destroying the main sources of supplies for the Abenakis. The final phase of warfare between the eastern Indians and New England was Dummer's War (named for Massachusetts Lieutenant Governor William Dummer), 1722 to 1725. The Abenakis, led by Sebastian Rasle, a Jesuit priest, caused terror all along the Maine frontier. In 1724, Massachusetts and New Hampshire militia attacked the largest Abenaki village in Maine, killing more than eighty Indians and Rasle. Another force under John Lovewell assaulted an Indian town on the Saco River. The New England colonies offered bounties of up to one hundred pounds for scalps of enemy Indians. Many of the Abenaki survivors made their way to an Indian refugee settlement set up by the French at the north end of Lake Champlain.

Local tribes and those allied with the Spaniards brought war to the Carolinas during the early eighteenth century. In 1702, nine hundred Apalachees accompanied a Spanish force on an invasion of South Carolina; in retaliation, a Carolina-Creek Indian expedition dealt the Apalachees a crushing defeat at the Flint River. Three years later Carolinians, assisted by Yamassee Indians, destroyed thirteen mission towns of the Apalachees, killing many of the Indians and taking 325 captives as slaves. The Yamassees and Creeks, about the Savannah and Altamaha rivers, provided a bulwark against the Spaniards in Florida.

In North Carolina, the Tuscaroras suffered from fraudulent trade practices and slave raids. Their lands were also encroached on by Swiss and German settlers under Baron de Graffenried in lower North Carolina between the Neuse and Trent rivers. The Tuscaroras, aided by the Corees, Pamlicos, and other lesser tribes, in 1711 went on the rampage. John Lawson, surveyor general of North Carolina, was tortured and burned to death by the hostiles. Sixty Englishmen and seventy German Palatines were killed in September. Colonel John Barnwell and James Moore led North Carolina and South Carolina militia in campaigns that destroyed the Tuscarora forts; one thousand Indians were killed. The surviving Tuscaroras moved northward to join the Iroquois. Moore also defeated several of the lesser tribes allied with the Tuscaroras, selling the captives into slavery.

The Yamassees, after numerous aggressions against them, suddenly turned on the South Carolinians in 1715. These Indians, too, had been viciously exploited by Carolina traders, who took lands and enslaved women and children; Indians were also impressed as burden bearers, carrying seventy-pound packs three to five hundred miles in trade with the southwestern Indians. The Yamassees, who at the time lived between the Savannah River and Beaufort Sound, in spring 1714 began a series of visits to Spanish St. Augustine, receiving ample presents. On Good Friday, April 15, 1715, the Yamassees went on the warpath, and by mid-June two hundred Carolinians had been killed. Creeks, Catawbas, and small Siouan tribes joined the Yamassees. Governor Charles Craven declared martial law and collected militia. He and Colonel Alexander Mackay routed the Yamassees, most of whom fled into Spanish Florida. Intermittently, the Yamassees returned to harass the southern frontier. At last the remnant Yamassees were crushed in 1727 by troops led by Governor Arthur Middleton. The Catawbas were forced into tributary status. The English victories in the Tuscarora and Yamassee wars cleared the area east of the Appalachians for settlement. Also significant is that those small Indian tribes, who had fought against the Carolinians, were amalgamated into the Creek Indian confederacy.

Fortunately for the English on the southern frontier, the French were kept occupied with periodic hostilities from the lower Mississippi Indians. From 1729 to 1763 wars with the Natchez Indians, occasionally aided by the Chickasaws, prevented the French from confronting the British along the Georgia and Carolina frontiers.

Relations with the Cherokees, who themselves warred with the Creeks between 1750 and 1752, deteriorated in the 1750s. The expansion of English settlements into the Cherokee country and the building of Fort Prince George (1753) on the Keowee and Fort Loudoun (1756) on the Little Tennessee were sources of friction. Trouble began when Cherokee warriors were killed on the far Virginia frontier for horse stealing or simply to collect the fifty-pound bounty per scalp of marauding Shawnees offered by Virginia—frontiersmen were not wont to distinguish between Indians of one tribe or another. In spring 1759, Cherokee warriors attacked settlers on the upper Yadkin and Catawba rivers in Rowan County, North Carolina.

Terror spread along the Carolina frontier; the Overhill Cherokees, the primary concern of Virginia, however, remained relatively neutral. The Cherokee hostiles besieged the two frontier forts. Fort Loudoun surrendered on August 9, 1760. The Indians killed several soldiers inside the fort, then massacred most of the others as they marched toward Fort Prince George; the commander of Fort Loudoun was scalped and mutilated and made to dance before he expired. Fort Prince George was able to hold out against the Indians. Virginia sent a regiment of troops, first under William Byrd III and then Adam Stephen, into the eastern area of the Overhill country. Stephen managed to arrange a truce. Meanwhile, Colonel Archibald Montgomery, with fifteen hundred British regulars and Carolinians, defeated the Indians and relieved Fort Prince George. Colonel James Grant and three thousand British and Carolina troops brought destruction to the southern Cherokee towns and burned Indian corn fields. The Cherokees finally sued for peace, ratified by treaty in Charleston in December 1761.

The French and Indian War brought the colonists for the first time into full confrontation with the Indians of the Ohio country. Indian allies of the French included the Chippewas, Ottawas, Miamis, Mingos, Wyandots, Shawnees, western Delawares, and Senecas (western Iroquois). The Shawnees conducted raids in western Virginia as far south as the Holston valley. From 1754 to 1758 a total of 177 Indian raids occurred along the frontier from the Holston to the Monongahela rivers. Settlements had to be evacuated. Great Lakes Indians (except the eastern Iroquois) and Ohio tribes assisted the French in their military campaigns. Especially in western Pennsylvania and Maryland, the Indian war parties kept up unrelenting attacks on frontier settlements and harassed military supply convoys. Tensions were still high at the war's end. In 1763 a Presbyterian minister, John Elder, organized about sixty men from his congregation (near present Harrisburg) to punish local peaceful Indians thought to be supplying aid to hostiles. In one of the most dastardly deeds in American Indian history, the so-called Paxton Boys massacred Christian Indians at a Moravian mission at Conestoga, a village in Lancaster County.

After the French and Indian War, the Ohio country Indians resented their treatment by the British, especially the abandonment of gift giving and having to go long distances to the new trading centers. Moreover, the Indians experienced a revitalization movement, inspired by the Delaware Prophet. This mystic told of his dream, in which he was conducted to a great white mountain and into the presence of the Master of Life, who declared that the Indians must undergo a moral regeneration and then the white men would be driven away. Pontiac, chief of the Ottawas, exploited this message to mean that the Indians must expel the English immediately. Pontiac rallied the western tribes, who almost simultaneously struck at the British western posts. During May and June 1763 every British fort west of the Alleghenies, except Forts Pitt and Detroit, fell to the enemy. The Indians terrorized the western valleys of Virginia, Maryland, and Pennsylvania. Delawares and Mingos joined in raids as far east as Fort Ligonier and Bedford in Pennsylvania. During the uprising more than two thousand whites were killed. Swiss-born Colonel Henry Bouquet, commanding British convoy troops, defeated the Indians on August 5, 1763, at Bushy Run, near the forks of the Ohio, and then proceeded to relieve the siege of Fort Pitt. In spring 1764, Bouquet led a force overland into the Ohio country, meeting with no opposition, while Colonel John Bradstreet secured the garrisons at Niagara and Detroit.

Ironically, at the end of the colonial period, the southern Indians, in comparison to their brethren of the Northwest, had much the greater population and military capabilities. But it was the small Ohio country tribes that would bring terror to the frontier in the future—from the 1770s through the 1790s, being finally defeated during the War of 1812.

22

The Colonial Wars

Rivalry for North American empire erupted serially in warfare, primarily in the context of European world wars. From the beginning of settlement, the northern colonies contended with New France (Canada) over Indian trade and fisheries. The southern colonies served as a barrier to Spanish and French expansion and influence over Indians east of the Mississippi.

In the long struggle with the French in North America, an English victory was inevitable. At the end of King William's War (1697), New France contained 12,000 persons; in 1713, it held 25,000. By 1760 the British colonies had a population of one and a half million, and New France, 65,000 (11,000 of whom lived in Quebec and Montreal); Louisiana's population of seven hundred in 1717 increased only tenfold by 1760. The French crown, unlike that of Great Britain, held to a restrictive immigration policy, forbidding Protestants, even during the great diaspora of Huguenots after the revocation of the Edict of Nantes in 1685, to settle in French territory in the New World. Indian wars, chiefly with the Iroquois during the seventeenth century and later involving the southern tribes, sapped the strength of the French colonies. The long delay in a final showdown can be attributed to two factors: separate, geographically defined spheres of interest and competition for resources rather than settlement. The Appalachian mountain ranges thwarted English westward movement, and the French controlled the two great interior waterways—the St. Lawrence River and Great Lakes system and the Mississippi River. The French mastered forest warfare and, on balance, could count on at least the neutrality of most of the Indians during the wars with the English colonists. But with the doubling of the English colonial population every generation, by the mid-eighteenth century the westward flow of pioneers, land speculation, and expansion of the English-Indian trade set the stage for a battle for the continent.

NEW FRANCE AND LOUISIANA

The expeditions of Jacques Cartier and Jean-François de la Rocque, Sieur de Roberval, into the St. Lawrence River between 1535 and 1543 failed to establish a permanent colony. The French returned to the St. Lawrence valley at the start of the seventeenth century. Samuel de Champlain in 1604 planted a small settlement, Port Royal, in Acadia at the Bay of Fundy and four years later established a post at Quebec. English settlers to the south quickly took notice of the French presence. In 1613, Samuel Argall, with a commission from the Virginia government, razed Port Royal and French posts at Mount Desert Island and the St. Croix River. The English government also laid claim to Acadia (Nova Scotia). In 1621, James I granted the peninsula to Sir William Alexander, who proceeded to establish a colony of Scots in 1629. By the Treaty of St. Germain en Laye (1632) upon the conclusion of the Anglo-French War (1626–1630), the English, however, agreed to evacuate "all the places in New France." Meanwhile, in 1627 the French king gave control of New France to the Company of Hundred Associates, organized by Cardinal Richelieu. In 1663 the crown revoked the charter and placed the colony under direct royal administration. The Treaty of Breda, ending the Anglo-French War of 1666–1667, recognized French sovereignty over Acadia.

The seigneurial system, in New France begun under the Company of Hundred Associates, was retained. Land was held as fiefs, subfiefs, and sub-subfiefs. Both a landed aristocracy and a social hierarchy prevailed. The noblesse, consisting of self-made men and younger sons of the French nobility, and seigneurs received large land grants, upon condition of paying a tax to the king and rendering military service. The vast majority of settlers were the habitants, who were established as tenants on the estates of the noblesse and seigneurs. The habitants, however, had few feudal obligations; members of all classes had equal rights under law. The crown also brought over indentured laborers, the *engagés*, who were bound to three years' service. It was estimated that one-eighth of all conferred land was owned by the Jesuits. To a much lesser degree the Franciscans, Sulpicians, and Ursulines had influence in New France. At the bottom of the social strata and often despised as society's rejects were the *coureurs de bois*, who sought furs in the wilderness, becoming in the eighteenth century a class of wage-earning canoe men working in the western trade. Of the lower classes, 94.3 percent of the population, only a few had their own land—9.9 percent of the total granted. The church and religious orders, 2.5 percent of the population, held 10.7 percent of the real estate; and the nobles, 3.2 percent of the population, had 70.8 percent of the landholdings. New France, with population outside the two cities dispersed in a thin line of settlement along the rivers, lacked demographic cohesiveness.

In Canada, for administrative purposes, the French king created the offices of governor, whose responsibility was chiefly military, and intendant, who had charge of various civil affairs. The bishop, assisted by an ecclesiastical court, had jurisdiction in such matters as moral discipline, missionary activity, divorces, and marriages. By 1710 there was also a council, consisting of the governor, bishop, and up to twelve other members, for implementing policy and exercising administrative duties. All laws, however, came from abroad, in the form of ordinances and edicts of the king and orders of the French Council of State. A measure of consultative government was nevertheless achieved by means of an annual public assembly held at Quebec that was open to all citizens. The divided responsibilities and the quarreling between the governor and the intendant confused policymaking in New France; however, the people were more unified, especially in wartime, than in the English colonies.

In the early eighteenth century, Louisiana became a separate entity in French colonial America. In 1717, John Law, a Scottish financier, persuaded the French king to bestow on his Company of the West (soon merged into the Company of the Indies) a proprietorship of Louisiana. The company's wild speculation, known as the "Mississippi Bubble," burst in 1720, and the crown took back Louisiana in 1731. The government of Louisiana (including the Illinois country) was similar to that of Canada, with laws and ordinances originating in France; administration was conducted by a governor, commissioner (mainly with financial responsibility), two lieutenant governors, and an attorney general, all of whom, with others, formed the Superior Council. No Canadian-style quasi-feudal system was inaugurated in Louisiana, where most of the early land grants to individuals were riverfront tracts only 350 to 475 feet wide and $1\frac{1}{2}$ miles deep.

KING WILLIAM'S WAR (1689–1697)

In May 1689, England joined the Grand Alliance (Spain, Sweden, the Netherlands, Austria, Bavaria, Denmark, Saxony, the Palatinate, and Savoy) in the War of the League of Augsburg (1688–1697) against France.

The conflict, known as King William's War in the colonies, was provoked by Louis XIV's invasion of the Palatinate. The fighting began in America in summer 1689 with an Iroquois massacre of French inhabitants of Lachine and subsequent raids on French outposts. Louis de Buade, Comte de Frontenac, upon returning as governor of New France in winter 1689–1690 sent three detachments of French and Indians against the New York, western Massachusetts, and New Hampshire–Maine frontiers. On February 8, 1690, French and Indians descended on Corlear (later called Schenectady), a little palisaded town of four hundred inhabitants and eighty houses fifteen miles west of Albany, leaving the village in ruins and killing sixty-two men, women, and children.

The northern colonies took forceful action in 1690 and 1691. Benjamin Church, with Massachusetts and Plymouth troops, successfully campaigned against the eastern Indians. An intercolonial conference held in New York City in May 1690 and attended by delegates from Massachusetts, New York, and Connecticut decided on a two-pronged action against Canada. By land, a force of 855 soldiers (160 from Massachusetts, 60 from Plymouth, 135 from Connecticut, 400 from New York, and 200 from Maryland) and 750 Iroquois was to attack Canada by way of the Lake Champlain–Richelieu River portage. Fitz-John Winthrop was made the commander. Everything conspired against the expedition: bickering between New England and New York troops; shortages of supplies, canoes, and munitions; and lack of manpower—only 150 New York and 135 Connecticut militia showed up, and of the Iroquois quota, 100 arrived, the rest being scared off by a smallpox epidemic in the Albany area. The expeditionary force, camping for a while at Wood Creek, near Lake Champlain, broke up, and the troops went home.

In May 1690, Sir William Phips, a Bostonian knighted for having salvaged treasure from a sunken galley in the Caribbean, and a New England force of eight hundred men and eight vessels captured the French garrison at Port Royal, the main seaport in Acadia. Three months later, Phips, with two thousand men on thirty-four ships, headed out of Boston for an assault on Quebec, not reaching his destination for eight weeks (three of which were spent going up the St. Lawrence). The siege of Quebec, however, lasted only four days. In some skirmishing across the St. Charles River, several dozen New Englanders and Frenchmen were killed. The investment of Quebec was called off because of a combination of factors: arrival of French reinforcements from Montreal, the miring of cannon in the mud, ineffectiveness of bombardment on the fortified city, only one-third of the troops fit for duty because of smallpox and other diseases, and depletion of provisions and munitions. Thus ended the first of a succession of land and sea offensives against Canada that would continue through the other colonial wars. In 1691, the French retook Port Royal.

After several years of stalemate, with only a few sorties by both sides in Maine and New York, the war again heated up in 1696. The French went on the offensive. Pierre Lemoyne, Sieur d'Iberville, led an attack that captured and destroyed Fort William Henry, a Massachusetts installation at the mouth of the Pemaquid River, and then followed up this victory with a sweep of English coastal villages in Newfoundland. At the same time, Frontenac carried raids against the Iroquois in central New York. In September 1697, d'Iberville, who had previously conducted successful expeditions against British trading posts in the Hudson Bay region, captured the strongest British post on Hudson Bay, Port Nelson.

The Peace of Ryswick of 1697, which ended the war, arranged for an antebellum status quo in America, except for French retention of Port Nelson and the provision for future adjudication of territorial rights at Hudson Bay by a commission (an effort that failed in 1699). The French held on to Acadia. The war in America had cost at least 650 English and 300 French lives. King William's War witnessed the first joint effort by American colonies against a foreign enemy, meager though it was; significantly, the English colonists fought on their own, without aid from Great Britain.

QUEEN ANNE'S WAR (1702–1713)

Queen Anne's War elicited more intercolonial cooperation from the colonies than King William's War, encouraged by the expectation of England's providing men and supplies to aid the war effort in America. The British government also assigned the colonies quotas of provincials to be raised, as it had done in the previous war.

The War of the Spanish Succession, as it was called in Europe, was another round of Hapsburgs versus Bourbons. In 1700, Charles II of Spain, a Hapsburg, died, willing the throne to Philip, duke of Anjou (Philip V of Spain), grandson of Louis XIV. Hapsburg claimants to the Spanish throne were Emperor Leopold I and Archduke Charles (later Emperor Charles VI). Most European states feared a dynastic union of France and Spain. When James II, former king of England, died in 1701, Louis XIV proclaimed James III rather than William III as the rightful wearer of the English crown. With France sending troops into the Spanish Netherlands, England and France declared war on each other in May 1702. England, the Netherlands, and most of the German states were aligned against France, Spain, Bavaria, Portugal, and Savoy.

Queen Anne's War embroiled the southern and northern colonial frontiers. Governor James Moore of South Carolina and a provincial naval force in 1702 captured St. Augustine but failed in the siege of the town's fortress, Castillo de San Marcos. The next year Moore's troops brought devastation to the Apalachee Indians of Florida. In 1706 a Franco-Spanish fleet assaulted Charleston, but its landing parties suffered heavy losses, and it soon withdrew. The eastern Indian allies of New France ravaged the eastern and western New England frontiers but were soon subdued by New England militia. A New England force, assisted by British naval units, attacked Port Royal in 1707, but largely due to lack of heavy artillery, the siege did not succeed. Actually, very little was accomplished by either the British or the French during the first seven years of the war.

One man who most influenced the British government's decision to conduct a major invasion of Canada was Samuel Vetch, a wealthy Indian trader and smuggler who had married into the Livingston family. Vetch lobbied successfully in England in 1708 for a land and sea offensive against Canada, involving a substantial military contribution from England. Provincials would march overland to attack Montreal, and a British fleet would assault Quebec. In early summer 1709, Colonel Francis Nicholson took charge of militia (800 from New York, 150 from Pennsylvania, 200 from New Jersey, and 300 from Connecticut) at Wood Creek. In October, Nicholson learned that the British fleet would not arrive because it was needed elsewhere; the provincial troops were immediately disbanded.

In 1710, Nicholson led a force of four hundred British marines and fifteen hundred militia in the capture of Port Royal, which was renamed Annapolis Royal. The next year another two-pronged invasion of Canada was staged. Nicholson again collected provincial troops at Wood Creek. This time a British naval force of 6,500 men and sixty-eight vessels (including fifteen warships) entered the St. Lawrence, commanded by Admiral Hovender Walker and General Jack Hill. But this expedition was called off when eight ships sank amid the hidden rocks near Anticosti Island, with the loss of 884 lives. Nicholson was so furious when he heard this news that he threw his wig on the ground and trampled on it. He then led his troops back to Albany, where they were discharged. Twice an invasion of Canada had failed.

Under the Treaty of Utrecht (1713) the French ceded Hudson Bay, Newfoundland, and Acadia (now renamed Nova Scotia) in North America and St. Kitts and Nevis islands in the West Indies; Spain surrendered Minorca and Gibraltar to England. The French recognized British sovereignty over the Iroquois and acknowledged that the Indian trade was open to the English colonists. France retained Cape Breton Island, islands at the mouth of the St. Lawrence, and fishing rights off Newfoundland. In Europe, the Austrian Hapsburgs received the Spanish Netherlands, and France recognized William III as king of England; the British did the same regarding Philip V of Spain. The Asiento (contract) for sending 4,800 slaves to the Spanish West Indies was transferred from France to the English South Sea Company for a period of thirty years, along with the privilege of putting into a Spanish port one trading ship annually.

The war deterred frontier settlement, which contributed to a greater population density in the colonies. It also produced a strain in colonial-British relations, due to the failure to comply fully with manpower quotas requisitioned by the British government and colonial disappointment with British assistance. One accomplishment, however, from the colonial point of view, was that the peace settlement relieved the pressure of the French and Indians along the northern and eastern frontiers. Yet the French seemed all the more secure in Canada and in their interior territory.

WAR OF JENKINS'S EAR (1739–1742)

The founding of Georgia posed the threat of borderland warfare with the Spaniards in Florida. Governor Oglethorpe's establishment of Ft. Frederica on St. Simons Island, several forts on Cumberland Island, and also one at the mouth of the St. Johns River encroached on Spanish territory. Meanwhile, relations between Spain and England deteriorated over commercial rivalry. The English abused the privileges conferred by the Asiento. The Spanish insistence on the right to search and seize vessels increased the prospect of armed conflict. On April 9, 1731, a Spanish *guardacosta* plundered an English trading vessel, the *Rebecca*, on its way from Jamaica to London. During the fray the Spanish captain, Juan de León Faudino, cut off an ear of the master mariner of the English ship, one Robert Jenkins. In England, Jenkins made known the event, but it was forgotten until political opposition mounted against the weak Spanish policy of the British ministry led by Robert Walpole. The Jenkins mishap (the ear had been carefully preserved) became a rallying point of the war party in Parliament. Walpole, for political expediency, finally agreed with the war party in demanding that Spain relinquish its right to intercept English ships. When Spain refused, England declared war on October 19, 1739. Captain Edward Vernon, a member of the parliamentary war faction, was commissioned vice-admiral, with orders to "destroy the Spanish settlements in the West Indies, and to distress their shipping by any method whatever." Vernon captured Porto Bello at the bend of the Isthmus of Panama, a terminus for shipping headed for Spain. He then returned to Jamaica to supervise preparations for an attack on Cartagena, a Spanish port 550 miles to the south in the Gulf of Darien (Colombia), opposite the Isthmus of Panama. Plans included participation by an American regiment of 3,500 troops. Young men in the colonies were eager for adventure and glory at the Spanish Main.

In eleven colonies, recruitment was vigorous for the four battalions and thirty-six companies of the American regiment. Each company was promised its own colony identity. A study of Massachusetts enlistees shows that one-third of the volunteers of that colony were artisans, one-half farmers, seventeen percent immigrants, and less than twenty percent laborers—most recruits were probably experiencing hardship, especially in light of the shortage of land. In Virginia many wealthy planters' sons eagerly sought commissions. Governor William Gooch of Virginia (replacing Alexander Spotswood, who died in 1740) was appointed commander of the American force. The Virginia legislature even passed a law that county courts could impress vagrants to make up any deficiency in the colony's quota.

After a long wait at Jamaica, the British-American expeditionary force, under the joint command of Admiral Edward Vernon and General Thomas Wentworth, made its way to Cartagena. On March 23, 1741, the English naval batteries reduced a Spanish fort at the head of the channel before Cartagena. The fleet then entered the harbor, depositing six thousand troops (only three hundred of them Americans) before the fortress city. The invaders, meeting fierce resistance from the Spaniards, were repulsed at great loss. Yellow fever and other sickness caused scores of deaths each day. At last the expeditionary force embarked, on April 17, and returned to Jamaica. Of the original American contingent, only thirteen hundred lived to see their homes again. One of the Virginians who came back sickly but a hero to his half-brother, George, was Lawrence Washington. George Washington later named his plantation on the Potomac, inherited after Lawrence's death in 1752, Mount Vernon, in honor of the British admiral at Cartagena.

The War of Jenkins's Ear gave Governor Oglethorpe an opportunity to invade Florida. In May 1740 he conducted a force of Georgia and South Carolina militia and British regulars to the mouth of the St. Johns River and then overland to St. Augustine. A five-week siege, however, came to naught, and the arrival of Spanish reinforcements prompted a return march to Georgia. The Spaniards counterattacked by landing at St. Simons Island in 1742 in expectation of advancing on Ft. Frederica. Oglethorpe routed a Spanish detachment in the woods. British regulars and Indians exacted a toll of two hundred Spaniards killed at the Battle of Bloody Marsh, after which the enemy sailed homeward. The War of Jenkins's Ear elsewhere settled mainly into a quasi-war of confrontation among ships in the West Indies. It nevertheless served as a testing experience for the colonies for the larger war to follow. The War of Jenkins's Ear was never formally ended. A new Franco-Spanish alliance, cemented by the signing of the second Family Compact in October 1743, augured an impending broader conflict.

KING GEORGE'S WAR (1744–1748)

King George's War was an extension of the War of the Austrian Succession, which began in 1740. European states again took sides: Spain, France, and Bavaria joining Prussia and England, Holland, and Saxony allying with Austria. France declared war on England on March 5, 1744. The war in America began in the same month with a French attack on the British post of Canso, on the northern tip of Nova Scotia.

War fever ran at a high pitch in New England. For the purpose of attacking Louisbourg on Cape Breton Island, Governor William Shirley organized a New England militia force of four thousand men, supported by fifteen ships carrying 210 guns. William Pepperrell, a wealthy timberman and merchant and also a Massachusetts councilor, was entrusted with the command of the expedition. The New Englanders also had the assistance of a British fleet of eleven warships under Commodore Sir Peter Warren. The defenses of Louisbourg, at the gateway to the St. Lawrence, had weaknesses. Its outer walls were only five feet high, and the ramparts, thirty feet high and thirty-six feet thick, were loosely constructed. The French neglected to make defense preparations on the surrounding hills, and the Grand Battery, two miles across the harbor, had its guns pointed only at the harbor and not at the land approaches from the rear of the fortress. The debarkation of colonial troops on Cape Breton Island was completed by the end of May. A detachment by land seized the Grand Battery, and British naval artillery neutralized other enemy harbor installations. For nearly seven weeks, Louisbourg underwent heavy bombardment. The French surrendered on June 17.

The New England and New York frontiers again erupted with Indian warfare. In November 1745, four hundred Canadians and two hundred Abenakis destroyed Saratoga, killing thirty persons and taking one hundred prisoners. The Iroquois, however, remained neutral, except for several raids by the Mohawks on French outposts along the Richelieu River.

Campaign plans for 1746, formulated in England, called for a two-pronged invasion: a land and sea attack on Quebec by forces under Warren and Sir John St. Clair and another expedition to be led by Governor William Gooch of Virginia against Crown Point and then Quebec. A delay caused by the Scottish Rebellion resulted in the cancellation of these operations. In the South, a scheme of Governor James Glen of South Carolina to coordinate an Indian attack on the French in Louisiana also failed to materialize. The Treaty of Aix-la-Chapelle in October 1748 angered Americans by its provision for a reciprocal restoration of all conquests. Thus Louisbourg was returned to France.

FRENCH AND INDIAN WAR (1754–1763)

A battle for a continent began in the American wilderness two years before the outset of the Seven Years' War (1756–1763), which in Europe pitted England, Prussia, and Hanover against Austria, France, Russia, Saxony, and Sweden. The previous wars had not solved the question of possession of the Ohio country. In the 1740s, Pennsylvania traders fanned throughout the region, and land companies sought entry into the trans-Appalachian territory. For the French to protect their western fur trade, they needed to make three moves: close the trade route through New York; destroy the English trading centers in the Ohio country, especially Pickawillany; and secure the trade route from Lake Erie to the Allegheny River. The English based their claims on the sea-to-sea provisions of the colonial charters and the Lancaster Treaty (1744), whereby the Iroquois surrendered the area west and north of the Ohio River. The Iroquois themselves had based their claim to the Ohio valley on conquest; the French, moreover, by the Treaty of Utrecht, had recognized the Iroquois as British subjects. The French insisted on their right of possession of the Ohio country by virtue of early exploration, dating back to La Salle's reaching the Ohio in 1679. Neither the French nor the English had settlements in the disputed region, though the French villages and posts in the Illinois country and along the Great Lakes bolstered the French claim.

The French physically took the initiative to establish the Ohio country as part of New France. The governor general of Canada, Roland-Michel Barrin, comte de La Galissonière, in 1749 sent Captain Pierre-Joseph Céleron de Blainville at the head of a party of two hundred Frenchmen and thirty Indians from Lake Erie down the Allegheny and Ohio rivers as far as the junction of the Ohio and Miami rivers. Along the way they put in the ground and nailed to trees lead plates bearing the arms of the French king.

By 1750 the Americans had succeeded in extending their influence over many of the Ohio Indians, thanks largely to the leadership of two chieftains, the Half-King (Monacatoocha) of the Senecas and Old Briton (La Demoiselle), the head of a branch of the Miami Indians. Old Briton had established the trading village of Pickawillany, one hundred miles up the Miami River; here the British carried on trade with the Delawares, Miamis, Shawnees, Mingos, and Wyandots. In 1752, Pierre-Jacques de Tafanel, marquis de Jonquière, now the governor general of New France, decided to use force in the Ohio country. Charles-Michel Langlade and a party of 240 Chippewa and Ottawa Indians captured Pickawillany; fifteen Miamis and one English trader were killed. The victorious Indians boiled and ate Old Briton and also the heart of the slain trader before they retreated northward with five white prisoners. Ange de Menneville, marquis de Duquesne, becoming the governor of New France in July 1752 upon the death of Jonquière, continued the aggressive policy. In 1753, three forts were constructed along the Pennsylvania frontier: Presqu'Isle (Erie, Pennsylvania), Le Boeuf (Waterford, Pennsylvania), and Venango (called Machault by the French, now Franklin, Pennsylvania). The southernmost post at the confluence of the Monongahela and Allegheny rivers and the Ohio, Fort Duquesne, was completed the next year.

The British ministry ordered all colonial governors to resist the French intrusion, and Governor Robert Dinwiddie of Virginia was instructed to build two forts on the Ohio. The two independent companies of regulars in America (one from New York and one from South Carolina) and thirty cannon were sent to the aid of the Virginians. Dinwiddie needed no prompting, since he regarded the French invasion as an encroachment on Virginia territory. Dinwiddie sent presents to the western Indians and also "one of the adjutants of the militia," 21-year-old George Washington, to the commanders of the new French forts, for the purposes of demanding a French withdrawal and ascertaining the further intentions of the enemy. Returning from his journey of November and December 1753, Washington reported that the French refused to abandon the posts. Dinwiddie called up volunteer militia, promising them 200,000 acres of land for service in the Ohio region, and dispatched Colonel William Trent in January 1754 to the Ohio River to erect a fort near the site where the French were building Fort Duquesne; instead Trent's men reinforced an existing Ohio Company post near the selected location. A French detachment, led by Captain Claude-Pécaudy de Contrecoeur, compelled the surrender of the thirty-two Virginia troops. Without a shot, an undeclared war began.

Meanwhile, Dinwiddie had sent 150 troops under Lieutenant Colonel George Washington to relieve Trent's fort. At Little Meadows, Washington and forty of his men, assisted by friendly Indians, surprised a French reconnaissance party commanded by Ensign Joseph Coulon, Sieur de Jumonville, killing ten of the Frenchmen. The Indian chief, the Half-King, "split the head" of Jumonville, and "then took out his Brains, and washed his hands with them. And then Scalped him." Twenty-one prisoners were conducted back to Virginia. But the Half-King's Indians soon deserted Washington, and the French had their revenge. The enemy appeared at Great Meadows, where Washington had constructed Fort Necessity (sixty miles from Fort Duquesne at present Uniontown, Pennsylvania). The French sent a deadly fusillade from the nearby hills against the small fort (only fifty-three feet in diameter), and on July 3, 1754, Washington surrendered. The captured Virginians were allowed to return home on condition of not returning to western service for a year.

The British ministry, headed by the duke of Newcastle, dispatched the 44th and 48th regiments, commanded by Major General Edward Braddock, from Ireland to assist the provincials in the wilderness war. At Alexandria, Virginia, in February 1755, Braddock met with Governors Dinwiddie, Shirley of Massachusetts, Sharpe of Maryland, and Robert Hunter Morris of Pennsylvania, Lieutenant Governor James De Lancey of New York, and Commodore Augustus Keppel to map out a military campaign—Braddock to take Fort Duquesne; Shirley, Niagara; and Wil-

Braddock's Defeat by E. W. Deming, 1903. Courtesy of the State Historical Society of Wisconsin

liam Johnson, Crown Point. Braddock assembled a force of 2,200 men—the two British regiments, the independent companies, and provincials (mainly Virginians but also some Maryland and North Carolina troops).

After cutting a road from Fort Cumberland, at Wills Creek on the Potomac, toward Fort Duquesne, Braddock and 1,460 of his troops camped two miles from the Monongahela just below the French fort. The rest of the army, under Colonel Thomas Dunbar, conveying supplies, had dropped behind because of the heavy wagons. On the morning of July 9, nearly 900 of the enemy (290 French regulars and militia and 600 Indians), led by Captain Liénard de Beaujeu, stealthily approached the vanguard of the British army, commanded by Lieutenant Colonel Thomas Gage. These troops were soon caught in enemy crossfire from the hills and ravines; the rest of the British troops came up, jamming the thoroughfare and making themselves easy targets. When the three-hour battle was over, of the British force, 456 had been killed and 421 wounded—two-thirds of Braddock's men engaged in the action; of 86 officers, 63 were killed or wounded. Braddock, dying from his wounds four days later, was buried on the road so that the Indians would not discover the body. Washington, only an aide-de-camp on Braddock's staff at the time, lost two horses, and his clothes were riddled by bullets. The vanquished British-American troops retreated to Fort Cumberland. A dozen British regulars and seven women who had been taken prisoner by the French Indians were tortured to death.

Braddock and the British troops came under severe criticism for the disaster along the Monongahela. Lieutenant Colonel Adam Stephen of the Virginia regiment said that the only way to fight Indians was to

> go against them light & naked, as they came against Us creeping near and hunting Us as they would do a Herd of Buffaloes or Deer; whereas you might as well send a Cow in pursuit of a Hare as an English Soldier loaded in their way.

Actually, the British veteran regulars had been experienced in bush fighting. The cause of the British defeat can be assigned mainly to Braddock's errors in judgment: lack of adequate reconnaissance on the day of the battle, failure to march by manageable platoons, not occupying the hillsides, not waiting for the rest of the army to catch up, and neglecting to build blockhouses along the way to fall back on.

From 1755 to late 1758 the British could boast of little success in the war. In May 1755, however, Lieutenant Colonel Robert Monckton at the head of a mixed force of 2,900 regulars and militia compelled the French to surrender two forts that they had constructed on the neck of land connecting Nova Scotia with the mainland, Forts Beauséjour and Gaspereau. The Niagara campaign failed. Although William Shirley arrived at Fort Oswego with an army in August 1755, the expedition was called off because of food shortages and delays in receiving supplies and boats. The French had also gathered a large force at Fort Frontenac on Lake Ontario at the entrance to the St. Lawrence River and were ready to reinforce Fort Niagara. The French captured and razed Fort Oswego on August 14, 1756.

William Johnson's army of New England and New York provincials and Indians set out to drive the French from their Lake Champlain posts. At the end of August 1755, Johnson made a fortified camp at the southern tip of Lake George. A French army of three thousand under Major General Jean-Armand, baron de Dieskau, attacked Johnson's camp on September 8 in the Battle of Lake George. The French were defeated, and Dieskau was captured. Johnson did not follow up his advantage to pursue the enemy and to attack the enemy's new fort under construction, Ticonderoga, or Crown Point, twelve miles farther north. Johnson finished building Fort William Henry at his camp, which post, along with Fort Edward on the upper Hudson, was expected to check any further advance of the French into New York.

In 1756, Lieutenant General John Campbell, the earl of Loudoun, was made commander in chief of His Majesty's troops in America, replacing Governor William Shirley, who had acted in this capacity since the death of Braddock. Loudoun did not arrive until July 1757. In the interim, Major General Daniel Webb took charge of the British military forces in America.

Louis-Joseph, marquis de Montcalm, having succeeded the captured Dieskau, in July 1757, with six thousand regulars and militia and eighteen hundred Indians laid siege to Fort William Henry. Webb had divided the troops available in New York between that post and Fort Edward. Outmatched, Colonel George Monro, commandant at Fort William Henry, surrendered to the French on August 9, on terms that his men would be marched to Fort Edward and not serve again for eighteen months. The Indians, however, fell on the prisoners, butchering about two hundred of them and taking away two hundred more as captives. The remaining sixteen hundred British-American troops made their way to Fort Edward.

The new commander in chief, the earl of Loudoun, disliked taking risks. As a result, the British military situation in America during 1757 and early 1758 was largely one of inaction. Loudoun's lengthy preparations for an assault on Louisbourg allowed time for a French fleet and new troops to reinforce that bastion. Because of the lack of will in prosecuting the war in America by British generals, William Pitt, secretary of state and sharing the prime ministry with the duke of Newcastle, was entrusted with the responsibility of guiding the war effort. In late December 1757, Pitt recalled Loudoun, giving the American command to Major General James Abercromby, who turned out to be even more inept than his predecessors. As one author has put it, he was "a doddering old fellow, so pettifogging that the colonial troops dubbed him 'Mr. Nambycromby.'" The strategy for 1758 called for three expeditions—one each against Ticonderoga, Louisbourg, and Fort Duquesne.

At Lake George, Abercromby assembled for an assault on Fort Ticonderoga the largest force yet in the field—6,300 regulars and 5,900 provincials. The French were ready, having placed outside the fort an abatis of large tree trunks with sharpened branches. Not waiting for artillery, at noon on July 8, Abercromby attacked, at the cost of heavy casualties—464 British and American troops killed and 1,117 wounded. The survivors retreated to Fort Edward.

Despite the Ticonderoga catastrophe, the fortunes of the war suddenly changed. Jeffery Amherst, in command of an expedition consisting of a British fleet and nine thousand regulars and five thousand provincials, gained the surrender of Louisbourg, after a siege lasting from May 28 to July 26, 1758. Lieutenant Colonel John Bradstreet and 3,600 provincials took Fort Frontenac on September 27 of that year.

Brigadier General John "Ironhead" Forbes, assisted by probably the most competent of the British field officers in America, Colonel Henry Bouquet, assembled six thousand troops (sixteen hundred of whom were provincials, mainly Virginians) at Raystown (Bedford, Pennsylvania). The destination was Fort Duquesne. The expeditionary force advanced slowly, engaged in the herculean task of road building across steep hills and mountains and erecting forts along the way. Except for a French ambush

Fort Ligonier (Loyalhanna) scale model. Courtesy of the Fort Ligonier Association, Fort Ligonier, Pennsylvania

of a forward detachment under Colonel James Grant on September 14, 1758, in which three hundred British-Americans were killed or captured, the Forbes expedition proceeded without opposition, although Indians harassed supply convoys and the road building. On November 26, 1758, the army entered the smoldering ruins of Fort Duquesne, which the French had evacuated. The French also abandoned their three other western Pennsylvania forts.

The year of decision was 1759. The only major offensive action by the French was an attack on Fort Loyalhanna, along the Forbes road, in August, but it was repelled in this last battle of the war on the western frontier. Fort Niagara, on July 25, 1759, surrendered to Brigadier General John Prideaux's three thousand regulars and one thousand Iroquois led by William Johnson. The French pulled out of Ticonderoga and Crown Point. Pitt's strategy of 1759 also called for destroying the enemy's power along the trunk of New France—the St. Lawrence. A British force, without any provincials, laid siege to Quebec, beginning in June 1759. At last, bringing his troops up the cliffs two miles above the city, Brigadier General James Wolfe met the French army of Montcalm on the Plains of Abraham. The English victory led to the surrender of Quebec on September 17. Amherst, now the British commander in chief in America, with troops coming up from New York, captured Montreal on September 8. A French effort to retake Quebec, lasting from April 26 to May 16, 1760, ended with the arrival of a British fleet.

By the Treaty of Paris (1763), the French ceded all claims to Nova Scotia, Cape Breton, Canada, and the islands of the St. Lawrence River;

however, they retained fishing rights off Newfoundland and received the islands of St. Pierre and Miquelon off the southern coast of Newfoundland. The British received East and West Florida, for which Spain was compensated with the return of Cuba and the Philippines. France ceded Louisiana to Spain. Islands in the West Indies were also involved in trade-offs and adjustments.

IMPACT OF THE FRENCH AND INDIAN WAR

The war greatly affected the social, political, and economic lives of colonial Americans. While pulling the people together for a common cause, it also unleashed disintegrative forces in society, enhancing the power of the rabble and seemingly promoting greed and immorality; thus there was an increased awareness of the need for finding means of promoting law and order in the future. The large numbers of British soldiers brought through the major ports allegedly had corrupting influences. Yet Americans learned that war could relieve social distress. Virginia drafted vagrants, and in that colony half of the enlistments in the Virginia regiment were foreign-born, much older than native recruits, and apparently down on their luck. Most other soldiers were very young; on balance, with the older inductees included, the average age upon joining the service in Virginia was between twenty-four and twenty-five years old, in Massachusetts, twenty-three. War profiteering was rampant, often to the deprivation of the citizenry, as merchants preferred to sell commodities for the handsome prices offered by army contractors. Impressment of goods in the countryside and the quartering of troops caused resentment of the British army.

Militarily, the war had a broad impact beyond arousing patriotism and linking arms to America's claim to manifest destiny and the protection of liberty. For one thing, the young colonial officers gained professional military experience in their association with British army units and in service in the field. From the ranks of these colonial soldiers came the officers of the American Revolution.

Colonial and British soldiers held each other in mutual contempt. An observation in the British *Public Advertiser* in November 1755, regarding Braddock's defeat, offered a contrast between the colonial and British troops serving in America: "Our American Countrymen have shewn us" what could "very reasonably" be expected from militia. "They had Property to lose, and that gave them Spirit to defend it. They were not dragged from Home to be exposed to the Fire of Foreign Invaders for . . . a very scanty Subsistence"; they "voluntarily took up Arms, and went to seek that Enemy who threatened their Neighbours and themselves with Destruction." The colonists resented the haughtiness of British officers and the raucous and lewd behavior of the British enlisted men. Of course, the

British came to hold Americans' military capacities in low esteem—a view that would contribute to fateful decisions in the later imperial contest. General James Wolfe wrote in 1758: "Americans are in general the dirtiest, the most contemptible, cowardly dregs that you can conceive. . . . There is no depending upon them in action. They fall down dead in their own dirt and desert by battalions." Forbes was of the same opinion as to the Virginia and Pennsylvania troops:

> [except for a] few of their principle Officers . . . all the rest are an extream bad Collection of broken Innkeepers, Horse Jockeys, & Indian traders, and . . . the Men under them, are a direct copy of their Officers, nor can it well be otherwise, as they are a gathering from the scum of the worst of people.

Sharp practices by British recruiting parties stirred hostility in the colonies, even provoking violence, as when in 1756 in Philadelphia a mob seized recruiters, killing the sergeant and releasing the enlistees. In all, eight thousand Americans served in British units, but only for three years or the duration of the war, and they were usually assigned to menial tasks. Because of the growing resentment of the British soldiery, colonial enlistments in the British service dwindled from about 2,500 in 1756 to 1,200 in 1757 and 670 in 1762.

The war made for tensions in imperial relations. Smuggling goods to the enemy occurred throughout the war and especially after 1759 when the outcome was known. The several embargoes imposed by British military commanders and colonial governors led to gluts of export commodities in colonial ports and depressed prices. In voting military appropriations, the lower houses of assembly enhanced their control over finances. Parliament's reimbursement of the colonies for two-fifths of their military outlay in addition to sending over arms, tents, ammunition, utensils, and other supplies tended to make Americans think that their defense should be the burden of Great Britain.

The war encouraged western settlement, not the least because of the military road building. It brought about some cooperation among the colonies while at the same time acerbating colonial jealousies. The southern colonies below Virginia, New Hampshire, Rhode Island, New Jersey, and Delaware did little to support the war effort. Yet the service of so many colonial soldiers far afield contributed to a broader geographic awareness.

The colonies and Great Britain were now forced to reassess their relationship. With the French and Spanish presence removed, the colonists could feel less dependence on the mother country. From the imperial viewpoint, however, the British government could be freer to strengthen British-colonial ties. "Perhaps the single most important result of the war in terms of the metropolitan [mother country]-colonial relationship," writes Jack P. Greene (1980), "was the vivid enhancement of awareness on both sides of the Atlantic of the crucial significance of the colonies to Britain both economically and strategically" (p. 85). The war brought attention to the advantage of the colonies to the empire and the problems in imperial relations, especially "the structural weakness of the empire and the fragility of metropolitan authority in the colonies" (p. 87). Because of its voting huge expenditures and other commitments to the war effort in America, Parliament was now prepared to assume a direct role in colonial affairs.

23

The Rise
of an American
Nationality

The long experience of the colonists in British North America slowly brought forward perceptions of community and self that eventually, with the aid of the independence movement, would mold a sense of American nationality. A nationality, to many writers, as Karl W. Deutsch (1969) has pointed out, is "a term which may be applied to a people among whom there exists a significant movement toward political, economic, or cultural autonomy" (p. 17). Deutsch also quotes John Stuart Mill, that "the strongest cause for the feeling of nationality . . . is identity of political antecedents; the possession of a national history, and consequent community of recollections; collective pride and humiliation, pleasure and regret, connected with the same incidents in the past." Although essentially Britons overseas, colonial Americans were beginning to recognize distinctions between themselves and the people of Great Britain and also their own interests, habits, and goals.

AMERICAN IDENTITY

The distance from England, challenges of the American environment, and patterns of economic, social, political, and cultural development all helped to forge a distinctiveness that was evident by the time of the

American Revolution. Sheer space contributed to a separateness between the mother country and the North American colonies. By 1700 the majority of the colonists were American-born. As stated in issue 106 of *Cato's Letters* (December 8, 1722, published in London and written by John Trenchard and Thomas Gordon) in reference to the American colonies, "No Creatures suck the Teats of their Dams longer than they can draw Milk from thence ... Nor will any Country continue their Subjection to another, only because their Great-Grandmothers were acquainted."

Although colonial American society and culture were Anglicized, the New World ethnic mix nevertheless led to complexities that lent distinctiveness to much of American society. Wrote Michel-Guillaume St. Jean de Crèvecoeur in his *Letters from an American Farmer* (1782), from a "promiscuous breed, that race now called Americans have arisen." Furthermore, "the American is a new man, who acts upon new principles."

Economic life helped to shape the new American. Thomas Dale, from Virginia, commented in 1611: "Take foure of the best kingdomes in Christiandome and put them all together, they may no way compare with this countrie either for commodities or goodness of soil." As Jack P. Greene (1988) notes:

> [The] distance from the metropolis, the laxity of British controls, the relative breadth of economic opportunity not just in land but in occupations catering to the needs of an increasingly complex economy, and incorporation into the larger Atlantic economy [combined] to produce levels of prosperity sufficient to support societies that were everywhere becoming more differentiated, pluralistic, and improved. (p. 174)

The rapid increase in population and rising standard of living, creating a large independent middle class, stimulated an awareness of common interests. Also, in contrast with the mother country, the colonies had greater class mobility, and landholding and inheritance were more flexible. As Jack P. Greene (1988) points out, a "similarity of situation and conditions" brought forward a "similitude of society and values" (p. 174).

Colonial Americans gave their stamp to cultural achievements and by the eighteenth century, in their writings, had established a historical memory of their origins and the subduing of the wilderness. The colonial historians especially sought to create a usable past that would confer identity on colonial Americans. "Foundation and corner stones, though buried," wrote William Hubbard, "ought not to be out of mind, seeing they support and bear up the weight of the whole building." America should also have its heroes, as Cotton Mather said in his *Magnalia* (1702): "Let it be known that America can *embalm* great persons, as well as produce them."

"Ideological unity," notes John Higham (1974), "assumed its special importance in America at the outset"; indeed "one large part of early

American society was founded upon an ideology" (p. 11). But in time the colonists sought a more secular context for their sense of purpose. As Russell B. Nye (1966) has observed, into the eighteenth century there was a necessity to redefine American purpose—from the Puritan sense of providential mission to a new identity of American purpose—establishing a land of freedom, not just a New Jerusalem. The expansion of society, along with its multiethnic elements, also called forth efforts to renew the faith in American destiny. As Higham (1974) writes, the Great Awakening marked "the moment in American history when ideology undertook the task of forging a new solidarity among individuals who had lost through migration and competition any corporate identity" (p. 12).

Colonists in the eighteenth century acquired a broader perspective of the American environment. Thomas Prince's book, *The Vade Mecum for America; or, A Companion for Traders and Travellers* (1732), was a guide to towns, counties, roads, and place names from the Kennebec River to the James. Maps encompassing all the British North American colonies, such as those by John Mitchell and Lewis Evans (both published in 1755) and Peter Jefferson's and Joshua Fry's map of Virginia, Maryland, and parts of North Carolina, Pennsylvania, and New Jersey (1751) were advertised in newspapers and sold by booksellers.

But the term *American* was beginning to convey more than mere geography. Clergymen in the mid-eighteenth century and especially during the French and Indian War increasingly invoked *America* in the sense of "my country." Though the early colonists were most apt to style themselves as "Britons," "British-Americans," or "Virginians" and the like, there were infrequent references to being an American; for example, Cotton Mather, in one essay published in 1691, called himself a "rude American" and in another (1701), "An American." Eliza Pinckney insisted in 1750 that at the British court she be introduced as an American. *America* could evoke feelings of affection and attachment. Thus John Dickinson, in England, could write his mother in 1754:

> I shall return to America with rapture. There is something surprizing in it, but nothing is more true than that no place is comparable to our native country. It is some strange affection nature has implanted in us, for her wise ends. America is, to be sure, a wilderness, and yet that wilderness to me is more pleasing than this charming garden. I dont know how, but I dont seem to have any connections with this country; I think myself only a traveller, and this the inn. But when I think of America, that word produces a thousand pleasing images; it is endeard by my past pleasures there, by my future prospects; that word includes my Honoured Parents, my dear relations, my friends and every thing that makes life valuable. I can bear a comparison between it and any other place. Tis rude, but it's innocent. Tis wild, but it's private. There life is a stream pure and unruffled, here an ocean briny and tempestuous. There we enjoy life, here we spend it. And

indeed, till I see it again, I shall not be so happy as I think it possible to be on earth.

War indeed served to sharpen negative perceptions of the British toward Americans and vice versa. British officers during the Cartagena expedition called colonial soldiers "Americans" contemptuously, and disdain toward provincial troops during the last war was even more pronounced. Yet in both wars, the colonists were proud to fight for their country, which, of course, still meant their colony but also increasingly referred to British North America as distinct from the empire as a whole. George Washington, who said that the only reason for not resigning his commission during the French and Indian War (he did anyway) was the imminent danger "to my Country," was beginning to think continentally. During the Revolutionary era, though the pull of sectional and provincial attachment had first claim on patriotism, the idea of country often had the wider connotation of being an American rather than merely suggesting loyalty to a colony or a region. Christopher Gadsden of South Carolina, in the Stamp Act Congress in 1765, proclaimed that "there ought to be no New England man, no New Yorker, known on the Continent, but all us Americans"; Patrick Henry expressed the sentiment in 1774 at the Continental Congress: "The distinctions between Virginians, Pennsylvanians, New Yorkers, and New Englanders are no more. I am not a Virginia, but an American."

Attention patterns in local news, as Richard L. Merritt (1966) has shown from examination of newspapers in Boston, New York, Charleston, Philadelphia, and Williamsburg for the period 1735–1775, increasingly referred to American place names and symbols at the expense of those of Great Britain and other nations. The American share of names and symbols rose from 13.2 percent for 1735–1744 to 34.3 percent for 1765–1775, with the American data also being used in more favorable contexts and those regarding Great Britain less favorable.

AMERICAN TRAITS

A modification of British English in the colonies indicated a growing Americanization of language. Social and geographic mobility in America made for more uniform and standardized verbal expression. Unlike England, in America there was almost no linguistic distinction according to social status. Similarly, dialects did not develop to any degree, although on a regional basis—north, south, and backcountry—language did reflect colloquialisms. The melting pot process in America also aided standardization of language, as immigrants were expected to adapt to Anglicized culture. A fascinating aspect of early American language, however, is the spelling of those who were undereducated; such persons added their own unique interpretations of phonetic sounds. The Revolutionary War pension applications afford a wealth of information on the phonetic rendering of language.

Different ethnic groups contributed words to American English. Many localities retained their Indian designations, and a variety of agricultural and animal names were borrowed from the natives, such as *persimmon, squash, succotash, raccoon, opossum,* and *skunk.* The colonists made "Indian loan words" more descriptive, such as *muskrat, chipmunk,* and *woodchuck.* From the Dutch, also in addition to place names, came such familiar words as *boss, scow, sloop, spook, crib, coleslaw, cookie,* and *sleigh.* Few New World words entered English from French and Spanish, during the colonial period; the most common ones from Spanish were probably *tomato, barbecue, savannah,* and *chocolate.*

The colonists had a tendency to combine English words to produce new descriptive meanings, for example, *backcountry, bullfrog, catfish, peanut, eggplant, groundhog,* and *lightning bug.* Some English words were also used differently, such as *pond* for a small lake or *pie* as a fruit pastry instead of a meat dish. John Witherspoon, Presbyterian clergyman and president of the College of New Jersey (Princeton), was among the first to analyze American "violations" of the king's English. In the column "The Druid," published in 1781 in the *Pennsylvania Journal and the Weekly Advertiser,* he discussed and gave examples of the American vernacular under the headings of "vulgarisms," "local phrases or terms," "common blunders arising from ignorance," "cant phrases," "personal blunders," and "technical terms introduced into the language."

Another kind of Americanism was a personality trait exhibiting tension, anxiety, and ambivalence. Americans were troubled by a sense of failure to live up to the expectations of one's forefathers or to one's own full potential. The jeremiads of the later Puritan clergy sounded the theme that hope had turned into despair. Among those who were religious, as Michael Zuckerman (1977) has stated, a person faced a "double requirement"—an "ardor of intimacy" within a fellowship and a "heat of hostility" outside it (p. 205). Growing contentiousness and antisocial behavior left a yearning for stability and order, yet "civilized virtue stood always in awful temptation of descending into savage vice" (p. 201). Zuckerman also contends that colonial Americans formed their own identities partly through negative appraisals of others; they "exhibited a disposition to conceive the world in dualistic terms, as though to redeem their own enigmatic identities by disparaging the identities of others, in the peculiar logic of negation and self-salvage imposed by the identity struggle" (p. 200). Michael Kammen (1972) similarly describes the strains reflected in the colonial American character; paramount is the attraction to "biformity"—a disjunctive state of mind, with the tendency to embrace, at the same time, opposite ideas and styles. American character traits posed a contrapuntal theme. On one hand were the ideals of morality, equality, and rule of law and on the other the realities of corruption, discrimination, violence, and savagery.

PROVIDENTIAL DESTINY

By the eve of the Revolution, civil millennialism had become an integral part of the emerging American conception of nationality. The motif of America as God's New Israel had been strongly expressed by the New England Puritans. Millennial expectations were grounded in the belief that Providence would guide the early settlers into creating conditions for establishing pure reformational communities. The Great Awakening reinforced the idea that God could reach out and favor a whole people. The patriotic fervor of the last two colonial wars, however, helped to give the millennial theme a new dimension: rather than a people attaining salvation through the course of history, victory against the Antichrist was also important in maintaining a society deserving of God's blessings and protection. Americans now viewed themselves in a collective role in the battle against Satan (in the form of their French-Catholic enemy). But victory against the French was not only a question of religion but one also of preservation of constitutional liberties. Religion and defense of country formed a dual patriotism. Though most colonial troop units were not like those of the Louisbourg expeditionary force in 1745, when most of the officers were church deacons, provincial soldiers fought for both God and country.

Increasingly, too, there was the idea that the defense of liberty, God-given and cherished by a free people, entailed sacrifices of blood against external enemies—a theme coming fully into its own as the "Spirit of '76" at the beginning of the American Revolution. Thus Rev. Samuel Davies, who preached a double-edged patriotism of Christianity and country, told Virginia troops during the French and Indian War, in his sermon, "Religion and Patriotism: The Constituents of a Good Soldier" (August 1755):

> You are engaged in a cause of the utmost importance . . . to secure the inestimable blessings of liberty . . . from the chains of French slavery . . . to guard your religion . . . against ignorance, superstition, idolatry, tyranny over conscience, massacre, fire and sword . . . to secure the liberties conveyed to you by your brave forefathers, and bought with their blood, that you may transmit them uncurtailed to your posterity.

Only during the Revolution, the Antichrist was not the French but the English.

The ousting of the French from North America gave cause for exuberance and confidence in colonial Americans that they were the bearers of true liberty and civilization. The providential mission was now one of fulfillment during a civil millennium. Such a view of America's destiny was not lost on Andrew Burnaby, an English clergyman touring the colonies, who wrote in 1759 that

> an idea strange as it is visionary, has entered into the minds of the generality of mankind, that empire is travelling westward; and every one is looking forward with eager and impatient expectation to that destined moment, when America is to give law to the rest of the world.

INTERCOLONIAL TIES

Ever widening spheres of activity and communication beckoned colonists to think of themselves in a continental rather than a merely provincial context. Intercolonial cultural and social ties were formed. Colonists traveled for purposes of health, pleasure, and business. Religious groups, chiefly Jews and Quakers, kept close association with their brethren among the colonies. The Great Awakening had an intercolonial dimension— especially the outreach of New Light ministers and then later the Separate Baptists. The Quakers engaged in extensive intervisitation, and their public Friends logged long journeys; one, Joshua Fielding, reported to the London yearly meeting in 1729 that he had traveled 21,000 miles and attended 480 meetings in 952 days. Local fraternal organizations, such as the Masonic order and the Sons of St. George, and learned societies kept in touch with one another. At the end of the colonial period, southern planters began sending their sons to northern colleges. Lawyers had intercolonial connections. One-half of the delegates at the Albany Congress in 1754 were of this profession. Kinship ties among families whose members lived distant from each other furthered a broader sense of American society.

Expansion of publication and activity in the arts underscored a growing American cultural consciousness. All kinds of printed materials, especially almanacs and newspapers, circulated beyond colonial borders. As Lawrence H. Gipson (1967) has pointed out, there were 4,467 colonial publications, from broadsides to books, published between 1763 and 1774 (including the forty-three newspapers printed during this period).

Intercolonial business ties greatly increased. Ships plying the coastal ports brought not only an exchange of goods and services but also news and familiarity with people from different colonies. Especially during the French and Indian War, mercantile firms supplied provisions and equipment to troops in the field outside their own colonies. Merchants had business connections and agents at different ports. Businesses with partners at separate locations, land companies, trade organizations, and itinerant peddlers made for greater intercolony awareness.

A regular postal service improved intercolonial communication. As early as 1672, Governor Thomas Dongan of New York attempted to establish a postal system between Boston and New York; it never fully succeeded for lack of a good road between the two cities. From 1685 to 1689, Edward Randolph headed the postal service set up by the government of the Dominion of New England. In 1691, William III appointed Thomas Neael, master of the mint in England, to hold a 21-year patent to carry the mail in the colonies; Neale named Andrew Hamilton, an Edinburgh merchant residing in New Jersey, as the deputy postmaster for the colonies. Weekly delivery was inaugurated between Portsmouth, New Hampshire, and Philadelphia. The crown took over the colonial postal service in 1711, which was supervised by deputies appointed by the postmaster general in England. Although in 1717 a postmaster was appointed for Virginia and Maryland, these colonies, on grounds that their taxing powers were being invaded, resisted implementing the service in their colonies. With the appointment of former governor Alexander Spotswood as postmaster in 1732, Virginia finally acquiesced in supporting the postal system. In 1753, Benjamin Franklin and William Hunter of Virginia became joint postmasters general for the colonies. Delivery was speeded up, with postal riders carrying the mails in shifts; a letter could now go between Boston and Philadelphia in six days. In 1764 newspapers were accepted at fixed rates. Eight years later a second postal district was established for colonies south of Virginia.

Negligence and rivalries diminished effective cooperation among colonial governments in wartime; nevertheless, colonial leaders increasingly depended on conferences and consultations for synchronizing planning of military campaigns and determining quotas in men, materiel, and funds to be expended. Major conferences during each of the colonial wars were convened, mostly on a regional basis. War councils among officers and special delegates from different colonies were also held. Governors and other officials from several colonies occasionally assembled to coordinate Indian affairs and treatymaking, assisted in the late colonial period by the Indian district superintendents who had been appointed by the crown. In some instances commissioners from colonies sought to arbitrate boundary disputes, though the final determination usually had to be made by the Privy Council in England. Not until after almost continuously meeting from 1750 to 1764 did Pennsylvania and Maryland commissioners finally settle the boundary between the two colonies on the Chesapeake-Delaware Bay peninsula; then the westward boundary was likewise extended.

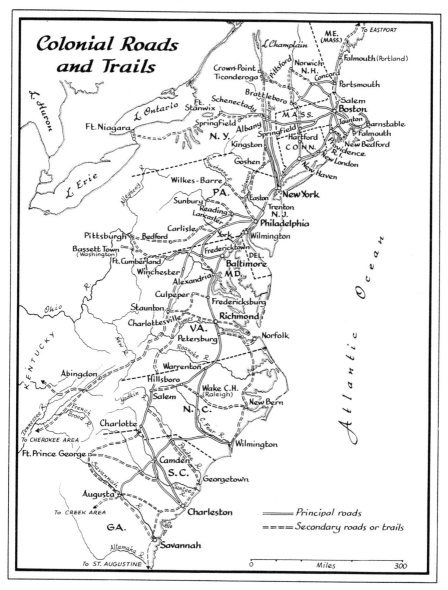

Colonial Roads and Trails

To EASTPORT

ME.
(MASS.)

L. Champlain

Pittsford
Crown Point
Ticonderoga

Norwich
N.H.
Concord

Falmouth (Portland)

Portsmouth

Brattleboro

Salem
Boston

Ft.
Stanwix

Schenectady

MASS.

Taunton
Barnstable
Falmouth
New Bedford

Ft. Niagara

L. Ontario

Springfield

Albany
N.Y.

Springfield
Hartford
CONN.

Providence

Kingston

New London

Goshen

New Haven

L. Erie

Wilkes-Barre

PA.

Sunbury
Reading
Lancaster

Easton
Trenton
N.J.

New York

Carlisle

Philadelphia

Pittsburgh
Bedford

York
Wilmington

Bassett Town
(Washington)
Ft. Cumberland

Fredericktown

DEL.

Winchester

Baltimore
MD.

Alexandria

Ohio R.

Culpeper

Staunton

Fredericksburg

Charlottesville

Richmond

VA.

Petersburg

Norfolk

Roanoke R.

KENTUCKY

New R.

Warrenton

Abingdon

Hillsboro

Yadkin R.

Wake C.H.
(Raleigh)

Salem

N. C.

New Bern

French
Broad R.

Charlotte

C. Fear R.

Tennessee R.

To CHEROKEE AREA

Wilmington

Ft. Prince George

Pedee R.

Camden

S.C.

Savannah R.

Georgetown

Santee R.

Augusta

To CREEK AREA

GA.

Charleston

Altamaha R.

Savannah

To ST. AUGUSTINE

Atlantic Ocean

========= Principal roads

==== Secondary roads or trails

0   Miles   300

Colonial Roads and Trails. Reprinted from Hofstadter, Miller, and Aaron, *The American Republic.* Englewood Cliffs, N.J.: Prentice Hall, © 1959. Used by permission.

The colonial agents in England during the late colonial period assumed more the responsibility of representing the mutuality of interests of different colonies rather than those of a single colony. In effect, as Michael Kammen (1968) notes, the agents were both lobbyists and "diminutive ambassadors" who appeared before various British government officials, including the Privy Council and the Board of Trade, and also met with members of the House of Commons and the House of Lords. The first agent was probably John Pountis, who in 1624 was sent by Virginia to England "to solicite the generall cause of the Countrey to the King and the Counciel." During the seventeenth century, agents most often represented a single colony on special missions, such as securing a charter. Not only looking after the interests of a colony, the agents also performed liaison duty in communicating information and news. The colonial agents, many of whom had once resided in the colonies, were usually retained by the lower houses of assembly. Among prominent agents who represented more than one colony were Jeremy Dummer, the "agent for New England," who served the colonies of Massachusetts, New Hampshire, and Connecticut intermittently from 1712 to 1730; Richard Partridge, agent for Rhode Island for forty-five years before 1759 and also at different times for New York, New Jersey, Massachusetts, Pennsylvania, and Connecticut; and Benjamin Franklin, agent for Pennsylvania (1757–1762 and 1764–1775), Georgia (1768–1774), New Jersey (1769–1774), and Massachusetts (1770–1774).

PLANS OF UNION

The two experiments in colonial union took place in the seventeenth century—the New England Confederation and the Dominion of New England. Representing two extremes, neither was destined for long-term success. From the end of the seventeenth century to the Revolution, nevertheless, ideas were introduced for bringing the colonies together into some kind of cooperative establishment.

From the viewpoint of imperialists, colonial union offered the advantages of coordination of defense measures, improved enforcement of trade regulation, and what Michael Kammen (1972) calls "singular standards of legitimacy" in such areas as the currency and uniform laws. The crown never abandoned the idea of imperial reform in regard to the colony governments, but given an intensification of political partisanship and wartime crises in the eighteenth century, there were only feeble efforts toward this end. To the colonists, any union, particularly one involving a superimposed executive appointed by the crown, was viewed as a threat to local liberties.

While imperialists gave attention primarily to administrative reform, proponents of union from the colonial viewpoint stressed limited fusion of provincial legislative authority. William Penn's plan, *A Brief and Plain Scheme for Union*, presented to the Board of Trade on February 8, 1697, became a prototype for later proposals for colonial union. Penn proposed the establishment of a congress, consisting of two delegates from each of the ten colonies; sessions would be held once a year in wartime and biennially during peacetime. The crown would appoint a "king's commissioner," who would preside over the intercolonial assembly and in time of war would command the colonial military forces "against the common enemy." The legislature could "hear and adjust all matters of complaint or difference between province and province" and set "quotas and charges" for defense; it would have no power, however, to levy troops or tax the colonies for their support.

Selectively, several other plans are of interest. Sir Charles D'Avenant's *Discourses on the Public Revenues and on the Trade of England* (London, 1698) suggested an intercolonial council of trade for the northern colonies, appointed by Parliament; the council would be assisted by an intercolonial assembly. John Usher, a former lieutenant governor of New Hampshire and councilor of the Dominion of New England, recommended in 1698 in a letter to William Blathwayt, a member of the Board of Trade, the creation of two northern regional unions: a consolidation of the governments of all of New England and also those of New York, Pennsylvania, and the Jerseys. Similarly, Robert Livingston of New York proposed in a letter to the Board of Trade on May 13, 1701, a tripartite union, consisting of "three distinct governments": one for Virginia, Maryland, North Carolina, and South Carolina; another for part of Connecticut, New York, East and West Jersey, Pennsylvania, and Delaware; and one for New Hampshire, Rhode Island, Massachusetts, and the rest of Connecticut. *An Essay upon the Government of the English Plantations on the Continent of America* (1701, probably written by Robert Beverley of Virginia) advocated a national assembly with representation proportionate to population. The governor of the colony where a meeting was held (the site to be rotated among five towns) would have executive powers.

Suggestions for imperial reform without union continued. For example, Caleb Heathcote, a New York councilor and surveyor general of customs for the Northern Department, in 1716 called on the British government to require customs and excise duties from the colonies to cover the cost of the civil service and of naval units protecting colonial ports, with the crown setting the rates and disbursing the revenue; "all the Governors, & other officers" would therefore "Receive their Bread, & support, from the Hands of the King, without a slavish dependence for it, on the uncertain Humours of assemblys."

The last effort in England toward completing the royalization of the colonial governments came in the early 1720s. Quo warranto proceedings were initiated against the charters of the corporate and proprietary colonies, though soon abandoned. In anticipation of such a change, the Board of Trade had gone ahead and drawn up a proposal, known as the Earl of Stair Plan, for a centralized administration for the colonies from Nova Scotia to South Carolina, largely for military purposes. A crown-appointed official as captain general and governor in chief, assisted by an advisory council of two delegates from each colony named by the assemblies, would take over the executive powers of the governors pertaining to defense and would have sole power for dispensing funds raised for this purpose.

Daniel Coxe, a New Jersey politician and son of one of the Carolina proprietors, in *A Description of the English Province of Carolana* . . . (1722) called for a union of all the colonies on the continent, chiefly for the purpose of defense; a governor general would have veto power over acts of a "grand council," which would consist of two delegates from each colony. Martin Bladen, a member of Parliament and the Board of Trade, in 1739 proposed the appointment of a captain general for the colonies, who would also be the governor of Massachusetts and New York. He would be assisted by an intercolonial advisory council representing all the colonies and by an assembly; the selection of members of both bodies would be in numbers proportionate to a colony's population, although New York, with the seat of government to be in New York City, would have several extra members. Bladen's supracolonial government would be concerned mainly with levying taxes and appropriating moneys for military purposes. The earl of Halifax came up with a similar plan in 1752. Archibald Kennedy, receiver general of New York, in *Importance of Gaining and Preserving the Friendship with the Indians, &c* (1752) also recommended union for general defense: Intercolonial commissioners would meet annually at Albany for the purposes of setting defense quotas, allotting lands on the frontier, and erecting forts.

On the eve of the French and Indian War, the British government hoped that the colonies would establish a common fund for military defense and find means to coordinate Indian affairs. The Board of Trade in September 1753 in a circular letter ordered all the northern governors to send commissioners to be appointed by the assemblies to a conference to be held at Albany. Seven colonies (from New Hampshire southward to Maryland) sent twenty-five delegates; 150 Iroquois also attended. The Albany Congress voted unanimously that some form of colonial union was expedient. A committee of one delegate from each attending colony drew up a plan of union, based largely on a draft by Benjamin Franklin but also on proposals submitted by Thomas Hutchinson, Richard Peters, and Thomas Pownall. The Albany Plan of Union advocated that a limited union of the colonies should go into effect upon enactment by Parliament and ratification by the colonies. The plan called for a president general, with veto powers, appointed by the crown, and an intercolonial legislature, to be chosen by eleven assemblies (Delaware and Georgia not included). Delegations were to consist of two to seven members, proportionately according to a colony's population, totaling forty-eight. The king could disallow any measure within three years. This intercolonial government would have jurisdiction over the regulation of trade, Indian affairs, import duties and taxes to be used for military defense, and all military affairs, including the appointment of officers.

The Albany Plan was rejected by all the colonies, chiefly on grounds that the powers of colonial assemblies would be lessened, the president general would have too much authority, and such a governing body would be subject to the influence of special interests, such as those of the land companies. Nevertheless, the Albany Congress had brought together representatives of the colonies to consider union. It also underscored common interests among the colonies. Both the Congress and the Plan of Union provided valuable precedents for the future.

From across the Atlantic, in 1757 a proposal by an English commercial writer suggested a lack of realism in discussions in the mother country as to reform of imperial administration. Malachi Postlethwayt, in *Britain's Commercial Interest Explained and Improved*, recommended making "the whole British Empire" a "complete union." All the colonies should "be united under a legal, regular and firm establishment, settled and determined by the wisdom of a British legislature." A lord lieutenant, who could be assisted by a "great council" of two delegates from each colony, should be appointed by the crown "as supreme governor" over the colonies, "to act in subordination to the voice of a British parliament."

1763: TOWARD INDEPENDENCE

The colonists in 1763 surveyed the world about them with new eyes. It was a year of harsh realities and apprehension for the future. In some ways it was a year of shock—war demobilization, postwar depression, the Indian uprising in the northwest, the announcement of creating a military establishment for the colonies and stationing ten thousand troops in North America, the notice by the Grenville ministry of new measures to be placed on the colonies, and the Proclamation of 1763 denying further westward expansion. Rumors still persisted that an Anglican episcopate would be established in America.

For the first time there was no foreign enemy along the colonial frontiers. With the end of military procurement and the rise of the prices of food, firewood, and taxes, especially in the seaport towns, craftsmen and laborers saw their standard of living threatened. Unemployment had increased. Prominent merchant firms, such as those of Daniel Clark and

William Griffiths, John Reed, Samuel Wallace, and Scott and McMichael in Philadelphia, had failed in the past two years. The depression spread. In Virginia, with the restriction of new credit and demand for payment of debts, planters were on the verge of bankruptcy. William Allason, a merchant at Falmouth, Virginia, in 1764 ordered a pair of pistols because "it is sometimes Dangerous in Traveling through our wooden Country, Particularly at this time when the Planters are pressed for old Balances." Political rivalry in the colonial governments had reached a high pitch. There were even indirect insults to royal authority, such as a Virginia court in 1763 defying the king in the famous "Parsons Cause" in returning only one shilling in back pay to a clergyman who had sued for full recompense on grounds of the king's disallowance of Virginia's Two-Penny Act.

Despite their anxieties, colonists had a new confidence in the future. Benjamin Franklin had written to Henry Home, Lord Kames, in 1760

> that the Foundations of the future Grandeur and Stability of the British Empire, lie in America; and tho', like other Foundations, they are low and little seen, they are nevertheless, broad and Strong enough to support the greatest Political Structure Human Wisdom ever yet erected.

Although colonial and British writers discounted any colonial movement for independence, as J. M. Bumsted (1974) has shown, the idea was very much in their minds, if for only feeling the necessity to refute such a possibility. The debate of 1759 and 1760 on whether Great Britain should receive either Guadeloupe or Canada in the peace settlement elicited concerns that the American colonies, without a common enemy in Canada, might turn on Great Britain itself. Franklin, who doubted that the American colonies would be inclined to separate from the British Empire, nevertheless sounded a warning in *The Interest of Great Britain Considered, with Regard to the Colonies, and the Acquisition of Canada and Guadeloupe* (1760): "When I say such a union [of the colonies against England] is impossible, I mean without the most grievous tyranny and oppression. . . . The waves do not rise, but when the winds blow."

The relationship between Great Britain and its North American colonies approached a constitutional crisis. The colonies had brought their own governments to maturity, with the locus of power in the assemblies, and viewed their political systems as coequal to that in Great Britain. The colonists cited their charters and their free choice of coming to America, bringing with them all the rights of Englishmen, not the least being that of making their own laws.

In 1763 the colonists looked forward to a return of the antebellum status quo in regard to their relations with Great Britain—a continuance of "salutary neglect," with lax enforcement of the navigation and trade acts, grants of western lands, and control of their own internal affairs. A difference in constitutional perspective is seen in the 1764 writings of James Otis and Richard Bland, who sought definition of the colonial position, and Francis Bernard, governor of Massachusetts (1760–1769), who in a letter that was widely circulated and praised in England suggested how to make the colonies a more integral part of the imperial system.

The Colonel Dismounted, which Bland wrote in response to the Two-Penny Act controversy in Virginia and Lyon G. Tyler called "the great initial paper of the American Revolution," distinguished between the right of the colonies to control their internal government and Parliament's regulation of external affairs relating to the colonies; an assembly's power to tax, therefore, was unabridged. James Otis, in *The Rights of the British Colonies Asserted and Proved* (1764), while conceding Parliament's right to legislate for the colonies, stated that any such statutes contrary to natural law were void. Americans had the same rights as Englishmen, and Parliament could not infringe on American liberties; certainly there could be no taxation of the colonists without their consent. In general, colonial writers were beginning to attack the theory of virtual representation— that Parliament represented the interests of all British subjects, if not directly the people themselves. The colonial American view was that in the Lockean sense, the social contract was not one of rulers and the ruled but of individual persons in a state of nature anterior to the formation of government.

Bernard's *Principles of Law and Polity, Applied to the British Colonies in America* (1764, published in 1774) argued that "the King *in Parliament*, is the sole and absolute Sovereign of the whole British Empire"; Parliament had the "right to make laws for, and impose taxes upon, its subjects in its external dominions, although they are not represented in such *Parliament*"; however, "taxes imposed upon the external dominions ought to be applied to the use of the people, from whom they are raised." Interestingly, Bernard recommended establishment of an American nobility, which could be formed into a colonial House of Lords, thereby making for a "real and distinct third Legislative power mediating between the *King* and the People."

In the 1760s, English public servants, lacking interest in America and often misinformed, failed to apprise themselves of the depth of the constitutional and political situation in the colonies. Factions in Parliament were more concerned with dividing the spoils of patronage than facing tough decisions. Many British departments, in addition to the branches of government, overlapped in responsibility for colonial administration. Furthermore, as Sir Lewis Namier (1931/1966), a British historian, has observed, "all conceptions" regarding the future of the colonies and Canada centered on questions of trade and finance. "Thus economic considerations impelled British statesmen to take action with regard to the Empire at a time when, even for constitutional reasons, a true settlement could not be attained" (p. 37).

The program of George Grenville (prime minister, 1763–1765) sought to relieve burdens on the British taxpayers, who themselves were suffering from a postwar depression. The British national debt, largely accrued from the war, in 1763 stood at 146 million pounds, and 350,000 pounds was the estimated annual cost of administration for the American colonies. The Sugar Act of 1764, by placing import duties for the purpose of revenue, intruded on the colonial claim of self-taxation. The fury of the colonists in opposition to taxation without representation, however, would not be unleashed until the passage of the Stamp Act. Rev. Ezra Stiles declared in summer 1765 that the Stamp Act "Diffused a Disgust thro the Colonies And laid the Basis of an Alienation Which will never be healed. Henceforth the *European* and *American* Interests Are Separated Never More to be joyned."

The decisions in 1763 and 1764 to tighten procedures against smuggling, to require British customs commissioners to reside in the colonies, to enlarge the jurisdiction and powers of the admiralty courts, and to provide naval assistance to customhouse officers further alarmed the colonists regarding British intrusion. To the colonists, a corrupt government abroad now conspired to deprive Americans of their true British liberties, rooted from the beginning of settlement and nurtured for nearly two centuries.

Suggested Reading

The works listed for one chapter may be relevant to other chapters as well.

CHAPTER 1

ANDREWS, K. R., CANNY, N. F., AND HAIR, P. E. H., eds. *The Westward Enterprise.* Detroit: Wayne State University Press, 1979.

BOLAND, CHARLES M. *They All Discovered America.* New York: Doubleday & Company, 1961.

BRIDENBAUGH, CARL. *Vexed and Troubled Englishmen, 1590–1642.* New York: Oxford University Press, 1967.

CHIAPPELLI, FREDI, ed. *First Images of America: The Impact of the New World on the Old.* 2 vols. Berkeley: University of California Press, 1976.

DENEVAN, WILLIAM M. *The Native Population of the Americas in 1492.* Madison: University of Wisconsin Press, 1976.

ENTERLINE, JAMES R. *Viking America: The Norse Crossings and Their Legacy.* New York: Doubleday & Company, 1972.

GIBSON, ARNELL M. *The American Indian: Prehistory to the Present.* Lexington, Mass.: D. C. Heath and Company, 1980.

GOLDSTEIN, THOMAS. "Impulses of Italian Renaissance Culture Behind the Age of Discoveries." In Chiappelli, Fredi. *First Images of America: The Impact of the New World on the Old.* vol. 1. Berkeley: University of California Press, 1976.

HALE, J. R. *Renaissance Exploration.* New York: W. W. Norton & Company, 1968.

HULTON, PAUL. *America, 1585: The Complete Drawings of John White.* Chapel Hill: University of North Carolina Press, 1984.

JACOBS, WILBUR R. "The Tip of an Iceberg: Pre-Columbian Indian Demography and Some Implications for Revision." *William and Mary Quarterly,* 3d ser., 31 (1974): 123–32.

JONES, GWYN. *The Norse Atlantic Saga, Being the Norse Voyages of Discovery and Settlement to Iceland, Greenland and America.* New York: Oxford University Press, 1964.

KEHOE, ALICE B. *North American Indians: A Comprehensive Account.* Englewood Cliffs, N.J.: Prentice Hall, 1981.

KUPPERMAN, KAREN O. *Roanoke, the Abandoned Colony.* Totowa, N.J.: Rowman & Allanheld Publishers, 1984.

LOWERY, WOODBURY. *The Spanish Settlements within the Present Limits of the United States, 1513– 1561.* New York: Russell & Russell, 1959.

MEGGERS, BETTY J. *Prehistoric America: An Ecological Perspective.* New York: Aldine Publishing Company, 1972.

MORISON, SAMUEL E. *The European Discovery of America: The Northern Voyages, A.D. 500–1600.* New York: Oxford University Press, 1971.

NEWCOMB, WILLIAM W., JR. *North American Indians: An Anthropological Perspective.* Pacific Palisades, Calif.: Goodyear Publishing Company, 1974.

O'GORMAN, EDMUNDO. *The Invention of America.* Bloomington: University of Indiana Press, 1961.

OLESON, TRYGGVI J. *Early Voyages and Northern Approaches, 1000–1632.* New York: Oxford University Press, 1964.

PARRY, JOHN H. *The Age of Reconnaissance.* Cleveland: The World Publishing Company, 1963.

POHL, FREDERICK J. *The Viking Settlements of North America.* New York: Clarkson N. Potter, 1972.

QUINN, DAVID B. *England and the Discovery of America, 1481–1620.* New York: Alfred A. Knopf, 1974.

————. *North America from Earliest Discovery to First Settlements: The Norse Voyages to 1612.* New York: Harper & Row, 1975.

————, ed. *The Roanoke Voyages, 1584–1590.* 2 vols. London: The Hakluyt Society, 1955.

SAUER, CARL O. *Sixteenth-Century North America: The Land and the People as Seen by the Europeans.* Berkeley: University of California Press, 1971.

SCAMMELL, G. V. *The World Encompassed: The First European Maritime Empires, c. 800–1650.* Berkeley: University of California Press, 1981.

WASHBURN, WILCOMB E. "The Meaning of 'Discovery' in the Fifteenth and Sixteenth Centuries." *American Historical Review,* 68 (1962): 1–21.

CHAPTER 2

ANDREWS, MATTHEW P. *The Founding of Maryland.* New York: Allen & Unwin, 1933.

BARBOUR, PHILIP L., ed. *The Complete Works of Captain John Smith.* 3 vols. Chapel Hill: University of North Carolina Press, 1986.

————. *The Three Worlds of Captain John Smith.* Boston: Houghton Mifflin Company, 1964.

BILLINGS, WARREN M., SELBY, JOHN E., AND TATE, THAD W. *Colonial Virginia—A History.* White Plains, N. Y.: KTO Press, 1986.

CRAVEN, WESLEY F. *Dissolution of the Virginia Company: The Failure of a Colonial Experiment.* New York: Oxford University Press, 1932.

————. *The Southern Colonies in the Seventeenth Century, 1607–1689* (Vol. 50 of *A History of the South*). Baton Rouge: Louisiana State University Press, 1949.

EARLE, CARVILLE V. "Environment, Disease, and Mortality in Early Virginia." In *The Chesapeake in the Seventeenth Century: Essays on Anglo-American Society,* ed. Thad W. Tate and David L. Ammerman. Chapel Hill: University of North Carolina Press, 1979.

GETHYN-JONES, ERIC. *George Thorpe and the Berkeley Company: A Gloucestershire Enterprise in Virginia.* Gloucester, England: Alan Sutton Publishing Limited, 1982.

HALE, NATHANIEL C. *Virginia Venturer: A Historical Biography of William Claiborne, 1600–1677.* Richmond: Dietz Press, 1951.

IVES, J. MOSS. *The Ark and the Dove: The Beginning of Civil and Religious Liberties in America.* New York: Cooper Square Publishers, 1969. Originally published in 1936.

Jamestown 350th Anniversary Historical Booklets. Williamsburg, Va.: Virginia 350th Anniversary Celebration, 1957.

KUPPERMAN, KAREN O. "Apathy and Death in Early Jamestown." *Journal of American History,* 66 (1979): 24–40.

LAND, AUBREY C. *Colonial Maryland: A History.* Millwood, N.Y.: KTO Press, 1981.

MERENESS, NEWTON D. *Maryland as a Proprietary Province.* New York: Macmillan and Company, 1901.

MORGAN, EDMUND S. "The Labor Problem at Jamestown, 1607–1618." *American Historical Review,* 76 (1971): 595–611.

MORTON, RICHARD L. *Colonial Virginia. Vol. 1: The Tidewater Period, 1607–1710.* Chapel Hill: University of North Carolina Press, 1960.

NEWMAN, HARRY W. *The Flowering of the Maryland Palatinate.* Washington, D.C.: Baltimore: Genealogical Publishing Company, 1985. Originally published in 1961.

QUINN, DAVID B., ed. *Early Maryland in a Wider World.* Detroit: Wayne State University Press, 1982.

ROUNTREE, HELEN C. *The Powhatan Indians of Virginia: Their Traditional Culture.* Norman: University of Oklahoma Press, 1989.

RUTMAN, DARRETT B. "The Virginia Company and Its Military Regime." In *The Old Dominion: Essays for Thomas Perkins Abernethy,* ed. Darrett B. Rutman. Charlottesville: University Press of Virginia, 1964.

SHEEHAN, BERNARD W. *Savagism and Civility: Indians and Englishmen in Colonial Virginia.* Cambridge, England: Cambridge University Press, 1980.

STEINER, BERNARD C. *Beginnings of Maryland, 1631–1639.* Baltimore: The Johns Hopkins Press, 1903.

VAUGHAN, ALDEN T. *American Genesis: Captain John Smith and the Founding of Virginia.* Boston: Little, Brown and Company, 1975.

WILLISON, GEORGE F. *Behold Virginia: The Fifth Crown.* New York: Harcourt, Brace and Company, 1951.

WOODWARD, GRACE S. *Pocahontas.* Norman: University of Oklahoma Press, 1969.

CHAPTER 3

ADAIR, JOHN. *Founding Fathers: The Puritans in England and America.* London: J. M. Dent & Son, 1982.

ANDREWS, CHARLES M. *The Colonial Period of American History.* Vols. 1 and 2. New Haven, Conn.: Yale University Press, 1934–1936.

ARNOLD, SAMUEL G. *History of the State of Rhode Island and Providence Plantations.* Vol. 1. Spartanburg, S.C.: The Reprint Company, 1970. Originally published in 1858.

BATTIS, EMERY. *Saints and Sectaries: Anne Hutchinson and the Antinomian Controversy in the Massachusetts Bay Colony.* Chapel Hill: University of North Carolina Press, 1962.

BRADFORD, WILLIAM. *History of Plymouth Plantation, 1620–47.* 2 vols. Boston: Houghton Mifflin Company, 1912. Reissued edited by Samuel E. Morison in 1952 and 1967.

BROCKUNIER, SAMUEL H. *The Irrepressible Democrat: Roger Williams.* New York: The Ronald Press Company, 1940.

CALDER, ISABEL M. *The New Haven Colony.* New Haven, Conn.: Yale University Press, 1934.

CARROLL, PETER N. *Puritanism and the Wilderness: The Intellectual Significance of the New England Frontier, 1629–1700.* New York: Columbia University Press, 1969.

COLLINSON, PATRICK. *The Elizabethan Puritan Movement.* Berkeley: University of California Press, 1967.

DEMING, DOROTHY. *The Settlement of the Connecticut Towns.* New Haven, Conn.: Yale University Press, 1933.

DUNN, RICHARD S. *Puritans and Yankees: The Winthrop Dynasty of New England, 1630–1717.* Princeton, N.J.: Princeton University Press, 1962.

ELLIS, GEORGE E. *Puritan Age and Rule in the Colony of the Massachusetts Bay, 1629–1685.* New York: Burt Franklin, 1970. Originally published in 1888.

ERNST, JAMES. *Roger Williams: New England Firebrand.* New York: The Macmillan Company, 1932.

GURA, PHILIP F. *A Glimpse of Sion's Glory: Puritan Radicalism in New England, 1620–1660.* Middletown, Conn.: Wesleyan University Press, 1984.

HALLER, WILLIAM. *The Rise of Puritanism.* New York: Harper & Brothers, 1957. Originally published in 1938.

HALLER, WILLIAM, JR. *The Puritan Frontier: Town-Planting in New England Colonial Development, 1630–1660.* New York: AMS Press, 1968. Originally published in 1951.

HEATH, DWIGHT B., ed. *A Journal of the Pilgrims at Plymouth: Mourt's Relation . . .* New York: Corinth Books, 1963.

HOSMER, JAMES K., ed. *Winthrop's Journal: "History of New England."* 2 vols. New York: Charles Scribner's Sons, 1908.

JAMES, SYDNEY V. *Colonial Rhode Island: A History.* New York: Charles Scribner's Sons, 1975.

JENNINGS, FRANCIS. *The Invasion of America: Indians, Colonialism, and the Cant of Conquest.* Chapel Hill: University of North Carolina Press, 1975.

JONES, MARY J. A. *Congregational Commonwealth: Connecticut, 1638–1662.* Middletown, Conn.: Wesleyan University Press, 1968.

LABAREE, BENJAMIN W. *Colonial Massachusetts: A History.* Millwood, N.Y.: KTO Press, 1979.

LANGDON, GEORGE D., JR. *Pilgrim Colony: A History of New Plymouth.* New Haven, Conn.: Yale University Press, 1966.

LEACH, DOUGLAS E. *Flintlock and Tomahawk: New England in King Philip's War.* New York: W. W. Norton and Company, 1958.

McINTYRE, RUTH A. *Debts Hopeful and Desperate: Financing the Plymouth Colony.* Plymouth, Mass: Plimoth Plantation, 1963.

MILLER, PERRY. *Errand into the Wilderness.* Cambridge, Mass. Harvard University Press, 1956.

MORGAN, EDMUND S. *The Puritan Dilemma: The Story of John Winthrop.* Boston: Little, Brown and Company, 1958.

MORISON, SAMUEL E. *Builders of the Bay Colony.* Boston: Houghton Mifflin Company, 1930.

MORTON, THOMAS. *New English Canaan.* New York: Burt Franklin, 1967. Originally published in 1637.

NOTESTEIN, WALLACE. *The English People on the Eve of Colonization, 1603–1630.* New York: Harper & Row, 1954.

OSGOOD, HERBERT L. *The American Colonies in the Seventeenth Century.* Vol. 1. Gloucester, Mass.: Peter Smith, 1957. Originally published in 1904.

POMFRET, JOHN E. *Founding of the American Colonies, 1583–1660.* New York: Harper & Row, 1970.

SIMPSON, ALAN. "How Democratic Was Roger Williams?" *William and Mary Quarterly,* 3d ser., 13 (1956): 53–67.

SMITH, BRADFORD. *Bradford of Plymouth.* Philadelphia: J. B. Lippincott Company, 1951.

VAN DEVENTER, DAVID E. *The Emergence of Provincial New Hampshire, 1623–1741.* Baltimore: Johns Hopkins University Press, 1976.

VAUGHAN, ALDEN T. *New England Frontier: Puritans and Indians, 1620–1675.* 2d ed. New York: W. W. Norton Company, 1979.

WALL, ROBERT E., JR. *Massachusetts Bay: The Crucial Decade, 1640–1650.* New Haven, Conn.: Yale University Press, 1972.

WILLIAMS, ROGER. *The Complete Writings of Roger Williams.* 7 vols. New York: Russell & Russell, 1963.

WILLISON, GEORGE F. *Saints and Strangers.* New York: Reynal & Hitchcock, 1945.

WINSLOW, OLA E. *John Eliot: Apostle to the Indians.* Boston: Houghton Mifflin Company, 1968.

ZIFF, LARZER. *The Career of John Cotton: Puritanism and the American Experience.* Princeton, N.J.: Princeton University Press, 1962.

CHAPTER 4

ASHE, SAMUEL A. *History of North Carolina.* Vol. 1. Spartanburg, S.C.: The Reprint Company, 1971. Originally published in 1908.

BRONNER, EDWIN B. *William Penn's "Holy Experiment": The Founding of Pennsylvania, 1681–1701.* New York: Temple University Publications, 1962.

CHILDS, ST. JULIEN R. *Malaria and Colonization in the Carolina Low Country, 1526–1696.* Baltimore: The Johns Hopkins Press, 1940.

CONDON, THOMAS J. *New York Beginnings: The Commercial Origins of New Netherland.* New York: New York University Press, 1968.

ENDY, MELVIN B. *William Penn and Early Quakerism.* Princeton, N.J.: Princeton University Press, 1973.

ETTINGER, AMOS A. *James Edward Oglethorpe: Imperial Idealist.* Hamden, Conn.: Archon books 1968. Originally published in 1936.

JACKSON, HARVEY H., AND SPALDING, PHINZEY. *Forty Years of Diversity: Essays on Colonial Georgia.* Athens: University of Georgia Press, 1984.

JOHNSON, AMANDUS. *The Swedish Settlements on the Delaware, 1638–1664.* 2 vols. Baltimore: Genealogical Publishing Company, 1969. Originally published in 1911.

KEITH, CHARLES P. *Chronicles of Pennsylvania from the English Revolution to the Peace of Aix-la-Chapelle, 1688–1748.* Vol. 1. Philadelphia: Patterson & White Company, 1917.

KESSLER, HENRY H., AND RACHLIS, EUGENE. *Peter Stuyvesant and His New York.* New York: Random House, 1959.

LEFLER, HUGH T., AND POWELL, WILLIAM S. *Colonial North Carolina.* New York: Charles Scribner's Sons, 1973.

MCCORMICK, RICHARD P. *New Jersey from Colony to State, 1609–1789.* Newark, N.J.: New Jersey Historical Society, 1981.

MCCRADY, EDWARD. *The History of South Carolina under the Proprietary Government, 1670–1719.* New York: The Macmillan Company, 1897.

MOWRER, LILIAN T. *The Indomitable John Scott: Citizen of Long Island, 1632–1704.* New York: Farrar, Straus and Cudahy, 1960.

NISSENSON, S. G. *The Patroon's Domain.* New York: Octagon Books, 1973. Originally published in 1937.

O'CALLAGHAN, E. B. *History of New Netherland.* 2 vols. New York: The Reprint Company, 1966. Originally published in 1845–1848.

PEARE, CATHERINE O. *William Penn: A Biography.* Ann Arbor: University of Michigan Press, 1956.

POMFRET, JOHN E. *Colonial New Jersey.* New York: Charles Scribner's Sons, 1973.

———. *The Province of East New Jersey, 1609–1702.* New York: Octagon Books, 1981.

———. *The Province of West New Jersey, 1609–1702.* Octagon Books, New York: 1976.

RAESLY, ELLIS L. *Portrait of New Netherland.* Port Washington, New York: Ira J. Friedman, 1965. Originally published in 1945.

REESE, TREVOR R., ed. *The Clamorous Malcontents: Criticisms and Defenses of the Colony of Georgia, 1741–1743.* Savannah, Ga.: The Beehive Press, 1973.

———. *The Most Delightful Country of the Universe: Promotional Literature of Georgia, 1717–1734.* Savannah, Ga.: The Beehive Press, 1972.

RINK, OLIVER A. *Holland on the Hudson: An Economic and Social History of Dutch New York.* Ithaca, N.Y.: Cornell University Press, 1986.

SIRMANS, M. EUGENE. *Colonial South Carolina: A Political History, 1663–1763.* Chapel Hill: University of North Carolina Press, 1966.

VAN DER ZEE, HENRI, AND VAN DER ZEE, BARBARA. *A Sweet and Alien Land: The Story of Dutch New York.* New York: The Viking Press, 1978.

VER STEEG, CLARENCE L. *Origins of a Southern Mosaic: Studies of Early Carolina and Georgia.* Athens: University of Georgia Press, 1975.

WARD, CHRISTOPHER. *The Dutch and Swedes on the Delaware, 1638–1664.* Philadelphia: University of Pennsylvania Press, 1930.

WEIR, ROBERT M. *Colonial South Carolina.* Millwood, N.Y.: KTO Press, 1983.

WESLAGER, C. A. *Dutch Explorers, Traders and Settlers in the Delaware Valley, 1609–1664.* Philadelphia: University of Pennsylvania Press, 1961.

WILDES, HARRY E. *William Penn.* New York: Macmillan Publishing Company, 1974.

CHAPTER 5

AKAGI, ROY H. *The Town Proprietors of the New England Colonies.* Philadelphia: University of Pennsylvania Press, 1924.

BALL, D. E., AND WALTON, G. M. "Agricultural Productivity Change in Eighteenth-Century Pennsylvania." *Journal of Economic History,* 36 (1976): 102–117.

BENSON, ADOLPH B., ed. *Peter Kalm's Travels in North America: The English Version of 1770*. 2 vols. New York: Wilson-Erickson Inc., 1937.

BIDWELL, PERCY W. *A History of Northern Agriculture, 1620 to 1840*. Washington, D.C.: Carnegie Institution of Washington, 1925.

BLISS, WILLARD F. "The Rise of Tenancy in Virginia." *Virginia Magazine of History and Biography*, 58 (1950): 427–441.

BOND, BEVERLEY W., JR. *The Quit-Rent System in the American Colonies*. New Haven, Conn.: Yale University Press, 1919.

BREEN, T. H. *Tobacco Culture: The Mentality of the Great Tidewater Planters on the Eve of the Revolution*. Princeton, N.J.: Princeton University Press, 1988.

BRIDENBAUGH, CARL. *Fat Mutton and Liberty of Conscience: Society in Rhode Island, 1636–1690*. Providence, R.I.: Brown University Press, 1974.

BRUCE, PHILIP A. *Economic History of Virginia in the Seventeenth Century*. Vol. 2. New York: Peter Smith, 1935. Originally published in 1895.

CARMAN, HARRY J., ed. *American Husbandry*. Port Washington, N.Y.: Kennikat Press, 1964.

CARRIER, LYMAN. *The Beginnings of Agriculture in America*. New York: McGraw Hill Book Company, 1968. Originally published in 1923.

COON, DAVID L. "Eliza Pinckney and the Reintroduction of Indigo Culture in South Carolina." *Journal of Southern History*, 42 (1976), 61–76.

CRAVEN, AVERY O. *Soil Exhaustion as a Factor in the Agricultural History of Virginia and Maryland, 1606–1860*. Urbana: University of Illinois Press, 1926.

CRONON, WILLIAM. *Changes in the Land: Indians, Colonists, and the Ecology of New England*. New York: Hill and Wang, 1983.

EGLESTON, MELVILLE. *The Land System in the New England Colonies*. Baltimore: Johns Hopkins Press, 1886.

ELIOT, JARED. *Essays upon Field Husbandry in New England, and Other Papers, 1748–1762*, ed. Harry J. Carman. New York: Columbia University Press, 1934.

FORD, AMELIA C. *Colonial Precedents of Our National Land System as It Existed in 1800. Bulletin of the University of Wisconsin*, no. 352. Madison: 1910.

GRAY, LEWIS C. *History of Agriculture in the Southern United States to 1860*. Vol. 1. Washington, D.C.: Carnegie Institution of Washington, 1933.

GREENE, JACK P., ed. *The Diary of Colonel Landon Carter of Sabine Hall, 1752–1778*. 2 vols. Charlottesville: University Press of Virginia, 1965.

HARRIS, MARSHALL. *Origin of the Land Tenure System in the United States*. Ames: Iowa State College Press, 1953.

JACKSON, DONALD, AND TWOHIG, DOROTHY, eds. *The Diaries of George Washington*. Vols. 1–3. Charlottesville: University Press of Virginia, 1976–1978.

JONES, E. L. "Creative Disruptions in American Agriculture, 1620–1820." *Agricultural History*, 48 (1974): 510–528.

LIVERMORE, SHAW. *Early American Land Companies: Their Influence on Corporate Development*. New York: Oxford University Press, 1939.

KIM, SUNG BOK. *Landlord and Tenant in Colonial New York Manorial Society, 1664–1775*. Chapel Hill: University of North Carolina Press, 1978.

KLINGAMAN, DAVID. "The Significance of Grain in the Development of the Tobacco Colonies." *Journal of Economic History*, 29 (1969): 268–278.

LAING, WESLEY N. "Cattle in Early Virginia." Ph.D. diss., University of Virginia, 1952.

LEMON, JAMES T. *The Best Poor Man's Country: A Geographical Study of Early Southeastern Pennsylvania*. New York: W. W. Norton and Company, 1972.

MARK, IRVING. *Agrarian Conflicts in Colonial New York, 1711–1775*. New York: Columbia University Press, 1940.

MERRENS, HARRY R. *Colonial North Carolina in the Eighteenth Century: A Study in Historical Geography*. Chapel Hill: University of North Carolina Press, 1964.

POWELL, SUMNER C. *Puritan Village: The Formation of a New England Town*. Garden City, N.Y.: Anchor Books, Doubleday & Company, 1965.

PRUITT, BETTYE H. "Self-sufficiency and the Agricultural Economy of Eighteenth-Century Massachusetts." *William and Mary Quarterly*, 3d ser., 41 (1984): 333–364.

RUTMAN, DARRETT B. *Husbandmen of Plymouth: Farms and Villages in the Old Colony, 1620–1692*. Boston: Beacon Press, 1967.

SIMLER, LUCY. "Tenancy in Colonial Pennsylvania: The Case of Chester County." *William and Mary Quarterly*, 3d ser., 43 (1986): 542–569.

SKAGGS, JIMMY M. *Prime Cut: Livestock Raising and Meatpacking in the United States, 1607–1983.* College Station, Texas: Texas Agricultural and Mechanical University Press, 1986.

STIVERSON, GREGORY A. *Poverty in a Land of Plenty: Tenancy in Eighteenth-Century Maryland.* Baltimore: Johns Hopkins University Press, 1977.

THOMPSON, JAMES W. *History of Livestock Raising in the United States, 1607–1860.* Wilmington, Del.: Scholarly Resources, Inc. 1973. Originally published in 1942.

WALCOTT, ROBERT R. "Husbandry in Colonial New England." *New England Quarterly*, 9 (1936): 218–252.

WOODWARD, CARL R. *Ploughs and Politics: Charles Read of New Jersey and His Notes on Agriculture, 1715–1774.* New Brunswick, N.J.: Rutgers University Press, 1941.

CHAPTER 6

ALBION, ROBERT G. *Forests and Sea Power: The Timber Problem of the Royal Navy, 1682–1862.* Cambridge, Mass.: Harvard University Press, 1926.

BAILYN, BERNARD, AND BAILYN, LOTTE. *Massachusetts Shipping, 1697–1714.* Cambridge, Mass.: Harvard University Press, 1959.

BINING, ARTHUR C. *British Regulation of the Colonial Iron Industry.* Philadelphia: University of Pennsylvania Press, 1933.

———. *Pennsylvania Iron Manufacturing in the Eighteenth Century.* Harrisburg: Pennsylvania Historical Commission, 1938.

BLACK, ROBERT C. *The Younger John Winthrop.* New York: Columbia University Press, 1966.

BOLLES, ALBERT S. *Industrial History of the United States.* New York: Augustus M. Kelley, 1966. Originally published in 1878.

BRIDENBAUGH, CARL. *The Colonial Craftsman.* New York: New York University Press, 1950.

BRUCE, KATHLEEN. *Virginia Iron Manufacture in the Slave Era.* New York: The Century Company, 1931.

BRUCE, PHILIP A. *Economic History of Virginia in the Seventeenth Century.* Vol. 2. New York: Peter Smith, 1935. Originally published in 1895.

CLARK, VICTOR S. *History of Manufactures in the United States.* Vol. 1. Washington, D.C.: Carnegie Institution of Washington, 1933.

GOLDENBERG, JOSEPH A. *Shipbuilding in Colonial America.* Charlottesville: University Press of Virginia, 1976.

HARTLEY, E. N. *Ironworks of the Saugus: The Lynn and Braintree Ventures of the Company of Undertakers.* Norman: University of Oklahoma Press, 1957.

HINDLE, BROOKE, ed. *America's Wooden Age: Aspects of Its Early Technology.* Tarrytown, N.Y.: Sleepy Hollow Restorations, 1975.

HODGES, GRAHAM R. *New York City Cartmen, 1667–1850.* New York: New York University Press, 1986.

INNES, STEPHEN, ed. *Work and Labor in Early America.* Chapel Hill: University of North Carolina Press, 1988.

INNIS, HAROLD A. *The Cod Fisheries: The History of an International Economy.* Revised ed. Toronto: University of Toronto Press, 1954.

LAWSON, MURRAY. *Fur: A Study in English Mercantilism, 1700–1775.* Toronto: University of Toronto Press, 1943.

MALONE, JOSEPH J. *Pine Trees and Politics: The Naval Stores and Forest Policy in Colonial New England, 1691–1775.* Seattle: University of Washington Press, 1964.

McCUSKER, JOHN J., AND MENARD, RUSSELL R. *The Economy of British America, 1607–1789.* Chapel Hill: University of North Carolina Press, 1985.

McKEE, SAMUEL, JR. *Labor in Colonial New York, 1664–1776.* Port Washington, N.Y.: Ira J. Friedman, 1963. Originally published in 1935.

MOLONEY, FRANCIS X. *The Fur Trade in New England, 1620–1676.* Cambridge, Mass.: Harvard University Press, 1931.

MORRIS, RICHARD B. *Government and Labor in Early America.* New York: Columbia University Press, 1946.

NORTON, THOMAS E. *The Fur Trade in Colonial New York.* Madison: University of Wisconsin Press, 1974.

PEARSE, JOHN B. *A Concise History of the Iron Manufacture of the America Colonies.* New York: Burt Franklin, 1970. Originally published in 1876.

PHILLIPS, PAUL C. *The Fur Trade.* Vol. 1. Norman: University of Oklahoma Press, 1961.

QUIMBY, IAN M. G. *The Craftsman in Early America.* New York: W. W. Norton and Company, 1984.

ROBBINS, MICHAEL W. *The Principio Company: Iron-making in Colonial Maryland, 1720–1781.* New York: Garland Publishing Company, 1986.

ROBERTS, WILLIAM I. "American Potash Manufacturing before the American Revolution." *Proceedings of the American Philosophical Society,* 116 (1972): 383–395.

Seafaring in Colonial Massachusetts: A Conference. Boston: The Colonial Society of Massachusetts, 1980.

SEYBOLT, ROBERT F. *Apprenticeship and Apprenticeship Education in Colonial New England and New York.* New York: Arno Press, 1969. Originally published in 1917.

TRYON, ROLLA M. *Household Manufacturers in the United States, 1640–1860: A Study in Industrial History.* Chicago: University of Chicago Press, 1917.

TUNIS, EDWIN. *Colonial Craftsmen and the Beginning of American Industry.* Cleveland: World Publishing Company, 1965.

WEEDEN, WILLIAM B. *Economic and Social History of New England, 1620–1789.* 2 vols. Boston: Houghton Mifflin and Company, 1890.

WEISS, HARRY B., AND SIM, ROBERT J. *The Early Grist and Flouring Mills of New Jersey.* Trenton: N. J. Agricultural Society, 1956.

CHAPTER 7

ANDREWS, CHARLES M. *The Colonial Period of American History. Vol 4: England's Commercial and Colonial Policy.* New Haven, Conn.: Yale University Press, 1938.

BAILYN, BERNARD. *The New England Merchants in the Seventeenth Century.* New York: Harper & Row, 1955.

BARROW, THOMAS C. *Trade and Empire: The British Customs Service in Colonial America, 1660–1775.* Cambridge, Mass.: Harvard University Press, 1967.

BEER, GEORGE L. *The Commercial Policy of England toward the American Colonies.* New York: Peter Smith, 1948. Originally published in 1893.

———. *The Old Colonial System, 1660–1754.* 2 vols. Gloucester, Mass.: Peter Smith, 1958. Originally published in 1913.

BROCK, LESLIE V. *The Currency of the American Colonies, 1700–1764: A Study in Colonial Finance and Imperial Relations.* New York: Arno Press, 1975.

BRUCHEY, STUART, ed. *The Colonial Merchant: Sources and Readings.* New York: Harcourt, Brace & World, 1966.

CLEMENS, PAUL G. E. *The Atlantic Economy and Colonial Maryland's Eastern Shore.* Ithaca, N.Y.: Cornell University Press, 1980.

COLEMAN, DONALD C., ed. *Revisions in Mercantilism.* London: Methuen and Company, 1969.

DAVIS, RALPH. *The Rise of the Atlantic Economies.* Ithaca, N.Y.: Cornell University Press, 1973.

DICKERSON, OLIVER M. *The Navigation Acts and the American Revolution.* 2d ed. Philadelphia: University of Pennsylvania Press, 1951.

ERNST, JOSEPH. *Money and Politics in America, 1755–1775.* Chapel Hill: University of North Carolina Press, 1973.

HALL, MICHAEL G. *Edward Randolph and the American Colonies, 1676–1703.* Chapel Hill: University of North Carolina Press, 1960.

HARPER, LAWRENCE A. *The English Navigation Laws: A Seventeenth-Century Experiment in Social Engineering.* New York: Octagon Books, 1964. Originally published in 1939.

HEMPHILL, JOHN M. *Virginia and the English Commercial System, 1689–1733.* New York: Garland Publishing Company, 1985.

JENSEN, ARTHUR L. *The Maritime Commerce of Colonial Philadelphia.* Madison: The State Historical Society of Wisconsin, 1963.

JOHNSON, EMORY R., VAN METRE, T. W., HUEBNER, G. G., AND HANCHETT, D. S. *History of Domestic and Foreign Commerce of the United States.* Vol. 1. Washington, D.C.: Carnegie Institution of Washington, 1915.

JOHNSON, RICHARD R. *Adjustment to Empire: The New England Colonies, 1675–1715.* New Brunswick, N.J.: Rutgers University Press, 1981.

MIDDLETON, ARTHUR P. *Tobacco Coast: A Maritime History of Chesapeake Bay in the Colonial Era.* Newport News, Va.: The Mariners' Museum, 1953.

NETTELS, CURTIS. *The Money Supply of the American Colonies before 1720. University of Wisconsin Studies in the Social Sciences and History,* no. 20. Madison: 1934.

PARES, RICHARD. *War and Trade in the West Indies, 1739–1763.* London: Frank Cass and Company, 1963. Originally published in 1936.

PERKINS, EDWIN J. *The Economy of Colonial America,* 2d ed. New York: Columbia University Press, 1988.

PRICE, JACOB M. *Capital and Credit in British Trade: The View from the Chesapeake, 1700–1776.* Cambridge, Mass.: Harvard University Press, 1980.

SHEPHERD, JAMES F., AND WALTON, GARY M. *Shipping, Maritime Trade and the Economic Development of Colonial North America.* London: Cambridge University Press, 1972.

STEELE, IAN K. *The English Atlantic, 1675–1740: An Exploration of Communication and Community.* New York: Oxford University Press, 1986.

THOMAS, ROBERT P. "A Quantitative Approach to the Study of the Effects of British Imperial Policy upon Colonial Welfare: Some Preliminary Findings." *Journal of Economic History,* 25 (1965): 616–638.

WALTON, GARY M., AND SHEPHERD, JAMES F. *The Economic Rise of Early America.* London: Cambridge University Press, 1979.

WEEDEN, WILLIAM B. *Economic and Social History of New England, 1620–1789.* 2 vols. Boston: Houghton Mifflin and Company, 1890.

CHAPTER 8

"American Council of Learned Societies Report of Committee on Linguistic and National Stocks in the Population of the United States." In *Annual Report of the American Historical Association for the Year 1931.* Appendices by Howard F. Barker and Marcus L. Hansen. 1: 126–441.

BAIRD, CHARLES W. *History of the Huguenot Emigration to America.* Vol. 2. Baltimore: Genealogical Publishing Company, 1985. Originally published in 1885.

BITTINGER, LUCY F. *The Germans in Colonial Times.* New York: Wadsworth Publishing Company, 1968. Originally published in 1901.

BROCK, WILLIAM R. *Scotus Americanus: A Survey of the Sources for Links between Scotland and America in the Eighteenth Century.* Edinburgh: Edinburgh University Press, 1982.

BROWNING, CHARLES H. *Welsh Settlement of Pennsylvania.* Philadelphia: W. J. Campbell, 1912.

BUTLER, JON. *The Huguenots in America: A Refugee People in a New World Society.* Cambridge, Mass.: Harvard University Press, 1983.

CUNZ, DIETER. *The Maryland Germans.* Princeton, N.J.: Princeton University Press, 1948.

DICKSON, R. J. *Ulster Emigration to Colonial America, 1718–1775.* London: Routledge & Kegan Paul, 1966.

DUNAWAY, WAYLAND F. *The Scotch-Irish of Colonial Pennsylvania.* Chapel Hill: University of North Carolina Press, 1944.

FAUST, ALBERT B. "Swiss Emigration to the American Colonies in the Eighteenth Century." *American Historical Review,* 22 (1917): 21–44.

GIUSEPPI, M. S. *Naturalizations of Foreign Protestants in the American and West Indian Colonies. The Publications of the Huguenot Society of London.* Vol. 15. Manchester, England: 1921.

GRAHAM, IAN C. C. *Colonists from Scotland: Emigration to North America, 1707–1783.* Ithaca, N.Y.: Cornell University Press, 1956.

HAWS, CHARLES H. *Scots in the Old Dominion, 1685–1800.* Edinburgh: J. Dunlop, 1980.

HIRSCH, ARTHUR H. *The Huguenots of Colonial South Carolina.* Durham, N.C.: Duke University Press, 1928.

HUHNER, LEON. *Jews in America in Colonial and Revolutionary Times.* New York: Gertz Bros., 1959.

KETTNER, JAMES H. *The Development of American Citizenship, 1608–1870.* Chapel Hill: University of North Carolina Press, 1978.

LEYBURN, JAMES G. *The Scotch-Irish: A Social History.* Chapel Hill: University of North Carolina Press, 1962.

MACLEAN, J. P. *A Historical Account of the Settlements of Scotch Highlanders in America prior to the Peace of 1783.* Baltimore: Genealogical Publishing Company, 1978. Originally published in 1900.

MARCUS, JACOB R. *Early American Jewry: The Jews of New York, New England and Canada, 1649–1794.* Vol. 1. Philadelphia: Jewish Publication Society of America, 1951.

MARSHALL, WILLIAM F. *Ulster Sails West: The Story of the Great Emigration from Ulster to North America in the Eighteenth Century.* Baltimore: Genealogical Publishing Company, 1979.

McDONALD, FORREST, AND McDONALD, ELLEN S. "The Ethnic Origins of the American People, 1790." *William and Mary Quarterly*, 3d ser., 37 (1980): 179–199.

MEYER, DUANE. *The Highland Scots of North Carolina.* Raleigh: State Department of Archives and History, 1963.

MYERS, ALBERT C. *Immigration of the Irish Quakers into Pennsylvania, 1682–1750.* Baltimore: Genealogical Publishing Company, 1969. Originally published in 1902.

ROEBER, A. G. "In German Ways: Problems and Potentials of Eighteenth-Century German Social and Emigration History." *William and Mary Quarterly*, 3d ser., 44 (1987): 750–774.

START, CORA. "Naturalization in the English Colonies of America." *Annual Report of the American Historical Association for the Year 1893:* 317–328.

WEAVER, GLENN. *The Italian Preserve in Colonial Virginia.* New York: Center for Migration Studies, 1988.

WAYLAND, JOHN W. *The German Element of the Shenandoah Valley of Virginia.* Baltimore: Genealogical Publishing Company, 1978. Originally published in 1907.

CHAPTER 9

BAILYN, BERNARD. *Voyages to the West: A Passage in the Peopling of America on the Eve of the Revolution.* New York: Alfred A. Knopf, 1986.

BALLAGH, JAMES C. *White Servitude in the Colony of Virginia.* Baltimore: *Johns Hopkins University Studies in Historical and Political Science.* Vol. 13, numbers 6–7. 1895.

BILLINGS, WARREN M. "The Cases of Fernando and Elizabeth Key: Status of Blacks in Seventeenth-Century Virginia." *William and Mary Quarterly*, 3d ser., 30 (1973): 467–474.

BOSKIN, JOSEPH. *Into Slavery: Racial Decisions in the Virginia Colony.* Philadelphia: J. B. Lippincott Company, 1976.

CAMPBELL, MILDRED. "Social Origins of Some Early Americans." In *Seventeenth-Century America*, ed. James M. Smith. Chapel Hill: University of North Carolina Press, 1959.

COUGHTY, JAY. *The Notorious Triangle: Rhode Island and the African Slave Trade, 1700–1807.* Philadelphia: Temple University Press, 1981.

CURTIN, PHILIP D. *The Atlantic Slave Trade: A Census.* Madison: University of Wisconsin Press, 1969.

DAVIES, KENNETH G. *The Royal African Company.* New York: Atheneum, 1957.

DUNN, RICHARD S. "Servants and Slaves: The Recruitment and Employment of Labor." In *Colonial British America*, ed. Jack P. Greene and J. R. Pole. Baltimore: Johns Hopkins University Press, 1984.

EKIRCH, A. ROGER. *Bound for America: The Transportation of British Convicts to the Colonies, 1718–1775.* New York: Oxford University Press, 1987.

GALENSON, DAVID W. "The Social Origins of Some Early Americans: A Rejoinder." *William and Mary Quarterly.* 3d ser., 36 (1979): 262–286.

———. *Traders, Planters and Slaves: Market Behaviour in Early English America.* Cambridge: Cambridge University Press, 1986.

———. *White Servitude in Colonial America: An Economic Analysis.* Cambridge: Cambridge University Press, 1981.

GEMERY, HENRY A., AND HOGENDORN, JAN S., eds. *The Uncommon Market: Essays in the Economic History of the Atlantic Slave Trade.* New York: Academic Press, 1979.

HAMM, TOMMY T. "The American Slave Trade with Africa, 1620–1807." Ph.D. diss., Indiana University, 1975.

HERRICK, CHEESEMAN A. *White Servitude in Pennsylvania: Indentured and Redemption Labor in Colony and Commonwealth.* Freeport, N.Y.: Books for Libraries Press, 1970. Originally published in 1926.

HORN, JAMES. "Servant Emigration to the Chesapeake in the Seventeenth Century." In *The Chesapeake in the Seventeenth Century,* ed. Thad W. Tate and David L. Ammerman. Chapel Hill: University of North Carolina Press, 1979.

JERNEGAN, MARCUS W. *Laboring and Dependent Classes in Colonial America, 1607–1783.* New York: Frederick Ungar Publishing Company, 1965. Originally published in 1931.

JORDAN, WINTHROP D. *White over Black: American Attitudes toward the Negro, 1550–1812.* Chapel Hill: University of North Carolina Press, 1968.

KILSON, MARTIN L., AND ROTBERG, ROBERT I., eds. *The African Diaspora: Interpretative Essays.* Cambridge, Mass.: Harvard University Press, 1976.

KLEIN, HERBERT S. *The Middle Passage: Comparative Studies in the Atlantic Slave Trade.* Princeton, N.J.: Princeton University Press, 1978.

LAUBER, ALMON W. *Indian Slavery in Colonial Times within the Present Limits of the United States.* New York: AMS Press, 1969. Originally published in 1913.

LITTLEFIELD, DANIEL C. *Rice and Slaves: Ethnicity and the Slave Trade in Colonial South Carolina.* Baton Rouge, La.: Louisiana State University Press, 1981.

LYDON, JAMES G. "New York and the Slave Trade, 1700–1714." *William and Mary Quarterly,* 3d ser., 35 (1978): 375–394.

MENARD, RUSSELL R. "The Africanization of the Lowcountry Labor Force, 1670–1730." In *Race and Family in the Colonial South,* ed. Winthrop D. Jordan and Sheila L. Skemp. Jackson: University Press of Mississippi, 1987.

———. "From Servants to Slaves: The Transformation of the Chesapeake Labor System." *Southern Studies,* 16 (1977): 356–390.

MORGAN, EDMUND S. *American Slavery/American Freedom: The Ordeal of Colonial Virginia.* New York: W. W. Norton and Company, 1975.

MORGAN, KENNETH. "The Organization of the Convict Trade to Maryland: Stevenson, Randolph and Cheston, 1768–1775." *William and Mary Quarterly,* 42 (1985): 201–227.

OSTRANDER, GILMAN M. "The Making of the Triangular Trade Myth." *William and Mary Quarterly,* 3d ser., 30 (1973): 635–644.

POPE-HENNESSY, JAMES. *Sins of the Fathers: A Study of the Atlantic Slave Traders, 1441–1807.* New York: Alfred A. Knopf, 1968.

RAWLEY, JAMES A. *The Transatlantic Slave Trade: A History.* New York: W. W. Norton and Company, 1981.

SALINGER, SHARON V. *"To Serve Well and Faithfully": Labor and Indentured Servants in Pennsylvania, 1682–1800.* Cambridge: Cambridge University Press, 1987.

SCHMIDT, FREDERICK H. "British Convict Servant Labor in Colonial Virginia." Ph.D. diss., College of William and Mary, 1976.

SMITH, ABBOT E. *Colonists in Bondage: White Servitude and Convict Labor in America, 1607–1776.* Gloucester, Mass.: Peter Smith, 1965.

SMITH, WARREN B. *White Servitude in Colonial South Carolina.* Columbia: University of South Carolina Press, 1961.

VAN DER ZEE, JOHN. *Bound Over: Indentured Servitude and American Conscience.* New York: Simon & Schuster, 1985.

WESTBURY, SUSAN A. "Colonial Virginia and the Atlantic Slave Trade." Ph.D. diss. University of Illinois, 1981.

CHAPTER 10

APTHEKER, HERBERT. *American Negro Slave Revolts.* New York: International Publishing Company, 1963.

BINGHAM, ALFRED M. "Squatter Settlements of Freed Slaves in New England." *Connecticut Historical Society Bulletin,* 41 (1976): 65–80.

BREEN, T. H., AND INNES, STEPHEN. *"Myne Owne Ground": Race and Freedom on Virginia's Eastern Shore, 1640–1676.* New York: Oxford University Press, 1980.

BROOKES, G. S. *Friend Anthony Benezet.* Philadelphia: University of Pennsylvania Press, 1937.

DAVIS, DAVID B. *The Problem of Slavery in Western Culture.* Ithaca, N.Y.: Cornell University Press, 1966.

DAVIS, THOMAS J. *A Rumor of Revolt: The "Great Negro Plot" in Colonial New York.* New York: The Free Press, 1985.

DRAKE, THOMAS E. *Quakers and Slavery in America.* Gloucester, Mass.: Peter Smith, 1965.

GREENE, LORENZO J. *The Negro in Colonial New England.* New York: Atheneum, 1968. Originally published in 1942.

HEUMAN, GAD, ed. *Out of the House of Bondage: Runaways, Resistance and Marronage in Africa and the New World.* London: Frank Cass and Company, 1986.

HIGGINBOTHAM, A. LEON, JR. *In the Matter of Color: Race and the American Legal Process. The Colonial Period.* New York: Oxford University Press, 1978.

HORSMANDEN, DANIEL. *The New York Conspiracy,* ed. Thomas J. Davis. Boston: Beacon Press, 1971. Originally published in 1741 and 1810.

JORDAN, WINTHROP D. *White over Black: American Attitudes toward the Negro, 1550–1812.* Chapel Hill: University of North Carolina Press, 1968.

KLINGBERG, FRANK J., ed. *The Carolina Chronicle of Dr. Francis Le Jau, 1706–1717. University of California Publications in History.* Vol. 53. Berkeley: 1956.

KULIKOFF, ALLAN. *Tobacco and Slaves: The Development of Southern Cultures in the Chesapeake, 1680–1800.* Chapel Hill: University of North Carolina Press, 1986.

MCMANUS, EDGAR J. *Black Bondage in the North.* Syracuse, N.Y.: Syracuse University Press, 1973.

———. *A History of Negro Slavery in New York.* Syracuse, N.Y.: Syracuse University Press, 1966.

MORGAN, PHILIP D. "Colonial South Carolina Runaways: Their Significance for Slave Culture." In Heuman, Gad. *Out of the House of Bondage* (see prior listing).

MULLIN, GERALD W. *Flight and Rebellion: Slave Resistance in Eighteenth-Century Virginia.* New York: Oxford University Press, 1972.

NASH, GARY B. "Slaves and Slaveowners in Colonial Philadelphia." *William and Mary Quarterly,* 3d ser., 30 (1973): 223–256.

PIERSON, WILLIAM D. *Black Yankees: The Development of an Afro-American Subculture in Eighteenth-Century New England.* Amherst: University of Massachusetts Press, 1988.

PORTER, KENNETH W. "Negroes on the Southern Frontier, 1670–1763." *Journal of Negro History,* 33 (1948): 52–78.

RUSSELL, JOHN H. *The Free Negro in Virginia. Johns Hopkins University Studies in Historical and Political Science.* Vol. 31, number 3. Baltimore, 1913.

SCHERER, LESTER B. *Slavery and the Churches in Early America, 1619–1819.* Grand Rapids, Mich.: William B. Eerdmans Publishing Company, 1975.

SCHWARZ, PHILIP J. *Twice Condemned: Slaves and the Criminal Laws of Virginia, 1705–1865.* Baton Rouge, La.: Louisiana State University Press, 1988.

SCOTT, KENNETH. "The Slave Insurrection in New York in 1712." *New York Historical Society Quarterly,* 45 (1961): 43–74.

SMITH, JULIA F. *Slavery and Rice Culture in Low Country Georgia, 1750–1860.* Knoxville: University of Tennessee Press, 1985.

SODERLUND, JEAN R. *Quakers and Slavery: A Divided Spirit.* Princeton, N.J.: Princeton University Press, 1985.

WATSON, LARRY D. "The Quest for Order: Enforcing Slave Codes in Revolutionary South Carolina, 1760–1800." Ph.D. diss., University of South Carolina, 1980.

WINDLEY, LATHAM A. "A Profile of Runaway Slaves in Virginia and South Carolina from 1730 through 1787." Ph.D. diss., University of Iowa, 1974.

WOOD, BETTY. *Slavery in Colonial Georgia, 1730–1775.* Athens: University of Georgia Press, 1984.

————. " 'Until He Shall Be Dead, Dead, Dead': The Judicial Treatment of Slaves in Eighteenth-Century Georgia." *Georgia Historical Quarterly,* 71 (1987): 377–398.

WOOD, PETER H. *Black Majority: Negroes in Colonial South Carolina.* New York: Alfred A. Knopf, 1974.

WRIGHT, JAMES M. *The Free Negro in Maryland.* New York: Octagon Books, 1971. Originally published in 1921.

CHAPTER 11

BEALES, ROSS W., JR. "In Search of the Historical Child: Miniature Adulthood and Youth in Colonial New England." *American Quarterly,* 27 (1975): 379–398.

CALHOUN, ARTHUR W. *A Social History of the American Family: The Colonial Period.* New York: Barnes & Noble, 1960. Originally published in 1917.

CALVERT, KARIN. "Children in American Family Portraiture, 1670 to 1810." *William and Mary Quarterly,* 3d ser., 39 (1982): 87–113.

CARR, LOIS G., AND WALSH, LORENA S. "The Planter's Wife: The Experience of White Women in Seventeenth-Century Maryland." *William and Mary Quarterly,* 3d ser., 34 (1977): 542–571.

COTT, NANCY F. "Divorce and the Changing Status of Women in Eighteenth-Century Massachusetts." *William and Mary Quarterly,* 3d ser., 33 (1976): 586–614.

DEMOS, JOHN. "Families in Colonial Bristol, Rhode Island: An Exercise in Historical Demography." *William and Mary Quarterly,* 3d ser., 25 (1968): 40–57.

————. *A Little Commonwealth: Family Life in Plymouth Colony.* New York: Oxford University Press, 1970.

DEXTER, ELISABETH A. *Colonial Women of Affairs: A Study of Women in Business and the Professions in America before 1776.* Boston: Houghton Mifflin Company, 1924.

DRINKER, SOPHIE. "Women Attorneys in Colonial Times." *Maryland Historical Magazine,* 56 (1961): 335–351.

EARLE, ALICE M. *Child Life in Colonial Days.* New York: Macmillan Company, 1899.

GREVEN, PHILIP J., JR. "Family Structure in Seventeenth-Century Andover, Massachusetts." *William and Mary Quarterly,* 3d ser., 23 (1966): 234–256.

————. *Four Generations: Population, Land, and Family in Colonial Andover, Massachusetts.* Ithaca, N.Y.: Cornell University Press, 1970.

————. *The Protestant Temperament: Patterns of Child-rearing, Religious Experience, and the Self in Early America.* New York: Alfred A. Knopf, 1977.

GUNDERSON, JOAN R., AND GAMPEL, GWEN V. "Married Women's Legal Status in Eighteenth-Century New York and Virginia." *William and Mary Quarterly,* 3d ser., 39 (1982): 114–134.

HASKINS, GEORGE L. "The Beginnings of Partible Inheritance in the American Colonies." In *Essays in the History of Early American Law,* ed. David H. Flaherty. Chapel Hill: University of North Carolina Press, 1969.

HOLLIDAY, CARL. *Woman's Life in Colonial Days.* Williamstown, Mass.: Corner House Publications, 1968. Originally published in 1922.

HOWARD, GEORGE E. *A History of Matrimonial Institutions, Chiefly in England and the United States.* Vol. 2. New York: Humanities Press, 1964. Originally published in 1904.

KEYSSAR, ALEXANDER. "Widowhood in Eighteenth-Century Massachusetts: A Problem in the History of the Family." *Perspectives in American History,* 8 (1974): 83–119.

KOEHLER, LYLE. *A Search for Power: The "Weaker Sex" in Seventeenth-Century New England.* Urbana: University of Illinois Press, 1980.

LEONARD, EUGENIE A. *The Dear-bought Heritage.* Philadelphia: University of Pennsylvania Press, 1965.

LEWIS, JAN. "Domestic Tranquillity and the Management of Emotion among the Gentry of Pre-Revolutionary Virginia." *William and Mary Quarterly,* 3d ser., 39 (1982): 135–149.

LOCKRIDGE, KENNETH A. *A New England Town: The First Hundred Years.* New York: W. W. Norton & Company, 1970.

MATHER, COTTON. *Diary.* 2 vols. Ed. Worthington C. Ford. Boston: Massachusetts Historical Society, 1912.

MORGAN, EDMUND S. *The Puritan Family: Essays on Religion and Domestic Relations in Seventeenth-Century New England.* Revised ed. New York: Harper & Row, 1966. Originally published in 1944.

NORTON, MARY B. "The Evolution of White Women's Experience in Early America." *American Historical Review,* 89 (1984): 593–629.

PINCKNEY, ELISE, ed. *The Letterbook of Eliza Lucas Pinckney, 1739–1762.* Chapel Hill: University of North Carolina Press, 1972.

SALMON, MARYLYNN. *Women and the Law of Property in Early America.* Chapel Hill: University of North Carolina Press, 1986.

SCHOLTEN, CATHERINE. *Childbearing in American Society, 1650–1850.* New York: New York University Press, 1985.

SHAMMAS, CAROLE, SALMON, MARYLYNN, AND DAHLIN, MICHAEL. *Inheritance in America from Colonial Times to the Present.* New Brunswick, N.J.: Rutgers University Press, 1987.

SMITH, DANIEL B. *Inside the Great House: Planter Family Life in Eighteenth-Century Chesapeake Society.* Ithaca, N.Y.: Cornell University Press, 1980.

SPRUILL, JULIA C. *Women's Life and Work in the Southern Colonies.* New York: W. W. Norton & Company, 1972. Originally published in 1938.

SEWALL, SAMUEL. *Diary.* 2 vols. ed. Thomas M. Halsey. New York: Farrar, Straus and Giroux, 1973.

ULRICH, LAUREL T. *Good Wives: Image and Reality in the Lives of Women in Northern New England, 1650–1750.* New York: Alfred A. Knopf, 1982.

WELLS, ROBERT V. *Revolutions in Americans' Lives: A Demographic Perspective on the History of Americans, Their Families, and Their Society.* Westport, Conn.: Greenwood Press, 1982.

CHAPTER 12

BAILYN, BERNARD. "Politics and Social Structure in Virginia." In *Seventeenth-Century America,* ed. James M. Smith. Chapel Hill: University of North Carolina Press, 1959.

BEEMAN, RICHARD R. *The Evolution of the Southern Backcountry: A Case Study of Lunenburg County, Virginia.* Philadelphia: University of Pennsylvania Press, 1984.

BILLINGS, WARREN M., SELBY, JOHN E., AND TATE, THAD W., *Colonial Virginia—A History.* White Plains, N.Y.: KTO Press, 1986.

BONOMI, PATRICIA U. *A Factious People: Politics and Society in Colonial New York.* New York: Columbia University Press, 1971.

BRIDENBAUGH, CARL. *Myths and Realities: Societies of the Colonial South.* New York: Atheneum, 1963.

———. *Rebels and Gentlemen: Philadelphia in the Age of Franklin.* New York: Reynal & Hitchcock, 1949.

BRUCE, PHILIP A. *Social Life of Virginia in the Seventeenth Century.* Lynchburg, Va.: J. P. Bell Company, 1907.

CARSON, JANE. *Colonial Virginians at Play.* Williamsburg, Va.: Colonial Williamsburg, 1965.

COOK, EDWARD M., JR. "Social Behavior and Changing Values in Dedham, Massachusetts, 1700 to 1775." *William and Mary Quarterly,* 3d ser., 28 (1970): 545–580.

DAVIS, HAROLD E. *The Fledgling Province: Social and Cultural Life in Colonial Georgia, 1733–1776.* Chapel Hill: University of North Carolina Press, 1976.

DAVIS, THOMAS R. "Sport and Exercise in the Lives of Selected Colonial Americans: Massachusetts and Virginia, 1700–1775." Ph.D. diss., University of Maryland, 1971.

EARLE, ALICE M. *Colonial Days in Old New York.* New York: Charles Scribner's Sons, 1896.

———. *Customs and Fashions in Old New England.* New York: Charles Scribner's Sons, 1893.

———. *Stage-Coach and Tavern Days.* New York: Benjamin Bloom, 1969. Originally published in 1900.

EKIRCH, A. ROGER. *"Poor Carolina": Politics and Society in Colonial North Carolina, 1729–1776.* Chapel Hill: University of North Carolina Press, 1981.

FREEMAN, DOUGLAS S. *George Washington: A Biography.* Vol. 1. New York: Charles Scribner's Sons, 1949.

GALLAY, ALAN. "Jonathan Bryan's Plantation Empire: Land, Politics, and the Formation of a Ruling Class in Colonial Georgia." *William and Mary Quarterly,* 3d ser., 45 (1988): 253–279.

GORN, ELLIOTT, JR. " 'Gouge and Bite, Pull Hair and Scratch': The Social Significance of Fighting in the Southern Backcountry," *American Historical Review,* 90 (1985): 18–43.

HAWKE, DAVID F. *Everyday Life in Early America.* New York: Harper & Row, 1988.

HENRETTA, JAMES A. "Economic Development and Social Structure in Colonial Boston." *William and Mary Quarterly,* 3d ser., 22 (1965): 75–92.

———. *The Evolution of American Society, 1700–1815: An Interdisciplinary Analysis.* Lexington, Mass.: D. C. Heath and Company, 1973.

HERVEY, JOHN. *Racing in America, 1665–1865.* Vol. 1. New York: The Scribner Press, 1944.

JONES, ALICE H. *Wealth of a Nation to Be: The American Colonies on the Eve of the Revolution.* New York: Columbia University Press, 1980.

LAND, AUBREY C. "Economic Base and Social Structure: The Northern Chesapeake in the Eighteenth Century." *Journal of Economic History,* 25 (1965): 639–654.

MAIN, GLORIA L. *Tobacco Colony: Life in Early Maryland, 1650–1720.* Princeton, N.J.: Princeton University Press, 1982.

MAIN, JACKSON T. *Society and Economy in Colonial Connecticut.* Princeton, N.J.: Princeton University Press, 1985.

NASH, GARY B. "Urban Wealth and Poverty in Prerevolutionary America." *Journal of Interdisciplinary History,* 4 (1976): 545–584.

RUTMAN, DARRETT B., AND RUTMAN, ANITA H. *A Place in Time: Middlesex County, Virginia, 1650–1750.* New York: W. W. Norton & Company, 1984.

SINGLETON, ESTHER. *Social New York under the Georges, 1714–1776.* New York: D. Appleton and Company, 1902.

SMITH, BILLY G. "The Material Lives of Laboring Philadelphians, 1750 to 1800." *William and Mary Quarterly,* 3d ser., 39 (1982): 163–202.

WRIGHT, LOUIS B. *The First Gentlemen of Virginia: Intellectual Qualities of the Early Colonial Ruling Class.* Charlottesville: University Press of Virginia, 1964. Originally published in 1940.

CHAPTER 13

BLAKE, JOHN B. *Public Health in the Town of Boston, 1630–1822.* Cambridge, Mass.: Harvard University Press, 1959.

BRIDENBAUGH, CARL. *Cities in Revolt: Urban Life in America, 1743–1776.* New York: Alfred A. Knopf, 1955.

———. *Cities in the Wilderness: The First Century of Urban Life in America, 1625–1742.* New York: Capricorn Books, 1964. Originally published in 1938.

———, ed. *Gentleman's Progress: The Itinerarium of Dr. Alexander Hamilton.* Chapel Hill: University of North Carolina Press, 1948.

DANIELS, BRUCE C. *Dissent and Conformity on Narragansett Bay: The Colonial Rhode Island Town.* Middletown, Conn.: Wesleyan University Press, 1983.

DUFFY, JOHN. *Epidemics in Colonial America.* Baton Rouge: Louisiana State University Press, 1953.

ERNST, JOSEPH A., AND MERRENS, H. ROY. " 'Camden's Turrets Pierce the Skies!' The Urban Process in the Southern Colonies during the Eighteenth Century." *William and Mary Quarterly,* 3d ser., 30 (1973): 549–574.

FOGLESONG, RICHARD. *Planning the Capitalist City: The Colonial Era to the 1920s.* Princeton, N.J.: Princeton University Press, 1986.

FRIES, SYLVIA D. *The Urban Idea in Colonial America.* Philadelphia: Temple University Press, 1977.

GILJE, PAUL A. *The Road to Mobocracy: Popular Disorder in New York, 1763–1834*. Chapel Hill: University of North Carolina Press, 1987.

GRIFFITH, ERNEST S. *History of American City Government: The Colonial Period*. New York: Oxford University Press, 1938.

JAMES, SYDNEY V. *A People among Peoples: Quaker Benevolence in Eighteenth-Century America*. Cambridge, Mass.: Harvard University Press, 1963.

JONES, DOUGLAS L. "The Strolling Poor: Transiency in Eighteenth-Century Massachusetts." *Journal of Social History*, 8 (1975): 28–54.

_____. *Village and Seaport: Migration and Society in Eighteenth-Century Massachusetts*. Hanover, N.H.: University Press of New England, 1981.

LEMISCH, JESSE. "Jack Tar in the Streets: Merchant Seamen in the Politics of Revolutionary America." *William and Mary Quarterly*, 3d ser., 25 (1968): 371–407.

LEMON, JAMES T. "Urbanization and the Development of Eighteenth-Century Southeastern Pennsylvania and Adjacent Delaware." *William and Mary Quarterly*, 3d ser., 24 (1967): 501–542.

MAIER, PAULINE. "Popular Uprisings and Civil Authority in Eighteenth-Century America." *William and Mary Quarterly*, 3d ser., 27 (1970): 3–35.

MOHL, RAYMOND A. "Poverty in Early America—a Reappraisal: The Case of Eighteenth-Century New York City." *New York History*, 50 (1969): 5–27.

NASH, GARY B. *The Urban Crucible: Social Change, Political Consciousness, and the Origins of the American Revolution*. Cambridge, Mass.: Harvard University Press, 1979.

PETERSON, ARTHUR E., AND EDWARDS, GEORGE W. *New York as an Eighteenth-Century Municipality*. New York: Longman, Green & Company, 1917.

REPS, JOHN W. "$C^2 + L^2 = S^2$? Another Look at the Origins of Savannah's Town Plan." In *Forty Years of Diversity: Essays on Colonial Georgia*, ed. Harvey H. Jackson and Phinzey Spalding. Athens: University of Georgia Press, 1984.

_____. *The Making of Urban America: A History of City Planning in the United States*. Princeton, N.J.: Princeton University Press, 1965.

_____. *Tidewater Towns: City Planning in Colonial Virginia and Maryland*. Charlottesville, Va.: University Press of Virginia, 1972.

ROACH, HANNAH B. "The Planting of Philadelphia: A Seventeenth-Century Real-Estate Development." *Pennsylvania Magazine of History and Biography*, 92 (1968): 3–47, 143–194.

ROTHMAN, DAVID J. *The Discovery of the Asylum: Social Order and Disorder in the New Republic*. Boston: Little, Brown and Company, 1971.

RUTMAN, DARRETT B. *Winthrop's Boston: Portrait of a Puritan Town, 1630–1649*. Chapel Hill: University of North Carolina Press, 1965.

TINKCOM, MARGARET B. "Urban Reflections in a Trans-Atlantic Mirror." *Pennsylvania Magazine of History and Biography*, 100 (1976): 287–313.

TRATTNER, WALTER I. *From Poor Law to Welfare State: A History of Social Welfare in America*. New York: The Free Press, 1974.

ZUCKERMAN, MICHAEL. *Peaceable Kingdoms: New England Towns in the Eighteenth Century*. New York: Alfred A. Knopf, 1970.

CHAPTER 14

BAILYN, BERNARD, Ed. *Pamphlets of the American Revolution*. Vol. 1. Cambridge, Mass.: Harvard University Press, 1965.

BECKER, CARL. *The History of Political Parties in the Province of New York, 1760–1776*. Madison: University of Wisconsin Press, 1960. Originally published in 1909.

BISHOP, CORTLANDT. *History of Elections in the American Colonies*. New York: AM Press, 1970. Originally published in 1893.

BONOMI, PATRICIA U. *A Factious People: Politics and Society in Colonial New York*. New York: Columbia University Press, 1971.

BROWN, ROBERT E. *Middle-Class Democracy and the Revolution in Massachusetts*. Ithaca, N.Y.: Cornell University Press, 1955.

———, AND BROWN, KATHERINE B. *Virginia, 1705–1786: Democracy or Aristocracy?* East Lansing: Michigan State University Press, 1964.

BUSHMAN, RICHARD L. *From Puritan to Yankee: Character and the Social Order in Connecticut, 1690–1765.* New York: W. W. Norton & Company, 1967.

CHUTE, MARCHETTE. *The First Liberty: A History of the Right to Vote, 1619–1850.* New York: E. P. Dutton & Company, 1969.

COOK, EDWARD M., JR. *The Fathers of the Towns: Leadership and Community Structure in Eighteenth-Century New England.* Baltimore: Johns Hopkins University Press, 1976.

DANIELS, BRUCE C., ed. *Power and Status: Officeholding in Colonial America.* Middletown, Conn.: Wesleyan University Press, 1986.

DICKERSON, OLIVER M. *American Colonial Government: A Study of the British Board of Trade.* New York: Russell and Russell, 1962. Originally published in 1912.

DINKIN, ROBERT J. *Voting in Provincial America: A Study of Elections in the Thirteen Colonies, 1689–1776.* Westport, Conn.: Greenwood Press, 1977.

GREENE, EVARTS B. *The Provincial Governor in the English Colonies of North America.* Gloucester, Mass.: Peter Smith, 1966. Originally published in 1898.

GREENE, JACK P. "Changing Interpretations of Early American Politics." In *The Reinterpretation of Early American History,* ed. Ray A. Billington. San Marino, Calif.: The Huntington Library, 1966.

———. *Peripheries and Center: Constitutional Development in the Extended Polities of the British Empire and the United States, 1607–1788.* Athens: University of Georgia Press, 1986.

———. *The Quest for Power: The Lower Houses of Assembly in the Southern Royal Colonies, 1689–1776.* Chapel Hill: University of North Carolina Press, 1963.

HENRETTA, JAMES A. *"Salutary Neglect": Colonial Administration under the Duke of Newcastle.* Princeton, N.J.: Princeton University Press, 1972.

JAMESON, J. FRANKLIN. *The American Revolution Considered as a Social Movement.* Boston: Beacon Press, 1926.

KATZ, STANLEY N. *Newcastle's New York: Anglo-American Politics, 1732–1753.* Cambridge, Mass.: Harvard University Press, 1968.

KLEIN, MILTON M. *The Politics of Diversity: Essays in the History of Colonial New York.* Port Washington, N.Y.: Kennikat Press, 1974.

LABAREE, LEONARD W. *Royal Government in America: A Study of the British Colonial System before 1783.* New York: Frederick Ungar Publishing Company, 1958. Originally published in 1930.

LANGDON, GEORGE D., JR. "The Franchise and Political Democracy in Plymouth Colony." *William and Mary Quarterly,* 3d ser., 20 (1963): 514–526.

LEDER, LAWRENCE H. *Robert Livingston and the Politics of Colonial New York.* Chapel Hill: University of North Carolina Press, 1961.

LOKKEN, ROY N. "The Concept of Democracy in Colonial Political Thought." *William and Mary Quarterly,* 3d ser., 16 (1959): 568–580.

LOVEJOY, DAVID S. *Rhode Island Politics and the American Revolution, 1760–1776.* Providence: Brown University Press, 1958.

MAIN, JACKSON T. *The Upper House in Revolutionary America, 1763–1788.* Madison: University of Wisconsin Press, 1967.

McCORMICK, RICHARD P. *History of Voting in New Jersey: A Study of the Development of Election Machinery, 1641–1911.* New Brunswick: Rutgers University Press, 1953.

McKINLEY, ALBERT E. *The Suffrage Franchise in the Thirteen English Colonies in America.* Philadelphia: Ginn & Company, 1905.

MORGAN, EDMUND S. *Inventing the People: The Rise of Popular Sovereignty in England and America.* New York: W. W. Norton & Company, 1988.

NASH, GARY B. *Quakers and Politics: Pennsylvania, 1681–1726.* Princeton, N.J.: Princeton University Press, 1968.

POLE, J. R. *The Gift of Government: Political Responsibility from the English Restoration to American Independence.* Athens: University of Georgia Press, 1983.

PURVIS, THOMAS L. *Proprietors, Patronage, and Paper Money: Legislative Politics in New Jersey, 1703–1776.* New Brunswick, N.J.: Rutgers University Press, 1986.

RAINBOLT, JOHN C. *From Prescription to Persuasion: Manipulation of Eighteenth-Century Virginia Economy.* Port Washington, N.Y.: Kennikat Press, 1974.

ROSSITER, CLINTON. *Seedtime of the Republic: The Origin of the American Tradition of Political Liberty.* New York: Harcourt, Brace and Company, 1953.

SYDNOR, CHARLES S. *Gentlemen Freeholders: Political Practices in Washington's Virginia.* Chapel Hill: University of North Carolina Press, 1952.

THAYER, THEODORE. *Pennsylvania Politics and the Growth of Democracy, 1740–1776.* Harrisburg: Pennsylvania Historical and Museum Commission, 1953.

CHAPTER 15

ALDERFER, E. G. *The Ephrata Commune: An Early American Counterculture.* Pittsburgh: University of Pittsburgh Press, 1985.

BOYER, PAUL, AND NISSENBAUM, STEPHEN. *Salem Possessed: The Social Origins of Witchcraft.* Cambridge, Mass.: Harvard University Press, 1974.

BROWN, RICHARD M. *The South Carolina Regulators.* Cambridge, Mass.: Harvard University Press, 1963.

BURG, B. R. *Sodomy and the Perception of Evil: English Sea Rovers in the Seventeenth-Century Caribbean.* New York: New York University Press, 1983.

CAPORAEL, LINNDA R. "Ergotism: The Satan Loosed in Salem?" *Science,* 192 (April 2, 1976): 21–26.

CRANE, VERNER W. "A Lost Utopia of the First American Frontier." *Sewanee Review,* 27 (1919): 48–61.

DEMOS, JOHN P. *Entertaining Satan: Witchcraft and the Culture of Early New England.* New York: Oxford University Press, 1982.

————. "Underlying Themes in the Witchcraft of Seventeenth-Century New England." *American Historical Review,* 75 (1970): 1311–1326.

GOLLIN, GILLIAN L. *Moravians in Two Worlds: A Study of Changing Communities.* New York: Columbia University Press, 1967.

GREENBERG, DOUGLAS. *Crime and Law Enforcement in the Colony of New York, 1691–1776.* Ithaca, N.Y.: Cornell University Press, 1974.

————. "Crime, Law Enforcement, and Social Control in Colonial America." *American Journal of Legal History,* 26 (1982): 293–325.

HANSEN, CHADWICK. *Witchcraft at Salem.* New York: George Braziller, 1969.

HOLLOWAY, MARK. *Heavens on Earth: Utopian Communities in America, 1680–1880.* 2d ed. New York: Dover Publications, 1951.

HOOKER, RICHARD J., ed. *The Carolina Backcountry on the Eve of the Revolution: The Journal . . . of Charles Woodmason, Anglican Itinerant.* Chapel Hill: University of North Carolina Press, 1953.

HULL, N. E. H. *Female Felons: Women and Serious Crime in Colonial Massachusetts.* Urbana: University of Illinois Press, 1987.

JAMES, BARTLETT B. *The Labadist Colony in Maryland.* Baltimore: Johns Hopkins University Press, 1899.

KARLSEN, CAROL F. *The Devil in the Shape of a Woman: Witchcraft in Colonial New England.* New York: W. W. Norton and Company, 1987.

KLEIN, WALTER C. *Johann Conrad Beissel: Mystic and Martinet, 1690–1768.* Philadelphia: Porcupine Press, 1972.

KOEHLER, LYLE. *A Search for Power: The "Weaker Sex" in Seventeenth-Century New England.* Urbana: University of Illinois Press, 1980.

LEAMING, HUGO P. "Hidden Americans: Maroons of Virginia and the Carolinas." Ph.D. diss., University of Illinois, 1979.

LEE, ROBERT E. *Blackbeard the Pirate: A Reappraisal of His Life and Times.* Winston-Salem, N.C.: John F. Blair, 1974.

LOVEJOY, DAVID S. *Religious Enthusiasm in the New World: Heresy to Revolution.* Cambridge, Mass.: Harvard University Press, 1985.

POWERS, EDWIN. *Crime and Punishment in Early Massachusetts.* Boston: Beacon Press, 1966.

PREYER, KATHRYN. "Penal Measures in the American Colonies: An Overview." *American Journal of Legal History,* 26 (1982): 326–353.

RANKIN, HUGH F. *Criminal Trial Proceedings in the General Court of Colonial Virginia.* Charlottesville, Va.: University Press of Virginia, 1965.

————. *The Golden Age of Piracy.* New York: Holt, Rinehart and Winston, 1969.

REDIKER, MARCUS. *Between the Devil and the Deep Blue Sea: Merchant Seamen, Pirates, and the Anglo-American Maritime World, 1700–1750.* Cambridge: Cambridge University Press, 1987.

RITCHIE, ROBERT C. *Captain Kidd and the War against the Pirates.* Cambridge, Mass.: Harvard University Press, 1986.

SACHSE, JULIUS F. *The German Sectarians of Pennsylvania, 1708–1800.* 2 vols. New York: AMS Press, 1971. Originally published in 1899–1900.

SCOTT, ARTHUR P. *Criminal Law in Colonial Virginia.* Chicago: University of Chicago Press, 1930.

SCOTT, KENNETH. *Counterfeiting in Colonial America.* New York: Oxford University Press, 1957.

SEMMES, RAPHAEL. *Crime and Punishment in Early Maryland.* Montclair, N.J.: Patterson Smith, 1970. Originally published in 1938.

SPINDELL, DONNA J. *Crime and Society in North Carolina, 1663–1776.* Baton Rouge, La.: Louisiana State University Press, 1989.

WEISMAN, RICHARD. *Witchcraft and Religion in Seventeenth-Century Massachusetts.* Amherst: University of Massachusetts Press, 1984.

WEISS, HARRY B., AND WEISS, GRACE M. *An Introduction to Crime and Punishment in Colonial New Jersey.* Trenton, N.J.: The Past Times Press, 1960.

CHAPTER 16

BILLIAS, GEORGE A., ed. *Selected Essays: Law and Authority in Colonial America.* Barre, Mass.: Barre Publishers, 1965.

BILLINGS, WARREN M. "Pleading, Procedure, and Practice: The Meaning of Due Process of Law in Seventeenth-Century Virginia." *Journal of Southern History,* 47 (1981): 569–584.

BOWLER, CLARA A. "Carted Whores and White Shrouded Apologies: Slander in the County Courts in Seventeenth-Century Virginia." *Virginia Magazine of History and Biography,* 75 (1977): 411–426.

BURANELLI, VINCENT, ed. *The Trial of Peter Zenger.* New York: New York University Press, 1957.

CHAFEE, ZECHARIAH, JR. "Colonial Courts and the Common Law." *Massachusetts Historical Society Proceedings,* 48 (1947): 132–159

————. *Freedom of Speech in the United States.* Cambridge, Mass.: Harvard University Press, 1967. Originally published in 1941.

CRESS, LAWRENCE D. *Citizens in Arms: The Army and the Militia in American Society to the War of 1812.* Chapel Hill: University of North Carolina Press, 1982.

CUDDIHY, WILLIAM, AND HARDY, B. CARMON. "A Man's House Was Not His Castle: Origins of the Fourth Amendment to the United States Constitution." *William and Mary Quarterly,* 3d ser., 37 (1980): 371–400.

CURRY, THOMAS J. *The First Freedoms: Church and State in America to the Passage of the First Amendment.* New York: Oxford University Press, 1986.

DARGO, GEORGE. *Roots of the Republic: A New Perspective on Early American Constitutionalism.* New York: Praeger Publishers, 1974.

DUNIWAY, CLYDE A. *The Development of Freedom of the Press in Massachusetts.* New York: Longmans, Green and Company, 1906.

FLAHERTY, DAVID H., ed. *Essays in the History of Early American Law.* Chapel Hill: University of North Carolina Press, 1969.

————. *Privacy in Colonial New England.* Charlottesville: University Press of Virginia, 1972.

GOEBEL, JULIUS, JR. "King's Law and Local Custom in Seventeenth Century New England." *Columbia Law Review,* 31 (1931): 416–448.

————, AND NAUGHTON, T. RAYMOND. *Law Enforcement in Colonial New York: A Study in Criminal Procedure.* Montclair, N.J.: Patterson Smith, 1970. Originally published in 1944.

HANDLIN, OSCAR, AND HANDLIN, LILIAN. *Liberty and Power, 1600–1760.* New York: Harper & Row, 1986.

HASKINS, GEORGE L. *Law and Authority in Early Massachusetts.* New York: The Macmillan Company, 1960.

_____. "The Legal Heritage of Plymouth Colony." In Flaherty, David H., ed. *Essays in the History of Early American Law.* Chapel Hill: University of North Carolina Press, 1969.

HILKEY, CHARLES J. *Local Developments in Colonial Massachusetts, 1630–1686.* New York: Columbia University Press, 1910.

KONIG, DAVID T. *Law and Society in Puritan Massachusetts: Essex County, 1629–1692.* Chapel Hill: University of North Carolina Press, 1979.

KUKLA, JON, ed. *The Bill of Rights: A Lively Heritage.* Richmond: Virginia State Library, 1987.

LEVY, LEONARD W. *Emergence of a Free Press.* New York: Oxford University Press, 1985.

_____. *The Establishment Clause: Religion and the First Amendment.* New York: Macmillan Publishing Company, 1986.

_____. *Origins of the Fifth Amendment.* New York: Oxford University Press, 1968.

_____. *Treason against God: A History of the Offense of Blasphemy.* New York: Schocken Books, 1981.

_____. *Blasphemy in Massachusetts: Freedom of Conscience and the Abner Kneeland Case—a Documentary Record.* New York: Da Capo Press, 1973.

MCLOUGHLIN, WILLIAM G. *New England Dissent, 1630–1833: The Baptists and the Separation of Church and State.* 2 vols. Cambridge, Mass.: Harvard University Press, 1971.

MILLER, HELEN H. *The Case for Liberty.* Chapel Hill: University of North Carolina Press, 1965.

MURRIN, JOHN M. "Magistrates, Sinners, and a Precarious Liberty: Trial by Jury in Seventeenth-Century New England." In *Saints and Revolutionaries: Essays on Early American History,* ed. David D. Hall, John M. Murrin, and Thad W. Tate. New York: W. W. Norton & Company, 1984.

NELSON, HAROLD L. "Seditious Libel in Colonial America." *American Journal of Legal History,* 3 (1959): 160–172.

NORTON, MARY B. "Gender and Defamation in Seventeenth-Century Maryland." *William and Mary Quarterly,* 3d ser., 44 (1987): 3–39.

PURVIS, THOMAS L. "Origins and Patterns of Agrarian Unrest in New Jersey, 1735 to 1754." *William and Mary Quarterly,* 3d ser., 39 (1982): 600–627.

RACKOW, FELIX. "The Right to Counsel: English and American Precedents." *William and Mary Quarterly,* 3d ser., 11 (1954): 3–27.

REINSCH, PAUL S. *English Common Law in the Early American Colonies.* New York: Da Capo Press, 1970. Originally published in 1899.

ROWLAND, JOHN K. "Origins of the Second Amendment: The Creation of the Constitutional Rights of Militia and of Keeping and Bearing Arms." Ph.D. diss., Ohio State University, 1978.

ST. GEORGE, ROBERT. " 'Heated' Speech and Literacy in Seventeenth-Century New England." In *Seventeenth-Century New England,* ed. David D. Hall and David G. Allen. Boston: The Colonial Society of Massachusetts, 1984.

SHALHOPE, ROBERT E. "The Ideological Origins of the Second Amendment." *Journal of American History,* 69 (1983): 599–614.

SMITH, M. H. *The Writs of Assistance Case.* Berkeley, Calif.: University of California Press, 1978.

ZIMMERMAN, JOHN J. "Governor Denny and the Quartering Act of 1756." *Pennsylvania Magazine of History and Biography,* 91 (1967): 266–281.

CHAPTER 17

ANDREWS, CHARLES M., ed. *Narratives of the Insurrections, 1675–1690.* New York: Barnes & Noble, 1967. Originally published in 1915.

ARCHDEACON, THOMAS J. *New York City, 1664–1710.* Ithaca, N.Y.: Cornell University Press, 1976.

BARNES, VIOLA B. *The Dominion of New England: A Study in British Colonial Policy.* New York: Frederick Ungar Publishing Company, 1951. Originally published in 1923.

BOOTH, SALLY S. *Seeds of Anger: Revolts in America, 1607–1771.* New York: Hastings House, 1977.

CARR, LOIS G., AND JORDAN, DAVID W. *Maryland's Revolution of Government, 1689–1692.* Ithaca, N.Y.: Cornell University Press, 1974.

CRAVEN, WESLEY F. *The Colonies in Transition, 1660–1713.* New York: Harper & Row, 1968.

DANIELL, JERE R. *Colonial New Hampshire: A History.* New York: KTO Press, 1981.

HALL, MICHAEL G., LEDER, LAWRENCE H., AND KAMMEN, MICHAEL G. eds. *The Glorious Revolution in America: Documents of the Colonial Crisis of 1689.* Chapel Hill: University of North Carolina Press, 1964.

JORDAN, DAVID W. "John Coode, Perennial Rebel." *Maryland Historical Magazine,* 70 (1979): 1–28.

KAMMEN, MICHAEL G. "The Causes of the Maryland Revolution of 1689." *Maryland Historical Magazine,* 55 (1960): 293–333.

LEWIS, THEODORE B., JR. "Massachusetts and the Glorious Revolution, 1660–1692." Ph.D. diss., University of Wisconsin, 1967.

LOVEJOY, DAVID S. *The Glorious Revolution in America.* New York: Harper & Row, 1972.

REICH, JEROME R. *Leisler's Rebellion: A Study of Democracy in New York, 1664–1720.* Chicago: University of Chicago Press, 1953.

RITCHIE, ROBERT C. *The Duke's Province: A Study of New York Politics and Society, 1664–1691.* Chapel Hill: University of North Carolina Press, 1977.

SANBORN, FRANKLIN. "Edward Gove and His Confiscated Estate." *Proceedings of the Massachusetts Historical Society,* 45 (1912): 628–640.

SHERMAN, RICHARD P. *Robert Johnson: Proprietary and Royal Governor of South Carolina.* Columbia: University of South Carolina Press, 1966.

SOSIN, JACK M. *English America and the Restoration Monarchy of Charles II.* Lincoln: University of Nebraska Press, 1980.

———. *English America and the Revolution of 1688.* Lincoln: University of Nebraska Press, 1982.

WASHBURN, WILCOMB E. *The Governor and the Rebel: A History of Bacon's Rebellion in Virginia.* Chapel Hill: University of North Carolina Press, 1957.

WEBB, STEPHEN S. *1676: The End of American Independence.* Cambridge, Mass.: Harvard University Press, 1985.

WERTENBAKER, THOMAS J. *Torchbearer of the Revolution: The Story of Bacon's Rebellion and Its Leader.* Gloucester, Mass.: Peter Smith, 1965. Originally published in 1940.

CHAPTER 18

BACKUS, ISAAC. *A History of New England with Particular Reference to the Baptists.* 2 vols. New York: Arno Press, 1969. Originally published in 1777–1796.

BONOMI, PATRICIA U. *Under the Cope of Heaven: Religion, Society, and Politics in Colonial America.* New York: Oxford University Press, 1986.

BRIDENBAUGH, CARL. *Mitre and Sceptre: Transatlantic Faiths, Ideas, Personalities, and Politics, 1689–1775.* New York: Oxford University Press, 1962.

BUMSTED, J. M. "Religion, Finance, and Democracy in Massachusetts: The Town of Norton as a Case Study." *Journal of American History,* 57 (1971): 817–831.

COALTER, MILTON J. *Gilbert Tennant, Son of Thunder.* New York: Greenwood Press, 1986.

COFFMAN, RALPH J. *Solomon Stoddard.* Boston: Twayne Publishers, 1978.

DE JONG, GERALD F. *The Dutch Reformed Church in the American Colonies.* Grand Rapids, Mich.: William B. Eerdmans Publishing Company, 1978.

ELLIS, JOHN T. *Catholics in Colonial America.* Baltimore: Helicon Press, 1965.

GAUSTAD, EDWIN S. *The Great Awakening in New England.* New York: Harper & Brothers, 1957.

GEWEHR, WESLEY M. *The Great Awakening in Virginia, 1740–1790.* Durham, N.C.: Duke University Press, 1930.

GOEN, C. C. *Revivalism and Separatism in New England, 1740–1800.* New Haven, Conn.: Yale University Press, 1962.

HALL, DAVID D. *The Faithful Shepherd: The History of the New England Ministry in the Seventeenth Century.* Chapel Hill: University of North Carolina Press, 1972.

_____. "On Common Ground: The Coherence of American Puritan Studies." *William and Mary Quarterly*, 3d ser., 44 (1987): 193–229.

HEIMERT, ALAN. *Religion and the American Mind From the Great Awakening to the Revolution.* Cambridge, Mass.: Harvard University Press, 1966.

_____, AND MILLER, PERRY, eds. *The Great Awakening: Documents Illustrating the Crisis and Its Consequences.* Indianapolis: The Bobbs-Merrill Company, 1967.

ISAAC, RHYS. *The Transformation of Virginia, 1740–1790.* Chapel Hill: University of North Carolina Press, 1982.

JACKSON, HARVEY H. "Hugh Bryan and the Evangelical Movement in Colonial South Carolina." *William and Mary Quarterly*, 3d ser., 43 (1986): 594–614.

JONES, JAMES W. *The Shattered Synthesis: New England Puritanism before the Great Awakening.* New Haven, Conn.: Yale University Press, 1973.

JONES, RUFUS M. *The Quakers in the American Colonies.* London: Macmillan and Company, 1911.

LUCAS, PAUL R. *Valley of Discord: Church and Society along the Connecticut River, 1636–1725.* Hanover, N.H.: University Press of New England, 1976.

MACMASTER, RICHARD K. *Land, Piety, Peoplehood: The Establishment of Mennonite Communities in America, 1683–1790.* Scottsdale, Pa.: Herald Press, 1985.

MAXSON, CHARLES H. *The Great Awakening in the Middle Colonies.* Gloucester, Mass.: Peter Smith, 1958. Originally published in 1920.

McGIFFERT, MICHAEL. "American Puritan Studies in the 1960s." *William and Mary Quarterly*, 3d ser., 27 (1970): 36–67.

MIDDLEKAUF, ROBERT. *The Mathers: Three Generations of Puritan Intellectuals, 1596–1728.* New York: Oxford University Press, 1971.

MILLER, PERRY. *The New England Mind: From Colony to Province.* Boston: Beacon Press, 1966.

_____. *The New England Mind in the Seventeenth Century.* Boston: Beacon Press, 1961. Originally published in 1939.

MORAIS, HERBERT M. *Deism in the Eighteenth Century.* New York: Columbia University Press, 1934.

PILCHER, GEORGE W. *Samuel Davies: Apostle of Dissent in Colonial Virginia.* Knoxville: University of Tennessee Press, 1971.

POPE, ROBERT G. *The Half-Way Covenant: Church Membership in Puritan New England.* Princeton, N.J.: Princeton University Press, 1969.

QUALBEN, LARS P. *The Lutheran Church in Colonial America.* New York: Thomas Nelson and Sons, 1940.

SWEET, WILLIAM W. *Religion in Colonial America.* New York: Cooper Square Publishers, 1965.

TANIS, JAMES. *Dutch Calvinistic Pietism in the Middle Colonies.* The Hague, Netherlands: Martinus Nijhoff, 1967.

TRINTERUD, LEONARD J. *The Forming of an American Tradition: A Re-examination of Colonial Presbyterianism.* Philadelphia: The Westminister Press, 1949.

WINSLOW, OLA E. *Jonathan Edwards, 1703–1758: A Biography.* New York: The Macmillan Company, 1940.

WOOLVERTON, JOHN F. *Colonial Anglicanism in North America.* Detroit: Wayne State University Press, 1984.

WRIGHT, CONRAD. *The Beginnings of Unitarianism in America.* Boston: Starr King Press, 1955.

CHAPTER 19

BAINE, RODNEY M. *Robert Munford: America's First Comic Dramatist.* Athens: University of Georgia Press, 1967.

BECK, JOHN B. *An Historical Sketch of the State of Medicine in the American Colonies: From Their*

First Settlement to the Period of the Revolution. Albuquerque, N.M.: Horn and Wallace Publishers, 1966. Originally published in 1850.

BELL, WHITFIELD J. *Early American Science: Needs and Opportunities for Study.* Williamsburg, Va.: Institute of Early American History and Culture, 1955.

BERKELEY, EDMUND, AND BERKELEY, DOROTHY S. *Dr. John Mitchell: The Man Who Made the Map of North America.* Chapel Hill: University of North Carolina Press, 1974.

————. *John Clayton: Pioneer of American Botany.* Chapel Hill: University of North Carolina Press, 1963.

BLANTON, WYNDHAM B. *Medicine in Virginia in the Eighteenth Century.* Richmond: Garrett & Massie, 1931.

————. *Medicine in Virginia in the Seventeenth Century.* Richmond: The William Byrd Press, 1930.

BUSHMAN, RICHARD L. "American High-Style and Vernacular Cultures." In *Colonial British America: Essays in the New History of the Early Modern Era.* ed. Jack P. Greene and J. R. Pole. Baltimore: Johns Hopkins University Press, 1984.

COLONIAL SOCIETY OF MASSACHUSETTS. *Music in Colonial Massachusetts, 1630–1830.* 2 vols. Boston, 1985.

COMMAGER, HENRY S. *The Empire of Reason: How Europe Imagined and America Realized the Enlightenment.* Garden City, N.Y.: Anchor Press/Doubleday, 1977.

CRAVEN, WAYNE. *Colonial American Portraiture: The Economic, Religious, Social, Cultural, Philosophical, Scientific, and Aesthetic Foundations.* New York: Cambridge University Press, 1986.

DAVIS, RICHARD B. *Intellectual Life in the Colonial South, 1585–1763.* Vols. 2 and 3. Knoxville: University of Tennessee Press, 1978.

EWAN, JOSEPH, AND EWAN, NESTA. *John Banister and His Natural History of Virginia.* Urbana: University of Illinois Press, 1970.

FLEXNER, JAMES T. *History of American Painting. Vol. 1: The Colonial Period.* 2d ed. New York: Dover Publishers, 1969.

FOOTE, HENRY W. *Robert Feke: Colonial Portrait Painter.* Cambridge, Mass.: Harvard University Press, 1930.

FRANKENSTEIN, ALFRED, AND THE EDITORS OF TIME-LIFE BOOKS. *The World of Copley, 1738–1815.* New York: Time-Life Books, 1970.

FRICK, GEORGE F., AND STEARNS, RAYMOND P. *Mark Catesby: The Colonial Audubon.* Urbana: University of Illinois Press, 1961.

HINDLE, BROOKE. *The Pursuit of Science in Revolutionary America, 1735–1789.* Chapel Hill: University of North Carolina Press, 1956.

HOOD, GRAHAM. *Charles Bridges and William Dering: Two Virginia Painters, 1735–1750.* Williamsburg, Va.: Colonial Williamsburg Foundation, 1978.

KENNEDY, ROGER G. *Architecture, Men, Women and Money in America, 1600–1860.* New York: Random House, 1985.

KIMBALL, FISKE. *Domestic Architecture of the American Colonies and of the Early Republic.* New York: Charles Scribner's Sons, 1927.

LEMAY, J. A. LEO. *Ebenezer Kinnersley: Franklin's Friend.* Philadelphia: University of Pennsylvania Press, 1964.

LOKKEN, ROY N., ed. *Meet Dr. Franklin.* Philadelphia: The Franklin Institute, 1981.

McNAMARA, BROOKS. *The American Playhouse in the Eighteenth Century.* Cambridge, Mass.: Harvard University Press, 1969.

MILLER, LILLIAN B. "The Puritan Portrait: Its Function in Old and New England." In *Seventeenth-Century New England: A Conference Held by the Colonial Society of Massachusetts, June 18–19, 1982.* Boston: The Colonial Society of Massachusetts, 1984.

MOLNAR, JOHN W. *Songs from the Williamsburg Theatre: A Selection of Fifty Songs Performed on the Stage in Williamsburg in the Eighteenth Century.* Charlottesville: University Press of Virginia, 1972.

MORRISON, HUGH. *Early American Architecture: From the First Colonial Settlements to the National Period.* New York: Oxford University Press, 1952.

PIERSON, WILLIAM H. *American Buildings and Their Architects. Vol. 1: The Colonial and Neoclassical Styles.* Garden City, N.Y.: Doubleday & Company, 1970.

RANKIN, HUGH. *The Theater in Colonial America.* Chapel Hill: University of North Carolina Press, 1960.

ST. GEORGE, ROBERT B., ed. *Material Life in America, 1600–1860.* Boston: Northeastern University Press, 1988.

SAUNDERS, RICHARD H., III. "John Smibert: Anglo-American Portrait Painter." Ph.D. diss., Yale University, 1979.

SAVELLE, MAX. *Seeds of Liberty: The Genesis of the American Mind.* New York: Alfred A. Knopf, 1948.

SCHOLES, PERCY A. *The Puritans and Music in England and New England.* New York: Russell & Russell, 1962. Originally published in 1934.

SHURTLEFF, HAROLD R. *The Log Cabin Myth: A Study of the Early Dwellings of the English Colonists in North America.* Cambridge, Mass.: Harvard University Press, 1939.

SHRYOCK, RICHARD H. *Medicine and Society in America, 1660–1860.* New York: New York University Press, 1960.

SONNECK, OSCAR G. *Early Concert Life in America (1731–1800).* Wiesbaden, West Germany: M. Sändig, 1969. Originally published in 1907.

STEARNS, RAYMOND P. *Science in the British Colonies of America.* Urbana: University of Illinois Press, 1970.

VAN DOREN, CARL. *Benjamin Franklin.* New York: Viking Press, 1938.

WRIGHT, LOUIS B., TATUM, GEORGE B., McCOUBREY, JOHN W., AND SMITH, ROBERT C. *The Arts in America: The Colonial Period.* New York: Charles Scribner's Sons, 1966.

CHAPTER 20

AXTELL, JAMES. *The School upon a Hill.* New Haven, Conn.: Yale University Press, 1974.

BEVERLEY, ROBERT. *The History and Present State of Virginia,* ed. Louis B. Wright. Charlottesville: University Press of Virginia, 1968. Originally published in 1947.

COHEN, EDWARD H. *Ebenezer Cooke: The Sot-Weed Factor.* Athens: University of Georgia Press, 1975.

COHEN, HENING. *The South Carolina Gazette, 1732–1775.* Columbia: University of South Carolina Press, 1953.

COWELL, PATTIE, AND STANFORD, ANN. *Critical Essays on Anne Bradstreet.* Boston: G. K. Hall & Company, 1983.

CREMIN, LAWRENCE A. *American Education: The Colonial Experience, 1607–1783.* New York: Harper & Row, 1970.

CRESSY, DAVID. *Literacy and the Social Order: Reading and Writing in Tudor and Stuart England.* Cambridge: Cambridge University Press, 1980.

DE ARMOND, ANNA J. *Andrew Bradford: Colonial Journalist.* Newark: University of Delaware Press, 1949.

EMERSON, EVERETT, ed. *Major Writers of Early American Literature.* Madison: University of Wisconsin Press, 1972.

FORD, PAUL L., ed. *The New-England Primer.* New York: Teachers College, Columbia University, 1962. Originally published in 1897. Includes facsimile reproduction of 1727 edition.

FROST, J. WILLIAM. *The Quaker Family in America.* New York: St. Martin's Press, 1973.

JERNEGAN, MARCUS W. *Laboring and Dependent Classes in Colonial America, 1607–1783.* New York: Frederick Ungar Publishing Company, 1960. Originally published in 1931.

JONES, HOWARD M. "American Prose Style, 1700–1750." *Huntington Library Bulletin,* 6 (1934), 115–151.

KELLER, KARL. *The Example of Edward Taylor.* Amherst: University of Massachusetts Press, 1975.

KEMP, WILLIAM W. *The Support of Schools in Colonial New York by the Society for the Propagation of the Gospel in Foreign Parts.* New York: Arno Press, 1969. Originally published in 1913.

KILPATRICK, WILLIAM H. *The Dutch Schools of New Netherland and Colonial New York.* New York: Arno Press, 1969. Originally published in 1912.

KOBRE, SIDNEY. *The Development of the Colonial Newspaper.* Gloucester, Mass.: Peter Smith, 1960. Originally published in 1944.

LEFLER, HUGH T. "Promotional Literature of the Southern Colonies." *Journal of Southern History*, 33 (1967): 3–25.

LEMAY, JOSEPH A. *Men of Letters in Colonial Maryland.* Knoxville: University of Tennessee Press, 1972.

LOCKRIDGE, KENNETH A. *The Diary, and Life, of William Byrd II of Virginia, 1674–1744.* Chapel Hill: University of North Carolina Press, 1987.

_____. *Literacy in Colonial New England.* New York: W. W. Norton and Company, 1974.

MATHER, COTTON. *Magnalia Christi Americana.* New York: Russell & Russell, 1967. Originally published in 1702.

MIDDLEKAUF, ROBERT. *Ancients and Axioms: Secondary Education.* New Haven, Conn.: Yale University Press, 1963.

MILLER, JOHN C., ed. *The Colonial Image: Origins of American Culture.* New York: George Braziller, 1962.

MORGAN, EDMUND S. *The Puritan Family: Essays on Religion and Domestic Relations in Seventeenth-Century New England.* Revised ed. New York: Harper & Row, 1966. Originally published in 1944.

MORISON, SAMUEL E. *Harvard College in the Seventeenth Century.* 2 vols. Cambridge, Mass.: Harvard University Press, 1938.

_____. *The Intellectual Life of Colonial New England.* Ithaca, N.Y.: Cornell University Press, 1965. Originally published in 1935.

RICHARDSON, LYON N. *A History of Early American Magazines, 1741–1789.* New York: Thomas Nelson and Sons, 1931.

ROBSON, DAVID W. *Educating Republicans: The College in the Era of the American Revolution, 1750–1800.* Westport, Conn.: Greenwood Press, 1985.

SEELYE, JOHN. *Prophetic Waters: The River in Early American Life and Literature.* New York: Oxford University Press, 1977.

SEYBOLT, ROBERT F. *The Evening School in Colonial America.* New York: Arno Press, 1971. Originally published in 1925.

_____. *The Public Schools of Colonial Boston.* Cambridge, Mass.: Harvard University Press, 1935.

SILVERMAN, KENNETH. *The Life and Times of Cotton Mather.* New York: Harper & Row, 1984.

SLOTKIN, RICHARD. *Regeneration through Violence: The Mythology of the American Frontier, 1600–1860.* Middletown, Conn.: Wesleyan University Press, 1973.

STOWELL, MARION B. *Early American Almanacs: The Colonial Weekday Bible.* New York: Burt Franklin, 1977.

THOMAS, ISAIAH. *The History of Printing in America, with a Biography of Printers.* 2 vols. New York: Burt Franklin, 1972. Originally published in 1874.

TYLER, MOSES C. *A History of American Literature, 1607–1765.* Williamstown, Mass.: Corner House Publishers, 1973. Originally published in 1878.

WARCH, RICHARD. *School of the Prophets: Yale College, 1701–1740.* New Haven, Conn.: Yale University Press, 1973.

WECHSLER, LOUIS K. *The Common People of Colonial America: As Glimpsed through the Dusty Windows of the Old Almanacks, Chiefly of New-York.* New York: Vantage Press, 1978.

WHITE, PETER. *Benjamin Thompson: Colonial Bard.* University Park: Pennsylvania State University Press, 1980.

WRIGHT, LOUIS B. *The Cultural Life of the American Colonies, 1607–1763.* New York: Harper & Brothers, 1957.

_____. *The First Gentlemen of Virginia: Intellectual Qualities of the Early Colonial Ruling Class.* Charlottesville: University Press of Virginia, 1964. Originally published in 1940.

_____, ed. *Prose Works of William Byrd of Westover: Narratives of a Colonial Virginian.* Cambridge, Mass.: Harvard University Press, 1966.

WROTH, LAWRENCE C. *The Colonial Printer.* Portland, Maine: The Southworth-Anthoensen Press, 1938.

CHAPTER 21

ALDEN, JOHN R. *John Stuart and the Southern Colonial Frontier. A Study of Indian Relations, War, Trade, and Land Problems in the Southern Wilderness, 1754–1775.* New York: Gordion Press, 1966.

AQUILA, RICHARD. *The Iroquois Restoration: Iroquois Diplomacy on the Colonial Frontier, 1701–1754.* Detroit: Wayne State University Press, 1983.

AXTELL, JAMES. *The Invasion Within: The Context of Cultures in Colonial North America.* New York: Oxford University Press, 1985.

BAILEY, KENNETH P. *The Ohio Company of Virginia and the Westward Movement, 1748–1792.* Glendale, Calif.: Arthur H. Clark Company, 1939.

BRICELAND, ALAN V. *Westward from Virginia: The Exploration of the Virginia-Carolina Frontier, 1650–1710.* Charlottesville, Va.: University Press of Virginia, 1987.

CLARK, CHARLES E. *The Eastern Frontier: The Settlement of Northern New England, 1610–1763.* New York: Alfred A. Knopf, 1970.

CORKRAN, DAVID H. *The Cherokee Frontier: Conflict and Survival, 1740–1762.* Norman: University of Oklahoma Press, 1962.

———. *The Creek Frontier, 1540–1783.* Norman: University of Oklahoma Press, 1967.

CORRY, JOHN P. *Indian Affairs in Georgia, 1732–1756.* New York: AMS Press, 1980. Originally published in 1936.

COTTERILL, R. S. *The Southern Indians: The Story of the Civilized Tribes Before Removal.* Norman: University of Oklahoma Press, 1979. Originally published in 1954.

CRANE, VERNER W. *The Southern Frontier, 1670–1732.* Ann Arbor: University of Michigan Press, 1959. Originally published in 1929.

CUTLIFFE, STEPHEN H. "Colonial Indian Policy as a Measure of Rising Imperialism: New York and Pennsylvania, 1700–1755." *Western Pennsylvania Historical Magazine,* 64 (1981): 237–268.

DE VORSEY, LOUIS, JR. *The Indian Boundary in the Southern Colonies, 1763–1775.* Chapel Hill: University of North Carolina Press, 1966.

FERNOW, BERTHOLD. *The Ohio Valley in Colonial Days.* New York: Burt Franklin, 1971. Originally published in 1890.

GIPSON, LAWRENCE H. *The British Empire before the American Revolution.* Vols. 4, 5, and 9. New York: Alfred A. Knopf, 1939, 1942, and 1956.

GOODWIN, GARY C. *Cherokees in Transition: A Study of Changing Culture and Environment Prior to 1775.* Chicago: University of Chicago Department of Geography, 1977.

HANN, JOHN H. *Apalachee: The Land between the Rivers.* Gainesville: University of Florida Press, 1988.

HANNA, CHARLES A. *The Wilderness Trail, or the Ventures and Adventures of the Pennsylvania Traders on the Allegheny Path.* New York: G. P. Putnam's Sons, 1911.

JACOBS, WILBUR R. *Wilderness Politics and Indian Gifts: The Northern Colonial Frontier, 1748–1763.* Lincoln: University of Nebraska Press, 1950.

JENNINGS, FRANCIS. *The Ambiguous Iroquois Empire: The Covenant Chain Confederation of Indian Tribes with English Colonies from the Beginnings to the Lancaster Treaty of 1744.* New York: W. W. Norton, 1984.

KEGLEY, FREDERICK B. *Kegley's Virginia Frontier: The Beginning of the Southwest—The Roanoke of Colonial Days, 1740–1783.* Roanoke, Va.: Southwest Virginia Historical Society, 1938.

LEACH, DOUGLAS E. *The Northern Colonial Frontier, 1607–1763.* New York: Holt, Rinehart and Winston, 1966.

MERIWETHER, ROBERT L. *The Expansion of South Carolina, 1729–1765.* Kingsport, Tenn.: Southern Publishers, 1940.

MERRELL, JAMES H. *The Indians' New World: Catawbas and Their Neighbors from Europe.* Chapel Hill: University of North Carolina Press, 1989.

———. "Some Thoughts on Colonial Historians and American Indians." *William and Mary Quarterly,* 3d ser., 46 (1989): 94–119.

PECKHAM, HOWARD H. *Pontiac and the Indian Uprising.* Chicago: University of Chicago Press, 1947.

RAMSEY, ROBERT W. *Carolina Cradle: Settlement of the Northwest Carolina Frontier, 1747–1762.* Chapel Hill: University of North Carolina Press, 1964.

REID, JOHN B. *A Better Kind of Hatchet: Law, Trade, and Diplomacy in the Cherokee Nation during the Early Years of European Contact.* University Park: Pennsylvania State University Press, 1976.

SLICK, SEWELL E. *William Trent and the West.* Harrisburg: Archives Publishing Company of Pennsylvania, 1947.

SOSIN, JACK. *The Revolutionary Frontier, 1763–1783.* New York: Holt, Rinehart and Winston, 1967.
VAUGHAN, ALDEN T. "From White Man to Redskin: Changing Anglo-American Perceptions of the American Indian." *American Historical Review,* 87 (1982): 917–953.
WAINWRIGHT, NICHOLAS B. *George Croghan: Wilderness Diplomat.* Chapel Hill: University of North Carolina Press, 1959.
WESLAGER, WES. *The Delaware Indians: A History.* New Brunswick, N.J.: Rutgers University Press, 1972.

CHAPTER 22

ALDEN, JOHN R. *Robert Dinwiddie: Servant of the Crown.* Williamsburg, Va.: Colonial Williamsburg Foundation, 1973.
ANDERSON, FRED. *A People's Army: Massachusetts Soldiers and Society in the Seven Years' War.* Chapel Hill: University of North Carolina Press, 1984.
CALDWELL, NORMAN W. "The Southern Frontier during King George's War." *Journal of Southern History,* 7 (1941): 37–41.
DOWNEY, FAIRFAX. *Louisbourg: Key to a Continent.* Englewood Cliffs, N.J.: Prentice Hall, 1965.
ECCLES, WILLIAM J. *The Canadian Frontier, 1534–1760.* Albuquerque: University of New Mexico Press, 1974.
FERLING, JOHN E. *A Wilderness of Miseries: War and Warriors in Early America.* Westport, Conn.: Greenwood Press, 1980.
FREEMAN, DOUGLAS S. *George Washington.* Vol. 2. New York: Charles Scribner's Sons, 1949.
FRÉGAULT, GUY. *Canada: The War of the Conquest.* New York: Oxford University Press, 1969.
GIPSON, LAWRENCE H. *The British Empire before the Revolution.* Vols. 6–8. New York: Alfred A. Knopf, 1946, 1949, and 1954.
GODFREY, WILLIAM G. *Pursuit of Profit and Preferment in Colonial North America.* Waterloo, Ont.: Wilfrid Laurier University Press, 1982.
GREENE, JACK P. "The Seven Years' War and the American Revolution: The Causal Relationship Reconsidered." In *The British Atlantic Empire before the American Revolution,* ed. Peter Marshall and Glyn Williams. Totowa, N.J.: Frank Cass, 1980.
HAMILTON, EDWARD P. *The French and Indian Wars: The Story of Battles and Forts in the Wilderness.* Garden City, N.Y.: Doubleday & Company, 1962.
HAMILTON, MILTON W. *Sir William Johnson: Colonial American.* Port Washington, N.Y.: Kennikat Press, 1976.
IVERS, LARRY E. *British Drums on the Southern Frontier: The Military Colonization of Georgia, 1733–1749.* Chapel Hill: University of North Carolina Press, 1974.
JENNINGS, FRANCIS. *Empire of Fortune: Crowns, Colonies, and Tribes in the Seven Years' War in America.* New York: W. W. Norton Company, 1988.
KNOX, JOHN. *The Siege of Quebec and the Campaigns in North America, 1757–1760,* ed. Brian Connell. Mississauga, Ont.: Pendragon House of Mississauga, 1980.
KOONTZ, LOUIS K. *The Virginia Frontier, 1754–1763.* Baltimore: Johns Hopkins Press, 1925.
KOPPERMAN, PAUL E. *Braddock at the Monongahela.* Pittsburgh: University of Pittsburgh Press, 1977.
LEACH, DOUGLAS E. *Arms for Empire: A Military History of the British Colonies in North America, 1607–1763.* New York: Macmillan Company, 1973.
———. *Roots of Conflict: British Armed Forces and Colonial Americans, 1677–1763.* Chapel Hill: University of North Carolina Press, 1986.
O'MEARA, WALTER. *Guns at the Forks.* Englewood Cliffs, N.J.: Prentice Hall, 1965.
PARKMAN, FRANCIS. *The Old Regime in Canada.* 1897. 1 vol. *A Half Century of Conflict.* 1898. 2 vols. *The Conspiracy of Pontiac and the Indian War after the Conquest of Canada.* 1899. 2 vols. *Pioneers of France in the New World.* 1902. 1 vol. *The Jesuits in North America.* 1902. 1 vol. *La Salle and the Discovery of the Great West.* 1903. 1 vol. *Count Frontenac and New France under Louis XIV.* 1903. 1 vol. New Library edition, Boston: Little, Brown, and Company.

PECKHAM, HOWARD H. *The Colonial Wars, 1689–1762.* Chicago: University of Chicago Press, 1964.

ROGERS, ALAN. *Empire and Liberty: American Resistance to British Authority, 1755–1763.* Berkeley: University of California Press, 1974.

RUSSELL, PETER E. "Redcoats in the Wilderness: British Officers and Irregular Warfare in Europe and America, 1740 to 1760." *William and Mary Quarterly,* 3d ser., 35 (1978): 629–652.

SCHUTZ, JOHN A. *William Shirley: King's Governor of Massachusetts.* Chapel Hill: University of North Carolina Press, 1961.

SHY, JOHN. *Toward Lexington: The Role of the British Army in the Coming of the Revolution.* Princeton, N.J.: Princeton University Press, 1965.

STANLEY, GEORGE F. G. *New France: The Last Phase, 1744–1760.* Toronto: McClelland and Stewart Limited, 1968.

STOTZ, CHARLES M. *Outposts of the War for Empire: The French and English in Western Pennsylvania—Their Armies, Their Forts, Their Peoples, 1749–64.* Pittsburgh: University of Pittsburgh Press, 1985.

WALLER, G. M. *Samuel Vetch: Colonial Enterpriser.* Chapel Hill: University of North Carolina Press, 1960.

WARD, HARRY M. *Major General Adam Stephen and the Cause of American Liberty.* Charlottesville: University Press of Virginia, 1989.

ZOLTVANY, YVES F. *Philippe de Rigaud de Vaudreuil: Governor of New France, 1703–1725.* Toronto: McClelland and Stewart Limited, 1974.

CHAPTER 23

BARROW, THOMAS C. "The American Revolution as a Colonial War for Independence." *William and Mary Quarterly,* 3d ser., 25 (1968): 452–468.

BERENS, JOHN F. *Providence and Patriotism in Early America, 1640–1815.* Charlottesville: University Press of Virginia, 1978.

BLOCH, RUTH H. *Visionary Republic: Millennial Themes in American Thought, 1756–1800.* Cambridge: Cambridge University Press, 1985.

BOORSTIN, DANIEL J. *The Americans: The Colonial Experience.* New York: Vintage Books, 1958.

BRIDENBAUGH, CARL. *The Spirit of '76: The Growth of American Patriotism before Independence.* New York: Oxford University Press, 1975.

BULLION, JOHN L. "'The Ten Thousand in America': More Light on the Decision on the American Army, 1762–1763." *William and Mary Quarterly,* 3d ser., 43 (1986): 646–657.

BUMSTED, J. M. "'Things in the Womb of Time': Ideas of American Independence, 1633–1763." *William and Mary Quarterly,* 3d ser., 31 (1974): 533–564.

CADBURY, HENRY J. "Intercolonial Solidarity of American Quakerism." *Pennsylvania Magazine of History and Biography,* 60 (1936): 362–374.

CARTER, CLARENCE E. "The Office of Commander in Chief: A Phase of Imperial Unity on the Eve of the Revolution." In *The Era of the American Revolution,* ed. Richard B. Morris. New York: Harper & Row, 1965. Originally published in 1939.

CHRISTIE, IAN R., AND LABAREE, BENJAMIN W. *Empire or Independence, 1760–1776.* Oxford: Phaidon Press, 1976.

DEUTSH, KARL W. *Nationalism and Social Communication: An Inquiry into the Foundations of Nationality* (2d ed.). Cambridge, Mass.: The M. I. T. Press, 1966.

GIPSON, LAWRENCE H. *The British Empire before the American Revolution.* Vol. 10. New York: Alfred A. Knopf, 1967.

GREENE, JACK P. "Martin Bladen's Blueprint for a Colonial Union." *William and Mary Quarterly,* 3d ser., 17 (1960): 516–530.

———. *Pursuit of Happiness: The Social Development of Early Modern British Colonies and the Formation of American Culture.* Chapel Hill: University of North Carolina Press, 1988.

HARKNESS, ALBERT, JR. "Americanism and Jenkins' Ear." *Mississippi Valley Historical Review,* 37 (1951): 61–90.

HIGHAM, JOHN. "Hanging Together: Divergent Unities in American History." *Journal of American History*, 61 (1974): 5–28.

KAMMEN, MICHAEL G. *People of Paradox: An Inquiry concerning the Origins of American Civilization.* New York: Oxford University Press, 1980.

———. *A Rope of Sand: The Colonial Agents, British Politics, and the American Revolution.* Ithaca, N.Y.: Cornell University Press, 1968.

KOEBNER, RICHARD. *Empire.* Cambridge: Cambridge University Press, 1961.

KRAUS, MICHAEL. *Intercolonial Aspects of American Culture on the Eve of the Revolution.* New York: Columbia University Press, 1928.

LEDER, LAWRENCE H. *Liberty and Authority: Early American Political Ideology, 1689–1763.* Chicago: Quadrangle Books, 1968.

MATHEWS, M. M., ed. *The Beginnings of American English: Essays and Comments.* Chicago: University of Chicago Press, 1931.

MERRITT, RICHARD L. *Symbols of American Community, 1735–1775.* New Haven, Conn.: Yale University Press, 1966.

NAMIER, LEWIS. *England in the Age of the American Revolution.* New York: 1966. Originally published in 1931.

NEWBOLD, ROBERT C. *The Albany Congress and the Plan of Union of 1754.* New York: Vantage Press, 1955.

NYE, RUSSELL B. *This Almost Chosen People: Essays in the History of American Ideas.* East Lansing, Mich.: Michigan State University Press, 1966.

SACHS, WILLIAM S. "Interurban Correspondents and the Development of a National Economy before the Revolution." *New York History*, 36 (1955): 320–335.

SLOTKIN, RICHARD. *Regeneration through Violence: The Mythology of the American Frontier, 1600–1860.* Middletown, Conn.: Wesleyan University Press, 1973.

SMITH, WILLIAM. "The Colonial Post Office." *American Historical Review*, 21 (1916): 259–275.

TUVESON, ERNEST L. *Redeemer Nation: The Idea of America's Millennial Role.* Chicago: University of Chicago Press, 1968.

VARG, PAUL A. "The Advent of Nationalism, 1758–1776." *American Quarterly*, 16 (1964): 169–181.

WARD, HARRY M. "The Search for American Identity: Early Historians of New England." In *Perspectives on Early American History*, ed. Alden T. Vaughan and George A. Billias. New York: Harper & Row, 1973.

———. *"Unite or Die": Intercolony Relations, 1690–1763.* Port Washington, N.Y.: Kennikat Press, 1971.

ZUCKERMAN, MICHAEL. "The Fabrication of Identity in Early America." *William and Mary Quarterly*, 3d ser., 34 (1977): 183–214.

Index

Anatomy, 287, 289, 292
  study of, 293
Andover, Mass., 156, 162
Androboros, a Biographical Farce . . . (1714),
  308
Andros, Sir Edmund, 234, 254–56
Angel of Bethesda (1723), 292
Anglican Church. *See* Church of England;
  Anglicans
Anglicans, 62, 65, 208, 281
Anglo-Dutch Wars:
  1652–54, 54
  1664–67, 60, 66
  1672–74, 61, 249
Anglo-French War:
  (1626–30), 348
  (1666–67), 348
Aniello, Tommaso ("Masaniello"), 258
Annapolis, Md., 143, 155, 181, 204, 314
  urban design of, 181
Annapolis Royal (Port Royal), 352
Anne Arundel County, Md., 262
Annesley, James, 127
Anticosti Island, 352
Antinomianism, 50
Anti-Quartering Act (1679), 239
Antislavery movement, 145–49, 209–13
  and religious groups, 209–10
Apalachee Indians, 339, 343, 352
Apothecaries, 293
Appalachian Mountains, 87, 111, 329–31,
  237
Appomattox River, 330
Apprentices (apprenticeship), 92, 97–98,
  123, 125–26, 188
Aquidneck Island, R.I., 50, 54
Arawak Indians (Haiti), 10
Arbella (ship), 36, 46
Archbishop of Canterbury, 233, 271
Archbishop of York, 39
Archdale, John, 310
Architecture, 298–302
  Dutch, 301
  Georgian, 302
  neo-Palladianism, 302
  Palladianism, 301
  Philadelphia townhouses, 300
  Renaissance neoclassicism, 301
  public buildings, 301
Areopagitica (1644), 233
Argall, Samuel, 348
Aristotle, 290
Arithmetic, Vulgar and Decimal (1729), 326
Arizona, 12
Ark (ship), 32
Arkansas, 12
Arkansas River, 329
Arlington, Henry Bennet, earl of, 73, 249
Arlington-Culpeper land grant, 73–74
Armagh County, Ire., 112
Arminianism, 275, 283
Arminius, Jacob, 283
Army:
  British troops in America, 102, 239–40,
    251–52, 256, 258, 357–63
  desertion, 218
  military establishment in the colonies, 377
  standing armies, 238
  See colonial wars; French and Indian

War; militia; quartering troops;
  Virginia regiment
Arson, 210
Arthur, Gabriel, 330
Ash, Thomas, 310
Ashley River, S.C., 65, 143–44
Asia, 1, 3, 9–10, 12, 14, 16, 96
Asiento, 133, 352–53
Assembly, freedom of, 236–37
Assistants: Mass., 46–48. *See* individual New
  England colonies
Astronomical Diary and Almanack, 322
Astronomical Observatory (Norriton, Pa.),
  289
Astronomy, 287, 325
Atherton Company, 114
Atkin, Edmund, 342
Augsburg, Ger., 8
Augusta County, Va., 205
Augusta, Ga., 70, 330
Austin and Laurens, firm of, 134
Australia, 57
Austria, 349, 355
Avalon (Newfoundland), 30
Avilés, Menéndez de, 14
Axtell, James, 323
Ayllón, Lucas Vasquez, 63
Azores (islands), 9, 11
Aztecs, 5

Bacchanalian Revel (painting), 297
Bachelors, 156
Backus, Rev. Isaac, 282
Bacon, Nathaniel, Jr., 250–52
Bacon, Nathaniel, Sr., 250
Bacon's Rebellion, 232, 248–53, 318
Badger, Joseph, 298
Baffin Island, 6
Baffin Bay, 16
Bahamas, 10, 86, 132, 220
Bailyn, Bernard, 192, 206
Balboa, Vasco Nuñez de, 11
Baltimore, Md., 79, 177
Banister, John, 290
Baptists, 38, 49, 62, 115, 147, 228, 230,
  275–76, 281–82, 327, 371
  English Baptists, 275–76; becomes
    Regular Baptists, 276
  General, Free Will, Particular, Six
    Principle, and Seventh Day Baptists,
    275
  German Baptists. *See* Dunkards
  London Confession, 275
  persecution of, 228
  Philadelphia Association, 275, 282
  Separate Baptists, 222, 275–78, 281–82
  Warren Association, 282
  Welsh Baptists,, 275–76
Barbados, 30, 65–66, 148, 166, 179, 220
  Barbadians settle in Carolina, 64–65
Barbour, Arthur, 17
Barcelona, Spain, 10
Barker, William, 126
Barnes, Richard, 231
Barnwell, Col. John, 315, 344
Barre and the Cubb (ca. 1665), 307
Barrington, R.I., 115
Barrow, Henry, 38
Barton, Andrew, 308

Boylston, Dr. Zabdiel, 183
Braddock, Gen. Edward, 341, 357–59
Braddock's expedition and defeat, 239,
    357–59, 362
Braddock's road, 332, 358
Bradford, Alice, 156
Bradford, Andrew, 319–20
Bradford, Cornelia, 323
Bradford, Gov. William, 39–40, 43, 310,
    312
Bradford, William (the printer), 234–35,
    319, 321
Bradstreet, Anne, 156, 304, 315–16
Bradstreet, Col. John, 346, 360
Bradstreet, Gov. Simon, 256, 315
Bradstreet family, 168
Braintree, Mass., 85, 89, 158
Branford (New Haven-Conn. colonies), 52
Brattle, Rev. William, 289
Brattle Street Church (Boston), 283
Bray, Rev. Thomas, 69, 147, 271
Brazil, 11
Brent, George, 250
Brent, Margaret, 215
Brethren, Churches of, 274
Brethren of the Separation of the First
    English Church, 39
Brewster, Sackford, 330
Brewster, William, 39
Bridenbaugh, 16
Bridges, Charles, 298
*Brief History of the War of the Indians in New-
    England* (1676), 312
Brief Meditations (1711), 311
Brief and Plain Scheme for Union (1697), 375
Brief and True Report . . . (by Hariot, 1588),
    17
Bristol, Eng., 7, 44, 46, 124, 220
    merchants of, 20, 44
Bristol, Pa., 201
Bristol, R.I., 133
*Britain's Commercial Interest Explained and
    Improved* (1757), 377
British merchants, 107–8, 152, 179. *See*
    listed cities and trading companies
British navy, 102. *See* colonial wars
Britton, James, 213
Broad Bay, Va., 18
Broadsides, 321–22, 271
Brockunier, Samuel, 50
Brooklyn (L.I.), 60–61
Brothels, 185–86
Brown, Charlotte, 156
Brownists. *See* Separatists.
Brown, Josias, 259
Brown, Katherine B., 203
Brown, Richard, 46
Brown, Robert E., 203
Brown University, 281, 327. *See also* College
    of Rhode Island
"Brutal filter," 110
Bryan, Hugh, 280
Bry, Théodor de, 17
Bubble Act of 1720, 107
Bucks County, Pa., 199
Bull, Gov. William, Jr., 143, 195
Bull Bay, S.C., 65
Bumsted, J.M., 279, 378
Bureau of American Ethnology, 4

Burgess, Jane, 154
Burglary, 210
Burlington, N.J., 149, 204, 271
Burling, William, 148
Burman, 1
Burnaby, Rev. Andrew, 371
Burnet, Gov. William, 174
Burroughs, Rev. George, 216
Burton, Mary, 145
Burwell, Lewis, 157
Burwell, Lucy, 157
Burwell, Robert, 170
Bushman, Richard L., 207
Busy-Body (1709), 307
Bushy Run, battle of, 346
Business (retail), 154–55, 219–20
Byllynge, Edward, 62
Byrd, Mrs. Lucy Parke, 315
Byrd, Ursula (Mrs. Robert Beverly), 157,
    326
Byrd, William I, 114, 166, 326
Byrd, William II, 65, 138, 142, 148,
    156–57, 160, 170, 172–73, 179, 185,
    198, 221, 293–94, 310, 312, 314–15;
    writings of, 314–15
Byrd, William III, 170, 175, 345

Cabot, John, 12, 15, 19
Cabot, Sebastian, 7, 12, 15, 19
Cabral, Gonçalo Velho, 7
Cabral, Pero Alvarez, 11
Caciques, 64
Cahokia, 329
Calcutta, India, 9
Calvert, Benedict, 262
Calvert, Cecilius, second baron of
    Baltimore, 31–33, 260
Calvert, George, first baron of Baltimore,
    30
Calvert, Gov. Charles, third baron of
    Baltimore, 260–62
Calvert, Gov. Leonard, 32–33, 152, 260
Calvert, Gov. Philip, 34, 260
Calvin, John, 8, 162, 273
Calvinism, 8, 58, 275, 283, 317
Cambridge Agreement (Mass. Bay Co.), 44
Cambridge, Mass., 51, 234, 289, 321–22
Cambridge Platform, 268–69
Cambridge University, 37, 48, 293
Camisards (French Prophets), 225
Campbell, John, 318
Campbell, Mildred, 124–25
Campbelltown, N.C. *See* Fayetteville
Canada, 7, 103, 120, 240, 330, 378, 379;
    French surrender, 361. *See* New
    France; colonial Wars
Canary Islands, 9, 11, 84
*Candidates; or, the Humours of a Virginia
    Election* (ca. 1770), 206, 308
Canso, Nova Scotia, 355
Cape Anne, 44
Cape Breton Island, 12, 85, 103, 352, 355,
    361
Cape Charles, Va., 20. *See* Chesapeake Bay,
    Capes
Cape Cod, 6, 40–41, 57, 207
Cape Fear, 63–64, 220
Cape Fear River, 20, 339
Cape Fear Valley and region, 87, 114, 208

Cape Finisterre (Spain), 100, 139
Cape Hatteras, 63
Cape Henry, Va., 20. *See* Chesapeake Bay, Capes
Cape Verde Islands, 9, 11
Caporael, Linnda R., 217
Card games, 174
Careful and Strict Enquiry into . . . Freedom of the Will (1754), 286
Carey (Dragon) plow, 80
Carolina, 4, 13, 78, 87, 97, 101, 111, 115
 coasts—Outer Banks, 17, 20
 charter, 63–64, 229
 frontier, 79
 piedmont, 113, 333
 promotion of, 310
 proprietors, 65, 77, 79, 116
 Separation of N.C. and S.C., 65
 See North Carolina, South Carolina, Albemarle region
Carpenter, Mary, 156
Carpenters Company of Philadelphia, 93
Carroll, Bishop John, 276
Carroll, Thomas, 325
Cartegena (Columbia), 353–54; British-American expedition, 368
Carter, London, 76, 78, 81, 138, 162–63, 170, 200, 289, 305, 315
Carter, Lucy, 305
Carter, Robert "King," 133, 198
Carter, Robert "Bob" (son of Robert Carter of Nomini Hall), 157
Carter, Robert (of Nomini Hall), 157, 305
Carter, Robert Wormeley, 162, 170
Carteret, Sir George, 62–64
Carteret, John (earl of Granville), 65, 73
Cartier, Jacques, 14, 348
Carver, John, 39, 41, 43.
Carver, William, 252
Cary, Thomas, 263–64
Castiglione, Baldassare, comte, 170
Castle Island (Boston harbor), 48
Castle William (Boston harbor), 186, 256
"Catalog of Plants, Fruits . . . Virginia," 291
Catawba Indians, 179, 338–39, 344
Catawba River, 102, 339, 344
Catesby, Mark, 291
Catholics, 8, 30–34, 37, 69, 115–118, 199, 204, 214, 228–29, 255, 261, 270, 276
 anti-Catholicism, 257
 Catholic-French conspiracy (alleged), 247
 German Catholics, 276
 "Great Fear" in Maryland, 261–62
 vicar apostolic of London, 276
 See Jesuits
Cato's Letters, 192, 366
Catskill Mountains, 331
Cattle, 77, 78, 105
 plague of 1672 in Virginia, 249
 range cattle industry, 79
 rustling, 79–80
 See also livestock husbandry
Cavan County, Ire., 112
Cayuga Indians, 4, 336
Céleron de Blanville, Pierre-Joseph, 356
Censorship, 255
Centlivre, Susanna, 307
Chaco (Indian boy, Virginia), 28
Chafee, Zechariah, Jr., 226–27, 232
Chalmers, Dr. Lionel, 293
Champlain, Samuel de, 14, 348

Chancellor of the Exchequer, 193
Charitable Irish Society (Boston), 190
Charles, Duke of Albany, 20
Charles I, 28, 30–31, 48, 53, 61, 88, 192
Charles II, 51, 53, 60, 63, 66, 68, 73, 117, 133, 228, 248, 252
Charles II of Spain, 351
Charles VI (emperor, Holy Roman Empire), 351
Charles County, Md., 262
Charles City County, Va., 29, 248
Charles River (Mass.), 44
Charles River County, Va., 29. *See also* York County
Charleston, S.C., 65, 79, 91, 99–100, 114, 116, 141, 143, 155, 169, 177, 179, 203, 220, 222, 280, 291, 319
 fire of 1704, 183, 1740, 301
 Indian trade, 330
 merchants, 104
 social clubs, 176
 urban design, 181
Charlestown, Mass., 212
Charterhouse School, Eng., 48
Charter of Liberties and Privileges (N.Y., 1683), 61, 230, 239, 243, 257
Charter of Privileges (Pa., 1701), 68–69
Charters (colonial), 226. *See* listings for individual colonies
Chattahoochee River, 339
Chauncey, Nathaniel, 306
Chauncy, Rev. Charles, 280, 283
Cheever, Exekial, 326
Chemistry, 287, 289–90; phlogiston theory, 290
Cherokees, 4, 224, 330, 339, 340, 344–5
Cherokee War (1759–61), 137, 225, 344–45
Cherry Valley, N.Y., 332
Chesapeake Capes, 220
Chesapeake Bay, 17, 19, 63, 68, 89, 223, 259. *See* Chapter 2
Chesapeake colonies:
 aristocracy, 166–67
 Society, 159, 163
Cheseldyne, Kenelm, 262
Chesepiooc Indian village (Va.), 17–18
"Chester" (Hymn), 306
Chester, Pa., 199, 201
Chicheley, Sir Henry, 250
Chickahominy River, Va., 21
Chichasaw Indians, 339–40, 344
Child, Dr. Robert, 48, 227
Child, Josiah, 96
Childbearing (slave women), 139
Childbirth, 159–60
 infant mortality, 160
Children, 152, 159–62
Children of Light. *See* Quakers
Chilton, Edward, 313
China, 1, 3, 10, 15
Chippewa Indians, 336, 345, 356
Choctaw Indians, 4, 339
Choptank Indians (Md.), 34
Choptico Indians (Md.), 34
Chowan County, N.C., 221
Chowan River, 221
Christiaensen, Hendrick, 57
Christian Commonwealth (1659), 234
Christian History, 320
Christian Philosopher (1720), 285–86

Cotterill, R. S., 339
Cotton, 91, 96, 132
Cotton, Rev. John, 52, 173, 285, 303, 326
Council (colonial government), 197–98
Council for Foreign Plantations, 193
"Council for the Safety and . . . of the
    Peace" (Mass.), 256
Council of New England, 40, 44, 59–60,
    254–55
Council of State (Parliament), 97
Counsel, right to, 243–44
Counter Blaste to Tobacco (1604), 26
Counterfeiting, 210, 212
County courts, 202–3
County government, 202–3
Courts (England):
    Assize, 61
    Chancery, 254
    Common Pleas, 227
    Exchequer, 227
    King's Bench, 28, 48, 68, 227
    Wards and Liveries, 46
    See also Old Bailey
Courtship, 157–58
Couture, Jean, 330
Covenant of grace, 37–38, 268
Cowle's Tavern, Va., 307
Coxe, Daniel, 376
Craftsmen (artisans), 92–93, 124, 154, 204,
    295
    protest action, 93
    standard of living, 377
    See also Apprentices
Cranfield, Gov. Edward, 195, 253
Craven County, S.C., 65
Craven, Gov. Charles, 344
Craven, William, earl of, 63
Credit and marketing, 103–4. See also
    commission agents
Creek Indians, 4, 339, 343
Cress, Lawrence D., 239
Cresswell, Nicholas, 173
Cressy, David, 323
Crevecoeur, Michel-Guillaume Jean de (also
    known as Crevecoeur, J. Hector St.
    John de), 120, 366
Crimes, 27, 33–34, 184–85, 209–14
    capital offenses, 24, 127–28, 130, 143,
    231, 243
    clemency, pardon, amnesty, 210–11
    criminal codes, 209–11
    sexual crimes, 157–58, 213–14, 225
    wife beating, 152
    See also benefit of clergy, executions,
    punishments, slaves, witchcraft, and
    individual listings of certain crimes
Criminals: intercolonial gangs, 211–12, 222
Croatoan Indians, 17–18
Croghan, George, 332
Cro-magnon man, 3
Cromwell, Oliver, 29, 60, 66, 88, 97, 113,
    227, 233, 248, 260, 270
Cronon, William, 77
Crops, 75–76. See agriculture and
    individual listings
Cross Creek, N.C., 179
Crown Point. See forts
Crusades, 1
Cuba, 10, 362
Culloden, Moor, Scotland, battle of (April
    1746), 112

Culpeper, John, 263
Culpeper, Thomas, baron of Thoresway,
    73–74, 197, 221, 249
Cumberland County, Pa., 199, 332
Cumberland Gap, 331
Cumberland Island (Ga.), 353
Cumberland Mountains and valley, 331–32,
    339
Cunningham, Waddell, 242
Curaçao, 58
Curles Neck (James River), 250
Currency Act of 1751, 108
Currency Act of 1764, 108
Currituck County, N.C., 221
Currituck Inlet, N.C., 221
Cushman, Robert, 40, 156
Customary (local) law (Eng.), 227
"Custom of the country," 126
Customs officials, 97, 240–41, 375, 380
    Commissioner of the Customs, 97, 193
Cuyahoga River, 332

Daingerfield plantation, Va., 158
Dale code, 24, 213, 231
Dale, Sir Thomas, 24, 366. See Dale code
Dancing, 156, 173
Danes, 58
Danforth, Rev. Samuel, 36, 289
Daniel, Gov. Robert, 263
Dankarts, Jasper, 222
Darnall, Henry, 262
Dartmouth (New Bedford, Mass.), 85
Dartmouth College, 281, 327
D'Avenant, Sir Charles, 375
Davenport, Rev. James, 280
Davenport, Rev. John, 52
Davie, Edmund, 293
Davies, Rev. Samuel, 280, 370
Davis, John, 15
Davis Strait, 16
Dawson, Elizabeth, 155
Day, John, 7
Daye, Stephen, 321–22
Day of Doom . . . the Great and Last Judgment
    (1662), 316–17
Dean George Berkeley and His Family
    (painting), 296
Debtors, 69, 126, 207
Decennium luctuosum (1699), 315
Declaration of Independence, 135
"Declaration . . . Inhabitants of Boston and
    the Country Adjacent" (1689), 255
"Declaration of the People" (Bacon's
    Rebellion), 251
"Declaration of the Protestant Association"
    (Md.), 262
Declaration of 1646 (Mass.), 227
Decorative arts, 295
Dedham, Mass., 156, 163, 322
Deerfield, Mass., 343
Defamation, 215, 231
Deism, 283–84, 286
    deistical societies, 284
De Lancey, Lt. Gov. James, 357
De Lancey family, 115, 166, 171, 207, 235
Delaware, 20, 56, 61, 68–69, 91, 101, 229
Delaware Bay, 57, 60, 68
Delaware Indians, 5, 297, 336, 340,
    345–46, 356
Delaware Prophet, 345

Geneva, Switzerland, 8, 162
Genoa, Italy, 8–9, 12
Gentleman's Magazine, 128, 319
Gentlemen:
  behavior, 170
  qualities of, 170–71 *See* social structure
Geology, 287
George II, 241
Georgia:
  aristrocracy, 166–67
  founding of, 56–57, 69–70, 353
Georgia–Creek treaty of 1768, 333
German Baptist Brethren, 273–74. *See* Dunkards
Germanna, Va., 89, 111
German Reformed churches, 110, 273
Germans, 58, 68, 70, 78–79, 110–13, 115, 118–19, 125, 158, 225, 273, 295, 332–33, 343–44
Germantown, Pa., 110, 147–48, 223, 274, 305, 319, 325
Germany, 109, 115, 119, 223, 273–74, 290
Gibbes, Henry, 296
Gibbes, Margaret, 296
Gibbes, Robert, 296
Gibralter, 352
Gibson, Arnell, 4
Gibson, Lawrence H., 371
Gilbert, Bartholomew, 20
Gilbert, Humphrey, 15, 17, 19
Gilbert, Raleigh, 44
Gilje, Paul A., 185
Gist, Christopher, 331
Glasgow, Scotland, 104
  University of, 272
Glass manufacturing, 91, 295
Glen, Gov. James, 355
Glorious Revolution (England), 88, 247, 255–57
  in New England, 247
  in New York, 247
  in Maryland, 248
  See Leisler's Rebellion
Gloucester County, Va., 158, 236, 248, 252, 290
Gloucester, Mass., 84
Glover, John, 293
Glover, William, 263
Godfrey, Thomas, 308
God's Controversy with New England (1873), 317
Godspeed (ship), 20
Godwin, Morgan, 147
Goebel, Julius, Jr., 227
Goldstein, Thomas, 7–8
Golf, 174
Gooch, Gov. William, 78, 354–55
Goode, John, 251–52
Goodhue, Sarah, 156
Good News from New England (1624), 310
Gookin, Daniel, 312
Goose Creek (S.C.) men, 65, 143, 264. *See* also Barbadians
Gordon, Thomas, 192, 366
Gorges, Sir Ferdinando, 44, 48
Gorton, Samuel, 51, 231
Gosnold, Bartholomew, 20
Gouverneur, Abraham, 259
Gove, Edward, 254
Government:
  imperial relations, 192, 378–80,

See also individual listings
Governor, role and duties of, 97, 195–97
Graffenried, Christopher baron de, 343
Grand Alliance, 349
Grand Banks (Newfoundland), 83–84
Grand Ohio Company, 335. *See also* Indiana Company
Grant, Col. James, 137, 345, 361
Grant, Temperance, 155
Graphic arts, 295
Gravesand, L. I. 60, 155
Great Awakening, 158, 190, 207, 229, 272, 275–81, 320, 367, 370–371
  effects of, 280–81
  enthusiasm, 277
  Middle colonies, 277
  New England, 277–80
  Southern Awakening, 280
Great Danger Swamp, Va., 252
Great Lakes 4, 87, 329, 338, 348. *See* individual listings
Great Lakes Indians, 345
Great Meadows (Pa.), capture of Virginia regiment, 357. *See also* Fort Necessity
Great Migration (Mass.), 46, 68
Great Plains (U.S.), 12
Great Swamp fight (1675), 55
Great Valley of Virginia, 74, 113. *See also* Shenandoah Valley
Great Wagon Road, 79, 333
Greeks in America, 116
  Greek-Corsicans, 116
Green, Jonas, 319
Green, Samuel, 234
Greenberg, Douglas, 211
Greenbrier Company, 334
Greenbrier River, 334–35
Greene, Ann Catherine, 154
Greene, Evarts B., 136
Greene, Jack P., 192, 363, 366
Greenland, 6, 16
"Green Spring" faction (Va.), 249
Greenwich, New Haven-Conn. colony, 52, 114
Greenwood, Isaac, 326
Greenwood, John (artist), 297
Greenwood, John (English Separatist), 38
Grenville, George, 116, 377, 380
Greven, Philip J., Jr., 161–63
Gridley, Jeremiah, 241, 320
Griffiths, William, 378
Gristmills, 90
Gronovius, John Frederick, 290–91
Groseilliers, Médard Chouart, Sieur des, 329
Groton Manor (Eng.), 45
Grymes, John, 198
Guadeloupe, 378
Gualdo, John, 305
Guale Indians, 339
Guardian, 318–19
Guild Hall (London), 202
Guilford, New Haven-Conn. colony, 52
Gulf of California, 12
Gulf of Darien (Columbia), 353
Gulf of Mexico, 12, 330
Gulf Plains (U.S.), 4, 12, 16
Gulf of the St. Lawrence River, 14, 84
Gunpowder Plot (1605), 172. *See also* Pope's Day

Ministry Act (N.Y., 1693), 230
Minnesota, 6
Minorca, 352
  Minorcans, 116
Minuit, Peter, 57
Miquelon Island, 362
Mississippi (state), 339
"Mississippi Bubble," 349
Mississippi Company, 335
Mississippi River, 4, 12, 63, 329, 335–36,
  347–48
Mitchell, Dr. John, 291, 293, 367
Mittelberger, Gottlieb, 111
Modell of Christian Charity (1629)
Modest Enquiry into the Nature and Necessity of
  Paper Currency (1729), 108
Mohawk Indians, 4, 336, 341, 355. See also
  Iroquois
Mohawk River, 114, 332
  Mohawk valley, 111
Mohican Indians, 5
Molasses, 90, 97–98, 102
Molasses Act (1733), 98
Monck, George, duke of Albemarle, 63
Monckton, Lt. Col. Robert, 359
Money, 104–8
  bills of credit (government promissary
    notes), 106–8
  bills of exchange, 106
  commodity money, 105
  coins in Mass., 105
  cropping of coins, 105
  exchange rate, 107
  foreign coins, 105
    specie and coins, 151
  paper money, 106–8
  tobacco (warehouse) notes, 106
  wampum, 105
  See Land banks; Silver banks
Monmouth grant, N.J., 62, 236
Monmouth, James Scott, duke of, 127
Monocacy River (Md.–Pa.), 111
Monongahela River, 340, 345, 357–59
Monopolies, 93–94
Monro, Col. George, 360
Montauk Indians, 5
Montcalm, Gen. Louis-Joseph, marquis de,
  360–61
Montgomery, Col. Archibald, 345
Montreal, 14, 347, 350, 352
Moody, Lady Deborah, 155
Moore, Gov. James, 330, 351
Moore, James, Jr. (revolutionary governor),
  265, 344
Moore, William, 219
Moors, 9
Moravia, 223
Moravians, 70, 110, 223–24, 273, 306, 333
Moray, Rev. Alexander, 271
Morgan, Edmund S., 22, 130, 323
Morgan, Philip D., 142
Morison, Samuel E., 6
Morris, Chief Justice (N.Y.) and Gov. (N.J.)
  Lewis, 195, 235
Morris family, N.Y., 166, 207
Morton, Nathaniel, 312
Morton, Rev. Charles, 289–90, 311
Morton, Thomas, 42–43, 310
Moses His Judicialls (written 1636), 52
Mosquito Inlet, Fla., 116
Mount Airy, N.C., 222

Mount Desert Island, 348
Mount Vernon, Va., 78, 354
Mourt's Relation (1622), 41–42, 310
Mozambique, 9
Muhlenberg, Henry Melchoir, 273
Müller, Heinrich, 319, 333
Mullin, Gerald W., 138, 142
Mundus novus (1507), 11
Munford, Robert, 206, 308
Munford, William, 308
Murphy, James, 130
Murrin, John M., 245
Muscovy Company, 15, 18
Music, 175–76, 303–307
  composition, 289
  concerts, 306
  instruments, 289, 304–305
  opera, 306
  Puritans and, 303–305
  singing, 303–6
Muskinghum River, 331
Muskogean (Muskhogean) Indian stock, 4,
  339
Musschenbrock, Pieter van, 387
Mutiny, 210, 218, 255
Mutiny Act (1689), 239–40
"My Days Have Been So Wondrous Free"
  (song), 306
Myles, Rev. John, 115
Myrick, Timothy, 307

McCormick, Richard P., 203–4
McDonald, Ellen Shapiro, 109
McDonald, Forrest, 109
McDougall, Alexander, 235–36
McKinley, Albert E., 203

Namier, Sir Lewis, 379
Nanfan, Ltd. Gov. John, 340
Nansemond County, Va., 117
Nansemond River, 23
Nantucket, 85
Naples, Italy, 10
Narragansett Bay, 13, 49
Narragansett Indians, 5, 49, 55
Narrative of the Troubles with the Indians of
  New-England (1677), 312
Narváez, Panfilo de, 12
Nash, Gary, 187
Nassau (Bahamas), 220
Natchez Indians, 344
Natick Indians, 5
National Geographic, 10
Natural history, 290–91
Natural History of Carolina, Florida and the
  Bahama Islands (1731 and 1743), 291
"Natural History of Virginia" (Banister),
  290
Naturalization, 116–18
Natural philosophy, 287–90
Naumkeag, Mass., 44, 46. See also Salem
Nautical technology, 1, 9
Nautilus (submarine), 16
Naval stores, 85–87, 97, 100, 102, 105, 111,
  119
Navigation Acts, 56, 68, 96–98, 100, 219,
  254–55
Nazareth, Pa., 111, 224
Neale, Thomas, 372
Necotowance (Indian chief), 29
Needham, James, 330

Recruiting Officer (1706), 307
Redemptioners, 110, 123, 125–26, 128, 273. See also Indentured servants
Rediker, Marcus, 218–19
Redwood Library, Newport, R.I., 302
Reed, John, 378
Referendum, 51
Reformation (Protestant), 8, 36, 38. See Puritans; Separatists; Chapter 18
Reformed churches (Europe), 8, 276. See Dutch Reformed Church; German Reformed Church
Regicides, 53
Regulators (N.C.), 265
Regulators (S.C.), 222
Rehoboth, Plymouth-Mass. colonies, 115
Reinsch, Paul S., 227
Relación que Dio Alvar Nuñez, Cabeça de Vaca . . . (1542), 12
Religion, Chapter 18, baptism, 160
  freedom of worship (toleration), 31, 33–34, 58, 62, 64, 69, 228–30
  separation of church and state, 48–49
  tithes, 112
Rembert, Peter, 225
Remonstrance of 1646, 48
Renaissance, 7, 171
Rensselaerswyck, 155
Repartimientos, 11
Restoration (Eng.), 56, 88, 115, 193, 229, 233, 253, 260
Revere family, 115
Revere, Paul, 93
Revolutionary War, 230, 282, 293, 308, 321, 335, 368
  pension applications, 369. See also American Revolution
Rhett, Col. William, 220
Rhineland, 37, 68, 111
Rhine River, 39
Rhode Island, founding of, 48–51, 229
  charter, 51, 229
  government, 51
Ribaut, Jean, 14
Rice, 65, 75–77, 80, 97, 100, 105, 122, 131
Richardson, Elizabeth, 215
Richelieu, Armand Jean du Plesis, Cardinal-duc de, 348
Richelieu River, 350, 355
Richmond County, N.Y., 257
Richmond, Va., 21, 88, 114, 177, 179, 308
Rights of the British Colonies Asserted and Proved (1764), 379
Rights (liberties) of Englishmen, 226–28
Rind, Clementine, 154, 323
Rio de la Plata (South America), 13
Rio Grande River, 4, 12
Riot Act (Eng., 1714), 236
Riots, 185–86, 205, 236–37, 363. See also Assembly, Freedom of
Rising, Johan, 58
Rittenhouse, David, 289
Roanoke Island ("Lost" colony), 17–19, 63, 310
Roanoke River, 250, 331, 339
  valley, 331
Roberval, Jean-François de la Rocque, Sieur de, 14, 348
Robie, Thomas, 289
Robins, Aaron, 79

Robinson, John (Va., Speaker of House of Burgesses), 334
Robinson, Rev. John, 39
Rogers, Robert, 308
Rogers, Gov. Woodes, 220
Rolfe, John, 25–26
Rolfe, Thomas, 26
Rope maing, 85, 91
Rose, Rev. Robert, 77
Rosewall plantation, Va., 289
Rosicrucians, 223
Rossiter, Clinton, 203
Rotterdam, Neth., 110
Rousby, Christopher, 262
Rowan County, N.C., 344
Rowe, Nicholas, 307
Rowlandson, Mrs. Mary, 156, 315
Roxborough (Pa.), 91
Roxbury, Mass., 46, 51
Royal Academy, 299
Royal African Company, 133–34
Royal disallowance, 68, 135, 194
Royal Navy, 218
Royal Society for Improving Natural Knowledge (Eng.), 195, 286–87; *Transactions* of, 290
"Rule of 1756," 102
Rules of Civility and Decent Behavior in Company, 170
Rumsey, Nancy, 155
Russia, 355
Rut, John, 15
Rutgers University, 281, 327. See Queens College.

Sabbath observance, 37, 49, 184, 201, 255
Saco River, Maine, 343
Sagadahoc River, 44
St. Andrew's Society, 176, 190, 344
St. Augustine, Fla., 14, 63, 143, 351, 354
St. Brendan, 5
St. Charles River (Canada), 350
St. Clair, Sir John, 355
St. Clement's (Blakiston) Island, 32, 34
St. Croix River, 332, 348
St. George, Robert, 231
St. George's Md., 34
St. Helena's Parish, S.C., 280
St. James's Palace (London), 26
St. Johns River, Fla., 70, 353–54
St. Kitts (St. Christopher) Island, 352
St. Lawrence River, 4, 14, 348, 350, 352, 355, 359, 361
St. Martin's Island, 58
St. Mary's County, Md., 34
St. Mary's, Md., 32, 34, 154, 234, 260, 262
St. Mary's River (St. George's), 32
St. Michael's Church, Philadelphia, 273
St. Michael's, Md., 34
St. Pierre Island, 362
St. Simons Island, Ga., 353
St. Stephen's Church, London, 52
Salem, Mass., 46, 48–49, 84–85, 121, 187, 245
  Salem church, 49, 232
  Salem Town, 217
  Salem Village, 217
Salem, N.J., 91
Salem, N.C., 224
Salisbury Iron Works, 89
Salisbury, N.C., 333

Tugaloo River, 339
Tule Springs, Nevada, 3
Tull, Jethro, 81
Turkey, 21
   Turks, 263. *See also* Levant
Turnbull, Dr. Andrew, 116
Turner, Thomas, 173
Turnstall, Martha, 155
Tuscarora Indians, 4, 264, 315, 336, 339,
   343–44
Tuscarora War (1711–12), 264, 343
Twightwee Indians, 338. *See* Miami Indians
Two Penny Act, Va., 378–79
Tyler, Lyon G., 379
Tynte, Gov. Edward, 264

Ulster County, N.Y., 258
Ulster Province, Ire., 112
Underhill, John, 53, 314
Union Fire Company (Philadelphia), 183
Uniontown, Pa., 357
Unitarianism, 283
United Colonies of New England. *See* New
   England Confederation
United States Magazine, 321
University of Franeker (Franeker, Neth.) 58
Urania (1761), 306
Urban conditions and life, 177–90
   law enforcement, 184
   urban government, Chapter 13
   urban and town planning, 177–82
Ury, John, 145
Usher, John, 375
Ursulines, 348

Vaca, Alvar Nuñez Cabaza de, 12, 78
Vade Mecum for America . . . (1732), 367
Vagrancy, 27, 79, 123, 189, 362
   laws, 123, 126
Vance, Hugh, 107
Van Cortlandt family, 166, 171
Van Cortlandt, Maria, 155
Van Cortlandt, Stephanus, 73
Vandalia, 335
Van Dam, Rip, 235
Vane, Sir Henry, 50
Van Rensselaer, Jeremias, 155
Van Rensselaer, Kiliaen van, 57
Vaughan, Alden T., 339
Vaughan, Lord Chief Justice John, 68
Venice, Italy, 12
Verrazzano, Giovanni da, 13–14
Vernon, Admiral Edward, 353–54
Vespucci, Amerigo, 10–11
Vestry Act (Eng.), 263
Vetch, Samuel, 352
Villafana, Angel de, 63
Vikings, 3, 5–7
*Vindication of the Government of New-England
   Churches* (1717), 191
Vinland, 6
Virginia, founding, Chapter 2
   Great Charter, 27
   becomes royal colony, 29. *See* Virginia
      Company
Virginia Company, 20, 24, 26–27, 30–31,
   40, 44, 63, 73, 121
   charters, 20, 24, 27–28, 30
Virginia (ship), 85

Wabash River, 335
Wachovia, N.C., 224

Waldseemüller, Martin, 11
Wales, 90, 115
Walker, Admiral Hovenden, 352
Walker, Dr. Thomas, 331
Wallace, Samuel, 378
Walley, John, 315
Walloons, 57, 114
Walpole, Sir Robert, 353
Walton, Gary M., 99–100
Walter, Thomas, 306
Wampanoag Indians, 5, 41, 49, 55
War of 1812, 346
War of the Austrian Succession (1740–48),
   354. *See* King George's War
War of Jenkins's Ear (1739–42), 144, 224,
   353–54
War of the League of Augsburg (1688–97),
   111, 349. *See* King William's War
War Office (British), 193
War of the Spanish Succession (1701–14),
   111, 351. See Queen Anne's War
Warm (Berkeley) Springs, Va., 170, 185
Warning out, 186–88
Warning Out Book (Boston), 187
Warrasqueake (also Warrasqueoc, etc.)
   County (later Isle of Wight County),
   Va., 29
Warren, Commodore Sir Peter, 355
Warren, R.I., 115, 282
Warrior's Path, Ky., 331
Wars of Religion (France), 8, 14
Wars of the Roses (1455–85), 7
Warwick, R.I., 51
Warwick River County, Va., 29
Warwick, Robert Rich, earl of, 28
Washington, Col. John, 166, 215, 250
Washington, George, 155, 163, 170,
   173–75, 215, 217, 315, 333, 335, 354,
   357
   burgess candidate, 205
   in French and Indian War, 357, 368
   as planter, 78, 81
Washington, Lawrence, 354
Wateree River, 338
Waterford, Pa., 356
Watertown, Mass., 46
Waverley (1814), 127
Weaver, Nathaniel, 253
Webbe, John, 320
Webb, Gen. Daniel, 240, 359–60
Weber, Jacob, 225
   "Weber heresy," 225
Weeden, William B., 105
Weedon, George, 173
Welde (or Weld), Thomas, 304, 327
Wells, Robert V., 157
Wells, Maine, 343
Welsh, 68, 115, 118
"Welsh Tract," Pa., 115, 275
Wentworth, Gov. Benning, 195
Wentworth, Gen. Thomas, 354
Wesley, Rev. John, 280, 282, 306
Wessaguset (Weymouth, Mass.), 42
West, Benjamin, 298
West Church (Boston), 192, 283
Westchester County, N.Y., 73, 114, 215,
   230, 257
Westfield, Mass., 318
West Florida, 333, 362